ISBN 978-0-265-15048-1
PIBN 10925979

Forgotten Books is a registered trademark of FB &c Ltd.
Copyright © 2018 FB &c Ltd.
FB &c Ltd, Dalton House, 60 Windsor Avenue, London, SW19 2RR.
Company number 08720141. Registered in England and Wales.

For support please visit www.forgottenbooks.com

English
Français
Deutsche
Italiano
Español
Português

www.forgottenbooks.com

Mythology Photography **Fiction**
Fishing Christianity **Art** Cooking
Essays Buddhism Freemasonry
Medicine **Biology** Music **Ancient
Egypt** Evolution Carpentry Physics
Dance Geology **Mathematics** Fitness
Shakespeare **Folklore** Yoga Marketing
Confidence Immortality Biographies
Poetry **Psychology** Witchcraft
Electronics Chemistry History **Law**
Accounting **Philosophy** Anthropology
Alchemy Drama Quantum Mechanics
Atheism Sexual Health **Ancient History**
Entrepreneurship Languages Sport
Paleontology Needlework Islam
Metaphysics Investment Archaeology
Parenting Statistics Criminology
Motivational

REPORTS OF TAX CASES

ÚNDER

The Act 37 Vict. cap. 16.

AND UNDER

The Taxes Management Act.

VOLUME I.

1875—1883.

REPORTED AND PRINTED FOR OFFICIAL USE UNDER THE
DIRECTIONS OF THE BOARD OF INLAND REVENUE.

1884.

TABLE OF CASES.

REPORTED IN THIS VOLUME.

NOTE.—*Mode of Citation.* For official purposes this volume may be referred to as 1 T. C.; *e.g.* Bent *v.* Roberts, 1 T. C. 199. In the following table references are also given to the published Law Reports.

PART I.

No. 1.—In the Exchequer, Scotland.—First Division.
30th January 1875.

Income Tax.—Coal and Iron Masters not entitled to deduction from profits of per-centage claimed for pit sinking and for depreciation of Buildings and Machinery.

CASE stated on the Appeal of Messrs. Addie & Sons.

At a meeting of the Commissioners for General Purposes acting under the Property and Income Tax Acts for the Middle Ward of the County of Lanark, held at Hamilton upon the 12th October 1874, for the purpose of hearing and disposing of Appeals under the said Acts, for the year ending 6th April 1875.

Messrs. Robert Addie & Sons, Coal and Iron Masters, carrying on business at Langloan and elsewhere, in the Parish of Old Monkland and County of Lanark, appealed against the assessment made on them under Schedule D. of the Act 5 & 6 Vict. cap. 35, intituled "An Act for granting Her Majesty Duties on "Profits arising from Property, Professions, Trades, and "Offices," and subsequent Income Tax Acts referring thereto, in respect of the profits arising from their business for the year preceding in so far as the said assessment includes two sums of 5,525l. 19s. 9d. and 4,435l. being a per-centage which they claim to deduct for pit sinking and for depreciation of buildings and machinery respectively, and for which they maintain they were not assessable.

Messrs. Addie & Sons stated that they carry on, and have for a number of years past carried on business as coal and iron masters. They manufacture pig-iron at their works at Langloan, and they hold a number of mineral fields under leases of 31 years, which leases are in various periods of their currency. The minerals wrought under these leases are coal, ironstone, and fire-clay. As such lessees Messrs. Addie have sunk at their own expense the pits from which the minerals are raised. They also require to erect, and do erect at their own expense, machinery and buildings of various kinds, including winding and pumping engines, pithead buildings, and the like.

The Appellants submitted that in ascertaining the profits upon which they are liable to be assessed under the said Act, there

ought to be deducted from the gross annual receipts derived from
their business (1), a sum in respect of the cost of sinking the
pits; and (2), a sum in respect of the cost of buildings and
machinery.

1. With respect to their pits, they explained that most of them
are sunk and used for working ironstone, and are wrought only
for comparatively short periods, as the ironstone seams are
wrought out more speedily than seams of coal usually are, and
that when a pit has ceased to be wrought they do not receive any
payment from the landlord or anyone else in respect of it, and
that they are not recouped in the cost of sinking their pits in
any other way than out of the gross annual returns derived from
the minerals raised from them. There is scarcely any year in
which the Appellants are not engaged in sinking one or more
pits. In these circumstances they contended that the share
of the gross annual receipts corresponding to the proportion of
the cost of sinking the pits effeiring to the current year (regard
being had to the number of years during which the several pits
have been and will still continue to be wrought) was in no sense
a profit, and that, therefore, it ought to be deducted from the
gross annual receipts in arriving at the assessable profit.

2. With respect to machinery and buildings the Appellants
explained, that where a pit is wrought out, the price or value
obtainable for the machinery and buildings thereat is very small
as compared with the original cost, being what is generally
known as breaking up value, and that they are not recouped in
the difference between the original cost of the machinery and
buildings and the price or value obtainable, therefore, when the
pits are exhausted otherwise than out of the gross annual
receipts derived from working the minerals.

They therefore contended that this difference is in no sense a
profit, and that consequently in arriving at the profits upon
which they are assessable there ought to be deducted from the
gross receipts of each year a sum corresponding to the share of
that difference effeiring to such year.

The surveyor stated that the Income Tax is an annual tax
existing for one year only.

5 & 6 Vict.
c. 35. s. 60.,
Sch. A.
No. III.
Rule 3rd,
and 29 Vict.
c. 36. s. 8.

That by the Acts and sections quoted, the profits from ironworks are assessable according to the profits of the preceding
year.

That by section 159 of the Act 5 and 6 Vict. cap. 35., it is not
lawful in computing the profits under this Act to make any deductions except such as are expressly enumerated therein.

That Messrs. Addie & Sons, in estimating the balance of
profits for which they are assessable for the year 1874-5,
deducted the two sums mentioned, being a percentage or proportion of the sum expended by them on *pit sinking* in previous
years, and a similar percentage for the depreciation or deterioration of their buildings and machinery, in order to recoup themselves for the capital expended on their works.

That these deductions are expressly forbidden, as they are not enumerated in the Acts, that the only deductions authorised are those referred to in section 100, rule 3rd of the Act 5 & 6 Vict. cap. 35, and rules applying thereto; and that no allowance can be granted for the sum originally expended in pit sinking or in erecting buildings and machinery.

That the assessment on Messrs. Addie and Sons has been made according to the profits of the preceding year, in conformity with the Acts of Parliament, and that no sum can be legally deducted in estimating these profits, except such as are actually expended in realising the profits of the year according to which the assessment has been made, and all these deductions the Messrs. Addie have been allowed.

The Commissioners dismissed the appeal, being of opinion that the deductions claimed were not admissible under the Income Tax Acts, and that, upon a sound construction of these Acts, no deduction ought to be allowed in respect of such pit sinking or depreciation of buildings.

Upon said appeal being dismissed, Messrs. Addie and Sons, being dissatisfied with the determination of the Commissioners, as being erroneous in point of law declared their dissatisfaction, and required a case for the opinion of the Court.

JUDGMENT.

The Lord President.—The Appellants, Messrs. Addie and Sons, have been assessed under Schedule D of the Income Tax Act in respect of profits arising from their business as ironmasters, and they say there ought to have been deducted from the amount of profits upon which they were so assessed two sums of 5,525*l.* and 4,435*l.*, being a per-centage for pit sinking and for depreciation of buildings and machinery, and this they maintain upon the ground that the sinking of new pits, although it be only an occasional thing, is still part of what may fairly be called the annual expenditure which they necessarily incur in realising the profits from their trade. I think there is only one point to be determined here, and not two, as represented, because the machinery and building connected with a pit appear to me to be just part of the pit itself. It is one compound structure, necessary for the working of the mine, and the question comes to be, whether under the special rules of the Income Tax Act, they are entitled to deduct something on account of the amount expended in making a new pit. Now, I am quite clear that the making of a new pit in a trade of this kind is in every sense of the term just an expenditure of capital. It is an investment of money, of capital, and must be placed to capital account in any properly kept books applicable to such a concern. Now, if that be so, it seems to me that the provision of the third rule under the first head of section 100 of the Property Tax Act is conclusive upon the question before us, because it is provided that in estimating the balance of profits and gains chargeable under Schedule D., or for the purpose of assessing the duty thereon, no sum shall be set against or deducted from, or allowed to be set against or deducted from such profits or gains on account of any sum employed or intended to be employed as capital in such a trade. It seems to me that it is quite unnecessary to go beyond that one part of the statute. No doubt some support may be had also from the 159th section, but I think this rule is in itself perfectly conclusive. As soon as you ascertain that this is an expenditure of additional capital, there is an end to any proposal to deduct anything in respect of it; and on that simple ground I think the judgment of the Commissioners right.

Lord Deas.—I am of the same opinion, and I think it is better not to run the risk of making any confusion in the grounds of Judgment by adding anything to what your Lordship has said.

Lord Ardmillan.—I am of the same opinion. I think the two sections taken together are quite conclusive.

Lord Mure.—I think the 3rd rule of section 100 is quite conclusive on the point.

Judgment of Commissioners affirmed.

Part II.

Nos. 2 and 3.—In the Exchequer, Scotland.—First Division.

21st January 1875.

Inhabited House Duty.—Proprietory Life Assurance Company and Mutual Life Insurance Society not within the exemption of 32 & 33 Vict. c. 14. sec. 11.

Case stated on the appeal of the Edinburgh Life Assurance Company.

At a Meeting of the Commissioners for executing the Acts relating to the Inhabited House Duties for the County of Edinburgh, held at Edinburgh the 3rd day of December 1874, the Edinburgh Life Assurance Company, 22, George Street, Edinburgh, appealed against the charge of 13l. 2s. 6d. made upon them for Inhabited House Duty, at the rate of 9d. per pound on 350l., the annual value of the premises occupied by them at the above-mentioned address. The Edinburgh Life Assurance Company (which is a proprietory Company) occupy the premises in question for the purpose of carrying on their business of life insurance.

The area flat, consisting of four apartments, having internal communication with the offices above, is occupied as a dwelling-house by a servant of the company, who goes messages, superintends the cleaning of the premises, and acts as a clerk to the company, to the extent of addressing and booking letters, and with whom reside his wife and a female servant, whose wages are paid by the company.

The Appellants claimed relief from the assessment under the Act 14 & 15 Vict. c. 46., and under the 11th section of 32 & 33, Vict. c. 14., on the ground that they were a proprietory company engaged in trade; that the business carried on for the benefit of and at the risk of the shareholders, of insuring lives, buying and selling annuities, reversions, &c., was essentially a trading business; that the part of the tenement occupied by them in 22, George Street, was used for the purpose of "trade only;" and that the person dwelling in the area flat lived there "for the protection thereof," and to take care of the premises.

The Appellants maintained that an insurance office was as little liable as a bank (which the surveyor admitted was not liable unless where it was also used as a dwelling-house), and that an insurance company could be sequestrated as well as a

A

bank or any other trading company. That in regard to the
duties performed by their servant or messenger they never could
be held to be of such a nature as to entitle him to have the
designation of a clerk, but were merely of a purely mechanical
or subordinate description such as are invariably performed by
any bank or insurance messenger, and that it was frivolous to
attempt to magnify the importance of such services by designat-
ing the person who discharged them as a clerk. The Appellants further contended that the case of the National Bank of
Scotland (1,115) was totally different from theirs, because the
upper stories of the bank were inhabited by the cashier and his
family. The surveyor contended that the premises did not fall
within the exemption quoted:—1st. Because the business
carried on by the Appellants was not of the nature of trade in
the meaning of the Act, and that the premises were not therefore
used "for the purpose of trade only." The surveyor stated
that, so far as he was informed, it had been universally held by
the Commissioners throughout Scotland, and also in London,
that the business of an insurance company was not of the nature
of trade, and their offices were therefore subject to assessment.
The Act makes a clear distinction between trades and professions, and under it the offices of writers, accountants, &c. are
charged, although a considerable part of their business is akin
to that of banking, inasmuch as they lend money, purchase
shares, &c.; but it is maintained that their offices are not solely
used for the purposes of trade, and they are therefore taxed.
The surveyor contended that life insurance was not a trade,
there was neither a buyer nor a seller, but, for an annual
payment, the company guaranteed a sum at death. And 2nd,
because, even if the business carried on was of the nature of
trade, the premises did not come under the exemption claimed,
inasmuch as the person residing in them did not dwell there
solely for the protection thereof, but was otherwise occupied,
sometimes in discharging the duties of a messenger, and at
other times the more important duties appertaining to the
position of a clerk. The surveyor cited the English case
(No. 2,850), the Atlas Assurance Company, and the Scotch case
(No. 1,115), the National Bank of Scotland.

The Commissioners were of opinion that the business carried
on was not of the nature of trade, and that therefore the premises
did not come within the exemption granted by the statute, and
they accordingly refused the appeal and confirmed the assessment. But the Appellants, being dissatisfied with this decision,
craved that a case might be stated for the opinion of the Court.

No. 3.

CASE stated on the Appeal of the Scottish Widows' Fund and
Life Assurance Society.

AT a Meeting of the Commissioners for executing the Acts
relating to the Inhabited House Duties for the County of
Edinburgh, held at Edinburgh 3rd December 1874, the
Scottish Widows' Fund and Life Assurance Society, 9, St.
Andrew Square, Edinburgh, appealed against the charge of
24l. 7s. 6d. made upon them for Inhabited House Duty, at
the rate of 9d. per pound on 650l., the annual value of the
premises occupied by them at the above-mentioned address.

The society occupy the premises in question for the purpose
of carrying on their business as a "mutual" life assurance
society. A house of five apartments in the area flat of the
building, and having internal communication with the society's
offices above, is occupied by one of their messengers, with his
wife, three children, and servant.

The Appellants contended that their premises were exempt,
under the 11th section of 32 & 33 Vict. cap. 14, being used solely
for the purposes of trade, and the messenger dwelling therein
"for the protection thereof."

The surveyor maintained that the premises did not fall within
the exemption quoted: 1st, because the business of a mutual
life assurance society was not of the nature of trade, and that
therefore the premises were not occupied "for the purposes of
"trade only;" and 2nd, because, even if the business should be
found to be of the nature of trade, the person residing on the
premises did not dwell there solely for the protection thereof,
but was engaged during the day in delivering messages and
attending the directors at their meetings.

The surveyor cited the English case (No. 2,850), the Atlas
Assurance Company, which he held to be analogous.

The Commissioners were of opinion that the business carried
on was not of the nature of trade in the meaning of the Act,
and that therefore the premises did not come within the exemption, and they accordingly refused the appeal and confirmed the assessment; but the Appellants, being dissatisfied
with this decision, craved that a case might be stated for the
opinion of the Court.

JUDGMENT.

Lord President.—In the case of the Edinburgh Life Assurance Company, the company claim exemption from the Inhabited House Duty, upon the ground that they are within the

meaning of the 11th section of the statute 32 and 33 Vict. c. 14, and the Commissioners have refused to sustain that exemption because they are of opinion that the business carried on by the company is not of the nature of a trade, and therefore the premises do not come within the exemption of the statute.

Now, in order to determine whether the business carried on by this company is of the nature of a trade, it is necessary of course to ascertain what is the meaning of the term trade as used in this statute. But, for that purpose, again it seems to me to be necessary to attend to the legislative history of this Inhabited House Duty,—what it is in itself, and how the exemptions have arisen and been introduced into the statute. The duty itself was imposed originally in the year 1808 along with a great many other taxes, and there cannot be much doubt, I think, reading that 48 Geo. 3, that it was intended to assess all houses or tenements which were occupied not merely by persons residing, but also by persons occupying them during the day for business purposes. In short, although it was called an Inhabited House Duty, it really was something more expansive than that, because an inhabited house, in the popular sense of the term, is a house in which persons dwell, reside, and spend the night as well as the day. But the tax in its original conception, under the 48 Geo. 3, was of a more comprehensive description than that. But after it had been in operation for some time there was first one exemption introduced by the Act of 57 Geo. 3, c. 25, and afterwards another by the 5 Geo. 4, c. 44. The first of these, the 57 Geo. 3, c. 25, introduced this exemption. (*Reads*.) Now this is an exemption applied to trade premises solely and confined entirely to that, and the words used in this statute are extremely important. It must be a house used for the purpose of trade only, or a warehouse for the sole purpose of lodging goods, wares, and merchandise, or a shop or counting-house, and it must be occupied only during the day for the purposes of such trade, and not occupied during the night as a dwelling-house. Now, *prima facie*, certainly under that statute, the word trade is used there as the trade of a merchant or shopkeeper, that is to say, of one who buys and sells as a merchant does, on a large scale, or of one who deals in retail like a shopkeeper; and certainly, reading that statute alone, one would be very much disposed to come to the conclusion that the exemption was not intended to extend beyond either a merchant in the proper sense of the term or a shopkeeper. But then we have the next statute, 5 Geo. 4, which extends the exemption to another class, c. 44, s. 4, and it is not immaterial to observe that that section 4 has a special preamble referring back to the 57 Geo. 3. (*Reads*.) Now, here is the interpretation of the previous statute in this preamble. The exemption extends to persons in trade in respect of houses used solely for the purposes of trade. That is the meaning of the clause in the 57 Geo. 3, as construed by the Parliament which passed the Act of 5 Geo. 4, and it extends that provision and enacts—(*Reads*).

Now, it seems to me that the question we have to solve in the present case is whether the Edinburgh Life Assurance Company is within the first statute or the second, whether it is a trader within the meaning of the 57 Geo. 3., or is a Company carrying on a business or calling within the meaning of the 5 Geo. 4. In these two statutes the two classes of persons are placed exactly in the same position. They are equally exempt, but the necessity of distinguishing between the two in this case arises from the provisions of the 11th section of the recent statute 32 & 33 Vict. which provides—(*Reads*).

The persons who are exempted under the 57 Geo. 3. have this additional privilege under the statute of the 32 and 33 Vict., that they may enjoy their exemption although they have a servant dwelling in the house for the purpose of protection, and this is not extended to those who enjoy their exemption under the 5 Geo. 4., and thence arises the necessity of determining to which class of exempted persons this insurance company belongs. Now, I am of opinion that the term trade is used in the first of these statutes in its strict meaning, and that there are a great many businesses which may be regarded as falling within the description of trading that are not trading within the meaning of that statute. I am satisfied, taking these two statutes together conferring the exemptions, that the distinction intended to be made between the two is that the one exemption is confined to traders in the proper and legitimate sense of the term, merchants and shopkeepers, and that the exemption is extended to all other persons who are carrying on any other kind of business for profit, not being traders in that proper sense; and as the 11th section of the 32 and 33 Vict. repeats the very words of the 57 Geo. 3. in giving the additional privilege, that additional privilege must be confined to the persons within the meaning of the 57 Geo. 3., and I am therefore of opinion, with the Commissioners, that this insurance company is not a trader. That renders it quite unnecessary to enter upon the question whether the servant whom they had in charge of their premises is within the meaning of the 11th section of the recent statute either for the purposes of protection and for no other purpose. That might raise some little difficulty, but it is not a question of the same importance as the other. It is sufficient for our judgment, I think, to adopt the same ground that has been adopted by the Commissioners, and in which, I think, they are quite right.

With regard to the case of the Scottish Widows' Fund, it is not necessary to say much, because, if a proprietory company, like the Edinburgh Life Assurance Company, are not traders, still less are the mutual society called the Scottish Widows' Fund. I think if we had held that a proprietory office was a trader in the meaning of the statute, a very serious question would have arisen whether the same construction of the statute would have applied to the case of a mutual office, but it is not necessary to enter on that question. I think we can fairly dispose of both cases upon the same ground which has been taken by the Commissioners.

Lord Deas.—I am of opinion, with your Lordship, that neither of these companies are to be held as carrying on a business of the nature of trade so as to entitle them to come within the exemption in the sense of these statutes. I cannot say I see any substantial difference between them. There may be more difficulty in regard to the Scottish Widows' Fund than in regard to the other, but it is not necessary to go into that, and I cannot see at present that any distinction can be taken between them. It is sufficient to hold that neither of them are carrying on a trade in the sense of the statute.

Lord Ardmillan.—When a court of law is called to decide a question affecting the incidence and distribution of taxation, the question is necessarily important. We have been told that a taxing statute must be construed liberally and favourably to the subjects. In one sense that is true, and the remark is well founded, but on the other hand equality and impartial justice in the incidence of taxation are of greater moment, and the statute should be construed so as to promote that equality and that impartiality of justice. There is no presumption in favour of the exemption of the few from the incidence of the general tax. I think the presumption is for equality, and rather against the partiality which is involved in special exemptions. Therefore, in deciding any presumption I would consider the question on the statutes according to their true meaning. So viewing the case I arrive at the conclusion that these insurance companies are not traders within the meaning of the 32 & 33 Vict., construing that statute by the aid of the preceding statutes, imposing and regulating taxation; and that the premises which they occupy are not houses for the purposes of trade only. The question is one of difficulty. I have felt it to be so, but on the whole I am quite satisfied with the construction which your Lordship in the chair has adopted and explained of the series of these Acts, and I have come to the same conclusion that neither of these insurance companies are the occupants of premises used for trade only. There is a distinction between the two, and I do not undervalue it. I think there was a great deal of ingenious argument about it, and if we had come to the conclusion that the proprietory company were engaged in trade there might have been a doubt whether a mutual insurance society, where every man insures himself as well as the others, is a proper trading company. There may be subtle and delicate questions involved in that. I do not know it is the trade for a man to insure himself with himself; I do not know it is sale when a man sells to himself and buys for himself. But it is not necessary to enter upon those questions. Holding, as I concur with your Lordship in doing, that both societies are liable and not within the exemption, it is not necessary to consider whether one is more liable than the other.

Lord Mure.—I concur with your Lordships, that the Commissioners have pronounced a correct deliverance in this case, and on the grounds explained by your Lordship in the chair.

Judgment of Commissioners affirmed in both cases.

No. 4.—IN THE EXCHEQUER, SCOTLAND.

LORD SHAND, LORD ORDINARY.

5th February 1875.

Inhabited House Duty.—A Proprietory Fire and Life Insurance Company not within the exemption of 32 & 33 Vict. c. 14. sec. 11.

CASE stated on the Appeal of the Scottish National Insurance Company.

AT a Meeting of the Commissioners for executing the Acts relating to the Inhabited House Duties for the County of Edinburgh, held at Edinburgh the 3rd December 1874, the Scottish National Insurance Company, 22, St. Andrew Square, Edinburgh, appealed against the charge of 9l. made upon them for Inhabited House Duty, at the rate of 9d. per pound on 240l., the annual value of the premises occupied by them at the above-mentioned address.

The Scottish National Insurance Company occupy the premises in question solely for the purpose of carrying on their business of fire and life insurance. A portion of the area flat, consisting of two small apartments, having internal communication with the remainder of the flat and with the offices above, is occupied by a servant of the company, who acts as messenger, cleans the premises, and collects premiums, and with whom his wife and three young children reside.

The Appellants claimed relief from the assessment under the 11th section of 32 & 33 Vict. cap. 14., on the ground that they were a proprietory trading company; that the business carried on by them for the benefit and at the risk of the shareholders, of insuring lives, insuring against loss by fire, buying and selling annuities, reversions, &c., was essentially of the nature of trade; and that the person living in the premises dwelt there expressly and solely for the protection thereof, although he might also perform other services to the company not requiring his residence on the premises.

The surveyor contended that the premises did not fall within the exemption quoted; 1st, because the business carried on by

the Appellants was not of the nature of trade in the meaning of
the Act, and that their premises were therefore not used "for
"the purposes of trade only;" and 2nd, because, even if the
business carried on was of the nature of trade, the person
residing in the premises did not dwell there solely "for the
protection thereof," but was otherwise occupied, sometimes in
the menial duties of a servant, and sometimes in the more
responsible ones of collecting premiums. The surveyor referred
to the English case (No. 2,850), the Atlas Assurance Company,
and the Scotch case (No. 1,115), the National Bank of Scotland.

The Commissioners were of opinion that the business carried
on was not of the nature of trade, and that the premises did not
therefore come within the exemption granted by the statute;
and they accordingly refused the appeal, and confirmed the
assessment. But the Appellants, being dissatisfied with this
decision, craved that a case might be stated for the opinion of
the Court.

Judgment of the Commissioners affirmed.

No. 5.—In the Exchequer, Scotland.

Lord Shand, Lord Ordinary.

5th February 1875.

---

*Inhabited House Duty.—A Proprietory Fire and Life In-
surance Company not within the exemption of 32 & 33 Vict.
c. 14. s. 11.*

Case stated on the Appeal of the Caledonian Fire and Life
Insurance Company.

At a Meeting of the Commissioners for executing the Acts
relating to the Inhabited House Duties for the County of
Edinburgh, held at Edinburgh the 3rd December 1874, the
Caledonian Fire and Life Insurance Company, 19, George
Street, Edinburgh, appealed against the charge of
10*l.* 2*s.* 6*d.* made upon them for Inhabited House Duty, at
the rate of 9*d.* per pound on 270*l.*, the annual value of the
premises occupied by them at the above-mentioned address.

The Caledonian Insurance Company (which is a proprietory
company) occupy the premises in question for the purpose of
carrying on their business of fire and life insurance. A house
of three apartments on the area flat, having internal communication with the offices above, is occupied by a man, as caretaker, and his wife. The former is a servant of the company,
who acts as messenger, takes charge of cleaning the premises,
books, letters with copying press, and collects premiums.

The Appellants claimed relief from the assessment under the 11th section of 32 & 33 Vict. c. 14., on the ground that the business carried on by them of insuring lives, insuring against risk by fire, buying and selling annuities, reversions, &c., was essentially of the nature of trade; and that the person dwelling in the premises were there "for the protection thereof," although he might be otherwise occupied during the day in the service of the company.

The surveyor contended that the premises did not fall within the exemption quoted: 1st, because the business carried on by the Appellants was not of the nature of trade in the meaning of the statute, and that their premises were not, therefore used "for the purposes of trade only;" and 2nd, because even if the business carried on was of the nature of trade, the person residing in the premises did not dwell there solely for the protection thereof, but was otherwise employed, sometimes in the menial duties of a servant, and sometimes in the more responsible ones of collecting premiums, &c. The surveyor referred to the English case, No. 2,850 (the Atlas Assurance Company), and the Scotch case No. 1,115 (the National Bank of Scotland).

The Commissioners were of opinion that the business carried on was not of the nature of trade, and that, therefore, the premises did not come within the exemption granted by the statute, and they accordingly refused the appeal, and confirmed the assessment. But the Appellants, being dissatisfied with this decision, craved that a case might be stated for the opinion of the Court.

Judgment of the Commissioners affirmed.

No. 6.—IN THE EXCHEQUER, ENGLAND.

5th June 1875.

Inhabited House Duty.—Building occupied for offices and residence having internal communication with warehouse. Warehouse portion not liable.

---

*CASE stated on the Appeal of the British and Foreign Bible Society.

AT a Meeting of the Commissioners for the General Purposes of the Income Tax Acts and for executing the Acts relating to the Inhabited House Duties, held at the Land Tax Rooms, Guildhall Buildings, in the City of London, on the 8th October 1874.

The Rev. Charles Jackson appealed on behalf of the Committee of the British and Foreign Bible Society against an assessment to the Inhabited House Duties, for the year ending the 5th of April 1871, of 3,200*l.* at 6*d.* in the pound upon their premises in Queen Victoria Street, in the ward of Castle Baynard, and claimed exemption under the Act 32 & 33 Vict. c. 14. s. 11.

The premises comprise a basement with cellars. A ground floor containing offices communicating with the warehouses, which are shut off by an iron door at night. A first and second floor containing committee rooms, a large library, and offices for secretaries and clerks. Also a third floor occupied by one of the clerks (Mr. Eckerstein), who is in receipt of a salary of 195*l.* per annum, his wife and two servants, who assist in the cleaning of the entire establishment.

Mr. Eckerstein occupies the whole of this floor, which consists of three bedrooms, a sitting-room, two kitchens, a storeroom, lavatory, and lumber-room partly furnished.

The access to this floor is by a private entrance from Wardrobe Place by means of a circular staircase, and from this staircase there is a communication with the main offices by a door leading into the passages on the second floor.

The warehouses and packing-rooms form part of the main building, assessed as a whole at 3,200*l.*, but they have no communication with the rest of the building occupied as offices, &c., and by Mr. Eckerstein, except by the iron door on the ground floor only, which is closed at night. The party wall between the warehouses and offices runs to the roof as required by the provisions of the Buildings Acts.

The Appellant claimed total exemption on the grounds that Mr. Eckerstein occupies the rooms only as a caretaker within the meaning of the 11th section of the Act 32 & 33 Vict. c. 14., but contended further that under any circumstances the duty ought to attach only to that portion occupied as a residence by Mr. Eckerstein, which the society allege is a separate building in conformity with the requirements of the Building Act. The Commissioners considered the premises to be occupied as an inhabited house, and that the internal communication with the warehouses rendered the whole building liable, and confirmed the assessments, whereupon the Appellant declared his dissatisfaction with their decision, and duly required them to state and sign a case for the opinion of the Court of Exchequer.

At the hearing of the case, counsel for the Appellants abandoned the objections raised by the Appellants at the appeal, but contended that the assessment was wrong, inasmuch as the portion of the building used as a warehouse came within the exception contained in rule 3 of 48 Geo. 3. c. 55., Schedule B., in favour of "such warehouses as are distinct and separate "buildings, and not parts or parcels of such dwelling-houses, "or the shops attached thereto, but employed solely for the "purpose of lodging goods, wares, and merchandize, or for "carrying on some manufacture (notwithstanding the same "may adjoin to or have communication with the dwelling-"house or shops)."

JUDGMENT, 5th June 1875.

The Court held that the assessment to the Inhabited House Duties of the premises stated in the said case at the sum of 3,200*l.* was not correct, and ordered that the assessment should be reduced by the value of the warehouse portion thereof.

No. 7.—IN THE EXCHEQUER, ENGLAND.

3rd June 1875.

Inhabited House Duty.—Weavers Hall, occupied partly by solicitors and other professional persons, not within the exemption of 32 & 33 Vict. c. 14, s. 11.

CASE stated on the Appeal of Mr. Thomas Newson, Weavers Hall.

AT a Meeting of the Commissioners for the General Purposes of the Income Tax Acts and for executing the Acts relating to the Inhabited House Duties for the City of London, held at the Land Tax Rooms, Guildhall Buildings, in the said city, on Thursday, the 8th October 1874.

Mr. Thomas Newson appealed against an assessment to the Inhabited House Duties for the year ending the 5th day of April 1873 upon the premises known as the Weavers Hall, No. 70, Basinghall Street, in the ward of Bassishaw, and contended that the premises were exempt under the Act 32 & 33 Vict. c. 14, s. 11, upon the grounds that they were occupied as offices and counting-houses for merchants and professional men, except the two rooms occupied by the housekeeper and his family, who lived on the premises solely for the protection thereof.

The premises are occupied by four accountants, two solicitors, stated also to be scriveners, thirteen merchants. one wine-shipper, and one shorthand writer, all of whom use the rooms they respectively occupy as offices, and by the housekeeper, his wife, and two children, and a servant, who occupy two rooms on the top story as a residence rent-free.

The housekeeper and his wife are employed by the various occupiers to clean the offices, for which they are remunerated by them.

The surveyor contended that as the premises were partially occupied by solicitors and other professional men. they were not used solely for trade, and therefore liable to Inhabited House Duty. He also referred the Commissioners to the Judge's Case 2,848 respecting the assessment on the same premises in the year 1869. ending April 1870. when they were held to be liable, and the Appellant admitted that the facts of the case in the years 1869 ending 1870, and 1872 ending 1873, were identical.

The Commissioners discharged the assessment, on the grounds that the greater portion of the premises were occupied for the purposes of trade, whereupon the surveyor for the Crown declared his dissatisfaction with their decision, and duly required them to state and sign a case for the opinion of the Court.

JUDGMENT.

Kelly, C.B.—It appears to me that this case does not raise the question whether some portion of Weavers Hall which has been assessed to this tax is not by law exempted from assessment; and even if it be supposed that it is raised by the case, still there is no statement in the case which enables me to determine whether the assessment now complained of is in respect of the value or rental of that portion which is so exempted from assessment, or only in respect of the value or rental of the portion which is undoubtedly liable to assessment. Under these circumstances, in the form in which the case has come before us, and lamenting much personally that it has come in such a form, I am of opinion that, inasmuch as it is perfectly clear that this building is liable to assessment, whether for the entire amount of the assessment or whatever that might be, I cannot pretend to say how that is, but I am of opinion that still it is liable to assessment for some amount or other, and therefore I am quite content to give judgment for the Crown.

Bramwell, B.—I really think that this case states every fact which is necessary, and raises every question which is necessary for us to form or express an opinion upon. It does not raise the point which Mr. Finlay would like to have argued, which is, that there should be a separate assessment upon each of these merchants, attornies, shorthand writer, and others. It does not raise that, as it never was intended to raise it, and ought not to raise it, because that is an after-thought; but I say that the real question that it does raise is that which Mr. Finlay has in fact admitted that he cannot maintain, that his house is used for the purposes of trade only, or any other of the things mentioned in the Act. He admits that the attorney uses his chambers and the shorthand writer uses his chambers for purposes other than trade. Then the house is not used for the purposes of trade only.

Then that brings me to this other point, which is, whether he can make any use of this expression, " any tenement or part of " a tenement occupied as a house for the purposes of trade." Mr. Finlay suggests that he can in this wise, that coupling these words with what comes afterwards, " any tenement or part of a " tenement used as a house for the purposes of trade only," and so on, " shall be exempt from Inhabited House Duties," he says means that a part of a tenement shall be exempt from Inhabited

House Duties and that that can only be sustained by supposing
that the house is to be assessed by the Commissioners assessing
it with an abatement for that part which is occupied for the
purposes of trade. That is what I understand to be the argument, briefly put. I think that that argument is erroneous, and
that it is indefensible on this construction of the Act of Parliament. I think that in truth this Act of Parliament must be
read as though these words, "or part of a tenement," were not
there. I think they make no alteration in the effect of the
Act of Parliament. I know very well that it is desirable, if
possible, to give effect to all the words that are put in; it is not
to be supposed that they are put in idly or uselessly; but my
opinion is that they have been put in there idly and needlessly
for a variety of reasons, which I think it right to state perhaps
at some more length than the importance of the case deserves.

Of course you cannot read these words, "or part of a tenement," without those words which immediately follow in that
sentence, "any tenement occupied as a house for the purposes
"of trade only," or "any part of a tenement occupied as a house
"for the purposes of trade only," but it is to be part of a tenement occupied as a house, the meaning of which is, that it is
what may be called a part of a tenement which is separately
assessable to the house duty (if I make myself understood), part
of a tenement which would come under rule 14 of the other Act
of Parliament, the 48th of Geo. 3, which in some way or another
would be separately assessed. And I am fortified in this conclusion by the words at the end of section 11, which say,
"although a servant or other person may dwell in such tene-
"ment or part of a tenement for the protection thereof." Well,
now then, if that were to be read as Mr. Finlay would have us
read it, it would read thus,—"Any room in a house used for
"purposes of trade shall be exempted from Inhabited House
"Duties, although a person may sleep and dwell in that room
"for the protection thereof." There clearly was not an intention to exempt a house, or a separately assessable tenement used
as a house for the purposes of trade only, although somebody
slept in it.

I think one can find a justification for this conclusion in the
previous Act of Parliament, to which my Brother *Cleasby* has
referred. That Act begins by reciting what would be very
favourable to Mr. Finlay's argument if you looked at that alone.
The statute recites that it has become very customary for people,
either separately or in partnership, "to occupy a dwelling-house
"or dwelling-houses for their residence, and at the same time
"one or more separate and distinct tenements or buildings, or
"parts of tenements or buildings, for the purposes of trade. or
"as warehouses for lodging goods, wares, or merchandise there-
"in, or as shops or counting-houses, and to abide therein in the
"day-time only." Surely that recital would, in general terms,
comprehend a case where a man had a dwelling-house in one
place, and had a room in another house not separately assessable

for the purpose of his trade. But we must see how it goes on.
" And it is expedient in such cases to exempt from the said
" duties such tenements or buildings, or parts of tenements or
" buildings, as are, or shall be, solely employed for the purposes
" therein mentioned. Be it therefore enacted, ' That from and
" ' after the 5th April 1817, on due proof made that any
" ' person, or any number of persons in partnership together
" ' respectively occupy a tenement or building, or part of a tene-
" ' ment or building,' (still the same words are used,) ' which
" ' shall have previously been occupied for the purpose of resi-
" ' dence, wholly as a house for the purposes of trade only, or as
" ' a warehouse for the sole purpose of lodging goods, wares, or
" ' merchandise therein, or as a shop or counting-house,' no per-
" son inhabiting, dwelling, or abiding therein, except in the
" daytime only for the purpose of such trade, such person or
" each of such persons in partnership respectively residing in a
" separate and distinct dwelling-house, or part of a dwelling-
" house charged to the duties under the said Act. It shall
" be lawful for the said Commissioners, according to the pro-
" visions of this Act, to discharge the assessment made for that
" year in respect of " what? " in respect of such tenement or
" building." The words " part of a tenement " being there
dropped, so that it is clear that in the Act of Parliament the use
of the words " part of a tenement " really is equivalent to " a
" tenement," and it is intended to meet such a case as this one
which comes within section 14 and to discharge it. Then it
goes on further in the 2nd section,—" Provided always, and be
" it further enacted, that all such tenements or buildings,
" whether employed wholly for the purposes of trade or as ware-
" houses," and so on. I rather think that from that time forth
the words " part of a tenement " are dropped, and therefore in
my mind that expression is father to the origin of the introduction of the words " part of a tenement " in section 11 under the
Act which we are construing.

When it is said that that would be a very harsh construction,
it is a sort of argument which it is difficult to deal with. Possibly
in one sense it is, but in another sense it clearly is not. The
Legislature had said originally that all inhabited houses should
be subject to the duty, and it was held, and properly held no
doubt, that a house which was not occupied at night, but was
occupied in the day-time for the purposes of trade, was an inhabited house, and subject to duty. It was pointed out that
that really was (I think it very likely, it was pointed out), in
truth, a taxing of the instruments of trade, and perhaps was as
injudicious as a tax upon machinery, or a tax upon tools, and
other means by which trade was carried on, and thereupon the
Legislature thought that it was reasonable to exempt buildings
which was solely used for purposes of trade, and for the other
purposes mentioned here. But they at the same time did not
exempt parts of buildings that were once used for such purposes,
and other parts which were used only as a dwelling-house,

because they could not go into nice distinctions as to the loss of revenue that might be sustained if the question could be raised as to one part of the house being used as a dwelling-house, and the other being used for the purposes of trade only. Therefore they determined not to give the benefit of that exemption, for the reason that I have suggested, that the houses were partly used for one purpose and partly used for another. Then the Act of 32 & 33 years of the Queen determined upon a liberality to the persons carrying on trade, and they said that what had been true of a house where nobody dwelt at night before should be true of it, although persons dwelt in it to take care of it for its protection, might sleep there, and therefore in one sense there is no hardship or injustice in the terms of this section, it is simply extending a boon which had been to a certain extent conferred before. In one sense it may be heard, that is to say it may be expedient in such a case as this that I have pointed out, that the Legislature should say that in assessing a house partly used for the purposes of trade, and partly used for other purposes, the Commissioners should make allowance for the value of that part of the house which was used for the purposes of trade only. I do not say that that would not be a very reasonable thing. The Attorney General seems to think it would be, and I confess I think so too rather, provided there was no danger to the revenue from such being the case. Whether there would be or not, I cannot say, but we have got nothing to do with such considerations as those of hardship, except this, that no doubt when a case of hardship is pointed out in a statute, it makes the construction which leads to it more improbable than if it led to a reasonable and just condition of things. But in my mind the construction of this statute is plain, and that the Crown is entitled to judgment, that Weavers Hall should be assessed to its full value as a house, without any abatement in respect of those parts that are occupied for the purposes of trade only.

Cleasby, B.—I am of the same opinion. We are construing here an exemption from a liability which was a severe burden, and there ought not to enter into the. consideration of this matter at all the question whether the exemption might or might not be intended liberally or otherwise. We see what the exemption is. The liability was no doubt there before. and it ought not to be extended further than its proper construction would extend it. I think in the present case if there be a burthen anywhere, one would say it is to show that the case comes within the exemption clauses. The facts here are precisely the same as in the case No. 2.848, which was stated. and which was referred to. They are precisely the same, and the question was the same; but the Commissioners thought proper, because they say in this case that as it appears now that the greater part of the building is occupied for the purposes of trade, we choose to take upon ourselves to determine, for that it substantially would be, to make that a condition of exemption

that a part of that which is assessed is occupied for the purposes
of trade only. They were not justified in doing that.

Upon the case generally, I must say that it appears to me
tolerably clear that the exemption does not apply, except where
the subject matter of assessment is that to which the exemption
applies. Although my Brother *Bramwell* has referred somewhat
fully to this statute of the 57th of George the Third, there is one
part which perhaps he did not dwell upon as much as I think he
might in the earlier part of the recital, and it is this. After the
recital of that section, which becomes involved by introducing
several persons, and so one, that a person may dwell in one house,
and at the same time occupy one or more separate and distinct
tenements and buildings, or parts of tenements and buildings,
for the purposes of trade, these are the words which I think are
so important here, "which have been charged with the said
"recited duties." I can only read these words as meaning that
parts of tenements so occupied for purposes of trade have
been charged with the said recited duties. Then, although the
Commissioners determined that there was an assessment here,
so far as I can see that is the only meaning that can be attached
to it, because it goes on, "although no person shall inhabit or
"dwell therein in the night-time," in what?—In the part of a
tenement, of course the very words point to the fact, that
although no person shall dwell therein in the night-time, still
they had been assessed for part of the tenement; then it goes on
to say that a portion has been assessed either as "a tenement or
"building, or part of a tenement or building, which shall have
"previously been occupied for the purpose of residence wholly,
"as a house for the purposes of trade only," and afterwards as
a shop or counting-house, and so on, and then the assessment
shall be discharged. That seems to me to point clearly to this,
that what was intended here was to extend this section so far as
this. Formerly the exemption had only been where no person
dwelt therein during the night-time; but that carries it further.
it is the same words, "tenement or part of a tenement," but it
shall make no difference whether a person does dwell therein,
and is therein at night-time, provided the occupation is such as
is mentioned. I think that "tenement" and "part of a tenement" have the same meaning, and therefore that the decision
of the Commissioners was wrong.

Decision of Commissioners reversed.

Nos. 8 AND 9.—IN THE EXCHEQUER, SCOTLAND.

25th May 1875.

Inhabited House Duty.—Premises occupied in several Tenements assessable as an entire House.

CASES stated on the Appeals of James Brebner and John Walker.

AT a meeting of Commissioners for General Purposes, acting for the County of Aberdeen, for hearing and determining Appeals against Property and Income Tax and Inhabited House Duty, held at Aberdeen, on the 8th day of December 1874, James Brebner, Warehouseman, appealed against an assessment of 1l. 3s. 3d., being Inhabited House Duty at 9d. per 1l. on 31l. rent or annual value of a dwelling-house belonging to and partially occupied by him at No. 67, Bonaccord Street.

The house was stated to consist of a sunk floor, street floor, upper floor, and attics, having one lobby and stair shut in by one street door, kept on latch during the day and locked at night. The rooms on the street floor and a kitchen in the sunk flat are let to Miss Murdoch at a rent of 15l. The apartments on the street floor are enclosed by a door entering from the stair, but which door does not shut in the stair leading down to the kitchen and other accommodation in the sunk floor. The rooms on the upper floor, which are also enclosed by a door on the stair landing, are occupied by the Appellant, who also occupies a cellar or store in the sunk flat; the annual value of this portion of the house is stated at 12l. The attic rooms, which are not enclosed in any way from the stair or lobby, are let to Miss Bridgeford at the rent of 4l. In the sunk flat there is a washing-house common to all the occupiers, access to which is by the stair and passage leading to Miss Murdoch's kitchen.

From the stair landing, between the street and upper floors, there is access to a green behind the house.

The Appellant claimed to be relieved from the assessment on the ground that the house was divided and separately occupied by three parties, none of whose rents amounted to 20l., and that each tenant should therefore be dealt with as the occupier of a separate house entering from a common stair.

He maintained that each occupier's part of the house was completely separate: one having the street floor and the habitable part of the sunk floor, another the upper floor, and a third, the attics; and that the fact of the wash-house on the sunk floor being common to the occupiers was not sufficient to take away the separate character of the premises occupied by each, the occupiers being in no way related to or connected with each

B

other, and each being separately assessed on the rents named to the poor rate and other local rates.

In support of his appeal he referred to the English appeal case No. 1,427, and also to the Scotch cases Nos. 15, 719, 843, and 888.

In support of the assessment the surveyor maintained that although inhabited by three occupiers the house was not so divided as to entitle any of them to claim his or her own portion, as a distinct and separate house, the entire premises of none of the occupiers being separately enclosed, and the whole house being shut in by the front door, the assessment was correctly made, in conformity with Rule VI., Sch. B., 48 Geo. III., cap. 55.

The surveyor also referred to Scotch case No. 1,077, decided by the judges 11th March 1865.

JOHN WALKER, clerk, also appealed against a similar assessment made upon him as proprietor of the house No. 69, Bonaccord Street, on the same grounds as in the preceding case. The house was stated to be in all respects similar to that belonging to James Brebner above described, the apartments on the street and upper floor being similarly enclosed, the only difference being that the house is inhabited by two occupiers instead of three, the value of each occupation being also under 20*l.*

The grounds of assessment were also stated by the surveyor to be the same as in the preceding case, and it was agreed that the decision of the Court in the first case should rule the second.

The Commissioners, being of opinion that the circumstances of the cases as above set forth were such as to entitle the Appellants to relief, sustained the appeals; but with this determination the surveyor declared his dissatisfaction, and required cases for the opinion of the Court.

JUDGMENT.

25th May 1875.—I am of opinion that the determination of the Commissioners is wrong.

(Signed)   A. B. SHAND.

NOTE.—In coming to this conclusion I have been mainly influenced by the previous decisions in the Scotch cases Nos. 659 and 1,077.

(Initd.)   A. B. S.

PART III.

Income Tax.—Harbour Mooring Commissioners entitled to a deduction for revenue applied under Act of Parliament for repayment of money expended in the renewal of works..

Case stated on the Appeal of the Harbour Moorings Commissioners of the Borough and Port of King's Lynn.

At a Meeting of the General Commissioners of Income Tax for the borough of King's Lynn, in the county of Norfolk, held at the Inland Revenue Office in the said borough on the 4th February, 1875.

Mr. John Osborne Smetham, as clerk to and on behalf of the Harbour Moorings Commissioners of the Borough and Port of King's Lynn, appealed against a charge of 444*l*. 0*s*. 10*d*. made upon Mr. Lewis Whincop Jarvis, the Commissioners' treasurer, in the assessment under Schedule "D" for the parish of Saint Margaret in the said Borough (Jew's Lane Ward, No. 2), for the year 1874–5, in respect of mooring dues.

The Appellant put in the King's Lynn Harbour Moorings (Local) Act (4th Vict. c. 47., a print of which marked A accompanies, and is to be taken as part of this case), with which is incorporated the Act 13 Geo. 3. c. 30., appointing the Commissioners, and particularly quoted sections 25, 26, 30, 8, 52, and 33 of the first-named Act.

Appellant then explained that the Moorings Commissioners some years since, on the requisition of the Corporation, took up 16 or 17 mooring chains in the harbour to enable the harbour to be dredged. After the dredging had been effected the present screw moorings were put down in substitution for the chains, and the expenditure thereby incurred caused the Commissioners' account with Mr. Jarvis, their banker, to be overdrawn by a 1,000*l*. or 1,500*l*. Interest being charged at 5*l*. per cent. at the bank the Commissioners deemed it expedient to avail themselves of the borrowing power given them by their Act. and raise the money required to pay off the bank debt by bonds at the lower rate of interest 4½*l*. per cent.

Appellant contended that no profits could arise until every charge directed by the Act had been paid. and that the Act

A

prohibits the Commissioners from making any profit and only authorises them to raise sufficient money to cover their annual outgoings.

Appellant next contended that the surplus shown by the treasurer's balance sheet for the year 1873 cannot be regarded as profits, inasmuch as the Act compelled it to be applied in liquidation of the bond debt, such debt being incurred in putting down moorings and thereby raising the revenue.

Appellant admitted the Commissioners' obligation to pay upon actual profits, but stated there were no profits, the annual income sufficing only to meet liabilities.

Appellant alleged that if one screw mooring had been put down each year, a deduction would have been allowed from that year's income for labour and materials to moorings, and contended that the fact of the moorings having been put down together, and the expenditure incurred in one year instead of being spread over several years, made no difference in principle.

A further contention by Appellant was that the alterations in the moorings were not improvements, but merely restorations.

Appellant argued that the rates and duties leviable under section 30 of the King's Lynn Harbour Moorings (Local) Act being " shipping rates," and imposed on all vessels entering the port irrespective of whether they use the moorings or not, the liability to income tax did not attach to them, but that they were exempt in the same manner as poor and other corresponding rates, and stated that the moorings dues, in respect of a vessel were analogous to poor rates on a house.

Mr. Hall, the inspector on the part of the Government, put in the Acts 5 & 6 Vict. c. 35, 16 & 17 Vict. c. 34., and 29 & 30 Vict. c. 36., which are to be referred to as part of this case, and after quoting section 60 of 5 & 6 Vict., c. 35., rule 3, No. 3, he referred to section 40 of the same Act, and section 1 of 16 & 17 Vict. c. 34., under which last-named provisions he submitted the Moorings Commissioners were liable to income tax in the same manner as any person would be chargeable; he also quoted section 8 of 29 & 30 Vict. c. 36., transferring the charge to Schedule " D."

The inspector quoted the cases of Attorney General v. Black, 24 L. T. 371, and Attorney General v. Scott, 28 L. T. 302.

The inspector contended that the Moorings Commissioners were not exempted by the Income Tax Acts, but that the surplus shown by the printed account then put in by him, which is hereunto annexed marked B, and is to be taken as part of this case, was before its distribution amongst the bondholders chargeable with duty.

The Commissioners were of opinion that the dues raiseable under the Moorings Act are not such rates as are exempted from income tax, and determined that the only liability of the Moorings Commissioners to income tax arises in respect of the tax deducted by them on paying the interest to bondholders regarding the 400l. appearing in the treasurer's account for the year 1873 as a payment to bondholders, although not strictly

PORT OF KING'S LYNN.

LEWIS W. JARVIS, ESQ., Treasurer, in Account with THE LYNN HARBOUR MOORINGS COMMIS-
SIONERS for the year ending Christmas, 1873.

(THE MOORING DUES ACCOUNT.)

Dr.	£ s. d.	Or.					
Balance due to the Commissioners..	199 14 0	**SALARIES AND WAGES.**					
To cash received :		By cash paid :—				s. d.	£ s. d.
From sale of old materials	0 15 0	Mr. M. R. Garland				0 0	
Of Mr. Self for one year's collection on 48,403 tons of coals, and on 156,323 tons of goods at 1½d.	1,155 8 5	Mr. Robert Eggett				0 0	
		Mr. Edward Self				0 0	
		Mr. L. O. Smetham..				10 0	
		Mr. Francis Coe				0 0	
		Mr. Simpson (carpenter)..				18 8	
		Mr. Wales (boatman)				12 0	
		Mr. Huggins (pension)				£ 15 0	
		Master of Sloops				195 0 0	553 13 8
		RENTS, RATES, AND TAXES.					
		Rent of buoy warehouse..				10 10 0	
		Rent of mooring dues office				8 0 0	
		Poor rate for buoy warehouse.. ..				2 9 6	
		Poor rate for pilot office				5 10 10	
		Income Tax				1 1 0	27 11 4
		BONDS AND INTEREST.					
		By cash bonds :—					
		47 and 50, repaid				400 0 0	
		Paid Mr. Robert Cook one year's interest on £600 at 4½ per cent., less income tax..				26 12 2	
		Paid Mr. H. H. Cook one year's interest on £200 at 4½ per cent., less income tax..				8 7 5	
		Paid Mr. Edward Walker one year's interest on £200 at 4½ per cent., less income tax..				8 17 5	
		Paid interest on bonds discharged ..				4 12 3	448 19 0
		MISCELLANEOUS CHARGES.					
		By cash paid :—					
		Labour at moorings, &c...				21 17 8	
		Materials for ditto				12 5 0	
		Materials for buoy ship				34 16 9	
		Materials for chain, boats, and skiff..				17 15 6	
		Mooring dues office, coals, candles, and cleaning				4 18 0	
		Furniture for ditto				7 0 0	
		Receipt stamps				0 10 0	
		Self, dues returned				2 1 7	
		Oil for pilot sloops and repairing lamp				7 12 1	
		Gas for pilot office				0 14 4	
		Chadwick's bill for ditto.. ..				0 18 0	
		Watson, Expenses, Lowestoft ..				2 5 0	
		Sydal for pilot sloops' moorings ..				10 10 0	
		Stationery, printing, and advertising				8 10 6	
		Mr. Smetham's bills				25 0 8	
		Gibson (messenger)				2 13 6	
		Brunning (hall-keeper)				3 0 0	162 8 7
							1,172 13 10
		Balance due to the Commissioners				..	113 4 7
	1,355 17 5						1,355 17 5

PORT OF KING'S LYNN.

LEWIS W. JARVIS, ESQ., Treasurer, in Account with THE LYNN HARBOUR MOORINGS COMMIS-
SIONERS, for the year ending Christmas, 1873.

(THE NORFOLK ESTUARY ACCOUNT.)

Dr.	£ s. d.	Or.	£ s. d.
To balance due to the Commissioners	258 2 6	By cash paid two instalments of the Norfolk Estuary contribution	105 14 4
		Balance due to the Commissioners	152 8 2
	258 2 6		258 2 6

belonging to the annual revenue account, nevertheless to be a proper deduction, inasmuch as it had been applied in the repayment of money expended in the *renewal* of works necessary, for raising the income of the Moorings Commissioners.

The inspector declared to the Commissioners his dissatisfaction with their determination as being erroneous in point of law, and required a case for the opinion of the Court.

JUDGMENT.

The Court were of opinion that the 400*l.* appearing in the treasurer's account for the year 1873 as a payment to bondholders was a proper deduction to be made, as it had been applied in the repayment of money expended in the renewal of works, and affirmed the decision of the Commissioners of the income tax as to the aforesaid deduction.

No. 11.—IN THE EXCHEQUER.—ENGLAND.

9th June 1875.

Income Tax.—Corporation of Birmingham held to be correctly assessed for profits of market hall, fish market, vaults, and meat market, and not entitled to deduct and set against profits in one or more of the said matters any loss sustained in any other concern.

CASE stayed on the appeal of the Corporation of Birmingham.

AT a Meeting of Commissioners of Income Tax, acting for the Birmingham division of the hundred of Hemlingford, in the county of Warwick, held at the Revenue Offices, Birmingham, on the 7th of January 1875.

The town clerk of Birmingham appealed against the following items of assessment made on the municipal corporation by the title of mayor, aldermen, and burgesses of that borough, in conformity with 29 Vict. c. 36. s. 8., which in effect transfers tolls and other concerns described in No. 3 of Schedule A. of the 5 & 6 Vict. c. 35. to Schedule D. :

				£
The market hall	...	...	...	4,000
The fish market	...	...	...	800
The vaults ...	...	...	...	1,200
Meat market	...	...	...	250

The amounts of the several assessments were not questioned, but the town clerk contended that the corporation were not liable to be charged in respect of the profits arising from these sources, inasmuch as they suffered losses from the following concerns, to an amount which more than covered the profits arising from those on which they were charged, namely: —

	£
Utilisation and disposition of sewage	28,132
Industrial schools	478
Baths and parks	3,623

And in all other departments of the corporation of a similar character the annual accounts kept by the borough treasurer and duly audited invariably show a large excess of the expenditure over income.

In support of this view the town clerk contended that the corporation were within the meaning of the 101st section of the 5 & 6 Vict. c. 35., which enables a person carrying on two or more distinct trades, manufactures, adventures, or concerns in the nature of trade, the profits whereof are made chargeable under the rules of Schedule D., to deduct and set against the profits acquired in one or more of the said concerns the excess of the loss sustained in any other of the said concerns over and above the profits thereof in such manner as may be done where a loss shall be deducted from the profits of the same concern.

The receipts from the sources charged, as well as all other moneys received by the town council, after deducting the cost of collection, were carried to a general account, from which was deducted the whole expenditure of the corporation for the civil government of the borough, including the maintenance of police, repairing of streets, &c., the result showing a large deficiency, which had to be made up by the rates levied on the inhabitants.

Mr. Herd, the surveyor of taxes, on behalf of the Crown, contended that the corporation could not be considered as persons carrying on trades or adventures, and that the concerns from which they derived no profit were part of the authorised and legitimate expenditure of the borough provided for the benefit of the burgesses and other inhabitants, and that the profits derived from the sources charged were in aid of the rates which the burgesses were called upon to pay.

He referred the Commissioners to the case of the Attorney General v. Scott, in the Court of Exchequer, 16th January 1873, which decided that the profits of the corporation of the City of London derived from market tolls, corn and fruit metages, brokers' rents, mayor's court fees, &c., are liable to income tax under Schedule D., without reference to the purposes to which they are applied, and that the proper principle upon which the assessment should be made is to take each item or head of income separately, and assess the income tax upon the net produce of such item, after deducting from the gross receipts the expenses incurred in earning and collecting the same.

The town clerk contended that the case was not decisive, as the introduction by him of the particular items of loss was a new feature to which the attention of the Court has not been directed.

The Commissioners considered otherwise, and that the general principles of the Income Tax Acts were hostile to the town clerk's view; they therefore confirmed the assessments.

The town clerk, acting on behalf of the corporation, being dissatisfied with their determination as being erroneous in point of law, demanded a case for the opinion of the Court of Exchequer.

JUDGMENT.

. The Court held that the several subject-matters of the assessment to income tax made on the said Appellants, and mentioned in the said case, viz.:—

				£
The market hall	...	...	...	4,000
The fish market	...	...	...	800
The vaults ...	...	...	...	1,200
Meat market	...	...	...	250

are correctly assessed under the Income Tax Act, and that the Appellants are not entitled to deduct and set against the profits acquired in one or more of the said subject-matters any loss sustained in any other concern mentioned in the said case over and above the profits thereof, and affirmed the determination of the said Commissioners as to the said assessment made upon the said Appellants.

NO. 12.—IN THE EXCHEQUER, SCOTLAND.—FIRST DIVISION.

26th May 1875.

Income Tax.—Corporation of Glasgow not chargeable for Income Tax as on profits of Waterworks for moneys received from compulsory District Water Rate.

CASE stated on Appeal of the Commissioners acting under the Glasgow Corporation Waterworks Acts.

AT a Meeting of the Commissioners for General Purposes, under the Property and Income Tax Acts for the City of Glasgow, held at Glasgow on the 22nd day of February 1875.

5 & 6 Vict. cap. 35 sec. 60 No. III., Rule 3D; 29 Vict. cap. 26.

The Glasgow Corporation Water Commissioners appealed against a *supplementary* assessment made upon them under Schedule D. of the Income Tax Acts for the year 1872–73, in respect of the sum of 17,032*l.* 15*s.*, on the ground that they have been already charged in the first assessment for the annuities and interest which they pay, and from which they are entitled to retain the tax, and upon which alone. they were previously assessed, and that the sum charged, which is the surplus of the water rates, after payment of all other current expenses necessary for carrying on the undertaking, has been applied as directed by Act of Parliament, viz., towards the formation of a sinking fund in redemption of the annuities and mortgages, and the remainder of the sum carried forward to the following year's account, to be applied, as the Act directs, in reducing the domestic water rate, and not therefore assessable. 18 & 19 Vict
c. 118.

The facts are these :—By the Act 18 & 19 Vict. c. 118., the Lord Provost and magistrates of the city of Glasgow were appointed commissioners to obtain a supply of water for the city of Glasgow and its suburbs, and as such commissioners were empowered to acquire, and have acquired, by purchase the " Glasgow Waterworks " and the " Gorbals Gravitation Waterworks," the two joint stock companies by which the city of Glasgow and its neighbourhood were previously supplied with water, with all their properties, privileges, and obligations, together with power to introduce an additional supply of water from Loch Katrine.

For these purposes they were authorised to borrow money by annuities, mortgage, and otherwise, and. it is provided that the several sums so borrowed should be applied in defraying the expense of purchasing and acquiring lands and other property and of executing the authorised works.

They are required, by compulsory clauses in the Act, to furnish the city of Glasgow, *i.e.*, within the municipal boundaries, with a supply of water for domestic purposes, and to erect 32 public fountains from which the poorer classes may draw water, and the area within these boundaries is termed "the limits of compulsory supply."

They are also required to introduce a supply to the suburbs within a prescribed area, extending as far as Barrhead, in Renfrewshire, and embracing a very large population.

They are also empowered to sell water for the purposes of trade, manufacture, &c., either by measure or upon such special terms as may be agreed on between them and the consumer.

They are also authorised to let meters on hire to those parties who consume by measure, and make a charge therefor of 10 per cent. per annum.

Householders residing beyond the limits of compulsory supply are not required to take water, but having once done so, must continue to take it for three years, when they may cease doing so, and be no longer liable to pay for it.

To provide for the annual expense connected with carrying on these undertakings, the Water Commissioners are required to meet once a year to make an estimate of the probable expense, and having done so, are empowered to levy (1) a rate, to be called "the domestic water rate," from the occupiers of all dwelling-houses within the municipal boundaries, "limits of compulsory supply," according to their rents; (2) the "public water rate," not exceeding 1d. per pound on the full annual value of all dwelling-houses, shops, warehouses, buildings, &c. within the municipal boundary, and this rate is payable within these limits, whether the water supplied by the corporation be used or not, except where the mains or other pipes are not within 50 feet of the outer wall, fence, or boundary of the premises, in which case no rate can be levied on a proportion greater than one-fourth of the annual value of the premises; and (3) such rates as may be fixed by the Commissioners from all parties residing beyond the limits of compulsory supply who use the water; but these rates are not to exceed the rates previously charged by the old companies.

The rates are not payable beyond the limits of compulsory supply, unless the water be actually taken. The sum to be thus raised, together with the sums received from traders and others supplied under special agreement, and for the use of meters, must be sufficient to cover all the annual expenses, including a sum of not less than one per cent. on the money borrowed, to be set apart as a sinking fund for the redemption of the annuities and mortgages, and such sinking fund, it is declared, shall be from time to time applicable to the redemption of mortgages and annuities, and to no other purpose whatsoever; and the rates to be levied must be so regulated that such rates shall be sufficient to pay the interest on the money borrowed, and the annuities payable under the Act, together with all other charges and expenses and such other sums as shall be set apart for the purpose of the sinking fund. And if in any year the amount received shall be more than sufficient for all these purposes, the Commissioners are required to make a reduction in the domestic water rate of the next year.

The Appellants specially referred to sections 89, 90, 92, 109, 110, and 119 of the Act 18 & 19 Vict. c. 118., "Corporation "Waterworks Act, 1855," and they desire that these be held as part of their case.

It was argued on behalf of the Appellants that the case of the Attorney General v. Black. 17th June 1871, 6 Law Reports, Exchequer, 308, founded on by the Inland Revenue, was not analogous, because—(1.) The question in that case was whether the corporation of Brighton were liable to pay income tax in respect of a coal duty levied by them. By 13 Geo. 3. c. 30. a power was given to improvement commissioners for Brighton to levy a duty of 6d. upon every chaldron of coals landed on the beach or brought into the town, for the purpose of erecting and maintaining groyns against the sea. By subsequent Acts the duty was continued and increased, and by 6 Geo. 4. c. 179. it was, together with rates which the Commissioners were empowered to levy, market tolls, &c., to form a common fund for the general purposes of the Act, which included paving, lighting, and watching, and the maintenance of groyns and other sea works. It was held, affirming the judgment of the Court below, that the corporation who had succeeded to the rights of the commissioners were liable to pay income tax in respect of the coal duty.

(2.) The grounds upon which that decision proceeded do not exist here. In that case the duty was of the nature of a toll, and was levied from whatever persons landed coals, whether inhabitants of Brighton or strangers.

It was thus not a "district rate"—a rate levied from the inhabitants or owners or occupiers of property within a defined area. In its application it was not exclusively or at all appropriated in the same manner as a "district rate," but was applicable to the general purposes of the corporation. While the Court in that case held the coal duty to be taxable, they intimated clear opinions that any revenue which was truly of the nature of a "district rate" would not be taxable.

Thus Mr. Justice Blackburn, in commenting upon a passage from the opinion of Mr. Baron Martin, says "They" (a corporation) "would not be liable, except in respect of something "of the same nature and kind as what had been previously "mentioned, not, for instance, in respect of a burgh-rate or a "highway rate, because these are not within the analogy of the "property or profit previously described."

So Mr. Justice Keating says,—"the argument has been "brought within a narrow compass. Mr. Manisty does not "contend that harbour and port dues and other revenues 'of "that description are not taxable, and the Attorney General "admits that a 'district rate' is not. The question then is "does the rate in question partake more of the nature of the "one or of the other. I am of opinion that it does not partake "of the character of a 'district rate' imposed by the inhabitants "of a place upon themselves, and that, on the other hand, it is "very difficult to distinguish it from harbour dues."

The opinions of the other judges are to the same effect.

(3.) The question in the present case thus comes to be whether the moneys dedicated to the creation of the sinking fund and the surpluses truly are, in point of character, profits from carrying on the business of introducing water, or whether they are a "district rate." The Appellants submit that whether regard be had to their origin or application they are a "district rate."

The moneys in question are raised by rates charged upon the persons possessing property within a defined area, so that they have the primary attribute of a "district rate," that they are levied in the form of a rate from persons within a specified district, not from strangers, as were the coal dues in the Brighton case.

As regards appropriation, the moneys in question are stamped with the character of a "district rate."

The sinking fund is created to provide for reduction or repayment *pro tanto* of the sums borrowed for the purposes of the Act, these purposes being exclusively confined to the specified area or district.

There is not, as in the Brighton case, any discretion left as to how the funds shall be applied. If, instead of the money required for the purposes of the Act having been borrowed and expended in large sums shortly after the passing of the Act, it had been expended and provided for by an assessment in each individual year, it would have been clear that the assessment thus required for the expenses of the year was in no view property or profits, and it can make no difference that the nature of the works required a large original expenditure, which needed to be provided for at the time by borrowing, but which was to be paid off gradually by rates.

(4.). The rate is in the strictest sense for the public benefit within the particular district. It is not fixed with relation to the amount of water used by the different persons, although even this would not deprive it of the character of a district rate. If a highway rate, or a poor rate, are, as the judges in the Brighton case say, district rates, not taxable, a water rate is precisely in the same position; indeed, a considerable part of the water is applied in watering the streets or highways.

The money is not of the nature of "property or profits" for another reason, viz., that it does not belong to any one for his patrimonial benefit, and that no one is enriched by it. The Appellants are merely gratuitous trustees, who provide the machinery necessary for levying the rates from the inhabitants within the specified district, and apply it for the statutory purposes within that district.

In this matter they act as section 6 of the statute bears,—" As " representing, and for and on behalf of the community of the " said city " of Glasgow. They make no gain or profit by the exercise of their statutory powers or the performance of their statutory duties, neither do the inhabitants of the district.

The rate is, in the words of Mr. Justice Keating, " a district " rate imposed by the inhabitants of a place upon themselves."

If the views now submitted would have been well founded if the Appellants had been the first body who supplied the district with water, the case is not varied by the fact that the Appellants took over the undertakings of private water companies. These companies were undoubtedly commercial undertakings, established and carried on for the purposes of profit and for no other purposes; and accordingly their rates were fixed at such an amount as to yield a profit to the shareholders.

But all this is different in the case of the Appellants, who do not derive any profit from their performance of the duty of supplying water either for themselves or for any one else, and their statutes are framed for the express purpose of so adjusting income and expenditure that no profits shall arise.

The Acts of the private companies taken over, expressly mention the profits to be earned by the companies, although they set certain limits to the amount of the profits to be so earned, just as the Legislature impose upon railway companies the obligation of carrying passengers at certain specified rates, or at rates not exceeding certain specified sums.

This, however does not prevent such companies from being undertakings constituted for the purpose of making profits, and of consequence the profits which they actually make are assessable.

The fact that the Appellants' duties were formerly discharged by companies deriving a profit therefrom does not prevent the Appellants from being merely the hands by which the inhabitants of the specified districts levy from themselves a district rate, as it is plain that scarcely any of the purposes for which district rates are raised and applied could not be discharged by private persons or bodies for the purposes of profit.

Thus, although highway rates are taken by the judges in Black's case as illustrations of proper district rates, not assessable, there would be nothing to prevent the formation of a private company to make and maintain, for the purposes of profit, a road between any two places, charging tolls for its use —just as railway companies charge tolls for the use of their line. But although the profits derived from such tolls would be assessable in the hands of the owners of the private undertaking, if the road were by statute converted into a highway, in respect of which a district rate was leviable, that rate would not be assessable because levied by the successors of persons who made and maintained the road and levied tolls for its use with a view to profit.

Nor is the case affected by the fact that the profits of waterworks are mentioned as assessable in the Income Tax Acts.

The provisions of these Acts relate to waterworks established and conducted with a view to profit, while the Appellants' position is that they earn no profits.

The Appellants maintain that no valid argument against them arises from the fact that their statutes contain provisions for supplying water beyond the limits for compulsory supply. In a certain sense the supply of water even beyond these limits, but within the limits of the Act, is compulsory, inasmuch as section 86 of the Act of 1855 declares that the Appellants shall cause pipes to be laid down and water to be brought to every part of the places and districts within the limits of the Act beyond the limits for compulsory supply whenever a sufficient requisition upon them to do so shall be made, and they are not entitled to make profit by such supply beyond, any more than within, the proper compulsory limit.

Rates of limited and defined amount are to be levied in the one case just as in the other.

The income on which the City of London were held liable to be assessed in the case of The Attorney General v. Scott was different from the rates levied by the Appellants, and in that Attorney General v. Scott, January 1874, 28 Law Times. 302.

case the city were making large accumulations of money not
appropriated by statute or otherwise.

On behalf of the Inland Revenue it was replied,—(1.) That
the supply of water to the city of Glasgow until the year 1855
was in the hands of two joint stock companies,—"The Glasgow
"Waterworks Company," and the "Gorbals Gravitation Water
"Company" Sections 13, 31, and 33 of the Glasgow Water
Company's Act, 1 & 2 Vict. cap. 86., and sections 48, 49, 50, and
110 of the Gorbals Gravitation Waterworks Company's Act,
9 & 10 Vict. cap. 347., were referred to as authorising these
companies to levy rates, borrow money, provide sinking fund,
and reduce rates in certain circumstances, just as in the case of
the Appellants.

Both of these Companies were annually assessed for their
profits,—that is to say, the amount of the rates, after deduction
of the costs and charges of carrying on the undertaking under
the third case, No. III., Schedule A., of 5 & 6 Vict. cap. 35.

In the year 1855 the Glasgow Corporation Waterworks Act
came into operation. After this the assessment was restricted
to the tax on annuities and the interest of money payable out of
the water rates, until the supplementary assessment in question
was made.

(2.) Whatever name may be applied to the water rate, it is
certain that in its origin the water company was a commercial
undertaking. It is so still, except that payment of rates under
the old companies was not compulsory.

They enter into contracts with traders and others to supply
them with water on terms which may be mutually agreed on,
and also let meters on hire, which are transactions of a purely
commercial nature.

Formerly, if you took the water you paid for it, if not, you
did not pay; but now, within a certain "defined area," you
must pay the rate whether you use the water or not.

18 & 19 Vict.
cap. 118, secs.
82-86.
(3.) The rates are only compulsory within this certain
"defined area," viz., the municipality of Glasgow; without there
is a large area entitled to water privileges, comprising all the
suburbs of Glasgow, and towns so far distant as Barrhead in
Renfrewshire.

This area must contain 100,000 inhabitants; perhaps more.

Within the whole of this area the corporation is bound,
certain conditions being complied with, to introduce the water,
but no one is obliged to take it unless he agrees to do so.

Sec. 93.
(4.) The Appellants are empowered to fix from time to time
the rates to be levied without the limits of compulsory rating,
but the rights of limitation of rates obtained by certain districts
under the Acts of the companies existing in 1855 are still in
force. So far, therefore, as the extra-municipal districts are
concerned, the Glasgow Water Commissioners are undoubtedly
carrying on a purely commercial undertaking. They supply an
article which the inhabitants may or may not take, and they
have authority to make them pay an adequate price for it.

(5.) If any of the suburban districts do take the water they must engage to take it for three successive years, when they may cease to be customers of the corporation if it suits them. From this point of view, the position of the corporation in those districts is precisely that of the old companies, whose liability to pay income tax was never doubted.

Can a rate of this kind legally be deemed a "district rate"?

Reference is again made to the case of the Attorney General v. Black.

Mr. Justice Keating, in distinguishing the Brighton tax from a "district rate," says, "I am of opinion that it does not partake "of the character of a 'district rate' imposed by the inhabitants "on themselves." Mr. Justice Lush says, "A rate is a call "made by the local authority on a given class of inhabitants "from time to time as occasion requires."

(6.) The Appellants being merely trustees, and personally deriving no gain or profit from their office, does not seem to affect the question, which is, is there any surplus after deducting from the receipts all the ordinary expenses which are necessary for carrying on the undertaking? There are no grounds under the Income Tax Acts for exempting it because the undertaking is vested in a corporate body. By section 40 of 5 & 6 Vict. c. 35., bodies politic or corporate are chargeable as persons, and the chamberlain, or other such officer, is bound to do all the acts necessary for their due assessment.

In the Attorney General v. Scott, January 1874, 28 Law Times, 302, the City of London were held liable for the tax on their income, just like an individual.

In the case also of the Tyne Improvement Commissioners v. Overseers of Chirton (1 Ellis and Ellis, 516), and the Birkenhead Dock Trustees v. Overseers (2 Ellis and Blackburn, 148), provision was made by Act of Parliament for the application of the profits in the formation of a sinking fund or otherwise, on the repayment of principal moneys borrowed, and the Court did not regard that circumstance as affecting the question before it, but held that the profits constituted the income, which was the measure of the extent of the liability in respect of occupation for rating purposes.

The Commissioners, having considered the whole case, refused the appeal, and affirmed the assessment; but the Appellants, being dissatisfied with that decision, craved a case for the opinion of the judges. 37 Vict.
cap. 16, sec. 9.

The Solicitor General.—In this case the Crown seeks to bring within the operation of the Income Tax Act, and I contend that it does fall within the operation of that Act, certain revenue derived by the Glasgow Waterworks Commissioners. The concern is a trading concern just as much as it was in the hands of the public companies before the Commissioners held it. The expressions used in the income tax are very wide, and it has been observed in the authorities already quoted to your lordship that it is really a question of common sense, and not a question of mere strict law, whether you are to deal with a concern of this kind of property and profits within the meaning of the Act. The contention on the other side is chiefly based upon the exception which is indicated in the opinions of the learned judges who decided the case of the Attorney General against Black, to the effect that a district rate does not fall within the incidence of the income tax. That is a proposition which, as understood by the judges according to my view, I do not in the least degree dispute. Where you have a rate levied as in the poor law, for the support of a pauper, a burden upon the community, and a rate levied for the purposes of meeting the burden, and for the benefit and maintenance of a pauper; that is in no direct or proper source for the benefit of the ratepayer who pays. That is the plain incidence of a public rate levied within a particular district for the benefit of certain objects within it.

Lord President.—Is it not for the public benefit that a pauper is maintained?

Solicitor General.—Undoubtedly, but the one case is an arrangement to meet a real burden, it is not the produce of profit and property.

Lord President.—But it is the produce of a tax, and I question if this is.

Solicitor General.—Undoubtedly, that is what I contend for. The 17,000*l.* is what arises in relation to a certain stock-in-trade, it is produced by that stock-in-trade, because keeping up that stock-in-trade and supplying the water by means of distributing reservoirs, and the works at Loch Katrine are necessary to furnish and supply it. This the statute enjoins on the corporation as a condition of what they are entitled to levy.

Lord President.—Take out of consideration altogether the surplus over the income, and take the case of the income alone. Suppose the Commissioners levy a rate which is equivalent to the maintenance of their works and the ordinary expenses and payments into their sinking fund; you propose to charge income tax upon what is to go to the sinking fund?

Solicitor General.—Unquestionably.

Lord President.—That prevents them discharging the obligation under the 119th section to the full extent, because you take something off the sum.

Solicitor General.—But if they have to pay income tax they must provide for it, as they provide for the property tax, which they pay on the heritages they possess. That is one of their current expenses, and if there be an income subject to deduction of income tax, they must calculate on that deduction.

Lord President.—Then they must raise, in addition to what is required for the sinking fund, so much more as will be 2*d.* to the pound on the sinking fund.

Solicitor General.—Yes, just as they estimate income tax and other public burdens on the heritages they possess.

Lord Deas.—Would not that be ratepayers paying income tax on their own expeniture?

Solicitor General.—I do not think so.   That is what I am coming to speak to.   I say you must look at the substantial character of the transaction.

Lord President.—I do not see the distinction between that rate and a poor rate.   If the parochial board levied too much and carried a balance to the next year's account, would you not assess that as profits?

Solicitor General.—It goes to meet a burden as before.   I hardly think you can call it a profit.   I venture to say that the moneys which go to the sinking fund are not of that same character.

Lord President.—What do you say to the case of a highway board and a paving rate, a rate for the purposes of maintaining a road or street?

Lord Deas.—There is an obligation to spend that money on the street.

Solicitor General.—No doubt, but I think the difference lies here.   It is quite within my argument that where the fund comes from the public for the benefit of a particular district, that is looked on as a source of income granted by the Crown to that district, just as much as giving them money or property, or adding to the common good of the district.   On the other hand, where you lay a burden upon a particular section of the community, which is not for the benefit of individuals merely, but for the benefit of the whole world, or any person who goes upon the road, and a rate which is for the maintenance of a road within that district, that is looked upon as a public impost levied from a particular section of the community.

Lord President.—Does not water fall as much within that description as anything?

Solicitor General.—No, for this reason, that the water which is charged against the proprietor or tenant of a house is being furnished to that house, and thus to a certain extent increases its value, and is therefore for the individual uses of the parties.

Lord President.—And also for the uses of the whole people who come to the borough.

Solicitor General.—Well, it is right that people who clean themselves and wash themselves should take the use of the water, and be thereby safer from other consequences; but I contend that the purpose and object of it all is individual benefit, and not only so, but there is a trade carried on.   It is right, for instance, that people should have bread to eat and gas to burn: and a corporation may undertake the duty of supplying these.   They do in Glasgow undertake the duty of furnishing gas, and when they do that, they are merely doing what a private company did before by arrangement sanctioned by the

Legislature, an arrangement which is confined to the Corporation of Glasgow on the one hand, and to proprietors of lands and houses within certain limits on the other. The town council thus manufacture gas for them, and provide water for them, with this view that they may get it at cheaper and more moderate rates than private companies.

Lord President.—This body in question is not the municipal body.

Solicitor General.—It is a municipal body constituted of the corporation.

Lord President.—They have no funds excepting those derived from this assessment.

Lord Deas.—They are constituted for the ratepayers within the municipal district, and they are just the municipal ratepayers.

Solicitor General.—I do not know that it is; but they differ in one sense trustees for the ratepayers within their limits, but not for the public generally. They are not maintaining a highway for the public generally, but waterworks for certain persons within a given area.

Lord Deas.—But what the corporation pay out is nothing but the expenditure of the ratepayers.

Solicitor General.—I do not know that it is; but they differ in this way, that the ratepayers have no further control upon them. They are an elected body by the ratepayers; but once in the management they are not in the position of members of the company; I mean the public are not. I can quite see that the company is a corporation constituted undoubtedly for their benefit solely; and accordingly and by reason of the benefit conferred upon them by the Act; and only if these benefits are afforded to them in the manner contemplated by the statute, is it, that the right to levy the rate arises at all. Now, I say that that is totally different from the other case of laying it on a particular section of the community, a tax intended to benefit the whole population, or any portion of the public who may go there. It is totally different where, in order to supply one of the common necessaries of life to all the inhabitants within a particular limit, the Legislature empowered, of course in the belief that it is for the good of the community, and at the instance either of the community or those represented, the corporation to supply that common necessary of life, and reduce the charge they have to pay to a minimum cost, because, unquestionably, that is the purpose of the statute. I venture to say it is something exceedingly different from a poor rate. I quite admit that it is for the benefit of everybody that streets should be paved, and roads made for the use of any who may go on them, or pass over or frequent them without being the owner of houses or heritages. I can also say that it is for the benefit of particular districts that paupers should be cared for and housed and fed; but then, that is a different thing as regards the community. The one is a burden upon the private man as a ratepayer; but for the other he only gets *quid pro quo*, but more for his money than a private adventurer would give. No doubt a certain amount of cleanliness ensues, because there are persons who might not make such a liberal use of water if it were not forced upon them; but that is an advantage for which the ratepayer pays a small cost, without its being brought about by the limitation which the Act imposes on the rate or charge made; but then the rate or charge is for the thing supplied to each individual. As a corporation the gas company charge according to meter; for those who burn gas the charge is thus differently made. But the real meaning of the charge in the case before us is to substitute for the rate which the Gorbals Gravitation Company on the one side, and the Glasgow Water Company on the other side, were induced to levy from the inhabitants of those districts before the concerns were amalgamated and vested in this corporation by means of the statute. It is really and truly a rate in the one case, a deduction from the private fortune or means of the individual for the purpose of maintaining those who are burdened on the community and with which they are burdened for behoof of the community. It is a very different thing when there is no return made for the rate, which is really a moderate charge for that which is supplied; indeed the most moderate charge possible, because it is intended to be strictly a charge nearly at cost price, charging a cost price, or about a cost price, for what a private company or individual would charge additional profit upon in order to make a dividend. They are in reality making a purchase of their supply, just as in the other case they would purchase their gas supply upon favourable terms; because the trade of or manufacture in gas within the limits of that particular district is for the behoof and benefit of the inhabitants in that district alone. It is taken out of the hands of the private trader or the company trader, and put into the hands of a corporation constituted as representative of the public themselves. Now it is possible that a private company may trade without profits. A private company by reason of competition may charge so low a price for water or anything else as to make small profits, and the amount upon which they pay income tax, too, varies accordingly. But the question is, have you not here a property within the strict sense of the statute, a property from which, in this sense, profits may be derived, and profits which in this sense were derived? The water consumed by them in a given area may be improved beyond a moderate price, and become more than sufficient to meet the cost of production.

Lord Deas.—That is, taking it as a tax upon property?

Solicitor General.—Yes.

Lord Deas.—Do you think a tax on property can be levied on any other ground than the valuation roll?

Solicitor General.—I am taking it on the result of the operations of a water company. I say the profit is a profit arising within the meaning of the Income Tax Act, arising out of the carrying on of the waterworks, which form a property capable of yielding profits within the meaning of the Income Tax Act. The Income Tax Act under Schedule A. includes all lands, tenements, and so forth; and by the third rule of Schedule A., sec. 60., it is laid down that the produce of these waterworks, the clear produce as the statute 5 & 6 Vict. originally stood, the clear produce payable or divisible amongst the persons entitled to it, being the members of the company or the owners of the soil or property, or payable to any creditor, or other person whatever having a claim on or out of the said profits, "shall," &c. (reads).

Lord President.—I have the greatest difficulty of making anything of Schedule A. in connexion with this. You say you must levy so much more if you have not money to pay income tax, and charge that as one of your current expenses against revenue; but is not water the balance of the account after all the charges against the revenue have been made? I quite understand the property and every other tax which these Commissioners pay in respect of their property as a water company. Those form their annual expenses and they charge them in their accounts before this sum of 17,000*l.* was brought out.

Solicitor General.—No; with all deference I say that whatever is required is so provided for. This is not a deduction on a provision that must be made under the statute; it is somewhat the same as if this were the case. Take a private trading company, the partners of which resolve to pay off a certain amount of the capital of their debt, and they are quite entitled so to provide; but, in estimating the profits from the gross receipts, you cannot deduct any sum applicable to the payment of the debt; and if you were to treat these as profits, adjusting that according to the ordinary rule applicable under the Income Tax Acts, then, although for the purposes of levying they are entitled to charge against the ratepayers a sum for the purpose of forming a sinking fund, yet on a question of income tax, they are not entitled to deduct that sum so payable from the amount of profit. In other words, whatever goes to the sinking fund, and is available for the sinking fund is, within the meaning of the Income Tax Act, profit.

Lord President.—That raises a great difficulty in this statute, because if they are bound to pay a sum of not less than 1 per cent. on their debt into the sinking fund for the first 10 years, and 30*s.* per cent. per annum after that, they are bound to pay that, and are not entitled to levy any money except for such a purpose as that. If they happen, not by accident, to have any balance, they are told what to do with it; they are to appropriate that sum by the statute, and it is for that 30*s.* per cent per annum on which you propose to tax them.

Solicitor General.—It is not levied in that name or in that form at all.

Lord President.—But it is ascertained in that form.

Solicitor General.—It is estimated merely. If there be public rates exigible they have power under the statute to lower these on whatever part of the fund they may fall. In estimating the amount of the domestic rate or other rate chargeable for water the price of water is to be regulated by these considerations. They are not bound to do more than estimate. They must make such an estimate as will cover the amount necessary; but then the whole of it is to be raised by charging a higher price for water and in no other way. Now Schedule D. or the rules attached to Schedule D. govern the case of corporations and waterworks. They are transferred by the statute 29 Vict.; and the provision there made is, the said duty of 20*s.* in the pound " shall extend to every person " (*reads down to* " directed to be therein charged "). So that what Schedule D. deals with, amongst other things, is profits arising from a profit in connexion with a property, or the profits arising in any other manner or way not specified in the statute, or previously specified in the Income Tax Act. Now I venture to say that there is the greatest possible difference between the case of a ratepayer, for I don't object to the word, if the meaning of the thing be looked to, being supplied with water at a rate, and being repaid for the maintenance of the waterworks by having water so supplied, and the case of gas being supplied in respect of a rate by a corporation entitled to charge only the cost price, with an addition to meet their expenses; and the greatest possible difference between that and the case of maintaining a pauper. The one of these cases is a public benefit, and the other is recognised as a public burden, and is always so called. Who would speak of a water rate as a burden, or of a gas rate as a burden, when a thing is given in return for the rate?

Lord President.—I must confess I am not acquainted with the subject of gas rates.

Lord Ardmillan.—A gas ratepayer pays for what everyone consumes.

Solicitor General.—Well, you can use water in cooking and other purposes, if it is not drunk.

Lord Deas.—But you must pay for the water whether you drink it or not.

Lord Ardmillan.—And you don't do that in the case of gas.

Solicitor General.—But you don't make the consumption of gas compulsory. I cannot admit that it is a burden; I should think it a much greater burden in my case not to have it. Now in point of fact, what I maintain in the first place is this, that the Glasgow Corporation or Water Commissioners are in possession of a subject of the nature contemplated by the Income Tax Act, and which produces to them a certain revenue by and really through the sale of the commodity they produce. Now I think it is exceedingly material in this question to consider the sources from which that revenue is derived. They are set forth in the printed papers, and I shall not refer to them further, except in so far as they are set forth in the Appendix. There.:are at all events three sources. One is the compulsory rate, within the compulsory limits; the second is a rate leviable over a large area embraced in the limits of non compulsory application, that is to say,. non compulsory upon the consumer of the water.

Your Lordships are informed that there is a very large area, going as far as Barrhead in Renfrewshire, and extending even to .Renfrew itself. There is a special clause in the Act applicable to that town, and the payment they are to make for their supply beyond those limits, I mean the rule of assessment, is quite different from what it is within the limits of compulsory supply. Within the limits of compulsory supply there is a provision that on one side of the river they shall not exceed for the domestic water rate the sum of 1s. per pound. That is the limitation or maximum; but then I think your Lordships will find that the only obligation on the part of the Commissioners, where they have a surplus, or where they find that the expense of furnishing the water is diminishing, and that they can reduce the rate, is to give only those persons whom they more strictly represent the benefit of that reduction in the rate, namely, proprietors within the limits of compulsory supply. There is a limitation in their power to assess those beyond the limits of compulsory supply who are using the water. Section 93 you will find deals with the rates to be levied beyond the compulsory limits, and as I read the statute the Commissioners can give the benefit to the compulsory ratepayers of the whole reduction in the cost of the supply without relieving to any extent those who pay rates in terms of section 93. The only provision under section 93 is that the rates " levied shall not exceed " (reads down to "'Gorbals Gravitation Company ").

Lord President.—The people beyond the limits of compulsory supply have the benefit over those within the limits in one view on account of the maximum rate.

Solicitor General.—There is also a maximum in the case of those on the south side, within the limits of compulsory supply.

Lord President.—Yes, but the provision there is that the rates shall not be beyond those of the old companies.

Solicitor General.—On the north there is no limit on the domestic rate, but in the case of those on the south side, at the end of section 90 it is said " Provided always," (reads down to " annual value "). Then there is the equalising clause which follows section 92, which is important because it refers to the regulation of the water rate so as not to exceed the expenses and other charges requisite to be raised. It provides that they shall " from time to time regulate the rates to be levied for the supply " (reads down to " the full annual value "). That is to say, the first benefit goes to those within the limits of compulsory supply on the north, and then if they are paying more than the maximum rate exigible from ratepayers to those on the south. Then it is said, " Provided that such a rate shall not be more

" than 1s. in the pound, a reduction shall be made on the whole "
(*reads down to* " both sides of the river Clyde ").

Lord President.—Suppose the Commissioners found themselves in a position to act on the last proviso, and make a
reduction in the rate on both sides of the river, say 6d. or 3d. of
a reduction, would they be entitled at the same time to keep up
the old high rate upon the people beyond?

Solicitor General.—Most unquestionably they are entitled to
rate the non-compulsory consumers to the full amount authorised to be levied by the Glasgow Waterworks and Gorbals
Gravitation Acts. I conceive that it is not incompetent to rate
the non-compulsory ratepayers up to that limit. It is what
the statute contemplates, because the words of section 92 are
imperative that when they find the current rates admit of considerable reduction they are enjoined and required to give the
benefit of that reduction to those parties within the compulsory
limits who are paying the domestic rate. They are first to
apply the reduction so as to give those upon the north side of the
Clyde the benefit of it, and put them on a par with the householders paying the domestic rate on the south side, because
there is a limit of 1s. in the one case and not in the other. To
have the advantage of paying less than 1s. they must, under the
statute, receive an equal benefit from the reduction in cost or
charge. There is no provision in the statute, and nothing to
show that the Legislature contemplated that upon the water rate
requiring to be reduced the benefit of that reduction should be
given to those out of the non-compulsory limits. On the contrary, the Commissioners by the express words of the statute
" shall and are hereby required to make a reduction on the
" domestic rate within the compulsory limits."

Lord Ardmillan.—But then in regard to the compulsory
limits, there is a further qualification, that wherever no more
than 1s. is charged the reduction shall be equalised over the
whole within the compulsory limits on both sides. You have an
ultimate equalisation within the compulsory limits. Beyond the
compulsory limits you have no such equalisation. It is left to
stand on the prescriptive rates to be levied.

Solicitor General.—It is so; there is power to levy up to those
rates to which I referred, but the important part is this, that the
statute obviously recognises that in carrying out this work they
are carrying it on for the immediate benefit of the ratepayers
within the compulsory limits.

Lord President.—Have the inhabitants beyond the compulsory
limits any representation in this body?

Solicitor General.—I cannot answer that question precisely.

Mr. McLaren.—The Commissioners are the town council.
The non-compulsory ratepayers would be beyond the municipal
boundaries.

Solicitor General.—The inhabitants of Renfrew and Barrhead
would also be beyond the municipal boundaries.

Lord President.—I can understand that some of them would be beyond the limits, but I wanted to know if the whole of those beyond the compulsory limits were also beyond the municipal boundaries.

Mr. McLaren.—I shall find that out from the statute.

Lord President.—I think the proposition now maintained seems to be that these Commissioners, as representing the inhabitants within the compulsory limits, may make a very good thing of the concern, and out of the people beyond the compulsory limits, and that whenever the Commissioners get them into their hands they may use them for the benefit of the people within the compulsory limits.

Solicitor General.—That is the nature of the undertaking.

Lord President.—That is a thing that could be done under the statute, although I don't say that it has been done, or that it is likely to be done.

Solicitor General.—They have no representation beyond the second section, which provides that it shall include the city of Glasgow and the royal burghs of Rutherglen and Renfrew, and the burghs Partick, Pollockshaw, Govan, &c. (*Reads* section 93.)

Lord Armillan.—The sixth clause constitutes the magistrates and council of the city the Commissioners.

Solicitor General.—Yes.

Lord President.—Suppose the Commissioners, who represent the inhabitants within the compulsory limits, were so to deal with this assessment as to make the people beyond the compulsory limits contribute the whole sinking fund, that would be making a profit for the people within the compulsory limits, but that would require to be established as matter of fact.

Solicitor General.—Possibly, but I am not saying that that fact does exist. I am speaking to the character of the trade they are carrying on. I say they are carrying on a great work, the work of supplying water. They are supplying water, and the policy of the Act has been dictated by the consideration that water is required as a necessity in every house. The only other consideration which has entered into it is that the inhabitants of Glasgow and surrounding district would be better supplied with better water at a cheaper rate than by leaving the supply in the hands of those companies on the north and south sides of the river as they had existed. One object they desired to attain was the bringing in, as they are authorised to do by this Act, a large supply of fresher and purer water from Loch Katrine. It was not only intended to absorb previously existing companies and previously existing sources of supply, but to add a new and very great source of supply, and to do that if possible at prime cost to the inhabitants.

Lord President.—Do you suppose they use the old sources of supply?

Solicitor General.—I have no doubt they use them for manufacturing and other purposes, but not for domestic consumption.

Lord Ardmillan.—They save the fresh water by using the old water for manufacturing purposes, and that I think is quite legitimate.

Lord Mure.—The Gorbals Gravitation Company spent an enormous sum of money. The gravitation works on one estate alone cost them 40,000*l.*

Solicitor General.—In one of the agreements with the burgh of Renfrew, which had an agreement with the Gorbals Gravitation Company, the Commissioners are to be held liable and subject to like obligations and agreements as the Gorbals Gravitation Company would have been prior to the passing of this Act, and the said agreement is ratified and confirmed. It is provided that " it shall not be lawful to supply," &c. (*reads down to* " Glasgow Waterworks "). Then there is a power given to sell water for the purposes of trade by measure, or according to such terms as can be agreed upon between them and the consumer. Then the persons who are within the compulsory limits, and who are compelled to take the water and use it,—for it is hardly presumable, unless they have inveterate objections to the water, that they will not use it when obliged to pay for it,— are to receive the benefit of other powers conferred on the corporation for distributing the supply, because the statute contemplates that it is these ratepayers who are paying the domestic, which is the leading rate no doubt; those who pay the domestic rate within the ` compulsory limits are the persons under section 92, who are required to be benefited by the Commissioners if the receipts of the company are raised to such an extent as to make them exceed what is absolutely required to meet the annual expenses. Now, my Lord, my contention is this, that though called a rate, that is a consideration given for something supplied by a public company, constituted for the benefit of the ratepayers who are the beneficiaries. I admit that they are not members of the company, and that they have no control over the directors. The direction and management of the undertakings are vested in the corporation. Those interested as beneficiaries have no way of influencing the directory except by means of exercising their privileges in returning members from each ward. But these persons, the representatives in council, have been constituted into a separate corporation to give the supply to every house within the limits, upon the statutory consideration that it is only by joint action that the benefit can be secured, and with the limitation that it shall not be in the power of the company to charge beyond a certain rate, which represents little more than the cost of procuring it, and bringing it into the dwelling-houses of the ratepayers. And this differs entirely from the case of a rate for the purpose of meeting a public burden, in respect that the corporation should supply one of the necessaries of life at a reasonable price from year to year, and that if they themselves shall find that it is not a concern which is not exempted from the provision of the Income Tax, that it is not all a burden, that it is an advantageous arrangement for the ratepayers, that they are getting sufficient consideration for it, and that in any one year, on paying a reasonable price, that reasonable price exceeds the cost of production, that must be taken and dealt with as profit for the year.

Lord Ardmillan.—Your argument has a good deal of force as applied to that proportion of rates collected from the non-compulsory ratepayers; but supposing you are right there, has that the effect of making the whole income subject to the Income Tax?

Solicitor General.—My contention is that those within the compulsory limits are getting a consideration or paying it; and I say there is no distinction between an excess directed to be carried to the sinking fund, and that which is kept for the sinking fund; because if these are the profits you have first to determine whether the surplus, arising in a concern of this kind, is a surplus of the nature of profits. The purpose for which it is applicable settled by the case of the Attorney General *v.* Black is of no consequence whatever. It is immaterial whether applicable to general purposes or whether applied by the Legislature to particular purposes. What you have here is, as was contended in the case just mentioned, a special purpose. The Legislature does not allow us to deal with these profits as profits, and to dispose of them as we please. They are directed to be applied to a particular purpose. One of the judges in Exchequer, where the cases were subsequently decided, Baron Martin, said, " The consideration for the grant of the duties," &c. (*reads*). In the Exchequer Chamber, Montague Smith, now member of the Judicial Committee, said, " I am of the same opinion," &c. (*reads*). Whenever you get it, it is not the less of the nature of a profit because it is directed according to the ordinary rules of mercantile dealing. The surplus is dealt with as a profit, and as profits frequently are dealt with by public companies and private companies and traders, when a certain proportion of or the whole of the profits of a particular year are devoted to the extinguishing the capital debt of the company or trade or a certain portion of it. Therefore I say that the application of part of what they have made by the introduction of water and the keeping up of the supply is not the less a profit arising from their carrying on that particular kind of trade or business, it is not the less a profit, I say, because it is applied in extinction of the capital debt borrowed for the purposes of the undertaking; and on these grounds I have to submit that the determination of the Commissioners of Revenue is right.

JUDGMENT.

Wednesday, 26th May, 1875.

Lord President.—This is a case stated for opinion of the Court by the Commissioners of Property and Income Tax of the city of Glasgow. The Glasgow Corporation Water Commissioners were charged under Schedule D. of the Income Tax Act with duty upon profits to the amount of 17,032*l*. 15*s*. arising for the year 1872-3 upon their undertaking; and they maintain the sum of 17,032*l*. 15*s*. does not consist of profits arising upon their undertaking, and is not assessable to income tax under Schedule D. For the purpose of answering this case it is necessary to attend very particularly to the constitution of this Water Corporation Commission, and to the clauses of the statute by which it was brought into existence. It is a Local Act, 18 & 19 Vict. c. 18, an Act which was obtained by the citizens of Glasgow for the purpose of obtaining a liberal supply of good water for the city, as we all know by the importation into the city of the water of Loch Katrine. The Commissioners for executing the Act are the municipal corporation; but in so far as this question is concerned, and in so far as regards their powers as Water Commissioners, they are a separate corporation. The first step that was necessary in prosecution of the design of that statute was to buy up two old companies who had been in the habit of supplying the town with water, one on the north side and the other on the south side of the Clyde, and accordingly the new corporation not only bought up the whole works of these two companies, but they also bought up the stock of the companies, and paid for this acquisition in the form of annuities to the shareholders of the two companies. It became necessary also to provide money for the purpose of executing the necessary works for bringing in the water of Loch Katrine, and it seems to have been estimated that that would cost somewhere about 700,000*l*.; and accordingly a power is given to the commissioners to borrow money to that extent. The old companies were bought up, the annuities were granted, the money was borrowed, and the works have now been executed for several years and are in active operation. The next question to attend to is what is the revenue of the Commissioners under this statute. They are required by the Act of Parliament to meet once a year, and make up an estimate of the probable expense for the year of the whole undertaking; and for the purpose of meeting that, they are empowered to levy a rate, which is called the domestic water rate, from the occupiers of all dwelling-houses within the municipal boundary, which is otherwise called in the statute the limits of compulsory supply. That rate is laid on according to the rental of the dwelling-houses. Besides that they are empowered also to impose a public water rate, not exceeding a penny in the pound on the full annual value of all premises whatever, not dwelling-houses only, but every kind of premises within the same limits; and, as regards what are called the limits of compulsory supply, these rates are payable whether the inhabitants of the district within these limits choose to use the water or no. In addition to that the Water Commissioners are entitled also to deal with the inhabitants of a certain district beyond the limits of compulsory supply, and to give them water if they chose to have it; and if they chose to have it, they are also empowered to lay on a rate upon these parties; and the rates thus raised, whether within the limits of compulsory supply or beyond them, are to be applied in the first place for the payment of current annual expenses of keeping up the undertaking and conducting the supply of water to the city,—in short, all ordinary current expenses. They are also applicable, of course, to the payment of interest upon the money borrowed on mortgage, and to the payment of the annuities which have been granted to the shareholders of the old water companies. There is a further provision that after the lapse of ten years there shall be a sum at the rate of 1*l*. per cent. upon the total amount of the money borrowed upon mortgage, paid over into a sinking fund for the redemption of the debt, and after the lapse of 20 years a sum of 30*s*. per cent. is to be paid over into the sinking fund for the same purpose. If, after providing for all these purposes, there is any surplus of the income for any year, the Water Commissioners are required to apply it in making a reduction on the amount of the domestic water rate for the next year; and therefore, any surplus which they may have after providing for these purposes must be carried into the next year's account, so to be applied.

Now the sum of 17,032*l*. 15*s*., upon which the charge is made under Schedule D. of the Income Tax Act, comprehends the whole portion of the revenue of the Water Commissioners which is applied towards the formation of the sinking fund, in redemption of the annuities and mortgages in the manner that I have already mentioned, and also the balance, if any, which is carried forward to the following year's account to be applied as the Act directs in reducing the domestic water rate; and the question is whether income arising from this assessment which is appropriated to such purposes is assessable for income tax under Schedule D. as profits of this water undertaking. I am humbly of opinion that it is not. It seems to me that this is an Act of Parliament by which the citizens of Glasgow have undertaken, through this water corporation as their representatives, to assess themselves for a very important public purpose—a purpose very conducive to their own comfort and well-being—to obtain a good supply of water for the city. In so assessing themselves they had not in view certainly to make profit by the undertaking. On the contrary, what they have distinctly in view is, to pay money in order to obtain this particular benefit. They are not, therefore, trading in any commodity, nor are they entering into any undertaking for the use of property that is to be attended by a resulting profit, or a beneficial interest accruing to any individuals or to any corporation. The object of the assessment is to pay for bringing in the water, and when that is done the assessment and the authority to levy it come to an end. If in the progress of the operation of this Act the city of Glasgow is in so happy a condition that they can afford to reduce their assessments to a mere fraction of a penny, that must be done under the operation of the statute. If that fraction of a penny is sufficient to pay the current expenses of maintaining this Water Commission and the works under their charge, and I suppose, if by some wonderful scheme of good management, they should so contrive that they would be able to get water for nothing bye and bye, then the right to levy assessment would come to an end altogether. But one thing at least is perfectly certain, that it is made matter of absolute statutory regulation that the expense of supplying this water, including all the various items of expenditure that I have already mentioned, and the revenue, are to be kept actually commensurate and equivalent, as near as possibly can be, and that being practically impossible in every year, the way in which the same object is achieved is by carrying over any surplus of one year into the next year, and employing it in reducing the assessments, and so in reducing the revenue for the next year. Now, it seems to me, that it is not within the contemplation of Schedule D. of the Income Tax Act to charge any portion of a local rate raised for such a purpose as profit or as anything else falling within that Schedule D. The case is entirely different from those that have been cited, which have been decided in the Court of Exchequer in England, because in those cases the statute which gave the right to levy the assessment did not impose it upon the citizens of the particular burgh or locality which obtained the Act. It was not an authority to the citizens of a particular locality to assess themselves. On the contrary, it was a right and privilege given to a particular corporation to assess everybody—the whole public who happened to import in the one case coals into the burgh, and in another case to import something else, I forget what it was. But there it must be observed the corporation of the particular burgh, or the Commissioners—for it does not matter in the least degree which they were—were making a profit out of a tax levied upon the lieges generally, and were applying the proceeds of that tax for the benefit of the community which they represented; and, therefore, they were held, most justly, I think, to be making profit, no doubt not for individual benefit but for corporate benefit, and for the benefit of the community represented by the administrative body that levied the tax.

I have only farther to say that if any attempt had been made here to discriminate between that portion of the revenue which arises from the rates levied within the limits of compulsory supply, and that portion of the revenue which is raised in the district beyond the limits of compulsory supply, I should have been very glad to attend to any grounds which might have been urged for such a distinction. It was said no doubt in argument, but rather by way of illustration of the general claim than anything else, that this corporation does in a certain sense trade in water and sell it to those people who are outside the limits of compulsory supply,—that it is a matter of traffic with them, and what they derive from them in the shape of rates may perhaps be fairly represented as coming within the denomination of profit, —of revenue derived from the use of a certain subject of which they are the administrators. But it appears to me that that question does not arise here. We have not before us the means of seeing what the result of the transactions between the. Water Commissioners and the persons beyond the limits of compulsory supply are or have been. We don't know that any surplus has arisen from these transactions. Most certainly we know that the only sum which is here charged with income tax does not represent anything in the nature of profits derived from that special source, but on the contrary represents the whole part of the revenue of the Water Commission which is devoted by Parliament towards the formation of a sinking fund, and which has been directed *quoad ultra* to be carried forward to the next year's account. I therefore give no opinion upon any question which may arise perhaps hereafter as to the portion of the revenue of this Water Commission which may be derived from those parties who lie outside the limits of compulsory supply But as the case stands I am against the deliverance of the Commissioners, and I think it must be quashed and the assessment disallowed.

Lord Deas.—If there are any profits made here I think it quite clear they must be profits made by the ratepayers, because there are not two parties,—the corporation on the one hand and the ratepayers in the other. The corporation is the mere trustees, hand and instrument of the ratepayers. There is no room therefore for saying that the corporation can make profit. That is impossible. The whole question is, are the ratepayers making profit? Now, as your Lordship has pointed out, if you confine your attention, as it is right to do in the first instance at least, to the bounds of compulsory supply, I do not see how it is possible to say that the ratepayers are making any profit. They are paying for the water, and once the water is paid for, even if it becomes free, there is no profit made. If that be so, the only question that could well have been raised, would have been that which your Lordship has latterly alluded to, viz., whether the ratepayers were making profit by selling the water to parties beyond the compulsory bounds. Now, there is no evidence that they are making profit of that kind. If they be. it is certain that this 17,000*l*. odd does not represent that profit. That profit may be within the 17,000*l*. for anything I can tell, but that sum certainly does not represent the profit. I entirely concur with your Lordship that questions which may be raised about assessing the profit made beyond the bounds of the compulsory supply are not before us, and I am not prepared to give any opinion as to how far that may be liable for assessment. The assessment at all events could not be upon the 17,000*l*., but upon something very much smaller than that. I need hardly say that in coming to this result I would not be supposed to indicate an opinion against what was done in the poor law cases quoted, and more particularly in the case of Adamson against Clyde Navigation Trustees. I see that I wrote the opinion in that case, which was substantially adopted by all the Judges, with one exception, and affirmed in the House of Lords, and it would be very strange if I were to say anything against that opinion, and I certainly am not doing so. But the differences between that case and this are sufficiently clear from the explanation which your Lordship has given of the facts of this case. I entirely concur in the views stated by your Lordship, and I have nothing further to add.

Lord Ardmillan.—I have very little to add to what your Lordships have said, for I entirely concur. I have only two observations to make. Where the area of taxation and the area of distribution exactly correspond, where a rate is raised for a public purpose, and the whole of what is collected is applied to that public purpose, I take it that that is what is meant by the English judges when they speak of a distinct rating or assessment; and in that case there could be no income which could be chargeable with income tax. Further, where there is an excess of revenue over the necessary expenditure for distribution, if a company voluntary use that excess of revenue to pay off their debt by the formation of a sinking fund, a question might very well be raised whether that, being their voluntary use of funds which would have been profit if not so applied, they might not still be liable for income tax, but that is not the case here. The statute and not the will of the company applies the whole excess to the creation of the sinking fund, and the statutory result of the application of that money is the ultimate diminution, and it may be the ultimate extinction of the assessment; for if ever it came to this that the water could be got for nothing there would be no assessment. The statute therefore charges the appropriation of the money, and that being the case I do not think that this sum of 17,000*l.* applied under the powers of the statute and by direction of the statute to the purposes of the statute can be considered as income. A separate question might arise, but it is not now before us, in regard to the sum raised from the non-compulsory district, as it is called, *i.e.*, the district beyond the compulsory area, it being said to be used to some extent for the benefit of those in the compulsory district. A curious question may be raised as to whether the fund raised beyond the line and used for the benefit of those within the line does not to some extent partake of the nature of income as profit. All I say now is that that question is not raised here, and we are not at present called upon to deal with it. I have formed no opinion upon it and I reserve my opinion upon it. I think it is a nice point, but it is not now before us.

Lord Mure.—I concur in the result which your Lordships have arrived at, and substantially on the same grounds, reserving of course my opinion on the question which may possibly some day or other be raised as to money collected or profits made beyond the compulsory boundary. That is not before us in my view of the case now.

Determination of the Commissioners reversed. and assessment disallowed.

APPENDIX TO PART III.

COURT OF EXCHEQUER, ENGLAND, January 24 and 26, 1871.

ATTORNEY GENERAL, Informant, *v.* BLACK, Defendant.

Income Tax Acts, 5 & 6 Vict. cap. 35, Schedules A. and D.—"Rate or duty" on coal.—Local Improvement Acts.

A "rate or duty" on coal landed on the beach, or otherwise brought into the town of B., and originally directed to the maintenance of sea-walls, was granted by a local Act to the corporation of B. Coals which were sent beyond the limits of B. were exempt from the rate. By another Act the rate was increased, and it was enacted that any surplus from it should be devoted to aid the rate for paving, watching, lighting, &c., the town of B. A subsequent Act, repealing the former Acts, empowered the corporation of B. to buy lands, widen streets, build a town hall, raise a general district rate, and continue to impose the "rate or duty" on coal, and enacted that all rates, duties, assessments, and impositions authorised by the Act should be consolidated into one fund, and be applied to the general purposes thereof.

Held, that this "rate or duty" was a profit within Schedule (D.) of 5 & 6 Vict. c. 35, (quære, a profit arising out of an hereditament within Schedule (A.) of the same Act), and consequently liable to duty under the Income Tax Acts.

JUDGMENT.

KELLY, C.B.—I am of opinion that the Crown is entitled to our judgment. To arrive at a proper decision on the question before us we must discover the substantial effects of all the acts relating to it, and not allow ourselves to be guided by any one particular Act. The question here is, are the Income Tax Commissioners entitled to tax a rate or duty on coals granted under certain Acts of Parliament to the Corporation of *Brighton?* This duty is stated to be at the rate of 3s. on each chaldron of coals landed on the beach of, or in any other way brought or delivered within the limits of, the town of *Brighton*, and it is said that the duty amounts yearly to the sum of £10,000. Now *primâ facie*, such a sum, if granted to a private individual, viz., the Duke of *Norfolk*, would be subject to income tax, and, therefore, the question arises is there anything in the nature of the duty or the objects to which it is applicable that relieves it from the liability to income tax? Now, I am of opinion that if the nature of the duty and the objects to which it is applicable be good tests by which to solve this question there is nothing in them to free the duty from income tax. It is contended that the duty is to be applied to parochial purposes, and that money so applied is raised by rate, which rate is no doubt not subject to income tax, and it is further said that the money arising from the duty in question is amalgamated with the other moneys which are raised by way of rate from the town of *Brighton*; but this argument is met by the fact that this money is applicable, and has, in fact, been applied to much larger purposes, viz., the purchase of land, the extension of the market, the enlargement of streets, the erection of a town hall, &c. Now there can be no doubt that money raised for such purposes from other sources would be subject to income tax; why, therefore, should not this money be equally subject? Coupling this consideration with the nature of the duty itself, I feel no doubt that it comes within the express words of the income tax. The argument against the Crown, founded on the word "rate," which it was contended must mean a rate as now popularly understood levied by overseers and not chargeable with income tax, comes to nothing when we find that the word occurs in 12 Car. 2. c. 4. s. 6, and is there used as equivalent to custom dues. The only remaining question seems to be, is this "rate or duty" a rate in substance, that is to say, a tax on the inhabitants of *Brighton*, still more on those among them who are alone otherwise rateable? I think it is nothing of the sort. The incidence of the tax on each ton of coal landed on the beach at *Brighton* or brought by land and delivered within the town of *Brighton* is upon the importer of the coal and upon him alone. Let us follow the coal further; is it sold only to the inhabitants of *Brighton?* Certainly not; the importer doubtless sells much of it to persons residing out of the limits of *Brighton*, and although on such sales he is entitled to a return of the duty, yet it does not appear that there is any corresponding difference in the price charged by him to the consumers of coal in or out of *Brighton*; again, does he sell this coal to the rateable inhabitants of *Brighton* alone? Certainly not; he sells to all indiscriminately, and among the residents of *Brighton* a large proportion of the coal consumers are not rateable at all. It cannot, therefore, be argued that this "rate of duty" is a rate by which *Brighton* taxes herself in the same sense as she taxes her householders for the maintenance of the poor, the lighting her streets, and for her police force, but it is an annual profit to which the Corporation of *Brighton* is entitled, and is therefore, on every construction of the words of the Income Tax Acts, liable to duty under those Acts.

MARTIN, B.—I am of the same opinion. The first question is whether a rate levied on all coal delivered in *Brighton*, and granted by certain Acts to the corporation of that town, is chargeable with income tax? I say, without any doubt on the subject, that it is chargeable. The question depends on whether the sum levied by the rate is "property" or "profits" within the meaning of 5 & 6 Vict. c. 35. s. 1. By that Act the Legislature intended to include every description of property or profits whatsoever. There are five schedules to the first section. Schedule A. includes all land, tenements, and hereditaments. Now I think this tax is included in the word "hereditaments," but I will not enlarge on that point, as, on the view which I take on this question, it is unnecessary to decide. Schedule B. is directed to the "occupation" of lands, tenements, and hereditaments; Schedule C. speaks of profits coming from annuities, dividends, &c.; Schedule D. is about the annual profits or gains arising from any kind of property, or from any profession, trade, or employment; Schedule E. comprises all offices or employments of profit, and all annuities, pensions, &c., payable by Her Majesty. Now, all these Schedules taken together would seem a sufficiently large net to include every description of property; but to prevent any doubt we have section 100, which imposes a duty on every description of property or profit not contained in the foregoing schedules. In fact, the care displayed in embracing every possible source of profit is, I may say, carried to an almost ludicrous extent; it is practically impossible to escape the operation of the Act. Now, as to the authority for the levy of this tax, I think it depends on 13 Geo. 3. c. 34., and not on the later Act, 6 Geo. 4. c. 179., as *Mr. Manisty* contends. The preamble of the latter Act, after reciting the object of certain former local Acts, the appointment of local improvement commissioners, the improvements which they had effected, the increase of the town, the necessity of further improvements, and the necessity of imposing additional rates, repeals the former Acts, and under section 117 consolidates into one fund, applicable to the general purposes of the Act, all rates, duties, tolls, &c., authorised to be imposed under the Act. *Mr. Manisty* contends that, by virtue of the 117th section, the "rate or duty" here in question has become in its nature like those rates which are not subject to income tax, and has lost the quality of a "toll." But the consolidation effected by section 117 has not, in my opinion, at all altered the question of this "rate, duty," or toll; and in fact it appears from the special case that the corporation of *Brighton* do actually pay income tax on rent issuing out of their corporate lands, which rent is carried into the general fund. I am, therefore, of opinion that, as this rate is not affected by being brought into the general fund, we must look, not to the Act of Geo. 4., but to that of Geo. 3., to trace its origin and discover its object.

Now, by the Act the Commissioners are empowered to pave, light, and cleanse the streets, and are for these purposes to raise an assessment on the occupiers of property. They are empowered to purchase land for and establish a market in the town. It appears that the corporation has purchased land for and established a market in the town, and we know, as I have said, that on the property thus created by the Act the corporation does pay income tax; the Act further states that, for the purpose of repairing and preserving groyns to protect the town from the inroads of the sea, certain commissioners are to be appointed as trustees for such purpose, and in order that they may be duly supplied with money, it is enacted that after the 24th of June 1773, they should be empowered to receive 6d. for each chaldron of coal brought by sea or land into *Brighton* and there consumed. The commissioners are to appoint persons to receive this duty, and no collier ships are to leave the Port of *Brighton* without the discharge and receipt of such persons for the impost on the coal. It appears, therefore, to me that this "rate or duty" is a tax on property to which, if the erection or preservation of the "groyns" had not cost one farthing, the corporation of *Brighton* would be equally entitled. This tax may be compared to that levied on ships passing a certain light-house. I personally know of many instances in which corporations are entitled to levy sums of money of which the expenditure is not immediately connected with the subject-matter on which such sums are levied. I therefore think that *Mr. Manisty's* argument that, as this tax is levied for a particular and specific object, it is therefore not subject to the income tax, is untenable. I am therefore of opinion, that this is a "property or profit," coming within the meaning of 5 & 6 Vict. c. 35, and consequently that the corporation of *Brighton* must pay income tax upon it.

KELLY, C.B.—My Brother *Channell* has been called away by election petition business, but desires me to say that he entirely concurs in the judgments of my Brother *Martin* and myself.

EXCHEQUER CHAMBER, June 17, 1871.

ATTORNEY GENERAL *v.* BLACK.

Proceedings in error—Judgment affirmed..

BYLES, J.—After having paid every attention to the argument, I am of opinion that the judgment of the Court of Exchequer must be affirmed. These duties are at all events in the nature of tolls under 5 & 6 Vict. cap. 35. sec. 60., Schedule A., No. III., Rule 3; it is plain that they, in the first instance, fall on the importers. It is not necessary to enquire as to their ultimate incidence. They are levied for the relief of the taxpayers at Brighton. On this ground I am of opinion that the judgment of the Court of Exchequer was right, and that it ought to be affirmed.

BLACKBURN, J.—I am of the same opinion. The words of 5 & 6 Vict. cap. 35. ss. 60. and 100. are very wide, but I do not think that they attach to everything. I think they would not apply to a borough rate or to a highway rate. I do not consider the latter analogous to the classes of property alluded to in section 60, Schedule A., and in Section 100, Schedule D., but, in my opinion, the duties in the present case are similar to these classes of property; the words in Schedule A., No. III., Rule 3, "fishing, rights of markets and fairs, tolls, railways, and other ways, "bridges, ferries, and other concerns of the like nature," are worthy of remark. I do not think that the object with which the toll is levied makes a difference, and the duties are strictly within the words of Schedule A. I think, also, that the duties may be described as falling within the meaning of the word property, as used in Schedule D.

KEATING, J.—I am of the same opinion. How can these duties be said to resemble a district rate imposed by the inhabitants of a place upon themselves? It is difficult to distinguish these duties from harbour dues. I agree that the object with which the duties are levied can make no difference.

MELLOR, J.—I am of the same opinion. These duties are much more like harbour dues than district rates.

SMITH, J.—I am of the same opinion. These duties cannot be regarded as taxes; they are tolls. I am not satisfied that the contention on behalf of the corporation of *Brighton* is correct.

LUSH, J.—This is a profit within the meaning of the Income Tax Act. It has been granted by Parliament, and is payable by importers, whether it is needed for the purposes of the Act or not. I am clearly of opinion that these duties fall within the meaning of the terms "profit" and "property."

Judgment affirmed.

IN THE EXCHEQUER, 16th January, 1873.

THE ATTORNEY GENERAL *v.* SCOTT (CHAMBERLAIN OF THE CITY OF LONDON).

Income Tax Acts, 5 & 6 Vict. cap. 35, and 16 & 17 Vict. cap. 34.—Profits of Municipal Corporations under Schedule D.—Deductions.—Principle of Assessment.

The Corporation of the City of London derived a large annual income from renewal fines, profits of markets, corn and fruit metages, brokers' rents, and Mayor's court and other fees. The receipts from these several sources, after deducting the cost of collection, were carried to a general account from which was deducted the whole expenditure of the Corporation for the civil government of the city, including the maintenance of the police, &c., and the balance was returned by the Defendant (the proper officer of the Corporation) as the profits of the Corporation chargeable under Schedule D.

It was admitted at the trial that the renewal fines were chargeable in the ordinary matter under Schedule A., No. 2, Rule 5, of 5 & 6 Vict. cap. 35, but, with this exception, it was contended that the Defendant's return was correct.

Held by the Court (Lord Chief Baron *Kelly* and Barons *Martin*, *Bramwell*, and *Pollock*):—

That the profits of the Corporation derived from market tolls, corn and fruit metages, brokers' rents, Mayor's court fees, &c., are liable to income tax under Schedule D., without reference to the purposes to which they are applied; and that the proper principle upon which the assessment should be made is to take each item or head of income separately, and to assess the income tax upon the net produce of such item, after deducting from the gross receipts the expenses incurred in earning and collecting the same.

PART IV.

10th July 1875.

Income Tax.—Master marmer, trading between Glasgow and foreign ports, having a house for his wife and family in Glasgow, liable for assessment on salary, notwithstanding he is abroad for the greater part of the year.

CASE stated on the Appeal of Captain H. Young, Master Mariner.

AT a Meeting of Commissioners for General Purposes for the Lower Ward of Lanarkshire, under the Property and Income Tax Acts, held at Glasgow, on the 23rd April 1875.

Mr. H. Young, Master of the Steamship "Olympia," belonging to Henderson Brothers of Glasgow, appealed against an assessment for the year 1874–5 made upon him under Schedule D. of the income tax in respect of his salary as master mariner, on the ground that he had not been resident within the United Kingdom for a period of three months during the year of assessment.

5 & 6 Vict.
cap. 35. sec. 39.
16 & 17 Vict.
cap. 34. sec. 5.
37 Vict.
cap. 16. secs. 8, 9, and 10.

It was stated on behalf of the Appellant that he trades between Glasgow, the Mediterranean, and New York, and that the greater part of his income is earned upon the high seas, and beyond the limits of the United Kingdom; that his arrivals in and departures from the United Kingdom were as follows:

	Period of residence in United Kingdom.
He left Glasgow for New York on 20th March 1874 — — — — — Arrived from New York on 17th May 1874 —	11 days.
Left Glasgow for New York on 28th May 1874 Arrived from New York on 5th July 1874 — Left Glasgow for New York on 21st August 1874 — — — — — Arrived from New York on 28th September 1874 — — — — —	47 „
Left Glasgow for Mediterranean and New York on 13th October — — — Arrived from Mediterranean and New York on 19th January 1875 — — —	15 „
Left Glasgow for Mediterranean and New York on 3rd February 1875— Arrived from Mediterranean and New York on May 1875 — — — —	15 „
Total — — —	88 days.

And that his detention in the United Kingdom during the year of assessment was, on account of dull trade, double that of previous years.

That he was therefore only a temporary resident in the United Kingdom during the year of assessment, and as such entitled to exemption under the 39th section of the Act 5 & 6 Vict. c. 35.

It was further stated on behalf of the Appellant that he had been allowed exemption on these grounds in previous years, and that the Board of Inland Revenue had in several instances ordered repayment to persons charged under circumstances similar to those of the Appellant.

The surveyor replied that Captain Young is the tenant of a house in Glasgow, occupied by his wife and family, and by himself when in this country, and must therefore be held to be domiciled in Scotland. That, under the section of the Act referred to, he is only a temporary absentee, and "notwithstanding "such temporary absence," as that given above, "chargeable to "the duties granted by the Act as a person actually residing in "the United Kingdom upon the whole amounts of his profits or "gains, whether the same shall arise from property in the "United Kingdom or elsewhere, or from any profession, "employment, trade, or vocation in the United Kingdom or "elsewhere," and that, even if Captain Young were only a temporary resident within the meaning of the Act, and as such had claimed exemption, he would become chargeable to income tax if he returned to the United Kingdom on or before the 5th day of April next after such claim had been made.

The Commissioners having considered the whole case were of opinion that the Appellant was assessable, and therefore confirmed the assessment, with which decision the Appellant declared his dissatisfaction, and craved a case for the opinion of the Court of Exchequer.

JUDGMENT, 10th July 1875.

Lord President.—This assessment was laid on under Schedule D. of the Income Tax Act, and it is an assessment upon the annual profits or gains arising or accruing to any person residing in Great Britain from any profession, trade, or employment, whether the same shall be carried on in Great Britain or elsewhere, and the only question is whether the person assessed in this case is resident in Great Britain. There is no doubt that his case in every other respect is within the terms of Schedule D. Now the expression in the Schedule regarding residence is very simple. The words used are "a person residing in Great Britain "or elsewhere." There are a great many persons who do not leave their places of residence very often, but there is certainly a much greater number of persons who are constantly leaving their places of residence. These people belong to various classes, and I suspect that this latter class is increasing every

day with the activity and restlessness of the present time.
Therefore anything like continuous residence is not a thing that
this statute can be held to contemplate at all, if by continuous
residence were meant constant personal presence in one place.

I think, therefore, that all the cases that have been cited on
the construction of the 76th section of the Poor Law Act have
no application whatever to the present case; and that we must
deal entirely with this statute in reference to the natural and
proper meaning of the words. I have no doubt myself that if a
man has his ordinary residence in this country, it does not matter
much whether he is absent for a greater or a shorter period of
each year from that residence or from the country itself. That
is a thing that depends a good deal on a man's occupation, or it
may be on his tastes and habits, especially in the latter case, if
he is a man not requiring to be engaged in business for his maintenance. There are many people engaged in such business and
who are taken constantly away from home, such, for instance, as
travellers; and there is one class of people very well known in
the political or diplomatic world who would escape taxation
altogether if there was anything like permanent residence in
this country required for bringing them within the meaning of
the Act. I mean the Queen's messengers. I have not heard that
these people have not a residence in this country and are not
assessable under the income tax.

The class to whom this Appellant belongs is a very extensive
class, and the question raised here is one of very great importance. He is the master of a trading vessel, a trading vessel
belonging to this country and hailing from the port of Glasgow;
and when he is not at sea the Appellant resides in Glasgow, and
when he is at sea he is represented in that residence in Glasgow
by his wife and family. Now, that he has, in the ordinary and
plain meaning of the words, a residence in Glasgow is, in these
circumstances, I think, clear beyond all doubt, and it is equally
clear upon the facts stated that he has no residence anywhere
else, unless a ship can be called a residence, which I rather
think it never has. A residence, according to the ordinary
meaning of the word, must be a residence on shore, a dwelling
in a house. A residence is a dwelling-place on land, and the
only dwelling-place on land which this Appellant has is in
Glasgow, where, as I said before, he dwells when at home, and
where his wife and children dwell when he is at sea.

The 39th section of the statute consists of several parts, and I
think the only part of it which is of much importance in this
present question in the view of construction is the first, which
provides that any subject of Her Majesty, whose ordinary residence shall have been in Great Britain, and who shall have
departed from Great Britain and gone into any part beyond the
sea for the purpose of occasional residence at the time of the
execution of the Act shall be deemed, notwithstanding such
temporary absence, a person chargeable with the duties granted

by this Act as person actually residing in Great Britain. Now, a doubt has been raised whether that portion of the section applies to the present case, whether a man who trades between Glasgow and New York can be said, when he goes to New York in the course of business, to have departed from Great Britain and gone into parts beyond the seas for the purpose only of a place of residence. It is not necessary to determine that. I confess I should rather be inclined to say that he does fall within that description; but supposing that he does not and that this portion of section 39 does not apply to the case of the Appellant, still it affords most important light in construing the word "residence" in Schedule D., because it shows the meaning of residence in this statute is ordinary residence, an ordinary residence, the continuity of which may be broken by persons going elsewhere and having an occasional residence there, but who though they are held, while occasionally residing abroad, to be only temporarily absent are nevertheless held to be actually residing in Great Britain. These are the important words in this section, and I think they throw a great deal of light on the meaning of the word "residence" used in Schedule D.

I do not entertain the least doubt, in short, that the ordinary residence of a party in this country fixes his liability to this taxation, although his absence from that residence may be during any year, of a very prolonged description, although not being of a necessarily prolonged description, that is to say, not fixed in such a determinate way that his presence or residence in some other country is not more enduring than his residence in this.

In the present case we have it stated that the absence of the Appellant from the United Kingdom is, in one year as compared with another, longer or shorter on account of the briskness or dulness of trade, and therefore, it is a mere accident that calls on a captain to be absent from his residence in any one part of the year. All these, I think, are within the meaning of this statute temporary absences, because I do not think a temporary absence necessarily means something shorter than the presence of the party in this country. Temporary absence may be for a very long time, and I think it may be temporary because it may be in prosecution of some special purpose.

I think I have very little doubt on the construction of this statute taken by itself. I am struck with the appositeness of the case cited by my brother, Lord Ardmillan, a case which comes very near to this in principle. In that case the execution by a messenger was required by the statute to be made at the dwelling-house of the party cited. It was made by leaving a copy with the father of the party, "within his said father's said "dwelling-house in Newburgh, with whom he lives and resides "when not at sea, and was given to him because he could not "find himself personally." The Judges in that case sustained that execution as a good execution at the dwelling-house of the

party a term which I think is almost entirely synonymous with
residence. In that case the Lord President said, " where a man
" lives and resides in his dwelling-house. An execution bear-
" ing the citation so left at Blackhouse or Whitehouse where the
" debtor lives and resides would be clearly sufficient, and saying
" this is his father's house is only descriptive," &c. Lord Mackenzie said, " the construction I put upon it is that he has his
" residence at his father's house. Every sailor has a residence
" on land. We have no persons who are born and live and die
" upon the water," &c. Lord Jeffrey said, " there are many men
" whose businesses are peripatetic. They are less in the bosom of
" their families than less fortunate men," &c. Now these views
of the construction of the word dwelling-house are perfectly
applicable to the word " residence " under this statute ; but the
construction of the statute itself, apart from authority, is quite
satisfactory and conclusive, and I am, therefore, for affirming
the Commissioners' judgment.

Lord Deas.—The assessment is laid on under the words that
occur in the first section of the Act under Schedule D., in the
following terms : " The assessment is to be laid " (*reads down to*
" elsewhere "). Now the main question is whether the Appellant
is residing in Great Britain in the sense of the enactment, and
there is a second question, whether, if he does come under that
enactment, there is anything in section 39 to take him out of it.
My opinion is that he does come under that enactment, and
in considering that question, I look entirely at this particular
statute. The question is, what is the meaning of these words
according to this particular statute ? I am disposed to think
that the argument on both sides with reference to the Poor
Law Acts is only calculated, if it is calculated for anything at
all, to mislead. If you get any light from these decisions at all
it is very apt to leave you uncertain. As your Lordship observed
in the course of the discussion, the tax under the Poor Law Act
was not a tax identical with the present. The Poor Law Act
lays a tax on a particular class of individuals, but we are here
dealing with a statute which lays a tax on a whole population
who are in the particular position to which it refers, a war tax,
and, as we had occasion to find recently, a tax from which it is
unlawful to stipulate for exemption. That is the sort of tax I
take it to be, and, although a taxing Act upon particular classes
of individuals has to be very strictly construed, we must keep in
mind in administering an Act of this kind that the great
principle comes in that there is to be equality of liability among
all the parties for whose benefit it is laid on. Therefore,
although this is a taxing Act, I think there is no more inference
to be drawn from that in favour than against liability.
I do not see how it can be doubted that this man is residing
in Great Britain if he has a residence anywhere. He is residing
in Great Britain, and I do not think it requires the aid of
decisions or authority to come to the conclusion that he has a

residence. Then I think it is equally clear, though it requires a little more examination, that there is nothing in section 39 to exempt him. He does not come under the first part of the section 39, that is to say, he does not go into foreign parts beyond the seas for the purpose of occasional residence. He must live at the port he trades to for a considerable time. He may live on shore or on board the ship according to his mind, but he goes there, not for occasional residence, not for residence at all, but for the purposes of his trade. Therefore, I am clearly of opinion that he is not, within the meaning of these words, " a man who " goes beyond the seas to foreign parts for the purpose of occa- " sional residence." If I am right in that, that disposes of the first part of section 39, and if so, it is equally clear that the Appellant is not within the proviso, because it applies to gains from possessions in Ireland, secondly from foreign possessions, thirdly, to gains from securities in Ireland, and fourthly, to gains from foreign securities. Now none of these apply to this party, for his gains are not within the four things I have described. The result of this is that he can derive no benefit from section 39, and it is enough to remark that if any light is to be derived from that section it is in favour of the Crown, and not in favour of the Appellant. With these views of these two sections I entirely concur with your Lordship that there is no ground for differing from the deliverance of the Commissioners.

Lord Ardmillan.—I express my entire concurrence in the remark of Lord Deas on the subject of the construction of a taxing Act of this kind. There is no doubt that an Act which taxes is to be strictly construed. Where there is an Act taxing a particular body, or laying a tax upon a particular article, of course that Act is to be strictly construed, but where there is an Act taxing the whole of Her Majesty's subjects, and the question is, whether it is to be construed so as to sustain the equality of the incidence of the tax, I think there is no presumption in favour of that exemption and against the equality of the incidence of the taxation. It is the next and soundest principle of taxation to be as equal as possible, and I cannot recognize, as a presumption against that equality, what has been urged to-day, or that from what has been urged we are to favour the Appellant with exemption. In the next place, I agree in excluding from considerations the questions under the Poor Law Act as applicable to this case in the interpretation of the income tax. Captain Young is a British subject. He is in the service of a Clyde shipping company. He commands a Clyde ship, and while he is on the deck of that Clyde ship and discharges his duty in the service of that Clyde shipping company he is certainly doing nothing to weaken his connection with the Clyde, on the margin of which he leaves his wife and family. The ship hails from the Clyde and is registered there as a Clyde vessel, and Captain Young is a British captain doing duty on deck of a British ship belonging to a British shipping company.

In the next place he has done nothing to change his residence. He had no other residence in any part of the world except on the deck of the ship and in Glasgow, and in Glasgow he leaves in his house his wife and family. Now, I do not think we can recognize in a question of this kind that he lives so entirely on the sea as to have no residence on the land. A man living on the sea and having a house on shore, and if he is a married man his house is on shore, is shown by the case which I quoted in the course of the discussion to reside on the shore, although he might be at sea for a time. But, taking the first part of the statute only to be the subject, and that the party is not a resident elsewhere, the choice is betwixt his having no residence, and that residence which he has engaged for his wife and family, which I believe is his true residence, and I think, therefore, that the Appellant is liable to assessment.

Lord Mure.—I have had no difficulty in coming to the same conclusion.

It appears that this Appellant is a British subject, who derives salary from a British ship, from a company of merchants in Glasgow.

His wife and family have a residence there, and it is not said that his residence was not there at the date when he took command of that ship. His absences were such as occurred in the prosecution of his profession, in a vessel engaged chiefly in foreign service, but in the intervals between those absences he always resided personally in the house he rented for his wife and family in Glasgow, and during the period to which this case relates, it is admitted that he was in the house for a period of 88 days, or about three months out of 13 months, and that during the whole of that time he never resided elsewhere. Now, I am very clear that that is a residence which plainly brings this gentleman under the provisions of Schedule D. of the statute quoted by Lord Deas. In the circumstances, the only question we have to decide is, whether the 39th section exempts him from the provisions of Schedule D. I concur with your Lordships, and I think the counsel for Captain Young admitted that the proviso in this section does not in any respect affect the question. The question may, however, possibly be affected by the first paragraph of the 39th section, but, as I read it, so far from exempting a party in this situation, it contains language which stamps his liability, because it says : " be it enacted, that any " subject of Her Majesty whose ordinary residence shall be in " Great Britain," that is the position of the Appellant at the time he went away, " and who shall have departed from Great " Britain and gone into parts beyond the seas for occasional " residence." It is a nice question, in view of the words " occa- " sional residence," to say whether a man who takes command of a ship and takes it to another place goes there for that purpose. He may be going to one port or to another, but I assume in the meantime that he is to be held as a person under these words. The statute goes on to say, that he "shall be "deemed, notwithstanding such temporary absence, to be a "person chargeable thereby." By the express terms of the statute liability is imposed, and indeed this part of the statute seems to have been framed to meet such cases, and I am on these grounds clear that the judgment of the Commissioners is right.

Judgment of the Commissioners affirmed.

PART V.

No. 14.—In the Exchequer.—England.
29th January 1876.

HENRY FORDER (Surveyor of Taxes) ... ... Appellant,

and

ANDREW HANDYSIDE AND COMPANY, LIMITED ... Respondents.

Income Tax.—Company carrying on the business of Iron-founders not entitled to deduction of amount written off for depreciation of buildings, fixed plant, and machinery.

CASE stated on the Appeal of Andrew Handyside and Company, Limited, against an assessment under Schedule D., made on them by the Commissioners of Income Tax for the District of Morleston and Litchurch, in the county of Derby, 7th August 1875.

POINTS FOR ARGUMENT.

FOR THE APPELLANT.

1. That in estimating the nett profits earned by the company in their business as iron-founders, under the provisions of the Income Tax Acts, the Respondents are not entitled to make any deduction on account of the depreciation of their buildings, fixed plant, and machinery.

2. That the amount sought to be deducted by the Respondents on that account in fact represents a portion of the capital invested in the business, and as such is not allowed to be deducted by the express provisions of the third rule under the first case of section 100, Schedule D., of the Income Tax Act (5 & 6 Vict. c. 35).

FOR THE RESPONDENT.

1. That the Respondents' company not having been working more than one year, the Respondents were justified in assuming that the average outlay for repairs for three

For the year 1874-5 an assessment under Schedule D. was made by the Commissioners for the district above named upon Andrew Handyside and Company, Limited, a company carrying on the business of iron-founders in the parish of St. Alkmund in Derby. The assessment made upon the company was 8,642l., the amount taken from their own report, and therein specified at nett profits; but in this amount a sum of 1,509l. 7s. 6d. is shown as "amount written off for "depreciation of buildings, fixed "plant, and machinery."

The Appellants, on their appeal on the 29th June 1875, produced a balance sheet for the year ended on the 31st July 1874, being their first year of trading, and objected to the charge in respect of the 1,509l. 7s. 6d., and contended that, inasmuch as such sum had no real existence, but was

A

years would be greater than the amount actually expended in the first year. and that the sum of 1,509*l*. 7*s*. 6*d*. might be treated as added to the actual amount expended in that year to arrive at the average expenses on account of repairs.

2. It being assumed that the buildings, machinery, and plant having become of less value to the extent of 1,509*l*. 7*s*. 6*d*. than they were at the commencement of the year's work, that sum must be struck off the receipts of the company to arrive at the profits and gains which were made by the company during that year.

3. That the deduction of the said sum of 1,509*l*. 7*s*. 6*d*. was not a deduction in respect of capital.

written off in the accounts in accordance with the articles of association, as the works must of necessity depreciate. from year to year, and as the sum expended in repairs could not entirely replace such depreciation, they were justified in writing off that amount as a deduction.

The surveyor objected that the sum appealed against was a deduction in respect of capital, and as such was contrary to the provisions of the third rule of the 100th section of the Act 5 & 6 Vict. c. 35, that no allowance for depreciation was provided for in the said Act, and that section 159 prohibited any deductions being made except those expressly enumerated in the Act.

The majority of the Commissioners, however, being of opinion that persons in trade were equitably entitled to write off from their profits each year a sum of depreciation, and that the amount claimed was fair and reasonable, decided in favour of the company.

The surveyor, being dissatisfied with such decision, has requested that a case for the opinion of the Court should be stated.

The opinion of the Court is therefore desired as to whether the Appellants are justified in making, and should be allowed, the deduction of 1,509*l*. 7*s*. 6*d*. claimed by them for depreciation.

JUDGMENT, 29th January 1876.

Kelly, C.B.—Whatever we may think of the justice and fairness as regards commercial or manufacturing interests, as to some parts of the Act of Parliament upon which there is no case before the Court, and upon which I do not feel myself at all at liberty to comment, it is perfectly clear that upon this Act of Parliament, that is to say, upon the third rule in the first case as regards Schedule D., the Respondents, the traders, are not entitled to this deduction. It appears that by the articles of association there is a provision in the 138th article, at page 40, that a reserve fund is to be formed, and before recommending a dividend, and of course therefore before paying a dividend, the company, perhaps, very prudently and properly, agree to set aside a sum from the nett profits of the company, and bear in mind that it is out of the nett profits of the company, and that they are nett profits before they begin to set it aside, and this is merely the mode in which they think fit to apply a portion of what are admittedly by their own expression their nett profits,

they may set aside out of the nett profits such sum as a reserve
fund for the purpose of meeting contingencies. But what are
they? They are a variety of matters which they have no more
right to deduct from the nett profits, and say that the nett
profits are thereby diminished, and that they have not really
netted that amount of profits, than they would have a right to
deduct a sum which they might spend upon the purchase of a
house or of a carriage. What they say is, that it is " for the pur-
" pose of meeting contingencies, or of purchasing, improving, en-
" larging, rebuilding, restoring, reinstating, or maintaining the
" works, plant, and other premises or property of the company."
Now I leave out the word "repairing," because it is admitted
that they are entitled to deduct, and they have deducted, a certain
sum for repairs, and we must take it for granted, as there is
no appeal against that deduction on the one side or the other,
that it is a proper deduction according to the Act of Parliament.
Therefore, there being that deduction for repairs, they may set
aside a portion of those nett profits for the purpose of improving,
enlarging, and rebuilding the works and premises. They cannot
claim to deduct that amount from the nett profits. I will
suppose that they have realised 2,000l. nett profits in the year.
If they chose, instead of spending that sum upon their own
establishments, and upon the maintenance of their families, to
lay out half of it on some new building, so as to extend their
works, it is an expenditure of a portion of the nett profits. The
words of the article proceeds as follows : " or the erection or construction of new buildings, works, or plant, or for equalising dividends." If they have made a nett profit of 2,000l. in the year,
and if they set aside a portion of it for the purpose of equalising
dividends, it may be said that that is not to be taxed. They can
so set it aside, and apply it to any of these many purposes. They
are nett profits before they have a right to apply any portion of
them for any of the purposes named. Then the article says " or
in furtherance of any of the objects of the company," and then
they say, " the reserve fund, or such part thereof for the time
" being as is not invested as herein-after provided, may be used
" for the general purposes of the company. The interest of the
" reserve fund " (that is in case it should be invested) " shall
" be treated as annual profits of the company." That would be
this—if they choose to apply 500l. out of the 2,000l. by investing
it in the 3 per cents., and they get interest upon it, though that
interest would pay the income tax, the company may constitute
a portion for a child out of the profits, and yet, according to the
view of the Respondents, it is not to be treated as profits. It is
perfectly clear that they have set aside 1,509l., or thereabouts, as
applicable to all these purposes, and how that money has been
actually applied we know not from the case. It is clearly
against the Act of Parliament to allow this deduction; for what
says the Act of Parliament? The Act is quite explicit, and
can admit of no doubtful or difficult construction; it is, that

"in estimating the balance of profits and gains chargeable under
"Schedule D., or for the purpose of assessing the duty thereon,
"no sum shall be set against or deducted from—or allowed
"to be set against or deducted from—such profits or gains on
"account of any sum expended for repairs of premises occupied
"for the purpose of such trade, manufacture, adventure, or con-
"cern, nor for any sum expended for the supply of repairs or
"alterations of any implements, utensils, or articles employed
"for the purpose of such trade, manufacture, adventure, or
"concern beyond the sum usually expended for such purposes,
"according to an average of three years preceding the year in
"which such assessment shall be made." Now just let us suppose
that this business had been carried on for three or four years,
and that the average sum actually expended for the necessary
and usual repairs had been 500l. a year, they would then be
entitled to deduct from the amount of nett profits 500l. The
average of the expenditure upon the repairs for the past three
years would be about the same amount in the year to come, and
therefore that would be very fair and just, because what was the
average of three years they would expect to expend in the ensuing
year to the year in question, and that would be deducted from
their profits. Here it is said that the case is different because
they have been in business for one year. There being no specific
provision applicable to that the result is this, that if you are to
take the average of the three years to determine how much may
be expected to be expended in repairs in the year to come, and if
there are not three years, and not even two years, but only one
year, you must get the best information that you can, and must
judge from what has been done during that one year what will
be the probable amount expended in the ensuing year. If there
be any special provision it is the one which has been referred
to, where it becomes a matter of inquiry before the Commissioners: but here it is perfectly clear that that is not the question, because the question is not what sum has been expended
upon repairs, inasmuch as it is admitted that a sum is set aside
as a deduction from the nett profits in respect of the repairs in
the ensuing year, and therefore the question remains whether the
Respondents are entitled to deduct this entire sum of upwards of
1,500l., which may be applied anywhere or at any time they
please for a great variety of purposes which are actually forbidden, directly as well as indirectly, by this provision of the Act
of Parliament. All that they are entitled to deduct they have
deducted, namely, the reasonably probable amount of repairs in
the ensuing year, and no other deduction is allowed by the terms
of this Act.

Pollock, B.—I am of the same opinion. The only question
here is whether the amount written off for the depreciation of
buildings, fixed plant, and machinery, 1,509l. 7s. 6d., can be
properly deducted in estimating the income tax payable by
the company. Now, in my judgment, upon no construction of
the Act of Parliament can that deduction be made. Strictly

speaking, there is no difference between what is called an equitable construction of an Act and any other construction. It appears to me that upon the most favourable and just construction of this Act of Parliament for the Respondents, they are not entitled to this deduction. Now there are three modes to which this fund to meet the depreciation of machinery may be dealt with—one is by adding to the company's original capital what is called a depreciation fund; the second is by laying aside out of the annual ·profits which would be otherwise divisible among the shareholders a certain sum to meet the estimated depreciation; and the third is by waiting until the depreciation occurs, and then either repairing or reinstating the machinery so as to make it of equal value and efficiency to what it before was. Now it is not worth while to consider all the different cases in which the matter is applicable, and the varying degree in which it is applicable. It is unnecessary to say that there are cases where there is a renewal from week to week, and sometimes from day to day, but there are cases in which certain machines employed, or certain parts of machines, may cost many hundreds of pounds, and the depreciation of which does not occur actually from day to day, or is not appreciable from day to day; but it is in the case of breakage, or of other events occurring, and as to which there may be a statement from year to year. Now the way in which that would practically be met under this Act is this, whether the depreciation was small or great, and the consequent reinstatement small or great, it would all in the long run, supposing the concern to be a going one, be met justly and fairly under this Act of Parliament when the money was actually expended, because the words of the third rule under the first case of Schedule D. in the Act of the 5th & 6th Vict. c. 35. are, " nor for " any sum expended for the supply of repairs or alterations of " any implements, utensils, or articles employed for the purpose " of such trade, manufacture, adventure, or concern beyond the " sum usually expended for such purposes." Therefore, where drilling machines are employed it may be usual to have so many new drills per week, or at the end of a year, and then this provision would come in; it would be necessary and usual, as of course when a breakage occurs that breakage comes in the average of three years, however large the amount may be. In that way perfect justice would be done between the parties. Now, it may be said, that supposing it is not a going concern, and that there is a sale, there is a very great depreciation, but that depreciation does not affect any question arising under this Act of Parliament. A depreciation always takes place when a concern is sold, not as a going concern, but as a thing which has failed, and for some reason or other has stopped. Therefore justice is done in the matter, and the only question at the end is, whether this estimated amount laid aside from year to year as written off for the depreciation of buildings, fixed plant, and machinery comes within the words of the section. I think it quite clear that it does not, and that therefore the Commissioners in this case were wrong, and that consequently our judgment should be for the Crown.

Huddleston, B.—I am of the same opinion. It is quite clear, on reading the case, that the sum 1,509*l*. is a sum which a prudent person, no doubt, would put by or lay aside for the purpose of meeting what might be called the expenses of renewal. The articles of association clearly contemplate that it should be carried into the capital account as a reserve fund. The articles of association contemplate that the company might make use of this money, but if they did it would be in the capital account, appearing on one side as drawn or expended in the capital account, and it is quite clear that it would be treated for all purposes of book-keeping and for all usual purposes as capital. The Scotch case which has been referred to clearly includes that view, because of the two sums 5,000*l*. was to have supplied the building necessary for the new pit, which would be capital, and 4,000*l*. was there, as here, written off for the depreciation, and the Scotch Court thought that that clearly would be capital. Then, if it be so, it is quite clear that that comes within the third rule, and cannot be taken into account, and that third rule is rendered still more imperative by the 159th section of the Act, which says that no deduction shall be made other than those expressly enumerated in this Act. Therefore, this sum of 1,509*l*. 7*s*. 6*d*. ought not to be allowed, and therefore the company will have to pay income tax on 10,151*l*. 7*s*. 6*d*., which is the sum which they enter as profits, namely 8,642*l*. plus the amount which they claim to deduct, and which they otherwise have deducted, 1,509*l*. 7*s*. 6*d*. I therefore think that the decision of the Commissioners cannot be upheld, and that our judgment must be for the Crown.

No. 15.—IN THE EXCHEQUER.—ENGLAND.
29th January 1876.

THE IMPERIAL FIRE INSURANCE COMPANY   ... Appellants,
and
WILLIAM WILSON (Surveyor of Taxes) ...   ... Respondent.

Income Tax.—Fire Insurance Company not entitled to deduction from profits on account of "unearned premiums."

CASE stated on appeal of the Imperial Fire Insurance Company to the Commissioners for Special Purposes, Somerset House, 16th March 1875.

POINTS FOR ARGUMENT.

FOR THE APPELLANTS.

1. That the determination of the Commissioners is erroneous.
2. That upon the true construction of 37 Vict. c. 16. s. 4., and 16 & 17 Vict. c. 34, the Appellants are entitled to make yearly the deduction claimed.
3. That inasmuch as insurances are effected with the Appellants at all periods of the year, and their liabilities thereunder do not expire with the expiration of each year, the gross amount of premiums paid to the Appellants in any one year ought not to be credited to them as profits actually realised in that year.
4. That in estimating their annual profits the Appellants are entitled to deduct from the gross amount of the premiums paid to them within the year 35 per cent., in order to make fair allowance for the premiums so unearned at the expiration of the year, and to enter such per centage among the profits realised in the succeeding year.
5. That in estimating their annual profits the Appellants are entitled to deduct from the gross amount of premiums paid to them within the year such a sum as it would cost to re-insure those premiums which have not been exhausted during the year.

The directors of the Imperial Fire Insurance Company, of No. 1, Old Broad Street, in the city of London, gave notice of appeal to the Special Commissioners through Messrs. Oliver and Sons, their solicitors, by letter dated the 3rd of September 1874, against an assessment of 67,927l. made on them by the Commissioners for General Purposes, for the year ending 5th April 1875.

The Special Commissioners issued their precept, requiring statements of accounts for the three years preceding the year of assessment, and in reply thereto a statement was sent in, of which a copy marked A. is annexed.

The appeal was heard at this office on the 12th of February 1875, when Mr. Cozens Smith, general manager, Mr. Johnson, clerk in the accountant's office, and Mr. Oliver, solicitor, attended on behalf of the Imperial Fire Insurance Company, Mr. W. Wilson, the surveyor of taxes for the district, also attended on behalf of the Crown.

Mr. Oliver, the Company's solicitor, was informed that he could take no part in the proceedings, but

1. That for the purpose of assessing the income tax th° whole of the annual premiums received by the Appellants in any year ought to be taken into account as profits or gains of that year, notwithstanding that the risks covered by a portion of such premiums may extend into the subsequent year.

2. That the Appellants are not justified by the provisions of the Income Tax Act (5 & 6 Vict. c. 35), Schedule D., 3rd and 4th Rules, in making any deduction in respect of what is termed by the Appellants "unearned premiums."

that there was no objection to his remaining in the room.

The company originally returned a loss, or rather put in a statement instead of a return, dated the 19th of November 1874, showing a deficiency of 45,559*l.*, but afterwards they consented to pay on 42,340*l.*

The books of the company were produced (by Mr. Johnson), and showed that the accounts are made up to the 31st of December in each year, and that no notice is taken therein of unearned premiums; in other respects the figures in the statement corresponded with the books, and showed an average profit of about 67,000*l.* The Commissioners would not allow the introduction of the unearned premiums as they did not appear in the books, and as this was the first year in which they were taken into account by the company in making their return for income tax, the Commissioners confirmed the assessment on 67,927*l.*

Mr. Smith, being dissatisfied with the determination of the Special Commissioners, declared his dissatisfaction, and duly required the Commissioners to state and sign a case for the opinion of the Court of Exchequer.

A.

STATEMENT of PROFIT and LOSS for the years 1871, 1872, and 1873.

INCOME, 1871.	£ s. d.	£ s. d.	EXPENDITURE, 1871.	£ s. d.
Premiums	609,184 4 10		Losses	
Do. unearned in 1870	151,808 0 0	760,992 4 10	Expenses	
			Dividends to proprietors	
Interest on investments, &c.			Unearned premiums, 25%	201,000 0 0
	Balance			
		801,583 14 9		801,583 14 9

INCOME, 1872.	£ s. d.	£ s. d.	EXPENDITURE, 1872.	£ s. d.
Premiums	718,846 14 2		Losses	
Do. unearned in 1871	201,030 0 4	919,876 14 2	Expenses	
			Dividends to proprietors	60,000
Interest on investments, &c.			Unearned premiums, 28%	207,250 0 0
	Balance	41,768 16 1		
		1,006,307 19 5		1,006,307 19 5

INCOME, 1873.					EXPENDITURE, 1873.			
	£	s.	d.	£ s. d.		£	s.	d.
Premiums	663,526	10	5		Losses	575,335	2	6
Do. unearned in 1872	287,219	0	0		Expenses	231,097	7	1
				919,745 10 5	Dividends to proprietors	60,000	0	0
Interest on investments, &c.	45,793	17	8		Unearned premiums, 33%	225,283	0	0
					Balance	83,873	18	6
				965,539 8 1		965,539	8	1

	£	s.	d.
The company is assessed for the year 1874 on the average profits of the above three years at	55,973	1	4
Interest on investments, 1873, on which tax has not been paid	11,954	18	4
	67,927	19	8

	£	s.	d.
Should be	30,385	17	6
Interest on investments	11,954	18	4
	42,340	15	10

Imperial Fire Insurance Company,
1, Old Broad Street, London.

(Signed) E. COZENS SMITH,
General Manager.

JUDGMENT.

Kelly, C.B.—In the case of the Imperial Fire Insurance Company versus the Surveyor of Taxes, it is with some reluctance that I feel that we ought to give judgment in favour of the Crown. I say with reluctance, because it is impossible not to see that perfect justice cannot be done by giving our judgment in favour of the Crown, and, on the other hand, it is not to be forgotten that the scheme or mode of making out and settling the accounts suggested by the Insurance Company seems substantially, though it is not really unobjectionable, and perhaps it is the most reasonable mode that could be determined on in most cases, but it really would not be according to law. There is nothing in the Income Tax Acts which enables the parties in such a case, the Crown on the one side, and the Insurance Company on the other, to determine with certainty what is the amount or value of the risk which continues after the end of the year, while a number of policies upon which a year's premiums have been paid are exhausted, and where they may or may not be upon one, or two, or more, or all, losses to a large amount or a smaller amount, or no losses at all. Therefore, in the mode suggested on the part of the company, they are obliged to resort to a speculative mode of ascertaining the probable amount of the risks which continue, and I see no warrants in the Income Tax Acts, nor indeed in the principle of the law, which will enable us thus to act; and under these circumstances it seems to me that the case stands thus, unless we resort to the 133rd and 134th section of the Act which have been referred to, and which do not apply to this case. I mean the section, for example, which refers to cases in which the company do not carry on their business, but cease to act altogether, and are dissolved within the year in which the income tax is paid; but, as I have said, with the exception of those sections it appears to me that the case stands thus: The only mode in which you really can say what is

nett profit is by taking on the one side the actual receipts, and on
the other side the actual expenditure or disbursements; all that
remains is, at least for the time, profit; and, therefore, taking
the sum of 600,000*l.* as having been paid to the company and
received by them in the year 1873, and taking, on the other
hand, losses during that year to the amount of 300,000*l.*, expenses to the amount of 100,000*l.*, and interest upon the capital,
or some further disbursement which, it is admitted, should be
allowed, and which reduced the sum to 50,000*l.*, their profit at
that moment is 50,000*l.*; and if everything were to stop at once,
and if nothing further were done by the company, 50,000*l.* would
be the amount of the profit. It is open to this observation, however, and that is why this mode does not do, and I do not know
any mode which can do, perfect justice: it is this, that the
company remain under the liability of paying the amount of any
losses in respect of these policies upon which they have received
the 600,000*l.* premiums which may occur in the course of the
year, and if they do occur it is quite clear that they diminish
the amount of profit upon which the income tax has been
assessed and paid. But there is a provision for that in the Act.
and if they leave off business, the 134th section applies, and then
a calculation is made in which perfect justice upon the figures is
done. If, upon the other hand, they continue their business,
then at the end of the year 1874 they again take the amount of
the premiums which they have received on the one side, and they
take the expenses and any other sums properly set off against
the amounts received, and they take the amount of the losses
against which the 600,000*l.* has been received in the year before,
so that year by year, as they go on, there is an absolute balancing
of accounts; and it is only when the last year comes, if a last
year does come, when the company are about to cease to carry
on their business, that although they will have paid the income-
tax upon the same sum, 600,000*l.*, of premiums, they may leave
off business within a month, but they are liable to make good
any losses which may happen upon the policies in respect of
which the 600,000*l.* has been paid. But that, as I have said,
can happen only in the last year of the business being carried on,
and if that should happen, then by the 134th section there is a
provision for the fact being ascertained and the matter being
made clear in some way or other, and, if necessary, a deduction
being made. Therefore, looking at the very nature of the case,
and to the absolute impossibility of doing perfect justice, because
even if you were to take it upon an estimate on the report of
an actuary, which might be fair enough, if you take into account
the number of policies and the amount of premiums paid upon
them, amounting to some hundreds of thousands of pounds, it
would cost more money to get the calculations made by an
actuary, or by somebody else, than perhaps double the amount
of the income tax which has to be paid. I say, under these
circumstances, seeing that at the moment it is profit and that

if any wrong be done by losses afterwards occurring, that will be taken into consideration in the next year's account, it seems to me that the only way in which something as near to exact justice as possible can be carried into effect in a case of this nature is by taking the accounts as they are made out and adjusted and the income tax assessed. Under these circumstances judgment will be for the Crown.

Amphlett, B.—I am of the same opinion. I certainly was struck in the first instance with what seemed to me to be an apparent injustice in this mode of assessing the duty, but I saw, on further consideration, that the injustice, if any, was really confined to the first year when the company commenced business. In the first year there would no doubt be this injustice which has been pointed out by my Lord. They would be charged upon all the premiums,' though, as to some or most of those premiums, there would be a liability of loss, and in strictness that loss ought to have been taken into account in the first year when the business commenced. Not very much in*·*ry arises, because in the very next year, one year too late as f. as strict justice is concerned, those losses are all brought into he account, and are allowed as deductions to the company; it is ʌ ' a recurring loss. ·After you have once begun that system there is really no injustice at all for the subsequent years, unless it should happen that the business was an increasing business, and then, with regard to the increase of business done in any subsequent year, there would be a slight modicum of loss, the same as there was in the first year; but, on the other hand, if in any subsequent years the business diminished, this way of keeping the account would be in favour of the company; and I observe that in these three years there was in the last year a not inconsiderable reduction in the premiums received; in that case it is actually rather an advantage to the company than otherwise. Therefore, taking three years together, and taking the average, supposing that the business remains stationary, there is no recurring loss at all; the only thing is this, which my Lord has pointed out, if the business was stationary, the account would be perfectly accurate for this year, upon the average of the three years in this way of taking it; but assuming for the moment that the business did remain stationary, the only possible further injury which could be done would be after the last year. After the last year the company would have paid income tax upon the whole amount of the premiums, and then there would be some loss which would remain unaccounted for in consequence of their having ceased business. I have no doubt that under the section of the Act which has been referred to, if this Insurance Company should happen to come to an end of their undertaking, an allowance would be obtained from the Commissioners in respect of that loss which had not been taken into account during the year in which the premiums upon the policies were paid, and which would be a loss never brought into the account in favour of the

Insurance Company. I cannot, therefore, help thinking that really the inconvenience, at least now after the Insurance Office has been started for some years, is extremely small, and when you consider the inconvenience of having recourse to estimates and averages for the purpose of ascertaining how much contingent loss ought to be taken into account during the year in which the premiums are paid, I think that the Insurance Company themselves would find that they would gain nothing by now making any change of plan. If they find it to their interest to adopt a new system I by no means intend to say that if they choose at a future time to alter the mode of taking the accounts, and set aside, for instance, some fund to answer the contingent losses in the next year, if they choose to do that, and make it intelligible, I by no means say that they may not oblige the Commissioners to accept the accounts in that amended form. But they have not done so; they have kept the accounts, I have no doubt, in the most convenient way, taking the premiums as receipts in the year, and taking the actual losses incurred in that year as a payment, and striking the balance and calling the balance profit. It is not exactly accurate, but that is the way in which they have found it most convenient to keep their books between themselves and their own shareholders; and I therefore think that as long as they keep their books in that way the Commissioners have a right to apply the same rule in estimating the amount upon which they ought to be assessed. Under these circumstances I think that we ought to give our judgment for the Crown.

Huddleston, B.—I should have thought that the most convenient way for the Insurance Company to have kept the accounts would have been to have debited themselves first of all with the amount of premiums applicable to the risks of the year; that is to say, they might very readily have ascertained when the premium was paid, in whatever month it was paid, how much was applicable to the current year, and how much would be applicable to the risks to be incurred in the succeeding year, assuming them to be annual payments, and they might very readily have carried out a figure which would really represent the amount applicable to the risks of that year; that is to say, they might either in the first instance have taken the gross sum of the premiums received, deducting from it such proportion as would be applicable to the succeeding year, and having debited themselves with the balance, or they might have done it in the way in which it is suggested by the company that they do it here; they might have debited themselves with the gross sum, and then have credited themselves with the actual sum which would be applicable to the next year, and, in that case, I think that they probably would have got at the right gross profits. I do not see that in fire insurance such a course would be as difficult as in the case of life insurance. They have not, however, done so. What they have done is this: under these three years they have debited themselves first with the gross sum of the year, they have then added to it the sum with which they say they have credited themselves in the previous year, and then, adding to that the sum receivable from interest, they carry to the other side of the account, first their losses, next their expenses, and then their dividends, which are all proper items of deduction, and then they take an arbitrary sum which they say (we have no evidence of the fact whatever) would represent the unearned premiums, and they take that as something like 33 per cent. We have to decide whether the difference between the two sides of the account as stated by the company is " the " full amount of the balance of the profits or gains of such trade " upon a fair and just average of three years." They do it with reference to the three years. It is quite clear to me, looking at this arbitrary sum which they put on the credit side of the account, that they have not arrived at " the full " amount of the balance of the profits or gains of such trade " upon a fair and just average of three years." They have not kept their accounts in that way (that is found by the case) as between themselves and their shareholders, and I find it also stated in the case that " this was the first year in which they " (the unearned premiums) were taken into account by the com- " pany in making their return." Now an obvious inconvenience would arise, supposing at the expiration of the next three years the company should feel themselves justified in establishing a different mode of account; it might be that they would not carry to the debit of the first year of the three years that sum which they had carried to their credit in the years previous to the first of the three years, and then justice would not be done. I cannot help thinking that as the company have not in their accounts adopted this method of computation, as this was the first year in which they made this attempt at changing the accounts, they must be bound by their accounts, and really, as pointed out by my Lord and by my brother Amphlett, in the result, *communibus annis*, no injustice would be done. If they find that in one year there are great losses, they may, under the 133rd section, get the matter put right by the Commissioners. If they stop business they may, under the 134th section, obtain the proper return of what they have over-paid. On the whole I think, looking at the case as stated before us, that our judgment must be for the Crown.

Kelly, C.B.—I may add that it is not unworthy of consideration that the company have in their hands during the whole of the year, say 1873, from the time of the receipt of each premium, the premiums upon the whole of these policies, and so they have in the year 1874, until the losses with respect to the policies begin to be sustained. They possess the advantage, which is a great advantage to them. We do not think that this is a case for costs. Each party must pay its own costs.

[Judgment for the Crown.]

No. 16.—In the Exchequer.—England.

Octavius Jepson   ...   .   Appellant,
                      and
Frederick Wynne Gribble (Surveyor
   of Taxes) ...   .   Respondent.

*Inhabited House Duty.—Resident Medical Superintendent of a
Lunatic Asylum not liable in respect of the House provided
for him within the Grounds of the Asylum.*

Case stated by the Commissioners for executing the Acts
relating to the Inhabited House Duties, under and in pursuance of " The Customs and Inland Revenue Act, 1874,"
37 Vict. c. 16.

Points for Argument.

For the Appellant.

1. That the Appellant is not liable
to be assessed to the inhabited
house duty for the house
which he occupies as medical
resident superintendent of the
lunatic asylum.
2. That the said resident is part
of the City of London Lunatic
Asylum, and therefore not
liable to be assessed to the
inhabited house duty.

For the Respondent.

1. That the dwelling-house in
which the Appellant resides
is altogether separate and distinct from the buildings which
constitute the City of London
County Lunatic Asylum, and
consequently does not fall
within any of the exemptions
from house duty contained in
Case 4 of Schedule B. of the
Act 48 Geo. 3. c. 55.
2. That if the Appellant or other
medical superintendent of the
asylum resided in a house
situate beyond the precincts
of the asylum he would unquestionably be liable to be
assessed to the inhabited house
duty, and that the mere fact
of the Appellant's house being
situated within the grounds
of the asylum does not exempt
him from payment of the
duty.

1. Octavius Jepson, the Appellant, is the medical resident superintendent of the City of London
County Lunatic Asylum, situated
at Stone, near Dartford, in the
county of Kent.
2. The Respondent is the surveyor of taxes for the district in
which the said asylum is situate.
3. The said City of London
Lunatic Asylum is a lunatic
asylum established under an Act
of the 16th and 17th Vict. c. 97.,
and is a hospital and house provided for the reception and relief
of poor persons, that is to say, for
the " lodging, maintenance, medi-
" cine, clothing, care, and treat-
" ment of pauper lunatics."
4. The committee of visitors of
the asylum duly appointed the
Appellant to be the medical resident superintendent of such
asylum, under section 55 of the
last-mentioned Act, and by which
section he is compelled to reside
in the asylum. His duties are
defined by the Act.
5. The Appellant lives in a
separate and detached house built
upon ground within the boundary
of the asylum, as shown on the
accompanying plan, as the servant
of the committee, and which house is suitable and convenient

for the performance of his duties, and is allotted to him for that purpose. From the rear of the house the Appellant has ready and convenient access to the main buildings of the asylum by passing through a portion of the grounds of the asylum through a door or gate in the wall which encloses his garden on that side. The front part of the garden of the Appellant's house abuts immediately upon the public lane, so that he has direct communication with such lane without passing through the asylum. (The garden is enclosed on the right and left by brick walls, and in each of these walls is a door or gate leading into the asylum grounds.) The plan marked A., attached to the case, accurately shows the relative positions of the main buildings of the asylum, entrance lodge, and of the Appellant's house. The house is occupied by and was specially built as the residence of the medical resident superintendent of the asylum, and does not contain more accommodation than is reasonably necessary for himself and family.

6. The Appellant has been assessed for the year 1874, ending 5th April 1875, to the inhabited house duty upon 50l. at 9d. in the pound, making a tax of 1l. 17s. 6d. for such year in respect of the house in which he lives, under 14 and 15 Vict. c. 36.

7. Section 2 of the Act last aforesaid enacts that all exemptions contained in or enacted by any Act or Acts relating to the duties of assessed taxes with reference to the duties on inhabited dwelling-houses, according to the value thereof, as set forth in the Schedule marked B., annexed to the Act of the 48th year of King George the Third, and which were in force in regard to the said last-mentioned duties at the time of the repeal of such duties by an Act of the 4th and 5th William IV., c. 19, except as in the said Act of 14th and 15th Vict. c. 36. excepted, shall severally and respectively be and become in full force and effect with respect to the duties thereby granted, and shall be severally and respectively duly observed, applied, practised, and put in execution in the respective parts of Great Britain for assessing, raising, levying, collecting, receiving, accounting for, and securing the said duties by the said Act granted, and otherwise in relation thereto, so far as the same are or shall be applicable, and are not repealed or superseded by and are consistent with the express provisions of the said Act of the 14th and 15th Vict. c. 36. as fully and effectually, to all intents and purposes, as if the same exemptions were particularly repeated and re-enacted in the Act last aforesaid with reference to the duties thereby granted.

8. Case 4 of the exemptions in the Schedule B. annexed to the said Act of 48 Geo. 3. c. 55. is to the following effect: —
" Any hospital, charity school, or house provided for the recep-
" tion or relief of poor persons."

9. Such exemption was in force in regard to the duties under the said last-mentioned Act at the time of the repeal of such duties by the said Act of 4 & 5 W. 4. c. 19.

10. The Appellant contended before us that his said residence formed part of the said City of London Lunatic Asylum, and was therefore part of a hospital and house provided for the reception and relief of poor persons, and was exempt from house duty under case 4 of the exemption before mentioned.

11. The Respondent, on the other hand, contended that the residence of the Appellant was a separate and distinct house from the said asylum, although it was situated upon the asylum land, and therefore did not fall within the said exemption.

12. We decided, on the 18th November 1874, that the Appellant was not entitled to the above exemption with respect to his residence, but was liable to pay the sum of 1l. 17s. 6d. for such year that he has been assessed to the inhabited house duty. The Appellant, immediately upon our determination being given, declared his dissatisfaction to us, and duly gave us notice in writing to state and sign a case for the opinion of this Honourable Court, under section 9 of 37 Vict. c. 16, which we now do accordingly. The Court to be at liberty to draw inferences of fact if they think fit to do so.

13. The question for the opinion of the Court is—

> Whether the Appellant is liable with respect to his said residence to be assessed to the inhabited house duty?
>
> If he is liable judgment is to be given for the Respondent, but if he is not liable, then judgment is to given for the Appellant.
>
> Costs to be in the discretion of the Court.

H. B. RASHLEIGH.
FREDK. HEBERDEN.

JUDGMENT.

Kelly, C.B.—We must really look at these cases with the eye of common sense. A hospital means a lunatic asylum, or any house of that description " provided for the reception and relief of poor persons." This asylum is strictly within those words, and the question is, whether the residence of the medical superintendent is a part of the premises.

The point may be raised that it is necessary for it to be so; but whether it is necessary or not, here the house is really made a part of the premises; it is within the walls; it is part of the curtilage, in the language of the old law, and it is for the residence of a person whose attendance may be required at any moment, and who ought therefore to be at hand, and for that purpose it is put within the grounds; it is a part of the premises themselves, and with a ready, rapid, and almost instantaneous communication with the building which contains the lunatics. Under these circumstances, unless there were some decision upon argument in a public court decidedly against it, I should hold that there can be no manner of doubt that this is one of those cases in which the Legislature intended that that which is, substantially speaking, part and parcel of an asylum, or a hospital, shall be exempt from duty; and whether it happens to be worth a little more, or a little less, depends entirely upon the nature of the institution. With regard to any case which has been cited by the Attorney-General, the only one which seems at all to approach the present case is that in which the residence of some such officer was on the other side of the public highway, which it is clear formed no part of the premises themselves; it was no part of the asylum, and it was the same as if it had been at a distance from the property, and as if it had been necessary to cross a public highway, and the most ancient highway in the kingdom, to get to a place a mile off. There it was a matter of degree; here it is no matter of degree at all. Here I hold the house in question to be part and parcel of the asylum itself, and, as such, exempt.

Amphlett, B.—I am of the same opinion as my Lord, and for the reasons which he has given. I really should have had no doubt upon the question if there had not been authority; but I cannot help referring to the case of Congreve v. the Overseers of Upton. That was a rating case, and it has a very strong bearing upon the present case, because there the chief question turned upon whether the medical superintendent's house was in the asylum or not. It is very much the same case as here, where the question is, whether or not this house forms part of the asylum. I observe that in that case there were two appeals against the rate, one by the chaplain and one by the medical superintendent. They both had a house assigned to them in the asylum. The Court held, with regard to the chaplain, that it was not necessary that he should be resident; they could hardly say that his residence, though upon the grounds of the asylum, was a part of the necessary buildings of the asylum, but it was a mere matter of accommodation to him. But with regard to the medical superintendent, Mr. Justice Blackburn says, "The statute expressly directs that he shall be resident "in the asylum"; and then Mr. Justice Blackburn says, "Mr. Welsby argued that the words 'in such asylum' must be "construed to mean strictly within the curtilage of the building "where the patients sleep at night, a place which might be so "laid in an indictment for burglary. But that is not a "reasonable meaning of those words. They mean that his "residence must be in grounds appropriated to the asylum, so "as to be reasonably within it. Now, looking at the position "of the building as described in this case, we cannot say that "it was not *in the asylum*, if we once assume that it need not "be under the actual roof." For the same reason here, inasmuch as it is necessary for the proper conducting of the asylum that there should be a resident medical officer, whether that medical officer is accommodated by private rooms or by a house, and whether that house happens actually to form part of the building or not, it is a necessary adjunct to the asylum, and therefore it is a part of the asylum, and as the asylum is exempted, I think that this house must be exempted. The opinions of the judges have been cited. There is no case which exactly fits this case. The nearest, perhaps, is the one of the jailer's house. That was under different circumstances. It was not under any exemption, properly speaking, unless it was that a jailer's house should be considered as belonging to Her Majesty. Under the circumstances, there the judges seem to have thought that it did not fall within the exemption. That does not appear to me to have a very direct bearing upon this case. The question here is, whether this house is a part of the asylum premises, and I think that it is.

Huddleston, B.—I am of the same opinion. I think that the Appellant is entitled to our judgment. No doubt, as the Attorney-General has argued, under 14 & 15 Vict. c. 36, *primâ facie* duty would be payable on this house; and the question now arises, Does it come within the fourth case of the exemptions in the 48th of George the Third, c. 55, which exempts "any hospital, charity school, or house provided for the recep-"tion or relief of poor persons?" Upon that point it is not like the case to which Mr. Poland has called our attention. The case finds that the asylum established in this case was a hospital, and was a house provided for the reception or relief of poor persons. Then the only question which remains is, Was, in fact, this house, although a separate house, occupied by the medical officer, within the asylum? Now I agree that the whole of the grounds of an asylum form a portion of the asylum. The case finds that the house was built upon grounds within the boundary of the asylum; and the gardens and the recreation grounds, in the modern view taken as to the care of lunatics, are almost as essential for their care as the dormitories or the infirmaries or the other offices. Then I am satisfied, looking at the subject in a common sense view, and taking actually the strict words, that this house of the medical officer was within the asylum, and was a part of the asylum. I listened with respect to the cases cited by the Attorney-General. For one I wish to enter my protest against cases of that description being absolutely binding upon us. We have not the guarantee of a public reporter (no doubt they would be accurately reported, looking at the place from which they come), nor a guarantee that these cases have been laid before the public, where errors or mistakes might be corrected, and where we should have the sanction of a judicial decision upon argument, with the reasons stated to us. If those cases are to be referred to, I do not myself feel inclined to look at them; I do not think that any of them are conclusive in this case; they would not alter my view upon the case as stated before us, and upon the Act of Parliament; and I think that the Appellant is entitled to our judgment.

PART VI.

No. 17.—In the Exchequer.—England.
2nd February 1876.

The Calcutta Jute Mills Company, Limited - Appellants,

and

Henry Nicholson (Surveyor of Taxes) - - Respondent.

*Income tax.—Company registered under the Joint Stock
Companies Acts in England, where the Directors hold their
Meetings, and exercise the powers conferred on the Company by
those Acts and the Articles of Association, liable as a person
residing in the United Kingdom in respect of the whole of the
profits, whether made in England or elsewhere.*

At a Meeting of the Commissioners for the general purposes
of the Income Tax Acts, and for executing the Acts relating
to the Inhabited House Duties, for the City of London, held
at the Land Tax Rooms, Guildhall Buildings, in the said
City, on Thursday, the 18th day of March 1875, for the
purpose of hearing Appeals.

Mr. Maurice Bibby, secretary of the Calcutta Jute Mills
Company, Limited, appealed against an assessment under
Schedule D. of the Income Tax Acts, in respect of the profits
of the said Company for the year 1874, ending 5th April 1875,
in the sum of 25,000l., being the entire and aggregate gains and
profits made and realised by the Company as spinners and
manufacturers of jute as aforesaid in India.

It was contended, on the part of the Company, that the assessment should be merely upon that portion of the profits which
is remitted to this country and distributed among the shareholders in the United Kingdom, viz., 8,497l.

Case.

Points for Argument.

For the Appellants.

1. That under the circumstances
stated the Calcutta Jute Mills
Company is not a company
resident within the United
Kingdom within the meaning
and for the purposes of the
Income Tax Acts.
2. That the trade of the said Company is not exercised or carried

1. The Calcutta Jute Mills Company, Limited (herein-after called
the Company), was formed for the
purpose of taking over the business,
good-will, and plant of certain jute
mills at Ishera, near Calcutta, in
India, belonging to and then
carried on by a firm of merchants,
Messrs. Borradaile, Schiller, & Co.,
resident there.

on within the United Kingdom within the meaning and for the purposes aforesaid.

3. That under the said Acts the Appellants are liable to pay income tax only upon so much of the profits as are received by them for distribution amongst the shareholders in this country.

FOR THE RESPONDENT.

1. That the Calcutta Jute Mills Company, Limited, being an English Company registered in England, and having the registered office of the Company in England, is in the same position as a person residing in the United Kingdom, and is liable to income tax under Schedule D. of the Act 16 & 17 Vict. c. 34. in respect of the whole of the annual profits and gains of the Company, whether made in England or elsewhere.

2. That on the facts of this case the Company resides in the United Kingdom and not in India.

3. That the provisions of section 10 of 16 & 17 Vict. c. 34., relied on by the Appellants, apply only to the case of dividends payable by a foreign company or concern to shareholders residing in the United Kingdom, and have no application to the present case.

4. That the return made by the secretary of the Company, as stated in paragraph 14 of the case, is bad in law.

2. The Company was incorporated under "The Companies Acts, 1862 and 1867," on the 16th April 1872, with a capital consisting of 120,000l. in 6,000 shares of 20l. each.

3. By the articles of association (a copy of which accompanies and forms part of this case) the Company, so far as its affairs in the United Kingdom are concerned, is managed by a board consisting of not less than five directors. The directors have, *inter alia*, power to appoint one or more persons resident in Calcutta as "the Calcutta directors." As a matter of fact, there is at the present time one Calcutta director, Mr. George Muirhead Struthers, who is a large shareholder in the Company, and the acting partner of the firm of Messrs. Borradaile, Schiller, & Co., of Calcutta, the former proprietors of the mills.

4. On or about the 1st May 1872 the Company commenced business as spinners and manufacturers of jute at Ishera, near Calcutta aforesaid, and not elsewhere.

5. The buying of the raw material and the manufacture and sale of the same, as well as all the operations connected with the business of the Company in all its branches, are wholly and exclusively carried on in India, where alone the gains and profits of the concern (if any) are earned.

6. At the time of the purchase of the said mills the Company adopted an agreement whereby Messrs. Borradaile, Schiller, & Co., of Calcutta aforesaid, were constituted their managing agents in India, and they have had the entire control of its business and works at Ishera, near Calcutta. At the same time they guarantee the solvency of those with whom they deal, and receive a *del credere* commission from the Company in return.

7. There is an Indian as well as an English share register, and the largest amount of capital, as well as the greatest number of shares, are owned by persons residing in India.

8. On the 31st day of December last the share register stood as follows:—3,843 shares, representing a capital of 76,860l., were held in India and entered on the Indian share register, while only 2,157 shares, representing a capital of 43,140l., were held

by persons residing in this country and entered on the English share register.

9. The Company has no office or other place of business in the United Kingdom, although, for the purpose of registration, its address here is No. 4, St. Helen's Place, in the City of London. This is in fact the office of Mr. Ferdinand Schiller, one of the directors of the Company, and when meetings of the English members of the Company are held there it is entirely by his leave and favour.

10. All the Company's books of accounts, papers, and other documents, as well as its moneys, are kept, received, and dealt with by the management in India.

11. As a matter of fact, the Company has no property whatever in this country. Nothing comes into the hands of the English directors excepting what is remitted from Calcutta from time to time to defray their necessary expenses. In addition to this, such proportion of the profits realised in India as is divisible amongst the shareholders in the United Kingdom by way of dividend passes through their hands.

12. After receiving such proportion of the profits as is mentioned in paragraph 11, all that then takes place in England is that the directors call a meeting of the shareholders and declare the amount that is to be distributed by way of dividend amongst them for the then current year.

13. For the year 1874 the sums received by the directors in this country, as the proportion of the profits wholly made and acquired by the business of the Company in India, and payable to the shareholders in the United Kingdom, amounted to 8,497l.

14. In the said year the secretary of the Company duly made a return of that amount to the Commissioners for putting into execution the Income Tax Acts for the City of London as the true and proper amount upon which the Company was ready and willing to be assessed to the income tax. To the said return there is appended a statement of the manner in which the same was made or estimated, as follows:—"This return is made by "me as secretary of the Calcutta Jute Mills Company, Limited. "It includes the whole amount of the dividends or profits paid "or payable to shareholders residing in the United Kingdom "for one whole year, on a fair computation or average from "the commencement of the business of the Company on the 1st "May 1872, but not the dividends or profits paid or payable to "shareholders resident in the East Indies, and whose names are "entered on the Company's Indian share register. The trade "of the Company is that of jute spinners and manufacturers. "The only place of manufacture, as well as the place of sale, is "at Ishera, Calcutta. The Company neither buys, manufactures, "nor sells in the United Kingdom. The raw material is all "purchased in India, manufactured there, and sold there, where "also the entire profits are made."

15. The assessment to tax is leviable under Schedule (D.) of the Acts 5 & 6 Vict. c. 35., and 16 and 17 Vict. c. 34. Under

the former of these Acts (*see* section 1, Schedule D.) certain
duties " are granted to Her Majesty upon the annual profits
" or gains arising or accruing to any person residing in Great
" Britain from any kind of property whatever, whether situate
" in Great Britain or elsewhere . . . . and upon the annual
" profits or gains arising or accruing to any person residing in
" Great Britain from any profession, trade, employment, or
" vocation, whether the same shall be respectively carried on in
" Great Britain or elsewhere."

16. By section 40 of the first-mentioned Act it is enacted that
all bodies politic, corporate or collegiate, companies, fraternities,
&c., whether corporate or not corporate, shall be chargeable with
such and the like duties as any person would under and by
virtue of the said Act be chargeable with.

17. By 16 & 17 Vict. c. 34. the like duties as are referred to
in paragraph 15 are granted to " Her Majesty upon profits
" arising from property, professions, trades, and offices (*inter*
" *alia*), section 2, Schedule (D.), for and in respect of the annual
" profits or gains arising or accruing to any person residing
" within the United Kingdom from any profession, trade, em-
" ployment, or vocation, whether the same shall be respectively
" carried on in the United Kingdom or elsewhere."

18. By 5 & 6 Vict. c. 80. s. 2. persons entrusted with the payment of foreign dividends or annuities are required to deliver,.
for the use of the Commissioners of Taxes, true and perfect
accounts of the amount of the annuities and shares payable by
them respectively, and the said Commissioners are empowered
to make an assessment thereon under Schedule (C.).

And by section 10 of 16 & 17 Vict. c. 34., the provision so
made by the last-recited Act is extended to the assessing and
charging of the duties granted by the Act as well on such
dividends and shares of annuities as aforesaid as on all interest,
dividends, and other annual payments payable out of or in
respect of the stocks, funds, or shares of any foreign company,.
society, adventure, or concern, and which said interest, dividends, or other annual payments have been or shall be entrusted
to any persons in the United Kingdom for payment to any
persons, corporations, companies, or societies in the United Kingdom; and all persons entrusted with the payment of any such
interest. dividends. or other annual payments as aforesaid in
the United Kingdom. or acting therein as agents or in any
other character, are required to perform all such acts and things
in order to the assessing of the duties on such interest, dividends,
or other annual payments as are required to be done by persons
entrusted with the payment of annuities or any dividends under
5 & 6 Vict. c. 80., above referred to; and the assessment of the
duties on all such interest, dividends, and other annual payments
as aforesaid shall be made by the Commissioners for Special
Purposes under Schedule (D.).

19. By section 5 of 16 & 17 Vict. c. 34. the duties thereby
imposed are directed to be assessed under the regulations of the
statute 5 & 6 Vict. c. 35.

20. The duties granted by 16 & 17 Vict. c. 34. have been
continued at various rates by a series of subsequent Acts, and
the Act imposing the duty for the year 1874 is the 37 Vict. c. 16.

21. The Commissioners having regard to the articles of
association accompanying the case, and to the certificate of incorporation signed by the Registrar of Joint Stock Companies,
and also to the fact that the registered office of the Company
is in England, where the directors meet and direct and control
the main operations of the Company, were of opinion that the
Company is an English company formed under the Joint Stock
Companies Acts for carrying on an undertaking abroad, and is
by virtue of sections 40 and 192 of 5 & 6 Vict. c. 35. in the
same position as a *person* residing in the United Kingdom, and
liable, under the provisions of 5 & 6 Vict. c. 35. s. 1., and
16 & 17 Vict. c. 34. s. 2., to make a return of the whole of the
profits of any trade, whether the same shall be carried on in the
United Kingdom or elsewhere.

The Commissioners further were of opinion that the decision
in the case of the Imperial Ottoman Bank, in the Court of
Exchequer, is not adverse to, but, on the contrary, is confirmatory
of, the Crown's contention herein, the Court having decided that
the residence of a corporation must be regarded as the place
of its incorporation, which in the case of the Calcutta Jute Mills
Company, is within the United Kingdom.

That the 5 & 6 Vict. c. 80. s. 2., and section 10 of 16 and 17 Vict.
c. 34., referred to by the Appellants in this case, do not bear
upon the question at issue, the said enactments applying only
to agents or other persons *entrusted* with the payment of dividends or other annual payments payable out of or in respect of
stocks, funds, or shares of any foreign company, society, or
concern.

22. The assessment was accordingly confirmed upon the whole
of the profits of the Company, whereupon the Appellants expressed their dissatisfaction with such decision as being erroneous in point of law, and duly required the said Commissioners,
by notice in writing addressed to their clerk, to state and sign
a case for the opinion of the Court of Exchequer according to
the said statute 37 Vict. c. 16. s. 19, which we have stated and
signed accordingly.

23. The question for the opinion of the Court therefore is,
whether the Company is bound to make a return in respect of
all annual profits wholly made by its business in India, including the portion paid there to the Indian shareholders, and
is chargeable to income tax thereon, or whether, as is contended
on the part of the Company, the London directors are bound
only to make a return and to pay income tax in respect of so
much of the profits made abroad as actually pass through their
hands for distribution among the shareholders residing in the
United Kingdom.

No. 18.—In the Exchequer.—England.
2nd February 1876.

The Cesena Sulphur Company, Limited - Appellants,

and

Henry Nicholson (Surveyor of Taxes)   -   Respondent.

*Income Tax.—Company registered under the Joint Stock
Companies Acts in England, where the Directors hold their
Meetings, and exercise the powers conferred on the Company by
those Acts and the Articles of Association, liable as a person
residing in the United Kingdom in respect of the whole of the
profits, whether made in England or elsewhere.*

At a Meeting of the Commissioners for the general purposes
of the Income Tax Acts, and for executing the Acts relating
to the Inhabited House Duties, for the City of London, held
at the Land Tax Rooms, Guildhall Buildings, in the said
City, on Thursday, the 18th day of March 1875, for the
purpose of hearing Appeals.

Mr. Robert Larchin, Secretary to the Cesena Sulphur Company, Limited, appealed against an assessment of 5,834*l.* under
Schedule D. of the Income Tax Acts in respect of the profits of
the said Company for the year 1874, and realised by the Company in their business of sulphur miners and manufacturers, at
Cesena, in the Province of Torli, in the Kingdom of Italy.

It was contended, on the part of the Company, that the assessment should be restricted to that portion of the profits which is
distributed amongst the shareholders of the United Kingdom.

CASE.

POINTS FOR ARGUMENT.

FOR THE APPELLANTS.

1. That the Company is not a person residing within the United
Kingdom within the meaning
of Schedule D. to the Acts
5 & 6 Vict. c. 35. and 16 &
17 Vict. c. 34 respectively.
2. That residence in the United
Kingdom cannot be predicated
of a company within the meaning of the said Act.
3. That there is no one within the
United Kingdom who receives
any profits in respect of the
said Company's business other
than the amount of dividends
required for the shareholders
in this country.
4. That the profits, other than the
aforesaid amount of dividends

The Cesena Sulphur Company,
Limited (herein-after called "the
Company"), was founded for the
carrying on the trade or business
of sulphur miners, manufacturers,
or merchants at Cesena, in the
Kingdom of Italy.

2. The Company was incorporated under the Companies Acts,
1862 and 1867, on the 27th day of
October 1871, with a capital of
350,000*l.*, divided into 35,000 shares
of 10*l.* each, and was subsequently
registered in Italy for all purposes
in the following year, namely, on
the 1st day of November 1872.

3. By the articles of association (a copy of which accompanies

accrue outside the United Kingdom, and are received by persons not resident within the United Kingdom.

5. That no part of the profits of the said Company is liable to income tax except the amount of dividends distributed among shareholders in the United Kingdom.

FOR THE RESPONDENT.

1. That the Cesena Sulphur Company, Limited, being an English corporation registered in England under the Companies Acts, 1862 and 1867, and having also a registered office in England, is in the same position as a person residing in the United Kingdom, and is liable to income tax under Schedule D. of the Act 16 & 17 Vict. c. 34, in respect of the whole of the annual profits and gains of the Company, whether made in England or elsewhere.

2. That on the facts of this case the Company resides in the United Kingdom and not in the Kingdom of Italy.

3. That the provisions of section 10 of 16 & 17 Vict. c. 34, apply only to dividends payable by foreign companies to shareholders residing in the United Kingdom, and have no application to the present case.

4. That the contention of the Appellants, stated in paragraph 14 of the case, is bad law.

and forms part of this case) the Company, so far as its affairs in the United Kingdom are concerned, is managed by a board of eight directors, holding their meetings at the registered office of the Company in England. There is an Italian delegation, consisting of two or three members of the board resident in Italy, by whom all the practical management of the Company's properties and affairs is carried on.

One of the Italian directors is managing director of the Company, and resides at Cesena.

4. All the operations connected with the manufacture and sale of sulphur and wholly and exclusively carried on at Cesena, where the profits of the Company (if any) are earned, but the Italian members of the board are in constant correspondence with their co-directors resident in France and in England, who meet at the English registered office, No. 84, King William Street, in the city of London.

5. Transcripts and copies of the Company's books of accounts are sent to London, where the register of the shareholders prescribed by English law is kept, but all the original books of accounts of the Company and all its moneys are kept in Italy; the dividends required for the English shareholders being the only part of its profits which are sent to this country. The principal banking accounts of the Company are kept at Turin and at Paris; the London banking accounts being kept for the payment of offices and administrative expenses, and of dividends here.

6. The shares of the Company are divided between the English and foreign shareholders in the proportion of 8,924 held in England to 26,076 held abroad.

7. The assessment is made under Schedule D. of the Acts 5 & 6 Vict. c. 35., and 16 & 17 Vict. c. 34.: "Under the former " of these Acts (*see* section 1, Schedule D.) certain duties are " granted to Her Majesty upon the annual profits or gains arising " or accruing to any person residing in Great Britain from any " kind of property whatever, whether situate in Great Britain " or elsewhere, and upon the annual profits or gains arising " or accruing to any person residing in Great Britain from any

"profession, trade, employment, or vocation, whether the same
"shall be respectively carried on in Great Britain or elsewhere."

8. By section 40 of the first-mentioned Act it is enacted that
all bodies politic, corporate or collegiate, companies, fraternities,
&c., whether corporate or not corporate, shall be chargeable with
such and the like duties as any person would under and by
virtue of the said Act be chargeable with.

9. By 16 & 17 Vict. c. 34. the like duties as referred to in
paragraph 7 are granted to Her Majesty upon profits arising from
the property, professions, trades, and offices (*inter alia*), section 2,
Schedule D., "for and in respect of the annual profits or gains
"arising or accruing to any person residing within the United
"Kingdom for any profession, trade, employment, or rotation,
"whether the same shall be respectively carried on in the United
"Kingdom or elsewhere."

10. By 5 & 6 Vict. c. 80. s. 2. persons entrusted with the
payment of foreign dividends or annuities are required to deliver
for the use of the Commissioners of Taxes, true and perfect
accounts of the amount of annuities and shares payable by them
respectively, and the said Commissioners are empowered to make
an assessment thereon under Schedule C.

And by section 10 of 16 & 17 Vict. c. 34. the provision so made
by the last-recited Act is extended to the assessing and charging
of the duties granted by the Act as well on such dividends and
shares as aforesaid, as on all interest, dividends, and other annual
payments payable out of or in respect of the stocks, funds, or
shares of any foreign company, society, adventure, or concern,
and which said interest, dividends, or other annual payments have
been or shall be entrusted to any person in the United Kingdom
for payment to any persons, corporations, companies, or societies
in the United Kingdom so acting as agents, or any other character, are required to perform all such acts and things in order
to the assessing of the duties on such interest, dividends, or other
annual payment as aforesaid, as are required to be done by the
persons entrusted as aforesaid as are required to be done by the
under 5 & 6 Vict. c. 80., above referred to; and the assessment of
the duties on all such interest, dividends, and other annual payments as aforesaid shall be made by the Commissioners for
Special Purposes under Schedule D.

11. By section 5 of 16 and 17 Vict. c. 34. the duties thereby
imposed are directed to be assessed under the regulations of the
statute 5 & 6 Vict. c. 35.

12. The duties granted by 16 and 17 Vict. c. 34. have been
continued at various rates by a series of subsequent Acts, and
the Act imposing the duty for the year 1874-75 is the 37 Vict.
c. 16.

13. The Commissioners, having regard to the articles of
association accompanying the case, and the certificate of incorporation signed by the Registrar of Joint Stock Companies, and

also to the fact that the registered office of the Company is in England, where the directors' meetings are generally held, though the main operations of the Company are directed and controlled by the Italian members of the board, were of opinion that the Company is an English Company formed under the Joint Stock Companies Acts for carrying on an undertaking abroad, and is by virtue of sections 40 and 192 of 5 & 6 Vict. c. 35. in the same position as a person residing in the United Kingdom, and liable, under the provisions of 5 & 6 Vict. c. 35. s. 1., and 16 & 17 Vict. c. 34. s. 2., to make a return of the whole of the profits of any trade, whether the same shall be carried on in the United Kingdom or elsewhere.

The Commissioners further were of opinion that the decision in the case of the Imperial Ottoman Bank, in the Court of Exchequer, is not adverse to, but, on the contrary, is confirmatory of, the Crown's contention herein, the Court having decided that the residence of a corporation must be regarded as the place of its incorporation.

In the case of the Cesena Sulphur Company it was originally incorporated within the United Kingdom, though subsequently registered in Italy as an Italian Company.

That the 5 & 6 Vict. c. 80. s. 2. and section 10 of 16 & 17 Vict. c. 34., referred to by the Appellants in this case, do not bear upon the question at issue, the said enactments applying only to agents or other persons entrusted with the payment of dividends or other annual payments payable out of or in respect of stocks, funds, or shares of any foreign company, society or concern.

14. The assessment was accordingly confirmed on the whole of the profits of the Company, whereupon the Appellants expressed their dissatisfaction with such decision as being erroneous in point of law, on the ground that the only sums properly assessable here under Schedule D. are the dividends payable to shareholders in the United Kingdom, and duly required the said Commissioners, by notice in writing addressed to their clerk, to state and sign a case for the opinion of the Court of Exchequer according to statute 37 Vict. c. 16. s. 9., which we have stated and signed accordingly.

15. The question for the opinion of the Court therefore is, whether the Company is liable to make a return in respect of all the annual profits wholly made by its business in Italy, and is chargeable to income tax thereon, or whether, as is contended on the part of the Company, the London directors are only to make a return and to pay income tax in respect of so much of the profits made abroad as is remitted to this country for distribution among the shareholders residing in the United Kingdom.

JUDGMENTS.

Kelly, C.B.—I think that the Crown is entitled to the judgment of the Court, I will first deal with the case of the Calcutta
Jute Mills Company, which has been most admirably argued,
and I may say, without speaking invidiously, especially so by
Mr. Matthews, who in his zeal has certainly said and done
all that could be effected to overcome those difficulties with
which he was environed.   But we have very carefully considered these cases, and the great principles of the law upon
which we think they ought to be decided, and we proceed at
once to pronounce our decision.   They are both cases of great
importance, because they raise, and I believe for the first time,
a very important question—important in the extent of its operation as well as in its nature—and involve most important principles of great weight as affecting the law of England, and I
may almost say as affecting the international law of the world;
and I should be very glad (an observation which I made before
when one of the previous cases was argued) if in both cases I felt
it consistent with my duty, or possibly consistent with the view
which I take of the law of this country, that I could decide the
question otherwise; because it is quite in vain to deny that
whatever may be directly the terms or effect of our decision, the
result in both cases that the Parliament of this country tax
foreigners, not natives of this country, not inhabitants of this
country, and with the exception of what relates to India, although
the same thing may almost be said of India, not within the
jurisdiction of its laws, and under these circumstances I would it
were otherwise.   But we must look at the principles of the law,
and we must look to what decisions have been pronounced upon
these Acts of Parliament, and, above all, we must look to the
precise terms and the real meaning of every word of the one Act
of Parliament, the parent of the others, as it may be called, upon
which this and the other case must be decided.

Now the question in the case is this, whether this Company,
which is called the Calcutta Jute Mills Company, can be held
liable to the income tax upon the entirety of its profits.   It is
a company undoubtedly incorporated in England, and under and
by virtue of the law of England, namely the Joint Stock Companies Act; it has a local position in England; it occupies, or
rather is permitted to occupy, an office, and therefore I may say
that it occupies an office within the city of London, and there it
transacts its business, and there it exercises the very large and
extensive powers with which it is invested by the Act of Parliament; while, on the other hand, it is equally true that the whole
property, in which the whole capital of the Company is invested,
is not in England, but in India, and in India alone.   It is true
also that the mills are worked and the property is made available and the whole profits of the Company are earned in India,
and in India alone.   It likewise appears (and it is here that the
question, not indeed of the law, but we may say, if I may venture

to use such an expression, what ought to be the law, arises) that out of the whole of its profits, amounting in the year in question to 25,000*l*., which was the amount of the entire annual profits of the Company, fully two-thirds, or about two-thirds, become payable, not to inhabitants of England, not to persons having any connection with England, save that they happen to dwell, happily for them, under the same Crown and under the same rule, but fully two-thirds, or thereabouts, of the dividends and the profits of the Company are payable, under the constitution of the Company, to persons resident out of England, and resident chiefly, if not entirely, in India. And, again, what has not incorrectly been called the whole business of the Company, the actual business of the Company, is actually transacted in India, and not in England. But then, on the other hand, when we look to the constitution of the Company, to the case as it is stated to us, and to the articles of association, the articles of the Company under and by virtue of which it exists, and by which it is governed, we find that it is entirely under the actual control, and I may say in the actual possession, but at all events under the control and the free and uncontrolled disposition of the Company, that is to say, the governing body of the Company and the Company itself in England. We find by the case (and this it is which raises the objection with which we have to deal) that the Company, so far as its affairs in the United Kingdom are concerned, is managed by a board consisting of not less than five directors. The directors have, *inter alia*, power to appoint one or more persons resident in Calcutta as "The Calcutta directors." As a matter of fact, there is at the present time one Calcutta director, Mr. George Muirhead Struthers, who is a large shareholder in the Company, and the acting partner of the firm of Messrs. Borradaile, Schiller, and Company, of Calcutta, the former proprietors of the mills.

Now thus far we begin with this, that first of all the Company is incorporated in England, under the laws of England, by virtue of the Joint Stock Companies Act, and therefore its first origin and existence is in England, and in England alone; that the governing body is in England, that is to say, the directors, and that these directors have power to appoint it; it is not that there exists by virtue of the constitution of the Company a director having power himself to act and conduct the affairs of the Company in India, but it is that the governing body, the directors in England, have power to appoint one or more persons resident at Calcutta directors, and they have accordingly done this; the Company have done this; the Company in England have made the appointment; they have appointed Mr. Struthers to be the resident director and the manager—the governor, as it were, of the Company in India—and he it is who directs and controls the whole conduct of the business there. But he is merely the appointee—merely the agent of the governing body of directors in England. Then we see that " the buying of the raw material, " and the manufacture and sale of the same, as well as all the " operations connected with the business of the Company in all

" its branches, are wholly and exclusively carried on in India,
" where alone the gains and profits of the concern (if any) are
" earned " ; and further on, without going further into what
relates to the property itself, we find this, that " the Company "
(these are the parts and passages relied upon chiefly on the part
of the Appellants) " has no office or other place of business in
" the United Kingdom, although, for the purpose of registration,
" its address here is No. 4, St. Helen's Place, in the city of
" London. This is in fact the office of Mr. Ferdinand Schiller,
" one of the directors of the Company, and when meetings of the
" English members of the Company are held there it is entirely
" by his leave and favour." If that is so (and it is a part of the
case) it really signifies little whether the office in which the
very important business of holding meetings at which everything
is or may or can be done by the Company is determined is an
office hired at a rent from any other person in the city of London,
or whether it is a place lent for that purpose by one of the
directors of the Company for the use of this Company, at the
disposition of the Company, and for that purpose alone, that
can make no difference. There is their location, there is their
residence, if I am to apply the terms of the Act of Parliament,
and there it is that the directors accordingly meet when they
have occasion to meet—the Company meet; that is to say, the
great body of shareholders, or such of them as choose to attend,
hold their general meetings and their extraordinary meetings
there. It is, therefore, for all the purposes of this case, the office
of the corporation. Then, as a matter of fact, the Company has
no property whatever in this country. Nothing comes into the
hands of the English directors excepting what is remitted from
Calcutta from time to time to defray their necessary expenses.
In addition to this, such proportion of the profits realised in India
as is divisible amongst the shareholders in the United Kingdom
by way of dividend passes through their hands.

Now, as this is the first of the paragraphs upon which great
reliance is placed by the Appellants, and to which our attention
has been called, it may be convenient to refer to the basis of the
whole argument, and what must be the basis of our decision in
this case, namely, the words of the Act of Parliament.

Now, by the fifth section of the statute of 16 & 17 Vict. c. 34.,
we find that it is thus provided : " The said duties hereby granted
" shall be assessed, raised, levied, and collected under the regu-
" lations and provisions of the Act passed in the Session of
" Parliament, held in fifth and sixth years of Her Majesty, c. 35.,
" and of the several Acts therein mentioned or referred to, and
" also of any Act or Acts subsequently passed explaining, alter-
" ing. amending, or continuing the said first-mentioned Act;"
and by Schedule D. there is this provision, that the companies
or persons are to be assessed " for and in respect of the annual
" profits or gains arising or accruing to any person residing
" in the United Kingdom from any kind of property whatever,
" whether situate in the United Kingdom or elsewhere; and

"for and in respect of the annual profits or gains arising or
"accruing to any person residing in the United Kingdom from
"any profession, trade, employment, or vocation, whether the
"same shall be respectively carried on in the United Kingdom
"or elsewhere, and to be charged for every twenty shillings of
"the annual amount of such profits and gains." Now the first
word here which becomes important is that the tax is imposed
upon "any *person* residing in the United Kingdom." By other
Acts of Parliament, for the word "person" here may be substituted a corporation or joint stock company, and therefore
we may read this word "person" as if it were a joint stock
company, "for and in respect of the annual profits or gains
arising or accruing to any joint stock company." Then follow
the words "residing in the United Kingdom," and so forth.
Now a great deal has been said as to how a person might be
assessed if entitled himself, and in his own right, to property of
the description of property of this Corporation, but it really
leads only to complication, and at last to confusion, to attempt
to enter into all the cases which might well be applied to the
tax as imposed upon a person—a single individual—and attempt
to apply them to a tax imposed upon a joint stock company.
I pass away from that, and I consider it only, as we are at liberty
to do, as if the words "joint stock company" were here used
instead of the word "person." Then come the important words
"residing in the United Kingdom," and therefore it must be,
in order to come within these words, a joint stock company residing in the United Kingdom; and a question of law arises,
independently of the particular provisions of these articles of
association, and the particular terms of the case now before us,
Where does a joint stock company reside? What is the meaning
of the term "residing," as applicable to a joint stock company,
and as applicable to this case? The answer is whether (whether
there may or may not be two places at which one and the same
joint stock company or corporation can reside, and upon which
I do not propose at the present moment to express or even to
suggest any opinion) the answer to the question, Where does a
joint stock company reside? is, where its place of incorporation
is, and where its governing body is to be met with and found,
and where its governing body exercises the powers conferred
upon it by the Act of Parliament, and by the articles of association, where it meets and is in bodily and personal presence for
the purposes of the concern; and where is that in the present
case? I deny that the whole case presents a single act which is
done in Calcutta, otherwise than in England or elsewhere than
in this very office, which can be truly called the act of the Company. That acts of the highest importance affecting the well-
being of the Company, the operation of its business, and the
realising and disposing of its funds, are done in India is perfectly
true; but they are all done by mere agents, whether they be
directors or not directors—by mere agents appointed under the
sole authority of the governing body in this country, appointed

by the Corporation, representing the Corporation, and so making their acts the acts of the Corporation. Therefore, within these words, if a company can be said to reside anywhere (and we must suppose that a company can reside, in order to give any effect at all to the Act of Parliament touching joint stock companies), this joint stock company undoubtedly, in my opinion, resides at the office or place of dwelling, wherever it may be (I think that it is in Bishopsgate Street or Great Saint Helen's), where the directors meet, where other meetings even of the whole Company, or those who represent the whole Company, are held, and where they transact their business and exercise the powers conferred upon them by the laws of the country and by the articles of association.

I need not go into the cases about "residing." The question has arisen, as it did in the Nottingham case, whether it could be said that the acts of a single member of a firm made the firm liable, which firm consisted of several partners who carried on an extensive business in New York, and which single member happened to reside in Nottingham, and represented the firm there and purchased goods, thus commencing the operation, and performing a part of the operation, in the name of the firm, that is to say, purchasing goods which were afterwards sent to America and purchased and paid for by the firm. The question arose whether it could be said that that made the firm liable. There it was held that this gentleman, this one individual, did not represent the firm, that the firm were not liable to be assessed to the income tax in his person by reason of his carrying on a portion of the business, if it can be called a portion of the business, namely, merely that of buying goods and consigning them or transmitting them to America, because, first, no one complete transaction of business was ever effected by him, but also because the principal seat of business, the place at which, and at which alone, the great body and bulk of the business of the firm was carried on, was in New York, and in New York alone. There are a variety of other cases, those arising under the County Court Acts; there the question has arisen as to where do the corporations reside who in fact constitute the great railway companies of this Kingdom. Where does the Great Western Railway Company reside? Why everybody who knows anything of those affairs, directly you ask the question, will tell you at Paddington; and the London and North-Western Railway Company resides at Euston; and that was held again upon the same principle, though in a minor case, and in a minor point of view, which was applicable to the other case to which I have referred, namely, the Nottingham case. The railway company resides there because that is the principal seat of its business; it is there that their directors meet; it is there that the directors assemble and exercise their powers; it is there that their books are kept; it is there, or rather thence, from which almost all their great railways emanate, or begin or end, and it may be properly called the principal place of business—the seat of the company.

I need not go into any other authority; there is no authority,
and no shadow of authority, quoted, which goes to show that the
place in which the directors, who are the governing body, meet,
and in which the shareholders at large hold their meetings, their
special meetings or extraordinary meetings, or general meetings,
and exercise the power of transacting their business, is not the
principal seat of business, and the place at which, in the language
of the Act of Parliament, the Company may be said to " reside."
I am therefore clearly of opinion in this case, upon these principles and for these reasons, that this joint stock company resides
at St. Helen's Place, if that be the name of the place, in Bishopsgate Street, where, as I have said before, the governing body of
the Company meets, and where all the business of the joint stock
company which is carried out, effected, or performed by the
Company itself is actually done, and where the authority is
created and conferred which alone authorises the carrying on of
the great bulk and body of the business in India.

Now it is said that the whole business is transacted in India,
that " nothing " comes into the hands of the English directors
excepting what is remitted from Calcutta from time to time to
defray their necessary expenses; in addition to which, such proportion of the profits realised in India as is divisible amongst
the shareholders in the United Kingdom by way of dividend
passes through their hands." All that is true; but every act
which is done, the working of the mills, the realising of the profits, the transmission of the proportion of the profits in question to
England, and the distribution of the rest of the profits in the
form of dividends to the different shareholders; all that, if not
done by the Company directly in India, is done by them indirectly, because it is done by the person appointed by them,
whom they may appoint at their pleasure, whom they may recall
at their pleasure, and who has no power to do a single act, and no
authority to interfere in any degree in the affairs of the Company,
except the authority conferred upon him by the governing body
at home.

Then comes the other statement: " After receiving such pro-
" portion of the profits as is mentioned in paragraph 11, all that
" then takes place in England is that the directors call a meeting
" of the shareholders and declare the amount that is to be distri-
" buted by way of dividend amongst them for the then current
" year." And then the case gives a statement of the amount of the
profits payable to the shareholders in the United Kingdom. Now
it is true that all they actually do in England with respect to the
dividend is that, having received a certain proportion of the
profits, about one-third, they apportion it among the shareholders
who are in England, and distribute and pay over to each of those
shareholders the dividend. That is all that is done. But the
payment of the dividends to those gentlemen who are in India
and elsewhere, though not actually done by the hands of the
governing body is done under the authority, and by law; no
one can doubt that if they could learn, that on any given day

25,000l. nett profits was in the hands of whoever represented the
Company in India, and therefore to be distributed in dividends,
whether with or without any deduction for a reserve fund, is
immaterial; if they were to hear by telegram that there was such
a sum in hand, they might by telegram direct that sum to be
remitted to England.   If it was improperly withheld by anyone,
by a banker into whose hands it had been paid, they might bring
an action for money had and received against that banker, after
demand, and recover it back against him.   They, therefore, are
the persons who in contemplation of law are the possessors as of
right of the money in question; and it is only because it would
be a very expensive and useless and sometimes, with the failures
of agents and banks, a very hazardous proceeding to desire the
acting director in India to remit the two-thirds in question to
the governing body in England for them to remit it back again
to him in order to pay it out to the shareholders in India, that
that is not done.   They might arrange to do so; they clearly
have the power to do so; it is their money, and they only do not
do so because it would be expensive and might be hazardous,
and for no other reason.

There may be other statements made in the case to which
reference had been had.   I do not propose to refer to any others,
because they will all be found to fall within the same principle,.
and to be open to the same observation.   Though the property
is in India, and so the whole capital is invested in India, and
though the produce of the property is in India, and so the whole
of the money which the Company are ever entitled to receive,
whether as profits or in any other shape or way, or for any other
purpose, is earned in India, yet it all belongs to the Company,
and the Company might at any moment virtually (I do not mean
by the whole of the directors going over as a body to India) take
possession of it; and if they were to find anybody in India,
against their will and without their consent, had taken possession
of one of these jute mills they might immediately bring an action
of ejectment against him, and there would be no defence to such
an action.   Everything therefore is the property of the Company, and it is the Company which is thus located in England
in the way which I have pointed out that alone can deal with
the property or authorise the dealing with it in any way
whatever.

Now, when we look at the articles of association, it again
becomes perfectly clear (it really cannot realise a doubt in anyone's mind) that all this property, and all these powers and
functions, belong to this corporation, that is to say, belong to
the joint stock company.   The memorandum of association begins in this way: " The name of the Company is the ' Calcutta
" Jute Mills Company, Limited.'   The registered office of the
" Company will be situate in England."   We find that it is situate
in England, namely, at St. Helen's Place.   " The objects for which
" the Company is established are," first, " the purchasing of the
" jute mills, land, business, works, machinery, plant, and stock-in-

" trade of the present proprietors of the Ishera Jute Mills, Bengal,
" with all the rights, privileges, and appurtenances thereto
" belonging, the carrying on there of the trade or business of buy-
" ing, selling, and manufacturing jute in all its branches, and the
" extending of the said business and works, or either of them.'
Who is it that purchases the property? Is it the director who
has been sent over there? Is it any number of shareholders, or
the whole of them, who are resident in India, or the majority?
No, the purchasers are the Company themselves here; and we
have the direct statement that this is one of the objects of the
Company, and that object is effected by the purchase of the jute
mills on the part of this Company, that is to say, by the Company,
not by any member or members of the Company, the Indian members or others. Then what else is to be done? " The carrying
" on in all branches of the trade or business of dealers in jute and
" other similar materials, including their purchase, preparation,
" pressing," and so forth. That means the carrying on of
the business of the manufacture of jute in India by which
at last considerable profits are expected to be realized. Who
is to do that? Why, this very article says that it is something to be done; by whom? Not by people in India, though it
must be done by the hands chiefly of labourers in India; not, in
contemplation of law, by anybody in India, but by the Company,
or by the persons authorised by them to do the acts in question,
in India. The same as to " the purchasing or otherwise acquiring
" of any total or partial or contingent interest in or the taking
" out in Great Britain, British India, or elsewhere, and the
" working of letters patent for inventions which may be con-
" ducive to the advancement of the businesses aforesaid." No one
can do that but the Company; and it will be found, without
dwelling too much upon any one or upon any number of these
articles of association, that every single act which is to be done
from the beginning to the end, from the coming into existence
of the Company down to (wherever and whenever it is to happen) the ultimate dissolution of the Company, everything is
to be done by the Company, and by the Company alone, which
means by the governing body of the Company as representing
the Company, or by meetings of the shareholders again representing the Company—all in England, and nowhere else.

Then we come to this object, " The establishing and regulating
" of agencies for the purposes of the Company, whether in the
" United Kingdom, British India, or elsewhere." Now there is
the key to the whole of the proceedings on behalf of this Company upon which the Appellants rely. The learned Counsel
contends that all that is done in India by a director over there,
who may do as he pleases, and by certain persons under his
authority, who alone carry on the business of the Company.

How is it? It is under this article of the memorandum of
association. " The establishing and regulating of agencies for the
" purposes of the Company, whether in the United Kingdom,
" British India, or elsewhere." Under this article the Company

language of the Act of Parliament, is included in the same
category as property actually in this country, are they or not,
under the express terms of the Acts of Parliament, to be treated
in the same way with respect to the application of the principle
of law as if the property had been situate in the county of
Gloucester? It appears to me that the true principle of the law
is that they are. I only say in conclusion, and I say it with
regret, that there can be no doubt that, inasmuch as this is a tax
upon what is called, and truly called, the earnings of this
Company, and as two-thirds of those earnings, except anything
which may be set aside as a reserve fund, which is not in
question here, belong to persons not within this country, and not
subject to the taxation and the laws of this country, it certainly
is an infringement upon one of the principles on which taxation
is levied by the laws of any country, that those two-thirds
should be thus taxed. On the other hand it may be an answer
to that (and it is not for me, still less for any member of the bar,
to say whether or not it is a sufficient answer), that if a foreigner
residing abroad, and having no property, or interest in this
country, and no connexion with this country, thinks fit to come
and invest his money in this country, and so to obtain the broad
shield of protection of the law to his property, he must take it
with the burdens belonging to it. It is exactly as if a man
thinks fit, because he will not trust any foreign state, to come
and invest his fortune, or a portion of his fortune, in the English
funds. It is very hard indeed to tax that man upon his whole
income. If a Spaniard or a Dutchman, who never set foot in
England in his life, and never intends to do so, should give
credit to the law of England for protecting what property he
possesses here, he must therefore pay the cost of it; and if there
be a tax of a penny, or twopence, or threepence, or more, in the
pound upon his income or dividends, he must submit to the
payment of that tax.

It appears to me therefore on these grounds that this assessment is well made, and that the Crown is entitled to the judgment
of the Court. I might say more, and might deal with the latter
argument, so very ably urged by Mr. Matthews, but it goes to
show that there may be cases in which persons in this country may
be taxed in relation to property abroad, and that therefore there
is something like a reciprocity of injustice, if it be injustice.
I do not, however, dwell upon those cases or upon that argument
at all, because it is founded upon a clause or clauses which have
no relation to the matter now before the Court, which is as to
the property and the gains or income of a joint stock company.
If the words "joint stock company" had been thrown into
those clauses which lastly Mr. Matthews referred to, then his
argument would have been entitled to much consideration, but
I find nothing in any Act of Parliament, or in any one of the
numerous authorities which have been cited, which interferes
with the plain and direct operation of the clause to which I
have called attention; and under which I hold that this Company

is liable to be assessed in respect of the whole amount of its annual profits.

*   *   *   *   *   *   *

Huddleston, B.—I am of the same opinion, and I hope that I may be permitted to offer my thanks to the learned Counsel who have argued these cases for the very great assistance which they have given us in coming to the determination at which we have arrived, and I must not omit from that the few observations which Mr. Wright was called upon suddenly to make in replying in the Cesena case. I own, that as far as I was concerned, I had every possible inclination to yield to the very able arguments which were offered to me by Sir Henry James and Mr. Matthews, and it is with the greatest reluctance that I am compelled to come to a contrary conclusion. Now I think that· the whole question here will, as indeed it has been argued on all sides, turn upon what we should consider the interpretation of the word "residence" as applicable to a company. The income tax is only imposed upon a person who· is resident in the United Kingdom in respect of property which he has there, and which he receives from foreign sources. A corporation for the purpose of paying the income tax is a "person," and then we have to see what interpretation we should give to the word "residence" as applied to a person, when it is to be made applicable to a corporation. Now the definition of the word "residence" is founded upon the habits and relations of a natural man, and is therefore inapplicable to the artificial and legal person whom we call a corporation. But for the purpose of giving effect to the words of the Legislature an artificial residence must be assigned to this artificial person, and one formed on the analogy of natural persons. You do not find any very great difficulty in defining what is the residence of an individual; it is where he sleeps and lives. We understand perfectly well what is the residence of a natural person. Then what is the residence of this artificial person? I think that all the Counsel are agreed here, that the residence of an artificial person, like a trading corporation, must be considered to be where he carries on his business, where the real trade and business is carried on. I adopt the powerful suggestion which was made by Mr. Matthews, that the Income Tax Act of the 16 & 17 Vict., when it speaks of a residence, does not mean an artificial residence. It means an actual residence. Mr. Matthews argues, therefore, that when you come to deal with a corporation it does not mean the place where they carry on the form or the shadow of business, but means the place where they really carry on their business; and that seems to be a definition which is almost conceded by all the Counsel. It is one which is perfectly well understood; it is understood in foreign jurists. There is a German word which is applicable to it, which means the middle point of the business carried on. The French term, adopted from Saugne, is " le centre de l'Entreprise," the central point of business, that is to say, the real place where the business is carried on. Now all the cases which have been quoted support that view. In the Keynsham Blue Lias Company v. Barker, although the Court held that Keynsham was the place of business they did so because the real business was carried on there; that was the judgment of the Court. It is not to be forgotten that in that case the Company itself, which had an office in London, was in liquidation, and their real, substantial business was carried on at Keynsham. In the case of Taylor v. The Crowland Gas Company, the judgment of the Court was put upon the question of the place where the corporation carried on its business. In Adams v. The Great Western Railway Company, for a similar reason it was held that the place where the Company carried on its business was Paddington. In Brown v. The London and North-Western Railway Company it was held that the place where the Company carried on its business was in London, and not in Chester, where it was contended that it did. The same rule is applied in Shields v. The Great Northern Railway Company. And then there is a very strong authority, namely, the case of the Aberystwith Promenade Company v. Cooper, in which it was held that the place of business was in London, although the pier was built in Wales and the tolls were taken there. There, again, the decision was that that was its place of business. Mr. Matthews satisfied me, and distinguished the case which was quoted by Sir Henry James, of the Kilkenny Railway Company v. Fielden. The decision in Sulley v. the Attorney General was to the same effect; and in the last case in this Court, namely, the Attorney General v. Alexander, the judgment at least of two of the learned Judges, the Lord Chief Baron and Mr. Baron Amphlett, pointed out that Constantinople, where the corporation was incorporated (that was a case where there was no charter of incorporation in England), was, as they say in both their judgments, the seat of business; that is to say, the place where it was carried on.

Now the Attorney General put a proposition which I for one, with great deference, cannot assent to; the Attorney General suggested that the registration of a company was conclusive of its residence; that if a company was registered in England it must be held to reside in England. I think that Sir Henry James's answer was a good one; he said, "Registration, like the " birth of an individual, is a fact which you may take into " consideration in considering the question of his residence, " because if you find that a man is born in a place, and eats " and drinks and lives in that place, it is a very strong circum- " stance to show that it is the place of his residence, but it is " only a circumstance." So you may say here. The birth is not conclusive of the residence; it would be idle to say that it is. Taking the analogy between a natural and an artificial person, in the case of a corporation you say that the place of its regis- tration is the place of its birth; but it is not because it is the place of its birth that the residence must be there; it is a fact

which you must take in connexion with all the other facts, and
if you find that it is registered in a particular country, and acts
in that country, and has its office in that country, and receives
dividends in that country, you may say that those are all acts,
coupled with the registration, which lead you to the conclusion
that that country is the seat of its business.

If I am right, Mr. Matthews quoted on the former occasion
many American authorities as applicable to the individual
States; he yesterday pointed out a case, which he got from Brock-
enbrough's Reports, of the difference between a corporation
created merely by the Act of a State, and a corporation created by
an Act of Congress.   That case was the Bank of the United States
v. Mackenzie.   He also showed that it is not at all consistent
with the English view that a corporation cannot be a corporation
except in a particular State, and he founded that on the authority
of Newby v. The Colts Patent Fire Arms Company.   I therefore
do not think (the case has been argued at considerable length)
that the principle of law is in dispute.   I think that we may
take it now for granted that the place of business is the sort
of artificial residence which you would give to this artificial
person to make him a person resident in the country within the
meaning of the Income Tax Act.   Now comes the very great
difficulty which I have found all along, and that is in applying
the facts of each of these individual cases to the principal.   I
admit that the onus to prove the residence lies upon the Crown;
that is put by Baron Cleasby in his judgment in the Attorney
General v. Alexander; and if the Crown fails to satisfy the
Court that the place of residence is within the jurisdiction, or
within the area of taxation, you cannot say that the Company
should be taxed.   I admit that.   Then I have to ask myself, in
both these cases, where really was the centre of the operation,
where was the substantial and real place of business which was
le centre de l'Entreprise, or the middle point?   I am afraid
that I must answer that question, looking at the facts in both
these cases, by saying that it was in England.

Now I do not think it necessary to go at any great length into
the facts of either of these cases, because they have been minutely
examined by my Lord.   But Sir Henry James's argument with
reference to the Cesena Company was put in the most captivating
form, and I am bound to say that, until the Attorney General
had called my attention carefully to the articles of association,
it had, if I may make use of the expression, caught me.   Sir
Henry James said this, " I am not going through the different
" clauses of the case, but in substance they amount to this: in
" this case of the Cesena Sulphur Company the trading is in
" Italy: the unrealized property is in Italy; everything is sold in
" Italy, the fixed property is in Italy; the case states that no
" goods are ever sent to England; the majority of the share-
" holders are either in Italy or France, and a small minority
" only, about one-third, are in England; the original books are
" kept in Italy: the managing director is in Italy; he is residing

" in Italy; he is at Cesena; and therefore (said Sir Henry James)
" you have almost everything in Italy—books, profits, manufac-
" tures—altogether." At first I began to think that it appeared
that the centre of business was in Italy; but when we came to
look at the articles and the memorandum of association, and
when we find that the object of the memorandum of association
is, no doubt, to purchase sulphur from a company or firm established at Cesena, but that they contemplate " taking concessions
of any lands wherever sulphur is likely to be obtained," and that
it is not confined to Italy, and when we find that the general
powers of the Company are for " selling, leasing, letting, and
" disposing of any of the lands, mines, and property acquired by
" the Company," we see by the memorandum, at all events, that
the operations of the Company are not to be confined to Italy;
and when we take the articles of association, the very first
article of association is that " the Company is formed for the
" purpose of developing and working the mines of sulphur at
" Cesena aforesaid, and carrying on the business mentioned or
" included in the memorandum of association;" that is, carrying
on the business of a Sulphur Company wherever sulphur may be
found. When we look to see what the power is which is to be
exercised by the directors, by the office in London, we find
what the " board " is; it is " a meeting of the directors duly
called and constituted." What is the business? " The working
" of the Company's mines, the mode of the disposal thereof, and
" the general business of the Company shall be wholly under
" the order, direction, and management of the directors, subject
" only to such control of general meetings as is hereafter pro-
" vided for." Then the directors have power to register the
Company, which they exercised; they registered it in Italy; they
have power to accept promissory notes, and so on. " The office
" shall be at such place in London as the board shall from time
" to time appoint." A London bank is to be their " first and
" present bankers." It is true that they had a banker at Turin
and a banker at Paris. They may invest their money in a
reserve fund. General meetings are to be held; and those
meetings which are described as ordinary or extraordinary are to
be held in London, some of them by some particular means, but
all certainly in London. There is the power of adjourning from
place to place, no doubt, given to them. But when we come to
consider what the board may do, we find that they may do
everything with reference to the Company, and that their minutes
recorded in their books are to be evidence. Now it is quite true
that it is not said anywhere that the directors must hold their
board meetings in London; but is quite obvious from the
facts which are found in the case, and from all the requirements
of the articles of association, that the books must be kept at
the office, and the office, according to the articles of association, must be in London; and, inferentially, you arrive at the
conclusion from the facts stated, and from the case, that the
directors are to meet in London.

Without going through the other different clauses of the articles of association, it seems that almost every act of the Cesena Company connected with the administrative part of its business is to be done in London. No doubt the manufacturing part may be done and was done in Italy; so supposing that in another part of the world they found sulphur and carried on their business there, the manufacturing part of the business would be carried on there, no doubt; but the administrative part of the business would be carried on at the place from which all the orders came, from which all the directions flowed, and where the appointments were made, where the appointments of the officers were revoked, where the agents were nominated, where their powers were recalled, where the money was received (whatever may have been sent), where the dividends were payable, and where the dividends were declared. We find that all those Acts are performed in London. I cannot help thinking that the main place of business of the Company is in England, and that Cesena is merely an agency, as it were, of the principal house; that agency being confined to the manufacture and sale of sulphur, but under the direction of the principal house.

Then I approach the other case which has been so fully gone into by my Lord, namely, the case of the Calcutta Jute Mills Company. I am bound to say that I thought at first that was a very strong case, and when Mr. Matthews, having put it very strongly, summed up his argument as to the result of the case in words which comprised everything which was stated in the case, I thought it could not be put in terser language. He said in fact this—the only transaction in England is the receipt of the amount transmitted for English expenses and dividends, and the declaration of that amount, and its division among the English shareholders. He put it really in a most captivating way. I again look at the articles of association and the case. The office, no doubt, was one lent to them for the purpose, or allowed to be used by them for the purpose; from that office would issue all the orders to the managing director in Calcutta. No doubt, until he received orders to the contrary, he would have full power and discretion to do what he liked in Calcutta; but at any moment, from this head office, they might have revoked his authority, or altered any arrangement which he had made connected with the working of the Company. The meetings were held in London. The operation of the Company in London was, not to divide the amount sent among the shareholders, but it was to "declare" the amount; and I apprehend that, within the meaning of that clause, the directors in London, who had full power, might say, "Well, we do not approve of this system upon which the division "has been made, and we shall require a different dividend for "the future," or something of that kind,—showing plainly that they exercise the authority, and that they are the persons who are the principal body, while the Calcutta Company is only their agent for the purpose of the manufacture and the sale of the jute, as the Cesena Company is the agent of the London Company for the purpose of the manufacture of the sulphur.

For these reasons I cannot help coming to the conclusion that the principal place of business of both these corporations is in London, and that therefore they are within the provisions of the Income Tax Acts. I am bound to say that I listened with a great deal of pleasure—a pleasure which I have not derived for the first time—to the very ingenious argument put forward by Mr. Matthews, the scope of which I hope I understood; if not, it must have been for want of intelligence on my part, and not from the want of clearness with which he put it. He said, assume that the place of business is in England, still the only division of the profits is to be a division of the profits earned by the English shareholders, which was a very ingenious way of arguing it. He argued that if this were a partnership, then, on the authority of Sulley's case, the English portion of the partnership would only be liable to pay on the profits which they received, whereas the Indian portion would not have to pay on theirs. If you could make this artificial being, namely, a corporation, a partnership, and say that every shareholder was a partner, probably Mr. Matthews' argument would be in accordance, as he said, with natural justice, and it would be very striking; but I am afraid that the answer is this, in a single word,—they are not partners; it is a corporation. I believe that that is an answer, although I am not by any means satisfied that I have given the true answer to Mr. Matthews' argument. I am bound to say that I cannot follow him in it altogether, but, as far as I do follow him, the answer in my mind is, "This is a corporation; it is not a partnership."

PART VII.

No. 19.—In the Exchequer.—Scotland.
16th March 1876.

Income Tax.—Deer Forest in Scotland to be assessed under Schedule B. The Basis of the Assessment to be the Value charged under Schedule A.

Case for Sir George Nathaniel Broke Middleton, Bart., under The Customs and Inland Revenue Act, 1874, (37 Vict. cap. 16.) for the opinion of the Court.

At a Meeting of the Commissioners under the Property and Income Tax Act, 5 and 6 Vict. Cap. 35., and subsequent Acts, for the county of Inverness, held at Inverness on the 2nd December 1875,—

Sir George Nathaniel Broke Middleton, Bart., appealed against the assessment of 4*l.* 15*s.* duty, under Schedule B., on 1,520*l.*, made on him as occupier of the deer forest of Invermoriston, &c., for the year ending 5th April 1876.

The Appellant pays a rent of 2,000*l.* for the furnished house of Invermoriston, with deer forest, including the privilege of shooting deer thereon, and certain grouse shootings and fishings; and the assessor, in fixing the assessable amount at 1,620*l.*, allowed a deduction of 480*l.* in respect of the houses, with the furniture, and the grouse shootings,—without, however, admitting that grouse shootings are not assessable.

On behalf of the Appellant, it was stated that the house, with furniture, and the grouse shootings, were under-estimated, and the assessor agreed to a further reduction of 320*l.*, thus making the estimated rent of the deer forest, with the privilege of killing deer thereon, and the Schedule B. assessment, 1,200*l.*

The Appellant objected to this assessment, in respect that it included the portion of the rent paid by him for the privilege of killing deer within the forest, which portion of the rent, he maintained, was not assessable under Schedule B., and claimed to have it reduced to the annual grazing value of the forest. He stated—and this was admitted by the surveyor—that the rent paid for the forest, including the privilege of killing deer thereon, was much above the rent that would be paid for it as a sheep farm. He referred to rule 7, under which the Schedule B. duty is charged, and Rule No. 1, Schedule A. of 5 and 6 Vict., where the properties to be charged are declared to be those "capable of actual occupation," and maintained that the forest was capable of actual occupation only in so far as the land was concerned (the mere privilege of shooting deer, for which so much was paid, not being capable of occupation), and that nothing beyond the ordinary value of the land could be charged for profits of occupation, the duty under Schedule B. being really chargeable in respect of profits only.

In support of the assessment the surveyor referred to rule 7, which provided for the Schedule B. duty being charged in addition to the duty to be charged under Schedule A. " according to " the general rule in number 1, Schedule (A.), before mentioned, on " the full amount of the annual value thereof." That rule extended to all lands, " *for whatever purpose occupied or enjoyed;* " and under the property Tax Acts (and Valuation of Lands Acts, which rule the Property Tax valuations), the rent, where a *bonâ fide* rent is paid, is held to be the annual value.

The Appellant had the exclusive use or occupation of the forest, and the rent paid by him was its agreed-on actual value. He maintained, therefore, that the Appellant was chargeable on the rent he actually paid under his lease, without reference to the rent the forest might bring in if let as a sheep farm or otherwise.

The Commissioners found that the assessment appealed against was made according to the amount of rent fixed in terms of the lease between the Appellant and the Trustees of the late James Murray Grant, of Glenmoriston, dated the 18th June and 2nd July 1872. They therefore refused the appeal; but in respect that the assessor consented to allow the sum of 800*l.* as a deduction from the actual rent payable by the Appellant to the said trustees, restricted the amount of the assessment to 1,200*l.* But the Appellant was dissatisfied with this decision, and required a case to be stated for the opinion of the Court of Exchequer.

JUDGMENT, 16th March 1876.

The Lord President.—My Lords, it appears from the case before us, that the Appellant, Sir George Broke Middleton, pays a rent of 2,000*l.* for the furnished house of Invermoriston, with a deer forest (including the privilege of shooting deer), and certain grouse shootings and fishings, and the assessor, in fixing the assessable amount at 1,520*l.*, which was his original charge, " allowed a deduction of 480*l.* in respect of the houses with the " furniture, and the grouse shooting, without, however, admitting " that grouse shootings are not assessable."

The Appellant maintained before the Income Tax Commissioners that the house, with the furniture and grouse shootings, were under-estimated, and that the deductions should be larger, and it appears that the assessor agreed to a further deduction of 320*l.*, thus making the assessable rental 1,200*l.*

Now, it is to be taken into consideration in this question that that rent of 1,200*l.* is paid for a deer forest; that is to say, it is a rent paid for the occupation of the ground of which that deer forest consists, and for the exclusive occupation of that ground for the purposes of sport; and the question is whether the Appellant is assessable under Schedule B. of the income tax for that forest. Schedule B. grants to Her Majesty a duty for "all "lands, tenements, and heritages in Scotland, in respect of the "occupations thereof for every 20s. of the annual value thereof, "the sum of 2½d." You will observe that it is in respect of the *occupation* of lands, &c. in Scotland.

In Schedule A. there is a corresponding sum charged against the owner of the land, "in respect of the property thereof, for "every 20s. of the annual value thereof, the sum of 7d." So that every acre of land in Scotland is made the subject of assessment in this way to the amount of 7d. in the pound for every owner, and to the amount of 2½d. in the pound for every occupier of such subject. The two assessments plainly go together. They are intended to apply and do apply to the same subjects, and the tax is payable as assessment upon the annual value.

Now, the way in which these assessments are to be laid on is regulated by the 60th and 63rd sections of the statute. The first rule under the 60th section is this: "The annual value of "lands, tenements, hereditaments, or heritages charged under "Schedule A. shall be understood to be the rent by the year at "which the same are let, at rackrent if the amount of such rents "shall have been fixed by agreement, commencing within the "period of seven years preceding the 5th day of April next "before the time of making the assessment; but if the same are "not so let (at rackrent), then at the rackrent at which the "same are worth to be let by the year, which rule shall be con-"strued to extend through all lands, tenements, hereditaments, "and heritages capable of actual occupation of whatever nature "and for whatever purpose occupied or enjoyed, and of whatever "value," excepting certain subjects which are specified in rules Nos. 2 and 3 which are not applicable to the present case.

The 63rd section has this rule No. 7: "The duties last before "mentioned shall be charged in addition to the duties to be "charged under Schedule A. on all properties in this Act directed "to be charged with the said duties. according to the general "rule in No. 1, Schedule A. before mentioned, on the full amount "of the annual value thereof, estimated by this Act as per "annum."

In laying on these duties under this statute the subject is to be considered. What is a heritage? And there can be no doubt that according to the description of the statute, the ground in question falls within that description. Then in the second place the annual value is to be ascertained by the actual rent, if it is the full rent of the subject. And we have in this case the rent ascertained in quite a satisfactory way. That, the Act says, is to be taken as the annual value; and the owner is to pay on that annual value 7d. in the pound. and the occupier is to pay 2½d. Now. surely all that is very clear and plain, and admits of no difficulty of construction at all. The only question raised here, as I understand it, is, whether this gentleman, Sir George Middleton, is the occupier of a heritage subject within the meaning of the statute. Now, I should not have thought that a great deal could be made of the question, unless some distinction could be shown between this statute and the Poor Law Amendment Act, because the question has been settled under the Poor Law Amendment Act, by the case of *Stirling Crawford v. Stewart*, and settled upon this precise ground, that the tenant of a shooting is a person in the occupation of land, and is assessable as such. He is assessable as a tenant or occupier under the Poor Law Amendment Act; and the occupier is a person to be assessable under this Act also. Therefore, unless some distinction can be pointed out between the one Act and the other, the present case is perfectly hopeless, for Mr. Mackintosh with all his ingenuity has been unable to point out any distinction unless it consists in this. He says the present Act is intended as a tax upon profits, whether they arise from lands or from trades and professions. And that is quite true; but there is a material distinction between the provisions of the Act as regards profits arising from the one source, and as regards profits arising from the other. In the case of profits arising from trades and professions, the Act says that there shall be an estimate made of what the profits are; and we know that it is a very rough and round kind of estimate that can be made even in that case. But in the case of lands, the statute requires no such estimate of profits. It fixes the mode in which the profits are to be estimated, a statutory mode of proving what the profits are, and that is by taking the actual annual value of the land which it defines to be the rent payable, if it be the full rent, or the rack-rent, as the statute calls it, or what the rent would be if it be not let. That is precisely the rule which is to be applied. So that as far as land and heritages are concerned, the rule of assessment under this statute, and the rule of assessment under the Poor Law Act are precisely identical; and therefore, I think the determination of the Commissioners is sound.

Lord Deas.—There is, I think, some distinction between the Poor Law cases and the present case. Poor rates are required to be payable upon the annual value, taking one year with another, one half by the landlord and the other half by the tenant. The first thing to be ascertained in such a case was of course, what was the annual value of the lands and heritages. That could only be ascertained by taking the rent. When it was required that one half should be paid by the landlord and the other half by the tenant, there was a division of liability between them upon the annual value; the annual value being what was paid by the tenant. But this, you observe, was not a tax upon the profits made by the tenant; it was a tax upon the whole annual value of the subject.

In the present case the one-half was not payable by either the

landlord or the tenant. There is a larger tax put upon the
landlord, and a smaller one upon the tenant. The question,
however, I think comes to be, notwithstanding the mode of
division between the two, whether it is not really a division of
the tax between the two of the whole annual value, just as
under the Poor Law Act, with this difference, simply that in the
one case the assessment is equally divided, while in the other
case it is unequally divided. Although there is that difference,
the assessment is laid on as in the Poor Law Act itself; and if
that be sound, it is no matter whether the tenant makes profit
out of it or no. It is not on the footing of the amount of profit
that the liability is laid on; but on the footing that the lands
are of a certain annual value, and has to be divided in certain
proportions between the landlord and the tenant. I have come
to the same result as your Lordship in the chair.

Lord Ardmillan.—I read from the print that " This case has
" been brought by Sir George Middleton on appeal against the
" decision of the Inland Revenue Commissioners," &c. (*reads*):
I read that merely to show the policy and intention of the
parties, and to show that some amount of discretion has been
shown in the way in which the charges have been enforced by
the Commissioners. I don't know that I need go into that; but
I think upon the whole the Commissioners have been very light
upon the tenant of the grouse shootings.

In the case before us I don't think there is any difficulty at
all. The tax is partly on the profits of the property and partly
on income. Schedule A. is distinct as to its being a tax on " all
" lands, tenements, hereditaments, and heritages in respect of
" property for every 20*s.* of the annual value thereof 7*d.*" Sche
dule B. is in the same terms in regard to the occupation of lands.
tenements, hereditaments, and heritages. the amount in that
case, however, being only 2½*d.* in the pound. Then. when
you proceed to the more detailed enactments on the subject, you
have section 60, when the rules for estimating lands mentioned
in Schedule A., that is, for the ascertainment of the tax on the
property, are laid down.

You have it there again put expressly on the ascertainment of
the annual value; and under section 63, which gives the detailed
enactment for assessing and charging properties under the Act
(Schedule B.) on the occupant, you have again the very same
words—the annual value. Whatever the thing be it is a tax
both in regard to the proprietor and in regard to the occupant.
Now, if there is in this case a rent accruing to the proprietor of
the deer forest, it is the annual value of the property. so far as it
is paid for the deer forest. The rent is, besides, the annual value
of the deer forest to the occupant. Both landlord and tenant are.
therefore. within the enacting words of the statute. The time
was when a difficulty was raised, which does not occur here at all,
whether game was a fit subject of such enactment, or of assessment at all, on the ground that game, or the shooting of game,

was a personal privilege or enjoyment. That question has long ago been settled. There is a whole string of cases, and I think the case in which the subject was perhaps most deliberately and satisfactorily dealt with was the case of *Menzies v. Menzies*. So that considering the numerous cases we have on that subject, it cannot be doubted that game let is property let. The privilege of shooting game let to a tenant is part of a right of property, unlet game raised a different question, and unlet game must be estimated as of so much annual value. The case of *Crawford v. Stewart* was of much the same character.

The fact that under the Poor Law the landlord pays one half does not raise a different principle; for where the landlord pays on the annual value, and the tenant does the same, you may call it one half or the other half which each pays, but it is the annual value still. It is the criterion of the landlord's and of the tenant's liability.

In regard to a deer forest, it is obvious that there is this other consideration, that there is no means of ascertaining, except by pure, hypothetical conjecture, the rent of the land apart from the deer shooting. In the case of a grouse shooting, there may not be a very great sheep stock upon it; but there is a sheep stock often put upon it; and it is capable of being let for pasture for cattle and sheep, whether it is so or not. But in the case of a deer forest everything else is excluded. In order to make it a deer forest it is made a desert, where "nothing but the antlered monarch roams." That is the very reason why it is impossible to reach the rent of the land, if it is merely a deer forest, otherwise than by taking the rent as the annual value, and the annual value as the rent.

The only difficulty suggested in dealing with the case is an attempt to say, that if it is not done in regard to grouse, why assess in regard to deer? But we have not that before us. There have been distinctions drawn in such matters; and even in this case the assessor has very handsomely, if I may so say, lowered the assessment as far as he could go.

Lord Muir.—I agree with your Lordship in the chair, that there is no substantial distinction between the circumstances of this case, and the case of *Stirling Crawford v. Stewart* which has been referred to, and which was tried under the regulations of the Poor Law Act. The only argument that Mr. Mackintosh used was that, strictly speaking, in the matter of deer, there is no profit, and that this Act being made for the purpose of levying a tax upon profits, deer did not fall within its general principle. Then he said that the Appellant did not occupy in the ordinary sense of occupation. I don't think that is a sound distinction; because in regard to property, the income tax is laid on the annual value as well as upon occupancy, and it is levied whether the occupant makes a profit or not. He is supposed, taking one year with another, to make a profit out of his occupation, but if he makes no actual profit he still pays, because it is presumed that whatever the rent may be, a profit is really made. So, in this case, the tenant of a deer forest is presumed to get some benefit out of the forest when he pays a particular rent for it. He makes some profit out of it in the shape of the enjoyment of the privileges of the deer forest. A deer forest appears to me to fall under the very words of section 60 of the Act, because section 60, to which we refer in dealing with section 63, uses not merely the word "occupy," but for whatever purpose "occupied or enjoyed." I am thus of opinion that a man who enjoys the privileges of the tenancy and occupancy of a deer forest, falls within the very words of section 60.

Lord Deas.—I should explain that in what I said about the application of the decision in the Poor Law case, I am quite aware that the division there between the landlord and the tenant is not between individual landlords and individual tenants, but landlords as a class and tenants as a class. But that makes no difference in the principle, or in the result at which I arrived, as the principle I go upon is this, that it is a tax upon the whole of the annual value, and divided between the two in certain proportions. It does not therefore matter what the proportions are, whether one half or some other proportion. So that, although I did not use the word "classes," it comes to precisely the same thing.

The Lord President.—We affirm the determination of the Commissioners, and find the assessor entitled to expenses.

APPENDIX.

Lease of Invermoriston Shootings, between the Trustees of
the late James Murray Grant, Esq., of Glenmoriston, and
Sir George Broke Middleton, Bart., dated 18th June and
2nd and 19th July 1872.

It is contracted, agreed, and ended between the parties following, viz., James Chadwick, Esquire, of Manchester, and Patrick
Grant, Esquire, formerly of the Madras Civil Service, and presently residing at 98, Cornwall Gardens, South Kensington,
London, the surviving, accepting and at present the only acting
trustees of the deceased James Murray Grant, Esquire, of Glenmoriston and Moy, nominated and appointed by and acting under
his trust-disposition and deed of settlement, dated the 15th day
of October 1867, and recorded in the books of Council and
Session, on the 21st day of August, 1868, on the one part, and
Vice-Admiral Sir George Broke Middleton, Baronet, Shrubland
Park, Needham, Suffolk, on the other part, in manner following;
—that is to say, the said trustees have set and in tack and
assedation let to the said Sir George Broke Middleton and his
heirs, but expressly excluding assignees, and sub-tenants, both
legal and conventional, unless specially approved of in writing by
the said trustees or their successors,—declaring, however, that the
said Sir George Broke Middleton shall have the power of giving
four months' notice in writing to the proprietors or their factor,
previous to any term of Whitsunday during the lease, to assign
the lease provided the subject shall, in the first place, be offered
to the proprietors, and if declined by them, to an assignee to be
approved of by them,—all and whole the Invermoriston shootings,
comprehending the deer forest of Bean-en-Eofn, the grouse shootings of Achlain and Sluich, the deer forest of Inverwick, the low-
ground shootings on Easter and Wester Inverwick, the deer
forest of Blairy and Livisy, the hill-lands of Achnaconeran and
Strone, as now defined, with the low-ground and cover-shootings
of Easter and Wester Achnaconeran, inn lands, mains, farm, and
plantations of Craigian and others, near and around the mansion-
house of Glenmoriston, with the mansion-house, furniture, and
other effects therein contained belonging to the proprietors,
according to an inventory thereon signed by the parties as
relative hereto, and gardens and grounds attached to the said
mansion-house, the coach-house, stables, and servants' apartments let to the former tenant of these shootings; as also
the grass parks at Fasagh; as also the dwelling-houses and
crofts of land occupied by the keepers attached to the shootings; with the right to fish on Loch Ness and the River
Morriston; comprising all the shootings and fishings lately
occupied by Mr. Frank Morrison, but under the stipulation

after mentioned as regards said river and other lochs and streams *ex adverso* or within the bounds of the foregoing, in so far as it is competent for the proprietors to convey such rights, and that for the space of five years from and after the term of Whitsunday last, 1872, which is hereby declared to be the term of entry, notwithstanding the date hereof: and it is hereby provided and declared that at the term of Whitsunday, 1873, when the lease of the deer forest of Glenloyne, at present let to Earl Cowper, expires, the said deer forest will be added to the aforesaid subjects, and held as embraced in this lease, and shall from and after said term be occupied and possessed by the said Sir George Broke Middleton and his foresaids as tenants thereof : But this tack is granted always with and under the following reservations, viz.—1*st*, The right to fish with the rod by the proprietor and his brothers and friends during this lease on the River Morriston, and all other streams and lochs, including Loch Ness, whether within the range of these shootings and lands held as deer forests, or *ex adverso* of them, respectively, is reserved ; but whenever this right shall be exercised, previous notice shall be given to the tenant in writing, naming the persons to whom the permission is accorded, and the term of their coming and going : 2*nd*, The proprietors reserve the right to all mines, minerals, quarries, mosses, and metals of every description, as also to all the woods which now are or hereafter may be on the subjects let, with right of access thereto and egress therefrom, but under the limitation after mentioned as regards the lands let exclusively as deer forests : 3*rd*, The proprietors, as regards the woods that now are or may hereafter be on lands held exclusively as deer forests, reserve all right to cut, thin, or dispose of them in any manner of way, they in the first place obtaining the consent of the said Sir George Broke Middleton or his foresaids to do so; but reserving, nevertheless, to the proprietors the right to enter into, at suitable seasons, the woods growing on lands not let as deer forests, to cut, thin, or plant up the same, as also the woods surrounding, or in the neighbourhood of the mansion-house, to cut, thin, or plant up the same, during this lease : 4*th*, The proprietors having some time since sold and disposed of some of the fir trees standing in the deer forest of Inverwick, in virtue of which sale it was covenanted that the purchasers should remove the trees in the forest therefrom between 1st January 1872 and 30th May next following, and that in the event of the whole of the said forest trees not being so removed therefrom by the said 30th day of May 1872, then and in that event such remaining trees were to be left standing in the forest untouched until the 1st of January 1873, between which date and the 30th of May next following the said remaining trees were to be removed from the forest; and further they were bound to complete the manufacture of the timber thus disposed of to them by the close of the year 1873, and to do so at certain places or sites outside the forest; therefore the rights and

powers of the purchasers and sellers of said woods are reserved
entire: 5th, The proprietors further reserve the right to create
and erect the necessary structures at Morriston Falls, in the
immediate vicinity of the mansion-house, for the introduction
of salmon to the River Morriston above the falls, and if need
be, to blast and break down the falls; but in respect that
there are not at present any salmon in the said river above the
falls, therefore it is stipulated, that if, in consequence of said
operations or otherwise, salmon shall be successfully introduced
therein, the exclusive right to fish them shall remain with
the proprietors, and is hereby reserved, but subject to this
provision, that before letting the right of salmon-
fishings above the falls to any other person, they shall be
bound to give the first offer thereof, so far as the River
Morriston flows through or *as adverso* of the subjects before
described, to the said Sir George Broke Middleton and his
foresaids: 6th, The proprietors further reserve the right of
planting in season the slope of land facing Loch Ness, between
Auldsay Burn and Craigian; as also of killing rabbits by trap-
ping on that ground at all seasons, for the preservation of the
plants: 7th, The proprietors further reserve the dwelling-house
presently occupied by Malcolm Macdonald at Blairey, as also
the right to graze a cow on the lands of Blairey; but in the
event of the said Malcolm Macdonald or any of his family behav-
ing in a way obnoxious to the tenant of these subjects, the said
tenant shall have the right to move him or them: And 8th,
The proprietors further reserve to the tenant of Ceamcroe deer-
forest, and for the tenant of the farm of Achlain, the right to
cut, season, and remove peats from the peat-hags on the south
side of the River Morriston on these subjects, wherefrom they
have been in the habit of doing so heretofore, as also similar rights
to the tenants of Achnaconeran and Livisy in the peat-hags adjoining their land: Which tack, with and under the reservations
before specified, the said James Chadwick and Patrick Grant, as
trustees foresaid, bind and oblige themselves and their successors
to warrant to the said Sir George Broke Middleton and his foresaids at all hands and against all mortals: For which causes,
and on the other part, the said Sir George Broke Middleton binds
and obliges himself, and his heirs, executors and representatives
whomsoever, to make payment to the said trustees, and their
foresaids, or to their factor for the time, of the following yearly
rent or tack-duty, viz. the sum of 1,700*l.* on 2nd August 1872
for the first year's possession—that is, from Whitsunday 1872 to
Whitsunday 1873—at which latter term the said Sir George
Broke Middleton and his foresaids will have the right to the deer-
forest of Glenloyne; and of the sum of 2,000*l.* for the second
and subsequent years of this lease, payable, the second, third, and
fourth years' rents, in two equal instalments, on the second day of
August and 1st day of January yearly but the fifth year's rent
—that is, the rent for the year from Whitsunday 1876 to Whit-

sunday 1877—shall be payable in one sum on the 2nd August
1876; with a fifth part more of each year's rent of liquidate
penalty in case of failure, and the legal interest of the said rent
from the time of the respective terms of payment until payment:
And the said Sir George Broke Middleton further binds and
obliges himself and his foresaids, during the currency of this
lease, to pay the usual local, public, and parochial taxes exigible
by law from the tenant in respect of the subjects hereby let,
and also to pay annually, along with his rent, one half of the
annual premium of fire insurance on the mansion-house and
furniture; it being understood, in the event of injury or de-
struction by fire to the buildings and furniture, the same shall
be made good by the proprietors out of the sum to be recovered
from the company taking the risk, the proprietor insuring to the
full amount of the inventory and the value of the mansion-
house; but the proprietors shall not be bound to expend or make
good anything beyond what they may recover from the said company: And the said Sir George Broke Middleton accepts of
the mansion-house hereby let, and the stables and other outbuildings or office-houses, as in good tenantable condition; and
he hereby binds and obliges himself and his foresaids to deliver
the same at his outgoing in like good condition, ordinary tear
and wear excepted; the proprietors, however, being bound during this lease to maintain the external walls and roofs of the
said mansion-house, stables, and other outbuildings or office-
houses in good repair, the tenant being bound to maintain the
inside of the same in like good repair; and as the said Sir
George Broke Middleton hereby receives and takes over on
inventory as aforesaid the furniture and other effects in the
mansion-house belonging to the proprietors, he hereby binds and
obliges himself and his foresaids to deliver the same at his outgoing in the same condition as he receives them, ordinary tear
and wear excepted; and he also hereby binds and obliges himself
and his foresaids during his absence from the estate to have a
suitable person in charge of the mansion-house, and otherwise
to attend to it; and he further binds and obliges himself and
his foresaids to uphold the gardens and pleasure-grounds in the
same good order and condition as they are at present during the
currency of this lease, defraying the whole cost of so doing, and
continuing James Munro, now head gardener, in his place, at
his present wages and emoluments, he being, however, liable
to dismissal in case of misbehaviour: it is, however, understood
that the tenant shall not be required to spend a larger
amount than the sum of 150l. in any one year in upholding
the said gardens and pleasure-grounds; and on proof of having
so expended such sum, he shall be deemed to have satisfied the
requirements of this clause: And it is hereby provided that
the tenant of the home farm shall supply the said Sir George
Broke Middleton and his foresaids with such dairy produce as
the farm may yield, as also supply and cart farm manure as

heretofore to the gardens, for which he shall pay 4*s*. 6*d*. per
cubic yard, and also perform all reasonable cartings for the
mansion-house at the rate of 6*s*. per day for man and horse;
also to remove once in every week, free of charge, the refuse in
the arch near the mansion-house, he receiving it free of charge;
also to provide straw for the carriage horses free of charge if he
can supply the same, but on the understanding, if he does so, that
he shall be entitl d to the manure from the carriage stables without payment: And in respect the said Sir George Broke Middleton receives at his entry the wire fences now on and pertaining
to the subjects hereby let in good repair, he hereby binds and
obliges himself and his foresaids at the termination of this lease
to deliver them, as well as any other fences which may be
erected during its currency, in like good repair: And he further
binds and obliges himself and his foresaids during this lease
always to have a sufficient staff of keepers, as at present, on the
said subjects, and to retain Donald Maclean, now head keeper, in
his present charge, the said Donald Maclean being, however,
liable to dismissal in case of misbehaviour; and the said Sir
George Broke Middleton and his foresaids shall defray and pay
the wages and emoluments to the keepers during this lease:
And further the said Sir George Broke Middleton binds and
obliges himself and his foresaids to shoot, sport, and fish at all
times in a sportsmanlike manner, and that no shooting, hunting,
or fishing shall be exercised by him or them, or by their game-
keepers or others, after the 30th day of November in the last
year of this lease: And the said Sir George Broke Middleton
and his foresaids shall have power, at their own risk and expense,
to prosecute, in his or their names, or in the names of the proprietors, all persons found poaching or trespassing on the said
lands: And it is hereby declared that the said Sir George
Broke Middleton and his foresaids shall have full power to burn
heather, in proper season, on the subjects hereby let, but under
and subject to this declaration and agreement, that if any damage
or loss may arise to the woods or others through or by these
operations, he or they shall be bound to pay therefor, as the same
may be ascertained and fixed by arbiters to be mutually chosen,
or by an oversman to be named by the said arbiters if they should
differ in opinion: And farther the said Sir George Broke Middleton binds and obliges himself and his foresaids to remove with
his servants and others, from the possession of the subjects hereby let at the expiration of this lease, and that without any
previous warning or process of law to that effect: And both
parties bind and oblige themselves and their respective foresaids
to perform their respective parts of the premises to each other
under the penalty of 500*l*., to be paid by the party failing to the
party performing, or willing to perform, over and above performance: And they consent to registration hereof, for preservation and execution: In witness whereof these presents, written
upon this and the five preceding pages of stamped paper by

Thomas Gillies, clerk to Messrs. Adam and Sang, W.S., Edinburgh, are subscribed by the parties in duplicate as follows, viz., by the said Sir George Broke Middleton (subscribing himself " G.N. Broke Middleton," his full name being George Nathaniel Broke Middleton) at London, the 18th day of June 1872, before these witnesses, Harry Snow, solicitor, London, and Francis Richard Turner Bloxam, clerk to Messrs. Paterson, Snow, and Barney, solicitors, London; by the said Patrick Grant, at Glenbrittle, Skye, the 2nd day of July and year last mentioned, before these witnesses, Simon Fraser, his butler, and John M'Caskill, gamekeeper, at Glenbrittle aforesaid; and by the said James Chadwick, at Folkestone, the 19th day of July and year last mentioned, before these witnesses, Henry Waite, clerk, and Josiah Chasey, waiter, both in the Pavilion Hotel, Folkestone; declaring that the word " annual " on the sixth line from the top of page four was deleted before subscription. (Signed) JAMES CHADWICK. PATRICK GRANT. G. N. BROKE MIDDLETON. H. Waite, *witness.* Josiah Chasey, *witness.* Simon Fraser, *witness.* John M'Caskill, *witness.* Harry Snow, *witness.* Francis R. T. Bloxam, *witness.*

PART VIII.

No. 20.—In the Exchequer.—Scotland.—First Division.

20th June 1876.

Income Tax.—Corporation liable to Assessment in respect of Profits of Gasworks.

Case stated on Appeal of the Glasgow Gas Commissioners.

At a Meeting of the Commissioners for General Purposes under the Property and Income Tax Acts, for the City of Glasgow, held at Glasgow on the 24th April 1876,—

The Glasgow Corporation Gas Commissioners appealed against an assessment made upon them under Schedule D. of the Income Tax Acts, for the year 1875-6, on the sum of 62,083*l.*, the alleged profits of the gasworks—

1st. On the plea of *res judicata*, in respect it was alleged that, under an arrangement come to between the solicitors in Edinburgh acting respectively for the Inland Revenue and the Glasgow Corporation, it was agreed that the decision in the case of the Waterworks (The Glasgow Corporation Waterworks *v.* Inland Revenue, Exchequer, Scotland, First Division, 26th May 1875), should rule that of the Gasworks ; and,

[*marginal note:* Case, No. 12, p. 23.]

2nd. On the merits—that under the statutes and the decision just quoted, they are only assessable for their annuities, interest on mortgages and feu duties, from which they are entitled to retain the tax on payment.

[*marginal note:* 5 & 6 Vict. c. 65 s. 104,]

The facts are these :—By " the Glasgow Corporation Gas Act, 1869," the Glasgow Gaslight Company and the City and Suburban Gas Company of Glasgow, with all their privileges, obligations, and liabilities, were transferred to and vested in the Municipal Corporation of the city ; the former as at 31st May 1869, and the latter as at 30th June 1869.

That Act was amended by "The Glasgow Corporation Gas Act, 1871," and "The Glasgow Corporation Gas Act, 1873."

The Corporation are authorised to supply gas to the city of Glasgow and suburbs. They are also required to pay the shareholders of the original companies perpetual annuities to the extent of 34,762*l.* 10*s.*, and in the event of there being any deficiency of funds to pay these annuities, they are authorised to assess the occupiers of all lands and heritages situated within the parliamentary and municipal boundaries of the city of Glasgow at a rate not exceeding 6*d.* per pound on the real rent or yearly value of such lands and heritages.

The Corporation are also empowered to borrow money, not exceeding one million sterling, on mortgage for the purposes of their carrying the Act into execution. They are further required to set apart as a sinking fund a sum not less than one per centum per annum on the amount borrowed, which fund is to be applied in the redemption of the mortgages or annuities, and must never be less than 2,000*l.* They are further empowered to manufacture and sell gas, gas-pipes, and lamps, and carry on such operations and business as are for the time being usually carried on by gas companies. The price charged by the Corporation must not exceed 4*s.* 7*d.* per 1,000 cubic feet.

The moneys received under the Act (not being money borrowed) must be applied in the following manner, and not otherwise :—

First. "In payment of the expenses of and incidental to the "raising, levying, and recovering the rents, charges, and re- "venues, and the borrowing of moneys under this Act."

Secondly. "In payment of the expenses of managing and "maintaining the gasworks of the Corporation."

Thirdly. "In payment of the Glasgow Corporation Gas an- "nuities, and annuities to holders of funded debt, and interest "of money borrowed under this Act."

Fourthly. "In carrying the several powers and provisions of "this Act into execution, including any extension and improve- "ment of the gasworks and mains and may carry any balance "thereof to the credit of the Corporation for their general "purposes."

In support of their preliminary objection, the Corporation stated—

1st. That when the question first arose as to the basis of assessment in the case of the Water and Gas Trusts, it was agreed that joint cases should be stated by these trusts and the Board of Inland Revenue for the opinion of the Law Officers of the Crown, which opinion should be held to settle the case. That two cases were accordingly prepared and sent to the Solicitor of Inland Revenue for revisal, and that on 7th March 1874, he returned the draft case with a letter, in which he said : " I "have not dealt in the meantime with the case under the Gas "Acts, as I presume you will hold that the deliverance in "one case will regulate the other ; " and they alleged that a verbal arrangement to the same effect was made at a meeting which the Town Clerk and the Corporation's Edinburgh correspondent had with the late solicitor, and that the Gas and Water Trusts acquiesced in that arrangement.

In June 1874 an Act was passed making it competent to appeal from the District Commissioners to the Court of Exchequer ; and on 17th December 1874 the Solicitor of Inland Revenue intimated that the Board had recalled their order remitting the question to the Law Officers of the Crown, and referring to the recent statute, stated that the proper course now to test the validity of the decision of the District Commissioners was to ask them to formally rehear the appeal when the Corporation could crave a case for the Exchequer Court, which was accordingly done. No notice was sent that the case of the Gas Corporation was to be reheard with a view of its being taken to the Court of Exchequer, which it was argued showed conclusively that the Inland Revenue officials considered that the former arrangement was still in force ; and it was only after a decision against the Inland Revenue in the case of the Water Trust had been obtained, that the Corporation were informed that it was intended to bring up the gas case again. They further stated that their Edinburgh correspondent bore testimony to the arrangement in question having been entered into ; and from their correspondent's accounts against the Corporation, it appears that they divided the charges incurred in connexion with the case for Crown Counsel and the appeal between the Gas and Water Trusts. It was therefore submitted that the question is already decided, and cannot now be opened up. But this plea they reserved, and only urged it now to enable them to bring it up again, should the appeal be carried further.

2nd. The Corporation admit their liability to pay tax on the annuities, interest, and feu duties, as they did in years prior to 1872-73, and which amounts for the year 1875-76 to 59,712l. ; but they maintain that they are not liable for income tax on any surplus after payment of the working expenditure, nor for the sinking fund (which in the case of the Water Company were found not to be assessable), as such an assessment would be practically one on means and substance.

It was submitted that the case of the gasworks is substantially the same as that of the waterworks, in which it has been found by the Court of Exchequer that there can be no profits in the sense of the Income Tax Acts. The expenses and revenue are intended to meet each other, and if there happen to be a surplus it is simply carried forward to aid in reducing the price of gas in the succeeding year.

The charge for gas in this case is cost price as nearly as can be estimated, and is simply "a district rate" imposed by the Corporation upon themselves, and payable in proportion as they use the article. The object of the Corporation in taking over the undertaking of the old gas companies was to save profits, and give the inhabitants gas at cost price. There are no profits belonging to anyone for his patrimonial interest, and no individual is enriched by the exercise of the statutory powers of the Corporation, who are merely gratuitous trustees for the general community ; and though the Corporation have power to apply the surplus to their general purposes, they have never done so, and have refused to do it—any surplus being always carried forward to next year's account.

Reference was also made to the opinion of the Judge who took part in the decision of the water case, and to the cases and dicta of the English Judges there referred to.

It was answered on behalf of the Crown to the first plea of *res judicata*, that this case of the gasworks was never previously before the Exchequer Courts, and no decision ever given in it, and that the plea of *res judicata* could not therefore be entertained. It was admitted, however, that there was an arrangement as stated, that a joint case by the Commissioners of Inland Revenue and the Glasgow Corporation should be stated for the opinion of Crown Counsel in the matter of the income tax assessments for the Glasgow Gas and Water Works ; but in consequence of the Corporation wishing that opinion to receive a much wider application than the Board of Inland Revenue would consent to give it, the whole of the questions in dispute were remitted *pro forma* to the District Commissioners, with a view to obtaining the decision of the Court of Exchequer, under the Act 37 & 38 Vict. cap. 16., Part III.

The case of the waterworks was alone proceeded with. But the Board of Inland Revenue entirely repudiate the view maintained by the Corporation on that point.

In consideration, however, of the losses sustained by the Gas Company in recent years, in consequence of the high price of coals, the assessments for all past years were restricted, without prejudice, to the sums for which the Corporation admit they are liable, and the question now is, whether the circumstances of the Gas Corporation, who have been assessed for year 1875–76 for their surplus (including the sum set apart for the sinking fund), are precisely the same as those of the waterworks in 1872–73. But to hold that the decision in one case which was before the Court should be held as deciding another, although differing in principle, would be unreasonable, and would require a very distinct and specific agreement to that effect to make it legally or morally binding.

2nd. In reply to the second plea, it was argued that in the case of the waterworks the whole point was whether the moneys collected by means of a compulsory general district rate, under the authority of an Act of Parliament, could be regarded as profit ; and the Court held that they could not be so regarded, because the rate must be and was adjusted so as to cover the expense incident to the supply of water, and leave no surplus.

In the case of the gasworks, there is no obligation upon any householder in Glasgow to have pipes laid down to his house or to burn gas ; and the amounts paid by those to whom gas is supplied are in no respect general or compulsory rates, but are payments made according to the quantity consumed, and in conformity with contracts between the consumer and Corporation.

It was further submitted that it is a commercial undertaking. The Corporation purchased the works of two companies who carried on their works as commercial undertakings, and by section 54 of " The Glasgow Corporation Gas Act, 1869," they are " empowered to manufacture, purchase, supply, sell, let, lay " down, place, and maintain gas fittings, meters, pillars, pipes, " lamp-posts, lamps, burners, and other articles and things con- " nected with gasworks or with the supply of gas for public or " private consumption, in such manner as the Corporation think

"proper, and generally may carry on such operations and busi-
"ness as are for the time being usually carried on by gas com-
"panies."

Again, they compete beyond the municipal boundaries with
other gas companies, which are purely commercial undertakings,
and sell their gas at the same price as the Corporation do.

Further, by the last part of section 86 of the said Act the
Corporation are empowered to carry any balance or surplus to
the Credit of the Corporation for their general purposes, clearly
showing that it is anticipated that profits will be realized; and
these profits, when so realized, may be applied as part of the
common good.

No such powers and privileges as those conferred on the Corporation by sections 54 and 86 of the Gasworks Act are contained,
in the Waterworks Acts, so that the two cases are not the same
in principle, nor are they analogous.

It was therefore maintained that the assessment was correct,
and should be affirmed.

The Commissioners having considered the case were of opinion
that there was no difference in principle between the two cases;
and as the trust existed for the benefit of the community they
sustained the appeal, and restricted the assessment to the amount
of the annuities, interest, and feu duties—say 59,712*l*.

A case was then craved on behalf of the Crown for the opinion
of the Court of Exchequer.

JUDGMENT, 20th June 1876.

The Lord President.—In this case, the Income Tax Commissioners say that they have not found any difference in principle
between the present case and the case which we decided in regard
to the water assessments in Glasgow. If I could agree in that
opinion, I should be very glad to confirm the decision of the
Commissioners; but the distinction between the two cases is, I
think, very palpable and essential for the purposes of this question. The Glasgow Corporation Act of 1869 empowered the
magistrates and town council, the Corporation of Glasgow, to
purchase the undertakings of the two companies, which had been
previously authorised by Act of Parliament to supply Glasgow
with gas, and the 4th section of the statute transferred the
whole property of those two companies to the municipal
corporation.

The way in which the Corporation were authorized to pay the
price for this subject, which they so acquired, is provided by the
11th section of the statute, and it was by way of annuity to the
shareholders in the former gas companies corresponding to the
value of the interest which they held in those companies. The
Corporation were then empowered to manufacture and sell gas
to the inhabitants of Glasgow and suburbs, and the 83rd section,
among other things, provided that there should be a sinking
fund to pay off the debts which of course the Corporation were

Case No. 12, p. 46.

obliged to incur in the first instance for the purpose of erecting works and setting the concern going. The provision is (*reads*).

Now, as regards the other clauses of the Act, with respect to the conduct of this undertaking by the Corporation, it is only necessary to add that they have no power to compel anybody to take their gas. On the contrary, it is quite optional for any of the inhabitants to buy their gas from the Corporation or not, as they think fit, and the Corporation are put under a restriction as to the price which they are to charge for the gas by the maximum price of 4*s.* 7*d.* being allowed. Then, finally, the 86th section of the statute provides for the application of all moneys that are to go into the gas Corporation in the way of revenue (*reads*). Now the revenue of .'1e Corporation is applied in terms of this section, in the first place, in payment of the interest of mortgage debt, and in payment of the annuities ; and there can be no doubt that income tax is charged on that part of the revenue, not on this Corporation but on their creditors, the creditors of the mortgage debts and the holders of annuities, because the income tax, which is levied on the Corporation in the first instance, forms a deduction from the payment of these interests and annuities. But then the question has arisen and it comes to this very narrow point, whether, if there be anything beyond that, if there be any revenue beyond what is applied in this way, or in maintaining the work, and which goes into the sinking fund in terms of the 83rd section, or goes into the coffers of the Corporation for their general purposes under the 85th section, that is or is not liable for income tax. Now, my Lords, I answer that question in the affirmative. It seems to me that the Corporation of the city of Glasgow is, by virtue of this statute, empowered to enter into a speculation as traders in gas. No doubt it may have been for the benefit of the community—that is perfectly true—but they have all the character and attributes of a trading company. They acquired the works for the purpose of manufacturing gas ; they manufactured gas, and sold it to those who were willing to become buyers ; but they can't sell it to anybody, that is to say, they cannot compel anybody to take it who is not willing to do so, and willing to do so at their price. They are empowered and authorised, nay, bound to make provision for the paying off of the mortgage debt which they had incurred at the commencement of the concern, and after they have done that, whatever surplus there is belongs to the Corporation for its general purposes, that is to say, goes simply into the common good of the Corporation, which is, in other words, saying that the surplus belongs to this company—to this trading company—for its own uses and purposes. The distinction between this and the case which is argued by the Income Tax Commissioners is very clear. There never could be any surplus or balance of profit under the Water Trust Act, for this simple reason, that the statute made it imperative so to use every shilling of revenue that was levied under that statute, so far as it was not otherwise employed, as to reduce the rates paid by the ratepayers, and in that way there never could be any balance at all. There was no trading in the sense that, after paying the expenses and interest, the balance, which was not otherwise appropriated, was to be devoted to the special purpose in question. The further distinction which exists between the two cases is this, that by the Water Trust Act, the Commissioners thereby appointed were authorised to levy the assessment within a certain district, at a certain rate, according to the rental of the property within that district, and that they were to apply it for a public purpose; and all the money raised by means of that assessment was devoted exclusively to that public purpose—to the public purpose defined by the statute itself. In this case there is no authority to levy a rate at all, and therefore the case belongs to a different category. because that rate which is authorised to be levied by the 42nd section of the statute is really nothing more than the creation of security, or a guarantee for the annuitants—the shareholders of the companies—an arrangement for the benefit of the concern in turning it to as profitable account as possible, in order to enable the Corporation to continue to pay the annuity. That, however, is not to come into operation under ordinary circumstances, and forms no proper part of the scheme under which the Corporation are to conduct this business of manufacturing and selling gas. I think the distinction in this way between the cases is so clear that it is needless to waste more words upon it. The portion of the revenue which goes into the sinking fund is just a part of the income of this trading corporation, which is used by them for paying off their debt, and the portion of it beyond that which goes into the funds of the Corporation for their general purposes is just also something which they had gained in the way of profit or surplus revenue for corporate benefit: and it does not require that profits shall be for the benefit of individuals only in order to make them profits within the meaning of Schedule D. of the income tax. If they are for corporate benefit, they are just as much profit within the meaning of the statute, and I have no hesitation in setting aside the decision of the Commissioners and sustaining the assessment.

Lord Deas.—The grounds for the opinion of the judges in the former case mainly centred in this, that the Corporation were not in the position of an ordinary trading company, but in a very different position. I need not repeat what the judges said when the former case was before them, because their opinions have been referred to at length in the course of the argument. Your Lordship in the chair has stated the aspect of the present case clearly; and I am of opinion that no grounds have been stated for distinguishing between the position in which the Corporation now stands with reference to the sale of gas from the position in which the two trading companies stood. I hereby agree with your Lordship on this question.

Lord Ardmillan.—I am also of the same opinion, and have little to add to what has already been said. I think there are two grounds on which the distinction of this case from the case

of the Water Company rests; in the first place in the mode of
operation by which the funds come in. How do the funds come
in? In the case of the Water Company the funds come in by
an assessment over all the parties liable in a public assessment,
and every person had to pay that assessment whether he consumed the water or not. But in the case of the supply of gas,
every person is not bound to take it. Customers take it just as
much as any other article sold to them. The relation between
the Corporation and the ratepayers in regard to gas is the relation
between a Company or corporation selling and individuals purchasing. In regard to the mere use of the article, the water
supplied by the Water Company was in the same position as the
gas. If a person chose not to use the water so supplied, having
a supply in his back-garden or elsewhere, he was not *bound* to use
it; still he was assessed for it; but if he uses oil lamps in pre-
ference to the gas supplied by the Corporation, he may do so, and
be relieved from paying for the gas which the Corporation manufacture. Therefore, the distinction in the mode of operation as
to the manner in which the funds are gathered in is very obvious,
but the other distinction is just as obvious. What is the ultimate
result in administering the funds? In the case of the water rate
the ultimate result led by force of the statute to a diminution of
the water rate. There is no such result in the case of the gas.
The statute, after setting forth what may be done with the
funds, ends by saying that the balance shall be carried to the
credit of the Corporation for their general purposes. I have no
doubt these purposes are wise and beneficent purposes, but they
are purposes within their own control so far as this statute
goes. I cannot see any ground for dealing with this Company
as other than a company choosing to sell to those who buy; and
the profits they make, after complying with certain statutory
regulations about the payment of debt, is property at their own
disposal. The case of the Water Corporation is quite different,
for a statute law came in and gave them statutory powers and
imperative statutory directions for the ultimate application of
the fund for the benefit of all assessed.

Lord Mure.—I concur entirely with the distinctions your
Lordships have pointed out, and I have nothing to add to what
you have said.

The Lord President.—We reverse the decision of the Commissioners, and sustain the assessment to the full amount.

PART IX.

No. 21.—In the High Court of Justice, Exchequer Division.

24th January 1877.

W. G. KEEN (Surveyor of Taxes)   -   -   Appellant

and

PEYTON DASHWOOD   -   -   -   - Respondent.

Inhabited House Duties. — Premises occupied in the daytime for business purposes partly by Professional Men and partly by Persons in Trade, and at night by a caretaker, liable to duty, at higher rate of 9d. in the pound, on the whole building.

CASE stated on Appeal of the Surveyor of Taxes for the Opinion of the Court under 37 & 38 Vict. c. 16., Part 3.

POINTS OF ARGUMENT.

FOR THE APPELLANT.

1. That the premises in question, being partly occupied by professional men and other persons who are not traders, are not used solely for the purposes of trade and so do not fall within the exemptions granted by the 57 Geo. 3. c. 25. s. 1., and 32 & 33 Vict., c. 14. s. 11.
2. That the portions of the premises respectively occupied by the several traders and others mentioned in the case are not separately assessable to the house duty, but form part of one entire building which is liable to be assessed to such duty.
3. That premises in which a servant or other person dwells for the protection thereof are by the 11th section of 32 & 33 Vict. c. 14. only exempted from duty where such premises are used for the purposes of trade only, which the premises in question are not.
4. That the present case is governed by the decision of this Court in Rusby v. Newson, Law Reports, 10 ; Exchequer, p. 322.

At a meeting of the Commissioners for the general purposes of the Income Tax Acts, and for executing the Acts relating to the Inhabited House Duties, for the city of London, held at the Land Tax Rooms, Guildhall Buildings, in the said city, on Thursday, the 3rd day of August 1876, for the purpose of hearing appeals,—

Mr. Peyton Dashwood appealed against an assessment to the Inhabited House Duties of 2,000l. at 9d. in the pound, in respect of the premises 74 and 75, Mark Lane, for the years 1874 and 1875.

The premises were occupied by Mr. Dashwood, who is a land speculator as well as a land agent, and also by 14 traders, as well as by two solicitors, one engineer, and a naval architect, and by a caretaker at night.

The Appellant claimed exemption under the 11th section 32 & 33 Vict. c. 14., contending that the entire premises were occupied solely

FOR THE RESPONDENT.

1. That a building consisting of several separate sets of offices occupied for business purposes only partially by persons in trade and partially by professional men, no person dwelling thereon except in the daytime, is not liable to the payment of inhabited house duty.

2. That if the court should be of opinion that the said building is under the said circumstances exempt from such payment, the exemption is not forfeited by reason of a servant remaining upon the premises at night to watch and guard them, he not dwelling thereon as a residence.

3. That if the said building under the circumstances firstly-mentioned is exempt from payment of the said duty, the exemption is not forfeited by reason of a servant or other person dwelling in such building for its protection.

5th October 1876.

for the purposes of trade within the meaning of the above statute.

The surveyor objected that as Mr. Dashwood the owner, and the other professional men above referred to, occupied the premises they could not be considered to be used for the purposes of trade only.

The Commissioners, however, granted relief on the grounds that the 11th section of the 32 & 33 Vict. c. 14. must be read with and construed in harmony with 5 Geo. 4. c. 44. s. 4.

Whereupon the surveyor declared his dissatisfaction with their decision, and duly required them to state and sign a case for the opinion of the Exchequer Division of the High Court of Justice, which we have stated and signed accordingly in pursuance of the 9th section of the 37 Vict. c. 16.

G. R. BENGOUGH ⎫
W. H. HEATH   ⎬ Commissioners.
              ⎭

JUDGMENT.

Cleasby, B.—We have in this case to consider the 11th section of the 32 & 33 Vict., c. 14., and we are called upon to give a certain effect to that section by way of construction, although in doing so we are not to be guided simply by the words, but a reasonable and proper construction is to be applied to the subject matter in order to give a proper effect to the words. That may be no doubt carried to a certain extent, but, referring to a decision of my own before the Court of Appeal, which was a decision in a case from the inferior courts, I ventured to say, that, although the language of the Act of Parliament might fit exactly with the particular subject, yet where there has been a *casus omissus*, and it becomes necessary to extend the words to another subject, you may so extend them. I think that was a case in which the language of the Act admitted of a certain extension although it was pretty plain that it fitted in exactly with a more limited state of circumstances. Now, if that could be done in this case I should be glad to do it, but, as it appears to me, we have not sufficient materials to enable us to do it in this case. The language of the Act of Parliament is clear, and I should say precise and free from any ambiguity. It makes use of the words "for the purposes of trade only;" there is no ambiguity in that whatever. I mean there is no ambiguity in the meaning of the words "for the purposes of trade only," and there is no reason why there should be any ambiguity. It is desirable to encourage trade, and it is a matter of importance to give it that encouragement. But, without going into that, it is satisfactory to know that we can find a reason for it, and not only do I find here the words "for the purpose of trade only," and other purposes, but it goes on to other particulars, showing that there are purposes not only as coming within the words "for the purposes of trade only," but other matters connected therewith, which are also made the subject of observation and upon which we are called upon to decide. It appears to me to be a clear case on this ground, that by a previous statute an exemption had been granted to a limited extent and that was by the statute of 6 Geo. 4. c. 7. A larger exemption had been granted under different circumstances by the 6 Geo. 4., which relates to trades and professions. The 6 Geo. 4. is to be taken into consideration as giving certainly an extended exemption, not only to premises occupied for trade purposes but to any premises; and because we find in the subsequent statute the words "for the purpose of trade only" we are asked to say that it follows as a matter of necessity, without involving any absurdity, that the Legislature must have intended and expressed their intention that the exemption must be extended. I see no reason for it whatever. The words of the Act of Parliament, by the ordinary rules of construction, are clear, and there is no ambiguity about them; whether we see the reason or not, we say that so far as regards the 32 & 33 Vict., the intention of the Legislature was only to relieve premises occupied "for trade purposes only;" and as the case comes within that intention, it appears to me that the Commissioners in attempting to harmonise the 32 and 33 Vict. with the 6 Geo. 4 have gone beyond their authority, and therefore, that the appeal from the decision of the Commissioners must be allowed.

Pollock, B.—I am entirely of the same opinion, and I will only say a few words with reference to the mode in which Mr. Herschel has most clearly dealt with what he referred to as either a *casus omissus* on the part of the Legislature in the last Act, the 32 & 33 Vict. c. 14. s. 11., or the use of language which amounted to almost the same thing. As I gathered from Mr. Herschel's argument, he said, that being so, this question must be governed by the meaning which the words actually conveyed. I do not think that the Legislature can be charged with any omission. I believe it arises from the fact that it is not usual in modern times to give a preamble to an Act of Parliament or to a section of an Act of Parliament. In the old days it was so. According to the 57 Geo. 3. c. 25. you will find a provision there setting out " And whereas it is become usual in cities and large towns and " other places for one and the same person, or for each person " where two or more persons are in partnership, to occupy a " dwelling-house or dwelling-houses for their residences, and at

" the same time one or more separate and distinct tenements or
" buildings, or parts of tenements or buildings, for the purposes
" of trade or as warehouses for lodging goods, wares, or
" merchandise therein, or as shops or counting-houses." That
being so. it follows that where houses are occupied for the purposes of trade only, then there may be what I called roughly a
caretaker on the premises. But that extension is carried further
by the 5 Geo. 4. c. 44. s. 4., and is applied to instances where the
premises are so occupied for professional or other purposes. Now
where you get to the 6 Geo. 4. you for the first time get the
application of the same principle to the case where the caretaker
actually dwells on the premises, and I suppose if there had been
a preamble to that Act it would have been so said. Now these
warehouses are often so far from the residence of the merchant,
that the caretaker must sleep there, and therefore, for the furtherance of trade, they provide for that case. But in this instance
by the Act of 32 & 33 Vict. the words used are " for the purposes
of trade only." I suppose that means in the case of a trade only
where the people are required to dwell on the premises. On the
other hand, if you take the case of a profession, the circumstances
are different. As I stated in the course of the argument, it may
well be that a professional gentleman may have a residence in
the country somewhere in the suburbs, a long way from the place
where he carries on his business or his profession, and have his
professional chambers or rooms, which are really like a second
dwelling-house, in London, but in that case it cannot be said that
it is necessary for the purpose of trade to have another residence
occupied by one of his servants and be exempted from paying
taxes. I think that this is a reasonable view of the case, and that
we ought to come to the conclusion that judgment in this case
should be for the Crown.

(Judgment for the Crown.)

PART X.

Before The Lord Ordinary.

---

*Inhabited House Duty.—Dwelling-house and business premises
under one roof, but without internal communication between
them, liable as one house.*

CASE stated on the appeal of Mr. William Russell,
Draper, Leslie.

At a Meeting of the Commissioners for the General Purposes
of the Income Tax Acts and for executing the Acts relating
to the Inhabited House Duties, held at Kirkcaldy on the
13th January, 1877.

Mr. William Russell appealed against an assessment to the
Inhabited House Duties for the year ending the 24th day of
May, 1877, at 6d. per 1l. on 52l., the annual value of premises
occupied by him at Leslie.

The Appellant stated that the amount on which the assessment is laid consists of 35l. rent of shop, and 17l. rent of dwelling-house, and there being no internal communication whatever, and the house being under 20l., no duty is payable. The
house is entered by a roofed staircase of 18 steps, built within
the yard after referred to, but outside all the other premises.
The dwelling-house was let some years ago as such, separately
from the other premises, and there has been no structural alteration since. The nearest shop door is nine feet in the open air
from the foot of the covered staircase. None of Mr. Russell's
workers board or lodge on either of the premises.

Mr. Webber, the surveyor, stated that he had viewed the premises, which consist of a shop on the ground floor and house
above, with yard and offices behind. The entrance to the house
is from said yard, to which access is had by a "close" between
this and the adjoining property, but the shop has two back doors
entering upon same yard, so that the Appellant goes from shop
to house without coming into the street or the "close." In
support of the assessment the surveyor referred to Rule 3,
Schedule B., 48 Geo. 3. c. 55, which enacts that "all shops and
"warehouses which are attached to the dwelling-house or have
"any communication therewith shall in charging the said

A

"duties be valued together with the dwelling-house," and to
the case decided by the English judges, No. 2781, and contended that as the house and shop are under one roof, and as the
whole premises are in the occupation of the Appellant, and
there is communication throughout by the private yard, which
is a portion of the premises, the Appellent is liable to the assessment appealed against.

The Commissioners considering the question as being attended
with difficulty decided to relieve the Appellant, with·which
decision the surveyor expressed himself dissatisfied, and
requested that this case might be stated for the opinion of the
Court.

Edinburgh, 6th March, 1877.

I am of opinion that the determination of the Commissioners
is wrong.

(Signed)　JOHN MARSHALL.

NOTE.—The business premises are under the same roof as the
dwelling-house, and are undoubtedly attached thereto, although
there is no internal communication between them, and as both
are occupied by the same person they must be valued *in cumulo*
under the statute.

(Intd.)　J.M.

No. 23.—IN THE EXCHEQUER.—SCOTLAND.
6th March, 1877.

Before THE LORD ORDINARY.

---

*Inhabited House Duty.—Dwelling-house and business premises
under one roof, but without internal communication between
them, liable as one house.*

CASE stated on the Appeal of Mr. Robert Salmond, junior,
Grocer, Burntisland.

At a Meeting of the Commissioners for the General Purposes
of the Income Tax Acts and for executing the Acts relating to the Inhabited House Duties, held at Kirkcaldy on
the 13th January, 1877.

Mr. Robert Salmond, junior, appealed against an assessment
to the inhabited house duties for the year ending the 24th day
of May, 1877, at 6d. per 1l. on 36l., the annual value of premises
occupied by him at Harbour Place, Burntisland.

The Appellant stated that the amount on which the assessment is laid consists of 19*l.* 10*s.* rent of shop, and 17*l.* rent of dwelling-house; and · there being no internal communication, and the house being under 20*l.*, no duty is payable. The house and shop, though entering from the back yard, might be let to two separate tenants without any alteration, and were so let for some time.

Mr. Webber, the surveyer, stated that he had viewed the premises, which consist of a shop on the ground floor and house above, with yard and offices behind. Besides the shop door entrance there is an entrance from the street pavement to the passage which leads to the house, and at one time there had been within the shop a door which also led into this passage, but this door was built up between 15 and 20 years ago. There is still, however, a back door to the shop communicating with the yard, and a back door to the house also communicating with the yard, so that the Appellant goes from shop to house without coming into the street. In support of the assessment the surveyor referred to Rule 3, Schedule B., 48 Geo. 3. c. 55, which enacts that "all shops and warehouses which are attached "to the dwelling-house or have any communication therewith "shall, in charging the said duties, be valued together with the "dwelling-house," and to the case decided by the English judges, No. 2781, and contended that as the house and shop are under one roof, and as the whole premises are in the occupation of the Appellant, and there is communication throughout by the private yard, which is a portion of the premises, the Appellant is liable to the assessment appealed against.

The Commissioners considering the question as being attended with difficulty decided to relieve the Appellant, with which decision the surveyer expressed himself dissatisfied, and requested that this case might be stated for the opinion of the Court.

Edinburgh, 6th March, 1877.

I am of opinion that the determination of the Commissioners is wrong.

(Signed)   JOHN MARSHALL.

NOTE.—The business premises are under the same roof as the dwelling-house, and are undoubtedly attached thereto, although there is no internal communication between them, and as both are occupied by the same person they must be valued *in cumulo* under the statute.

(Intd.)   J. M.

No. 24.—In the Exchequer.—England.
12th June, 1877.

The Imperial Continental Gas Association -   -   -   -   -   - Appellant,

and

Henry Nicholson (Surveyor of Taxes)   -   Respondent

*Income Tax.—Incorporated English Company, having its
office in England, liable as a person in the United Kingdom for
the whole of its profits wherever made.*

CASE.

POINTS OF ARGUMENT.

FOR THE APPELLANTS.

The following are the points
intended to be insisted upon on
behalf of the Appellants on the
argument of this case :—
1. That the Appellants are not
liable to be assessed upon the
whole of their profits wherever
made.
2. That the assessment should be
confined to the profits, which
actually are received in England, and should not include
profits made and retained
abroad.
3. That the Appellants correctly
made their return in respect
of foreign possessions.

FOR THE RESPONDENT.

1. That the Imperial Continental
Gas Association being an
English Company, incorpo-
rated by Act of Parliament,
having its office in England, is
in the same position as a person
residing in the United Kingdom, and is liable to income
tax under Schedule D. of the
Act 16 & 17 Vict. c. 34, in
respect of the whole of the
actual profits and gains of the
Company derived from its
business, whether carried on
in the United Kingdom or
elsewhere.

1. The Imperial Continental Gas
Association having required to be
assessed to income tax by the
Special Commissioners made by
their secretary a return under Schedule D. for the year 1875 ending
the 5th April 1876 of 210,655*l.*
2. The said Association are a
Company originally established
under the provisions of a co-part-
nership deed bearing date 9th
March 1825 for the purpose of
supplying cities, towns, and places
in foreign countries with gas, and
were incorporated by an Act
16 & 17 Vict. c. 190, intituled "An
Act for consolidating and amending
the powers of the Acts of the Imperial Continental Gas Association."
The said Act was repealed by "The
Imperial Continental Gas Association Act, 1870," but the Association
remained incorporated by virtue of
the said last-mentioned Act.
3. The offices of the Association
are at 30, Clement's Lane, Lombard
Street, in the City of London and
the meetings of the directors of
the Association take place at such
offices.

2. That the Association being an English Company, incorporated by Act of Parliament, having its office in England, is liable to income tax under Schedule D. of the Act 16 & 17 Vict. c. 34, on the whole of the annual profits and gains derived from its business, whether carried on in the United Kingdom or elsewhere, and whether such profits or gains be remitted to the United Kingdom or not.

3. That on the facts of the case it appears that the Association resides in the United Kingdom.

4. That the case of the Cesena Sulphur Company v. Nicholson (Exchequer D. 428)* has decided that the Association being an English Corporation, resident in England, is assessable upon the whole of its gains and profits derived from its business, whether carried on in the United Kingdom or elsewhere.

5. That the return made on behalf of the Association as stated in paragraph (5) of the case is bad in law.

6. That the assessment made by the Commissioners as stated in paragraph (7) of the case is good in law.

4. The Association possess interests of various natures and tenures in gas works in France, Germany, Austria, Holland, and Belgium, the profits of which wholly arise in those foreign countries; and, in such of them as have a tax equivalent to the income tax, those profits are assessed to such tax.

5. The said sum of 210,665l. being the amount stated in the return made on behalf of the Association in respect of profits, is made up of two sums, videlicet, 208,805l. and 1,860l. The sum of 208,805l. was stated to be in respect of profits from foreign possessions, and the sum of 1,860l. was stated to be in respect of interest of money.

6. The reason given on behalf of the Association for confining the amount of the return to the said sums is that the said sum of 208,805l. represents the profits of the Association from foreign possessions actually remitted and which would have to be remitted to the United Kingdom to make up (together with 1,860l. interest of money lent in the United Kingdom) the interest on the debenture debt of the said Association, and the gross total amount found from time to time by the directors to be applicable for the purposes of dividend, including both the dividend paid to non-resident shareholders and that paid to resident shareholders. And further that the profits *ultra* such remittances, and wholly arising abroad as aforesaid, are never transmitted to this country at all, but are retained abroad in liquidation of charges and expenses arising abroad from the exigencies of contracts for lighting foreign places, and are not divided among the shareholders either in this country or abroad.

7. The Special Commissioners in making their assessment charged the Association in the sum of 258,668l. in respect of the whole of their profits. Assuming the assessment to be made on the right principle (which the Appellants deny), it is admitted for the purposes of this case that the Association ought to be assessed in the sum of 258,668l.

8. Against such assessment the Association gave notice of appeal, and the appeal was heard by the Special Commissioners at their office on the 27th July, 1876, when Mr. Albert F. Jackson, the secretary, attended with Colonel Wilkinson, one of the directors.

---

* *Ante*, page 88.

9. No accounts were produced, the secretary stating that the said Association contend that the assessment should be confined to profits accruing in the United Kingdom, and to so much of those accruing abroad as are received by them in the United Kingdom for distribution amongst the shareholders, whether residing in the United Kingdom or elsewhere.

10. The Special Commissioners decided that the Association were liable for the whole of their profits, and confirmed the assessment made by them on the amount thereof, 258,668*l.*, the secretary of the Association expressing his dissatisfaction at the decision.

11. On the 17th August the Association through the secretary required the Special Commissioners by notice in writing to state and sign a case for the opinion of the Exchequer Division of the High Court of Justice, which was stated and signed accordingly; and, in conformity with the order of Mr. Baron Huddleston, dated the 3rd January, 1877, the case has been amended, and we now sign such amended case.

The question for the opinion of the Court is whether the assessment made by the Commissioners is in principle correct.

(Signed)   R. M. LYNCH.
SUDLEY.

Dated this 9th day of May, 1877.

JUDGMENT.

Kelly, *C.B.*—In this case of the Imperial Continental Gas Association against Nicholson, which we are all agreed has been very admirably argued before us, and it certainly has raised considerable doubt in the mind of the Court, especially the very able argument of Mr. Charles, it appears to me upon an attentive consideration of the Acts of Parliament, and of the decisions of this Court in what we may call briefly the Cesena case, that the Crown is entitled to the judgment of the Court. In the first place, let me observe that there is really no substantial distinction of any kind, either in fact or in principle, between the case now before us and the Cesena case,* the one and the other, they are both cases in which a joint stock company incorporated an incorporated company under the Joint Stock Companies' Act existing in England, established in England, registered in England, and within the meaning of the language of the Acts of Parliament resident in England, happened to be possessed of very extensive works in a foreign country or in foreign countries, in which what may not be improperly called a manufactory

---

* *Ante*, page 88.

and trade is carried on, and carried on at a profit, but in which
all that is earned in the way of profits is earned, but when
earned and when the profit is ascertained, it becomes the property and is payable to the joint stock company established and
resident in this country, which is assessed for income tax in
respect of the whole of that profit; and the objection made to
the assessment is that it ought to be assessed only on that
portion of the profit accrued and received which is remitted to
this country and is received in this country by the joint stock
company in question.

Now the difference in fact, but it is scarcely a difference at
all, is this, that in the Casena Company's case the profits of the
company in the year in question, or the average of years, whichever it may have been, but I say in the year in question, consisted of a certain sum of money which became and was dealt
with in the form of a dividend payable to the whole of the
shareholders of the company, whereas in the present case the
profit which had been acquired by the company in question, by
means of its very extensive dealings in foreign countries, has
been applied not altogether in the form of a dividend and paid
as a dividend to the shareholders in the company, but a portion
of it though profit, and though a portion of it has undoubtedly
been made into a dividend and as a dividend paid to the shareholders of the company, another portion of the profit has never
been treated as or made into the form of a dividend, but has
been applied by the company in some way not very well defined
in the case, but in some manner in which the company were
entitled to apply it, it was profit received which might if they
had thought fit. It might have been appropriated to the dividend which was divisible and divided among the shareholders;
but they thought fit to apply it in some other way, in improving
their works or something of that description, but, whatever it
was, it existed in the shape of profit, it was made in the shape
of profit, a great portion and by far the greater portion became
a dividend and was distributed amongst the shareholders, but
another portion was disposed of according to the will of the
company and possible under some resolution or resolutions of
the company in some other manner, still it was all profit and
would only differ from the profits acquired in the Cesena case in
this, that in that case the whole of the profit acquired was distributed in the shape of a dividend among the shareholders,
whereas the profit here was distributed, one portion among the
shareholders and the other portion applied by the company at
their pleasure to some other purpose. But in both cases there
was this feature common to both cases, and which has raised the
question which was before this Court in the Casena case, and
which is before this Court now, that a portion only of the entire
profit acquired was remitted to this country, and was consequently ever received by the joint stock company in this
country. In the Casena case that occurred in this way:
a number of the shareholders of the company were resident in

this couutry, but a number, I believe a great number of the
shareholders in the Cesena case were resident in Paris, in Italy,
and in various parts of the continent, and consequently that
portion only of the profit which was payable to the shareholders
in this country was ever remitted to this country, and all the
other was paid to the shareholders resident in Paris and elsewhere on the continent of Europe. Here a portion only of the
money has been remitted to this country, that portion payable
in the shape of a dividend to the shareholders of this company.
The other portion was never remitted to this country at all.
On all these points, therefore, in everything which constitutes
the substance of the case, and indeed of the one and the other
case the two cases are identical. It was a joint stock company
formed, registered, and established, and ordinarily, I say, within
the meaning of the Acts of Parliament resident in this country,
the property, or the undertaking, or the works, whatever they
may be called, out of which the profits arose, and by means of
which the profits were made, all in the continent of Europe, all
belonging to them in this country, and a portion only of the
profits was remitted to this country in the one case as in the
other case. The other portion was applied in some other way
and applied on the continent of Europe. Under those circumstances, therefore, the two cases being substantially identical, if
we were to give effect to the very able argument, as I say again
and again, of Mr. Charles, we must in effect and decidedly overrule the decision of this Court in the Cesena case, which being a
decision of this Court of some two judges of this Court, would
be an act which I should be very unwilling to do ; but still if I
were perfectly satisfied not only that in point of law that decision was wrong, but that justice required, there being no appeal
in this case, that we should give effect to the argument which
has now been offered, I do not say I should not be prepared to
take that course, but upon full consideration of the Acts of Parliament it appears to me the objection of Mr. Charles or the
argument of Mr. Charles, even if it had been offered and brought
under the attention of the Court in the Cesena case, ought not
to have prevailed and ought not to prevail now. And it is on
these grounds the case comes before us. The question that that
argument raises is whether this case is for all purposes to be
treated as within Schedule A., not only whether these gas works
on the continent of Europe are to be considered as property
substantially speaking. as land on the continent of Europe,
not only in construing the different schedules, Schedule A.,
Schedule B., Schedule C., and Schedule D., but also in giving
effect to the cases and the rules for carrying the schedules into
effect to be found in various parts of the old Act, the 5th and 6th
of Victoria, and in the Act of the 16th and 17th of Victoria.

Now when we look to the Act of Parliament, Schedule A.
being in the first instance for lands, tenements, hereditaments,
and heritages, we certainly do find, when we refer to the 60th
section, and it is upon this section and all that follows that

reliance is placed by the learned counsel for the company, that the duties in Schedule A. are to be assessed and charged under the following rules, and shall be deemed and considered to be a part of the Act, and so forth. Then we find a general rule for assessing the annual value of the lands, tenements, hereditaments, or heritages charged under Schedule A., and which shall be understood to be the rent by the year, the rack rent or the average rent by the year of the land and tenements in question. Then we find in No. 2 the mode in which the tax is to be assessed in respect of tithes and certain other descriptions of property referred to. Then we find in No. 3 and No. 4 other provisions take place ; there are other cases and there are other rules, but finally we find that No. 3, the rule for estimating the lands, tenements, hereditaments, or heritages herin-after mentioned, which are not to be charged according to the preceding general rule, is substantially as follows :—the annual value of the properties (and all that is afterwards dealt with is certainly called "properties") herein-after described shall be understood to be the full amount for one year or the average amount for one year of the profits received within the respective times herein-after mentioned. Then they deal with limestone, chalk, and so on, which are made to be ·properties within this Schedule A., and then with mines of coal, tin, lead, and so forth, which are made properties within Schedule A. ; and, lastly, we find iron works, gas works, salt springs, and so on. Gas works are also to be made property or properties within Schedule A., and are to be dealt with ; and it is therefore contended that these gas works, though they are not strictly speaking land or landed property at all, but are in effect only works by which a certain manufactory and trade is carried on, ·the manufacture, namely, of gas, and the trade of supplying gas for money and for profit to various persons to whom it is supplied in various parts of Europe, we find, no doubt, that that is, for the purpose of this portion of the Act of Parliament, treated as property, and as property within and subject to the operation of Schedule A. and the cases and rules for carrying that Schedule into effect. But when we come to look carefully at the whole of the provisions in all these cases and rules touching Schedule A., and particularly those which relate to and include these gas works, we find they are all, and necessarily so, within this kingdom of England, and there is nothing to be found in any one of these rules, or in any one of these cases, carrying it to its utmost extent, of any dealing with gas works which can relate to and include gas works not in this country, but are gas works either in the colonies or on the continent of Europe. Under these circumstances, and as we find that these provisions which would treat these gas works as property within Schedule A. relate only to gas works in England, and that the whole of the provisions in the cases and in the rules here pointed out with reference to gas works and every other description of property which is within Schedule A., are all in the kingdom of

England, within this country, none of them are abroad, there is no provision at all applying, directly or indirectly, to gas works or any property of this description abroad. It appears to me the whole effect of this part or these parts and portions of the Act of Parliament relating to gas works in England has no application whatever to gas works which, like those under consideration in the present case, are on the continent of Europe. Under these circumstances, therefore, we have only to consider the law concerning them, treating them as within Schedule D., which undoubtedly they are, being gas works on the continent of Europe, and having regard to all the provisions concerning them. It is unnecessary to go through the different sections of the Act of Parliament, the different cases, and the different rules for expounding and carrying into effect the original provisions in the Act of Parliament touching Schedule D., and every description of property, or work, or undertaking within it, because in all respects that can apply to the present case, the present case as identical with the case of the Cesena Company. It is a joint stock company established and resident in England; the whole property of the Company, the whole of the sources of the profit of the Company, the whole of the works of the Company, are not in England, but on the continent of Europe. The whole profit of the Company is received and acquired on the continent of Europe, and a great portion of it is applied, distributed, and spent on the continent of Europe. Therefore in all these points the two cases are identical, and upon the ground to which I have adverted, that these provisions under section 60, and touching Schedule A., are not applicable to any but gas works in the kingdom of England, and have no application to a case like this, where they are altogether abroad, I think that the argument of Mr. Charles, able as it really is, and captivating as it seemed at first sight, ought not to prevail, and that under the circumstances of the case, this being a foreign undertaking, that is an undertaking in a country on the continent of Europe, but belonging to a joint stock company established and registered here in this kingdom, that the whole of the profits, whether that portion of them which has been remitted and received in this country, or any that has been applied on the continent itself, the whole of the profits are assessable to income tax in this country, and that consequently the right of the Crown is established, and the judgment should be in favour of the Crown.

I ought to add, at the request of my brother Cleasby, that, being a shareholder in this Company, he does not think he ought to be a party to the judgment given in this case.

Huddleston, B.—The real practical question in this case is whether the Imperial Continental Gas Company are to be assessed in this country, where their place of business is, on a sum of 258,668*l.* or a sum of 210,665*l.* The Company claims exemption as to 48,003*l.* on the ground that that sum is or are profits never transmitted to this country at all, but retained abroad in liquidation of charges of expenses arising abroad from the exigencies of contracts for lighting foreign places, and not divided among the shareholders, either in this country or abroad.

Now Mr. Charles says that if that is to be taken as part of the profits, as it undoubtedly is, as a trade, he concedes that it would be assessable; but he says you must not look at it in that light, because gas works are to be assessed in the way that real property should be assessed, namely, as he says, under the fifth case of section 100, Schedule D., and therefore it is not assessable, because it has not been actually received annually in this country. That raises the question for our consideration.

Now I want first of all to see whether this is really profits of a trade. They are clearly profits arising from something that has been carried on. They are profits arising from the sale and manufacture of gas abroad.

I cannot help thinking that in ordinary parlance that is a trade. The mere fact that it is gas does not distinguish it, as far as I can see, from any other trade. It is made, manufactured, and sold, and the profits, looking at it as a book-keeping concern, are what is received *minus* the outgoing expenses.

Now, if I look at the words of Schedule D. in the 16th and 17th of Victoria, chapter 34, it seems to be clear that those profits come within those words. They are the annual profits arising or accruing to a person (for this purpose we may hold a corporation to be a person) residing in the United Kingdom for some kind of property. The words are "from any kind of property "whatsoever, whether situate in the United Kingdom or else- "where, and for and in respect of the annual gains arising or "accruing to any person." They clearly are profits arising from or accruing to a person in the United Kingdom from property out of the United Kingdom, and therefore clearly come within the words of Schedule D. Mr. Charles does not deny that, but he says that they are assessable under case 5, and not under case 1. As I understand Mr. Charles' argument, and certainly it is not from any fault on his part one fails to understand it, for he argued it most ably, he says it may be it comes within Schedule D., but you must assess it under case 5 of Schedule D., and he says that that is so because in fact the works abroad are foreign possessions, and he says, " I say it is so by " referring to the Act of Parliament, and to the cases under " Schedule A., because under No. 3 of Schedule A. gas works are " placed in the category of lands, tenements, and hereditaments, " and the assessments are to be on the annual value of those " properties." That is what I understand Mr. Charles to argue; and he says, " These being foreign possessions you are only to " assess them under the fifth case for that money which is " actually received in this country." Well, I must say, that if his view is correct, that case of the Cesena Sulphur Works was wrongly decided, because it is exactly this case. There is no distinction between mines and gas works. Mines are mentioned specifically in the second subsection of No. 3 attached to Schedule

A., but gas works are in the third subsection, but all the rules with reference to them are applicable to the first, second, and third, and therefore as far as this case of the Cesena Company is concerned it is exactly on all fours, and so it is in its circumstances as pointed out by my Lord, and I do not wish to repeat that again. I recollect perfectly well in the Cesena case an argument was raised with reference to how far the profits would be assessable where a portion of them was paid to persons abroad and had never come to this country. Well, it is said that point was not raised in the Cesena case. The point that Mr. Charles suggests, it is said, was not raised in the Cesena case. It has been urged that he has argued this part of the case with great ability; I am bound to agree in that, but I think one word of praise must be awarded to Mr. Dicey, who no doubt furnished a complete answer to what was a captivating argument of Mr. Charles.

Now what is that argument? It is obvious that this Schedule D., which is with reference to trades and to gas works, is confined to gas works in the United Kingdom. It says in substance certain things shall be assessable; amongst those things gas works in England shall be assessable as real property. I cannot help thinking that it might have required a legislative interpretation to put that construction upon gas works. I really cannot see that the manufacture of gas is not a trade. I cannot understand that it is not just as much as a trade, although it is carried on with buildings and by pipes put in the ground, as a hotel business abroad is carried on, by means of buildings, gardens, and hotel premises. It could never be said a company formed in England for the purpose of carrying on the business of hotel-keepers all through the continent were not to be assessable in England, because it happened they carried on their business by means of houses or gardens. I say it required a legislative enactment to bring gas works within the category of property, and there is no legislative enactment with reference to gas works abroad. I cannot help feeling that gas works abroad are to be considered as the works used for the manufacture of gas, to be a trade, and are not within the view which Mr. Charles put forward as being possessions abroad, or in the nature of lands, tenements, and so on.

Now Mr. Charles certainly put two points very strongly no doubt to show that the first case under section 100 of Schedule D. would not be applicable to the gas works abroad, and he argued that under rule five, which applies to both cases one and two, there would be no power to charge the duties in one division, unless where the person is engaged in different concerns, in trade in different places. That no doubt at first raises a difficulty, but it says, "every statement of profits to be charged under this " schedule shall include every source so chargeable on the person " delivering the same on his own account, or on account of any " other person, and every person shall be chargeable in respect of " the whole of such duties in one and the same division, and by

"the same Commissioners (except in cases where the same person
"shall be engaged in different partnerships, or the same person
"shall be engaged in different concerns relating to trade or
"manufacture in divers places, in each of which cases a separate
"assessment shall be made in respect of each concern at the place
"where such concern if singly carried on ought to be charged as
"herein directed)." Where is the business concern of these gas
works? In England. If the concern was carried on in different
places it might be assessed in different places, but here, as
pointed out by Mr. Dicey, according to our decision in the Jute
Company's case, and the Cesena Company's case, the business is
carried on at the place where the orders emanate. That is the
central point where the business is carried on, where the directors meet, from whence the orders are issued, and where the
whole transactions occur, and according to the 5th part of this
clause it would be assessed there. Then Mr. Charles also called
our attention to the 108th section for the same purpose. If I am
right in my view that these gas works were not foreign possessions that section does not apply, because it only applies to
foreign possessions. On the whole I am clearly of opinion these
works are assessable for that sum of 48,003*l.*, and that therefore
our judgment should be for the Crown.

Mr. Dicey.—I ask your Lordship to make an order for costs.

Kelly, C.B.—Yes, it must be with costs.

Mr. Charles.—I should have asked your Lordships to follow
the Cesena Company's case, the point I have urged before the
Court being an entirely new one.

Kelly, C.B.—In the decision of the Cesena case, as it was the
first time the case came before the Court, I thought each party
ought to pay his own costs, but as this is the second time, though
upon a new point, it is an appeal from the Cesena case, and we
must order costs.

PART XI.

Before The Lord Ordinary.

Income Tax.—Where the Surveyor of Taxes is not appointed Assessor under the Lands Valuation (Scotland) Acts, the Valuation is not binding for the purposes of the Income Tax Acts; and the Assessment to Income Tax is to be made under the Rules in the Acts relating to that Tax.

Case stated on the Appeal of William Menzies, Farmer, Keilator, Killin, under "The Customs and Inland Revenue Act, 1874" (37 Vict. c. 16).

At a Meeting of the Commissioners under the Property and Income Tax Act, 5 & 6 Vict. c. 35, and subsequent Acts for the county of Argyll, held at Oban on the 11th May 1877.

William Menzies, farmer, Keilator, Killin, appealed against the assessment of 17l. 10s. duty under Schedule A., and also against the assessment of 7l. 5s. 10d. sterling duty under Schedule B., made on him for the year 1876–77, in respect of his being lessee of the farm and lands of Kinlochbeg, Blackcarries, Blackburn, and Corryvalloch, including the shootings and fishings thereon.

1st. The Appellant was represented by Mr. Alexander M'Arthur, writer, Oban, his agent, who stated that the Appellant's lease is for a period of 13 years, commencing at Whitsunday 1868 and the rent stipulated for and paid under said lease is 875l. per annum.

2nd. The surveyor of property and income tax for Argyllshire has charged the Appellant the above-mentioned sum of 17l. 10s. under Schedule A., on the ground that the real annual value of the subjects held by him under said lease is 1,400l. per annum, and that he is liable to be taxed under this schedule for this amount subject to a right of relief against the proprietor for the amount, which applies to the rent stipulated for in the lease.

3rd. The surveyor has also charged the Appellant the above-mentioned sum of 7l. 15s. 10d. under Schedule B., being the amount applicable to said valuation of 1,400l., chargeable against occupants of lands and heritages.

4th. The Appellant objected to these assessments in respect that he alleges he is only liable to be assessed under Schedule B., and that only on the sum of 875*l.*, the *bona fide* rent which he pays under his lease, and the appropriate tax under which schedule is 4*l.* 11*s.* 1*d.*

5th. The Appellant claimed that the case falls under the rule of valuing lands and heritages laid down by the "Lands Valua-"tion (Scotland) Act," 17 & 18 Vict. c. 91. s. 6, which pro-vides that "when land and heritages are *bona fide* let for a "yearly rent conditioned as the fair annual value thereof, with-"out grassum or consideration other than the rent, such rent "shall be taken as the yearly rent or value of such lands and "heritages in terms of this Act," &c.; and that the present being a short lease (or a lease the stipulated duration of which is less than twenty-one years) it falls under this rule, and that the *bona fide* rent is alone the basis of taxation, whether the lease be a profitable or a losing one. He declined entering on the question of whether the lease was a profitable one to the extent claimed by the assessor, as that was not necessary for the decision of the point raised.

The surveyor of taxes (Mr. Donald Lamont) submitted that the Appellant's arguments were wholly irrelevant to the Statutes under which the Property and Income Taxes are imposed and levied and referred.

Firstly. To the "Valuation of Lands (Scotland) Act Amend-ment," 20 & 21 Vict. c. 58. s. 3, which says:—"Provided "always, that if in any county or burgh the said Commissioners "or Magistrates shall not appoint the officers of Inland Revenue "to be such assessors as aforesaid, then no valuation made under "the said Act by any other assessor or assessors shall be conclu-"sive against or for the purpose of reducing, on appeal or "otherwise, any assessment, rate, or charge under any Act of "Parliament relating to the duties of excise, or the land tax, or "assessed taxes, or income tax, or any other duties, rates, or taxes "under the care or management of the Commissioners of Inland "Revenue." The Appellant replied: The section of the Act quoted by the surveyor only enables him to have entries that are wrong in the valuation roll corrected for imperial taxation pur-poses; he must still abide by the rules of valuing lands and heritages laid down by the first-recited Act, which is not repealed or altered by the section quoted by the surveyor.

Secondly. The surveyor referred to the Act 5 & 6 Vict. c. 35. s. 60, No. 1, declaring that "The annual value of lands, &c., "&c., &c. under Schedule A. shall be understood to be the rent "by the year at which the same are let at rackrent, if the "amount of such rent shall have been fixed by agreement com-"mencing *within the period of seven years preceding the 5th* "*day of April next* before the time of making the assessment, "but if the same are not so let at rackrent then at the rack-"rent at which the same are worth to be let by the year; which

"rule shall be construed to extend to all lands, tenements, and
"hereditaments."

He referred also to section 68, rule 7, of last-recited Act
imposing the duty under Schedule B, and contended that this
valuation was legal and in accordance with the provisions of the
two Acts last above quoted, on the ground that *eight years* of
the lease had expired at the term of Whitsunday 1876 before the
assessment appealed against was made; and that his valuation
would be found considerably under-stated, in the event of the
lands being valued by a person of skill in terms of the following
statutes, viz., 5 & 6 Vict. c. 35. s. 81, authorising the Commissioners to cause valuations to be made; and also the Act
16 & 17 Vict. c. 34. s. 47, empowering Appellants to require
a valuation by person of skill; but the Appellant declined to
crave such a valuation.

Thereupon the Commissioners refused the appeal, and confirmed the charges under both Schedules A. and B., on the ground,
inter alia, that the Appellant neither exercised his right to
claim a valuation, nor adduced any evidence in support of his
appeal. The Appellant expressed himself dissatisfied with the
decision. The surveyor maintained that the decision of the
Commissioners is final and conclusive under the Act 37 Vict.
c. 16. s. 9, which declares "that the Appellant or the in-
"spector or surveyor may, if dissatisfied with the determina-
"tion of the Commissioners as being erroneous *in point of law*
"declare his dissatisfaction to the Commissioners who heard the
"appeal."

Subsequently, the Appellant craved a case for the opinion of
the Court of Exchequer, which is here stated accordingly.

C. A. M'DOUGALL, *Com.*
NEIL M. MACDONALD, *Com.*

ADDITIONAL STATEMENT.

Edinburgh, 1st November 1877.—The Lords, having heard
counsel on the case for William Menzies, appoint the Solicitor of
Inland Revenue to transmit the case to the Commissioners, that
it may be amended by adding a statement of the value of the
subjects as appearing in the Valuation Roll; also a statement to
the effect that the assessor for the county of Argyll is or is not
the officer of Inland Revenue, and any other statement which
the Commissioners may think necessary or advisable in consequence of the above additions or otherwise.

JOHN INGLIS, I.P.D.

Oban, 13th November 1877.—The Commissioners for the Lorn
District of Argyllshire, in obedience to the above interlocutor,
beg to submit an excerpt from the Valuation Roll of the county
of Argyll for the current year 1877–78, in relation to the subjects

in question. The entries of the subjects in the Valuation Roll of the previous year (1876-77) were exactly the same. The Commissioners farther beg to state that the assessor for the county of Argyll is not the officer of Inland Revenue.

C. A. M'DOUGALL, Commissioner.
T. W. MURRAY ALLAN, Commissioner.

EXCERPT from VALUATION ROLL of COUNTY of ARGYLE for Year 1877-78.

No.	Description of Subjects.	Proprietor.	Occupier	Tenant.			Feu-Duty or Ground Annual	Feu-Duties, to whom Payable	Yearly Rent of Value after Appeals and Adjustments	No.
				Not under Lease of 19 Years or upwards.	Under Lease of 19 Years and less than 57 Years.	Under Lease of 57 Years or upwards, rent payable under Lease.				
6,510	Kinlochbeg Grazing.	Miss Downie of Appin.	William Menzies.	—	The heirs of A. C. Campbell of Monzie.	—	—	—	£ 350	6,510
6,511	Black Corries	"	"	—	"	—	—	—	75	6,511
6,512	Corryvallich Shealing.			—	"	—	—	—	60	6,512
6,513	Leven Bridge	"	"	—	"	—	—	—	34	6,513
6,514	Goul Shealing	"	"	—	"	—	—	—	65	6,514
6,515	Tartan Cottage fishings and shootings.	"	"	—	"	—	—	—	*157	6,515

* NOTE.—Kinlochbeg fishings and shootings sublet to G. W. Brewis, 18, Queen's Gate Gardens, London, for 300l.; and Black Corries to Percy L. Brewis for 500l.

A true copy from the Valuation Roll of the county of Argyll for year 1877-78.

C. A. M'DOUGALL, Commissioner.
T. W. MURRAY ALLAN, Commissioner.

JUDGMENT.

1 DIV. Friday, 18th January 1878.

Lord President.—Before disposing of this case we wish to be quite sure that we are right in supposing that only one question was intended to be raised, the question, namely, whether the rate was to be charged according to the Valuation Roll. Is there any other question intended to be raised?

Mr. McKechnie.—My understanding is that the only question is whether the principle of the Valuation Roll is to apply.

Lord President.—There is no question intended to be raised, I understand, as to the regularity of the assessment made under Schedule A.

Lord Deas.—In short, Mr. McKechnie, you don't found on the fourth head in the case. As I read the case, it seemed to me that they were two pleas, the one in the fourth head and the other in the fifth.

Mr. McKechnie.—The only point we argued was this, that what your lordships should decide, if you are for us, would be that whoever is the assessor, whether a Crown officer or not, he should take the rent in the lease.

Lord Deas.—But that is not the plea that was stated, nor the plea you are stating at this moment. You are stating only a plea on the Valuation Roll.

Lord President.—The fifth head of your case is (*reads it*). Now is that the question you intend to raise?

Mr. McKechnie.—That is the whole question.

Lord Deas.—Then that is not the rent. Observe what you are about. The fourth head is this: "The Appellant objected to these assessments in respect, &c." (*reads*). The plea that he is to be liable according to the Valuation Roll, is perfectly different, and is the only plea that I heard argued.

Lord President.—Now, are we to understand that the question that we are to dispose of is the one raised by the fifth head of the case? Is that so, Mr. McKechnie?

Mr. McKechnie.—That is so.

Lord President.—Then the only question which is raised by Appellant is stated in the fifth head of the case, in which he maintains that this charge of income tax falls under the rule of valuing lands and heritages provided by the Lands Valuation Act, 17 & 18 Vict., c. 91, and that the lease of the lands is under that to be taken as showing conclusively the annual value of the subjects, without taking into consideration whether the lease be a profitable one or the reverse.

The Appellant, that under fifth head of the case, is represented as stating that he declines "entering on the question whether "the lease was a profitable one to the extent claimed by the "assessor, and that was not necessary for the decision of the point "raised." The surveyor of income tax, on the other hand, the officer of Inland Revenue, maintains that he is entitled to charge the Appellant as upon a valuation of 1,400*l.* a year. The entry of the subjects in the valuation roll is 731*l.*, as we have it now stated in the amended case. The rent under the lease is 875*l.*, a considerably larger sum than that stated in the valuation roll; but the contention of the Appellant is, that either the entry in the valuation roll of 731*l.* is to be taken as the annual value, or that the amount of rent stipulated to be paid by the lease, viz., 875*l.*, is to be taken, that being, as he says, according to the principle of the Valuation of Lands Act, 17 & 18 Vict. Now, under the Income Tax Acts, there is a machinery provided for ascertaining the annual value of heritable subjects for the purpose of imposing and levying the tax. The 60th section of the 5 & 6 Vict. c. 35, No. 1 declares that the annual value of lands, &c. under Schedule A., shall be understood to be the rent

by the year at which the same are let at rackrent, if the amount
of such rent shall have been fixed by agreement, commencing
within the period of seven years preceding the 5th day of April
next before the time of making the assessment, but if the same
are not so let at rackrent, then at the rackrent at which the
same are worth to be let by the year. Now in the present case
the lease commenced eight years before the period preceding the
5th of April next before the making of the assessment; and therefore, if this rule applies, the officer of Inland Revenue was not
bound, or indeed entitled, to take the rent in the lease, but was
bound to ascertain what was the rent at which, one year with
another, this subject would let for; and he made his valuation
in the manner pointed out by the Act of Parliament. Of course
it was open to the Appellant to challenge that valuation.
He was entitled under the 5 & 6 Vict. to appeal to the
Commissioners of Income Tax and to satisfy them that the
valuation was excessive. The 80th section of the statute
5 & 6 Vict. gives the Commissioners of Income Tax the power
of having a valuation made upon appeal, so as to correct, if
need be, the valuation made by the surveyor. It is also within
the power of the Appellant in such an appeal to produce a lease
commencing within seven years, if he has a lease of that kind to
produce; and in a subsequent statute of the 16 and 17 Vict. c. 34,
likewise relating to the Income tax, there is a section (section 47)
which gives the Appellant right to demand a valuation, even if
it should not be proposed by the Commissioners, and the Commissioners are bound to grant him that valuation upon demand.
In the present case the Appellant declined to ask for such a
valuation. That is stated in the case by the Commissioners;
they say in the end of the paragraph, middle of p. 4, that the
Appellant declined to crave a valuation under the Act 16 & 17
Vict. c. 34. s. 47, and accordingly, unless the Appellant can make
out that he has got a rule of valuation under the 17 and 18
Vict., the Lands Valuation (Scotland) Act, he has, of course, no
ground of appeal here at all. Now, unless the Valuation Act
17 & 18 Vict. is to be held to repeal, in so far as regards
Scotland, the provisions of the Income Tax Acts, regarding
the ascertaining of the value of subjects upon which income
tax is to be imposed, I don't see very well how that statute can
affect the case. If the Income Tax Acts have provided a mode of
ascertaining annual value, and if that is still the rule as regards
the United Kingdom, how can a statute applicable to Scotland
only, which does not repeal those statutes in so far as Scotland is
concerned, impose upon the officer of Inland Revenue the duty
of following a different rule of valuation as regards Scotland
from that which he follows, or would have followed, in any other
part of the United Kingdom? It is very difficult to see how
that could be; but the truth is, all difficulty is put an end to
when the Valuation Act of 1854 is examined, because it is quite
obvious upon the face of that statute, and it is proved by a
number of its clauses, that it never was intended to apply to the

imperial taxation at all, but confined its operations entirely to valuing lands and heritages for the purpose of local assessment. And there is a very good reason why that should be so. The valuation of lands under that statute is entirely in the hands of local governing bodies, the commissioners of supply in the counties, magistrates of burghs, and so forth. They appoint their own assessor who is to value the different subjects within the locality, and his valuation roll, when completed and reported, is conclusive as regards all the assessments which are to be levied according to that rule. But the interest of a local community like that in making up a valuation roll is very different indeed from what may be stated to be the interest of the representatives of the Crown in valuing lands for the purposes of imperial taxation. In the case of local assessments, what is wanted is a certain sum of money, required it may be for the support of the poor for the year or for the maintenance of prisons. It does not matter what the object is, but it is always a certain estimated amount of money that is wanted; and what the governing body of the locality have to consider is, what rate according to the valuation of the county or burgh will produce that sum. It is obvious that for the purpose of such taxation as that it does not in the least degree matter whether the valuation of the county or the burgh be high or low, provided it is upon an equal principle and does justice as between the different ratepayers. A low valuation will produce the sum wanted as well as a high valuation; the rate only requires to be made a little higher in the event of the valuation being low. But in the case of imperial taxes the matter is quite different. It is not a certain sum of money that is to be levied in that case, but Parliament grants to the Queen a certain rate of taxation upon all subjects that are to be assessed, and the duty of the officers of the Crown is to get as much as they possibly can out of that tax. So that the interest of the Crown is to have the valuation of subjects that are to be rated, as far as possible; and therein the Crown and its officers have a perfectly different interest in the matter of valuation from that which the commissioners of supply or magistrates of burghs have in making up their valuation roll. Now it must be very obvious that it could never be the intention of Parliament to say that the valuation to be made for the purposes of imperial taxation should in England be in the hands of the officers of the Crown, and should in Scotland be in the hands of the commissioners of supply and magistrates of burghs. At all events, that is an extremely unlikely thing to have happened; and, accordingly, without going through the clauses of the Act, it is enough for me to say that I think it is impossible for anyone to read this statute with anything like care and attention without seeing that it is obviously intended to regulate only the local assessments which are to be imposed and levied according to the real rent. No doubt, by a subsequent statute of the 20 & 21 Vict. c. 58, there is a provision made for having one valuation to answer both purposes, the purposes both of imperial taxation and of local taxation, and the valuation roll of counties and burghs accordingly may be made available for the purposes of imperial taxation upon certain conditions, that is to say, that the surveyor of public taxes for the county or burgh shall be taken as the assessor under the Valuation Act, and if that be done by the commissioners of supply or the magistrates of burghs, then the valuation roll made up by that assessor may receive effect for regulating imperial taxes as well as local assessments. But then in the county of Argyll the Commissioners of Supply have not thought fit to appoint the officer of Inland Revenue to be the assessor for the county, and consequently they are not within the operation of the statute of 20 & 21 Vict. at all. They stand under the statute of the 17 & 18 Vict. alone, and under that statute certainly they have made up, according to the views I have stated of the Act, a valuation roll which never can be made available in any way whatever to regulate imperial taxation. I am therefore for affirming the deliverance of the Commissioners.

Lord Deas.—It would rather appear to me from reading this case, that there were two pleas stated on the part of Mr. Menzies, and consequently two questions raised, the one under the fourth head of the amended case and the other under the fifth head. There certainly was no argument upon the plea that may be raised under the fifth head of the case, and it has now been distinctly explained by Mr. McKechnie, on the part of Mr. Menzies, that the only question intended to be raised by this case is under the fifth head. That being so I am very clearly of opinion with your Lordship, that the statute there founded upon, viz., the Valuation Act, has no application to this case. I think it is quite clear that the Valuation Act is not applicable to imperial taxation. Almost every clause of it makes that to my mind clearer and clearer. It is quite true, as your Lordship has explained, that by the subsequent Act of 20 & 21 Vict. c. 58, there might be a certain event in which the Income Tax would be regulated by valuation under that Act, viz., where the commissioners of supply of the county or the magistrates of the burgh have appointed the Inland Revenue officer to be valuing officer. In that case, but in that case only, is the Valuation Act applicable to the income tax. Limiting the question therefore to the Valuation Act and the subsequent Act 20 & 21 Vict. which has nothing to do with it, the commissioners of supply or magistrates not having appointed the Inland Revenue officer to be assessor, I am clearly of opinion that the Valuation Act has no application to this case.

Under the fourth head of the case another and a very different and very important question might have been raised because then we should have had to examine the Income Tax Act, and to inquire whether this assessment was rightly made under the Income Tax Act. Mr. Menzies is assessed in two capacities. He is assessed as proprietor in the sum of 17*l*. 10*s*. under Schedule A. and he is assessed in a sum of 7*l*. 5*s*. 10*d*. as occupier under

Schedule B. If these assessments were under the Income Tax Act, he would be entitled to relief from his landlord to the extent, but only to the extent, of the rent which he actually paid to his landlord. The landlord would not be liable under the Income Tax Act to relieve him of the rest of the tax which is laid on in respect of his profitable enjoyment. He would only be liable to relieve him of the tax to an extent corresponding to the rent that is actually paid under his lease, leaving him to bear his own burden in so far as he is assessed substantially as proprietor. Now under Schedule A. of the Income Tax Act, the tax is payable for all lands, tenements, hereditaments, heritages, &c., for every 20s. of the annual value of 7d. of tax, it varies of course; and under Schedule B. in respect of the occupancy for every 20s. a similar sum. Then Schedule A. bears in substance that estimating the lands and heritages under that Income Tax Act, the rent for the year at which the subjects are let at rackrent, if paid by agreement commencing within seven years before the 5th of April before making the assessment, and if not let at rackrent then at the rackrent which they are worth. Article 9 of the same Schedule A. is that the occupiers are to recover from their landlords the 7d. in respect of property. Section 66 bears on production of the lease showing let within the seven years, and no other condition than the rent payable, the assessor may assess according to such rent. But that is not to be binding upon the Commissioners if it does not appear to be the rackrent. That may be said to mean—I don't give any opinion about it—that if the rent in the lease is not a rackrent, then that is not to be binding. The rent in this lease is not said to be other than a rackrent. The liability is said to arise from the improvements made upon the lands. That may be a very important question. It may be a very important question whether the tenant of a farm let at rackrent upon a lease, but which in the course of the lease becomes worth a great deal more than the rackrent, is liable to be assessed as proprietor without relief from his landlord. That question is not raised here. It is distinctly disclaimed, and therefore I give no opinion about it. All I say is that it is a very important question if it had been raised. I am very glad that it is not raised, because it would require very great consideration, and very considerable argument. I only allude to it in order to make it clear that I am not giving any opinion, either by inference or otherwise, upon any question of the kind. My opinion is clear, with your Lordship that the Valuation Act has nothing to do with this case, and that disposes of the only question which we are told was intended to be raised.

Lord Mure.—I agree with your Lordship, that the only question which we are here called upon to decide is that stated under the fifth head of the case, viz. whether the surveyor of income tax in making up his valuation for the purposes of the income tax collection is bound to adopt the rule of the 6th section of the Lands Valuation (Scotland) Act, 17 & 18 Vict. c. 91. That is raised in a pure and distinct shape under the fifth head

of this case, and that is the sole question which was argued
before us and which we have to deal with. Now upon that
point I have no difficulty whatever in concurring with your
Lordships in holding that the surveyor is not bound by the
6th section of the Valuation Act. He is bound to make up his
roll in terms of the directions in the Income Tax Act 5 & 6 Vict.
and any amendment which may be made on that Act. The
proceedings we are here dealing with are proceedings by the
Commissioners of Income Tax, who have nothing to do with the
Land Valuation (Scotland) Act at all, but must be regulated by
the Act of Parliament under which they are bound to act.
Those Acts of Parliament do provide a mode by which the Commissioners, if they are satisfied that the assessor has taken a
wrong step, may allow a party to get a remedy, and that is under
a clause mentioned in the case, where the Commissioners say
that an option was given to this Appellant to have a valuation
made in terms of the Acts under which they act, and that that
was declined by him. Therefore he declined to adopt the
remedy and the only remedy open to him under the Act of
Parliament. I am very clearly of opinion upon the general
terms of the Lands Valuation Act of 1854, and on the same
grounds which your Lordship has stated, that it is not intended
to regulate imperial taxation, but that it is intended to regulate
local taxation. The clauses of the Act make that quite clear,
and I think the clause bringing the Prison Act taxation under
the Valuation Act shows that it was necessary to make provision for that. But section 3 of the 20 & 21 Vict. appears to
me to be perfectly conclusive of itself against any such plea as
that maintained by the Appellant, because that is the Amendment
of the Valuation Act of 1854, which contemplates that in certain
circumstances a roll made up under the Valuation Act (that is
when the surveyor of taxes is made the party to make up that
roll) may to some extent be held to regulate the Income Tax
Commissioners in freeing the assessment. But it goes on
specially to provide that if they do not take the surveyor under
the option given by the statute, no valuation made up under
any Act of Parliament shall be conclusive of the assessment.
Now the argument submitted to us was that the valuation made
up in terms of the 6th section of the Valuation Act of 1854 was
conclusive. But the clause in the amendment of the Valuation
Act makes that plea utterly untenable, because it declares that
it shall not be conclusive, and therefore it leaves the matter to
be regulated by the usual rules applicable to the assessment for
the income tax, which are provided by the Income Tax Act
itself.

Lord Shand.—The only question which has been raised by the
Appellant, and to which I have applied my mind, is whether the
Surveyor of Property and Income Tax for Argyllshire is bound
to observe the rule enacted by sec. 6 of the Valuation Act in
the valuation which he makes for the purpose of the collection of
the property and income tax; and that question arises in this

state of matters, that the surveyor of property and income tax has not been appointed to be assessor for the making up of the ordinary valuation roll of the county. Upon that question the latest enactment which we have quoted in the case is contained in the 20 & 21 Vict. c. 58, s. 3, which provides that no valuation made under the said Act (*i.e.*, the Valuation Act of 16 & 17 Vict.) by any other assessor or assessors shall be conclusive against or for the purpose of reducing any assessment, rate, or charge under any Act of Parliament relating to the duties of excise, or the land tax, or assessed taxes, or income tax; that is to say, that where in any county or burgh the Commissioners have not appointed the officer of Inland Revenue to be assessor, then no valuation made under the Valuation Act is to have any application to the matter of income tax. It rather appears to me that by implication, and probably very direct implication, the force of this provision is that where the officer of Inland Revenue has been appointed assessor in any county, it is intended that one valuation shall then come to be operative, for not only local, but imperial taxation. But however that may be, I think it is clear from this provision of the statute, that in the case in which we are, there is a direct provision that the valuation under the Valuation Act shall not apply to the assessments for imperial purposes. It lies, therefore, with the Appellant to show that under previous statutes the rule under the 17 & 18 Vict. was binding upon the officer of Inland Revenue. Upon that question I have to observe, in the first place, that when the statute of 17 & 18 Vict. passed, there was a separate system of valuation for the purpose of imperial taxation. That system was regulated by two statutes, the 5 & 6 Vict. c. 35, s. 60, as modified by a statute passed the year before the Valuation Act (the 16 & 17 Vict. c. 34), and without detailing the effect of these provisions, I may just notice that they amounted to this, that where a subject was under lease for a period of years, and the lease had gone beyond its seventh year, the rent in the lease was not to be taken as the rule of valuation. Now the Valuation Act 17 & 18 Vict. contains no repeal of the clauses to which I have referred, which have hitherto regulated imperial taxation. If it had been intended to substitute an entirely new system in place of that which was in existence under those statutes, I think it would be reasonable to expect repealing clauses. But I agree with your Lordships, that an examination of the Valuation Act, in holding that taking the clauses as a whole, the purpose of it was to introduce a roll which has proved of great value, but which it was intended should regulate only the matter of local taxation, municipal and county rates, and rates of that kind. I don't think it necessary to go over the provisions of the statute, but there are many indications which satisfy me on an examination of the statute as a whole that is so. It is possible, then, to maintain that the roll provided under section 6 of that statute is to be binding, not merely on the assessor, but on the officer of Inland Revenue? I think the opening passage of section 6 shows that that was not to be so, for it there provided that in estimating the yearly value of lands and heritages under this Act, the same shall be taken to be the rent which one year with another, &c. If you once reach the conclusion that under this Act, you are only providing a valuation roll for county and local purposes, then the rule which the assessor is to follow is a rule to be followed with reference to what is being done under this Act, and so, I think, cannot go back to affect the rules under which the surveyor of income tax was bound to make up his valuations. Where the surveyor of income tax is named assessor for the county there may be only one roll for all purposes, but that is not the case here.

Lord President.—Affirm the determination of the Commissioners.

APPENDIX.

MINUTE of AGREEMENT between Donald Beith, W.S., Edinburgh, for Alexander Cameron Campbell, Esquire, of Monãie, Iverawe, on the first part; and Mr. James Menzies, residing at Luss, Dumbartonshire, on behalf of, and taking burden on him for his son, Mr. William Menzies, farmer, Auch, on the second part.

First. The first party hereby agrees to sublet to the second party, and the latter hereby agrees to become the sub-tenant of the farms of Kinlochbeg, Blackcarries, Blackburns, and Corryvalloch, belonging to Miss Downie of Appin and Benchrulist, belonging to the heirs of Mr. Macdonald of Dalness, with the whole shootings and fishings thereon, including the shootings on Benevrick, the property of Cameron of Lochiel, all as at present occupied and possessed by the said Alexander Cameron Campbell, and that for the space of two years as regards the shootings of Benevrick, 14 years as regards the lands of Benchrulist with the pertinents, and 13 years as regards Kinlochbeg, Blackcarries, Blackburn, and Corryvalloch, all from the term of Whitsunday 1868, and that at the rents following, viz., for the first and second years 900*l.*, for the following 11 years 875*l.*, and for the fourteenth and last years 70*l.* sterling, payable in equal portions at the terms of Martinmas and Whitsunday, and beginning the first payment at Martinmas 1868.

Second. The first party also hereby agrees to sell to the second party, and the second party agrees to purchase from the said Alexander Cameron Campbell, the whole sheep stock on the said several farms and possessions, and that at a valuation thereof to be made by Mr. Donald Stewart of Achallander, whom failing, such other person as the parties may agree upon, as sole referee and valuator chosen by the parties in the premises, the valuation and delivery to take place on the 29th day of May 1868, or such other day not later than ten days thereafter, as may be most convenient; and the price shall be payable on delivery, so far as the number of sheep has then been ascertained, discount at the rate of five per centum per annum being allowed for the period between Whitsunday and Martinmas, 1868; and as regards the remainder of the number of sheep, the price thereof shall be payable at Martinmas 1868.

Third. The second party hereby agrees to accept of the buildings, fences, fanks, and other erections on the farms as they shall be at Whitsunday, 1868, and to relieve the first party of all claims in connexion with the leases of said farms, at the instance of the proprietors of the said farms and possessions at the termination of the leases respectively, at which times respectively the second party hereby binds and obliges himself to remove from the said several farms and possessions.

Fourth. In respect of the rents paid by the first party to the proprietors of the said several farms are less by 74*l*. for the first 13 years of the present sub-lease than the several rents which the said second party hereby agrees to pay, the said second party agrees to redeem the said surplus rent of 74*l*. for the sum of 680*l*. being the value thereof as fixed by Thomas Martin Esquire, chartered accountant and actuary, Edinburgh, which price will also be payable at the said term of Whitsunday, or 26th day of May 1868, and provided the proprietors of the said several farms agree to accept the second party as their tenant in the said lands and possessions instead of the said first party, it is hereby agreed that, in so far as the first party is concerned, the second party shall be substituted in all respects in the room and stead of the first party, whom the second party shall be bound to free and relieve from all rents and prestations exigible by the landlords of the said several farms and possessions. The second party agrees to relieve the said Alexander Cameron Campbell of the wages of any shepherds or servants engaged by him in connexion with said farms since the 27th day of April 1868. In witness whereof these presents, written upon this and the preceding page of stamped paper, by Robert Peter Mitchell, clerk to M'Grigor, Stevenson, and Fleming, writers in Glasgow, are subscribed by the said Donald Beith and James Menzies, both at Glasgow, the 22nd day of May 1868, before these witnesses James M'Grigor, of the Queen's Hotel, Glasgow, and Robert Patzer, waiter at the said Queen's Hotel, Glasgow; this testing clause from and inclusive of the words, "the said Donald Beith," being written by the said Donald Beith, and it being declared that these presents have been extended by the said Robert Peter Mitchell for the said Donald Beith.

James MacGrigor, witness.
Robert Patzer, witness.

DONALD BEITH.
JAMES MENZIES.

PART XII.

No. 26.—In the High Court of Justice (England).— Exchequer Division.
23rd January 1877.

Andrew Knowles and Sons Limited - - - Appellants

and

James Kilby McAdam (Surveyor of Taxes) - - Respondent.

Income Tax.—In estimating the profits of mines a deduction may be allowed on account of the exhaustion of the stock of coal or minerals.

At a Meeting of the Commissioners for Special Purposes held at Somerset House on Friday, the 17th of December 1875, for the purpose of hearing appeals under the Income Tax Acts, for the year ending the 6th of April 1875.

Andrew Knowles and Sons (Limited), a company carrying on business as colliery proprietors at Pendlebury and elsewhere, appealed against an assessment in the sum of 226,824l. made on them under Schedule D. of the Act 16 & 17 Victoria, chapter 34, in respect of the profits of their business as colliery proprietors.

The Company was represented by Mr. David Chadwick, M.P., of the firm of Chadwick, Adamson, and Company, of 65, Moorgate Street, in the city of London, who is also one of the directors of the Company.

At the hearing of the appeal, the Commissioners were of opinion that the assessment should be reduced to the sum of 216,827l. 2s. 10d., but it was urged by Mr. Chadwick that a sum of 10,424l. 15s. 3d. should be deducted on the ground that in estimating the amount of assessable profits the Commissioners ought to allow as a deduction that sum which was claimed by the Commissioners as "depreciation," and which, as stated in the annual report for the year ending 31st December 1874, "is "based on a calculation of the extent of coal available and the "duration of existing leases, but it may be modified as future "circumstances require"; and he further explained that the term "depreciation" in the balance sheet was used to show to the shareholders the deterioration or difference in the value of their property at the end of the year and after the working out of a year's coal and the expiration of a year of their leases, as

A

compared with the value of such property at the beginning of the year; in other words, that a re-valuation of the property showed that it was worth, at the end of the first year, 10,424*l.* 15*s.* 3*d.* less than at the time of the purchase 12 months before.

The Commissioners were of opinion that they were precluded by the third rule applicable to the first case of Schedule D. in section 100 of the Act 5 and 6 Victoria, chapter 35, and by section 159 of that Act from allowing the deduction claimed, and determined to confirm the assessment in the said sum of 216,827*l.* 2*s.* 10*d.*

Mr. Chadwick thereupon expressed his dissatisfaction with the determination of the Commissioners, as being erroneous in point of law, and duly required the Commissioners to state and sign a case for the opinion of the Exchequer Division of the High Court of Justice, under the provisions of the Act 37 & 38 Victoria, chapter 16, which we have stated, and do now sign accordingly.

(Signed)   R. M. LYNCH }   Special
           D. O'CONNELL } Commissioners.

Somerset House, London,
    22nd March 1876.

NOTE.—A print of the Annual Report, with the balance sheet, accompanies this case(*a*).

AMENDMENTS by way of addenda to the case stated for the Opinion of the Court by the Commissioners for the Special Purposes of the Income Tax Acts, under the Act 37 and 38 Vict. cap. 16, as to Income Tax assessed under the Income Tax Acts, Schedules A. and D.

POINTS OF ARGUMENT.	CASE.

FOR THE APPELLANTS.

1. That the determination of the var· Commissioners is erroneous.
2. That the assessment upon the Appellants under the Income Tax Acts, in respect of the profits of their business as colliery proprietors, for the year ending the 6th April 1875, ought not to be in a sum including the sum claimed as a deduction by the Appellants.
3. That the sum claimed as a deduction by the Appellants is no part of the profits or of the balance of profits or gains upon which the Appellants are

The Company's colliery property comprises both freehold and leasehold mines, which were purchased by them, the price paid for the leasehold coal mines, subject to an average royalty rent of 7*d.* per ton, and having an average of 32 years to run, being 717,421*l.*, the purchase money for the freehold mines being 67,550*l.*

At the end of the first year's working, which is the year of the assessment in question, it was liable to be assessed under the Income Tax Acts, in respect of the profits of their said business, for the year ending the 6th April 1875, and ought not to be included therein.

4. That the assessment upon the Appellants ought not to be in a greater sum than 206,403l. 7s. 7d.

FOR THE RESPONDENT.

1. That the amount of duty chargeable upon the Appellants' colliery is to be calculated upon the full annual value of the profits of such colliery, on an average of the preceding five years, without making any deduction therefrom on the ground of its depreciation in value, either through the working out of the coal, or the expiration of any portion of the lease.

2. That the deduction claimed by the Appellants in the present case, from the amount of the profits or gains arising from their said colliery, is not such as the Appellants are justified in claiming under the provisions of the third rule of the first case of Schedule D. of the Income Tax Act (5 & 6 Vict. c. 35.), and is contrary to law.

3. That the case of the colliery in question does not differ in principle from the case of leasehold properties or annuities, in neither of which cases is any such deduction allowable as that now claimed by the Appellants.

ascertained that from the Company's leasehold collieries, 844,877 tons, and from their freehold pits 62,000 tons of coal had been wrought or gotten, and sold in that year, the total quantity therefore being 906,877 tons.

The Appellants allege that in ascertaining by a correct and accurate balance sheet, the profits made in that year, the Company valued their coal mines at 10,424l. 15s. 3d. less than the sum for which they had purchased them at the commencement of that year, which sum (as the Appellants allege) fairly represented the diminution in their value, by reason of the coal gotten as above mentioned, and which sum, for the purposes of such balance sheet, was technically, but perhaps incorrectly, referred to as depreciation. Of the said sum of 10,424l. 15s. 3d., the sum of 721l. 17s. 11d. represents the diminution in the value of the freehold mines, and the balance that of the leasehold.

The Appellants further allege that in ascertaining the profits of the freehold, no sum is set against or deducted from the gross receipts on account of any rent assumed to be paid in respect thereof.

Herschell, Q.C. (*Saunderson* with him), for the appellants.— The plaintiffs are a company which has purchased a number of mines; the freeholds of some, leases of others. They claim to be allowed a deduction for the diminution in the value of the mines by reason of the amount worked out each year. This is not a deduction under the third rule or under section 159, but it must be taken into account before you can ascertain what the profits are. In any ordinary case of trading you must see in estimating the profits how much less the stock was at the end than at the beginning of the year. A lease of a coal mine is in reality a sale of the coal which is taken away.

[*Pollock*, B.—If you overwork a market garden the same result of exhaustion will be produced.]

When you take the coal it is gone. The market garden may be made again as profitable as ever it was, but not the coal mine.

If a man bought a coal mine in which there was only one year's working left, gave 10,000l. for it, and made only that sum, the other side must logically contend that he would have 10,000l. profit.

[*Cleasby, B.*—You have made no profits because there are no-profits. You have spent as much as you have got.]

And I say that is the case in the present case.

You are not entitled to deduct on account of capital withdrawn. but capital withdrawn is a different thing to capital used up.

Sir John Holker,.A.G. (*Dicey* with him), for the respondent.— The Income Tax is a temporary tax, and a man has to pay on the amounts of profits which he may realise in any particular year. The idea of capital is kept separate from income, and it is upon the income that he has to pay. In principle the case is similar to that of leasehold buildings, and no deduction would be made for the exhaustion of the lease. The Act defines what deductions are not to be allowed, (reads 5 & 6 Vict. c. 35, third rule of first case, Schedule D.).

[*Pollock, B.*—We had this case in principle not very long ago, where a person sought, instead of incurring the expenses of keeping up a mill, to charge a sort of sinking fund.] (*b*)

I think that case is conclusive upon the matter.

[*Pollock, B.*—The difference is that in one case it would take so many tons of coal, and in the other that each spindle, each stone, each everything else is being gradually by attrition frittered away.]

The argument of the other side may be right, upon the principles recognised in political economy; but the very aim and object of the Income Tax Acts seem to have been to prevent the principles which a political economist would apply from applying to cases under those Acts.

[*Pollock, B.*—There is a case which occurs to my mind. If a man pay a lump sum for a mine he cannot according to your argument make a deduction, but if he pay a royalty then he gets a deduction. Practically, this case has arisen in a way, but not with regard to coal, in the Scotch case of Addie and Sons.] (*c*)

Case sent back for amendment.

5th December 1877.

Herschell, Q.C., for the appellant.—The first element to be determined is the full amount of the profits or gains. In an ordinary case of trade to arrive at the balance of profit you take into account the stock at the beginning and the end of the year. You must, before you arrive at the profits at all, not merely be able out of your receipts to pay your expenses, but to replace your exhausted capital; before that is done profit does

---

(*b*) *Forder v. Handyside. ante* p. 65. L. R. 1, Exch. Div. 233.
(*c*) *Ante* p. 1.

not begin. There is no difference in principle between the case of a colliery proprietor with a stock of coal under ground and a coal merchant with his stock above ground. Lord Cairns in Gowan v. Christie (d) distinguished between an agricultural lease and a lease of minerals, saying that the latter "is really "when properly considered, a sale out and out of a portion of "land. It is liberty given to a particular individual, for a "specific length of time to go into and under the land, and to "get certain things there if he can find them, and to take them "away just as if he had bought so much of the soil:" and therefore so much of the receipts as represents the diminution in the value of the mine by the exhaustion of the coal is not profit at all in any true sense of the word.

[*Pollock, B.*—You cannot take the word profit alone. The Act says "profit or gain." You cannot deny that if a man had 100,000l. worth of coal given to him and he sold it right off, it would be gain if not profit.]

I should deny that it was gain from this particular adventure, trade, or concern; it is only your property converted into another form. Would not the Court of Chancery interfere if the company were going to pay a dividend when, though it had made a sum of money, it had exhausted an amount of coal more than representing that sum of money? Would not the Court of Chancery stop the payment of the dividend because there had been no profit? The third rule of Schedule D. is not applicable, because this is not a case of "capital withdrawn" from the business, but of exhaustion of stock. Nor is the deduction barred by the 159th section, because the first thing to be done is to ascertain the profits, and you cannot do that until you have ascertained your loss too. In no proper sense of the word can you say that a man has made a profit when he has only that in another shape which he had before, namely, money instead of coal.

Dicey, for the respondent.—Mines are still under the rates of Schedule A., though for purposes of convenience the assessments on them have been transferred to Schedule D. Therefore the question is not about deductions to be made from profits, but about the annual value, and the annual value is what a person gets from a mine.

[*Kelly, C. B.*—It is the impression, I believe, of the whole Court that this case is regulated by the eighth section 29 & 30 Vict. c. 36, and that the question in this case is transferred altogether from Schedule A. to Schedule D.]

My contention is that the transfer is only as to the mode of assessment, and does not place mines within the rules of Schedule D., except so far as is not inconsistent with the rules of Schedule A.

(d) L. R. 2, Soo. App., 282.

But even under Schedule D. concerns are not treated by the
Act as a political economist would treat them, and the Act being
only yearly, it would be extremely difficult to do so. This
money set aside to meet the exhaustion of capital is really
" capital withdrawn " from the concern. A man who has leased
land for a term cannot be allowed a deduction; and the coal
being a product of the land, this question is distinct from the
case of coal bought when lying free out of the land. This case
has been decided by Forder v. Handyside (e). In estimating the
balance of profits and gains there must be taken in the first
place the gross profits, and from that sum no deduction is to be
made for capital withdrawn. We contend that this money is
capital withdrawn.

JUDGMENT.

Kelly,C. B.—This case comes before me and my learned brethren
under the disadvantage of my not having heard the former
arguments upon it, and not having had the same opportunity and
the same time for consideration as my learned brethren on either
side of me have had; but looking to the nature of the Income
Tax Act, and looking to the plain and simple, but clear and
undoubted meaning of the word " profits," I do not think this
case admits of the smallest doubt. The reference which has been
made to the case of Forder and Handyside, and again, the reference which has been made to one or two statutes passed before
the time when this question arose, may be disposed of almost in
a word. Under the 29th and 30th Victoria, chapter 36, section 8,
the precise terms of which I need not refer to, it appears to me
that the question in this case is transferred, to use a comprehensive expression, from Schedule A. to Schedule D.; and we have,
therefore, only in this case to consider, upon the question or
questions raised before us, the construction of Schedule D. and the
different rules to which reference has been made by the learned
counsel on either side.
  Now, in the first place, let us take the substantial leading and
commanding provision, that upon which the whole question turns,
unless the proposition which it contains is qualified by something
afterwards to be found in one or more of the rules. The first of
these rules is as to what it is, in respect of which the subject is to
be assessed, and we find it is this: " the duty to be charged in
respect thereof," that is, in respect of any trade, manufacture, or
adventure, which now must be taken to include a mine or minerals
in a coal mine. The duty to be charged in respect thereof shall
" be computed on a sum not less than the full amount of the
" balance of the profits or gains of such trade, manufacture, or
" adventure." Now what is " the balance of the profits or gains
of such adventure "? Now beginning at that point, let us take the

---

(r) *Ante*, p. 65 ; L.R., 1 Exch. Div., 233.

simplest case that can be imagined. If a man goes into a wholesale warehouse and purchases a bale of cotton or a chest of tea for the sum of 40*l*. and then passes into another town or place and sells to some retail dealer in the district (who has not the same facilities as himself for purchasing at wholesale prices at a wholesale warehouse) the bale of cotton or the chest of tea he has purchased at 40*l*. for 45*l*., what is his profit? I assume there are no expenses in passing from one place to another, or at all events of so trifling a nature as not to enter into the computation. He has bought an article for 40*l*. and sold it for 45*l*., and 5*l*. therefore is his profit. Now why is it his profit? Because it is the balance which remains to him, and is in his possession after having repaid himself everything he has expended, be it what it may, in order to obtain the price of 45*l*. Therefore deducting everything that he has expended in order to obtain that sum of 45*l*., and that being only 40*l*. and no more, 5*l*. is undoubtedly the net profit. In respect of that, if it stood simply by itself, it would be the whole of that man's yearly income, but if it were multiplied one hundred times by one hundred different transactions, his income would be 500*l*. a year, and in respect of one or the other (if so small a sum as 5*l*. could be assessed at all), he would be assessable for income tax.

Now let us go a little further, and suppose he had obtained possession and become the owner of a bale of cotton and a chest of tea of the value, I will say, of 20*l*. each, but the bale of cotton he had purchased for 20*l*., whereas the chest of tea had been made a present to him, or it may be that somebody had died and left it to him, but he begins business with those two articles, the bale of cotton for which he has paid 20*l*., and the chest of tea which is worth 20*l*., for which he has paid nothing, because it has been given to him, or been bequeathed to him. They are each of the value of 20*l*. He has paid the sum of 20*l*. for one, and the other is assumed or admitted to be of the value of 20*l*. He opens a shop, and he sells in the course of a week or more these two articles; it may be by retail, or it may be by wholesale, both to one person, or two persons, or sells them both together for 45*l*. Is not his profit the difference, the 5*l*. and the 5*l*. only? If the 20*l*., the value of the article which has been bequeathed to him, or given to him, is to be transmuted into profits, and to be treated as profits, I see no escape from the proposition that whether a man has a sum of 20*l*. left to him as having been an old servant of a family, or whether he has 100*l*. left to him in goods or money's worth, that is to be taken to be his income. Now what would be the consequence, first of all, if we take it in money? Suppose a father, who is not the possessor of land and freehold property or estates, but who is possessed, it may be, of half a million of money, has five sons or five daughters, and he leaves to each of them a fortune which he intends them to possess, and who would otherwise begin life at his death without a shilling except what they derived from him, and that upon his death they find themselves each possessed

of the sum of 100,000*l.* Now suppose that to be money; would
any human being contend in a court of law that that is income,
and that every one of the sons and daughters are to be assessed
with income tax upon 100,000*l.*, which would be the annual
income of a duke, or the owner of landed estates of great value,
in which case that sum would represent the year's produce of his
estates. No one would contend that it was so, if it was money.
It would be something startling, and almost ludicrous to contend
that, when a fortune is left to an individual, if it happened to be
in money, the whole fortune is to be taken as a year's income,
and the recipient is to pay income tax on it as the year's income?
If that were so, and it remained untouched and uninvested,
and none of it spent during the whole of his life, according to
that, he would be liable to be assessed at the same rate all his
life, and that surely could not be contended.

Now let us see. whether there is any difference between that
case and the case of goods, the latter being assessable under
Schedule D. of the Act of Parliament. Supposing that a
merchant or manufacturer dies and leaves to his son the whole
of the goods in his warehouse which do in fact, or may, at any
rate, at any given moment of time, constitute his entire fortune
—his entire capital if he be a trader—all that he possesses in
the world, and all that he has to leave to his son, who succeeds
to him, the whole of which the son upon his father's death,
receives or possesses, or continues to possess in the world. Supposing there to be a stock in a warehouse at Manchester of
10,000, or, it may be, 20,000 bales of cotton, and the son, succeeding to the business of his father, proceeds to sell them by
wholesale to retail dealers or export them to foreigners who
may become the purchasers of the commodities in which he
deals, bale by bale, and in the course of that year sells, I will
say 1,000 out of the 20,000 bales of cotton. What is his profit?
Why the profit is this.   What would it have cost him to
purchase at cost price, or perhaps wholesale prices, the 1,000
bales he has sold, and if that be, I will suppose, 10,000*l.*, and he
has sold them to other dealers in the kingdom for 12,000*l.*, what
is his profit? Is it the whole 12,000*l.*; because if so, if he sold
the whole 10,000 bales in the course of the year it would have
been the same as a legacy 100,000*l.* in money, and he must
have been assessed on the whole value of the amount of the
property that he had obtained as if it were a yearly income.
But what he has really gained in the way of a profit is the sum
for which he has sold the 1,000 bales of cotton, deducting from
it, or setting against it, in the words of the statute, the price he
has paid for it; or if he has paid no price for it, if he has had
it bequeathed to him, or become possessed of it without payment
of money, the market value, or that which he would have had
to pay for it if he had purchased it on the most favourable terms
in the market; and that difference alone is his profit.

Now, if that be so, let us apply the case which has been put
forward, and as it appears to me unanswerably, by Mr. Herschell

in this case in his argument. We must begin by supposing, as might well be, that this was the case of a lease to a man for one year only. A man wishes to experiment upon a coal mine, and he applies to some great landed proprietor who has some mines, under the surface of his land, or some mine that has been opened already, or is about to be opened, and asks him, " For what sum " will you let me have a lease of this mine for one year, and allow " me to take out as much coal as I can find means to take out " by ordinary fair working, and with the assistance of machinery " within one year," and he is told, "I will let you have it, for it is " a valuable mine, for 1,000l. For a payment of 1,000l. you shall " have the use of this mine, and free entry into the mine, and " liberty to win and take out of it and dispose of as much of the " coal as you can." What is the condition of that man at the end of the year? He takes, I will suppose, a quantity of coal which he sells altogether for 1,200l. What is the profit that he has earned in the course of the year? Well, he has paid 1,000l. for the lease which is gone; he has paid 1,000l. for the means by which he gets the liberty to enter the mine and take the coal, and by which means alone he could have acquired the right to dispose of the coal. I assume that the machinery and labour employed would have cost him during that one year 100l. more, and that he has sold the coal he has obtained for 1,200l. What is his profit? Why he has traded as a lessee of a coal mine, or coals during one year, and one year only, and he may then be disposed to leave that business and what has he paid for the articles he has sold for 1,200l.? He has paid 1,000l. for the lease of the mine, that is to say, for the power to enter the mine and the power to work the mine and win and take away, and sell the coal, and he has paid 100l. more for labour and for machinery. Therefore he has spent 1,100l. in acquiring the quantity of coal he has sold in the market, and he has sold that coal in the market for 1,200l. Now what is his profit? Is it the whole 1,200l.? The idea of applying the term " profit " to anything of that kind is an abuse to the English language. His profit is that which remains to him and which he can put into his pocket and spend, if he has not already spent it, as part or the whole of his year's expenditure. The amount he receives is 1,200l., and against that is to be set off his expenditure in order to enable him to acquire that 1,200l., namely 1,000l. for the lease and 100l. for the labour and machinery, and consequently 100l. only is his profit.

Now if that be the case with regard to one year, what is the case having regard to a lease for 32 years? If he proceeds for 32 years, from year to year to carry on the business of a lessee of a mine, or of the minerals in a mine, and takes from year to year various portions or parts of the mine, or takes so much coal as he can get from time to time it may be either a time specified as an average in the Act of Parliament, namely, three years, or a year, or so long a time as he continues working the mine. What is the result? Is there any difference in the mode of stating

the figures in order to gain a knowledge of the specific amount
of profit he has obtained? If the working has been equally
profitable from one year to another, and he has gone on in much
the same way paying the same rent for the mine, and the
royalty, and if there be, besides the rent, a premium, dividing
that premium over 32 years, and then adding beyond that the
expense of working, of labour, and of machinery, and if,
taking one year with another or taking the average of three
years, or if you will, for the whole 32 years, he has acquired
10,000*l.* a year that is if he has 10,000*l.* a year over and above
what he has paid for the working and acquiring of the coal
he has sold for, I will say, 100,000*l.* a year, that 10,000*l.* a
year is the net profit which he has a right to spend in any
way he pleases or put into his pocket. In order to arrive at
that profit of 10,000*l.*, or whatever it may be, he has a right
to set off against the gross receipts the whole expenditure
over the 32 years divided into 32 portions if all the years have
been alike in his dealings, just as he would, supposing it had
been a lease for one year and for one year only. Now, that
is the expenditure? It is, first, the rent paid for the lease
and the premium, and if it were a one year's lease, he would
have to set off the premium against the gross earnings, so if it
were a three years' lease or a 32 years' lease he would have to
divide it into three or 32 portions, as the case may be, in order to
ascertain what, if any, during the three years, or 32 years, is the
annual profit in respect of which he is assessable to the income
tax.

Such is the construction of this provision of the Income Tax
Act, in the first rule, supposing there were no qualification to
be found in another section of the Act of Parliament which I
will refer to by-and-by. When we look to the third rule, it is
this: " In estimating the balance of profits and gain chargeable
" under Schedule D. or for the purpose of assessing the duty
" thereon," no sum shall be deducted from it except several which
are here enumerated. Several of them are not material and
have no application to this case, but before coming to one, or it
may be, two, which are applicable to this case, and which have
been referred to, and properly referred to, by Mr. Dicey, and, as I
understand, more elaborately and amply referred to in the former
argument, I will first observe that we find it is, " that in
" estimating the balance of profits." Therefore, we must consider
what this is; is it to constitute something that is to be set
against the price obtained for the material sold and which is
not to be taken into consideration in ascertaining and making
up the balance of the profits? First it is this, " not on account
" of loss not connected with or arising out of such trade." That
is, something not in the way of trade. The man might have
speculated while working this coal mine by purchasing a quantity of coals, say, four or five cargoes of coal at Newcastle, and
sending them to London to be sold. He might have experienced
a loss, and a considerable loss, but that has nothing to do with

the trade in which he is engaged. Then we come to this, "nor "on account of any capital withdrawn therefrom." The meaning of that is perfectly plain. If a man begins to work this mine or to carry on any other trade or undertaking or adventure, with a capital of 40,000l., and in the course of a year he withdraws from that capital a sum of 10,000l., perhaps for the purpose of setting up a coal warehouse in a distant part of Manchester (if Manchester is the place in which he carried on his business), that would be a portion of his capital withdrawn, and he would find himself at the end of the year with 10,000l. less capital, but that is not to be taken into consideration in ascertaining the amount of his profits. There are various other ways in which capital might be withdrawn, and there are various other purposes to which it might be applied, or which might be taken into consideration, but they do not affect, inevitably, the calculation necessary to ascertain the amount of the net profits.

The other case may require a little more attention, and might for a moment breed a little difficulty in one's mind. The other words are "nor for any sum employed or intended to be "employed as capital in such trade." Now when we come to find the word "employed" coupled with "or intended to be employed," we have the alternative that it is something additional to the capital which has been actually employed in realising the profit that has been acquired during the year. If, for instance, during the year the lessee of the mines, in order to work the mines with greater success, had added to all his previous expenditure in the mines a sum of money, it might be 1,000l., in order to assist in working the mines in general, that would be a sum of 1,000l. which might add to the value of the mines, and in one sense it would be employed in the trade, because it would be employed to add to the value of the mines, but it must be estimated over, or divided over, or among, the whole of the years yet remaining of the lease. Therefore, although that would be really a sum of money employed in the trade, yet it would not be an element in ascertaining that year's profit, whereas anything that was actually paid and which would apply to that year is to be taken into consideration.

But then we come to another clause, the 159th clause, which is to this effect, as showing what deductions shall not be allowed in computing the duties to be charged under this Act. It says, "Be it enacted, that in the computation of duty to be made "under this Act in any of the cases before mentioned, either by "one party making or delivering any list or statement," and so on, "it shall not be lawful to make any other deductions there-"from than such as are expressly enumerated in this Act, nor "to make any deduction on account of any annual interest, "annuity, or any annual payment to be paid to any person out "of any profits or gains." The reason of that is this, it is the profits of a trade or of an undertaking which are substituted for the interest which it is presumed would otherwise be acquired upon that capital. A man begins with a capital, say of 10,000l., and it may be taken that if he had invested that in any ordinary mode of investment and never entered into trade at all, he would have made five per cent. of it, and that therefore the interest on 10,000l. would be 500l. a year. If, therefore, his profit comes to 500l. a year, it is not to be said that he has lost 500l. a year, or that the interest which he would probably have acquired can be set off against the profit which has actually been acquired; therefore no deduction can be made against the profit in respect to that interest; hence it is that no interest on capital is ever taken into consideration in estimating or ascertaining the amount of the year's profit. But then there are some further matters which are referred to "nor to make any "deduction from the profits or gains arising from any property "herein described, or from any office or employment of profit, on "account of diminution of capital employed or of loss sustained "in any trade, manufacture, adventure, or concern, or in any "profession, employment, or vocation." Diminution of capital is this, it is not a diminution of capital to purchase an article which afterwards you sell at a profit; hence in the cases which I have put there never would be any profit at all; but it is this, capital may be diminished in the first place by a fire. Supposing one half of the stock-in-trade which has been purchased by the capital or that goods to the value of 5,000l. have been burnt in an accidental fire, you cannot set that off against the profits; it is a loss or depreciation of the amount of capital, but it is not an element in the calculation of the amount of profits. So, supposing any other diminution to have taken place, as, for example, the company or trader may really think that his capital is too large and desire to reduce it. Assuming 20,000l. to be the amount of his capital or the amount invested in the purchase of various articles of trade in his possession, and supposing he chooses to reduce that capital from 20,000l. to 15,000l. he diminishes his capital 5,000l. either by placing so much money at his bankers, or by investing it in the purchase of stock, or in some other way; that is a diminution of capital, and one may suppose innumerable other ways in which capital may be diminished. But that diminution is not to be set off against the amount of his profits in estimating the balance of profits, in respect of which balance he is to be assessed to the Income Tax, but is quite of another character; it is a diminution in the amount of capital, but it in no respect is an element in the estimate of the amount of profits. Upon none of these grounds can it be contended under any of the provisions of these Acts of Parliament that the entire sum or any part of the entire sum, whether year by year, or during the whole 32 years, as in this case (happily in this case the figures are simplified) which has actually been paid and expended in order to enable a trader, or the lessee of a mine, in the case of a mine, to acquire by the sale of the article he deals in the excess or profit which constitutes his annual income can be treated as an element in the calculation of the estimate of the amount of profits. From the produce of the article he deals in he has to deduct all the expenses he has been put to, whether by the purchase of commodities of merchandise, or by payments for work or labour or machinery, or payments of any other kind. All that he has necessarily and actually paid in order to acquire possession and the' rights to dispose of the article he deals in, and which he has disposed of for a certain sum. If that of which he had a right to dispose be in excess of all he had paid upon it and of all his outgoings, that excess, and that excess alone, is his profit. But he has a right to take into consideration before the amount of the profit can be said to be ascertained, all that he has expended of every description in order to enable him to acquire the right to the article, that is, the right to dispose of it, and ·thus to obtain the sum in respect of which he is to be assessed. Under these circumstances I think the appellant is entitled to our judgment.

Cleasby, B.—The present case involving the application of the rules for assessing Income Tax appears to me to be of a class in which we must look at each case, and be careful not to generalise so as to.appear to include different cases. Now this is not the case of an owner of land opening a quarry or a mine and letting it at a royalty or working it himself. I do not say anything about such a case as that, for it must be understood, as far as I am concerned,. that.I am not dealing with that case at all. I take it to be quite clear in the present case.that the 8th section of the 29th of Victoria places the assessment under the rules prescribed in Schedule D. I say I take it to be quite clear, the words being " the several and " respective concerns described in No. 93 of Schedule A.," that is, mines, " shall be charged and assessed to the duties hereby " granted in the manner in the said No. 3 mentioned, according " to the rules prescribed by Schedule D. of the said Act, so far " as such rules are consistent with the said No. 3." Nothing can possibly be clearer, I think, than that language. Unless the enactment applies to the case of a colliery company formed for the purpose of carrying on the business of working coal mines, no case can be suggested, in my opinion, to which it can apply, and it must be struck out altogether. This is a case to. which it was intended to apply. I do not express any opinion whatever as to how far it applies to the case of an owner of land, as I said before, opening a quarry and letting or working it. You might say that that case ought to come under Schedule A., and it would be consistent with Schedule A. to bring it under Schedule D. It is possible; but I would not say whether that would be so or not, however, I think nothing can. be clearer than such a case as. I have put of a colliery company formed for the purpose of carrying on a trade being that very matter to which this section is intended to apply, correcting in that way the law as it stood before, making that which appeared to be property assessable as such. Now, having settled this point, we have only to apply the words of Schedule D., treating this. as it ought to be treated, as a trade or business. I think the words are " amount of balance of profits." Now, as soon as you get to this point it seems to me the case is perfectly free from difficulty. I think the whole may be summed up as it was stated by the learned counsel; how can you get at the balance of the profits of trade without stock-taking? How can you get at the balance of the profits of trade for a year without stock-taking at the beginning of the year and at the end of the year? It is impossible, I must say, that this was hardly disputed, looking to Rule 1 in the first part of it, because it does end with these words, "without any other deduction than is herein-after allowed;" therefore in this case the whole argument appears to me to turn upon the application of the language of Rule 3 as correcting the necessary application of the language of Rule 1, which prescribes that you are to take the balance of profits. No doubt there are some of these rules which are inconsistent with economics. No doubt there is some reason why in dealing with the Income Tax it was thought that it should not go by the ordinary rules, and if there is anything in Rule 3 which we can see applicable to the present case, we should be equally bound to adopt it; but we should be guided by the proper rule of taking the ordinary balance of profits. But I can find nothing in Rule 3 to call upon us in this case not to have that sort of stock-taking to which I have referred for the purpose of arriving at the balance of profits. I do not feel myself justified in going through the whole of the rule, and showing how each part of it does not apply. The only part of it, I think, on which anything can turn is the use of the words "capital withdrawn from the concern," and to call this "capital withdrawn from the concern," is entirely erroneous. The proper description of it is "capital consumed in "making the profits." There is not the idea of capital withdrawn from the concern in it. And with regard to the case which has been referred to of Forder and Handyside, there is no doubt the principle of the Income Tax is to take the result one year or an average of years, and every person must pay something, not necessarily out of what may result eventually from the transactions of that year, but he is called upon to pay something out of the profits of that year; and you cannot put by a sum of money for the purpose of meeting depreciation. All you are allowed to do is to deduct your own repairs and things of that sort which belong to the year or average of years. It seems to be quite obvious that if you do more than that you depart from the principle of the Income Tax Act, which forbids it. The case seems to me to be so inapplicable that I almost wonder it was brought forward. At all events it really has no bearing on this case, as it appears to me that the principle in that case was a person attempting to put by a sum for depreciation, and of course that was a thing he was not entitled to do. I think, therefore, under these circumstances that the appellant is entitled to our judgment.

Pollock, B.—I entirely agree with my learned brethren. The first point for us to determine is, under what Act of Parliament is this case governed. It appears to me clearly that it is governed by the 29th and 30th of Victoria, chapter 36, section 8, which provides that any concern such as this is to be "charged and "assessed with duty according to the rules laid down in "Schedule No. 3 of the earlier Acts, and according to the rules "prescribed by Schedule D. of the Act so far as such rules are "consistent with the said No. 3." It is not contended, and we do not for one moment assume, that there is any inconsistency between Schedule A. and those rules. That being so, the rest of the case seems to me really to have arisen, from a sort of mis-apprehension which often unfortunately arises, not only in matters of law, but still more perhaps, in matters of commercial accounts, by the nomenclature which is used. It so happens that in this Company giving their first return to their proprietors they use this phraseology showing the value of their freehold and leasehold colliery and so forth, and put down as their "deprecia-"tion for the year" the sum of 10,240l. 13s. 3d. That seems to have landed the Commissioners in the idea that that was necessarily in diminution of the sum of the balance of profits or gains. When they get before the Commissioners, Mr. Chadwick, who thoroughly understands this matter, explains it in this way: He says, "that the amount which was claimed by the Company as "depreciation and which as stated in the annual report for the "year ending 31st December 1874, is based on a calculation of "the extent of coal available, and the duration of existing "leases, but it may be modified as future circumstances re-"quire;" and he further explained "that the term depreciation "in the balance sheet was used to show to the shareholders the "deterioration or difference in the value of their property at "the end of the year, and after the working out of a year's "coal, and the expiration of a year." That was explained by Mr. Herschell as meaning that what they had done was this: they had overworked the proportion of the whole quantity of coal as compared with the whole number of years, that is to say, in proportion to the term of 32 years they had overworked the colliery to that extent. Can there be any doubt, then, that that throws you back upon the question, before you go into the question of deduction at all, of what has been the balance of profits or gains of the concern? If you have any rent to pay you must first ask yourselves, What is the rent? It may not be an annual rent, or it may be a small annual rent with a very heavy sum paid as premium. Of course in that case the premium must be distributed over the whole number of years. Of course, no person would argue for a moment that because a man paid 100,000l. as premium and only 500l. a year as rent, that 100,000l. should be treated as a nullity. So again in this case; supposing a larger proportion of coal, having regard to the number of years, were taken in any one year than would be taken if it were distributed over the whole number of years, I do not think that there can be any doubt that when these facts are apprehended, and when we ask ourselves what is the profit

or gain of this adventure, we must consider that term and estimate it, and therefore deduct it from the gross receipts of the
sale of the coal before we can arrive at the balance of profits or
gains. That being determined, I think the whole question is at
an end. That is the only way in which the case comes before
us. It was amended by the Company putting in their accounts,
and if it had been done originally in that way, it would never
have come to us at all. I quite agree that the appellant is entitled to our judgment.

Lord Chief Baron.—I ought to have said with costs.

APPENDIX TO KNOWLES *v.* McADAM.

(*See page* 162.)

ANDREW KNOWLES AND SONS, LIMITED.—DIRECTORS' FIRST ANNUAL
REPORT, YEAR ENDING DECEMBER 31, 1874.

To the Shareholders of Andrew Knowles and Sons, Limited.

Your directors have the pleasure to submit the duly audited balance
sheet showing the results of the first year's operations.

It will be seen that the total net profit for the year amounts to
136,560*l.* 14*s.* 9*d.*, being equivalent to 5*l.* 9*s.* 3*d.* per share, or 37½ per cent.
per annum on the amount of share capital paid up during the year.

Your directors recommend that a dividend at the rate of 12½ per cent.
per annum shall be paid, being the maximum sum authorised by the
Articles of Association to be distributed until the reserve fund amounts
to one fourth of the paid-up capital.

The proposed dividend amounts to 1*l.* 16*s.* 3*d.* per share. An interim
payment of 12*s.* per share has already been paid to the shareholders on
account of the year's profits, thus leaving 1*l.* 4*s.* 3*d.* per share to be received.
This sum your directors suggest shall be paid free of income tax.

This dividend will absorb 45,311*l.* 18*s.* 0*d.*, leaving 91,248*l.* 16*s.* 9*d.*
balance of profits to be carried to the reserve fund, in accordance with the
Articles of Association.

During the year your directors have purchased from the representatives
of the late William Scott, Esq., their one third share of the Stoneclough
Collieries, and the properties connected therewith.

They have also acquired from the representatives of the late Henry Hall,
Esq., their one fourth share of the Radcliffe and Bank Top Collieries, with
the accompanying properties.

The lease of the last-named collieries, situated on the estate of the Right
Hon. the Earl of Wilton, has also been renewed for the term of 21 years,
from September 29th last.

At these collieries it is intended to sink two new shafts to the mines now
in work, and to deepen three others in order that the lower seams may be
won.

Your directors have also purchased the mines under an estate of about
57 acres at Pendlebury, and negotiations are at the present time in
progress for the acquirement of the mines under an additional extent of
about 52 acres in the same locality. In this latter case it will be requisite
to purchase about 46 acres of the surface as the owners cannot dispose of it
and the mines separately.

Your directors have much satisfaction in saying that the get and sales
of coal during the past year have been quite equal to the average of former
years.

After the most careful consideration your directors have determined to set
aside annually the sum of 10,424*l.* 15*s.* 3*d.* for depreciation. This amount is

based upon a calculation of the extent of coal available and the duration of the existing leases, but it may be modified as future circumstances require.

Your directors have pleasure in announcing that considerable progress has been made in the transfer of the several freehold and leasehold estates purchased by the Company from Messrs. Andrew Knowles and Sons. The legal inquiries and the preparation of the proper deeds and legal documents for effecting the transfer of a property comprising such numerous and valuable estates necessarily occupy considerable time; from information, however, furnished by the solicitors engaged in this work, your directors hope to be able to report to the annual meeting about to be held that, with the exception of a few properties for which licences have not yet been obtained, the respective conveyances have been completed. In the meantime it should be stated that all the property has since the purchase been worked for the benefit of the shareholders.

The total expenses chargeable to the Company on its formation and establishment, including brokerage, stamp duty, counsel's fees, legal charges, valuation, and other expenses will amount to about 21,000l.; and it is proposed to provide for this sum out of revenue by an annual charge of 2,000l.

Your directors have further to report that the collieries, works, and machinery have been maintained in good working order during the year.

The following directors retire by rotation, but being eligible they offer themselves for re-election, viz.:—Thomas Vickers, Esq., and John Whitehead, junr., Esq.

ANDREW KNOWLES,
Pendlebury, 13th February, 1875.   Chairman.

ANDREW KNOWLES AND SONS, LIMITED.—BALANCE SHEET FOR THE YEAR ENDING DECEMBER 31ST, 1874.

Dr. Capital and Liabilities.		£ s. d.	£ s. d.	Cr. Properties and Assets.		£ s. d.	£ s. d.
To nominal capital 25,000l. shares of 50l. each 1,250,000l.				By freehold and leasehold collieries, estates, buildings, fixed plant, &c.		933,871 5 6	
To paid-up capital :— 25,000 shares, 17l. each paid	425,000 0 0			Add purchases since January 1st, 1874		34,071 19 2	
Less :—Calls unpaid	550 0 0					967,943 2 8	
	424,450 0 0			Deduct property sold since January 1st, 1874		3,735 3 5	
To amount received in advance of calls	46,119 0 0					964,207 19 3	
		470,569 0 0		Less :—Depreciation for the year		10,424 15 3	
„ liability on mortgage debenture bonds		500,000 0 0					953,783 4 0
„ amount owing on account of purchase of share of Radcliffe collieries		14,151 14 2		By stock of stores, waggons, carts, horses, and loose plant			64,441 16 11
„ amount owing on account of purchase of share of Stoneclough collieries		687 12 9		„ stock of coal			14,808 18 0
„ sundry creditors		21,854 11 5		„ over-paid mine rents			5,698 18 7
„ amount owing for rents		5,140 4 1		„ sundry debtors			79,292 15 7
„ „ „ for wages		3,559 18 1		„ preliminary expenses	21,372 16 3		
„ estimated amount due for royalties		14,027 3 10		Less written off this year	2,000 0 0		
„ amount owing for directors' and auditors' remuneration		2,400 0 0					19,372 16 3
„ profit and loss :—				„ Cash in banks and hand			15,403 1 9
Profit for the year	126,560 14 9						
Less :—Interim dividend already paid	14,999 8 0						
		121,561 6 9					
		£1,152,721 11 1					£1,152,721 11 1

Examined and found correct,

EBENEZER ADAMSON,
EDWIN COLLIER,
Manchester, February 12th, 1875.   Auditors.

PART XIII.

The Chartered Mercantile Bank of India,
London, and China   - - - - Appellants

and

William Wilson (Surveyor of Taxes)   - - Respondent.

---

*Inhabited House Duty.—Offices of a Telegraph Company,
within the exemption granted by 32 & 33 Vict. c. 14. s. 11.
Premises in different occupations, and having separate street
doors, but having a lobby in common, with access from it to
both premises during the daytime, one tenement.*

At a Meeting of the Commissioners for the General Purposes
of the Income Tax Acts and for executing the Acts relating
to the Inhabited House Duties, held at the Land Tax Rooms,
Guildhall Buildings, in the said city, on Wednesday, the
10th day of June 1874, for the purpose of hearing Appeals.

Mr. W. Ormiston, secretary to the Chartered Mercantile Bank
of India, London, and China, appealed on behalf of the bank
against an assessment to the Inhabited House Duties for the
year ended 5th April 1874 of 5,500*l.* upon and being the full
value of the whole of the premises Nos. 65 and 66, Old Broad
Street, in the city of London, and claimed exemption under the
Act 32 and 33 Victoria, chapter 14, section 11.

The premises constituting Nos. 65 and 66, Old Broad Street,
are rated to the poor as one building, and the ground floor is
occupied by the Appellants for the purpose of carrying on their
business as bankers. They also occupy certain rooms on the
third floor, in which a caretaker and his wife reside for the
protection of the premises.

The remainder of the building above the ground floor (with
the exception of the rooms in the occupation of the servant
employed and paid by the bank) are let to the Eastern Telegraph Company, Limited, and are occupied by them solely for
the purpose of carrying on the business of the Company, and are
known as No. 66.

The whole of the orders for the management of the business
are issued from these offices, and all the accounts between the
Company and their customers, and between the Company and

A

their own shareholders are kept on the premises. No person sleeps in that portion of the building occupied by the Telegraph Company, but there is internal communication throughout the entire premises.

The Appellants contend that the premises so occupied did not form an inhabited dwelling-house within the meaning of the statute 14 and 15 Victoria, chapter 36, section 2, and that even if they came within that section they would still be exempt under the provisions of the 11th section of the statute 32 and 33 Victoria, chapter 14, inasmuch as they were used for the purposes of trade only, &c., &c., &c.

The premises were similarly assessed for 1872-3, and an appeal was made against that assessment on the 12th June 1873, when it was contended on behalf of the Crown that this case should be governed by Case No. 2,845 decided by the judges, in which it was stated that in their opinion the booking offices, waiting-room, board-room, and other offices of the South-eastern Railway Company were liable as not being used for the purposes of trade, and as these premises were similarly occupied by the Telegraph Company and the bank they were also liable. The Commissioners confirmed the assessment on that occasion, and the duty for 1872 was paid.

Finding on the present occasion that the circumstances were unaltered the Commissioners again confirmed the assessment, whereupon the Appellants declared their dissatisfaction with the decision and duly required them to state and sign a case for the opinion of the Court of Exchequer, which we have stated and signed accordingly in pursuance of the 9th section, 37 Victoria, chapter 16.

Dated this 15th March 1875.

5th June 1875.

Whereas in pursuance of the statute 37 & 38 Victoria, chapter 16, a case has been stated and signed for the opinion of this Court, at the request of the above Appellants, by the Commissioners for the General Purposes of the Income Tax Acts and for executing the Acts relating to the Inhabited House Duties for the City of London, which case had been filed in the Office of the Queen's Remembrancer of this Court. Now upon the application of J. P. Benjamin, Esquire, one of Her Majesty's Counsel for the Appellants, and on reading the affidavit of Cyril Mortimer Murray Rawlans, it is ordered by the Court that the said case be sent back for amendment by stating the special mode in which the internal communication between the tenements exist, and to what extent and in what manner the occupants of Nos. 65 and 66 enjoy any means of communication which are stated to exist, including a statement of the mode of entrance into each tenement from the street.

W. F. POLLOCK,
Q.R.

AMENDED CASE.

1. At a Meeting of the Commissioners for the General Purposes of the Income Tax Acts and for executing the Acts relating to the Inhabited House Duties, held at the Land Tax Rooms, Guildhall Buildings, in the said city, on Wednesday, the 10th day of June 1874, for the purpose of hearing Appeals.

Mr. W. Ormiston, secretary to the Chartered Mercantile Bank of India, London, and China, appealed on behalf of the bank against the bank's assessment to the Inhabited House Duties for the year ending 5th April 1874 of 5,500l. upon and being the full value of the whole of the premises Nos. 65 and 66, Old Broad Street, in the city of London, and claimed exemption under the Act 32 and 33, Victoria, chapter 14, section 11.

2. The premises constituting Nos. 65 and 66, Old Broad Street, are situate at the corner of Old Broad Street and Austin Friars. They consist of a basement ground and upper floors, such upper floors running in part over the portion of the premises known as No. 65. There are two separate main entrances from the street, one in Old Broad Street known as No. 65 and the other in Austin Friars known as No. 66, as shown on the plan of part of the ground floor hereto annexed and marked A. (a)

3. The portion of the premises constituting and known as No. 65, is the ground floor (except that part marked B on the said plan), and the basement under such ground floor No. 65. The whole of the remainder of the premises, consisting of the first and upper floors with the portion of the ground floor marked B, and the basement thereunder, constitute and are known as No. 66. The portion of ground floor marked B consists of an entrance and staircase leading to the first and upper floors, and stairs leading to the basement thereunder, as marked on the plan. The basements respectively of Nos. 65 and 66 are completely severed by brick walls one from the other, and approached as shown on the plan by separate staircases, so that there is no communication between the two, and throughout the building there is no communication whatever between the premises No. 65 and No. 66, except the lobby communication herein-after mentioned.

4. The premises No. 65 are in the occupation of the Appellants and used by them as a bank, and for the purpose of carrying on their business as bankers.

5. The premises No. 66 are (with the exception of two rooms on the third floor occupied by a caretaker employed by the Appellants, and his wife, who reside there for the protection of the entire premises) let to the Eastern Telegraph Company, Limited, and are occupied by them solely for the purpose of carrying on the business of the Company. The whole of the

---

(a) • See opposite page.

orders for the management of the business of the Company are issued from the premises so occupied by the Company, and all the accounts between the Company and their customers, and between the Company and their own shareholders, are kept on such premises.

6. With the exception of the caretaker and his wife, no person sleeps on any portion of the premises No. 65 or No. 66.

7. The entrance No. 65 from Old Broad Street opens as shown on the plan into a lobby through which, by the doors therefrom on the right, is the access to the Appellant's bank premises.

The regular entrance to the premises No. 66 is by the door from Austin Friars, but during banking hours the iron doors shown on the plan by a blue line, giving an entrance from the portion of the ground floor marked B to the lobby, are allowed by the Appellants to be open so as to enable the Eastern Telegraph Company by crossing the lobby to have an access to their premises from Old Broad Street, which is to some more convenient than the entrance from Austin Friars. At the close of the bank business of the day these iron doors are with the entrance, No. 65, Old Broad Street, closed and locked by the bank porter, who keeps the keys of both doors, and when this is done the bank premises are completely shut off from the rest of the building, and the only approach to the premises No. 66 is by the street door, No. 66, from Austin Friars.

8. In the valuation list made for the city under the Valuation (Metropolis) Act, 1869, in the year 1870, the premises were valued as one building, and were thenceforth until 1875 rated to the poor as one building, but upon the appeal of the Appellants against the new valuation list made in the year 1875 the assessment has been divided, and Nos. 65 and 66 are now separately assessed and rated to the poor.

9. The Appellants contend, first, that no part of the premises so occupied form an inhabited dwelling-house within the meaning of the statute 14 and 15 Victoria, chapter 36, section 2, and that even if they came within that section, they would still be exempt under the provisions of the 11th section of the statute 32 and 33 Victoria, chapter 14, inasmuch as they were used for the purposes of trade only.

Secondly, they contend that the bank premises are occupied for the purpose of trade only, and that they are so structurally severed from the rest of the building as to be a different tenement for rating purposes, and that even if the premises in the occupation of the Telegraph Company are not exempt, and are not occupied as trade premises within the meaning of this statute, yet the assessment is wrong, inasmuch as the whole of the premises are rated therein.

Thirdly, whether this is so or not, the assessment is bad as being to the full value, although a considerable part, at least in their own occupation, is occupied for the purposes of trade only.

10. In the year 1870 the Appellants were assessed to the Inhabited House Duty for the year 1869 ending the 5th of April

1870, as the occupiers of the premises No. 65, and having by mistake paid the amount, it was on their application to the Board of Inland Revenue refunded, on the ground that the premises occupied by the appellants were exempt under the 11th section of the Act 32 and 33 Victoria, chapter 14.

During the whole of that year (1869-70) the premises No. 66 were unoccupied with the exception of the two rooms on the third floor occupied by the caretaker, but from that time the occupation has been as at present.

11. The premises were again assessed for 1872-3, and an appeal was made against that assessment on the 12th of June 1873, when it was contended on behalf of the Crown that this case should be governed by Case No. 2,845, decided by the judges, in which it was stated that in their opinion the booking offices, waiting-room, board-room, and other offices of the South-eastern Railway Company were liable as not being used for the purposes of trade, and as these premises were similarly occupied by the Telegraph Company and the bank, they were also liable. The Commissioners confirmed the assessment on that occasion, and the duty for 1872 was paid.

12. The Appellants, however, have taken the first opportunity of appealing against the assessment since the statute allowing an appeal was passed.

Finding on the present occasion that the circumstances were unaltered, the Commissioners again confirmed the assessment, whereupon the Appellants declared their dissatisfaction with the decision, and duly required them to state and sign a case for the opinion of the Court of Exchequer, which we have stated and signed accordingly in pursuance of the 9th section, 37 Victoria, chapter 16.

5th December 1877.

Meadows White, Q.C., for the Appellants.—These are two houses, and not one house within the meaning of the Inhabited House Duty Act. Both bankers and telegraph company are traders within the meaning of the Act. Each occupier should be separately assessed. The case is quite different from "The Attorney-General v. The Mutual Tontine Westminster Chambers Association, Limited" (a). There each block of buildings had only one street door, and had externally the appearance of a single house; but here there are two entrances from different streets, and if it were not for the iron door being allowed to be open for a limited period of the day, it would be perfectly clear that these were two houses. Again, a telegraph company is a trader. It carries on business for the purpose of profit, and the public for profit are allowed the use of the plant, and of the electricity, and the services of the staff. But even if the telegraph company's portion of the premises is liable the part

(a) L.R. 1, Exch. Div. 469.

occupied by the bank is exempt. The case of Rusby and Newsom (b) did not raise that point.

This case is not within the sixth rule of Schedule B., 48 Geo. 3. c. 55.

[*Kelly*, C.B.—Does this case come within the clause at all, as being a house let in different stories, tenements, &c. There is only one part of it let?]

There is only one part let to any dessee. The Appellants occupy part and let part.

Sir Hardinge Giffard, S.G., for the Respondent.—The Telegraph Company is not a trader. Trading involves of necessity the notion of buying and selling. (Reads judgment in the case of the Edinburgh Life Assurance Company. (c)) The statute imposing the duties was passed in 1808.

[*Pollock*, B.—We are looking at the 11th section of the Act of 1869.]

When the statute uses the word "trade" as applicable to an exemption from what was subject to taxation in 1808, the language must be understood in the sense in which it was then used. If the definition of the word "trader" is so wide as to include a telegraph office, what is the difference between a trade and a vocation? Both law books and statute books have preserved the distinction between traders properly so called, and persons engaged in mere handicraft.

6th December 1887.

The word "trade" must be regarded *juxta subjectam materiam*; in strictness it signifies buying and selling, not buying alone, not selling alone, but buying and selling coupled. Accountants are certainly not traders, but they carry on business in which they do work for people and receive money for doing it.

[*Kelly*, C.B.—Has there been any decision as to trading in respect of the business of a dyer?]

Apart from authority and apart from express statutory enactment, a dyer would not be a trader within the meaning for which I am contending.

[*Kelly*, C.B.—Is this in any sense of the word an "inhabited house"?]

An inhabited house does not mean, according to more than one decided case, a house in which people sleep at night. If it be used during the day only, that makes it an inhabited house. A house occupied solely for the purposes of trade may retain the exemption although somebody sleep in it at night, but not if it be occupied by persons carrying on businesses or vocations which are not trades.

(b) L.R. 10, Exch. 322 ; *ante*, p. 15. *Sub nomine* Weavers' Hall.
(c) *ante*, p. 7 ; 12 Sco. L.R. 275.

JUDGMENT.

Lord Chief Baron.—Mr. Solicitor-General, in the present state of the argument we think we are justified in at once putting an end to this case, and pronouncing our judgment. With regard to the question which has been argued on the other side, and which you have not yet argued, although speaking for myself alone, I might, independently of the authorities in this Court of more than one decision and even a unanimous decision, I might, I say, independently of those authorities, be disposed for myself to entertain some doubts whether this was really to be deemed one tenement and so to be liable to the duty in question; but my learned brethren are decidedly of opinion that it is to be deemed one tenement, and that therefore it is liable to duty, and on looking to the authorities and without looking very carefully into this lease which the Appellants counsel has been good enough to hand up to us, whatever doubts I might have been disposed to entertain I do not feel disposed to differ with my brethren, and therefore upon that point, so far as it can be important to you, you may consider the judgment of the Court as given in your favour. But with regard to the question of whether this tenement, or whatever it may be called, which is demised to and in the possession and occupation of the Telegraph Company is to be deemed as a tenement occupied as house for the purpose of trade only, I am disposed to hold myself and say that I am clearly of opinion that it is to be deemed a house or tenement occupied for the purposes of trade. And the main ground upon which I found that opinion is that in these days and in this great commercial country, the greatest and most commercial country in the world, we are bound to put a large and liberal construction upon any terms of any provisions to be found existing in any Act of Parliament where the construction proposed to be put upon it is in favour of the trade and commerce of the country. Undoubtedly, if we are to take the terms "for the purposes of trade" as relating only to an occupation or a business of buying and selling, no one can say that there is any buying or selling in carrying on of the business of a telegraph company. It was never the intention of the Legislature in a provision of this nature to so limit the meaning of the word "trade." It is not only the literal meaning of the word which is to be regarded. In literature of all descriptions, both in prose and verse, whether with regard to commerce or with regard to any other subject with relation to which the term may be used, we find that the word "trade" is often used in a much more extensive signification than merely the operation or occupation of buying and selling. And why are we to limit it in a case of this nature to buying and selling? When we find now that from improvements in machinery and the advancement of science and the vast accumulation of subjects and materials and operations which have come into practice and use in the world, and especially in this great commercial country, when we find the word "trade" used not singly and simply by itself, and where it is possible that under some circumstances it may be interpreted

to relate only to the operation of buying and selling ; but where
we also find it in a provision of this nature to which I next
propose to call attention, I cannot feel any doubt but that really
the object of the section was to protect the commerce of the
country and all the commercial business of the country. Whatever might be the precise nature of the occupation, if it was one
which was practised for the commercial benefit of the country it
was intended . to exempt those operatives from the liability to
this tax. We find it does not stand alone, but that the section
also says, "part of a tenement occupied as a house for the
purposes of trade only " ; that is the first exemption. Then
comes this, "or as a warehouse for the special purpose of lodging
goods, wares, or merchandise therein." Now I apprehend that
throughout a very great portion of the commerce of the country,
not only in the city of London and in the Metropolis, but in
Manchester, Liverpool, and all the great commercial towns of
this country, a warehouse is the scene of larger and more
numerous commercial operations than any description of building
that can well be imagined. There may well be warehouses
where there is nothing like buying and selling, but where
goods are deposited ; and there may be persons who may
be traders in other respects, and who likewise carry on
that business independently of their own particular trade,
and when we find the example given in the next provision "a
"warehouse for the purpose of lodging goods, wares, and mer-
"chandise therein," and where there is therefore nothing like
buying and selling referred to or at all pointed at, I think we
may apply the maximum "*noscitur a sociis*," and I say that we
must apply the earlier provision about a house used "for the
purposes of trade only " upon the same principle and upon the
same course of construction as the provision itself which next
follows, namely, the provision respecting warehouses where there
is nothing like buying and selling carried on, and which has
been adopted and given as an example by the Legislature. We
then come, again, to a "shop or counting-house." Now a shop,
undoubtedly, is a place in general in which nothing is carried on
but buying and selling. I say "in general" because it is not
always so. I have heard the expression repeatedly, and we find
it in books, and most of you have heard it in conversation, that
a banker's is a "shop"—the "banking shop of a bank"—and
there again there is nothing like buying and selling as generally
understood, but it is a trade or business of a description quite
sui generis and certainly quite apart from what is generally
understood by buying and selling. But when you come to a
counting-house, a counting-house is a building or apartment in
which every description of commercial business which can be
imagined is usually carried on. A tradesman doing any large
amount of business has, independently of his shop, a counting-
house in which the counting-house business of the concern is
carried on. Merchants have it who live by buying and selling,
and a variety of descriptions of commercial men—in fact almost
every description of man of business has something like a

counting-house in which he carries on his business or a portion of his business. Therefore, there again, we have one of the largest and most comprehensive terms which the English language contains introduced into this provision for exemption.

I think, therefore, applying the term *noscitur a sociis*, we may reasonably infer that the Legislature never intended by the use of this word " trade " to limit the business carried on, which is to exempt the occupier of the tenement from the tax in question, to purely buying or selling. We may reasonably say that it was intended to embrace a great variety of different operations though all of a commercial character, something, therefore, like a warehouse, like a shop, like a counting-house; all are to be construed, in my opinion, upon the same principle of construction, namely, to put a large and liberal interpretation upon the exemption which the legislative law provided for persons, whatever may be the precise occupation or vocation which they follow, who do carry on or assist in carrying on the commercial business of the country.

I have only a word to say about the Scotch case which has been cited. I have the greatest respect for the decisions of the Court of Session in Scotland, though, undoubtedly, not exactly for their decisions in general upon purely commercial questions. Now, however, that the trade and manufactures of Scotland have become of a vast degree of extent and importance I receive with great attention every decision we hear of in the Court of Session in Scotland, even upon commercial questions. But when we consider that the judgment of the learned Judges in that case related to a life assurance company, there is something so totally different in the life assurance company from anything in the nature of a telegraph company, that I cannot think the authority in question has any bearing upon the present case. The difference is substantial in every way. A life assurance company in one sense may be said to be a commercial undertaking, but, on the other hand, it is one of a very peculiar character, and indeed, of a very limited character—it is an agreement or contract which is made between one man and another, or between an individual and the company, that in consideration of an annual payment during his life the executors of the one party shall, at his death become entitled to a particular sum of money. I do not know that there is anything of a commercial nature or of a commercial character in a transaction of that kind; it is quite different from the business of a telegraph company. I content myself, therefore, with saying that in my opinion the difference is so manifest, both in principle as well as in fact, in the nature of the operations in question between those of a telegraph company and those of a life assurance company, that I do not consider the case of Scotland at all applicable to the case which is now before the Court. Under those circumstances, and without more, it appears to me that we are bound to put a large and liberal construction upon the exemption which I have now pointed out, and that therefore, upon these points, the Appellant is entitled to the judgment of the Court.

Mr. Baron Cleasby.—I confess I think that judgment ought to be given for the Crown, although I deemed it quite unnecessary to have any further argument, because we are all agreed upon the question which the learned Solicitor-General has raised. Now as to the first question, I do not entertain any doubt that these premises are to be regarded for the purpose of applying the law of inhabited house taxation as an inhabited house. It is a question of considerable difficulty when you read it by itself, but the question has. really been considered and decided already, and it is impossible, I cannot help saying, without great waste of time, in every case where no essential difference exists, to go back and have a difficult question which has already been settled by authority argued over again. Various cases have been referred to and I need not repeat them, namely, the Weavers Hall case, and the Westminster Buildings case. The question of part of a tenement was particularly considered in the Weavers Hall case, and I endeavoured to point out in that case, although I am afraid I did not do so as clearly as I might have done,—at all events it does not appear so on reading the report,—that if you refer to the 57th of George III., when it speaks of a tenement or part of a tenement you will find that it refers to that which might have been taxed as part of an inhabited house, and that part of a tenement was one tenement in that sense which was subject to taxation. That appeared to me to be decisive of the question that it becomes the same as one house with a separate private entrance altogether ; it was part of a tenement in the simple and ordinary meaning of the word, but it was an inhabited house for the purposes of taxation, no one can dispute that. That is the only explanation, in my opinion, of that term "part of a tenement"; we must read it with the recital, which I will not go through at length, of the 57th of George III., from which it appears that it must part of a tenement which was the subject of taxation as an inhabited house. Now in this case we have this morning seen the lease which has been referred to. I think it would be a waste of time to read the words of it, but the result is this, speaking generally, though perhaps not with perfect accuracy as to every point. All the upper floor is let, no doubt, but there is a common entrance during the day, that is a great feature of the case. The tenant had a right to go through the entrance of the bank to his premises during the day, and he has a right to put his plate upon the door of the bank, giving a character of unity as it were to the whole, but still more there is one person living in one part, that is the telegraph part, who has the care of the whole. Those circumstances give to this tenement the character of one house, and in a way which certainly has not occurred in any case which has been decided. There is one person living and sleeping in the apartments and having common access to the whole. I would particularly desire not to make a mistake upon that, "the premises No. 66 are (with the exception of two rooms on the third floor occupied by a caretaker"—the caretaker not being employed by the Telegraph Company but employed by the Appellants, by the bankers—"and his wife, who reside there for the protection of the entire premises) let to the Eastern Telegraph Company." But upon this a remark occurs which places the Appellant in an unfavourable position as regards a part, for if the learned counsel's argument is correct that these are separate tenements, it is then quite plain that the telegraph part must be assessed as an inhabited house, and for this reason, that assuming the opinion of my learned brother to be correct, as we will for the purpose, that this is a trade, that part is not exempt, because there is a person who lives there who is not a caretaker of those premises, but who takes care of other premises as well. You cannot have a person there for any purpose but for the purpose of taking care of that part of the premises whch is in question, and which claims exemption. Therefore, if that conclusion were really the correct one, it must, in my opinion, and without any possibility of answering it, convey the obligation to have that part of the premises assessed. I say no more upon that part of the question, and should hardly have dealt with it at such length, but that I thought it might be of advantage in explaining what had taken place before. Now we come to the next part of the case, and after what I have heard from my Lord, I cannot say that I come to the same conclusion as I do with regard to the other part of the case. I quite agree that the Scotch decision is not upon the same facts as the present case, because you can see a considerable distinction between an insurance society and a telegraph company, and passing by the case of the Mutual Assurance Society, it appears to me that the principles laid down in that case are quite correct, and that if you apply them to the present case, we should come to the conclusion that the Telegraph Company does not come within the exemption of the section. It is necessary, however, to go back to the history of the legislation upon the subject in order to see how one arrives at this conclusion, because it is to a certain extent a system of legislation, and you cannot take one part of it alone without regard to the rest. I will begin taking the learned Solicitor-General's suggestion that every house that is occupied is an inhabited house. Then you have an exemption made by the 57th of George III., and the importance of referring to this arises from the fact that the language of the 57th of George III. is the same as the language of the 32nd and 33rd Victoria. I have very little doubt that I am almost repeating the previous argument of the learned Solicitor-General; but not having had the advantage of hearing it, I must give it as my own view. It is said that there "Whereas it is become usual in cities and large " towns and other places for one and the 'same person, or for each " person where two or more persons are in partnership, to " occupy a dwelling-house or dwelling-houses for their residence, " and at the same time one or more separate and distinct tene- " ments or buildings, or parts of tenements or buildings, for the " purposes of trade, or as 'warehouses for lodging goods, wares, " or merchandise therein, or as shops or counting-houses, and to

" abide therein in the daytime only for the purposes of such
" trades respectively, which have been charged with the said
" recited duties." With regard to this question, the words which
are important are " for the purpose of trade," it does not say for
the purpose of trade only. There is clearly a difference between
that Act of Parliament and the one we are now considering,
though perhaps it may occur in the enacting part, but it does
not in the recital. A little further on it says, "as a house for
" the purposes of trade only, or as a warehouse for the sole pur-
" pose of lodging goods, wares, or merchandise therein, or as a
" shop or counting-house." Here we come to the enactment.
This enactment having been made and acted upon, it was felt to
be a grievance to a certain class of persons who did not occupy
premises for the purposes of trade, but who occupied premises for
the purpose of some employment by which they gained their
livelihood. This led to the enactment of the 5th George IV.,
chapter 44, section 4, of which is in these terms. After reciting
the Act of the 57th George III., it says, " Whereas by an Act
passed in the 57th year " of George III., " provisions is made for
granting exemptions "—I will not read them in detail—" And
" whereas it is expedient to extend the same exemptions to the
" cases herein mentioned : Be it further enacted, that upon all
" assessments to be made for any year commencing from and
" after the 5th day of April, 1824, the provisions in the said Act
" contained for granting exemptions from the said duties to
" persons in trade, in respect of houses, tenements, or buildings
" in the said Act described, shall and may be extended and
" applied by the respective commissioners and officers acting
" in the execution of the said Act, and of this Act, on due
" proof to all and every person, or any number of persons
" in partnership together, for and in respect of any house,
" tenement, or building, or part of a tenement or building, in
" the said Act described, which shall be used by such person
" or persons as offices or counting-houses for the purposes of
" exercising or carrying on any profession, vocation, business,
" or calling by which such person or persons shall seek a
" livelihood or profit." You have here, therefore, in reference to
this particular subject of taxation, a clear distinction drawn
between premises occupied for the purposes of trade, or as warehouses or counting-houses, or shops, and premises which are
occupied as offices or counting-houses for the purposes of carrying
on any business of profit. That is the way in which the law
stood until we come to the Act of the 32nd and 33rd Victoria.
This Act of Parliament did not allow any person to sleep on the
premises at all ; they must be upon the premises by day only.
When the enactment took place which we are now considering,
however, intentionally or unintentionally, it is not for me to say,
it may have been intended or it may not have been intended,
the enactment is made to apply only to these premises mentioned in the 57th of George III. ; that is to say, counting-houses
and so on, and it is not made to apply to those matters

enumerated in the 5th of George IV., where persons occupy offices or counting-houses for the purpose of carrying on any business whereby they obtain a livelihood. The language of the larger section which I am now considering is precisely the same as the language of the 57th George III., with the exception of the addition put at the end, but I do not think that can have any bearing upon the present question, " or being used as such," in addition to the words " being occupied as such." I do not think that can make any difference. It was upon this that they proceeded in the Scotch case, seeing that the Legislature had drawn a distinction between premises used for the purposes of trade, and offices or premises occupied for the purposes of carrying on any vocation or business. Those are the Acts of Parliament, and there is a distinction made, and there is nothing whatever to repeal it, and I should feel myself departing from the distinction which the Legislature itself has pointed out if I were to say that those premises, which would in my opinion clearly come within the 57th of George III. as being offices for the purpose of carrying on business, were offices or premises occupied for the purpose of trade only. I think we should say there is no distinction between the two, but the Act of Parliaments says there is, for these are plainly the offices of the Telegraph Company, and occupied by them, and would be exempt from taxation as an inhabited house if no person slept there by night, and if they were only used by day, but if a person does sleep there by night they do not come within the words of this exemption. For these reasons which I have stated, I think the Crown is entitled to our judgment.

Mr. Baron Pollock.—In my judgment the Appellant is entitled to our judgment, and inasmuch as there is no difference of opinion or any reasonable doubt, after so many decisions upon the same subject, with regard to the character of the premises, I think it will be quite sufficient for me to give my reasons for agreeing with my Lord upon the question of whether or not this Telegraph Company can be said to be using these premises for the purposes of trade. Now, no precise description of the business of this Company is given to us, and therefore there is something left, although not much that is material, for us to infer, as to what is the nature of the business; they are described in the case of a Telegraph Company, Limited. It is said that these premises are occupied by them solely for the purpose of carrying on the business of the Company. The whole of the orders for the management of the business are issued from the premises so occupied by the Company, and all the accounts between the Company and their customers, and between the Company and their own shareholders, are kept on such premises. Now, as I understand the business of a company like that, they have not merely to transmit by electric apparatus messages from one part of the world to the other, but they have also to do all those things which are conditions precedent to their doing so in the way of acquiring machinery and telegraphic communication by wires

and cables, and arrangements for the repairs of their cables,
involving either the direct purchase of the materials or the
entering into contracts for their repair by others who do purchase those materials, and they have also to keep up correspondence and communication with many parts of the world,
receiving money and paying money, and having clerks who keep
their accounts. Now, that being so, is this business which is
carried on by them such as can properly be said within the
meaning of this Act of Parliament, or these series of Acts of
Parliament (for I entirely agree with my brother Cleasby that we
must take them as a series with which we have to deal), to come
within the words, so that they can be said to occupy these premises for the purposes of trade. Now one is almost tired of citing
rules and principles whereby statutes are to be construed, but
there is one rule which I think is perfectly clear, and that I find
so well expressed by Mr. Benson Maxwell in his very able work
on the Interpretation of the Statutes, that I will take his words
rather than use my own. He begins his second chapter of the first
section in this way, " In interpreting a statute it is to be borne in
" mind at the outset that language is always used *secundam*
" *subjectam materiam*, and that it must therefore be understood
" in the sense which best harmonises with the subject matter"
that I think is a very good and a very clear proposition. Now,
that being so, what was the subject matter of this statute, and
what was the spirit of the *distinction* to be created? It was a
distinction between persons who inhabited houses for the purpose
of residence and persons who occupied " houses," as they were
then called, for the purpose of trade; and you find coupled with
the word " trade," as my Lord has said, such places as warehouses for lodging goods, wares, and merchandise therein, or
shops or counting-houses; thereby expressing that as the anti-
thesis, as it were, which it is the intention of the statute to
establish. Now I think if I am right in the construction which
I have put upon the statute and the spirit in which I construe
it, that it would be a somewhat dangerous rule to depart from
the meaning which the word would require upon that principle,
because I find in the subsequent statute other words introduced
for a more extended purpose by the Legislature. If it is for me
to choose between the two rules of construction, I would rather
prefer the construction adopted by my Lord than that which
had been adopted by my brother Cleasby in the construction of
the later statute. But I regard it as a very important matter; I
do not think that it is a matter to be treated lightly, nor do I
think it is a question which is perfectly free from doubt, but I
have applied my mind as best I can to see what is the fair and
reasonable meaning of the words " for the purpose of trade," in
the section. Now some citations were made in the course of the
argument from dictionaries, and I would only say that I would
personally avoid citing any word from dictionaries as implying
in any sense a definition, because such is dangerous; but one
may cite from a dictionary, or a work of good repute, to see

what is the common acceptation of a word. Yesterday two dictionaries, one Richardson's and the other Webster's, were cited for the purpose of giving us a definition of the term, but I have found a definition in Johnson which seems to me to be more near the spirit in which I am construing the words.   It is the second meaning which he gives in which trade is described as an "occupation or particular employment, whether manual or "mercantile, as distinguished from the arts or learned profes- "sions."   That is a very fair expression of the meaning of the word in common parlance when you are speaking of whether a person exercises a profession or whether he carries on a trade; and in the same way, whether a person occupies a house for the purpose of dwelling therein personally or whether he occupies it for the purpose of carrying on a trade.

Now another head of argument, and one of course to which we ought to attend with the greatest care, is that which is used by the learned Solicitor General in regard to the Bankruptcy Act, and no doubt the word trade was originally there intended as applying only to persons who either bought or sold or whose business was immediately cognate to the buying or selling of goods, but even then you find from time to time the words used in a much looser sense; and although we have no right to refer to the enlargement of the number of persons who have been made liable to become bankrupts by different statutes from time to time, we may look at these statutes to see in what sort of sense they used the word themselves.   I find in one statute as far back as James the First that a scrivener may be bankrupt. In the 21st of James the First, chapter 19, section 2   the words used are, "or that shall use the trade or profession of a scrivener "receiving other men's moneys or estates into his trusts or "custody."   Therefore even there you find the word used in a wider sense than that of mere buying or selling.   And in "Christian's Bankruptcy Law," you find 30 or 40 pages devoted to considering all the different cases in which, apart from the statute law, persons have been made bankrupts who have not actually been traders in the limited sense of buying, selling, or bartering.   I do not think, however, myself, that that is a true guide to our conclusion in this case.   I would rather say that although the statutes relating to bankruptcy present some analogy, they do not present a true analogy, because the comtemplation of the statute and the common law too was devoted to a very different purpose from that which was the object and intention of the statute which is now under consideration.   I thought it right to say so much because, as I said before, this is an important matter, and it is a matter in which one is desirous of giving the grounds of the conclusion at which we have come.   Upon these grounds I think the Appellant is entitled to our judgment.

Mr. Meadows White.—Do your Lordships give judgment with costs in this case for the Appellant ?

Lord Chief Baron.—Yes.

No. 28.—In the High Court of Justice.—England.—
Exchequer Division.

6th December 1877.

Keen   -   -   -   -   -   - Appellant
                        and
Fuller and Horsey   -   -   -   - Respondents.

Inhabited House Duty.—Offices of an Auctioneer within the exemption granted by 32 & 33 Vict. c. 14. s. 11.

Sir Hardinge Giffard, S.G., for the Appellant.—The next case in order is one which I should call your Lordships' attention to with reference to the decision which has just been pronounced. It is the case of Keen against Fuller and Horsey. Now, my Lords, with reference to that case, I should be very much in your Lordships' hands. It raises the question as to whether or not a firm carrying on business as auctioneers have a right to the exemption which we have been discussing in the last case, by reason that their premises are occupied for the purposes of trade.

[*Pollock, B.*—This case was amended, was it not?]
I do not think the amendment is very material. My Lords, as I say, I am quite in your Lordships' hands, I do not want to argue the whole question over again as to what is or what is not a trade. It seems to me that if a telegraph company is a trade, it would be very difficult to say that an auctioneer is not ; but I am quite in your Lordships' hands upon that matter.

[*Kelly, C.B.*—What are the words?]
They are the same words.

Cleasby, B.—No one can say that it is possible to apply the words "counting-house" to an auctioneer.

Waugh, for the Respondents.—The case begins by saying that their office is a counting-house.

Sir Hardinge Giffard, S.G.—If it turns upon that, I will argue it, of course. The question of whether it is a counting-house or not has not been touched upon in the last case.

Pollock, B.—The words are these : " They carry on the
" regular business of auctioneers, that is, they effect sales by
" auction and by private treaty or tender, some of the said sales
" being sales by sample, and samples are exhibited in the said
" offices above mentioned. They also do business as factors ;
" they receive bills of lading of goods, transfer notes, and delivery
" notes of goods, and make advances on such goods with which
" they are entrusted in such capacity, and which they sell and

" repay themselves out of the proceeds of sale, and render
" account sales to their principals. They also grant temporary
" loans and advances on houses, lands, machinery, and other
" property, the sale of which is entrusted to them. They also
" receive in their said offices tenders for old materials, which are
" entrusted to them for sale. They also arrange, lot, and assort
" goods of all descriptions."

Kelly, C.B.—I think we need not resort to the counting-
house to determine this case.

Sir Hardinge Giffard, S.G.—The counting-house question I
did not argue in the last case. If your Lordships think it is
governed by the question as to their being traders, I have no
more to say upon that subject than I said in the last case.

Cleasby, B.—It is not worth while to have this particular
case argued again for the purpose of seeing whether the
Court would be unanimous in this case. I cannot see that it can
be so.

Judgment for the Respondents.

No. 29.—COURT OF EXCHEQUER.—SCOTLAND.
FIRST DIVISION.

In Re THE UNION BANK OF SCOTLAND.

---

*Inhabited House Duty. — Banking-house and dwelling-house
under the same roof, but without internal communication;
dwelling-house occupied by the accountant of the Bank for the
protection of its property; held that the Bank was liable to one
assessment for the whole.*

AT Dumbarton, the 15th day of November 1877, at a Court
held by Commissioners for General Purposes for the West
District of Dumbartonshire, acting in the execution of the
Property and Income Tax Acts and Inhabited House Duty
Acts.

The Union Bank of Scotland appealed against an assessment
of inhabited house duty, at 9d. per 1l. on 80l., being the annual
value of new premises in Dumbarton belonging to them.

These premises consist of two storeys and attics under one
roof. The ground floor is used chiefly as a branch office of the
Bank, which is accessible only by a door opening to the public
street. A small portion of the ground floor, situated behind the
office (but without any internal communication therewith) and
the upper floor and attics form a dwelling-house, which is occupied
by the branch accountant of the Bank as the residence of himself
and family, the furniture in the house belonging to him. Access

B

to the dwelling-house is obtained by a door opening into a passage or close leading from the street, and by a back door opening into a court behind, which passage or close and court form parts of the premises attached to the dwelling-house, and are used solely by the occupiers thereof. The court is enclosed by walls, excepting at the end of the passage or close from the street. There is a door on this passage or close at the street entrance. There is no internal communication between the Bank office and the dwelling-house, or between the Bank office and the court behind or the passage or close. To go from the one to the other, it is necessary to enter upon and pass along the public street. There is a bolt leading from the Bank safe to, and controlled from, a room in the dwelling-house above.

It was contended for the Appellants —

1. That as the occupation of the dwelling-house forms the basis of an assessment for inhabited house duty, the Appellants cannot be liable in duty either on house or office, unless the Bank corporation occupy the dwelling-house.

The corporation does not occupy it. The accountant occupies the house as his private personal residence by himself and his family, and with his own furniture, to the exclusion of the Bank and of the branch agents and all other officers of the Bank so long as he, the accountant, is in lawful actual possession, however terminable that possession may be.

2. But even assuming the corporation to be occupants of the house, the office is not liable to inhabited house duty, seeing it is used solely as a place of business, and has no communication whatever with the house either internally within the fabric of the building itself, or externally over ground forming part of the same premises, as in the cases of Russell and Salmond hereinafter referred to, which cases therefore were different from the present. The circumstance that the office is under the same roof with the house does not of itself infer liability; if it did, every tenement consisting of separate flats in different occupation would be chargeable to duty as one house.

The surveyor, Mr. Forbes, contended that the Union Bank of Scotland are the occupiers of the whole premises, the accountant being in possession of the house merely as their servant, and removable at their pleasure. He instanced the fact that Bank officials had in the Registration Courts uniformly been refused the franchise as occupiers of official residences, and he referred to Exchequer cases Russell and Salmond, Nos. 22 and 23 of Reports, decided 6th March 1877, and maintained that under these decisions the premises fell to be valued for assessment *in cumulo*, and that the Bank are properly charged as the occupiers.

The Commissioners were of opinion that the accountant's occupancy is the Bank's occupancy, and in respect of the decisions in the cases referred to by the surveyor they confirmed the charge.

The Appellants being dissatisfied with the decision, craved a case for the opinion of the Judges, which is accordingly stated,

It was agreed that in the event of the Judges holding that the Appellants are not liable in inhabited house duty in respect of the whole tenement, the annual value of the Bank office shall be fixed at 45*l.*, and of the dwelling-house at 35*l.*

A. SMOLLETT.
JOHN M'AUSLAND.

2nd February 1878.

Lord President.—The enactment on which the pursuer founds here is the third rule of Schedule B. appended to the statute 48 George III., chapter 55, which enacts that all shops and warehouses which are attached to the dwelling-house, or have any connexion therewith, shall in charging the said duties be valued together with the house.

Now if it has been intended by the Appellant here to maintain that the business premises which we have to deal with are not within the meaning of the statute, that would have been required to be raised in the Court below, and brought up for review in the ordinary way. But it has not been so raised, and it is not now proposed to amend the case so as to embrace that question. The only point to decide is whether the Bank are liable to be assessed for the Bank premises and dwelling-house above as one tenement of which they are the proper occupiers in the statutory sense. The Bank's agent or accountant, who manages the affairs of the Bank in the business premises, lives in the dwelling-house which is situated partly above those business premises and partly at the back of them.

But upon two grounds the Bank maintain that they are not liable; in the first place on the ground that they are not occupants, and in the second place on the ground that the premises cannot be valued together, because there is no communication between one set of premises and the other—no internal communication of any kind and no external communication of any kind over the ground belonging to the same party.

Now as to the first of these questions—as to their being the occupants—I do not think any separate argument has been maintained on that; and I rather think if the second point was decided against the Bank, the first follows almost of necessity. The question is, what is meant by the statute by the words "attached to the dwelling-house or anything in communication therewith"? Does it mean that the business premises must be attached to the dwelling-house in such a way as to have communication therewith? or, does it mean on the other hand that if the two are attached then they are to be liable whether there is any internal communication at all? In short, are we to read these words as disjunctive, and hold that there will be liability for common assessment if the business premises and the dwelling-house are either attached to one another or have communication with one another? I am of opinion that the latter is obviously the sound construction of the statute. I think it is intended

that this rule should apply wherever the business premises and
the dwelling-house are attached to one another, although there
may not be internal communication. And I think it is also quite
possible under this section that business premises and a dwelling-
house may be liable to be assessed in the manner there provided
if they have a communication with one another, although they
may not be immediately attached to one another; in short, that
there are two separate things intended to be provided in that
statute. If that be so, then it is plain that these two subjects,
the business premises and the dwelling-house, are to be charged
as one set of premises and one occupation; and that they are
to be charged as one occupation and one set of premises it seems
to me quite obvious when the Bank are the occupiers, and not
merely their servant, but the person who carries on their
business for them. That is quite in consistency with all the
previous decisions on these statutes as regards the meaning of
the words which I have been commenting upon in the third
rule. I think the construction is extremely well stated by Lord
Curriehill, who was Ordinary in both of the cases referred to—
the cases of Russell and Salmond.

I am, therefore, for affirming the deliverance of the Commissioners.

Lord Deas.—It is contended for the Bank in the first place
that there is no liability because there is no internal communication. If your Lordship is right, and if I am right in
thinking that these places are not in communication internally,
there is an end of that part of the case, and the question comes
to be whether they are attached the one to the other. Now I
have no doubt that this dwelling-house and this office are
attached to each other. They are so physically, and then they
are attached moreover by that very important bolt, which is
important upon both branches of the argument. I cannot
imagine any kind of attachment more important than that
between the safe of the Bank in which they kept their money,
and the residence of the Bank's accountant. And then, upon the
other branch of it, it is of importance likewise, because it goes
very deep into the question whether there is separate and
independent occupancy of the house above and of the Bank. It
is out of the question to suppose that this gentleman can sublet
his house and still retain his connexion with the Bank. I think
the Bank would certainly have something to say to that. He is
put there for the safety of the Bank, and for the safety of the
Bank's safe, the most important purpose he is there for, and
therefore that goes to this question whether he is the servant of
the Bank, because it is said he pays rent as a separate and
independent tenant. In every point of view, therefore, I am of
opinion that those two places, the house and the office, are
occupied together in the sense of the statute. The occupancy
must cease the moment he ceased to be the servant of the Bank.

Lord Mure.—I am of the same opinion. According to my
recollection it was substantially decided by some of the older

decisions on the same point, and I find it was so in 1870, when various banks in various parts of the country tried every possible means to bring themselves under the exemption. In the case of the British Linen Company's Bank in Glasgow there was a communication from the tellers room to the lower part of the house where the porter lived, so there was internal communication. But here I agree with your Lordship in the chair that it is not necessary there should be internal communication if substantially it belonged to and was occupied by the Bank as it is here occupied by their accountant, and if the premises are all attached to each other in the sense of being one building, it would be a strange thing to say that if a man went out into the street and walked in at the back door he should be exempt, but if he walked down a passage internally the house should be liable to taxes. It is not sound in principle. I therefore agree with your Lordship in the chair.

Lord Shand.—I am of the same opinion.

Lord President.—We affirm the determination of the Commissioners.

NO. 30.—IN THE HIGH COURT OF JUSTICE.—ENGLAND.—EXCHEQUER DIVISION.

6th December 1877.

JAMES BENT   -   -   -   -   - Appellant

and

WILLIAM HENRY ROBERTS, Surveyor of Taxes - Respondent.

Inhabited House Duty, and Income Tax, Schedule A.—A police constable, compelled by the police authorities to live in a house having a communication with a police station by a doorway between the two yards, the residence there of the constable being necessary for police purposes, and the constable being liable to removal to another station at any time, not an occupier within the meaning of the Acts.

AT a meeting of Commissioners of Income Tax and Inhabited House Duty acting in and for the Division of Manchester, held at the Office of the said Commissioners on the 2nd Day of December 1875, for the purpose of hearing (amongst other things) the following appeal against an assessment under Schedule A. of the Income Tax and for Inhabited House Duty on the House occupied by James Bent of Old Trafford, in the township of Stretford, in the district of

Manchester, second superintendent of the police station there, which is assessed as follows :—

No. of Assesst.

36.　　　Superintendent Bent, House, Schedule A., £50
　　　　　　　　　　　　　　 ,,　　　　House Duty, £50

1. The county constabulary of the county of Lancashire was established under the statute of the 2nd and 3rd Victoria, chapter 93.

2. The county is divided into police districts or divisions, and station-houses and strong-rooms have been built and provided under the statute of the 3rd and 4th Victoria, chapter 88.

3. The force is annually inspected by a Government officer, and if his report is satisfactory a grant is made by the Treasury amounting to one half of the expenses of the pay and clothing of the force in aid of the police rates.

4. The house in which the Appellant resides is included within the boundary of certain premises known as the Old Trafford Police Station, which comprised other buildings and offices provided for the purposes of the Manchester police district.

5. In addition to the communication between the Appellant's house and the drill yard there is a further communication between the drill yard and the cell yard which adjoins, and into which the cells open.

6. It is necessary ·for the police purposes of the district of Manchester that the Appellant should reside in the house in question for the due performance of his official duties.

7. The Appellant is compelled to live on the premises in question, and the house in which he resides is liable to be used for such purposes connected with the police force as the chief constable of the county may direct, and the Appellant is further liable to be removed from station to station at any time.

8. There is no accommodation in the Appellant's residence beyond what is actually necessary for the requirements of himself and his family, and the transaction of his business as superintendent of police, and he would not be permitted to make use of the premises for any other purpose.

9. The Appellant is not assessed to the poor rate.

10. The Appellant admitted that the house which he occupied was separate from the police station, but added that there was a communication with the station yard by a doorway in his own yard wall. The front entrance was quite distinct. He said that he himself possessed the keys of the house, and that he and his family alone has access thereto ; that is was wholly occupied by himself and family, and furnished throughout with his own furniture ; that it might occasionally be used as a place of detention for prisoners, and that on one occasion he had admitted a female prisoner there for a few hours who was not

in very good health, and who was of a more respectable class
than prisoners ordinarily are.

11. He contended that he was not liable to house duty nor to
Schedule A. of the Income Tax beyond the amount of the rental,
10l. 8s. per annum, and the reasons assigned were that the
house was a part of the police station, it being included within
the boundary wall known as the Old Trafford Police Station,
which, in addition to the house occupied by the Appellant, comprises other buildings and offices provided for the police purposes
of the Manchester police division, that the force was annually
inspected by a Government officer, and that the whole of the
premises was used for the purposes of the county constabulary,
and being so used was used for Government purposes, and was
exempt from assessment as being occupied for the purposes of
the Crown, and that in any case the house in question ought not
to be separately assessed, but should be included in one charge
with the police station, some of the apartments of which were
occupied by police constables who paid rentals for them.

In support of his opinion he cited Regina v. St. Martin's,
Leicester, Queen's Bench, July 1867, Law Reports, volume 2,
page 493.

12. The Appellant admitted that he was the officer of the
county, and was paid out of the county fund.

13. The Surveyor submitted that the case referred to did not
apply, and that as the house in question was admittedly separate
and distinct from the police station, its front entrance facing the
street or road (formerly an ancient footpath), and the only communication with the station yard being by a doorway in the
wall of its yard, which doorway could easily be closed up, and
its being moreover furnished throughout by Mr. Bent as a
private residence, it was to all intents and purposes a private
house, and was separately assessable upon its full annual value,
for which Mr. Bent was liable, he being the beneficial occupier.

Judge's Case No. 2,827 was referred to in support of this
view.

14. The accompanying sketch or plan of the whole premises
clearly shows the respective position of Mr. Bent's house and the
police station.

15. After considering the statement of the Appellant and the
surveyor, the Commissioners were of opinion that the superintendent was the servant of the county and not of the Crown,
and that the house being separate and distinct from the police
station, the only communication being by a door in the yard
wall to the drill ground, and being furnished by the superintendent at his own expense, was liable to be assessed upon its
full annual value, and from its position was separately
chargeable.

Confirmed the assessment.

16. The Appellant being dissatisfied with this decision gave
due notice that he required a case to be stated for the opinion

of the Court of Exchequer, which we, the Commissioners who heard the appeal, hereby state and sign accordingly.

JAMES WORRALL.
J. W. WESTON.

6th December 1877.

Gorst, Q.C., for the Appellant.—It is necessary for police purposes that the Appellant should reside in the house in question. He is compelled to live there, and the house is liable to be used for such purposes as the chief constable of the county may direct; and the Appellant is liable to be removed from one station to another at any time. He is not assessed to the poor rate. He is not the occupier, and his position does not amount to what is technically called occupation, because he is compelled to live on the premises for the performance of his police duties. A man might be compelled to live upon premises for the performance of his duties, and yet possibly in the sense of the Inhabited House Duty Act be an occupier, but the seventh paragraph of the case goes further than that. This house is liable to be used for any purposes connected with the police which the chief constable may appoint. This is quite inconsistent with the idea of the Appellant being the occupier, because if anything is essential to the occupation of a house, it is that there shall be some kind of exclusive use. The Appellant might be made to turn his whole family out of their rooms in order to make room for the reception of prisoners, and from the 10th paragraph of the case it may be taken that it did actually happen on one occasion that a female prisoner was received and confined in this so-called dwelling-house. Moreover, he is liable to be removed at any time, and such an occupation would hardly be considered an occupation within the meaning of the Inhabited House Duty Act. In the Franchise case of *James William Clark v. The Overseers of the Parish of St. Mary, Bury St. Edmunds,* (a) Mr. Justice Cresswell said, " I apprehend the true " question to be whether the claimant occupied the premises as " tenant or as servant. It may be that he occupies it as tenant, " and that he is required to occupy, but it may also be that he " occupies as servant, and that he is required to occupy because " he is a servant. . . . . The case finds that it is necessary for " the discharge of his duties as hall-keeper that he should reside " in the house in question which was built for the residence of " the hall-keeper. . . . . I think, therefore, that we are justi-" fied in holding that the claimant occupied these premises as " servant and not as tenant."

Dicey, for the Respondent.—The case distinctly states that the Appellant is in the occupation of the house (*reads* paragraph 10). The case states as plainly as a case can state that he was in occupation, and a man who is in occupation is the

(a) 1 C. B. R. (N.S.) 23.

occupier. Occupation does not in all cases imply exclusive occupation, but it implies just such facts as are alleged here. The word occupier is not defined by the House Duty Act, and therefore we must take it in the ordinary current sense. The Parliamentary franchise is a different question. I now turn to the Income Tax Acts. Number IX., 5 & 6 Victoria, chapter 35, provides that the duty shall be charged on the occupier, and the person having "the use" not "the property" is to be considered the occupier, and whatever may be said under the House Duty Act, surely it is the fact that the Appellant has the use of this house; the Act does not say "exclusive use," but only "use."

JUDGMENT.

Lord Chief Baron.—The question in this case is whether the Appellant is the occupier of the premises in question within the meaning of the Inhabited House Duty Act, or within the meaning of the Income Tax Act, and it appears according to the statement of the case before us that the Appellant has been assessed in respect of both statutes, the Inhabited House Duty Act and the Income Tax Act, in respect of the year's occupation from the month of April 1875 to the month of April or to the end of the month of March 1876; and that the sums payable to the Crown in respect of which this assessment has taken place, if they could be sustained, would be payable on the 1st of January, or at all events in the month of January 1876; and the question which we have to determine is whether the occupation and the use of the premises by the Appellant in the manner and under the circumstances stated in this case render him liable to either the one or the other of these assessments. I am clearly of opinion that he is not liable to either the one or the other, either under the Inhabited House Duty Act or under the Income Tax Act. If the case were confined to what is stated in paragraph 10 of the Case, a question might well arise as to whether he might or might not be liable; for there it appears that "the "Appellant admitted that the house which he occupied was "separate from the police station, but added that there was a "communication with the station yard by a doorway in his own "yard wall. The front entrance was quite distinct. He said "that he himself possessed the keys of the house, and that he "and his family alone had access thereto; that it was wholly "occupied by himself and family, and furnished throughout with "his own furniture; that it might occasionally be used as a place "of detention for prisoners, and that on one occasion he had "admitted a female prisoner there for a few hours who was not "in very good health and who was of a more respectable class "than prisoners ordinarily are." Now if it had stopped there and had contained nothing · else to assist us in determining whether this was an occupation within either of these Acts of Parliament, the question might well have been arguable, but when we refer to another paragraph we find that the Appellant, who it appears is an officer of the constabulary of Lancashire, is by the duties of his office, and under the circumstances in which he holds that office, and is paid the salary for them, compelled to live on the premises in question, and that the house in which he resides is liable to be used for such purposes connected with the police force as the chief constable of the county may direct, and the Appellant is further liable to be removed from station to station at any time.

Now any one of these portions of this paragraph would, in my opinion, be perfectly fatal to the argument on the part of the Crown, that the Appellant has such an occupation of these premises as to render him liable to either of these assessments; and the first is, that he is compelled to live on the premises. A man who pays rents for premises has the right to live upon the premises under a contract between himself and the landlord to whom he is liable for the rent, who is entitled to distrain for the rent, and to whom, under the contract between them, he is bound to pay the rent, and is in return entitled to the occupation of the premises. No such case exists here. This, though it is called a rent in the statement of the case before us, is clearly no rent at all; it is stated that the Appellant is an officer of the constabulary under the authorities of the constabulary in the county of Lancaster, and that he is compelled to live upon these premises, but while he enjoys a lodging which probably saves him the rent of some lodging elsewhere, it amounts to nothing more than this, that the authorities by whom he is employed think fit to deduct from the salary that they pay him, a certain sum, namely, 8l. 10s. a year, in consequence of the benefit that he derives from lodging in this house with his family during whatever time they may compel him to remain there. That is not a rent at all; it is not a tenancy at all; it is not an occupation at all in respect of the Acts which regulate and determine either of these assessments; and, therefore, were it upon that ground alone, I should hold that it is not an occupation within the meaning of either of these Acts of Parliament. But it goes on with this, "that the "house in which he resides is liable to be used for such purposes "connected with the police force as the chief constable of the "county may direct." Under this power in the chief constable he might either upon a particular occasion, or on any number of occasions where the proper conducting of the business of the police officers might require it, send any number of persons who might be taken into custody, and who were to remain in custody until the following morning before they would be taken before the magistrate, into his house, and put half a dozen of them into half a dozen of the beds in the different rooms of this house; and they might, if they thought fit in order to do so (and it might be a public duty on their part that they should do so), confine him to a single bed in a room at the top of the house, or they might desire him to lie upon the floor all night in order that these several prisoners would be in safe custody. That alone is inconsistent with the beneficial occupation or use of the house by a tenant who is liable to assessment under these Acts of Parliament, and therefore if it stood alone upon this second clause of the seventh paragraph it also would be fatal to the question of occupation. But then when we come to the last provision in this seventh paragraph we find that the chief constable "may direct, and the Appellant is there- "fore liable to be removed from station to station at any "time." Here is a man assessed for the income tax for the year, and assessed to the Inhabited House Duty for the year who might, if it were thought fit, a week or a month, or even a single day after the assessment, which would render him liable to the Income Tax and to the Inhabited House Duty, be removed to another place altogether, and might not occupy the house for a single day after the notice or the command is issued to him to quit the station and remove himself to another station. It is not arguable whether or not this could be an occupation within the meaning of these Acts of Parliament. I am clearly of opinion, therefore, that he is not an occupier; he is merely a servant of the constabulary, put into the house for their purposes, and has liberty and permission to live in that house just as long as they think fit and no longer—just as long as it answers their purposes and suits their public duties to leave him there, or desire or compel him to remain there and no longer ; and again, just as long as they may think it expedient that he should remain an officer in their establishment, and not be removed to another station, and no longer. Under these circumstances it clearly is not an occupation within these statutes.

Mr. Baron Cleasby.—I must say that I was a good deal surprised at the statement of the learned Counsel for the Crown that the point intended to be raised here was a different one from that which we are now considering. I refer to the case, and I see that this is the only point upon which the case is stated, paragraph 15: "After considering the statement of the " Appellant and the surveyor, the Commissioners were of opinion " that the superintendent was the servant of the county and not " of the Crown, and that the house being separate and distinct " from the police station, the only communication being by a " door in the yard wall to the drill ground, and being furnished " by the superintendent at his own expense, was liable to be " assessed upon its full annual value." They state everything connected with the place to show in what way it is connected with the police station, and, not deciding anything upon the other question, the Commissioners decide that it is to be regarded as if he were living apart from the police station altogether in a street in the town. If it were so, although he is paid by the police authorities or there is an allowance made for it, he might be removable to a different station, which would be quite a different thing. Passing by that altogether, the Commissioners hold that in this case he occupies the premises so separated from the police premises, and furnishing them at his own expense, he is liable to be assessed. Upon that, which is mainly a question of fact, we come to a different conclusion. I will only say with reference to the case referred to, which case was not referred to in the Judge's case, that the question there considered was a totally different one ; what we have to consider is simply this : Is he to be regarded as a person occupying, or living upon these premises in any different manner from this, that he lives there upon part of the police premises and is allowed to live there upon part of the police premises. I apprehend that if the police premises were shut in by an outer door, and this man had the house (there seem to be other uses of the station here) within that outer door, no question whatever could possibly arise ; it would not be in his occupation in any sense of the word according to these Acts of Parliament ; but in a general way as he has the key of the house, you say that he occupies it. No one could contend, if it were all within the wall of the police premises, over which, of course, the police authorities would have the exclusive control, that he was the occupier of the house though he was the only person living in it. How can it be that it makes a difference if for the more convenient enjoyment by their servant of the particular house, to make it more comfortable for him as their servant because it is to their interest to have servants who are satisfied and pleased with the conveniences that they enjoy—I say, how can it make any difference that with all the internal communications requisite for the discharge of his duties they allow him to have an outer door into the footpath or street ? It appears to me not of the slightest importance. The Lord Chief Baron has fully gone into the statements of the case, and I will not repeat them. This is an application by the police authorities, and if this man is to efficiently discharge his duties as their servant he must have a place to live in, of course.

Mr. Baron Pollock.—I also think that there is ample material for a decision in this case contained in the argument alone addressed to us by Mr. Dicey, and which turns upon the meaning of the word "occupier" in Schedule B. of the 48th George III., chapter 55, and the facts stated in the case, upon which we have to draw inferences of fact as well as of law. It is sufficient to say that such a so-called occupation as is shown to exist in this case is not such an occupation as makes the man an occupier within the meaning of the statute, and after what has been said by my Lords I think it quite unnecessary to repeat the reasons given by them.

Lord Chief Baron.—The judgment will be for the Appellant.

Mr. Gorst.—With costs ?

Lord Chief Baron.—With costs.

No. 31.—COURT OF EXCHEQUER.—SCOTLAND.—
14th June 1878.

In re The Rev. GEORGE WALTER STRONG.

---

*Income Tax.— A gift of money, raised by voluntary sub-
scription, and made annually to a minister of religion by his
congregation, is assessable.*

AT a Meeting of the Commissioners for General Purposes for
the Kintyre District of the County of Argyll, under the
Property and Income Tax Acts, held within the Court
House, Campbeltown, on the 25th day of January 1878.

The Reverend George Walter Strong, Minister of the Second
Charge of the Parish of Campbeltown, appealed against an
assessment of 100*l.* for the year 1877-78, made upon him under
Schedule E. of the Income Tax, in respect to a sum paid to him
in the following circumstances, and alleged to be an emolument
of his office.

It was admitted on the behalf of the Appellant that since he
came to Campbeltown, about three years ago, he had received at
each Christmastide a pecuniary gift from his congregation of
100*l.*, as a token of their regard for him, and that at Christmas
last he received this gift, which was raised by voluntary subscription among his friends, the majority being members of the
congregation. The Appellant grants no receipt for this sum, the
contributors are under no obligation whatever to repeat the gift,
and it may never be repeated.

In these circumstances the Appellant contends that this gift
forms no part of his income within the meaning of the Income
Tax Acts. He pays income tax on his stipend, glebe rents, &c.,
being the full amount of the profit derived by him from his
public office or employment as one of the ministers of the parish
of Campbeltown. The gift referred to does not follow the office,
nor does it fall under any of the descriptions given in the Act as
" Salaries, fees, wages, perquisites, or profits whatsoever accruing
by reason of such offices or employments," and he therefore
craved to be relieved from the charge.

In support of the charge, the Surveyor referred to Schedule E.
16th and 17th Victoria, chapter 34, under which duties in respect
of every public office or employment of profit are granted, and
to the rules for charging the said duties contained in section
146 of 5th and 6th Victoria, chapter 35, the first rule of which
provides that the duties shall be annually charged on the persons
having, using, or exercising the offices or employments of profit
mentioned in Schedule E. "for all salaries, fees, wages, perquisites,
" or profits whatsoever accruing by reason of such offices or em-
"ployments," and by rule 3 it is provided that the duties shall
be paid in respect of *inter alia* " any office or employment of
profit held under any ecclesiastical body."

It was contended by the Surveyor that the Appellant being a minister of the Church of Scotland as by law established, his benefice was clearly within the description of "an office or employment of profit held under any ecclesiastical body" and so chargeable under Schedule E. ; that the sum of 100*l.* received annually by the Appellant in the circumstances herein set forth, though voluntarily paid, accrued to him by reason of his holding such office under the said ecclesiastical body, and was a pecuniary profit or perquisite liable to duty.

It was further maintained by the Surveyor that even although the sum in question should not be deemed a profit chargeable under Schedule E., the Appellant was nevertheless liable to assessment therefore as "annual profits or gains," under the general rule, Schedule D., 5th and 6th Victoria, chapter 35, which, by virtue of section 188 of the said Act, could be applied to the assessment in dispute.

The Commissioners, having considered the appeal, relieved the Appellant, with which decision the Surveyor declared his dissatisfaction and craved a case for the opinion of the Court of Exchequer, which is here stated accordingly.

> (Signed)   A. FORBES MACKAY, Commissioner.
>   „   DAVID McGIBBON, Commissioner.

INTERLOCUTOR and NOTE of the LORD ORDINARY in EXCHEQUER CAUSES in CASE for the SURVEYOR of TAXES on Appeal of Reverend G. W. STRONG as to INCOME TAX.

Edinburgh, 14th June 1878.

The Lord Ordinary in Exchequer having heard the Counsel for the Surveyor of Taxes, no appearance being made for the Appellant the Reverend Mr. Strong, finds that the determination of the Commissioners is wrong.

> (Signed)   JOHN MARSHALL.

NOTE.—Although this case has been heard *ex parte*, the Appellant not having appeared, I have not disposed of it as in absence, but only after carefully considering the argument for the Appellant stated in the case. It is with some reluctance that I have formed the opinion that the Commissioners are wrong, and that the Appellant is liable for Income Tax on the 100*l.* mentioned in the case. It is true that it is a voluntary contribution by the parishioners, one which they are under no obligation to make, and which they may withdraw at any time. But still it is a payment made to the Appellant as their clergyman, and is received by the Appellant in respect of the discharge of his duties of that office, which is one of public employment in the sense of the statutes. This being so, it follows that the payment must be regarded as erther "emolument" under Schedule E., or "gain" under Schedule D. of the Statutes 5th and 6th Victoria, chapter 35, and 16th and 17th Victoria, chapter 34, and that it is chargeable with duty.

> (Initialed)   J. M.

PART XIV.

No. 32.—In the Court of Appeal, Lincoln's Inn.

In re Henley & Co.

Income Tax, Schedule A.—Crown entitled to Priority over general Creditors of an Estate in Liquidation.

JUDGMENT, 29th July, 1878.

Lord Justice James.—It appears to me quite clear upon every principle of law in this country that the Crown is not bound by the Winding-up Acts, and that in respect of any Crown debt the Crown is not debarred from taking any proceedings whatever against the property of its debtor, and under this particular statute which has been cited * it has a right to distrain upon any chattels that were seized upon. Independently of that, a debt due for property and income tax is an absolute debt due from the person in possession of the property. Now the person in possession of the property in this case is the Company, although there is a liquidation; the Company is the tenant, and liable like any other tenant to pay the income tax. There was nothing to prevent the Crown from suing the Company for that income tax, and there was nothing to prevent the Crown from distraining upon any chattels which it could put its hands upon, because the Crown's right to distrain, I believe, is universal.

There being this right upon the part of the Crown, the Crown says, "Well, we do not want to go and tear this thing " to pieces. We have a right to be paid, but we are willing " to treat the thing as a matter of administration." I think it was a very proper thing of the Crown not to take proceedings which would result in useless expense. It appearing that there being a debt due to the Crown in respect of which the property of the Company might be seized or taken; the property being now subject to the supervision, and therefore under the administration of the Court, it was a right and proper thing for the receiver and for the Court to say to the parties, "This is a debt " due from you, and therefore you ought to pay it." Therefore, if it is treated as a question of priority in the administration of the assets, it seems to me that the cases referred to were conclusive upon that point, that wherever the Crown's right and the subject's right come into competition with one another, then the Crown's right is paramount, that is to say, in the particular case of debts, and it is laid down by very high authority that in the adminis-

---

tration of assets a debt due to the Crown takes priority of a debt of the same kind due to the subject. That principle ought to apply to these cases, and there being that priority to the Crown in respect of debts of the same character as debts due to the subject, the debt ought to have been ordered by the liquidator to be paid to the Crown.

Lord. Justice Brett.—It seems to me that there are two prerogatives in favour of the Crown; one is that the Crown is not bound by any statute unless it is named in it, and therefore, that being so, the Crown not being named in the Winding-up Acts, they do not apply to it. The other prerogative is that the Crown has in this case a debt in respect of which it can issue distress. That being so, the Crown might ask for an order, as if it had issued a distress. But supposing the Crown had had no right of distress, and this had been simply a contract debt, then in the administration that simple contract debt would have been in competition at the same time with the simple contract debts of other creditors, and then the other prerogative of the Crown would have taken effect, and the Crown would have had a right to be paid first, and if the Crown had a right to be paid first, it was right to ask for this order; in either view the Crown, in my opinion, is right in this case.

Lord Justice Cotton.—I am also of opinion that the decision of the Vice-Chancellor cannot be supported. It is a general rule that the Crown cannot be bound by a statute unless it is named in it. There are cases in which it must be held that the statute applies to the Crown; but in this case the Crown in respect of the taxes has a right of distress, and the question is whether or no that right is taken away by the Winding-up Acts. Now I am of opinion that there is no ground for supposing that these Acts do apply to the Crown. It has been laid down since the passing of the Winding-up Acts, and of the Acts of Insolvency, that the Winding-up Acts do not apply to the Crown. At the same time in my opinion this Act is binding upon all subjects, and takes away the rights and remedies that they had, and directs that as between them the property shall be divided *pari passu*. But then the Crown has in my opinion this right of distress, and can exercise it,—that is not taken away. Although the Crown has come here asking that this debt may be paid, yet that simply means this, " I do not wish to go in and exercise my " right of distraining ;" and the Court, seeing that there is no ground for saying that there is a defence to that distress, directs the liquidator to pay the Crown rather than cause the Crown to exercise such remedies as it has. But if we regard it as though the Crown has come in and taken the benefit of the Winding-up Acts as administering the assets of the Company—has come in therefore, as in the course of administration—in that case I think the rule prevails that in respect of debts due to the Crown where there are competing debts due to the subject the Crown is entitled to priority.

PART XV.

Court of Exchequer (Scotland).—First Division.
March 7th, 1879.

In re The Glasgow Coal Exchange Company, Limited.

Inhabited House Duty.—Hall and adjoining rooms erected by a Company for the purpose of profit or gain, and used principally as a Coal Exchange, members of the Exchange paying an annual subscription and being supplied with newspapers, the Hall being also let occasionally for balls, &c., within section 13 (2) of the Customs and Inland Revenue Act, 1878.

At a meeting of the Commissioners for General Purposes, acting under the Property and Income Tax and Inhabited House Duty Acts for the Lower Ward of the County of Lanark, held at Glasgow the 14th day of November 1878, for the purpose of hearing and disposing of appeals under the said Acts for the year ending 5th April 1879,—

The Glasgow Coal Exchange Company, Limited, 11, West Regent Street, Glasgow, appealed against an assessment of 1,660*l.* made upon them for inhabited house duty, at the rate of 9*d.* per pound for the year 1878–79.

Mr. William Burns Shand, writer, Glasgow, for the Appellants, claimed that they were entitled to exemption from assessment for house duty on their hall and side rooms, including hall-keeper's house, in terms of section 13 of the "The Customs and "Inland Revenue Act, 1878," and sub-section 2, and in support of this view he contended that the purposes for which the premises are occupied are such as fall within the limit of the exemption, in respect that the Glasgow Coal Exchange Company, Limited, is a proprietary limited company, formed for the purpose of profit or gain, and that the halls and adjoining rooms are occupied principally as an Exchange and pertinents thereto, in which coalmasters, coal merchants, coal brokers, and others meet, the membership subscription being one guinea and 10*s.* 6*d.* respectively: Farther, the said buildings are let for temporary purposes, such as balls, soirées, church bazaars, and entertainments of various kinds, but have never been occupied for such purposes for more than an evening at a time except in one instance, when a church bazaar occupied the halls and ante-room

A

for three days, and for such temporary lets money is paid to the company. They are further occupied daily by subscribers, who are supplied with newspapers and other periodicals, which is covered by the said annual subscription.

The surveyor of taxes for Glasgow second district, Mr. John Allan, contended that the assessment was correctly made, in respect that the subjects assessed, so far as in the occupancy of the Appellants, were not "occupied solely for the purposes of "any trade or business or of any profession or calling, by which "the occupier seeks a livelihood or profit." That, although the premises are let by the company with a view to profit, the exemption regards only the purposes for which they are occupied by the various persons to whom they are let, and that, as they are not in all cases occupied for purposes by which the temporary occupiers seek a livelihood or profit, they do not fall within the terms of the section under which exemption is claimed. In farther support of the assessment the surveyor quoted the Act 48 Geo. III. cap. 55. Schedule B., rule 5, by which it is provided that "Every hall or office whatever belonging to any person or "persons, or to any body or bodies, politic or corporate, or to "any company that are or may be lawfully charged with the "payment of any other taxes or parish rates, shall be subject to "the duties hereby made payable as inhabited houses, and the "person or persons, bodies politic or corporate, or company, to "whom the same shall belong, shall be charged as the occupier "or occupiers thereof."

The Commissioners, by a majority of two to one, confirmed the assessment, they being satisfied that the premises are so occupied as not to come within the exemption claimed.

Mr. Shand, for the Appellants, immediately upon the determination of the Commissioners being given, declared on behalf of the said Company his dissatisfaction therewith, as being erroneous in point of law, and now having duly intimated in writing his desire that a case be stated and signed for the opinion and decision of the Court of Exchequer, in terms of and under the provisions of the "Customs and Inland Revenue Act, 1874," such case is now stated accordingly.

A. CRUM MACLAE,
ROBT. WALKER, } Comrs.

Glasgow, 23rd January 1879.

Glasgow, 4th March 1879.—In terms of interlocutor by the Lords, dated 28th February 1879, the undersigned Commissioners for General Purposes, acting under the Property and Income Tax and Inhabited House Duty Acts for the Lower Ward of the county of Lanark, respectfully state an amendment to the foregoing case as follows :—(*First.*) That the assessment is made in respect of the Appellants' hall and side rooms, including hall-keeper's house, and that the admitted facts are, that the

Glasgow Coal Exchange Company, Limited, is a proprietory *In re* GLASGO' COAL limited company formed for the purpose of profit or gain, and EXCHANGE the halls and adjoining rooms on which they are assessed are COMPANY. occupied principally as an exchange and pertinents thereto, in which coalmasters, coal merchants, and coal brokers and others meet, the membership subscription being one guinea and 10s. 6d. respectively. Further, the said buildings are let for temporary purposes, such as balls, soirées, church bazaars, and entertainments of various kinds, but have never been occupied for such purposes for more than an evening at a time, except in the instance when a church bazaar occupied the halls and ante-room for three days, and for such temporary lets money is paid to the Company; they are further occupied daily by subscribers, who are supplied with newspapers and other periodicals, which is covered by the said annual subscriptions.

(*Second.*) The question of law for the opinion of the Court is, whether the facts set out in the foregoing statement are such as (having in view rule 5 of Schedule B. to the Act 48 Geo. III. cap. 55.) would bring the premises assessed within the terms of the exemption contained in section 13 and sub-section 2 of " The Customs and Inland Revenue Act, 1878."

A. CRUM MACLAE.
ROBERT WALKER.

Counsel having been heard.

Lord President.—The question raised in this case is whether March 18, 187: the Appellants fall within the exemption from the duty on inhabited houses and arises under the Customs and Inland Revenue Act, 1874, 37 & 38 Vict. c. 16. Part III. The inhabited house duty was in its institution originally very extensive, and may be described generally as being an assessment upon all occupied houses. That was in fact the meaning of the word " inhabited house " at the time of the original enactment on this subject. Subsequent Acts of Parliament narrowed the extent of that very much, and the question comes to be whether this Coal Exchange Company, who appeal against the deliverance of the Commissioners, fall within the list of those exemptions. The first exemption that was made from the tax was introduced by the 57 Geo. III., which exempted buildings occupied entirely for the purposes of trade. Trade was stated to mean the trade of merchants. It was held that the exemption was confined substantially to warehouses for the storing of goods belonging to wholesale merchants in the premises occupied by them in carrying on their business, and specially occupied by retail traders. A little later the Legislature thought fit to extend the exemption still further—by the 5 Geo. IV.—to premises which were occupied (as it was generally described) for business purposes, that is to say, for the purpose of carrying on

In re GLASGOW
COAL
EXCHANGE
COMPANY.

any profession, business, or calling. Taking these two statutes together, I think the fair result may be said to be that premises which were occupied exclusively for business premises, whether for the purposes of trade or for the carrying on of any profession or calling, were exempted from the tax.

But then there remained this peculiarity, that if anyone lived in the premises in which either trade or business was carried on that destroyed the exemption and brought the premises within the category of inhabited houses. To remedy that so far the Act of 32 and 33 Victoria provided that the presence of a person living in the house for the purpose of merely taking care of the premises should not prevent the exemption applying in the case of premises occupied for trading purposes. But that left the law in a very peculiar position, because premises occupied for trading purposes might have somebody there for taking care, and still be exempt, while premises occupied either for professional or business purposes would not be exempt if anybody dwelt in them even for the simple purpose of taking care of them. Now, it was to remedy this defect that the enactment of last year was passed; and I think the object is very plain on the face of it. It is to put premises, occupied for the carrying on of any profession, calling, or business in the same position as trading premises are placed by the 32nd and 33rd Victoria; and so the legislation, as far as this matter of exemption is concerned, is now complete. And it may be generally stated as resulting in this, that premises which are not dwelling-houses, but are occupied entirely for business purposes, whether trading purposes or professional purposes, or for the carrying on of any other business, shall be exempt, even although there be a caretaker dwelling upon the premises.

Now, the question comes to be, whether this Coal Exchange Company (Limited) is, in respect of the occupation of its premises, in the position contemplated by the law as it now stands. I am of opinion that it is. I think that upon the statement of facts before us, beyond which we cannot go, this Coal Exchange Company is carrying on a business in the rooms set forth as their premises, and a business of a perfectly intelligible kind; it is carrying on the business of a Coal Exchange. That is the primary purpose to which its premises are devoted. It furnishes accommodation to persons in the coal trade to meet together in its premises, and buy and sell, or to deal with one another in any other way they may think fit; and it provides them with accommodation of various kinds to make them comfortable in carrying on their business with one another. It was suggested in the argument for the Inland Revenue that the people who resort there, and who may be called members of this exchange, are in reality the partners of this Coal Exchange Company (Limited). If that were so it might introduce a totally different element into the case, but nothing of the kind has been stated by the Commissioners. And I take the facts as they are stated by the Commissioners to mean this. that the Coal Exchange Company (Limited) and its partners are entirely distinct and separate from the persons who resort there for the purpose of taking the benefit of the coal exchange. It may very well be, and I am quite willing to assume that it is so, that some of these members may be shareholders in this company. That wont make the least difference in the state of the case, but that the two are identical is not the fact before us at all and cannot be taken for granted.

Now, as I said before, this is quite an intelligible business for the company to carry on, and I do not think it matters in the least degree, this being a primary use they make of their buildings, that they also let them to be used for other and temporary purposes, that is to say, for a night. or two days, or something of that kind. Nothing is more common than for persons to have large premises, which they use for one purpose as their primary purpose, but yet let them out occasionally for other purposes. Take, for example, the ordinary case of a hotel-keeper who has large rooms in his hotel. His business is that of a hotel-keeper, but it is not the least degree inconsistent with his carrying on that business that he should also let his larger rooms for public meetings, and any similar purpose. And just so here. The Coal Exchange Company use these premises primarily as a coal exchange ; but at other times—at times of the day when they are not wanted for the coal exchange, or at times of the week or times of the year when they are not wanted for that purpose—they are let for balls, bazaars, and other temporary purposes of that description. Now, I do not think that interferes in the least degree with the central fact of this case, that the company are carrying on these premises for profit or gain, the business of a coal exchange, and they appear to me to fall clearly within the statutes as they now stand.

I am therefore for reversing the determination of the Commissioners.

Lord Deas.—I have arrived at the same opinion. It rather appears to me that this Exchange Company are either carrying on one calling in these premises, or they are carrying on two callings. If they are carrying on the business or calling of a Coal Exchange Company, then they are plainly exempted ; but if they are carrying on the calling or business of letting these premises for balls and amusements, I think they are equally carrying on a business. If they are exempted on each of these grounds, they must be exempted on both of them.

Lord Mure.—I have come to the same conclusion. The object of this clause of the statute was just to extend the exemption a little further than it had been extended in the case of the insurance company and others referred to by Mr. Balfour and reported in 6 Rettie. The words here are larger and more general, and I have no difficulty in coming to the conclusion, upon the facts stated, that this company are exercising the calling

or business of letting their premises for certain specific purposes.
Those premises they do not live in, though there is apparently a
person in them who looks after them at night and takes charge of
them ; but his position brings them within the express qualification that they shall be exempted if they are used for profit, although a servant or other person may dwell in such a house for its
protection. Now the party who dwells there is evidently there
merely for the purpose of taking charge of it, and therefore the
fact that he takes charge of it does not bring it within the
category of inhabited houses.

Lord Shand.—I have come to be of the same opinion. I
think, in order to the sound construction of the statute, one must
ascertain at the outset who are the occupiers of these buildings ;
and I think, within the meaning of the statute, the occupiers of
the buildings are plainly the Coal Exchange Company. They
occupy the greater part of the building by using it as a Coal
Exchange, where, as I understand, they provide their own
servant to take charge of it ; and they allow coal merchants,
coal brokers, coal masters, and others the privilege of resorting
to those premises, with the use of newspapers and periodicals,
and general use of the building as an exchange upon a return in
the shape of an annual subscription varying from a guinea to
10s. 6d. The persons who come in that temporary way now and
then cannot be represented as occupiers of the building in any
sense. The Coal Exchange Company are occupiers for the purposes of a Coal Exchange. Then with regard to the other uses
made of the building the Coal Exchange Company are also the
occupiers. Although they may give over the use of some of the
rooms, as has been explained, for an evening at a time, or a
day or two at a time, when the halls are occupied by a church
bazaar or the like, still those persons are there merely temporarily, not in any proper sense as occupiers of the building ;
and that being so the provision of the statute is this, that every
house or tenement which is occupied solely for the purpose of
any trade or business, or of any profession or calling, by which
the occupier seeks a livelihood or profit, shall be exempted. The
occupiers here being the Coal Exchange Company, they are
occupying those premises solely, so far as they are concerned,
for the purpose of earning profit, either in so far as the premises
are occupied as a coal exchange or in so far as there are other
temporary lets. I observe that the surveyor, in the argument
which has been submitted, and which seems to have weighed
with the Commissioners, puts the case thus ; that although the
premises are let by the company with a view to profit, the exemption regarded only the purposes for which they are occupied
by the various persons to whom they are let, and that, as they
are not in all cases occupied for purposes by which the temporary
occupier seeks a livelihood or profit they do not fall within the
terms of the section. But I do not think that what the statute
has regard to here is such use as may be made of the premises

by what the surveyor calls temporary occupiers. If that were so there would be considerable room for the argument maintained by the Crown; and if the words used in the statute had been "every house or tenement which is used solely for the purposes of any trade or business," it would have been different. But I think the statute has no regard to temporary occupiers having the use of premises in this way; it may be for two or three days or two or three evenings at a time. It regards rather the occupation of the trade or business of the person who is really the occupier, in this case the Coal Exchange Company, and as they occupy solely for the purpose of profit in making as large a return from their building as they can, I think they are within the terms of this clause of exemption.

Lord President.—Reverse the determination of the Commissioners and remit to them to disallow the assessment. Find the Appellants entitled to expenses.

No. 34.—In the High Court of Justice (England).— RILEY *v.* READ.
Exchequer Division.

March 4th, 1879.

John Riley   ...   .   Appellant
and
R. Read, Surveyor of Taxes...   ...   Respondent.

Inhabited House Duty.—A building occupied by a Working Men's Club, which occupied the ground floor for the ordinary purposes of a Club, and let the upper floor to an Auctioneer for an Office, no person sleeping on the premises, is not an Inhabited Dwelling-house, and is, therefore, not within the charge to Inhabited House Duty.

County of Lancaster.—Hundred of Blackburn.

AT a meeting of the Commissioners for the General Purposes of the Income Tax and for executing the Acts relating to the Inhabited House Duties held at the Office of the Clerk to the Commissioners, Shorrock Fold, Blackburn, on the 18th of July 1887,—

1. Mr. J. Riley appealed on behalf of the Working Men's Reform Club, William Street, in the township of Over Darwen, against an assessment to inhabited house duty for the year ending 5th April, 1877 at 9d. in the pound upon 40l. the annual value of the building occupied by the club.

RILEY v. READ.   2. Mr. Riley claimed exemption on the ground that the building was not an inhabited dwelling-house within the meaning of the Act 14 & 15 Vict. cap. 36, inasmuch as the place is not and never has been since its erection furnished as a dwelling-house or slept in at night and is used in the daytime for club and trade purposes only. He stated that the upper floor of the building was let to an auctioneer who used it during the daytime as a place for sale of goods, and, being a place used entirely for trade purposes, was not liable to inhabited house duty.

3. The surveyor of taxes, Mr. R. Read, stated he had seen the premises, and found the building to consist of two storeys. The ground floor was occupied by the Appellants as a Club and contained the usual rooms, namely, billiards, newsroom, lavatory, &c. The upper floor was let to an auctioneer and used by him as a place of trade. The club is open each day from 9 a.m. to 10.30 p.m., and is then closed for the night, no person remaining inside the premises. The surveyor contended that the building came within the scope of 48 Geo. III. cap. 55, Schedule B., No. 5, and that it was not necessary for a building to be slept in to render it liable to inhabited house duty. In support of these views he referred to case 2,760 decided by the Judges on 15th February, 1867, and contended that as the place was not used for trade, but in the manner above stated, it was not within any of the exemptions contained in the Acts.

The Appellant sought to distinguish the present case from the case No. 2,760, inasmuch as the present building had never acquired the character of a dwelling-house by reason of its never having been furnished or slept in as such.

The Commissioners were of opinion that the club was liable, and the Appellant thereupon expressed his dissatisfaction with their decision and demanded a case for the opinion of the Exchequer Division of the High Court of Judicature, and we the Commissioners by whom the appeal was heard hereby state and signed accordingly.

(L.S.)   RICHARD ECCLES,   } Commissioners.
(L.S.)   WM. HY. HORNBY, Jun., }

Blackburn, 20th October 1877.

Bush Cooper for the Appellant. — The point is whether a building which has not been used as a dwelling-house and slept in by the occupier is chargeable to the inhabited house duty. In one sense no doubt this house is inhabited, but nobody dwells in it, not even a caretaker.

Dicey for the Respondent.—The house is dwelt in from 9 in the morning till half past 10 at night. It is not necessary that any one should sleep in a house to make it a dwelling-house. Referred to 48 Geo. 3. c. 55 ; 57 Geo. 3. c. 25 ; 5 Geo. 4. c. 44 ; 6 Geo. 4. c. 7 ; 14 & 15 Vict. c. 36 ; and to *Rusby v. Newson* (a)

(a) L.R. 10 Exch. 322 ; 23 W. R. 632 ; *sub-nomine*, Weavers' Hall, *ante* p. 15

JUDGMENT.

The Lord Chief Baron.—It appears to me that the claim of RILEY *v.* BEA this inhabited house duty by the Crown cannot be sustained. The many Acts of Parliament which, in his able and elaborate argument, the learned Counsel who has just sat down has referred to, either taken separately or taken together, impose the tax upon inhabited dwelling-houses, and the question is whether the building in question is an inhabited dwelling-house within the meaning of the Act of Parliament, although no person sleeps in it. The whole building is either occupied as a club or for trade purposes, or both. Now all the statutes together say that what is taxable to the inhabited house duty is an inhabited dwelling-house within the meaning of the Acts. If the word "inhabited" only existed, we should have to consider whether there might not be an inhabitancy, and I am not prepared to say that there may not be an inhabitancy which would make the building an inhabited house within these Acts of Parliament, as far as the word "inhabited" goes, although no one ever slept in it; but when we find that all the Acts of Parliament, in order to make a building of any kind taxable, say that the building in question must be an inhabited dwelling-house, we must put a construction, not only upon the word "inhabited," but also upon the words "dwelling-house," or a house in which some one dwells. Is that the case here; is any part of it a dwelling-house in which one or more persons may dwell, unless one or more persons sleep within the house? I think it is not. In my judgment the meaning of the words "to dwell" is really to live in a house; that is, to live there day and night; to sleep there during the night, and to occupy it for the purposes of life during the day. Is there anything to show that that is not the natural meaning? We refer to dictionaries. I have referred to Richardson and to Johnson, and to all the dictionaries to which resort may be had for such a purpose, some of them containing quotations from legal and eminent men, men of learning and of good education, and amongst others there is a quotation from scripture, and in no one of these dictionaries do I find the word "dwelling" or "to dwell" used at all except in the way in which it can only be interpreted, namely, as living, actually residing and living in the place in question.

The learned Counsel who has last addressed us has not pointed to anything in any great English writer during the last two or three centuries to show that the term "to dwell" or "dwelling" has by any one of the writers been used in a manner so that it can be interpreted into anything else but as living, in the ordinary sense of the word. Why are we then for the first time to put a different interpretation upon it without being compelled to do so, either by an Act of Parliament or by a decision of a court of law?

There is something which at first sight appears to be very plausible in the recital here of the Act, and the first section of the Act of the 57th of George III., chapter 25; but it means no more than this (putting it even as the learned Counsel has submitted it to us, and urged it upon our attention) that the legislature has in this section used the word "dwelt" or "abided," whichever it may be, in the sense in which he contends for, that it is an authority to us as to its meaning in these Acts of Parliament; but when we look carefully at the language of this recital or preamble, it really only amounts to this, that besides the residence, in respect of which people have been assessed, there may have been separate buildings, in respect of which they have also been assessed, and they may have been charged with the duty and have paid the duty, though no one slept there, and they were not occupied at night; and if you could have before you the cases which have been decided as to which this preamble or recital refers, it would be found that in every case they were assessed in respect of the value or rental of these separate buildings in addition to the rental or value of the house in which they resided and lived. At all events, if it means anything else it is only because the framer of this Act of Parliament incautiously used a word which, as we find it, is bad grammar and not good English or good sense in any way; but, putting the most favourable interpretation upon it, he has misapplied the word, and that will not avail us in a case of taxation so as to impose the tax upon the subject, which has never been imposed under any Act of Parliament, or by any decision by any court that we can find in any report to which we are bound to give credence and treat as of value.

I think that the plain and natural meaning of the words is to dwell and live in a building day and night; to reside there and occupy it as a residence; and as this place has never been so occupied, in my opinion it is not a dwelling-house, and therefore the claim must be disallowed.

Mr. Baron Pollock.—In my judgment the members of the club who occupy for certain purposes this Working Men's Reform Club in William Street, Over Darwen, are not properly assessable to the Inhabited House Duty. If it were necessary to decide in all cases that in order to make a building assessable as an inhabited dwelling-house, some person or persons must sleep in that house, as well as occupy it by day, I should pause before I came to that conclusion, because although I agree with what has fallen from my Lord, and I am far from differing with him with respect to any words that he has used, I still see that the arguments that Mr. Dicey has pointed out to us certainly tend to show that there are some passages in the Statute relating to this matter which tend to support that view. There are also some dicta of the learned judges both here and in Scotland, which also may be said to have some effect, but I for my part think it unnecessary to decide this question here at all, and for this reason that the position of a gentleman or any person who occupies a place by day, either by himself, or by himself and his clerks or agents, in a warehouse or counting-house, and another place by night as his ordinary place of abode, where he resides with his family is entirely distinct from the present case. So again will be the case which is more analogous to the present case, of a gentleman who had a large domain where he lived, and slept in the ancient mansion-house of the domain, and had buildings for pleasure purposes in different parts for lunching at when he was out shooting or for many other purposes such as we have seen in many parts of the country; in all those cases the argument which Mr. Dicey has used would be properly and strictly applicable, but the present case is an entirely different one. It is the case of a great number of persons possibly, and probably some hundreds being members of a club, and using the building, not in any sense for the purpose of a dwelling-house, but merely as a place to which they may resort for the purposes of recreation and enjoyment during certain periods of the day and evening.

Now I am far from saying, and it is no part of my duty here (my duty being *jus dicere*, not *jus dare*) to say that such a place ought not to be taxed; sitting here I can form no opinion upon that, and I ought not to do so, but I am strongly of opinion that if it be the intention of the Legislature to tax a building which has for many years belonged, and at this present time belongs to a club, the purpose of which is thoroughly well known, and the character of the occupation and the object of which are thoroughly well known, I am clearly of opinion that words should be used which properly and clearly comprehend such a case, and there could be no possible difficulty in framing a clause which would apply to and include a building like this. But when I look at the ordinary meaning of the words "inhabited house" and "inhabited dwelling-house," it seems to me that it is altogether a misapplication of that language to say that it applies to the case of a club consisting of a great number of persons who have a house in order to carry out the objects of the club. Therefore upon these grounds I think that this assessment is wrong and can not be supported.

Judgment for the Appellant with costs.

No. 35.—COURT OF EXCHEQUER (SCOTLAND).

7th February 1879.

In re The Commercial Bank of Scotland.

*Inhabited House Duty.—Banking-house and dwelling-house
under the same roof, but without internal communication;
the use of the dwelling-house granted by the bank to its
agent, who with the consent of the bank lets it to a third
person. Held that the banking-house and dwelling-
house are attached to each other and are one property in
the occupation of the bank, which is chargeable for the
whole.*

At a meeting of the Commissioners for the General Purposes
of the Income Tax Acts and for executing the Acts relating
to the Inhabited House Duties, held at Dumbarton on the
21st day of November 1878.

The Commercial Bank of Scotland appealed against an assessment to the Inhabited House Duties for the year ending the
24th day of May 1879, at 9d. per pound, on 100l., as the annual
value of premises in Dumbarton belonging to the bank.

The premises are situated in the high street of Dumbarton.
They consist of one building of two storeys. The ground floor
is occupied almost entirely by the office for conducting the
business of the agency of the bank. A small portion of that
floor situated behind the office, and the whole of the upper floor
are a dwelling-house for the use of the agent of the bank.
There is no internal communication between the bank office and
the agent's house, but the lock of the safe in the bank is controlled by a bolt which is connected with a recess in the wall
of a bed room in the house above, which recess is shut in by a
locked door. The bank have unrestricted and exclusive access
through the house to that recess and bolt. The office and house
have each a separate entrance. That to the bank is by a door
opening from the street, and to the agent's house by a door in a
close or passage leading from the street.

The agent is removable at the pleasure of the bank. He does
not himself live in the house, but with the knowledge of the
bank lets it to a third party, who is also removable at pleasure.
The rent is drawn by the agent for his own profit.

The surveyor contended that the case is not distinguishable
from the case of the Union Bank of Scotland, No. 29, of
Exchequer Cases decided 2nd February 1878. (a)

The Appellants maintained that the inhabited house assessment ought to be restricted to the annual value of the agent's
house, which is the only part of the premises actually inhabited;
that the portion of the premises occupied exclusively for the

---

(a) *Ante* p. 195.

transaction of the bank business should be freed from assessmen in virtue of the provisions of the Customs and Inland Revenue Act of 1878, section 13, sub-sections 1 and 2, which relieve from Inhabited House Duty portions of a house therein designated as "tenements" which are occupied exclusively for business purposes.

The surveyor maintained that the Act referred to does not apply in respect, (1) that the premises are not "divided into and "let in different tenements," so as to come within the scope of the exemption granted by sub-section 1 of Clause 13 of the Act quoted by the Appellants, and (2) that the Bank office is not a "tenement which is occupied solely for the purpose of any trade "of business, or of any profession," &c., and does not fall within the exemption under sub-section 2 of said clause, but being attached to the dwelling-house and occupied therewith, must, in accordance with the Judges' decision before referred to in charging such duty, be valued together with the dwelling-house.

The surveyor further observed that the term "tenement," in the provision quoted by the Appellants, is a repetition of that contained in section 11 of 32 & 33 Vict. c. 14, which was in force when the decision above referred to was given.

The Commissioners, regarding the business office of the Bank as a tenement in the sense of sub-section 2. of Clause 13 of the Act, relieved the Appellants of duty corresponding to the annual value thereof, which by agreement with the surveyor, was fixed at 60*l*., thus restricting the assessment to Inhabited House Duty on 40*l*. as the annual value of the dwelling-house; but the surveyor being dissatisfied with this decision craved a case for the opinion of Her Majesty's Judges, which is now stated accordingly.

(Signed)   A. SMOLLETT, Preses.

I am of opinion that the decision of the Commissioners is wrong.

(Signed)   JOHN MARSHALL.

NOTE.—The present case does not in my opinion fall under the exemptions introduced by the 1st and 2nd sub-sections of section 13 of the Customs and Inland Revenue Act, 1878. The property, in respect of which the assessment of 100*l*. was laid on by the surveyor, is "one property" belonging to the Appellants. It consists of a dwelling-house and bank office, which, although they have no internal communication with one another, are yet attached to each other. Both dwelling-house and office are in the occupation of the Appellants through their agent, and it is immaterial to the case that the agent, with the knowledge of the Appellants, lets the dwelling-house to a third party and pockets the rent, as the party is removable at the pleasure of the Appellants, and his occupation is just the occupation of the Appellants; and, accordingly, the assessment is charged not against the agent or his tenant, but against the

Appellants as occupiers, and it is not disputed that in so far as the dwelling-house is concerned, the assessment is rightly so charged.

The statutory occupation in section 13, sub-section (1), is not, in my opinion, to take effect where the property, however sub-divided, is all in one occupation ; it is only to take effect where it is "divided into and let in different tenements." But that is not the condition of the present case.

Sub-section (2) does not, in my opinion, apply to the present case. I do not think it was thereby intended to exempt from assessment tenements "attached" to dwelling-houses, even although such tenements are used solely for the purpose of trade or business, &c., unless these can be shown to fall within the operation of sub-section (1). But wherever a tenement is ex-empted under either of the sub-sections in respect of its being occupied solely for trade or business, &c., it is not to lose the benefit of the exemption although a servant should reside on the premises for the protection thereof.

PART XVI.

No. 36.—COURT OF EXCHEQUER (SCOTLAND).—FIRST
DIVISION. June 28th, 1879.

Rogers *v*. Inland Revenue.

*Income Tax.—Master Mariner absent from the United Kingdom
the whole of the year, his wife and family living in the
United Kingdom, is liable to assessment under Schedule D.
of the Income Tax Act.
In re Young followed (a).*

AT a meeting of the Commissioners for General Purposes of
the Income Tax Acts, held at Kirkcaldy on the 26th day of
April 1879,—
Mr. David Rogers, master mariner, appealed against an assessment under Schedule D. of the Property and Income Tax Acts,
for the year ending 5th April 1879, on the sum of 240*l*., with
which, in absence of a return of his salary, he had been assessed
in respect of his income as shipmaster.
The Appellant appeared by his agent, who stated that the
Appellant is in command of the ship "Saint Magnus," of Glasgow, which sailed for the East Indies in July 1877, since which
month he had been absent from Great Britain in command of said
ship, and that he could not therefore be held to be a person residing in Great Britain during the year from April 1878 to April
1879, and liable to be assessed for that year to the duty imposed
by Schedule D. of the Act 5 & 6 Vict. cap. 35. The Appellant's
agent further stated that Appellant's wife could not supply the
return called for by the surveyor, because the amount of the
Appellant's income could not be stated either by her or his
employers, and it was impossible to say what arrangement may
be come to between him and them as to his salary for the past
two years, should he live to return to this country.
Mr. Webber, the surveyor, admitted that the Appellant had
not been in Great Britain since said month of July 1877, but
stated that he is a British subject, commanding a British ship,
and possessed, in his own name, of a dwelling-house at Inner-

---

(a) *Ante*, p. 57.

leven, in the county of Fife, wherein his wife and children had resided during the year from April 1878 to April 1879; that he had no dwelling-house in any other country, and that his absence from this country was only of the temporary nature contemplated by the 39th section of said Act 5 & 6 Vict. c. 35, seeing it was caused by following his vocation of master mariner; that he would return to Great Britain when ordered by his employers, and that he had no present intention of residing permanently out of Great Britain; and the surveyor maintained that therefore he was liable to be assessed to the duty referred to.

The Appellant's agent admitted the surveyor's statements as to the Appellant's house at Innerleven, and the residence of his wife and family therein during the period specified, and he also admitted that the Appellant was at present following his vocation of master mariner on board the ship referred to, and that he would return to Great Britain when ordered by his employers, and had no present intention of residing permanently out of Great Britain; but the agent maintained that absence from Great Britain, which had extended over the entire tax year, was not of the temporary character contemplated by said section 39 of the Income Tax Act, and that, not having been in Great Britain during the year assessed for, the Appellant was not amenable to the jurisdiction of the Commissioners, nor assessable for salary, which he might not live to claim and receive.

The Commissioners were of opinion that the Appellant's ordinary residence is in Great Britain; that he had departed from Great Britain and gone to the West Indies for the purpose only of occasional residence, and that he must be held to be liable to the duty assessed, and they decided accordingly; with which decision the Appellant's agent expressed himself dissatisfied, and requested that this case might be stated for the opinion of the Court.

PATRICK D. SWAN, } Comrs.
WM. DRYSDALE,

W. R. SPEARS, Clerk to Comrs.

Dean of Faculty (Fraser), *Scott* with him, for Appellant.— This case is not within Young's case (a), the Appellant here having been absent during the whole year of assessment.

The Solicitor General (Macdonald), *Rutherford* with him, *contra* was not called on.

Lord President.—I have no doubt about this case at all. It is ruled by the case of *Young*. Every sailor has a residence on land, as Lord Mackenzie very well puts it in the case of *Brown* v. *M'Callum* (b), and the question is, Where is this man's residence? The answer undoubtedly is that his residence is in Great Britain.

(a) *Ante*, p. 57.
(b) 14 Feb. 1845; 7 D. 23.

He has no other residence, and a man must have a residence somewhere. The circumstance that Captain Rogers has been absent from the country during the whole year to which the assessment applies does not seem to me to be a speciality of the least consequence. That is a mere accident. He is not a bit the less a resident in Great Britain because the exigencies of his business have happened to carry him away for a somewhat longer time than usual during this particular voyage.

Lord Deas, Lord Mure, and *Lord Shand* concurred.

Judgment for the Respondent.

No. 37.—COURT OF EXCHEQUER (SCOTLAND).—FIRST DIVISION. November 15th, 1879.

Young *v.* Douglas.

Inhabited House Duty.—A Hotel is not within the exemption granted by 41 & 42 Vict. c. 15. s. 13 (2)—the fact of the hotel-keeper and his family residing elsewhere is immaterial. Stables behind the hotel, occupied by the hotel-keeper, and used in connexion with his hotel business, regarded as belonging to, and occupied with, the hotel within Rule II., Schedule B., 48 Geo. 3. c. 55, notwithstanding that the hotel and stables were held under different leases at separate and distinct rents.

AT a meeting of the Commissioners for General Purposes of the Income Tax Acts, and for executing the Acts relating to the Inhabited House Duties, held at Campbeltown, on the 1st April 1879,—

Mr. John Douglas appealed against the charge of 3*l.*, being inhabited house duty at 6*d.* per £ on the hotel and stables occupied by him, rented at 120*l.* from the Duke of Argyll.

The Appellant claimed total relief from the assessment under sub-section 2 of 41 Vict. cap. 15, section 13, in respect that the premises assessed are occupied solely for the purposes of his trade or business as a hotel-keeper, by which he seeks a livelihood or profit, the Appellant having a separate residence for his family about three-quarters of a mile distant, the Appellant or his wife and servants remaining on the hotel premises only for the conduct of the business.

In the event of the premises not being held to come within the exemption granted by the sub-section 2, the Appellant alternately claimed relief from the assessment as far as it included the stables, on the ground that the hotel and stables are distinct tenements, and separately let to him at the rents of 80l. and 40l. respectively, as entered in the Lands Valuation Roll for the Burgh of Campbeltown, and therefore fell within the exemption granted by sub-section 1 of section 13 of 41 Vict. cap. 15.

The stables are separated from the hotel by a court or yard surrounded by houses, partly occupied by the Appellant and partly by other tenants. The stable-court is behind the hotel, with entrance by a gate from a side street, and the court is in the Appellant's occupation.

In answer to the first ground of appeal, the surveyor contended that the exemption granted by sub-section 2 of 41 Vict. cap. 15, read in the light of previous enactments, applied only to premises used for trade or business purposes during the day, and not used for residence; and that the house occupied by the Appellant being an hotel, was essentially an inhabited house used for residence, in which parties dwelt or resided during the night as well as the day, and therefore did not come within the exemption claimed.

In answer to the alternative contention of the Appellant the surveyor maintained that under Rule 2 of 48 Geo. III. cap. 55. Sch. B., the stables, offices, and yard, belonging to, and occupied with, the hotel fell to be included in the assessment. The stable court is behind the hotel and enclosed by walls, with entrance by a gate from a side street, and although they are separately entered in the Valuation Roll, and separate rents payable for the hotel and stables, the surveyor contended that these circumstances could not exclude the operation of the rule of the Act under which the assessment is made, and that the duty was chargeable on the full rent of the whole premises.

The Commissioners find that the hotel is occupied by the Appellant or his wife at night, and also by servants for management and for carrying on the business of the hotel throughout the year. The Appellant's separate residence is about three-quarters of a mile distant from the hotel, and in a house of four rooms and kitchen and conveniences. The Appellant's family consists of six children, and this house is occupied by Appellant and his family only.

The Commissioners being of opinion that the exemption granted by sub-section 2 of section 13 of 41 Vict. cap. 15, applied to the case, sustained the appeal, and relieved the Appellant from the charge, with which decision the surveyor expressed himself dissatisfied, and craved a case for the opinion of the Court of Exchequer, which is here stated accordingly.

H. MACNEAL,
C. B. MACALISTER, } Comrs.

Counsel for the Surveyor of Taxes having been heard.

(*Cur. adv. vult.*)

Lord President.—My Lords, in this case the Appellant in the Court below sought relief from the assessment under the Inhabited House Duties Act in respect of premises occupied by him as a hotel; and it is stated in the case that the hotel is occupied by the Appellant or his wife at night and also by servants for the management and carrying on the business of the hotel throughout the year. The Appellant has a residence about three-quarters of a mile distant from the hotel—a house of four rooms and a kitchen. The Appellant's family consists of six children, and this house is occupied by the Appellant and his family only. That is the only statement of fact we have in this case, and it is not by any means satisfactory. Still, this at least appears quite clear that the premises which are assessed are occupied as a hotel, by which of course we understand that they are occupied not as a tavern, or a place where the public receive refreshment during the day, but are occupied by guests at night, who sleep there as well as eat and drink. And the question comes to be whether such premises are entitled to be exempted under the second sub-section of section 13 of 41 Vict. cap. 15, which provides that " every house or tenement which is occupied " solely for the purposes of any trade or business, or of any " profession or calling, by which the occupier seeks a livelihood " or profit, shall be exempted from the duties by the said Com- " missioners upon proof of the facts to their satisfaction, and this " exemption shall take effect although a servant or other person " may dwell in such house or tenement for the protection " thereof."

Now it is contended that the case falls within the operation of this section, because the premises are occupied by the Appellant for the carrying on of the trade or business of a hotel-keeper, and not as a dwelling-house.

But it is necessary to read this clause of exemption in connexion with all the other legislation upon the subject. We had occasion to consider the whole series of statutes in the case of the Glasgow Coal Exchange Company; and I there stated, with the concurrence of all the other members of the Court, that the result of the whole legislation was that all premises which are not dwelling-houses, but which are occupied for the purposes of trade, or for exercising a professional business, avocation, or calling, from which profit is derivable, are exempt from this duty, even though occupied at night by a caretaker who dwells in them.

I think, therefore, the true question here comes to be whether the premises in this case are a dwelling-house within the fair construction of the statute. I am of opinion that this hotel is a dwelling-house within the meaning of the statute. I know of no other purpose to which this house is put except that of a dwelling-house, and it appears to me to be quite immaterial under the statutes to which I refer whether the person who occupies the house is himself the only dweller in the house or whether he entertains a great variety of guests for limited periods who pay for the accommodation which they receive. In short, I think the guests in a hotel are dwelling there in the proper sense of the term, and are not at the same time dwelling anywhere else; and therefore that these premises are occupied as a dwelling-house.

Now, in the original imposition of this tax, it was imposed by the 48th of Geo. III. upon dwelling-houses throughout Great Britain; and all exemptions which subsequent statutes have introduced must be read with special reference to that general enactment.

Upon the first point raised in the case I have, therefore, no doubt. But it is maintained further that the stables which are occupied by this hotel-keeper ought to be dealt with separately from the house, and that they being occupied for business purposes only, and not as a dwelling-house, ought to be exempted from the duty. Now the ground upon which that is maintained is the provision contained in the first sub-section of this same section 13, which I have already mentioned in reference to the first part of the case. But it appears to me that that sub-section has been mis-read; and in order to understand it fully it is quite necessary to go back to the enactments in the 48th of Geo. III., because in Schedule B., which contains the rules for charging the duties on inhabited houses, we have a provision in the first place for the case of houses let in separate apartments, and it is provided by the sixth of these rules that where houses are let in separate apartments they shall be assessed as one house. Then there is a provision also regarding stables and such like premises. Under the second rule every coach-house, stable, brewhouse, washhouse, woodhouse, and so forth, enumerating a great many other things, "gardens and pleasure grounds "belonging to, and occupied with, any dwelling-house, shall, in "charging the said duty, be valued together with such dwelling-"house."

Now, the section in the recent Act relied upon, the first sub-section of section 13, provides that "where any house being one "property shall be divided into and let in different tenements, "and any of such tenements are occupied solely for the pur-"poses of any trade or business, or of any profession or call-"ing by which the occupier seeks a livelihood or profit, or are "unoccupied, the person chargeable as occupier of the house "shall be at liberty to give notice in writing at any time dur-"ing the year of assessment to the Surveyor of Taxes for the "parish or place in which the house is situate, stating therein "the facts, and after the receipt of such notice by the Surveyor, "the Commissioners shall upon proof of the facts to their satis-"faction grant relief from the amount of duty charged in the "assessment so as to confine the same to the duty on the value "according to which the house should in their opinion have

"been assessed if it had been a house comprising only the   Young v.
"tenements other than such as are occupied as aforesaid, or are   Douglas.
"unoccupied."

Now, it appears to me very clear that the object of that provision is to alter the sixth rule, but not to interfere in any way with the second rule, which provides that stables and premises of that kind shall be assessed along with the house to which they are attached. Therefore that second rule remains untouched by subsequent legislation. But it is contended that the stables in this case are let for a separate rent from the hotel. But it does not appear to me that that makes any difference. They are occupied together and for one combined purpose, so far as we can gather from anything that is stated in the case, I can quite understand a person in the position of the Appellant here having an establishment of stables and coach-houses and so forth, which he occupied solely for a purpose not necessarily connected with his hotel, for the purpose of a great coaching establishment and the like; and I am not by any means prepared to say that such premises as these so occupied would necessarily be assessable along with a hotel merely because they were in the occupancy of the same person. But there is nothing here to lead us to suppose that the stables in question are anything but ordinary hotel stables; and therefore I think there can be no relief on that branch of the case any more than on the other.

Lord Deas.—My Lord, the first question is whether this house is to be regarded as an inhabited house and dwelling-house, and so liable to the inhabited house duty.

Now, it is not disputed that the house is a hotel in the full sense of that word, a hotel in which people are accommodated by day and by night, and, in short, in which they live and dwell, just as much as if it was their own house. So far as the business is concerned, it goes on by night as well as by day, and the servant or servants who are there are not there to take care of the premises, but in order to attend to the guests, and to carry on the business of the hotel. It would be a very remarkable thing if every hotel were to be exempted from this duty because the landlord or proprietor of the hotel, or the tenant of the hotel in the position of landlord, did not himself sleep in that hotel. We all know that many landlords are landlords of a number of hotels in different places in different parts of the country, sometimes in England as well as in Scotland. The landlord certainly cannot sleep in all these hotels, and it would be a very curious result if we must take the one he sleeps in and not the others. I don't know what would become in that case of the assessment upon the railway companies who have large hotels at different stations in which hundreds of people dwell and are accommodated. It would surely be very anomalous if, because the landlord was the railway company and did not sleep in any of them, that they were to be exempted from the inhabited house duty. I don't think that is at all a right construction, and I have therefore no doubt upon that point.

The other point is certainly a more delicate one. It depends, as your Lordship has put it, on whether the landlord is carrying on a separate kind of business in his stables and offices from that which is carried on in the hotel. That certainly, as your Lordship has remarked, is a thing that may quite well be. There may be a posting establishment quite separate from the hotel, and I should not be prepared, any more than your Lordship, to say that such an establishment, or the premises for such an establishment, would be liable to the inhabited house duty along with the house. But I agree with your Lordship that in this case the occupation of the stables and offices is so connected with the hotel, and the business carried on in the hotel, that they must be regarded as one and the same concern. I am of opinion on these grounds that these premises must be included in the valuation for liability for the inhabited house duty.

Lord Shand.—My Lord, I am of the same opinion. There can be no doubt that this hotel is occupied as an inhabited house or dwelling-house. The case does not show very distinctly whether the person charged with the duty himself resides in the house at night. There is a passage which might be read either that he or his wife resides in the house at night. But I do not think it of any consequence how that may be, because it is clear that there are servants permanently there, residing in the house by day and by night, and it is also clear that there are constantly a number of guests in the house who occupied it as a dwelling-house. It is a dwelling-house clearly, and in the ordinary sense of these terms. It might be that one of them was a manager of the house, and as such resided in it, but surely, although the person charged with the duty as occupier of the house does not happen personally to reside there, if he keeps it, using it as a residence for his servants and guests, it is nevertheless, an inhabited house, and accordingly the case falls plainly within the spirit and letter of the earlier Acts of Parliament. The only question that arises is whether the exemption in the statute of 41 Vict. cap. 15, can notwithstanding that this is the very kind of house that it was intended to make subject to taxation, be held to relieve the occupier of the house from the duty. That statute provides that in every house or tenement which is occupied solely for the purpose of any trade or business, or of " any profession or calling by which the owner seeks a livelihood " or profit, shall be exempted from the duties by the said Com- " missioners upon proof of the facts to their satisfaction," and then follow what I think are very important words : " And this " exemption shall take effect, although a servant or other person " may dwell in such house or tenement for the protection " thereof." My Lord, I think it is impossible to read that exemption in the way that seems to be contended for by the occupier here, as it would exempt from the duty a person who was carrying on, not a business of the ordinary class of a trade or profession, but a business the very purpose and object of which

is to make profit of the house as a dwelling-house. He is carry- YOUNG v
DOUGLAS
ing on a business there no doubt, but the business he is carrying
on is to use the building as a dwelling-house, being the very class
of house that these statutes are intended to include and strike
at. That is quite apparent when you look at the concluding
words, that the exemption is to have effect, although the servant
or other person may be there for the protection of the house—
showing that the exemption cannot on any reasonable construction of it be applied to a house which is obviously used as
a dwelling-house, and the success of the business carried on in
which depends on its being constantly used as a dwelling-house.
On that branch of the case, accordingly, I have no difficulty in
agreeing with your Lordships. I think the occupier of this house
is responsible for duty as an inhabited house, because he occupies
it as a dwelling-house through his servants and the guests he may
receive.

On the second point I have nothing to add. I think the case
shows that these stables are, in the first place, in connexion
physically to some extent with the hotel, and in the next place,
are used in connexion with the private hotel business. Taking
the case as of that kind, I am of opinion that no distinction can
be made between the hotel and the stables as a part of the
premises.

Lord Deas.—My Lord, as you have observed now and formerly,
there is want of precision in the statement of the case. There
are particularly the words alluded to by Lord Shand, which
might lead to a supposition that the man or his wife might sleep
in the hotel. Now, it is necessary it should be understood what
the judgment proceeds upon. I understand that neither the man
nor his wife sleeps in the hotel.

Lord Shand.—For my part I think that quite immaterial.

Lord President.—And so do I. I deal with the case as the
ordinary case of a hotel.

Reverse the determination of the Commissioners and remit to
them to affirm the assessment and dismiss the appeal.

No. 38.—COURT OF EXCHEQUER (SCOTLAND).—FIRST
DIVISION.   October 25th, 1879.

Campbell *v.* Inland Revenue.

*Income Tax (Schedule A.).—Inhabited House Duty.—Where a
lease is granted of heritable and moveable subjects at an
inclusive rent for the whole, the assessments must be
limited to so much of the rent as is payable according
to a fair valuation for the assessable subjects.*

At a meeting of the Commissioners under the Property and
Income Tax Act, 5 & 6 Vict. c. 35, and subsequent Acts, for
the District of Lorn, County of Argyll, held at Oban on the
18th April 1879,—

Dr. Donald Campbell, Ballachulish, as proprietor, and Alexander Campbell, hotel-keeper, Oban, as tenant of the Caledonian
Hotel there, appealed against the following assessments made
upon the said Alexander Campbell under Schedule A. of the
Property and Income Tax Act, 5 & 6 Vict. c. 35, and subsequent
Acts, and under the Inhabited House Duty Act, 14 & 15 Vict.
c. 36, for the year 1878-9 :—

Property under Schedule A.

No.	Occupier.	Resi-dence.	Description of Property.	Proprietor.	Gross Rent or Value.	Deduc-tions.	Net Amount Assessed.	Duty.
					£	£	£	£ s. d.
24	Alex.Camp-bell, hotel-keeper.	Oban	Hotel and stabling.	Dr. Donald Campbell, Ballachu-lish.	1,000	20	980	20 8 4

Inhabited House Duty.

At 6d.	Duty.
£	£ s. d.
1,000	25 0 0

1. The said Donald Campbell appealed against the assessment
of 20*l.* 8*s.* 4*d.*, duty under Schedule A., as proprietor of the
Caledonia Hotel, Oban, and stables in Tweeddale Street,
Oban.

2. The Commissioners of Property and Income Tax have
charged the Appellant the above-mentioned sum of 20*l.* 8*s.* 4*d.*

under Schedule A., on the ground that the real annual value of the said subjects is 1,000l. per annum.

3. The Appellants objected to this assessment, in respect that the *bonâ fide* rent payable under the existing lease of the subjects was 650l. In support of the objection, the Appellants produced the leases after mentioned, and which accompany this case.

4. Alexander Campbell, as tenant of the Caledonian Hotel, &c. aforesaid, appealed against the assessment of 25l. for inhabited house duty, on a rental of 1,000l. in respect of his being tenant of the said Caledonian Hotel and stables.

5. The Commissioners of Property and Income Tax have charged the Appellant, the said Alexander Campbell, the abovementioned sum of 25l. of inhabited house duty, on the ground that the real annual value of the said subjects is 1,000l. per annum.

6. The said Alexander Campbell objected to this assessment, in respect that he is only liable to be assessed upon the sum of 650l., being the *bonâ fide* rent which he pays under the said existing lease of the subjects.

7. In support of the said objection of Donald Campbell, the proprietor, and of the said objection of Alexander Campbell, the tenant, of the said Caledonian Hotel and stables in Tweeddale Street aforesaid, the following explanations were given on their behalf :—

In 1876 the parties entered into negotiations for a lease of the Caledonian Hotel, Oban, and a lease was executed between them for the period of 10 years, at the yearly rent of 500l., with entry at the term of Whitsunday 1876; and in respect of certain improvements to be executed by the proprietor, the tenant obliged himself to pay on the sum to be so expended interest at the rate of seven and one-half per cent. per annum, to be paid termly with the rent. In the course of the following year the improvements thus stipulated for were completed, and by the time of their completion the said parties, the Appellants, had entered into a second arrangement, whereby the proprietor, Donald Campbell, had disposed to the tenant, Alexander Campbell, of his whole interests in certain coach companies in the district, consisting of the stock of horses and coaches belonging thereto, and the stabling accommodation in connexion therewith. The parties deemed it advisable in the circumstances to cancel the then existing lease, and execute a new lease in which all the matters between them should be embodied, and a new lease was accordingly executed, in which an annual rent of 1,000l. sterling is stipulated to be paid by the tenant to the proprietor. The subjects included in this new lease were the Caledonian Hotel, the coaches and horses therein specified, and stables in Tweeddale Street, which were required by the tenant as additional stabling accommodation in connexion with the said coaching business. It was further explained that the stables in Tweeddale Street were in no way connected with the said hotel. The basis upon which the sum of 1,000l. of annual rent was fixed

CAMPBELL
INLAND
REVENUE

CAMPBELL *v.* INLAND REVENUE.

was explained to be as follows:—The former rent was 500*l.*, and the cost of the improvements was stated to be about 2,000*l.*, the annual interest of which, at seven and one-half per cent., yielded 150*l.*, which interest, being added to the rent stipulated in the first lease, made a total new rental for the Caledonian Hotel of 650*l.* The said Donald Campbell's interest in the said coaching business, consisting of 20 horses, harness, &c., a list of which was produced to the Commissioners, the value of the said coaches enumerated in the said lease, together with certain outlays amounting to 827*l.*, a note of which was also produced, made by the said Donald Campbell in connexion therewith, and also including the rental of the stables in Tweeddale Street for the nine years of the lease then to run, was estimated at about 3,000*l.*, and that this was the true value thereof the Appellants offered to prove. To cover this sum of 3,000*l.* it was agreed, in terms of the new lease, that a yearly sum of 350*l.* should be paid termly with the rent for the hotel; and it was stated that in order to save the expense of a separate agreement it was agreed between the parties to add the sum of 350*l.* to the said rental of 650*l.*, thus bringing out a total sum of 1,000*l.*, payable annually by the tenant to the proprietor, being the apparent rental due to that amount for the hotel and stables.

In reply to the objection of the said Donald Campbell, the proprietor, the assessor stated that it had already been decided that the value of the good will of a business fell to be included in any assessment made in terms of "The Property and Income Tax, and Inhabited House Duty Act."

And in reply to the objections of both the proprietor and the tenant, the assessor stated there was an unqualified obligation by the subsisting lease upon the tenant to pay the proprietor a yearly rent of 1,000*l.* for the subjects let, and that both the proprietor and the tenant fell to be assessed upon this sum.

No evidence was produced to the Commissioners of the values of the coaches, horses, and harness given over by Donald Campbell to Alexander Campbell, and no subsisting arrangement was alleged other than what is contained in the lease dated the 7th July 1877.

The Commissioners dismissed both appeals, and sustained the charges made, in respect there is in the lease of 1877 an obligation to pay a yearly rent of 1,000*l.* for the subjects let, and that they considered it incompetent to examine into the details of the arrangements whereby that sum was fixed by the parties as the annual rent. Subsequently the Appellant craved a case for the opinion of the Court of Exchequer, which is here stated accordingly.

C. A. M'DOUGAL,
JOHN CAMPBELL STEWART, } Comrs.

Oban, 26th June, 1879·

· APPENDIX.

1. LEASE between Dr. Donald Campbell and Alexander Campbell, dated 6th and 12th February 1877.

It is contracted, agreed, and ended between Doctor Donald Campbell, Ballachulish, heritable proprietor of the subjects after mentioned, on the one part, and Alexander Campbell, hotel-keeper, King's Arms Hotel, Oban, on the other part, in manner after mentioned : That is to say, the said Donald Campbell, in consideration of the tack duty and other prestations after stipulated, has set, and hereby in tack and assedation lets to the said Alexander Campbell, and his heirs, all and whole, the subjects situated in George Street, Oban, called the Caledonian Hotel, as formerly occupied by Miss Catherine Smith (excluding the stables, coach-shed, and yard), declaring that the portion of said yard and sheds on the west of said yard and adjoining said hotel premises, indicated on the plans prepared by Alexander Ross, architect in Inverness, as being enclosed to the hotel, shall also form part of the subjects hereby let, with this exception, that the space enclosed shall be nine feet of said yard instead of fifteen feet in breadth, and that for the space of ten years from and after the term of Whitsunday 1876, which is hereby declared to be the said Alexander Campbell's entry to the same notwithstanding the date thereof ; and from thenceforth to be peaceably occupied and possessed by the said Alexander Campbell and his aforesaids, during the whole foresaid period, reserving to the said Alexander Campbell and his foresaids the option of bringing this tack to a termination at the end of five years from the said entry, on giving twelve months' previous notice to that effect in writing to the said Donald Qampbell ; which tack the said Donald Campbell bind and obliges himself, his heirs and successors, to warrant to the said Alexander Campbell at all hands, and against all mortals ; and the said Donald Campbell binds and obliges himself and his aforesaids to expend the sum of 1,000l. sterling, or such other sum as may be agreed upon with the said Alexander Campbell, in making certain additions to, and alterations on, the said hotel, before the term of Whitsunday 1877 ; and the said Donald Campbell, having put the said premises in good tenantable order at entry he also binds and obliges himself and his foresaids to keep the same wind and water tight during the currency of this lease ; and the said Donald Campbell binds and obliges himself and his foresaids to work the said Alexander Campbell's current contract for conveying the mails between Oban and Easdale, from and after the said term of Whitsunday 1876, and to relieve the said Alexander Campbell of all responsibilities and obligations connected therewith, it being in the option of the said Donald Campbell to terminate said mail contract on giving the usual notice : For which causes, and on the other part, the said Alexander Campbell binds and obliges himself and his foresaids, to make payment to the said Donald Campbell and his foresaids of the sum of 500l. sterling yearly of rent and tack duty, at two terms in the year, Whitsunday and Martinmas, by equal portions, beginning the first term's payment thereof, being 250l. sterling at the term of Martinmas next 1876, and the like sum at the term of Whitsunday 1877 thereafter, for the year from Whitsunday 1876, and so forth, yearly and termly during the currency of this tack, with a fifth part more of each term's payment of liquidate penalty in case of failure, and the legal interest of the said termly payments, from the time the same becomes due during the nonpayment thereof ; further, the said Alexander Campbell binds and obliges himself and his foresaids to pay interest at the rate of 7l. 10s. sterling per cent. per annum, on the amount to be expended by the said Donald Campbell as aforesaid, in making and carrying through the said additions and alterations, which interest shall be payable along with the rent above stipulated, at Whitsunday and Martinmas, by equal portions, beginning the first term's payment thereof at the term of Martinmas 1877, and the next term's payment thereof at the term of Whitsunday 1878, and so forth yearly and termly thereafter during the currency of this tack; Declaring as it is hereby specially provided and declared, that the said Alexander Campbell shall be bound to give all reasonable and necessary facilities for making and carrying through the said additions and alterations, and he shall have no right or claim against the said Donald Campbell, or his foresaids, for any convenience or for any loss or damage which his furniture and other effects may sustain thereby, or on any ground whatever; Further, on the said additions and alterations being executed, the said Alexander Campbell binds and obliges himself and his foresaids to keep the said premises in good order during the currency of this lease and to leave them in a proper tenantable condition at the expiry hereof—ordinary tear and wear excepted—or in case the said Alexander Campbell shall fail or neglect so to uphold and repair the said premises, he shall be bound and obliged to pay to the said Donald Campbell the deficiencies thereon, as the same shall be ascertained by persons of skill mutually chosen; And, further, the said Alexander Campbell binds and obliges himself and his foresaids, that he shall not at any time, or to any extent whatever, directly or indirectly, engage in any posting or coaching business during the currency of this tack; and the said Alexander Campbell binds and obliges himself and his foresaids to remove at the end of this tack without any warning or process of removing; And both parties bind and oblige themselves and their foresaids to perform the premises to each other under the penalty of 100l. sterling, to be paid by the party failing to the party performing or willing to perform over and above performance; And they consent to the registration hereof for preservation—In witness whereof these presents, together with the marginal additions written on this and the preceding page of stamped paper, by Ewen Taylor Miller, clerk to Duncan Macniven, solicitor, Fort William, are subscribed by the parties as follows, viz.: by the said Alexander Campbell at Oban, upon the 6th day of February 1877, before these witnesses, Alexander Macarthur, solicitor, Oban, and James Steven, his clerk; and by the said Donald Campbell at Fort William, upon the 12th day of the said month of February and year last mentioned, before these witnesses, Duncan Macniven, solicitor, Fort William, and Ewen Cameron, bank agent, Fort William.

ALEXR. CAMPBELL.
D. CAMPBELL.

Dun. Macniven, *Witness.*
Ewen Cameron, *Witness.*
Alex. Macarthur, *Witness.*
James Steven, *Witness.*

---

2. EXTRACT REGISTERED LEASE between Dr. Donald Campbell and Alexander Campbell, dated 7th July, and registered in the Sheriff-Court Books of the county of Argyll, 30th October 1877.

At Inverary the 30th day of October 1877, the deed herein-after engrossed was presented for registration in the Sheriff-Court books of the county of Argyll for preservation, and is registered in the said books as follows: It is contracted, agreed, and ended between Doctor Donald Campbell, Ballachulish, heritable proprietor of the subjects after mentioned, on the one part, and Alexander Campbell, hotel-keeper, Oban, on the other part, in manner after mentioned; That is to say,—whereas, by a lease, dated 6th and 12th February last, entered into between the said parties, the said Donald Campbell let to the said Alexander Campbell the Caledonian Hotel, situated in George Street, Oban, for the period of ten years, from Whitsunday 1876, with a break in favour of the said Alexander Campbell at the end of five years, and that at a rent of 500l. sterling yearly; And further the said Alexander Campbell thereby bound and obliged himself to pay interest at the rate of 7l. 10s. sterling per centum per annum on the amount thereby agreed to be expended by the said Donald Campbell in making and carrying through certain additions to and alterations on the said hotel, which interest was to be payable along with the rent, all as therein more particularly mentioned; And now, seeing that the contemplated additions to and alterations on the said hotel have been executed by the said Donald Campbell, and that it has been mutually agreed between him and the said Alexander Campbell, that the present lease above referred to should be renounced and superseded, and that a new lease

should be entered into on the following terms and conditions, viz. : *First*, That
the said Donald Campbell should let along with the hotel as presently possessed by the said Alexander Campbell the stables belonging to him, situated
in Tweeddale Street, Oban : *Second*, That the said Donald Campbell should
give up and assign to the said Alexander Campbell his whole share, right,
and interest in the following coaches, viz., two saloon coaches, belonging to
the Tarbert and Oban Coach Company ; one stage coach, belonging to the
Oban and Brander Coach Company ; and two saloon coaches and three
omnibuses, belonging to the Oban and Dalmally Coach Company ; *Third*,
That the said Donald Campbell should give and forthwith deliver to the said
Alexander Campbell all the horses used in connexion with the coaches above
enumerated, being 20 in number, together with all the coach harness and
stable tools presently in use for the same ; the said horses, harness, and tools
to become the property of the said Alexander Campbell ; *Fourth*, That the
said Donald Campbell, so far as competent, should assign to the said
Alexander Campbell his right to stabling accommodation in connexion with
said coaching business, the said Alexander Campbell being bound to relieve
him of the rent for the same as Stonefield Farm, and of the taxes effeiring
thereto : *Fifth*, That the said Alexander Campbell should pay the said Donald
Campbell a rent of 1,000*l.* sterling yearly, for the said hotel and stables, and
that for a lease of nine years, from and after Whitsunday last, when the
former lease came to an end ; *Sixth*, That the said Alexander Campbell should
be allowed the privilege of using a portion of Stevenson's Terrace Yard, to be
pointed out by the said Donald Campbell, measuring 42 feet by 18 feet, and
also a passage through the yard to the same, which were specially reserved for
the above-named coaches in a lease granted by the said Donald Campbell to
Donald M'Gregor, posting-master, Oban ; the said Alexander Campbell not
being entitled to use the same for any other purpose whatever ; *Seventh*, That
the said Alexander Campbell's right to a share in the coach profits should
commence as at 2nd July current, he undertaking from said date all obligations and duties incumbent on the said Donald Campbell in connexion with
the Oban and Dalmally and Oban and Brander coaches, and to run the
coaches to and from Buchanan's coach office and otherwise to act for this
season neutrally, and for the joint interest of his partners, it being understood that the three new coaches built at Stirling this year, and not included
in the above list, fall to be paid by the said Alexander Campbell and his
partners in the usual way at the end of the season ; *Eighth*, That the said
Alexander Campbell should pay to the said Donald Campbell for the hay and
oats in hand for Tweeddale Street stables, and also for any hay and oats that
may be consumed there since 1st July current, and that according to invoice
prices ; and, *Ninth*, That the said Alexander Campbell should have the right
to run stage coaches, but he would not be entitled to engage in any posting
business, directly or indirectly, and he should give the posting connected with
the coaches to the tenant of the Caledonian posting establishment, and also
that of the hotel, so far as the same is expedient and possible, the tenant of
the said posting establishment being restricted from coaching, with the
exception of excursion coaches to Culfail and Brander, and the said Donald
Campbell hereby transfers his entire interest in, and connected with, the
coach business in Oban, and binds himself to abstain from coaching on the
routes of the said coaches, directly or indirectly, during the currency of this
lease, and if necessary, on renewing the lease of the said Donald M'Gregor
or again letting the posting business to another person, the said Donald
Campbell will insert a condition that the tenant shall not run coaches such as
is contained in the present lease of the said Donald M'Gregor : Therefore, and
in implement on his part of the said agreement and in consideration of the
tack-duty and other prestations and conditions before and after specified,
the said Donald Campbell hereby sets and, in tack and assedation, lets to the
said Alexander Campbell and his heirs, (*First*), All and whole the said subjects situated in George Street, Oban, called the Caledonian Hotel (excluding the stables, coach-shed, and yard), declaring that the portion of said
yard and sheds on the west of said yard, and adjoining said hotel, forms part
of the subjects hereby let, with the exception that the space enclosed shall be
nine feet of said yard in breadth ; and (*Second*), all and whole the said stables
situated in Tweeddale Street, Oban, as presently occupied by the said Donald

Campbell, declaring that the said Alexander Campbell shall be allowed the privilege of using the portion of Stevenson's Terrace Yard, and the passage through the yard to the same for coaches, as above mentioned, and for no other purpose whatever, and that for the space of nine years from and after the term of Whitsunday last, 1877, which is hereby declared to be the date of the said Alexander Campbell's entry to the said subjects, and from thenceforth to be peacefully occupied and possessed by the said Alexander Campbell and his foresaids during the whole period above mentioned; which tack the said Donald Campbell binds and obliges himself, his heirs and successors, to warrant to the said Alexander Campbell at all hands and against all mortals; and the said Donald Campbell binds and obliges himself to lay proper flag and curbstones opposite the hotel in Argyll Street, and further, to bear the expense of any additional papering requiring to be done in the hotel in winter or spring next, and also to keep the said premises wind and water tight during the currency of this lease; for which causes, and in implement of his part of the said agreement above narrated, the said Alexander Campbell binds and obliges himself, and his foresaids, to make payment to the said Donald Campbell and his foresaids of the sum of 1,000l. sterling yearly of rent or tack-duty, at two terms in the year, Whitsunday and Martinmas by equal portions, beginning the first term's payment thereof, being 500l. sterling, at the term of Martinmas next, 1877, and the like sum at the term of Whitsunday thereafter, and that for the first year's possession; and so forth yearly and termly during the currency of this tack, with a fifth part more of each term's payment of liquidate penalty in case of failure, and the legal interest of the said termly payments from the time the same becomes due during the nonpayment thereof: Further the said Alexander Campbell hereby accepts the said premises as in good and tenantable condition, and binds and obliges himself and his foresaids to keep them in the same condition during the currency of this lease, and to leave them in that state at the expiry thereof, ordinary wear and tear excepted: Declaring that in case the said Alexander Campbell shall fail or neglect to uphold and repair the said premises during the currency of the lease, he shall be bound and obliged to pay to the said Donald Campbell the deficiencies thereon, as the same shall be ascertained by persons of skill, mutually chosen; and the said Alexander Campbell binds and obliges himself and his foresaids to remove at the end of this tack, without any warning or process of removing; and both parties bind and oblige themselves and their foresaids to perform the premises to each other, under the penalty of 500l. sterling, to be paid by the party failing to the party performing, or willing to perform the same, over and above performance: And they consent to the registration hereof, for preservation.—In witness whereof these presents, written on this and the preceding page, are subscribed, together with the marginal addition on page second hereof (under this declaration that the words "the" and "above-named," both occurring on the thirteenth line, counting from the top of page second hereof, were deleted before subscription) by the said Donald Campbell and Alexander Campbell, both at Oban, upon the 7th day of July 1877, before these witnesses, Alexander Macarthur, writer, Oban, and James Stephen, his clerk.

D. CAMPBELL
ALEX. CAMPBELL.

Alex. Macarthur, *Witness.*
James Steven, *Witness.*

Extracted from the records of the Sheriff-Court Books of Argyllshire, on this and the eight preceding pages, by me, Depute Sheriff-Clerk of the said shire.

ARCH. HENDERSON, D.S.O.

a. 7 of pro.

3. LETTER, Dr. Donald Campbell to Alexander Campbell, with List of Horses &c., left in stables, dated 8th August 1877.

Ballachulish, 8th August, 1877.

DEAR SIR,

    I ANNEX list of horses, &c., left in stables on the date you took possession.

Yours truly,

A. Campbell, Esq., Caledonian Hotel, Oban.   D. CAMPBELL.

Tweeddale Street Stables, Oban.

20 horses.
2 sets 5-horse harness.
2 sets 4 „   „
Collars and bridles for same.
2 pails.
17 stall collars.
Tools and brushes.
Body of hay cart.

4. NOTE of EXPENSES of Horses, &c.

No. 8 of p

	£
Feeding of six horses for one year at 50*l.* each	300
Wages of one strapper for 12 months	52
Smith's a/c for shoeing six horses during year	21
Feeding of 14 extra horses for 15 weeks at 14*l.*	210
Wages of two extra strappers for 15 weeks	30
Smith's a/c for shoeing 14 extra horses	14
Saddlers a/c for repairs and renewals	10
Depreciation of stock	100
Rent, taxes, insurance, &c.	50
Management, travelling expense, and sundry expense	40
	£827

Counsel having been heard.

Lord President.—I think we must call for inquiry here. There is no doubt the Income Tax Act, and the Inhabited House Duty Act as well prescribe that where there is no existing lease by which the subjects are let at rackrent that is to be taken as the annual value of the assessable sum. But if upon the face of the agreement by which the subjects are let, it clearly appears that that which is called rent is payable in part at least for something that is not an assessable subject, then I apprehend the clauses of these Acts of Parliament do not apply. For example, if it should clearly appear on the face of an agreement that a heritable subject and a movable subject were both let, so to speak to the assessed party for a period of years, and that a cumulo rental was payable for both, it could never be said that that was to be taken as the rack-rent of an assessable subject, being the heritable portion of the subject let. Now applying that very obvious rule to the case in question, let us see what the agreement of the parties is, as disclosed on the face of the lease dated 30th October 1877. It is narrated that there was a previous lease between the parties, the rent under which was 500*l.* It is further stated that the tenant was to pay interest at the rate of 7½ per cent. upon money expended upon the improvements of the subject; and it appears that the money expended on the improvement of the subjects was of such an amount that the interest payable under this agreement would be 150*l.*, so that under the original lease the rent would be 650*l.* and no more. Now it has been arranged between the parties, as

PART XVII

No. 39.—COURT OF EXCHEQUER (SCOTLAND).—FIRST DIVISION, 22nd January 1880.

In re Cowan and Strachan.

Inhabited House Duty.—Shop in the occupation of Appellants, and flats extending over it and over a shop occupied by another person under the same roof, all the flats opening on one staircase. Two of them occupied by Appellants for their business, and one by their salesman. Held, that the Appellants were properly assessed for their shop and all the flats. The salesman not a " servant or other person " within 41 & 42 Vict. c. 15 s. 13 (2).

No. 40. *In re* The Scottish Widows Fund and Life Assurance Society (No. 2).

Inhabited House Duty.—Offices of the Society, over them a flat occupied by the cashier, access to it being by stairs under the roof of the next house. The Society chargeable for the whole.

At a meeting of the Commissioners for executing the Acts relating to the Inhabited House Duties for the county of Edinburgh, held at Edinburgh the 20th day of November 1879,—

Messrs. Cowan & Strachan, silk mercers, &c., No. 15, Princes Street, Edinburgh, appealed against a charge of 21*l.* 5*s.* made upon them for Inhabited House Duty at the rate of 6*d.* per £ on 850*l.*, the annual value of the premises occupied by them at the above-mentioned address.

The premises consist of a shop on the street or ground floor, and of three flats above (herein-after designated the first, second, and third flats), which extend not only over the shop occupied by the Appellants, but also over the adjoining shop owned and occupied by Messrs. Thomas Methven & Sons, seedsmen and florists. The first and third flats are occupied by the

A

ʼʀ ʀᵉ COWAN
ᵗ STRACHAN.
In re
SCOTTISH
WIDOWS
ʼᵁᴺᴰ(No.2).

Appellants as show and work rooms, and have internal communication with the shop below. The second flat is occupied as
a dwelling-house by William Douglas, who is a salesman of the
firm, paid by salary. In addition to his duties in that capacity,
he has to look after the premises over night and on Sundays, to
open them in the morning, and to superintend the cleaning,
to wait in the business premises until all goods were despatched,
to close the shop, and to keep the keys. For the discharge of
these duties he receives no additional salary, but is allowed
the occupancy of the house (unfurnished) as an equivalent.
By a separate contract Douglas provides dinner in the house for
certain of the employées of the firm, and for this he is paid
so much per head. This flat (which is separately assessed for
property tax at a rental of 50*l*.), has no internal communication
with the other parts of the building, but access is obtained to
it by means of a stair rising from a passage between the shops
occupied by the Appellants and Messrs. Methven & Sons. This
last-named firm has right to the use of the passage, from which
they have a side entrance to their shop. The Appellants, however, have the exclusive right to the stair, but which was
originally the common stair of the tenement.

The Appellants contended (*First*) that the shop on the
ground floor, and the first and third flats connected therewith,
and used exclusively as business premises, were not liable to
Inhabited House Duty; but that the second flat, having a
separate entrance by a passage common to Appellants and
the occupant of the adjoining shop, must be held to be a
distinct subject, liable to Inhabited House Duty on the annual
value thereof; and they craved that the assessment should be
restricted accordingly. And (*Second*) they contended alternatively, that if the premises were held to be in the occupation
of the Appellants through their servant, they were only so
occupied for the purpose of protection, and therefore came
under the exemption granted by the Act 41 Victoria, chapter 15,
section 13, sub-section 2.

In support of the assessment it was argued that the second
flat was really in the occupation of the Appellants through their
servant, and that although there was no internal communication, there was attachment, and that therefore the whole premises were chargeable under the Act 48 George III., chapter 55,
Schedule B., Rule 3. And further, that the premises did not
come under the exemption granted by the Act 41 Victoria,
chapter 15, section 13, sub-section 2, in respect that the terms
of the statute, "although a servant or other person may dwell
" in such house or tenement for the protection thereof," are not
applicable to the case of an employée holding a position such as
that held by Mr. Douglas, and reference was made to the case
(No. 1,115) of the National Bank of Scotland, decided by the
Judges in Scotland 26th July 1870.

We, the Commissioners, were of opinion that Messrs. Cowan &
Strachan were liable for Inhabited House Duty on the whole

In re COWA
& STRACHAI
In re
SCOTTISH
WIDOWS
FUND (No.2

premises as charged, and we accordingly refused the Appeal and confirmed the assessment; but the Appellants being dissatisfied with our decision, craved that a case might be stated for the opinion of the Court, and which is here stated accordingly, and signed by us this 31st day of December 1879.

(Signed) JAMES GARDINER BAIRD.
     ,, J. DON WAUCHOPE.
     ,, ALEX. W. INGLIS.

At a meeting of the Commissioners for executing the Acts relating to the Inhabited House Duties for the county of Edinburgh, held at Edinburgh the 20th day of November 1879,—

The Scottish Widows Fund and Life Assurance Society, 9, St. Andrew Square, Edinburgh, appealed against a charge of 40*l*. 13*s*. 9*d*. made upon them for Inhabited House Duty on a rental of 1,085*l*., the annual value of the premises belonging to them at the above-named address, at the rate of ninepence per pound.

The premises consist of three flats and an area or sunk flat. The ground or street flat and the one immediately above are occupied by the society for the purpose of carrying on the business of Mutual Life Assurance. The area or sunk flat is occupied as a dwelling-house by one of their messengers for the protection of the premises, and has internal communication with the two flats occupied as the offices of the Society. The *third* flat, being the one immediately above the office, is occupied as a dwelling-house by the cashier of the Society, who gets the house, unfurnished as part of his salary, and without any special arrangement as to his ceasing to occupy the house on his ceasing to hold office under the Society. It has no internal communication with the other flats, but it is entered from a stair, No. 10, St. Andrew Square, between the premises occupied by the Society and those belonging to Mr. William Christie, clothier, &c., No. 11. This stair, which is under the roof of No. 11 and not of No. 9, is common to the Appellants and to Mr. Christie and his tenants in the flats above his shop.

The Appellants objected to the assessment, and contended (*First*), that Schedule B., rule 3, of the Act 48 George III., cap. 55, does not apply to business premises such as those in the present case, and that consequently such business premises falling to be rated separately are within the exemption created by the Act 41 Victoria, chapter 13, section 13, sub-section 2, and the only assessable subject is the dwelling-house; and (*Second and separatim*), that the premises in question fall within the exemptions created by the combined action of sub-sections 1 and 2 of section 13 of the said Act, 41 Victoria, chapter 15, and the assessment ought to be restricted to that effeiring to the value of the dwelling-house alone.

In re COWAN
& STRACHAN.
In re
SCOTTISH
WIDOWS
FUND (No. 2).

In support of the assessment it was maintained (*First*), that the first objection was groundless, as offices are not charged under the *third* but under the *fifth* rule of the Schedule of the Act above quoted; and (*Second*), that although the *access* to the flat occupied by the cashier is by a common stair outside the building in which the offices of the Society are situate, the flat itself is under the same roof with, and is really attached to, and forms part of, the premises of the Society, and that being occupied by one of their officers, who does not reside therein for the protection of the premises, the whole building is thereby rendered liable to Inhabited House Duty, which is chargeable, *in cumulo* against the Society.

We, the Commissioners, were of opinion that the appeal fell to be decided in conformity with the judgment of the Court of Exchequer (Scotland) in the case of the Commercial Bank of Scotland (7th February 1879), and we accordingly refused the appeal and confirmed the assessment. But the Appellants being dissatisfied with our decision, craved that a case might be stated for the opinion of the Court, and which is here stated accordingly, and signed by us at Edinburgh this 31st day of December 1879.

JAMES GARDINER BAIRD.
J. DON WAUCHOPE.
ALEX. W. INGLIS.

Wallace, for Cowan & Strachan, in answer to the Lord President, stated that as a fact there was a door opening into each of the flats from the stair.

[*Lord President.*—Methven (the tenant of the other shop) has a right to the passage but not to the stair. The Appellants Cowan & Strachan have the exclusive right to the stair, and each of the three flats has a door opening on the stair. That is really the whole case.]

The business premises are not so connected with the dwelling-house as to make them accessible together. In the case of the Union Bank (*a*) the building had been erected for bank premises, here the occupation of the dwelling-house by a servant of the Appellants is not necessary; the house could be let to an independent person. Secondly, Appellants are entitled to the benefit of 41 & 42 Vict. c. 15. s. 13 (2).

[*Lord Shand.*—Do you say that Mr. Douglas, having a whole flat there, is a care-taker? Is that a servant?]

I think he is there simply as a care-taker. I cannot maintain that he has not other duties.

[*Lord President.*—He takes care of the entertainment of the people?]

That is a separate contract.

In re COWAN
& STRACHAN
In re
SCOTTISH
WIDOWS
FUND (No. 2

[*Lord Shand.*—It is a large house to give to a care-taker—perhaps the best flat in the house?]

It is there and ready to hand.

[*Lord President.*—This gentleman is described as a sales-man?]

Yes, he is so, undoubtedly; but it is not in that capacity that he has the house. His duties are watching the premises at night, &c.

Graham Murray, for the Scottish Widows Fund.—The state of facts is the same as in the case of the *Union Bank*(a), but that was argued and decided on the 3rd rule of Schedule B., 41 Geo. 3. c. 55. Cites *In re Scottish Widows Fund*(b) to show that the premises occupied by the Appellants are not a shop or warehouse, and are, therefore, not within that rule, but must be assessed under Rule V., in which there is no attachment clause. But if the premises fall within Rule III. they are exempt under sub-sections 1 and 2 of 41 & 42 Vict. c. 15. s. 13, refers to case of *The Glasgow Coal Exchange* (c).

Rutherford, for the Commissioners of Inland Revenue.—The Insurance Company must be regarded as occupiers of the whole block of building. Refers to *Attorney-General v. Mutual Tontine Westminster Chambers Association* (d) to show that the building is assessable as one house. The premises are not occupied solely for business purposes because the cashier occupies part of them.

Balfour, for the Scottish Widows Fund.—The Society is not chargeable under Rule III. but under Rule V.; and the building consists in two assessable units, "the hall or office" and the dwelling-house.

The Lord Advocate, for the Commissioners of Inland Revenue.—Rule V. means only that the class of building there defined by the uses to which it is put shall be subject to duty. Rule VI. shows that a dwelling-house is to be an assessable unit where it is not divided into separate tenements with separate owners. If the Scottish Widows Fund were to let their building to six different people, some of whom occupied it for business only and others resided there, the exemption in 41 & 42 Vict. c. 15. s. 13 (1), would apply, but this is not the case. If the part of this building occupied by the Society's cashier be a separate tenement the section is useless.

Lord President.—My Lords, the first case that was argued to-day is the case of Cowan and Strachan; and although we did not think it necessary to call for an answer on the part of the Crown, we thought it desirable to hear both cases before we decided either because they both depend in some degree upon the same Statutes; but we must take them separately now, because they undoubtedly depend upon different clauses of the Statutes, and upon different views of the same Statute.

(a) *Ante*, p. 195.   (b) *Ante*, p. 7.
(c) *Ante*, p. 211.   (d) L.R., 1 Exch. Div. 469.

In re COWAN
& STRACHAN.
In re
SCOTTISH
WIDOWS
FUND (No. 2).

Now in the case of Cowan and Strachan, the premises occupied by them consist of a shop on the street floor and of three flats above, extending over the shop below, and also over an adjoining shop occupied by another person. The first and third flats are occupied by the Appellants as show and work rooms, and have internal communication with the shop below, that is to say, you can from the shop below on the street floor, go up by a stair to the first and third flats. The second flat, between the first and third, is occupied as a dwelling-house by a person of the name of Douglas, who is the Appellants' salesman, and who is paid by a salary. He lives there apparently with his family. He takes charge of the premises undoubtedly, but he cannot be said, in any ordinary sense of the word, to be a mere care-taker. On the contrary, he has very large responsibilities laid upon him in connection with the conduct of the Appellants' business. He gets this dwelling-house as part of his remuneration for the services which he performs; and in that dwelling-house by a separate arrangement, we are told that he provides dinner for certain of the employées of the firm. Now, this house, as occupied by Mr. Douglas, enters from a stair. The passage leading from the street to that stair is common to the Appellants and their next door neighbour, Mr. Methven, seedsman; but the stair belongs exclusively to the Appellants. Mr. Douglas's house enters from that stair, and so do the first and third flats occupied as part of the business premises of Cowan and Strachan; so that the stair being exclusively in the occupation of the Appellants, the part of their premises occupied by Douglas, by means of that stair, communicates with the other portions of their premises occupied as show-rooms; and thus there is really internal communication between Mr. Douglas's dwelling-house and portions of the building—and indeed of all the building which is occupied as a shop or business premises.

Now, the question is whether under the construction of the 3rd Rule of Schedule B. of the Act 48 George III., chapter 55, the whole premises are assessable as a dwelling-house with business premises attached; and if there could have been any doubt on the construction of the statute I think it has been already decided by this Court in the case of the *Union Bank*. There was a point intended to be raised in the *Union Bank* case, but which we could not decide because it had not been properly brought out, but the point which we did decide was the construction and effect of that Rule 3, to which I have referred; and in accordance with that decision, I cannot say that I have the slightest doubt that the duty has been properly assessed in this case.

Then we come to the case of the Scottish Widows' Fund, which, undoubtedly, requires more careful consideration, in the first place, because we have no previous case deciding the point, and, in the second place, because it depends upon a different view of the Statutes altogether from that which applies to the case of Cowan & Strachan; and requires a very careful con-

In re COWA
& STRACHA
In re
SCOTTISH
WIDOWS
FUND (No. 2

sideration of the different clauses of the Acts, and a special consideration of the precise meaning of the words used in that series of Statutes.

As to what the conditions or this house or building belonging to the Scottish Widows' Fund would have been as an assessable subject under the Act 48 George III., I don't think there can be any doubt; the entire building, which belongs to the society, is an assessable subject under that Statute. The duty is laid upon inhabited dwelling-houses; but it must be observed, that, according to the construction put upon these words in the Statute itself, they comprehend, not merely houses in which people live, that is to say, in which they eat and sleep, but also houses which are occupied in different ways, although nobody eats or sleeps in them at all. The 5th Rule of the Schedule B. is that, undoubtedly, under which this house would have fallen, as regards the part of it occupied as business premises by the Scottish Widows' Fund Society, and the words are these:— " Every hall or office whatever, belonging to any person or " persons, or any body or bodies politic," and so forth, "that " are or may be lawfully charged," &c. Now, that is just as much as to say, a hall or office is, for the purposes of this Act, an inhabited house, an inhabited dwelling-house. Now, supposing that under this Act, 48 George III., a building, such as we are dealing with here, belonging to one proprietor, is used partly for living in, and partly for carrying on business in, I cannot in the least degree doubt that it is just one inhabited house within the meaning of this Statute; because a part of an inhabited house does not cease to be a part of an inhabited house when it is occupied as an office, but, on the contrary, is declared to continue to be an inhabited house, notwithstanding that there is no person living in it. And, therefore, to say that you must lay on two different duties under this Statute, one upon the portion of the house that the proprietor lives in, and another upon the portion of the house that he carries on his business in, is, I think, under this Act, an absurdity; and this is still further illustrated by a consideration of some of the other words which are not specially applicable to the case in hand. Suppose that a proprietor, instead of occupying the entire building himself, lets it out to a number of tenants. That case is provided for by the 6th Rule, which is as follows: (*Reads.*) And again, the 14th Rule provides for the other case, where an entire house or building like this, is divided into separate tenements, being different properties belonging to different owners; there the opposite rule prevails, and each owner becomes assessable, or the occupier under each owner, becomes assessable for his own tenement only. Now, all that I think under the Act 48 George III. is extremely clear and intelligible, and I don't think there can be the smallest doubt that, if we are here dealing with the present case under the Act 48 George III., or any of the subsequent Statutes, the assessment must be held to be good, for it is laid upon a property

In re COWAN
& STRACHAN.
In re
SCOTTISH
WIDOWS
FUND (No. 2).

which, in the whole, notwithstanding the different ways in which it is occupied by its proprietor, is one assessable subject. Then, under the Act 14 & 15 Victoria, I think, it will be found that the same result follows. The house duty, with which we are dealing, was repealed at one time in the reign of William IV., but it was re-imposed by the Statute of Her present Majesty, and in re-imposing the house duty at a different rate from the old Statute, this Act of 14 & 15 of Her Majesty's reign just re-enacted, in regard to that new duty, all the rules and regulations and penalties and forfeitures which had existed under the previous statute of 48 George III.; and, among other things, I think it revived and made applicable to the new duty the provisions of Schedule B., and the rules in that schedule. So that, without going through the provisions of that statute in detail, I content myself with saying that I think that is the result. No doubt there was a difference in the rate, and there are some particular provisions of that statute which created a difference in the rate as regards some particular premises. "Where a dwelling-house is occupied by a person in "trade, &c." (*Reads.*) Now, it must be observed that down to this time there were no exemptions whatever beyond those which existed in the old Act of 48 George III. The exempting clauses, with which we have become familiar, are of later date than this Act, 14 & 15 Vict., and under this Statute it appears to me, as under the Statute 48 George III., the building belonging to the Scottish Widows Fund would have been assessable as one single tenement, no part of it being occupied in such a way as to create any exemption. Well, then in the progress of legislation we see that while exemption was originally confined to persons in trade, shopkeepers, and occupants of warehouses, it came to be extended to business premises of a different kind, and without going through those exemptions, and the history of them, which would be of no manner of value here, we come down to the latest of those Statutes, which is really the rule for the exemptions upon which we must act now, the Customs and Inland Revenue Act, 1878. The 13th section of that Act provides that with respect to the duties on which inhabited houses after such and such a year, the following provisions shall have effect; and the first of these is, "where any house being one property," &c. (*Reads.*) Now, it is quite clear that this first sub-section deals precisely with the same case, that the 6th Rule of the Schedule B. of the Act 48 George III. dealt with. That is the case where the proprietor of an entire house lets it out in different portions to different tenants. Under the 48 of George III., he was held to be the occupier of the entire house, and was liable for the entire duty charged upon the whole house; but exemptions having been introduced in favour of trade or business premises since that Statute, it seemed reasonable that in such a case the person who is described here, or the person chargeable as occupier of the house, that is under Rule 6th of Schedule B. the proprietor of the entire house, should be exempted from duty in so far as portions of his house had been let out for and used as business premises only. Now, that is the object of the first sub-section or the first clause of exemptions in this Statute, and there is just one other, and that is the 2nd sub-section. It is expressed in very general terms undoubtedly, but its meaning, I think, after this examination of the Statute, is not doubtful:—" Every house or tenement," &c. (*Reads.*) Now, be it observed that this deals with a house or tenement as being the assessable subject. The assessable subject, apart from this exemption altogether, in the present case is the building, and the entire building, occupied by the Scottish Widows Fund; and the fair meaning of these words " Every house or tenement," I think, is every house or tenement belonging to one proprietor; because, if the house or tenement was divided between several proprietors, the unrepealed provisions of the Act 48 George III. would make each separate proprietor assessable for his own share of the duty. Now, taking it in that sense, every house or tenement belonging to one proprietor is to be exempt upon certain conditions. The first condition is, that it is to be occupied solely for the purpose of any trade or business, or of any profession or calling. If it is not occupied solely for that purpose, it is not within this sub-section. In the second place, while there is a provision that a care-taker may dwell in the premises without derogating from the condition that it is to be occupied solely for business purposes, it is quite clear that if anybody other than a care-taker, or higher in his position, or different in his character from a care-taker, occupies the premises, or part thereof, those premises are not within the exemption. Tested by that construction of the Statute, what have we here? I have no doubt a care-taker lives in the area flat of this building, and if he were the only occupant of the premises besides the persons who carry on the business of life assurance, why, that would be no objection at all to the application of the exemption; but part of this assessable subject is occupied by another man altogether, as a dwelling-house. No doubt he is an officer of the Company but it does not in the least degree alter the nature of the case that he is an officer of the Company because he occupies the upper floor of this building as a dwelling-house; and, therefore, it cannot be affirmed, in the words of this clause of exemption, that the tenement is occupied solely for business purposes. I think, therefore, that in this case also, the duty has been properly laid on.

Lord Deas.—Upon the first of these cases, Cowan & Strachan, I really have no doubt at all.

The second case is attended with more complexity, but after careful consideration of the arguments, I have come to the same conclusion as your Lordship.

Lord Mure.—My Lord, in regard to the first case, I think it is quite distinctly ruled by the decision in the *Union Bank* case referred to; I have no doubt upon that point.

In re COWAN
& STRACHAN.
In re
SCOTTISH
WIDOWS
FUND (No. 2).

The other case has been argued very fully. I come to the same conclusion as your Lordship, that, under the provisions of 48 Geo. III., and the rules and regulations there laid down, the property belonging to the Scottish Widows Fund is assessable as one subject. That being the case, the only point for consideration is, whether the 13th section of the Act 41 Victoria, chapter 15, exempts that property from the assessment to which it was subjected. Sub-section 2 is very precise, to the effect that the exemption is applied to tenements occupied solely for the purpose of any trade or business. That is not the case with this tenement. One of the flats of it is occupied simply as a dwelling-house by one of the officials, who gets that dwelling-house to live in, and so does not come within the description of the sub-section 2 of section 13, and, accordingly, it is not occupied solely for the purposes of trade.

Lord Shand.—I don't think it necessary to say anything about the case of Cowan & Strachan, as your Lordship has said it is ruled by that previous case to which reference has been made.

In regard to the case of the Scottish Widows Fund, the question seems to turn entirely upon the meaning to be attributed to the second sub-section of clause 13 of the Statute 41 Victoria. Now, I think, in the first place, in regard to the facts of this case, as appearing on the statement of the Commissioners that the building, the whole of this building, is plainly occupied by the Scottish Widows Fund Society. It is true that part of it is used as a dwelling-house by one of their servants; but that is not in the capacity of a tenant, but simply as representing them, and his occupancy could partly be brought to an end at any time they chose. Therefore you have this building entirely occupied by the Scottish Widows Fund.

In the next place, part of this building is certainly a dwelling-house; and that being so, it appears to me that the only question which remains is, whether the words "house or tenement," in sub-section 2, are not to be read as referring to the whole of this building in the circumstances in which the case arises. It is not a case in which a building is divided amongst different proprietors. It is a building which is the property and in the occupation of one proprietor; and that being so, it appears to me that the words "house or tenement" in this section must be read with reference to the whole building, and unless it can be predicated that that building, in its entirety, is occupied solely for the purpose of trade or business, or profession or calling by which profit is gained, the exemption does not apply. You cannot say that of this building, because part of it is used as a dwelling-house. I, therefore, agree in the result arrived at by your Lordships.

Lord President.—Affirm the determination of the Commissioners.

No. 41.—COURT OF EXCHEQUER (SCOTLAND).—FIRST DIVI-
SION. February 21st, 1880.

In re Campbell.

*Inhabited House Duty.—Rooms on ground floor of a building,
otherwise let for, and occupied as, a hotel, let to a club.
The owner assessable for the whole under Rule VI.,
48 Geo. 3 c. 55, Schedule B.*

AT a meeting of the Commissioners for General Purposes,
acting under the Property and Income Tax and Inhabited
House Duty Acts for the district of Bute, held at Rothesay,
on 18th November 1879, for the purpose of hearing and
disposing of Appeals under the said Acts, for the year
ending 5th April 1880,—

Mr. Nicol Campbell, advocate, Edinburgh, appealed against an
assessment of 410*l.* made upon him for Inhabited House Duty,
at the rate of 6*d.* per pound, for the year 1879-80, as proprietor of the buildings of which the following are an
account :—

A few years ago the Appellant became by succession the
owner of the Queen's Hotel, in the West Bay, Rothesay; and
being animated with a desire to benefit the town, he proposed
to erect an entirely new building adjacent, which should be
occupied as the head-quarters of the Royal Northern Yacht Club,
and in part as an extension of the hotel. Accordingly he built
an addition, which is referred to in the memorandum or articles
of agreement produced. On the street floor in the new addition
the Club occupy a reading-room, a committee-room, steward's
service and store rooms, and lavatory. From the entrance hall
leading to these rooms a stair leads to a billiard-room, also
occupied by the Club, in a wing behind the new addition (the
wing being part of the new addition). From this stair by a
landing, and by an ordinary two-leaved door with the usual
lock and fastenings, entrance to the dining-room, called in the
printed memorandum the dining-hall on the first floor, is
obtained. This is the dining-room of the hotel which the
members of the Club are entitled to use, and entrance to it from
the hotel is had by an ordinary door opening from the lobby of
the hotel. This room is entirely in the new addition, and
occupies nearly the whole space of the first floor of such addition.
There are bedrooms connected with the hotel in the floor
immediately above the dining-hall. The Club-house is open
during the whole year for the use of the members. The hotel

In re
CAMPBELL.

consists of the whole of the old building, the second flat of the new building, containing dining-room, &c., and the third flat of the new building, containing bedrooms; and the Yacht Club part consists of the ground-floor in the new building occupied as before-mentioned and billiard-room in wing.

The door by which there is internal communication between the portion of the building let to the Club and the hotel has bolts, and was not opened at all when members were absent, which was generally the whole winter. The hotel-keeper has nothing to do with the taking care of and cleaning the Club premises, that duty being attended to throughout the whole year by a resident steward in the employment of the Club.

There were produced—(1), lease by the Appellant to Mr. W. M. Whyte, for thirteen years from Whitsunday 1876, of the hotel and the dining-hall and bedrooms before mentioned in the new building adjoining, at an annual rent till 1883 of 270*l.*, by which it is declared that the tenant of the hotel should, as far as incumbent on him, implement Article 6 of the Articles of Agreement of lease of the club-house after mentioned; and that the dining-hall should be used in connexion with the hotel alone, "and that while the members of the Yacht Club may have "access thereto from their own premises, they shall not be "entitled to use it otherwise than as the dining-hall of the "hotel;" and (2), print of Articles of Agreement of lease by the Appellant to the Yacht Club, for 15 years from 1st April 1877, of the rooms of the Club, together with the use of the foresaid dining-hall, to which, as stipulated by the said agreement, the Club were to have a private access, at an annual rent for the first seven years of 140*l.*, by Article 6 of which it is provided "that the tenant of the hotel, or his servants, or any "one living in the hotel, unless he be a member of the Club, "shall have no right to the use of any of the rooms set apart for "the Club."

The occupancy was in accordance with the leases referred to, and both subjects let had separate and distinct entrances to the street, with the internal communication before explained.

Rough sketches of the elevation and plan of the buildings are herewith sent, with notes, indicating so far the parts occupied as hotel and the parts occupied as club-house.

Mr. Alexander Malcolm Scott, writer, Glasgow, commissioner and attorney for the appellant, claimed that he was entitled to exemption from assessment for house duty on the hotel and club-house in terms of the Act 48 Geo. III. chapter 55, schedule B, and particularly by rule 14 of said schedule, by which it is provided that 'where any dwelling-house shall be divided into 'different tenements, being distinct properties, every such 'tenement shall be subject to the same duties as if the same 'was an entire house, which duty shall be paid by the occu- 'piers thereof respectively.' He contended that as the proper- ties let were clearly distinct, and the tenants were the occupiers in the sense of the Act and schedule referred to, the landlord could not be held liable, and that rule 6 of the schedule referred to did not apply to the present case.

Mr. John Muat, the surveyor of taxes, on the other hand, contended that rule 6 of said schedule, which enacts that 'where any house shall be let in different stories, tenements, 'lodgings, or landings, and shall be inhabited by two or more 'persons or families, the same shall nevertheless be subject to and 'shall in like manner be charged to the said duties as if such 'house or tenement was inhabited by one person or family only, 'and the landlord or owner shall be deemed the occupier of such 'dwelling-house, and shall be charged to the said duties,' was applicable to the present case in respect that the buildings were let out to two different parties as before mentioned, and there was an internal communication between the portions let to the different parties by means of a door between the dining-hall and a lobby in the club-house; and that therefore the appellant, as landlord, was liable. Further, the buildings belong to one proprietor, and the parts occupied by the different tenants being attached, and having internal communication, were therefore not distinct properties chargeable under Rule XIV.

The surveyor in support of his contention referred to cases No. 1077, Scotch, and No. 9 of cases decided by the Court of Exchequer.

The Commissioners unanimously confirmed the assessment, they being satisfied, while admitting the hardness of the case to the appellant, that the surveyor could not do otherwise than assess him as landlord or owner.

Mr. Scott, for the appellant, immediately upon the determination of the Commissioners being given, declared on behalf of the appellant his dissatisfaction therewith as being erroneous in point of law, and now having duly intimated in writing his desire that a case be stated and signed for the opinion and decision of the Court of Exchequer in terms and under the provisions of the "Customs and Inland Revenue Act, 1874," such case is now stated accordingly.

J. A. MACKECHNIE, }
JOHN M'EWEN,   } Comrs.

Rothesay, 26th January, 1880.

Kinnear, for the Appellant.—The club rooms and the hotel are two houses. The means of access from one to the other is merely for convenience, and does not make the two houses into one. Rule VI. was intended to meet cases in which there would be difficulty in laying the tax on the several occupants. This case is distinguishable from that of the Scottish Widows Fund (a), because there the company in assessment was the actual occupant of part of the building.

(a) *Ante,* p. 245.

In re CAMPBELL.

Lord President.—Solicitor General, do you consider the door of communication here to be an essential part of your case?

Solicitor General.—No, certainly not.

Lord President.—I think it is immaterial.

The Solicitor General, for the Commissioners of Inland Revenue, was not called on to reply.

The Lord President.—My Lords, the case which has now been stated by Mr. Kinnear with his usual ability and ingenuity has never hitherto been determined, but I think it has been all but determined, by the cases which have been recently before us. We have had occasion to consider the 6th rule of Schedule B. in the 48th of Geo. III., and also the 14th rule, and upon these occasions I certainly made up my mind very clearly as to what was the meaning of both the one rule and the other; and whether I did upon the occasion of giving judgment in the Scottish Widows Fund case precisely interpret these rules as I am prepared to do in the present case, I think, at all events, the way in which we dealt with these rules in the Scottish Widows Fund case almost necessarily led to the conclusion in this case at which the Commissioners have arrived.

The 6th rule provides that, " where any house shall be let in " different stories, tenements, lodgings, or landings, and shall be " inhabited by two or more persons or families, the same shall " nevertheless be subject to and shall in like manner be charged " to the said duties as if such house or tenement was inhabited " by one person or family only, and the landlord or owner shall " be deemed the occupier of such dwelling-house." The 14th rule provides that " where any dwelling-house shall be divided " into different tenements, being distinct properties, every such " tenement shall be subject to the same duties as if the same was " an entire house, which duties shall be paid by the occupiers " thereof respectively." Now, in the first place, there is a clear distinction in both these rules between the word house or dwelling-house and the word tenement. The former is the larger and more comprehensive term, and signifies the entire building which is divided into different tenements occupied by different persons. A tenement is a portion of the dwelling-house separately occupied. These are plainly the statutory meanings of these two words. And that is borne out very strongly by the 13th section of the Customs and Inland Revenue Act of 1878, sub-section one, which I need not read because in the whole course of legislation on this subject the words which we are now construing have throughout one distinct and well ascertained meaning. Now that being so, what is the provision of Rule 6. and what is the provision of Rule 14, taking the two together? It simply comes to this, that where a dwelling-house, meaning an entire block of building, is the property of one individual, but is divided into different occupations or tenements let to different tenants, the landlord or owner of the entire block of building is to be taken as the occupier of the entire block of building, and assessed as if he occupied the whole himself, but where the entire block of building is divided into tenements in the same manner as is contemplated by the 6th section, but these tenements are distinct properties belonging to different owners, then the incidence of the duty is to be upon the occupant of each separate tenement. Now if that is the distinct and clear construction of these two rules there is an end of this case, because there cannot be the smallest doubt in the case before us that the entire building is the property of one owner, and it is let in separate parts to two distinct tenants. Therefore, I am clearly of opinion that the determination of the Commissioners is right.

Lord Deas.—I am entirely of the same opinion.

Lord Mure.—I quite concur, and I have nothing to add. The words of the 6th rule are quite distinct.

Lord Shand.—I am of the same opinion. If in order to make this one house within the meaning of Rule 6th of the Statute, so that the duty on that house should be chargeable against the landlord, as an entire subject, it were necessary to take into view the existence of the door of communication, I should have considerable difficulty in affirming the decision of the Commissioners. I do not say that I have made up my mind upon it, but I think the use is of a very limited kind, and it would require very serious consideration whether such a communication and such a use would make this one house, but I agree with your Lordship in thinking that really there is no difficulty under Rule 6th. The simple question to be solved is what is the meaning of the word "house" in the opening part of that rule? Does it or does it not mean building? And I am of opinion that it does mean building. We have it again occurring at the end of the rule—"house or tenement," and there the word "tenement" is used as meaning the same thing as "house." But taking it as house or tenement, it is a house or tenement let in "different stories, tenements, lodgings or landings" that is dealt with, and that is just the ordinary case of a large building consisting of different flats which the landlord or proprietor has let off in different flats. If he has done so, then he is to be regarded as the occupier, and he is the person who is made subject to the inhabited house duty. The practical result is, I think, that those who are imposing assessments of this kind, and collecting them, are entitled to treat him as the occupier of the whole; and, if it be intended, as in a question between tenants of particular flats and the landlord, that they ought to bear a proportion of the inhabited house duty, that must be made matter of arrangement or stipulation between them in order to secure that object, but in a question between the Crown and the landlord of such a

In re
CAMPBELL. house, I think the landlord is the occupier of the house as a whole.

The Lord President.—Then we affirm the judgment of the Commissioners.

Solicitor General.—And find the appellant liable in expenses.

Lord President.—Yes.

YEWENS *v.*
NOAKES. No. 42.—IN THE SUPREME COURT OF JUDICATURE BEFORE THE COURT OF APPEAL AT WESTMINSTER.

J. W. Yewens (Surveyor of Taxes), Appellant, and C. Noakes, Respondent.

Inhabited House Duty.—Exemption.—A clerk with a salary of 150l. a year is not a "servant or other person" within the meaning of 32 & 33 Vict. c. 14. s. 11, or 41 & 42 Vict. c. 15. s. 13 (2) (a).

AT a meeting of Commissioners for Division of Southwark Surrey, held at 9, Three Crown Square, Southwark, on the 16th day of February, 1877,—

Mr. C. D. Field appealed, as agent for Mr. C. Noakes, of 9, Southwark Street, Borough, Hop Merchant, against a charge for Inhabited House Duty of 500l. at 9d. per pound upon the houses Nos. 11 and 13, Southwark Street aforesaid, for the year 1876–7, such houses having an internal communication throughout, upon the ground that they were solely used for trade purposes and only otherwise occupied by a caretaker.

(a.) The 11th section, 32 & 33 Vict. c. 14, was as follows : "From and after the "5th day of April, one thousand eight hundred and sixty-nine, any tenement or "part of a tenement occupied as a house for the purposes of trade only, or as a "warehouse for the sole purpose of lodging goods, wares, or merchandise therein, "or as a shop or counting-house, or being used as a shop or counting-house, shall "be exempt from inhabited house duties, although a servant or other person may "dwell in such tenement or part of a tenement for the protection thereof."
It was superseded by 41 & 42 Vict. c. 15, section 13 (2), which enacts that "every house or tenement which is occupied solely for the purposes of any trade "or business, or of any profession or calling by which the occupier seeks a "livelihood or profit shall be exempted from the duties by the said Commis-"sioners upon proof of the facts to their satisfaction, and this exemption shall "take effect although a servant or other person may dwell in such house or "tenement for the protection thereof."
This provision came into force in April, 1878. The assessment under the consideration of the Court in *Yewens* v. *Noakes* was for the year 1876–7.

It appeared in evidence that Mr Kepell, a clerk in Mr. C. Noakes's employ at a salary of 150l. per annum, with his wife, five children, and a servant girl about 13 years old, occupied five rooms on the upper portion of the premises, three on the second floor, and two attics, coal and gas free, and that his wife and girl cleaned the offices in the building.

It appeared in evidence that Mr. Kepell was only occupying so many rooms until some of them with three others were let, although he had resided in them for two years and a half without being disturbed; it was also stated he had been placed there in consequence of a fire having occurred on the premises a short time before taking up his abode in them. Mr. Kepell admitted to have received 10l. advance of salary about 12 months before removing into the above premises but none since.

The Commissioners, considering that as the premises were solely used for trade purposes, and believing Mr. Kepell's position was simply that of a caretaker, allowed the exemption claimed, but the surveyor contended that Mr. Kepell was in a much superior position to that of a servant or other person referred to in the 11th section of 32 & 33 Vict. c. 14, which did not embrace the occupation of five rooms for the residence of himself, wife, five children, and female servant, in a building containing the offices of two hop merchants only, his residing on the premises was for other purposes than a caretaker, rendering him liable to assessment, and therefore declared his dissatisfaction with their decision, and required them to state and sign a case for the opinion of the High Court of Justice, Exchequer Division, which we hereby state and sign accordingly.

Dated this 22nd day of June 1877.

THOMAS B. SIMPSON.
CRAWFORD BURKETT.
FREDERICK SIMPSON.

In the Exchequer Division, the Court (Kelly, C.B., and Pollock, B.) affirmed the decision of the Commissioners.

Yewens appealed.

Sir Hardinge Giffard, S.G., and *Dicey*, for the Appellant.— The Act says "a servant or other person" in the singular, and the singular was intended. The whole policy of the Acts(a) shows that the other person must be a person ejusdem generis, and that it was not intended that exempted premises should be inhabited

(a) 57 Geo. 3. c. 25. s. 1. Tenements which have been occupied as dwelling-houses not to be charged when used solely for purposes of trade or as warehouses, provided that the occupier reside in a house charged to the duty.
5 Geo. 4. c. 44. s. 4. Extending the above exemption to professional offices, &c., with the same proviso.
6 Geo. 4. c. 7. s. 7. The Commissioners authorised to give a license to the occupier of any tenement within the above exemptions for one of his servants named in the license to abide in such tenement at night "for the purposes only "of watching and guarding the same."

by a person who would otherwise pay duty on a house of his own.

McIntyre, Q.C., and *Graham,* for the Respondent.—The Commissioners have found that the building is used for the purposes of trade and that the clerk is placed there for the purposes of protecting them. In *Bent* v. *Roberts* (a) the policeman had his family living with him. The clerk is a servant within the meaning of the Act. The restrictions in the former Acts are abolished by 32 & 33 Vict. c. 14, s. 11.

Bramwell, L.J.—I think this appeal must be allowed. Here is a building which is subject to the duty, unless it is within the exemption.

Now, I do not desire to rely too much upon the burden of proof, or the burden of making out the exemption being on the Defendant; and that this is not a case in which a tax is being imposed upon the subject, but a case in which a tax being imposed, the subject is endeavouring to get rid of it by exemption. I do not desire to rely too much upon that, as I never do on analogous rules; but I think one ought to try and get at the meaning of the Statute as well as we can, without considering on whom the burden of proof is. But still, so it is; it is for the Respondent to show that he is within the exemption. In my opinion he does not do so. I think if one looks at the Acts of Parliament passed one after another, one can see what the object of them was. The object of them was to remove that which was practically a tax upon the particular trades which were subject to this duty in the circumstances under which they were carried on. For instance, if a trade could not be carried on without a warehouse for the produce of the trader's manufacture, or of what the trader dealt in, and if the having of that warehouse involved the necessity of having a caretaker, why, to charge that warehouse when there would be no analogous tax upon a trade or produce which did not require such a caretaker would evidently be a tax upon a particular trade, just as though there had been a particular tax upon a hop merchant, say, for instance. The Legislature saw that; and from time to time they have recognised that there must be a caretaker in the day time, and that there must be a caretaker in the night time; and that in all reason, if a man is to take care, he must be at liberty to do what one would call dwell there; that is to say, it should not be necessary that he should have some other place for his true dwelling, at which first place, before an alteration was made, he would have had to go to sleep, or, afterwards, when he was at liberty to sleep where he took care, where he could go and take his meals. The Statute said, rather than that the trade should be taxed in this particular way which involved the having of a caretaker, and houses or dwellings, that would come within the Inhabited House Duty, they should not come within it if they had such a person there as a caretaker. A man is there, the caretaker; his wife is there; the servant is there; the family are there; and there are some children there; but how can it possibly be said that that is within the reason or the principle of legislation to which I have called attention? It is to be observed, that it is not legislation for the benefit of the caretaker, it is legislation for the benefit of the trade or trader. As was pointed out by the learned counsel, if the argument in favour of the Respondent could prevail, the Crown would lose the benefit of the tax on an inhabited house, which otherwise it would of necessity get, from the necessity of a person, a caretaker in this case, occupying an inhabited house, the whole or part of an inhabited house which would otherwise be subject to duty. Therefore it is a mistake, in my opinion, to construe these sections as though they were passed for the benefit of the caretaker, which they were not; they were passed for the benefit of the trade or the trader.

It may be said, Then what is the conclusion from that? Are married men not to be caretakers? I do not say that they are not to be; but what I say is that the house which they take care of must not be the dwelling of themselves and their family; and that if it is made the dwelling of themselves and their family, it is not within the exemption, which supposes an exemption in the case of a caretaker only. I think the meaning of the expression in the Act of Parliament is plain, it says "servant or other person," by which I understand this, that the "other person" may not exactly occupy the position of a servant, he may have undertaken the duty of taking care for the proprietor of the building, but not necessarily as a consequence of being a servant. A servant is a person subject to the command of his master as to the way he shall do his work. I think the statute means, that the person so employed shall be a person who has entered into a contract for that purpose, or who has entered into a contract of service for that purpose, and has agreed to do it. I use the word "contract," not as speaking of anything formal, but who has agreed to take care of the premises, either as a servant, or not as a servant. I think, therefore, that this case might be decided on the general considerations to which I have endeavoured to give expression.

But as to this particular case, with very great deference to those who thought otherwise, it does seem to me impossible to hold that this particular case can be within the intention or within the spirit, or even the words of the Act of Parliament. Here is a man and his wife, having a servant residing within this place which, as far as they are concerned, is as much an occupied dwelling house, to the extent to which they occupy it, and as far as the rooms they occupy, as a part of the house can be; and it is impossible not to see on the evidence, that this gentleman, I can only call him,—a clerk or a servant if you please,—it is impossible to say that he is not residing, or having the benefit of a residence with his family there. I think, therefore, that whether we look at those general principles to which I have adverted, or to the circumstances of this particular case, it is not within the Statute.

I did intend to make one further remark, and that is, that I really do not see where this is to stop. If, because a man may be there, his wife may be there, and his children may be there, and his servant may be there, why might he not have his father and his mother, if he was a good man and took care of them, and they were part of his family; because there is no magic in the children being his children; they might be the children of his wife, and not his children; and if he has his children and his wife's children, why not his father and mother, and why not her father and mother, and why not any number of their relations and friends that his sense of benevolence may induce him to make a part of his family. I really cannot see the limit.

Under these circumstances, in this case I think the appeal should be allowed.

Thesiger, L.J.—I agree that this appeal should be allowed, but not entirely upon the same grounds as those stated by Lord Justice Bramwell. I cannot bring myself to think that the exemption from inhabited house duty which trade premises enjoy is necessarily lost from the fact that the caretaker is put in possession and occupation of the house with his wife and family. And I found my view upon this point upon a consideration partly derived from previous legislation *in pari materia*, and the practice of the Commissioners under such legislation, and partly upon considerations derived from the views and habits of the community, with reference to which Acts of Parliament ought to be construed, and with reference to which also it appears to me that the practice of the Commissioners has been founded.

After referring at length to the various Acts which had been quoted in the arguments, his Lordship continued—It appears to me that if this were a case so far of an ordinary caretaker, the mere fact of that caretaker residing in the trade premises with his wife and family would not exclude the occupier of the trade premises from the exemption which is given by these Acts. But it appears to me that this is not, upon the facts stated to us by the Commissioners, the case of an ordinary caretaker at all. It is the case of a man who goes in, not merely into one or two rooms in the basement storey of the house, for the ordinary purpose of guarding the premises, and cleaning them up in the morning, but of a man who occupies, with his wife and family, a considerable portion of the dwelling, sitting rooms, and bed rooms, and occupies them also not merely with his wife and family, but with a servant, for the purpose of attending upon him and his family. Therefore, upon that ground alone, it appears to me there is sufficient ground upon which to allow this appeal.

But there is another ground also upon which I am of opinion
that this appeal should be allowed. The words of section 11,
leaf 14, of the 32nd and 33rd Victoria, include the case of a
" servant or other person." Now what is the meaning of the
Legislature when they use those words? It appears to me that
the Legislature, in using the term " servant," is using that term
in the ordinary and popular sense of it; that is to say, not in the
sense in which any clerk or manager is called the servant of his
employer, or in the sense in which the Judges might be said to
be the servants of the Crown, but in the sense of the ordinary
menial or domestic servants; and that is made more clear by the
Act of 6th George the Fourth, to which I have referred already,
which speaks of a man or woman putting into premises his or
her servant or servants.

Then if that be so, what is the meaning of the words " other
person "? Now definitions are proverbially dangerous, and I do
not propose to define exactly what the words " other person "
may mean; but this, I think, is obvious, that by the words
" other person " is intended some person of the same kind and
description as a servant standing somewhat on the same footing
and subject to the same conditions; and I think a very good
illustration was given by the Solicitor-General when he referred
to the not uncommon case of a policeman being put into an
unoccupied house or trade premises for the purpose of watching
and guarding them. But if that be the proper meaning, as I
think it is, of the words " servant or other person," then it is
obvious that a clerk with a salary of 150*l.* a year does not come
within such words. If he did, where are you to stop? The
manager of a bank, a foreman with high wages, persons in the
position almost of gentlemen, might be put in under this Act of
Parliament to take care of premises, and then it might be said
that those particular premises were subject to the exemptions
contemplated by the Act.

On these grounds, therefore, first on the ground that even if
this man had not been a clerk, he was not within the exemption,
because he was in the premises with his wife and family and a
servant; and upon the second ground that being a clerk with a
salary of 150*l.* a year, he is not in the position of a " servant or
other person " contemplated by the Act; upon both these grounds
it appears to me that this appeal should be allowed.

I would merely add, that with reference to the difficulty which
there must be of drawing the line between cases under this Act,
I would say that the Commissioners must no doubt decide the
points which come before them as regards these matters; and
if in this case they had distinctly found as a fact that the caretaker in this particular instance was simply the caretaker, and
was a " servant or other person " within the Act, although we
might think the decision was erroneous I do not think we
should be justified in interfering; but in this case, under the
terms of the special case, the object of the Commissioners appears
to be to submit to the Court the very question, and that being

YEWENS *v*
NOAKES.

so, we are justified notwithstanding their belief that this was
the case of a caretaker and not of a "servant or other person"
within the Act—we are justified in deciding in the way in which
we have done.

Baggallay, L.J.—I agree in thinking that this appeal should
be allowed, and I prefer to rest my decision upon the ground
that upon the facts stated in the Special Case, Mr. Keppel had
not been regarded as a "servant or other person," dwelling in
the tenement in question for the protection thereof within the
intention and meaning of the Statute.

Without expressing any opinion as to whether, if Mr. Keppel
could be regarded as a "servant or other person," his dwelling
upon the premises together with his wife and other members of
his family would deprive the Respondent of the right to claim
exemption, I should be disposed to doubt whether that circumstance alone would deprive him of his right to exemption.

I will not state the grounds upon which I hold that Mr. Keppel
was not a "servant or other person" within the meaning of the
Act, because they have already been stated by Lord Justice
Thesiger, with whose remarks upon this part of the case I
entirely agree.

Appeal allowed, without costs.

PART XVIII.

No. 43.—In the Supreme Court of Judicature; before the Court of Appeal at Westminster.

Jones (Surveyor of Taxes) v. The Cwmmorthin Slate Company.

Income Tax, Schedule A., No. III., first and second rules.—Works for getting slate, are slate quarries within the first rule, and the fact of their being carried on underground will not bring them within the words " other mines" in the second rule.

At a meeting of the Commissioners of Income Tax for the Division of Ardudwy Uwch, in the County of Merioneth, held at the " Griffin" Inn, Penrhyndeudraeth, on the 28th day of March 1878.

Mr. Albert Bromwich as cashier to and on behalf of the Cwmmorthin Slate Company, Limited, appealed against a charge of 6,373*l.* made upon the Company in the assessment under Schedule D. for the Parish of Festiniog, for the year 1877–8, in respect of profits as a Slate Company under Rule 1 of No. 3 of Schedule A., 5 & 6 Vict., cap. 35.

The appellant contended that the concern was a mine and claimed to be assessed on the average profits of the five preceding years under Rule 2 of No. 3 of Schedule A., 5 & 6 Vict., cap. 35, (*a*) and that the concern came under the title "and other mines."

The appellant then explained that originally the concern was worked in the open, but for some years the slates have been got by means of levels driven straight into the mountain to a distance of from 250 to 300 yards, those levels are about 5 feet wide and 7 feet high, the whole process was carried on underground. Under the Metalliferous Act they are deemed to be a mine, also for Poor Law and other purposes.

The annexed document was also put in by the appellant, in which Mr. Justice Blackburn held the concern to be a mine.[*]

Mr. Jones, the Surveyor of Taxes, on the part of the Government, held the concern to be a quarry, and that the wording of

---

(*a*) This rule provides that the profits of " mines of coal, tin, copper, mundic iron, and other mines," shall be assessed on an average of five years.

[*] " The annexed document" was the short-hand writer's notes of the judgment in the case of *Sims* v. *Evans*, see note (*b*) next page.

Rule 1, No. 3 of Schedule A., 5 & 6 Vict. cap. 35, as follows:
" of quarries of stone, slate, limestone, or chalk, on the amount of
" profits in the preceding year," is decisive of the question, and
that it is impossible to regard a slate quarry as a mine for
Income Tax purposes.

We, the Commissioners present, were of the opinion, that the
concern was a mine, and gave our decision accordingly, whereupon the surveyor being dissatisfied, requested a case for the
opinion of Her Majesty's Judges, which we hereby state and sign
accordingly.

Given under our hands this 26th day of April 1878.

JOHN JONES.
A. OSMOND WILLIAMS.

In the Exchequer Division, the Court (Kelly, C.B., and Pollock, B.) reversed the decision of the Commissioners.

The Cwmmorthin Slate Company appealed.

A. L. Smith, for the Cwmmorthin Slate Company, the appellant in this Court.—The slate is worked by mining operations,
and the Court of Queen's Bench has held that for the purposes of
the Metalliferous Mines Act, 1872, this concern is a mine (b).
An open air working is a quarry, but work under-ground is
mining, and comes within the words "other mines" in the
second rule of No. III. In the case of the *Duchess of Cleveland*
v. *Meyrick* (c), a testator by codicil bequeathed "all shares in
mines," of which he should die possessed to his wife absolutely,
and it was held by Malins, V.C., that shares in a concern which
had formerly been a slate quarry but was then worked as a slate
mine passed under that bequest.

[*Bramwell, L.J.*—Had he any other mining property? *The
Solicitor General.* No; and I think that is given as the reason
for the decision (d).]

There is no distinction between a vertical shaft to the centre
of a mine and a horizontal level to the same point.

[*Brett, L.J.*—The distinction in this Act is not between the
modes of getting the thing, but between the things got. The
judgments of the Lord Chief Baron and Mr. Baron Pollock seem
to be given on that ground.]

Sir Hardinge Giffard, S.G., for Jones, Surveyor of Taxes.—
Although for certain purposes this working might be considered

---

(b) *Sims* v. *Evans*, before Blackburn, Quain, and Field, J.J., on the 2nd June 1875,
not reported

(c) L.R., 37 Ch. (N.S.), 125.

(d) At the date of the codicil the testator does not appear to have possessed any other
mining shares, but he afterwards acquired some, which were in his possession at the time of his death. Malins, V.C., in his judgment said "I have
"no doubt that his (testator's) object was to give to his wife. the present
"plaintiff, an interest in this quarry, but the course of dealing having so
"completely altered the nature of the works, he considered it a mine, and
"properly designated it as such in the codicil, not having, so far as we can
"judge, any other mining property in contemplation at the time."

as a mine, yet in popular language, although it be underground, it is a quarry. Cites a book entitled " Slate and slate-quarrying, " scientific, practical, and commercial: " by D. C. Davies, F.G.S., 1878, in which underground quarries are fully described, but the word " slate-mine " is not used. The decision under the Metalliferous Mines Act had reference to the express language of that Statute. According to the contention on the other side this concern, which was begun as a quarry, was in the first instance chargeable under the first rule on the profits of the preceding year, but the moment a level was cut its character was changed and it became chargeable under the second rule on an average of five years. This shows the extreme inconvenience, and almost absurdity, of that construction of the Act. The Legislature took a broad and general view of the way in which these things are worked, and in substance it is said that stone works and slate works are to be assessed in such a way, and iron works, and lead works in such another way. The words " other mines " in the second rule cannot be extended into " all other mines," because in the third rule we find " alum mines or works."

A. L. Smith, in reply, cited *Rex v. Inhabitants of Sedgley* (e), in which it was held that the question whether an excavation in the earth from which limestone is obtained be a mine or not is a question of fact.

Bramwell, L.J.—I am of opinion that this judgment must be affirmed. I really think the case is a clear one. The question is not what is the meaning of the word " mine " or the word " quarry " in the abstract, but what is the meaning of those words in this particular Statute. I think the meaning of them there is this, that the rule as to mines applies to such mines as are there mentioned, and " other mines " *ejusdem generis*. The words " other mines " clearly do not mean all other mines because there is special mention afterwards of " alum mines." Whether there are any other mines, metalliferous or other mines, in England, than those enumerated, I do not call to mind at the present moment, but even if there were not there are other metals no doubt than those enumerated in the second rule, and the word " other mines " might be very prudently put in by the person who drew the rule, to comprehend such cases if they should arise. I think therefore the meaning of " mines " in that rule is mines *ejusdem generis*. This certainly is not; and it seems to me, if Mr. Smith's argument were a valid one, it would come to this, that he was not liable to be assessed at all because this certainly is not a mine within the second rule, and unless it is a quarry it would not be within any rule at all. But really in my judgment the best thing you can say of it is that it is a quarry

19 Dec. 1878

(e) 2 B. & Ad., 65.

worked to a certain extent somewhat in the way that mines are
worked. It is a quarry worked by mining operations, but it is
clearly a quarry. I do not want to go into derivations on the
precise meanings of words, but one understands by a quarry a
work in which something is cut out in a block or a large shape,
and not a work in which the material is got out without reference to its size or shape, or make, as iron stone or iron ore,
or coals are, accordingly you speak differently of different stone
works, you say a stone quarry and a stone pit, but a quarry is
where the material is cut out in blocks. This to my mind is
clearly a slate quarry, worked however, owing to its nature and
condition, with certain mining operations, or operations such
as are used in mines. I think it is clear that the judgment
must be affirmed.

Brett, L.J.—I am of opinion that the judgment should be
affirmed. I thought that Mr. Smith did make out that as a
matter of fact, looking at the mode of working, this slate was
obtained by mining operations, and that in that sense this might
rather be called a mine than a quarry. I doubt whether anybody who went to look at these works, using the ordinary mode
of describing the working, would say that this was a quarry. He
would rather say that it was a slate mine, and it seems to me
that the Court of Queen's Bench so held, and, I think, rightly
held, that is to say, that the operation by which this slate was
obtained was a mining operation, and that it was therefore, so
far as the workpeople were concerned, a mine, and for that reason
the people who so worked were entitled to the protection of
miners within the other Statute, but nevertheless I am of opinion
that this comes within the first class of the Statute under which
the question arises, and not within the second class. It seems to
me that this Statute which is imposing a tax, is imposing that
tax upon that which is worked and not upon the mode of working it. It is true that the Statute speaks of one class of produce
as being obtained at a quarry, and of another class of produce
as being obtained at a mine, but I apprehend that the true intent
of using the words "quarries" and "mines" is only to fix the
place at which the tax is to be imposed, or in other words, the
persons upon whom the tax is to be imposed; that is to say,
those who are obtaining the profits of certain produce are to be
taxed in one way, and those who are obtaining the profits of
certain other produce are to be taxed in another way; and I
should think myself that the reason of the difference of average
is on account of the mercantile differences between the sales of
the different kinds of product. It is to be noticed that the tax
is upon profits. That implies a sale and a deduction of expenses,
and the difference of average probably is to be accounted for in
this way, and that it is well known that the profits on those matters
which are in the first class are tolerably uniform, whereas it is
equally well known that the profits in the second class are
exceedingly varying from year to year. Therefore in the first

class the Legislature have taken the one year and in the second
class they have taken an average of five years. That seems to me
to show that the words "quarries" and "mines" are really only
to fix the place and the person, and have nothing to do really
with the mode of working, and certainly nothing to do with the
subject-matter of the taxation. Then if that be true the question
is whether the slates are within the first class or whether they
are *ejusdem generis* as those which are mentioned in the second
class. It cannot be doubted that they are named in the first
class and they are not intended to be named in the second.
Upon the proper construction of the Statute. I have no doubt
that the decision appealed from is right. .

Cotton, L.J.—I am of the same opinion. We have not here to
decide whether or no, as a matter of definition, this work is a
mine or whether it is a quarry—what we have to decide is
whether the profits made from getting the slate out of its original
bed in the earth are to be dealt with under one or the other rule.
We had quoted to us yesterday a book in which even the working of slate by mining operations is called the quarrying of slate,
and reference is there made to underground as well as above-
ground quarries. That being so, I think the true interpretation
of this Act of Parliament is to say that one rule refers to working and raising such substances as slate and limestone, and that
the other refers to such substances as coal, tin, lead, copper,
mundic, and iron, and that the distinction is as to the classes of
things raised from the earth, and not as the modes in which in
particular instances they happen to be worked and raised. Of
course the decision in the Court of Queen's Bench upon that
other Act which was referred to is not at all inconsistent with
this. There the matter in question was held to be a mine within
the meaning of the Act intended to provide for the safety of
those who were engaged in certain workings—in certain shafts
or levels—but that is entirely beside the question as to whether
or no the profits made by raising from the earth this slate come
under the one rule or the other rule.

Appeal dismissed with costs.

No. 44.—In the High Court of Justice (Exchequer
Division), March 1880.

Watney & Co. -   -   -   -   *Appellants,*

Musgrave (Surveyor of Taxes) -   *Respondent.*

---

*Income Tax, Schedule D.—A brewer paying a premium for the
lease of a public-house, for the purpose of letting it to a
tenant under covenant to buy beer brewed by him, is not
entitled to a deduction on account of the gradual exhaustion
of the premium.*

Knowles v. M'Adam (a) *distinguished.*

Case stated for the Opinion of the Court by the Commissioners
for the Special Purposes of the Income Tax Acts, under
"The Customs and Inland Revenue Act, 1874," 37 & 38
Vict. c. 16 s. 9. as to Income Tax Assessment under
Schedule "D."

1. At the meeting of the Commissioners for Special Purposes
held at Somerset House on January 31st and February 4th, 1879,
for the purpose of hearing appeals under the Income Tax Acts
for the year ending the 5th April 1879, James Watney and
James Watney the younger, partners in trade, carrying on the
trade and business of brewers, under the style of Watney and
Company, at the Stag Brewery, Pimlico, in the Parish of Saint
Margaret, Westminster, in the County of Middlesex, duly
appealed against an assessment made on them under Schedule
D. of the Act 16 & 17 Vict. c. 34, in respect of the profits of their
trade.

2. The appellants were represented by the said James Watney
the younger. At the hearing of the appeal the Commissioners
made a considerable reduction in the assessment, but they
refused to allow a further reduction of 4,466*l.* which was claimed
by the appellants under the following circumstances.

3. The appellants made their profits in trade by brewing beer

---

(a) *Ante,* p. 161.

and by selling it to persons who might think fit to buy it, but in order to increase their trade it has for years been their practice to buy the leases for various terms of licensed public-houses and beer-houses, and then to let such houses to tenants who covenanted to buy of the appellants all the beer to be sold in such houses.

4. In order to obtain such leases the appellants are obliged in many cases to pay large premiums and to covenant to pay a fixed rent for a term of years.

5. When the appellants have acquired such leases they let the houses to tenants, and make a profit by the sale of their beer to such tenants who, as before stated, covenant to buy beer solely of the appellants. The profits made by the sale of beer to these tenants are included in the assessment, and the appellants claim that for the purpose of arriving at the just balance of the profits and gains of their said trade, it is necessary each year to make an allowance in respect of a portion of the amount which was paid by them to acquire the leaseholds, and without which they would not have been able to make any profits in respect of the same, and that such allowance represents only the portion of their capital exhausted during the year in the earning of the said profits.

6. The following instance has been stated in writing on the part of the appellants as an example.

7. The appellants had recently bought the lease of a public-house for 30 years, for which they paid a premium of 1,300l., and covenanted to pay the landlord a rent of 105l. a year. Such lease contained the usual covenants for the lessees to repair, &c. The appellants let such public-house to a tenant, who under his agreement is bound to buy of the appellants all beer to be sold in the house, and assuming that their gross profit from such sale would amount to 60l., which profit they could not have made unless they had expended the 1,300l. in purchasing the lease, they claimed that the balance of profits and gains on which they were to be assessed should be less than that sum of 43l., being the portion of the said sum of 1,300l. which had been exhausted during the year by reason of one year of the term having run out, namely, one 30th of the said sum of 1,300l. In the assessment to the income tax the 60l. profit from the sale of the beer was included.

8. The said sum of 4,466l. consisted of the aggregate of various sums relating to the leaseholds in which capital of the appellants was invested as mentioned in paragraphs 4 and 5, and arrived at in the same manner as the sum of 43l. mentioned in the last paragraph.

9. But for the expenditure of the capital to pay the premiums the leaseholds out of which profit is made, as mentioned above, could not have been acquired, nor such profit made, and each year a portion of the premium paid is exhausted.

10. The Commissioners were of opinion that the claim to reduce the assessment by 4,466l. ought not to be allowed.

WATNEY
v.
MUSGRAVE

11. The question for the opinion of the court is whether the Commissioners were right in refusing the said allowance. If they were right the assessment is to. be confirmed, but if they were not right then it is requested that this case be remitted to the Commissioners with the opinion of the court thereon, in order that they may reduce the assessment accordingly.

12. The said James Watney the younger, immediately after the determination of the said appeal by the Commissioners, expressed his dissatisfaction with the same as being erroneous in point of law, and duly required the Commissioners to. state and sign a case for the opinion of the Exchequer Division of the High Court of Justice under the provisions of the Act 37 and 38 Vict. cap. 16, which we have stated and do now sign accordingly.

Dated 15th April 1879.

D. O'CONNELL, } Special
R. M. LYNCH, } Commissioners.

Somerset House, London.

NOTE.—*At the hearing of the case a difficulty having arisen from the fact that the case does not set forth the amount of rent received by the appellants, the Attorney-General for the respondent expressed his willingness to admit, for the sake of argument, that the rent received did not cover the exhaustion of the premium.*

Grantham, Q.C., for the appellants.—Where the appellants have sunk a sum of money in purchasing the lease of a house, in which they can make a profit, a proportion of the money so sunk should be allowed every year off the gross profits they make. They are entitled to deduct all expenses they are put to in order to make a profit. Whether it is by advertising, or by paying premiums which will be lost at the end of the term, the cost of increasing sales is a deduction from the gross profit.

[*Kelly, C.B.*—If any brewer chooses to give dinners to the publicans, and in return they say, " Well, we will buy a quantity " of beer from you," you might just as well deduct that.]

Brewers pay large sums of money for leases in order to get tenants compelled to buy their beer. It makes no difference whether they pay a sum down or a sum per annum for the right of selling beer at a particular place, and they are entitled to deduct the cost to which they have been put to be able to sell that particular beer. Before the publican can take the beer the brewers have to provide the house, and in providing the house they sink the premium.

Cites *Knowles* v. *M'Adam* (a) and quotes from judgment of *Kelly, C.B.* (b). "But he has right to take into consideration, "before the amount of the profit can be said to be ascertained, "all that he has expended of every description in order to enable "him to acquire the right to the article, that is, the right to "dispose of it, and thus to obtain the sum in respect of which "he is to be assessed." Now that is exactly the case here (c). The statute forbids any deduction "for any disbursements or "expenses whatever not being money wholly and exclusively "laid out or expended for the purposes of such trade" (d), and the converse must hold true that you are entitled to deduct money which is wholly and exclusively laid out for trade, and this money is so laid out and lost, never to be recovered, but to be completely exhausted.

Sir John Holker, A.G., for the respondent, was not called on to reply.

Kelly, C.B.—I am clearly of opinion that the Crown is entitled to the judgment of the Court. The distinction given to the costs and expenses, the aggregate of which is to be deducted from the price realised by whatever quantity of beer is made and sold in the course of the year, is that it is merely and only the costs and expenses of production of the article that are to be deducted. In this case it is claimed to deduct not the costs of production of the article, but expenses incurred and money disbursed to promote and increase the sale of the article after it has been produced and for the expenses of sale. I am not aware of any authority to be found in the statutes or any text book for deducting such expenses in ascertaining the amount of profit which is to be assessed under the Income Tax Act. I am not aware that there is any authority whatever for any deduction of any expenses whatsoever incurred after the beer is produced and really to promote or increase the sale. In the first and ordinary case, I do not go so far back as the imposition of the Income Tax during the administration of Pitt and Perceval and afterwards Lord Liverpool, but I take the cases and authorities and practice which have existed under the Act of Parliament from the time when Sir Robert Peel revived the Income Tax in 1842, from that time to the present day, that is a period of some 38 years; and I am not aware that in the whole of that period any exception or qualification has ever been introduced by law or under authority, or on the construction of the statutes, which at all affects the mode in which the profits of the trade of a brewer shall be assessed and taxed, and that is confined entirely

11 March 1880.

(a.) *Ante*, p. 161.   (b.) *Ante*, p. 173.
(c.) *See per* Kelly, C.B., *post*, p 278
(d.) 5 & 6 Vict. c. 35. s. 100 1st rule, 1st and 2nd cases, Sch. D.

WATNEY
v.
MUSGRAVE.

and exclusively to the costs and expenses incurred in the production of the article. I do not pretend to enumerate in detail
what all those costs and expenses are, but amongst other things,
the Attorney-General or the Solicitor-General in the course of
this argument alluded to one third, or in some cases it might
possibly be the whole, but in the case referred to it was one third
of the rent of the premises or building or buildings in which or
upon which the beer was produced. Without those premises and
paying for them the rent, the beer could not be produced. It
could not be produced in the open air; you must have a brewery,
and you must have building or buildings of some kind in a
case like this, a very large and spacious building in which the
beer is to be manufactured. The annual cost of that building,
whether it be one third of the supposed rent or any other proportion, is necessarily a deduction and a proper deduction. Then
there is also the cost of the raw material, without which the beer
could not be produced. That raw material in this case consists
of very large quantities of malt and hops, and the costs of those
large quantities of malt and hops to the brewer of course constitute a portion of the expenses of production. Besides that,
in a case like this, if there be, as I suppose there are, a great
many servants and labourers and persons of that description
employed in the manufacture, that is, in the production of the
beer, their wages must be taken into consideration. To put a
supposed case with regard to the precise amount of the profits of
these gentlemen in one year in which they carry on their trade,
supposing they sell beer, and the aggregate price of the whole
quantity sold is half-a-million of money in the course of the year;
and of that 400,000l. is spent in producing the beer, that is, in the
annual rent of the premises within which the beer is produced
and without which it could not be produced at all, the price of the
large quantities of malt and hops, and the wages of a great
number of labourers whom they may employ in assisting in the
manufacture of the beer, and there may be other expenses which
may be found enumerated sometimes in the statute or statutes,
and sometimes in books of authority, to which I need not refer,
whatever they may be; whenever in actual practice the question
has been considered, or where the question has been considered
in a court of law as in a case like this, they will be found to be
exclusively, simply, and merely costs incurred in the production
of the article which is sold. Now, for the first time, as far as I
am aware, I may say from the time of the income tax being first
laid on by Pitt until the present year, it is sought to include in
the sums to be deducted, so as to ascertain the balance which
would constitute the net profits of the concern, the amount of
profits liable to be assessed to the income tax. It is contended
that sums of money expended no matter how, not in the manufacture, but after the production of the article, and after the
completion of all that is necessary to determine what the expenses
of production are, and what the quantity of beer sold is, it is now
for the first time sought to deduct from the price of the beer, in

order to ascertain the net profits, the expenses incurred after the
beer is produced, and indeed after the beer is sold, or it may be
not after it is sold, but after it is produced and completely ready
for sale, in order to promote the sale or increase the quantity of
the sale. I myself by way of illustration put the case of advertisements. No doubt many houses, and the trade of brewers for
aught I know, and I believe it has been so, but many houses
engaged in the manufacture of various articles of trade, after
those articles are prepared, or while those articles are preparing,
with a view of increasing the quantity of the sale, spend a large
sum of money in advertisements. That practice has existed
more, perhaps, of late years than before; but in more than 30
years that have passed since Sir Robert Peel revived the income
tax I am not aware that any attempt has been made until the
present day in the present case to claim to deduct from the
amount received from the sale of the whole quantity of beer sold
during the year the costs of advertisements by means of which
the quantity of beer sold in the course of the year may be considerably increased, but which has no reference and bears no
part at all in the production of the article. The present case is
another instance not of advertisements, but of expenses incurred,
it may be, or a sum of money paid in order to induce a publican
or a class of publicans to purchase quantities of beer, which is
exactly of the same character as those incurred in advertisements.
It may be necessary to take those expenses into consideration in
ascertaining the net profits of a commercial firm during any
given year or time; but inasmuch as it has never been attempted,
or even suggested, that such expenses should be taken into consideration in ascertaining the difference between the cost of production and the money realised in the course of the year by the
sale of beer, I do not think we ought, even if the justice of
the case required it, to deal with this in the way suggested. No
doubt the sale of any commodity is promoted, so that the profits
of the trader are greatly increased, by means of incurring
expenses of this character, such as the expense of purchasing
leases and purchasing public-houses, and letting them to tenants
who become purchasers of the beer, by means of which, no doubt,
the beer sold in the course of the year may be considerably increased, and thus the profits during the year may be considerably
increased; but before I can admit any such anomaly, I shall
require that the title to deduct such expenses, such an outlay of
money, should have been affirmed by some court of appeal, or
expressly authorised by some Act of Parliament to meet the
justice of the case. Those expenses are of a totally different
character from the mere cost of production, and in the absence
of any Act of Parliament, I cannot myself be the party to admitting what would be an entirely new principle in relation to the
operation of the income tax, and which, whether it would be just
or not, would be a novelty to the law of England. Under these
circumstances, it only remains for me to observe that in the case
cited (a) the decision to which I was a party, and which has been

adverted to by my brother Hawkins in the course of the argument, was a totally different case. It was a case in which it was really a portion of the actual expenses incurred in the production of the article in question, it was a depreciation to a very considerable amount of the property which had been leased to the parties, and which had occurred in the course of the production and by means of the production of the article itself; and the mere *dicta* of the judge's casual expressions in half a sentence are not what should be regarded as a decision in favour of this appellant's contention. It appears that the expenses which are sought to be deducted here are of a character and description quite unconnected with the production of the article, and if they are to be allowed to be deducted, it must be by an Act of Parliament or a decision at least of a court of the last resort.

Hawkins, J.—I am also of opinion that the Crown is entitled to our judgment. I have listened very attentively, and I have thought a good deal over the matter, and the arguments of Mr. Grantham failed to convince me that there is any ground at all for allowing this deduction. The assessment is to be made on the profits of trade, and the Act under which the assessment is made prescribes the mode in which the assessment is to be made. It sets forth in the schedules those matters which may or may not be claimed by way of deduction, and I have failed to find in the Act itself any ground whatever for saying that a public-house which is bought for the purpose of inducing persons to deal with the occupier of it is to be considered as a trade deduction so as to diminish the amount of profit of trade which would otherwise be assessable. I fail to see anything at all which would justify such a contention. The house itself, it seems to me, is a matter totally apart from the trade. The trade consists to the brewer in manufacturing the beer, in selling it to the customer, and when it has got into the customer's hands at a fixed price, the price that is paid for the beer *minus* all those charges which are strictly incidental to the production of it which are clearly those matters which are to be deducted, then remains the profit which is liable to be assessed. As at present advised, I do not myself go to the extent of saying that under no circumstances could the costs of conveying the beer to the consumer be allowed as a deduction, as a legitimate trade expense, and for this reason: If the costs of conveying the beer to the customer were not incurred, the customer himself would be obliged to go to the brewery and fetch his own beer, and it stands to reason that the price paid at the brewery by the customer who carried it away and delivered it at his own house for himself, would be less than the price which it realised where the brewer himself conveys it to the public-house, and delivers it to his customer. It is not necessary, however, to determine that question, though I am far from saying myself that such a deduction as that might

(a.) *Knowles* v. *McAdam*, *ante* pp. 161 and 275.

not be allowed; but here there is a considerable expense incurred in carrying on the trade. I do not find the house in the least degree has anything to do either with the manufacture of the beer, with the conveyance of it from the brewery to the house, or with the price paid by the public for it. The house, it is true, is or may be a valuable adjunct to the brewery by increasing the number of customers; but the house, whether it yield a profit or a loss to the brewer, is not in the least degree connected with the trade profit of the brewery. The rent of the house is not taken into consideration by the brewer in considering what are the incomings of the trade, neither are the outgoings of the house to be taken into consideration when we come to consider the out-goings of the trade. If there is a lease and the rent does not equal that which the brewer has to pay for it, surely he cannot deduct the difference between the rent which he receives and the rent which he has to pay as an expense of trade, the trade of a brewer consisting of the manufacture of beer, and the selling it to his customer. I cannot myself, I confess, see the difference between this case and the illustration I put in the course of the argument. If a man has a piece of ground upon which he is minded to speculate and build for himself a brewery and carry on in that the business of a brewer, if in order to bring custom to his brewery he builds on that ground a couple of hundred houses, imposing upon each tenant of the houses he has so built the obligation of buying beer from him, and by the sale of the beer to his customers so obtained he makes a profit of 1,000*l.* or 2,000*l.* a year, I cannot see myself upon what possible grounds it can be said, if the tenants did not pay their rents to the landlord, that the rent which was so in arrear should be charged against the profits of the trade as being expenses incurred in the trade. I cannot myself see the difference between those two cases, and it seems to me that to contend it is right to deduct the rents from the profits of trade under such circumstances, because they have resulted in a loss, would be to contend that which was absolutely absurd. I think myself they are two distinct things, the trade and the house; they are generally distinct, and I think on that ground the expense incurred in respect of the house cannot be deducted, and therefore the Crown is entitled to the judgment of the Court.

The Attorney-General.—I presume the appeal will be dismissed with costs?

The Lord Chief Baron.—Yes.

PART XIX.

No. 45.—In the Court of Exchequer (Scotland).—First Division.

16th July 1880.

Clerk (Surveyor of Taxes) *v.* The Commissioners of Supply for the County of Dumfries.

Income Tax.—Schedule A. Police Stations, the property of the local authority, yielding no rent, are chargeable under the General Rule 5 & 6 Vict. c. 35 s. 60, Schedule A., No. 1.

At a meeting of the General Commissioners of Income Tax for the County of Dumfries, held in the Sheriff Court House, Dumfries, on the 12th day of May 1880.

Mr. Thomas Brisbane Anderson, treasurer, and for behoof of the Commissioners of Supply of the County of Dumfries, appealed against the following charges under Schedule A., made upon the Commissioners of Supply for the Police Committee in respect of premises belonging to them, and occupied as police stations in the following parishes and on the following valuations :—

						£
Carlaverock	-	-	-	-	-	9
Dunscore	-	-	-	-	-	6
Glencairn	-	-	-	-	-	10
Hoddam	-	-	-	-	-	5
Kirkmichael	-	-	-	-	-	4
Langholm	-	-	-	-	-	14
Moffat	-	-	-	-	-	15
Penpont	-	-	-	-	-	7
Annan	-	-	-	-	-	10
Dumfries	-	-	-	-	-	115

In whole, 195*l.* ; Duty, 1*l.* 4*s.* 3*d.*

The Appellant stated, as a preliminary ground of appeal, that at a meeting of Income Tax Commissioners, held at Dumfries on 1st May 1872, the Commissioners of Supply appealed against charges made on the premises in the parish of Dumfries belonging to them, and occupied as police stations, and relief was granted. He further stated that the police stations in Dumfriesshire had never been assessed, and that, except in the instance before referred to in 1871, no attempt had been made to assess them.

On the merits the Appellant stated that the Commissioners of Supply are bound by statute (21 & 22 Vict. cap. 72) to maintain a police force in the county for the public service; that, in order to fulfil the said statutory obligation, it is necessary to provide police stations at different police districts into which the county is divided, which stations are used partly as strong-rooms and partly as lodgings for the police constables serving in the several districts; that said stations yield no return, the strong-rooms being used for the temporary detention of offenders, and the lodgings and offices being given to the constables, as being necessary for the performance of their duties. The police force is annually inspected by a Government officer, and if he reports it efficient (as has always been done in the case of the Dumfriesshire force), the Treasury grants one-half of the expense of pay and clothing, and the rest of the cost of the establishment is defrayed by means of the "Police Assessment," which is a compulsory rate levied upon all lands and heritages within the county. He contended—(1) that the decision of 1st May 1872 should be taken as a precedent in the present case; (2) that the stations are not assessable, as they yield no rent; (3) that as the stations are provided by means of a compulsory rate, the assessing of them would be imposing a tax upon a burden. He referred to the following cases:—The Queen v. Inhabitants of St. Martin's, Leicester, and The Queen v. Inhabitants of Castle View; 2 Queen's Bench, 493.

The Surveyor of Taxes, Mr. John Clerk, replied.—*Preliminary* —That the decision of 1st May 1872 was by the Commissioners for General Purposes, and for a different year than the present, and did not prevent liability for the assessment for the present year being considered and decided by the General Commissioners, and a case taken by either party in the Court of Exchequer; at the time the former decision of 1872 was given by the General Commissioners, there was no appeal to the judges of the Supreme Court, that right having been introduced in 1874 by the Act 37 Vict. cap. 16. sect. 9.

On the merits, the Surveyor submitted:—(1.) That the stations are chargeable under the general rule Schedule A. of the Act 5 & 6 Vict. cap. 35, which provides that all heritages capable of actual occupation shall be charged on the annual value at which they are worth to be let, whatever may be the purpose for which they are occupied; that there is no exemption for such property as here forms the subject of appeal, in the said Act, or in any subsequent Act relating to Income Tax. (2.) The allowance by the Government is for pay and clothing and not in respect of such stations, and the duty, if the Commissioners are found liable, would not be payable by Her Majesty. (3.) That the decisions referred to by the Appellant applied to assessments for local rates only; that the Crown was not the owner or joint-owner of the stations, which belonged to and were upheld by the country.

The Commissioners were of opinion that they were bound by the decision of the Commissioners in 1872, and granted relief of the assessment, but the Surveyor, being dissatisfied with this decision, craved that a case might be stated for the opinion of the Court, and which is here stated accordingly.

DAVID BOYLE HOPE,

Chairman.

Counsel having been heard,

The Lord President.—In this case a charge has been made upon the Commissioners of Supply of Dumfriesshire for payment of Income Tax under Schedule A., in respect of certain premises belonging to them and occupied as police stations. The power of the Commissioners of Supply to erect these stations is contained in certain clauses of the Act 20 & 21 Victoria, the General Police, Scotland, Act ; and it is stated in the case that in order to fulfil the statutory obligations of the Commissioners in maintaining a police force in the county, it is necessary to provide police stations at different districts into which the county is divided, and these stations are used partly as strong rooms and partly as lodgings for the police constables serving in the several districts. The stations yield no return, the strong rooms being used for the temporary detention of offenders, and the lodgings and offices being given to the constables, as being necessary for the performance of their duties. Now under the statute 20 & 21 Victoria, the Commissioners of Supply perform very important functions in respect of the local government of the county in regard to matters of police, and they are no doubt acting in a public capacity. They acquire the property, which they use as police stations under the 55th and 56th sections of the statute which I have already cited. The 55th section provides that it shall be lawful for the Commissioners to order that station houses and strong rooms——(reads clauses). And to facilitate the acquisition of property for this purpose certain portions of the Lands Clauses Consolidation Act are incorporated with this Police Statute by section 56. Now in these circumstances it cannot admit of doubt that the Police Commissioners are the owners of this heritable property, and I think it is just as clear from the statement in the case that they are also the occupants. Some of the police constables reside at some of these stations, but they do so merely as the servants of the Commissioners of Supply or of the Police Committee, and they are liable to removal without any notice at all whenever it serves the convenience of the police management. The property therefore is acquired for the purpose of local government, and it is owned and occupied by the Commissioners of Supply. Now it is very difficult to see how property so situated should not come under the rule No. 1 in Schedule A. of the Income Tax Act. It must be kept in

mind that under Schedule A. the assessment is this, "for all lands,
"tenements, and hereditaments, or heritages in Great Britain,
"there shall be charged yearly in respect of the property thereof
"for every 20s. of the annual value thereof the sum of 7d.;"* and
then the first rule of Schedule A.† is this: "The annual value of
"lands, tenements, hereditaments or heritages charged under
"Schedule A. shall be understood to be the rent by the year at
"which the same are let at rack rent, if the amount of such
"rent shall have been fixed by agreement commencing within
"the period of seven years, &c., but if the same are not so let
"at the rack rent at which the same are worth to be let by the
"year, which rule shall be construed to extend to all lands,
"tenements, and hereditaments or heritages capable of actual
"occupation, of whatever nature, and for whatever purpose
"occupied or enjoyed, and of whatever value, except the pro-
"perties mentioned in No. 2 and No. 3 of this Schedule." Now
Nos. 2 and 3 of the Schedule have no sort of application to
property of this description, and it is needless to refer to them;
and there is not in this statute any clause that can be cited conferring an exemption on property held for such purposes as that
we are dealing with. We can find no ground of exemption
within this Income Tax Act of the 5th and 6th Victoria, nor in
any subsequent Act upon that subject. But it is said that this
is property occupied for the purposes of the Government of the
country, and in support of that contention reference is made to
those provisions of the Police Act which authorise the Treasury
to advance to the Commissioners of Supply a certain proportion of
cost of maintaining the police force. But it must be kept in
view that what the Treasury undertake, and are entitled to
undertake, to do in respect of these provisions, is to pay a certain
portion of the pay and clothing of the constables, and nothing else.
The cost of maintaining stations is not defrayed by the Treasury
at all, nor could any portion of the money advanced by the
Treasury be lawfully applied to such a purpose. On the contrary,
the Act (as I have already shown) by the 55th section provides
that all the cost of acquiring and maintaining the stations is to
be defrayed out of the police assessment, out of a local assessment. In these circumstances it appears to me that it is impossible to say that in charging income tax against this property
any charge is made against the Queen or the Queen's Government. The charge is made against a certain public body
administering the statute for local purposes and as part of the
local government, and I know no ground upon which it can be
said that property so occupied is exempt from income tax.

---

* His Lordship quoted the words in 5 & 6 Vict. c. 35. s. 1. which is repealed.
The words in 16 & 17 Vict. c. 34. s. 2. are, "Schedule A. For and in respect of
"the property in all lands, tenements, hereditaments, and heritages in the United
"Kingdom, and to be charged for every twenty shillings of the annual value
"thereof."

† 5 & 6 Vict. c. 35, s. 60. Schedule A. No. 1.

Indeed I should say it is impossible to hold that, unless you could find within the Income Tax Acts themselves some clause of exemption. I take no account of that class of cases which has been referred to, and upon which the argument of the Respondents mainly turned, viz., those cases in which certain premises have been found not liable in Poor Rates or other local assessments of that kind; because I think these cases have no application to a question under the Income Tax Acts. I don't think it necessary to inquire whether these cases are all reconcilable with the principles laid down in the House of Lords in the case of the Mersey Docks and in the case of the Clyde Navigation Trustees. That question may perhaps arise for consideration hereafter, and it would be very improper to prejudge it. The cases, I think, have no application to the present question. I proceed entirely upon the plain rule laid down in Schedule A. of the 5th and 6th of Victoria, and upon that ground I am of opinion that the deliverance of the Commissioners is wrong and must be reversed.

Lord Deas.—I am of the same opinion, and very clearly so. I think these Commissioners of Police are both the owners and the occupiers of these stations, and I do not know of any ground upon which it can be held that they are not liable for this assessment.

Lord Mure.—I am entirely of the same opinion. It appears to me that, looking to the nature of the property, and the nature of the occupation, its falls distinctly within the provision of rule No. 1 of Schedule A. which your Lordship has read; and the fact that the police force is to a certain extent supported by Government money, cannot, I apprehend, take the occupiers or owners of these premises in which the police force is located from time to time out of the provisions of the Act, more especially when, in addition to the rule which your Lordship has read, we find that in the 8th rule of No. 4 it is expressly provided how the income tax is to be levied from parties who occupy official houses, plainly contemplating that under this Income Tax Act there is no exemption of property occupied for such public purposes from the taxes laid on by that statute. In addition to what your Lordship has said with reference to the plain distinction which there is between the Poor Rate cases in England and in this country, I observe, in looking over the opinions of Lord Cranworth and Lord Chancellor Westbury in the Mersey Docks case, that the opinion of both these noble Lords proceeded upon this very special ground applicable to poor rating in England, viz., that in the particular statute that they were dealing with the name of the King is not mentioned at all. Lord Westbury says, at page 122, "The only occupier exempt from the operation "of the Act is the King, because he is not named in the statute." But I think your Lordship's observation that these cases apply to poor rating exclusively, and have nothing to do with income tax rating, is sufficient for us to hold that they are not authorities in dealing with a point of this sort.

Lord Shand.—I am of the same opinion. Regarding this as raising a question as to the property tax, and the property tax only, it appears to me that the statute by which that tax is imposed plainly includes this subject. I think the Surveyor, Mr. Clerk, in the propositions which he has submitted, and which form part of this case, states very clearly and succinctly the true argument in regard to this question, and I adopt entirely the propositions so stated by him as part of my judgment.

Lord President.—Then we reverse the decision of the Commissioners, and remit to them to sustain the assessment.

PART XX.

No. 49.—In the Court of Exchequer (Scotland).—First
Division.
6th February 1879 and 29th April 1880.
In the House of Lords.
7th April 1881.

Coltness Iron Company v. Black (Surveyor of Taxes).

*Income Tax.—Deduction not allowable for Expenses of Pit-
sinking.*
Knowles v. McAdam, No. 26, *overruled* (a).

At a Meeting of the Commissioners for General Purposes acting COLTNESS
under the Property and Income Tax Acts for the Middle IRON
Ward of the County of Lanark, held at Hamilton, upon the BLACK.
7th day of November 1878, for the purpose of hearing and
disposing of appeals under the Acts for the year ending
5th April 1879.

The Coltness Iron Company, carrying on business at Coltness,
in the parish of Cambusnethan, and elsewhere in the county of
Lanark, appealed against the assessment made on them under
Schedule D of the Act 5th and 6th Victoria, caput 35, intituled
"An Act for granting her Majesty Duties on Profits, arising
"from Property, Professions, Trades, and Offices," and subsequent Income Tax Acts referring thereto, in respect of the
profits arising from their business for the year preceding in so
far as the said assessment includes a sum of 9,027l., being the
cost incurred by them in sinking new pits; and for which they
maintained they were not assessable.

The Coltness Iron Company stated, and it is the fact, that for
a number of years they have carried on business as coal and iron
masters, and have opened up several mineral fields, sinking new
pits at their own expense from time to time as the old ones
have become exhausted; and they submitted that, in ascertaining the profits upon which they are liable to be assessed
under the said Act, there ought to be deducted from the gross
annual receipts derived from their business, the sums expended
by them in sinking the said pits.

They explained, and it is believed to be the fact, that when
a mineral field is wrought out, the pits on it become useless to
them, and they receive no compensation from the landlord or
any one else in respect of them, and that they have no means of

(a) *Ante*, p. 161.

compensating themselves for the cost of these pits other than out of the gross annual returns derived from the minerals worked from them. They contended that, until these outlays are allowed them, the profits of their business are not ascertained.

The Appellants further contended that, whatever might have been the interpretation of the law prior to the passing of the Customs and Inland Revenue Act, 1878, they were entitled, under the twelfth section of that Act, to the deduction they claimed.

The Surveyor of Taxes, Mr. Thomas Morton Black, maintained that the deduction claimed is not included, either expressly or by inference, among those allowed by the Act 5th and 6th Victoria, caput 35; that the cost of sinking new pits is an expenditure and investment of capital, and so cannot form a deduction from the annual profits of the concern; but, on the contrary, by the terms of the Act 5th and 6th Victoria, caput 35, section 100 (Rule Third for Schedule D), it is specially disallowed as a deduction.

The Surveyor farther maintained that the 12th section of the Customs and Inland Revenue Act, 1878, founded on by the Appellants, did not apply, as it only empowered the Commissioners to allow such deduction as they may think just and reaso .able, as representing the diminished value by reason of wear and tear during the year of "any machinery or plant used "for the purposes of the concern"; and he founded upon the judgment of the Court in the case of the appeal of Messrs. Addie & Sons, dated 30th January 1875, as an authority, to the effect that the expense of pit-sinking was a charge upon capital, and could not form a deduction in estimating profits under the Property and Income Tax Acts. He contended that the assessment on the Coltness Iron Company had been made in conformity with rules of the Acts of Parliament on the profits of the preceding year; that no sums could be legally deducted in estimating such profits, except those which had been actually expended in earning the profits for such year; and that the Coltness Iron Company had been allowed deduction for all such expenses, including an allowance for the depreciation of machinery and plant, under section 12 of 41 Vict., cap. 16.

The Appellants maintained, in answer, that there could be no profits until the expenditure of sinking was repaid, any more than there could be profits before the wages of the miner in working the minerals were repaid—that, in fact, the sinking of the pits was expenditure in winning the minerals, and not, as the surveyor stated, an investment of capital. In the case of wages expended in sinking, there is nothing, they contended, to represent capital, and the money so expended cannot be an investment, because it can never be recovered. The Appellants further stated that, in the case of Knowles and others v. M'Adam, the High Court of Justice in England (Exchequer Division) had allowed deduction even for the exhaustion of estate or capital by the working of minerals, and the Appellants claimed as a right that the whole cost of winning, of which the sinking of COLTNESS shafts is a part, should be allowed. IRON COMPANY v.

The Commissioners dismissed the appeal, being of opinion that BLACK. the deduction claimed was not admissible under the Income Tax Acts, and that, upon a sound construction of these Acts, no deduction ought to be allowed in respect of pit-sinking.

Upon said appeal being dismissed, the Coltness Iron Company, being dissatisfied with the determination of the Commissioners as being erroneous in point of law, declared their dissatisfaction, and required a case for the opinion of the Court, in terms of the Act 37 & 38 Vict., cap. 16, sec. 9, and the present case has been stated and signed accordingly.

JOHN MEEK, Commissioner.
G. A. LOCKHART, Commissioner.

Counsel having been heard.

The Lord President.—My Lords, the Appellants here, the Coltness Iron Company, carry on a very extensive business as coal masters in the county of Lanark, and they have been assessed for income-tax in respect of the profits arising from their business, but they complain of the assessment because the Surveyor of Taxes has failed to give them a deduction which they claim of no less than 9,027*l.*, which they state to be the cost incurred by them in sinking new pits. Now, they have not said, and it does not appear upon the face of this case, within what period that expenditure has been made, but that really does not affect the principle upon which our judgment must proceed. The state of the fact, as appearing upon the case, is that the Company have been carrying on business for a number of years, and have opened up several mineral fields, and sunk new pits at their own expense from time to time as the old ones have become exhausted. That is the statement of the case made to us by the Commissioners. Now, as has just been suggested by the Lord Advocate, it does not appear to me that that presents a different case in principle from this more simple case, that a tenant of a mineral field has sunk one pit, and one only, and has proceeded to work out the whole subject of the lease by means of that one pit. The only difference arises from the circumstance that the Coltness Company carry on this business upon a very large scale, and instead of having a small mineral field to work, as other people have, they have very large mineral fields, probably belonging to different proprietors, and they require in the prosecution of their business to sink half a dozen pits or 20 pits, where a smaller man would sink only one.

Now, what the Company maintain upon that state of the fact is, that in ascertaining the profits upon which they are liable to be assessed under the Act, there ought to be deducted from the gross annual receipts derived from their business the sum expended by them in sinking the said pits.

My Lords, if this case were new, it would be necessary to examine the clauses of the Income Tax Act, 5 & 6 Vict., but it appears to me that the case of Addie, which we decided in the year 1875, is directly applicable to the present. In that case, Messrs. Addie claimed a deduction of two sums, 5,525*l.* and 4,435*l.*, being a per-centage for pit sinking and depreciation of buildings and machinery, and that they maintained upon the ground that the sinking of new pits, though it was only an occasional thing, is still fairly to be considered as annual expenditure, and not expenditure of capital. The view that the Court took in that case was that the pit and the machinery and buildings connected with it were to be dealt with as a single subject, and that the creation of that subject—the pit with its machinery and buildings—was brought about by a proper expenditure of capital; and accordingly the deduction was there disallowed. Now, since that case was decided, there has been an alteration in the rule regarding deductions introduced by the Customs and Inland Revenue Act of 1878; and whereas formerly no deduction whatever was allowed for tear and wear of machinery and plant, it is now provided by the 12th section of that statute that, notwithstanding any provision to the contrary contained in the Income Tax Acts, the Commissioners shall, in assessing profits or gains of any trade, manufacture, adventure, or concern in the nature of trade, chargeable under Schedule D, or the profits of any concern, chargeable by reference to the rules of the Schedule, allow such deduction as they may think just and reasonable, as representing the diminished value, by reason of wear and tear during the year, of any machinery or plant used for the purposes of the concern, and belonging to the person or company by whom the concern is carried on. Of course, whenever the case occurs, we shall be quite ready—as I dare say the Surveyor of Taxes will be ready without appeal—to give effect to this new enactment; but there is no point raised here upon a deduction for machinery or plant. The deduction claimed here is a deduction in respect of the expense of sinking the pit. The case of Addie is certainly trenched upon by this new legislation to this extent, that it may be necessary in future to distinguish between the pit and the machinery and buildings connected with the pit, for the purpose of allowing a deduction on the ground of tear and wear of machinery and plant; but as regards the pit itself it does not alter the law in the slightest, and so far as the pit is concerned, and the expense of sinking the pit, the case of Addie, I apprehend, remains in full force.

I am therefore of opinion that we must follow the same course here, and affirm the decision of the Commissioners.

Lord Deas.—My Lords, after what we formerly decided, I think it quite unnecessary to say more than that I concur in what has been said by your Lordship.

Lord Mure.—I also concur. I think that the 12th section of the late Act plainly does not apply to the capital expended in

sinking the pit, but merely to the wear and tear of the machinery COLTNESS
used in that pit; and on the broad question, looking at the IRON
third rule in sec. 100 and at sec. 159 of the original Income Tax COMPANY *v.*
Act, I am of opinion that this is an expenditure of capital which BLACK.
falls within the provisions of those sections, which expressly
provide that those things shall not be a deduction from profit.

Lord Shand.—My Lords, this case is expressly decided by the
case of Addie; but, having taken no part in that decision, I
may add that I entirely concur in it. This case raises, I think,
a question of general principle, and not a question of what may
occur in any special case—the general question being whether
the expense of sinking shafts for the purpose of getting at the
minerals underground is an expenditure of capital, or is to be
treated like wages expended in working out the minerals themselves. It may be that special cases may arise which fall under
a different rule from the general rule. I can only say at this
moment that it does not occur to me that there are any special
circumstances of that kind here. On the matter of general
principle the question simply is, whether this is capital expenditure or not. I think it is matter of notoriety that such
operations are treated as capital expenditure, and that year after
year, as a company of this kind goes on, they write off part of
that capital expenditure, treating it as such. But whatever
may be the practice in that respect, I think that is a reasonable
course in itself. We have no information as to the depth of
these particular shafts. It may be that the minerals are at a
comparatively shallow depth, perhaps 90 or 100 fathoms, and
we know there are many mineral fields, if not here, at least in
England, where there is a great depth of sinking to be performed, 300, 400, or 500 fathoms, and it would be a very
extraordinary thing, if you had sinking of that kind, and a great
deal of it perhaps through hard rock, involving enormous expenditure, that that should be treated in any other way than as
expenditure of capital in order to reach the mineral you are
about to work. The case is obviously quite different from that
which was put in argument in reference to stirring the soil for
the purpose of getting at stone lying near the surface, in which
practically the whole operation is that of cutting the stone, and
where you have no expenditure which you can fairly distinguish
from ordinary expenditure. But I may further say this, that I
should even accept the test which the Appellant's Counsel has
put here upon the question whether this is capital expenditure
or not. Mr. Balfour in his argument suggested the view that
capital expenditure was really to be taken as only of that class
for which you would get a return when you came to sell the
subject. I know of no expenditure for which you will get a
better return in selling a subject than the expenditure in sinking
a mine. If a man who has taken a lease of minerals has not
begun to sink a shaft he gets so much for the subject if he comes
to sell it; but if he has sunk several shafts down to the minerals

he gets a direct return from that capital expenditure; so that even applying the Appellant's own test, it is demonstrable that this is a proper expenditure upon capital. I have only to add that I do not think the later Act of Parliament has the least bearing upon the question that we are now determining, I mean the clause relating to the tear and wear of plant and machinery.

Lord President.—Affirm the determination of the Commissioners, with expenses.

An appeal having been made to the House of Lords, the case was remitted by their Lordships to the Commissioners for amendment.

AMENDED CASE for the COLTNESS IRON COMPANY, under " The Customs and Inland Revenue Act, 1874 (37 and 38 Vict., cap. 16) "

For the Opinion of Court.

At a meeting of Commissioners for general purposes, acting under the property and Income Tax Acts for the Middle Ward of the County of Lanark, held at Hamilton, upon the 7th day of November 1878, for the purpose of hearing and disposing of appeals under the Acts for the year ending 5th April 1879.

The Coltness Iron Company carrying on business at Coltness, in the parish of Cambusnethan, and elsewhere in the county of Lanark, appealed against the assessment made on them under Schedule D of the Act 5th and 6th Victoria, caput 35, intituled " An Act for granting Her Majesty Duties on Profits, arising from Property, Professions, Trades, and Offices," and subsequent Income Tax Acts referring thereto, in respect of the profits arising from their business for the year preceding, in so far as the said assessment includes a sum of 9,027*l.*, being the cost incurred by them in sinking new pits; and for which they maintained they were not assessable.

The Coltness Iron Company stated, and it is the fact, that for a number of years they have carried on business as coal and iron masters, and have opened up several mineral fields, sinking new pits at their own expense from time to time as the old ones have become exhausted; and they submitted that, in ascertaining the profits upon which they are liable to be assessed under the said Act, there ought to be deducted from the gross annual receipts derived from their business, the sums expended by them in sinking the said pits.

They explained, and it is believed to be the fact, that when a mineral field is wrought out, the pits on it become useless to them, and they receive no compensation from the landlord or any one else in respect of them, and that they have no means of compensating themselves for the cost of these pits other than out of the gross annual returns derived from the minerals worked from them. They contended that, until these outlays are allowed them, the profits of their business are not ascertained.

The Appellants further contended that, whatever might have been the interpretation of the law prior to the passing of the Customs and Inland Revenue Act, 1878, they were entitled, under the twelfth section of that Act, to the deduction they claimed.

The surveyor of taxes, Mr. Thomas Morton Black, maintained that the deduction claimed is not included, either expressly or by inference, among those allowed by the Act 5th and 6th Victoria, caput 35; that the cost of sinking new pits is an expenditure and investment of capital, and so cannot form a deduction from the annual profits of the concern; but, on the contrary, by the terms of the Act 5th and 6th Victoria, caput 35, section 100 (Rule Third for Schedule D), it is specially disallowed as a deduction.

The surveyor farther maintained that the 12th section of the Customs and Inland Revenue Act, 1878, founded on by the Appellants, did not apply, as it only empowered the Commissioners to allow such deduction as they may think just and reasonable, as representing the diminished value by reason of tear and wear during the year of "any machinery or plant used for the purposes of the concern;" and he founded upon the judgment of the Court in the case of the appeal of Messrs. Addie and Sons, dated 30th January 1875, as an authority, to the effect that the expense of pit-sinking was a charge upon capital, and could not form a deduction in estimating profits under the Property and Income Tax Acts. He contended that the assessment on the Coltness Iron Company had been made in conformity with the rules of the Acts of Parliament on the profits of the preceding year; that no sums could be legally deducted in estimating such profits, except those which had been actually expended in earning the profits of such year; and that the Coltness Iron Company had been allowed deduction for all such expenses, including an allowance for the depreciation of machinery and plant, under section 12 of 41 Vict., cap. 15.

The Appellants maintained, in answer, that there could be no profits until the expenditure of sinking was repaid, any more than there could be profits before the wages of the miner in working the minerals were repaid—that, in fact, the sinking of the pits was expenditure in winning the minerals, and not, as the surveyor stated, an investment of capital. In the case of wages expended in sinking, there is nothing, they contended, to represent capital, and the money so expended cannot be an investment, because it can never be recovered. The Appellants further stated that, in the case of Knowles and others v. M'Adam, the High Court of Justice in England (Exchequer Division) had allowed deduction even for the exhaustion of estate or capital by the working of minerals, and the Appellants claimed as a right that the whole cost of winning, of which the sinking of shafts is a part, should be allowed.

The Commissioners dismissed the appeal, being of opinion that the deduction claimed was not admissible under the Income Tax Acts, and that, upon a sound construction of these Acts, no deduction ought to be allowed in respect of pit sinking.

Upon said appeal being dismissed, the Coltness Iron Company, being dissatisfied with the determination of the Commissioners as being erroneous in point of law, declared their dissatisfaction, and required a case for the opinion of the Court, in terms of the Act 37 & 38 Vict., cap. 16, sec. 9, and the present case has been stated and signed accordingly.

JOHN MEEK, Commr.
A. E. LOCKHART, Commissioner.

In terms of the order of the Court of Exchequer, of date 11th March 1880, pronounced on a petition, presented in pursuance of the remit made by an order of the House of Lords, of date 1st August 1879, to have the foregoing case amended and adjudicated on, and praying their Lordships to remit the case to the Commissioners, in order to the same being amended by adding thereto, in form of schedules or otherwise :—(1.) Statement of the amount expended by the Company in sinking pits, and charged to capital account, from 30th June 1858 to 30th June 1878; (2.) Statement of pits exhausted from 30th June 1858 to 30th June 1878, showing the total cost in sinking the pits, the depth of them, and the length of time they were in operation; (3.) Statement of the amount expended on pit-sinking, and charged to capital account, from January 1872 to 30th June 1878, giving the depth of each pit, (4.) List of pits exhausted from January 1872 to 30th January 1878, giving the depth of each pit, when the sinking of the pit commenced, when each pit was exhausted, and the cost of sinking each pit; (5.) List of pits at present working, giving the depth of each pit, when the sinking of each pit commenced, and when the output commenced, and the expense of sinking each pit; also by adding a statement as to the schedules and rules of the schedules of the Income Tax Acts on which the assessment of the duty was made on the Appellants; also by adding a statement explaining how the sum of 9,027l., claimed as a deduction from the assessment by the Appellants, is arrived at..

We, the Commissioners foresaid, amend the above case as follows :—

I. There are appended hereto statements and lists, Nos. 1, 2, 3, 4, and 5, containing the information required by the order of Court, as also a plan signed as relative thereto.

II. The mines and ironworks of the Appellants were charged and assessed to the duties, in the manner directed in Schedule A, No. III., of the Act 5 & 6 Vict. c. 35, and according to the rules prescribed by Schedule D of the said Act, as far as such rules

are consistent with the said No. III. (29 Vict. cap. 36. sec. 8).
The provisions of the said Schedule A, No. III., so far as
material, are as follows:—" The annual value of all the properties
"herein-after described shall be understood to be the full
"amount for one year, or the average amount for one year, of
"the profits received therefrom within the respective times
"herein limited. 1st. Of quarries of stone, slate, limestone, or
"chalk, on the amount of profits in the preceding year; 2nd.
"Of mines of coal, tin, lead, copper, mundic, iron, and other
"mines, on an average of the five preceding years, subject to the
"provisions concerning mines contained in this Act; 3rd. Of
"iron works, gas works, salt springs or works, alum mines or
"works, water works, streams of water, canals, inland naviga-
"tions, docks, drains, and levels, fishings, rights of markets and
"fairs, tolls, railways, and other ways, bridges, ferries, and other
"concerns of the like nature, from or arising out of any lands,
"tenements, hereditaments, or heritages on the profits of the
"year preceding: The duty in each of the last three rules to be
"charged on the person, corporation, company, or society of
"persons, whether corporate or not corporate, carrying on the
"concern, or on their respective agents, treasurers, or other
"officers having the direction or management thereof, or being
"in the receipt of the profits thereof, on the amount of the
"produce or value thereof, and before paying, rendering, or
"distributing the produce or the value, either between the
"different persons or members of the corporation, company, or
"society engaged in the concern, or to the owner of the soil or
"property, or to any creditor or other person whatever having
"a claim on or out of the said profits, and all such persons,
"corporations, companies, and societies respectively shall allow
"out of such produce or value a proportionate deduction of the
"duty so charged, and the said charge shall be made on the said
"profits, exclusively of any lands used or occupied in or about
"the concern."

The Schedule served on the Appellants, with a view to their
being assessed to the said duties, was in the form and in the
terms of the Schedule appended hereto.

III. The sum of 9,027l. claimed as a deduction from the
assessment by the appellants, does not represent the cost of pit-
sinking during the year, but is a sum arrived at by calculating
two shillings a ton on iron made, and a penny halfpenny a ton
on coal sold during the year; it being estimated that this will
properly represent the amount of capital expended on making
bores and sinking pits which has been exhausted by the year's
working. The cost of making bores and sinking pits is charged
in the books of the company to an account called "Sunk
Capital Account," and is written off annually by a sum computed
at the respective rates above specified, on the quantities of iron
made and coal sold in the year, as representing the capital
expended on pit-sinking, exhausted by the year's working. The
working charges deducted and allowed in ascertaining the

profits for assessment include the whole cost of getting and raising the minerals, after the pits are sunk, and of manufacturing the metal and selling the iron and coal, and the general expenses of the concern.

A. E. LOCKHART, Commissioner.
JOHN MEEK, Commissioner.

Hamilton, 16th April 1880.

STATEMENTS AND LISTS Nos. 1, 2, 3, 4, and 5, WITH RELATIVE PLAN BEFORE REFERRED TO.

I.—STATEMENT of the AMOUNT expended by the COMPANY in SINKING PITS, and charged to CAPITAL ACCOUNT, from 30th June 1858 to 30th June 1878.

	£	s.	d.
1859	5,808	5	9
1860	3,749	15	2
1861	7,839	11	10
1862	4,402	19	8
1863	5,702	2	0
1864	10,970	5	0
1865	9,857	13	9
1866	13,014	12	1
1867	11,320	3	2
1868	8,154	16	10
1869	6,708	3	3
1870	2,647	11	6
1871 and 1872	8,119	2	2
1873	22,555	9	1
1874	16,234	12	10
1875	11,307	1	2
1876	6,795	4	7
1877	5,990	11	5
1878	4,647	2	3
	£165,825	3	6

A. E. L.
J. M.

II.—STATEMENT of PITS exhausted from 30th June 1858 to 30th June 1878, showing the total cost of SINKING the Pits, the depth of them, and the length of time they were in operation.

COLTNESS
IRON
COMPANY v.
BLACK.

	£ s. d.	£ s. d.	Depth. Fthms.	In Operation. Years.
Exhausted in year ending:—				
June 30, 1859. No. 2 Whitestripe Pit	1,148 6 4		45	12½
"　　" 　*Bores	2,097 17 4	3,246 3 8		
"　1860. Eastfield Engine Pit	4,716 9 2		90	12
"　　" 　Langshaw No. 1 Pit	432 2 10		45	13½ 4½
"　　" 　Whitehill Nos. 1 & 2 Pits, say	680 0 0		30	Average 2½ each.
"　　" 　Newmills No. 1 Pit	321 16 0		25	1½
"　　" 　Birkenshaw Mines	969 5 2		—	2½
"　　" 　Bores	1,395 8 7			
"　　" 　†Conjoint Pit, pumping water	516 6 2	8,451 7 11		
"　1861. Woodend No. 3 Pit	951 2 0			··
"　　" 　Bores	1,402 10 11			
"　　" 　Conjoint Pit, pumping water	2,877 9 8	4,481 2 7		
"　1862. Woodend No. 4 Pit	805 12 10		20	Never in operation ⅔ths.
"　　" 　Mountcow Coal Pit	485 5 6		9	
"　　" 　Bores	1,631 7 6			
"　　" 　Conjoint Pit, pumping water	1,565 1 6	3,977 7 4		
"　1863. Hareshawmoor Pits	1,156 12 11		9	3½
"　　" 　Bores	2,074 9 6			
"　　" 　Conjoint Pit, pumping water	1,443 16 2	4,654 18 7		
"　1864. Goodockhill No. 2 Pit	363 11 11		30	3½
"　　" 　Bores	1,866 15 0			
"　　" 　Conjoint Pit, pumping water	1,234 7 7	3,464 14 6		
"　1865. Goodockhill No. 1 Pit	914 11 0		30	6
"　　" 　No. 3 Stonecraigs Pit	385 15 3		26	5
"　　" 　Bores	1,008 12 1			
"　　" 　Conjoint Pit, pumping water	1,356 2 6			
"　　" 　Westsidewood, Pool, &c.	855 12 9		—	9½
"　　" 　Eastfield No. 4 Pit, say	5,000 0 0		98	9½
"　　" 　Knowes No. 1 Pit	1,499 18 6	10,920 12 1	60	6½
"　1866. Bores	92 14 2			
"　　" 　Conjoint Pit, pumping water	1,813 4 6			
"　　" 　Woodend No. 1 Pit	942 5 10		54	12
"　　" 　Birkfield No. 3 Pit, say	500 0 0	3,348 4 6	13	7½
"　1867. Victoria Pit	355 17 8		40	8½
"　　" 　Muldron Nos. 1 and 2 Pits	455 18 2		10	3½ & 3½
"　　" 　Conjoint Pit, pumping water	2,255 5 6			
"　　" 　Bores	614 3 10			
"　　" 　Headsmuir No. 1 Pit, say	500 0 0		14	5½
"　　" 　Hunterfield No. 1 Pit, say	500 0 0	4,676 5 2	30	3½
"　1868. Conjoint Pit, pumping water	1,863 1 3			
"　　" 　Springhill Pit	745 7 10		24	5½
"　　" 　Bores	1,909 13 5			
"　　" 　Herdshill No. 1 Pit, say	500 0 0	5,018 2 6	16	11
"　1869. Crofthead Nos. 7 and 8 Pits	317 11 3		48 & 14	1½
"　　" 　Conjoint Pit, pumping water	815 9 10			
"　　" 　Bores	856 16 4	1,989 17 5		
Carried forward		54,150 16 3		...

* Bores are for the purpose of ascertaining the existence of minerals.

† This was a pit sunk by the Coltness Iron Company and Messrs. Dixon, the adjoining mineral proprietors, at mutual expense, for draining their respective mineral fields. The sums entered for pumping water represent the one-half of the cost of pumping paid by the Coltness Iron Company.

				Depth.	In Operation.
		£ s. d.	£ s. d.	Fthms.	Years.
Brought forward		.. .. ..	54,180 18 2		
Exhausted in year ending :—					
June 30, 1870.	Eastfield No. 5 Pit ..	1,164 3 4		110	9½
" "	Benthead Pit ..	68 6 0		65	4
" "	Nos. 3 and 4 Muldron Pits ..	394 8 7		12	3½ & 2½
" "	Burnbank Pit	685 8 7		26	25
" "	Bores	1,302 12 3			
" "	Conjoint Pit, pumping water	400 16 4			
" ♪	*Conjoint Pit	7,415 0 0		84	10½
			11,284 15 1		
" 1871.	Langshaw No. 3 Pit ..	562 2 11			
" "	Bores	77 1 5			
			639 4 4		
" 1872.	Falahall Pit and water Pit	6,095 18 8		100	7½
" "	No. 3 Father Air Pit ..	100 1 2		60	
" "	No. 4 Greenhead Blind Pit	116 6 11		34	
" "	Bores	13 12 5			
			6,332 19 2		
" 1873.	Knowes No. 2 Pit ..	420 4 3		14	3½?
" "	Muldron No. 5 Pit ..	250 16 11		13	4½?
" "	Foulskyes Air Pit ..	304 11 2		17	
" "	No. 6 Garriongill Air Pit	140 16 8		22	
" "	No. 1 do.	683 8 10		49	
" "	Garriongill Mine ..	155 0 5			
" "	Bores	206 14 5			
" "	Davisdykes No. 2 Pit ..	343 17 0		10	3½
			2,435 9 8		
" 1874.	Greenhead No. 4 Pit ..	1,026 4 8		34	6½
" "	Garriongill No. 8 Air Pit	75 11 0		22	
" "	Do. No. 9 do. ..	175 10 2		54	
" "	Hallcraig Communication Pit and Mine ..	610 1 3		24	
" "	No. 1 Duntilland Outlet	329 2 8			
" "	Bores	1,138 10 2			
" "	Garriongill No. 2 Pit ..	442 7 8		22	10
			3,797 7 7		
" 1875.	Muldron No. 6 Pit ..	489 11 1		14	4½
" "	Whitestripe No. 3 Pit ..	59 17 2		30	3½
" "	No 9 Garriongill Pit, Outlet	159 1 8		54	
" "	No. 9 do. Air Pit	415 13 11		54	
" "	No. 9 do. Stone Mine	222 8 4			
" "	No. 6 do. Air Pit	191 11 8		32	
" "	†Bores	4,505 10 3			
" "	Allanton Pit	412 12 6		12	5½
" "	No. 1 Duntilland, Outlet Mine	40 0 0			
			6,500 6 7		
" 1876.	No. 2 Royal George Pit	537 16 1		40	18½
" "	Harthill Blind Pit ..	155 10 0		36	
" "	Do. Communication Mine.. ..	192 0 6			
" "	Muirhead No. 2 Air Pit	963 15 1		114	
" "	Do. No. 3 do. ..	23 4 0		80	
" "	Bores	967 6 6			
" "	Garleton	2,100 14 10		28	5
			4,994 7 0		
" 1877.	No. 2 Stonecraigs Pit ..	1,129 1 1		56	23½
" "	Bores	170 1 6		30	20½
" "	No. 2 Bush Pit	801 12 5		34	11½
" "	Garriongill No. 3 Pit ..	414 0 0			
			2,514 15 0		
" 1878.	No. 2 Duntilland Pit ..	2,714 3 9		62	15½
" "	No. 4 Stonecraigs Escape Pit	116 5 7		24	
" "	Garpel	6,894 6 8			4½
" "	Bores	323 10 9			
			10,048 6 2		
			102,878 6 10		

* Sum paid by the Coltness Company as their share of sinking Conjoint Pit, which was not used by them after 1870.

† Includes 3,715l. 19s. 11d. for Bores at Bo'ness, where Minerals were not found.

A. E. L.

J. M.

III.—STATEMENT of the amount expended on PIT SINKING, and charged to Capital Account, from January 1872 till 30th June 1878, giving the depth of each Pit.

COLTNESS
IRON
COMPANY v.
BLACK.

Depth in Fathoms.	NAME OF PIT.	Amount.
		£ s. d.
	SALSBURGH—	
65	No. 1 Duntilland Pit	569 2 8
62	No. 2 do.	364 18 7
	COLTNESS—	
54	No. 4 Stonecraigs Pit	3,952 6 7
17	Foulsykes Pit	468 6 5
18	No. 3 Royal George Pit	1,237 19 8
46	No. 5 Greenhead Pit	2,511 16 0
76	No. 6 do.	2,349 19 6
4	Newmains Mine	65 10 11
56	No. 2 Stonecraigs Pit	16 19 10
40	No. 2 Royal George Pit	52 1 7
34	No. 4 Greenhead Blind Pit	38 19 0
60	Father Pit	98 2 2
49	No. 1 Garriongill Air Pit	553 1 3
54	No. 6 do.	4,351 2 3
84	No. 7 do.	3,006 19 11
19	No. 8 do.	2,493 1 3
54	No. 9 do.	4,421 4 0
42	No. 5 do.	61 7 0
	HALLCRAIG—	
46	Hallcraig Pit	1,946 2 2
	BRAIDWOOD—	
60	No. 2 Mayfield Pit	3,769 2 9
45	Wilton Pit	178 12 1
	BO'NESS (Bores)	1,540 á
	WOODEND—	
56	No. 5 Pit	26 15 7
	GARLETON	1,714 1 5
	HARTHILL—	
134	Harthill Blind Pit, Bores and Mine	1,405 5 11
126	Polkemmet Bores	776 6 5
114	No. 1 Muirhead Pit	12,336 10 5
80	No. 3 do.	10,295 15 0
	MULDRON—	
24, 16, 14	Nos. 7, 8, and 9 Pits	4,514 9 2
	GARPEL	6,894 6 3
	SUNDRY PLACES	61 2 0
		71,964 10 2*

* This sum includes 10,357l. 10s. 9d. applicable to Bores and Air Pits.

A. E. L.
J. M.

OLTNESS
RON
OMPANY c.
LACK.

IV.—LIST of PITS EXHAUSTED from January 1872 to 30th January 1878, giving the Depth of each Pit, when the Sinking of the Pit commenced, when each Pit was Exhausted, and the cost of Sinking each Pit.

Depth in Fathoms	NAME OF PIT.	Commenced Sinking.	Commenced Output.	Exhausted.	Cost of Sinking.
					£ s. d.
62	SALSBURGH—				
	No. 2 Duntiliand Pit	July 1862	July 1864	May 1876	2,714 3 9
	COLTNESS—				
56	No. 2 Stonecraigs Pit	May 1852	April 1854	November 1876	1,120 1 1
40	No. 2 Royal George Pit	October 1856	March 1856	November 1876	537 16 1
34	No. 4 Greenhead Pit	August 1865	June 1887	September 1873	1,026 4 8
32	No. 2 Garriongill Pit	October 1862	June 1864	June 1874	856 7 8
30	No. 3 do.	May 1865	August 1865	February 1872 }	801 12 5
	No. 2 Bush Pit ..	March 1854	July 1856	February 1877	
	No. 3 Whitestripe Pit	January 1853	August 1853	October 1874	89 17 2
	HARTHILL—				
100	Fallahill Pit .. }	Nov. 1863 {	January 1865 {	April 1872 }	6,003 18 8
100	Do. Water Pit }		January 1865 {	April 1872 }	
84	No. 1 Conjoint Pit }	June 1855 {	June 1859	March 1870 }	7,415 0 0
	No. 2 do. }		June 1859	March 1870 }	
14	No. 2 Knowes Pit ..	October 1866	February 1869	October 1872	499 4 3
	MULDRON—				
13	No. 5 Pit..	November 1867	November 1868	November 1872	250 16 11
14	No. 6 Pit..	February 1869	August 1870	October 1874	439 11 1
	GARPEL—				
	Garpel (two Pits) ..	August 1872	July 1873	December 1877	6,894 6 8
	GARLETON—				
	Garleton (two Pits)	May 1871 (Purchased this date).	May 1671	June 1876	2,166 14 10
	DAVISDYKES—				
12	No. Allanton Pit ..	February 1866	September 1866	February 1875 }	756 9 6
10	No. 2 Davisdykes Pit	February 1866	April 1869	September 1873 }	
	BONESS BORES	1870	No minerals found.	1876	3,715 19 11
	BORES AND AIR PITS..	—	—	—	8,617 8 5
					44,013 13 1

A. E. L.
J. M.

V.—LIST of PITS at PRESENT WORKING, giving the Depth of each Pit, when the Sinking of each Pit commenced, and when the Output commenced, and the Expense of Sinking each Pit.

COLTNESS
IRON
COMPANY v
BLACK.

No. on Plan.	Depth in Fathoms.	NAME OF PIT.	Commenced Sinking.	Commenced Output.	Expense of Sinking.
					£ s. d.
		SALSBURGH—			
1	52	Drumbowie Pit	July 1860	June 1861	1,006 10 9
2	58	Mountcow Pit	July 1860	June 1863	1,793 11 0
3	65	No. 1 Duntilland Pit	Jan. 1862	Jan. 1864	2,718 7 10
		COLTNESS—			
4	48	No. 1 Stonecraigs Pit	March 1849	December 1849	588 14 8
5	54	No. 4 Stonecraigs Pit	March 1867	June 1874	3,962 6 7
6		and Escape			
7	63	No. 3 Greenhead Pit	Nov. 1863	Nov. 1865	1,729 8 6
8	46	No. 5 do.	April 1872	May 1875	5,065 7 6
9	76	No. 6 do.	April 1874	June 1876	2,849 19 6
10	26	Orindledyke Pit	Dec. 1864	August 1865	869 7 7
11		and Escape			
12	17	Foulsykes Pit	May 1866	May 1872	713 6 5
13		and Escape			
14	54	No. 1 Garriongil Pit (purchased this date)	Sept. 1863	Sept. 1863	}
15		and Escape			
16	45	No. 4 do.	April 1865	April 1866	4,596 12 1
17	43	No. 5 do.	July 1865	Sept. 1866	
18	54	No. 6 do.	March 1866	Nov. 1872	4,794 0 2
19	94	No. 7 do.	March 1866	Nov. 1872	5,340 17 5
20	19	No. 8 do.	August 1870	Nov. 1872	2,635 7 4
21		and Air Pit			
22	54	No. 9 do.	Feb. 1873	Dec. 1874	4,421 4 0
23		and Escape			
24	60	Pather Pit	April 1866	Oct. 1866	1,805 6 4
25		and Escape			
26	18	No. 3 Royal George Pit	January 1873	August 1873	1,537 19 8
		HALLCRAIG—			
27	46	Hallcraig Pit	Nov. 1864	Sept. 1872	3,517 6 8
28		and Escape			
		BRAIDWOOD—			
29	45	Wilson Pit	March 1856	March 1857	1,726 12 1
30		and Escape			
31	46	No. 1 Mayfield Pit	Jan. 1857	Sept. 1857	650 0 0
32	60	No. 2 do.	March 1872	Jan. 1879	3,849 7 3
		WOODEND—			
33	54	No. 2 Pit	July 1857	Dec. 1858	980 0 0
34	56	No. 5 Pit	Feb. 1865	May 1866	1,397 10 0
		HARTHILL—			
35	134	Harthill Pit	Oct. 1865	April 1869	9,515 14 10
36	126	Polkemmet Pit	Jan. 1864	June 1867	9,184 10 5
37	114	No. 1 Muirhead Pit	Nov. 1871	April 1875	12,561 14 3
38		and Escape			
39	80	No. 3 do.	April 1876	April 1879	10,296 15 0
40		and Escape			
		MULDRON—			
41	24	No. 7 Pit	Sept. 1871	March 1873	}
42	16	No. 8 Pit	Sept. 1871	March 1873	4,514 9 2
43	14	No. 9 Pit	August 1872	Feb. 1874	}
					97,587 7 1

A. E. LOCKHART, Commissioner.

JOHN MEEK, <i>Comr.</i></div>

JOLTNESS
IRON
COMPANY v.
BLACK.

SCOTLAND.

No. 11 (B.)   INCOME TAX.   [Schedule D.]

For the Year 1878, ending 5th April 1879.

NOTICE requiring Return for Assessment for the year commencing 6th April 1878, and ending 5th April 1879, in respect of the Annual Value or Profits arising from the following concerns, viz.:—

1. Mines of Coal, Tin, Lead, Copper, Mundic, Iron, and other Mines;
2. Quarries of Stone, Slate, Limestone, or Chalk, Iron Works, Gas Works, Salt Springs or Works, Alum Mines or Works, Water Works, Streams of Water, Canals, Inland Navigations, Docks, Drains, and Levels, Fishing Rights of Markets and Fairs, Tolls, Ways (*except Railways, for which a special form of Return is provided*), Bridges, Ferries, and other concerns of the like nature.

To the Person named on the back hereof.

IN pursuance of the Acts of Parliament for granting to Her Majesty Duties on Profits arising from Property, Professions, Trades, and Offices, you are hereby required to fill up the following Statement of the Annual Value or Profits chargeable for the said Year, in respect of any Concern or Concerns above described carried on by

and deliver such Statement, under cover and sealed, at my Office, *indicated on the back hereof,* or at the office of the Commissioners at
within Twenty-one days from the date hereof, in default whereof you will incur a Penalty,—that is to say, TWENTY POUNDS and TREBLE DUTY if sued for before the Commissioners of the District, or FIFTY POUNDS if sued for in any of Her Majesty's Courts.

The sum chargeable as the Annual Value or Profits of a MINE of any description for the said Year, is to be returned on an average of the *Five preceding Years,* or if the working commenced within five years on an average from the period of commencing such Workings, either ending on the day of the year when the Annual Accounts of the Concern have been usually made up, or on the 5th day of April 1878. If the working commenced within the year of Assessment, the return should be according to the best of your knowledge and belief, and the grounds on which the amount shall have been computed should be stated for the information of the Commissioners.

The sum chargeable as the Annual Value or Profits of the several OTHER Concerns above described for the said Year is to be returned according to the Profits of the *preceding* year.

The Annual Value or Profits of these several Concerns is to be returned, and the duty charged, upon the Produce or Value thereof before paying rendering, or distributing such Produce or Value, either between the different Persons or Members of the Firm, Corporation, Company, or Society engaged in the Concern, or to the Owner of the Soil or Property, or to any other Person having a claim on or out of the said Profits;

COLTNESS IRON COMPANY v. BLACK.

No Deductions are allowed—

On account of Loss not connected with or arising out of the Concern;

Nor on account of Capital withdrawn therefrom;

Nor for any Sum employed or intended to be employed as Capital therein;

Nor on account of any Capital expended on Improvement or extension of such Concern;

Nor on account of any annual Interest, Annuity, or other annual Payment out of such Profits or Gains;

Nor for any Disbursements or Expenses which shall not be Money wholly and exclusively laid out in working the Concern:

Nor for any Disbursements or Expenses of Maintenance of the Parties, their Families, or Private Establishments;

Nor for any Sum paid as Salary to a Partner in any Concern, or for any Sum paid as Income Tax on the Profits or Gains of any Concern.

Deductions are allowable—

For the Supply or Repair of Implements, Utensils, or Articles employed, not exceeding the sum usually expended for such purposes according to an average of Five Years, or in the preceding year, as the case may be.

For Bad Debts, or such part thereof as shall be proved to the satisfaction of the Commissioners to be such, and Doubtful Debts according to their Estimated Value.

For any Average Loss not exceeding the Actual Amount of Loss after Adjustment.

For the Sum representing diminished Value by reason of wear and tear of Machinery or Plant. Amount to be stated.

DEPRECIATION OF MACHINERY OR PLANT.

Amount deducted in arriving at profits where the Machinery or Plant belongs to the Person or Company carrying on the Concern, or is let to such Person or Company so that the Lessee is bound to maintain and deliver over the same in good condition :—	Amount of Rent paid for the use of the Machinery or Plant where the burden of maintaining and restoring the same falls upon the Lessor, in which case no deduction for Depreciation is allowable to the Lessee :—
Amount £_____	Amount £_____

You may select whichever of the following modes of Assessment you think fit:—

1st. By the Commissioners of the District in the Ordinary Course.

2d. By the Commissioners of the District under a Number or Letter.

3d. By the Commissioners for Special Purposes appointed by the Crown.

If you elect to be assessed under a Number or Letter, or by the Special Commissioners, you will signify your desire in your Declaration. In the former case, the Return should be sealed up and directed to the Clerk to the Commissioners; in the latter, it should be directed to the Surveyor of the District, and endorsed "For Special Assessment." The Return, if not delivered at the Office of the Commissioners, should be delivered at my Office, to be forwarded to the Clerk to the Commissioners, or the Surveyor, as the case may require; your name and place of abode having been first superscribed thereon.

Given under my hand this   day of   1878.

DAVID PATRICK, *Assessor.*

STATEMENT.

Style of Firm, Company, &c., &c., carrying on the Concern.	If not a Public Company, state names and addresses of Partners.	Places at which the Business is carried on.	Profits chargeable *without deduction* of Rent or Royalty or other Payments, as above directed.
			£
			Whereof—
			Profits ... ... £
			Rent or Royalty ... £
			£

DECLARATION.

I,   do hereby declare, that all the particulars required in this Notice to be returned, as appertaining to me, in relation to the Duties arising in respect of the several and respective concerns mentioned or referred to in this Notice, are in every respect fully and truly stated herein, according to the best of my judgment and belief, and according to the Rules and Regulations of the Acts of Parliament in that behalf. *And I desire to be assessed by*†

Dated this   day of   1878.

Signed _____

† Here state whether you desire to be assessed by the Commissioners of the District under No. or Letter, or by the special Commissioners. If not, strike out the words (in Italics) "*And I desire*," &c.

First Division, January 7, 1881.

The Lord President.—In the case originally presented to the Court, on the 28th of January 1879, by the Coltness Iron Company, against the determination of the Commissioners of Income Tax for the Middle Ward of Lanarkshire, they maintained that, from the amount of the profits of their business for the year ending 5th April 1878, as assessed to the income tax, there ought to have been deducted a sum of 9,027l., being the cost incurred by them in sinking new pits. The case stated, as matter of fact, that for a number of years the Appellants have carried on business as coal and iron masters, and have opened up several mineral fields, sinking new pits at their own expense from time to time as the old ones have become exhausted; that, when a mineral field is wrought out, the pits on it become useless to them, and they receive no compensation from the landlord or any one else in respect of them; and that they have no means of compensating themselves for the loss of those pits, other than out of the gross annual returns derived from the minerals worked from them. Upon these facts, the Appellants maintained that there could be no profits till the expenditure of sinking was repaid, any more than there could be profits before the wages of the miners in working the minerals were repaid; that, in fact, the sinking of the pits was expenditure in winning minerals, and not an investment of capital; that in the case of wages expended in sinking, there is nothing to represent capital, and the money so expended cannot be an investment, because it can never be recovered.

On these statements and this contention, the Court gave judgment, on the 6th of February 1879, holding that the case thus presented to them did not in principle differ from the case of the tenant of a mineral field sinking one pit and one only, and proceeding by means of that pit to work out the whole minerals let to him. They therefore affirmed the determination of the Commissioners, and refused the proposed reduction on the grounds stated in the judgment and the authority of the earlier case of Addie v. the Solicitor of Inland Revenue, in which it was expressly decided that the cost of sinking a pit and carrying on the business of mining is an expenditure of capital, and it cannot be taken into account in assessing the profits of the business to the income tax.

The Coltness Company appealed to the House of Lords, and it appears that in the course of the Appellants' argument at the bar, facts and considerations were advanced and urged, which were not stated or suggested in the case on which the Court gave judgment. On the contrary, on the conclusion of the argument, the House of Lords, " being of opinion that the state-" ment of facts contained in the case submitted to the Court of " Sessions on this matter is not sufficiently full to enable this " House finally to dispose of the points of law on which its " decision is asked," was pleased to remit the case to this Court in order that it might be amended, "pursuant to the power "conferred for that purpose by the Act of Parliament of the "37th and 38th years of Her present Majesty, chap. 16, and "that an adjudication be had on such an amended case and "reported to this House."

The case has been amended accordingly, and the Court having heard a full argument from counsel, now proceed to give their judgment, in compliance with the order of the House.

The amended case contains the following new and important statements in addition to certain details as to pit sinking, which will be immediately noticed:—*First*, the working charges deducted and allowed in ascertaining the profits for assessment include the whole cost of getting and raising the minerals, after the pits are sunk, and of manufacturing the metal and selling the iron and coal, and the general expenses of the concern. *Secondly*, the sum of 9,027*l*., claimed as a deduction from the assessment, does not represent the cost of pit-sinking during the year, but is a sum arrived at by calculating 2*s*. per ton on iron made, and 1½*d*. per ton on coal sold during the year, it being estimated that this will properly represent the amount of capital expended in making bores and sinking pits which have been exhausted by the year's work. It will be observed that while in the original case the deduction asked by the Appellants was in respect of the cost incurred by them in sinking new pits, and it was contended that in fact the sinking of the pits was expenditure in winning the minerals, and not, as the Surveyor stated, an investment of capital, the Appellants no longer maintain that the deduction claimed does not represent capital invested or expended in carrying on the business of the Company. On the contrary, it is now distinctly stated that the sum proposed to be deducted from the profits represents the amount of capital expended on pits and exhausted by the year's working.

The facts regarding pit-sinking in the Appellants' mineral field, as now amplified and explained, may be summarized as follows:—*First*, during twenty years, from 30th June 1858 to 30th June 1878, the Appellants expended in sinking pits 165,825*l*. 3*s*. 6*d*., or on an average annually about 8,500*l*. This includes the cost of many pits used only as air pits, and pits for pumping water, as well as the expense of bores made in searching for minerals. *Secondly*, during the same period many pits have become exhausted. The total cost of sinking those pits, including air pits, pumping pits, and bores, as above, was 102,678*l*. 6*s*. 10*d*., being about an annual average of 5,000*l*., varying from 639*l*. 4*s*. 4*d*. in one year, being the lowest, to 11,234*l*. 15*s*. 1*d*. in another, being the highest. The depth of those pits varies from 9 fathoms to 114 fathoms. Their endurance in a state of usefulness varies from about one year to twenty-three years. *Thirdly*, taking a shorter period of about six and-a-half years, from January 1872 to June 1878, the total cost of pit-sinking is 71,964*l*. 10*s*. 2*d*. including 10,337*l*. 10*s*. 9*d*. for air pits and boring, or an average annual expenditure of about 11,000*l*.

These pits vary from 4 to 134 fathoms in depth. During the
period six years from January 1872 to January 1878, the nine-
teen pits which became exhausted had cost 44,013*l.* 13*s.* 1*d.*, or
about 2,300*l.* each pit on an average. They vary from 13 to
100 fathoms in depth, and lasted on an average about nine-and-
a-half years each. The pits at present working, that is, in June
1878, are forty-three in number, and cost 97,537*l.* 7*s.* 1*d.*, or an
average of about 2,250*l.* for each pit. They vary in depth from
14 to 134 fathoms, and were sunk, the earliest of them, in 1849
and the latest in 1876.

The question thus comes to be, whether the statutes authorise
any deduction to be made from profits on account of the capital
expended and exhausted in the conduct of the Company's
business. The general principle of the property and income tax
to which effect is given by the statutes is,. that everything of the
nature of income shall be assessed, from what source soever it
may be derived, whether from invested capital, or from skill and
labour, or from a combination of both and whether temporary
or permanent, steady or fluctuating, precarious or secure. Nor
does it make any difference on the incidence of the tax that the
income has been created by the sinking of capital, as in the case
of the purchase of annuities, instead of being merely the natural
annual product of an invested sum which remains unconsumed
and undiminished by the consumption of the income which it
yields. In applying this general principle to an assessment
on profits of trade, the Act 5 and 6 of Her present Majesty,
chapter 35, speaks in very clear language. The first rule,
section 100, Schedule D., provides that "the duty to be charged
"in respect thereof shall be computed on a sum not less than
"the full amount of the balance of the profits or gains of such
"trade upon a fair and just average of three years, and shall be
"assessed, charged, and paid without other deduction than is
"herein-after allowed." The third rule provides, that in estimating the balance of profits and gains no deduction shall be
allowed for any sum employed, or intended to be employed, as
capital in such trade, nor for any capital employed in improvement of premises occupied for the purposes of such trade, nor on
account of or under pretence of any interest which might have
been paid on such sums if laid out at interest. And the fourth
rule provides that no deduction shall be made on account of any
annual interest on any annuity or any annual payment payable
out of such profits or gains. The term "full amount of the
"balance of profits" in the first of these rules is something very
different from the amount of the net profits of the year which
would appear in the ordinary annual balance sheet of a trading
company; for in ascertaining net profits there falls to be
deducted, not only annual working expenses, but interest on
capital employed in the business, and every kind of annual
payment which either by the original constitution of the Company or by its subsequent obligations fall to be paid out of the
profits. So. also, in ascertaining the amount of net profits for

the purpose of division, the state of the capital account necessarily affects the balance sheet. If any part of the capital is
lost, or if, from the nature of the business, the capital employed
can never be recovered or restored, that is an element of primary
importance in fixing the financial condition of the Company and
the true amount of its net earnings. But the statute refuses to
take an ordinary balance sheet, or the net profits thereby ascertained, as the measure of the assessment, and requires the full
balance of profits, without allowing any deduction except for
working expenses, and without regard to the state of the capital
account or to the amount of capital employed in the concern, or
sunk and exhausted, or withdrawn. Any other construction of
the statute would not only be inconsistent with the leading
principle on which it is based and with its express words, but
would lead to very embarrassing consequences. A man who
employs his whole capital in the purchase of terminable
annuities increases his income, and is assessed to the income
tax for the full amount of the annuity; but after the step has
been taken, he is in practical effect living on his capital, and
when the account terminates it will all be gone. He might have
left his money on an ordinary investment, and have consumed
every year a portion of the capital in addition to the interest.
Nay, he might calculate the matter so nicely, that the whole
capital would be gone just at the same time that the annuity
would terminate. In this case this assessable income would be
only the interest accruing annually on the principal sum,
gradually diminishing year by year, and would not include the
portion of the capital which he chose to expend year by year.
But when he purchases an annuity he converts his whole estate
into an income which represents no capital but that which he
has paid away and exhausted to purchase the income. But the
statute takes no heed of his exhausted capital, and makes no
deduction from the actual amount of his income on that account.
In like manner, one may buy a business which is necessarily of
a temporary character, but the endurance of which may extend
over a series of years. He realises a large income from the
business, and in the end he may find that the profits derived
from the business while it lasted have repaid him the full
amount he paid for it, with interest, and left an ample margin
of gain beyond. On the other hand, he may find that though
he drew considerable profits from the business annually during
its continuance, the balance is the wrong way in the end, and
he has lost a great part of the money he paid for it. But the
statute is not concerned with the failure or success of his
speculation, and looks only to what is the income derived from
the business year by year.

To come nearer to the case before us, one man takes a lease
of the minerals under the ground of a certain estate, which have
never been wrought, and to which there is as yet no access by
pit or otherwise. Another buys from a former tenant the unex-
pired term of a lease of minerals, which are in the course of being
wrought by means of numerous and well-constructed shafts.

Are these two men to be assessed to the income-tax on different rules? Is the former to have such an allowance on deduction as is claimed in the present case on account of capital expended and exhausted in the sinking of pits, and is the other to have no such allowance when the pits sunk by his predecessor in the mine become exhausted and useless? Such a result would seem very unjust to the latter, for his pits have possibly cost him quite as much, in the shape of purchase-money of the lease, as the former has expended in actually sinking his.

And yet to give the latter the same kind of allowance as is now claimed for the former would involve such an inquiry as the legislature could never have contemplated, and as seems almost inextricable,—an inquiry into the manner in which the purchase-money of the lease ought to be apportioned between the minerals themselves and the pits, and the other advantages and conveniences of the going mine at the date of the purchase, including an estimate of the worth of each pit at that date, its probable continuance as a useful pit, and the expense of maintaining it. But, besides all this, the supposed claim of the purchaser of the lease would be nothing less than a proposal to deduct from the income arising from the subject purchased a proportion year by year of the purchase-money. This would be to establish a distinction between temporary and permanent income, in the mode of imposing the assessment, to which the Statute gives no countenance.

As already noticed, the contention of the Appellants in the original case was that the expenditure in respect of pit-sinking was not outlay of capital at all, but the ordinary working expenses of the mine. For the reasons given in our former judgment, we thought that argument unsound, and in the amended case it is abandoned, and the expense of pit-sinking is admitted to be outlay, or investment of capital. But the claim of the Appellants, as made in the amended case, though thus differing in form, does not differ in any material respect from the claim made in the original case. Capital expended in the sinking of pits must necessarily become exhausted and lost sooner or later, and that is foreseen when the expenditure is made. The only distinction between the two claims is that, in the original case, the deduction was asked of expenditure actually made in the year of assessment; while in the amended case the deduction is asked to be made in the year of assessment in which the pits created by the expenditure ceased to be useful. But it is not the less in the one case than in the other a deduction from annual profits of capital employed in the business of the Appellant's Company, which the Statute expressly prohibits.

A certain appearance of plausibility is given to the Appellants' argument by the great number and variety of pits sunk and worked by them. The constant employment of capital year by year in such sinking, by reason of the great extent of their business, gives to this expenditure a certain similarity to ordinary working expenses. But the likeness is merely on the surface.

If a man buys an unwrought mineral field, and sinks one pit, by means of which he works out all the minerals, he has converted the dormant, inaccessible, and unproductive subject into a going mine. He has made a new subject which differs from the unwrought mineral field just as a railway or canal is a different subject altogether from what the ground on which it is constructed originally was. The miner has invested his capital in creating the subject, which consists partly of the minerals and partly of the access by which the minerals are approached and worked; but the cost of the one, equally with the cost of the other, is an employment of capital, and it would be quite as reasonable to ask for an allowance for the general exhaustion and loss of capital embarked in paying the price of the mineral as of that employed in sinking the pit.

The Court had occasion, in the case of Miller v. Ferrie, to decide that no allowance could be made for depreciation of the subject, or the gradual extinction of the capital employed by the constant diminution of the quantity of minerals remaining to be won, and we have seen no reason to doubt the soundness of that judgment. But if these considerations are conclusive in a small amount, with a single pit, it seems impossible to dispute their equal applicability to a large subject of the same kind. Instead of 50 acres in the case supposed, the mineral field may extend to 1,000 acres; but the extension of the area, the multiplication of the strata worked, and of the pits sunk to reach them, do not alter the character of the subject, or the nature of the trade, and cannot make that in the latter case working expenses which in the former is employment of capital.

Having regard to the express words of the Statute, and the principle of assessment which runs through all its provisions, the Court are of opinion that the claims of the Appellants ought to be rejected, and the determination of the Commissioners ought to be affirmed.

I may mention that Lord Deas entirely concurs in the judgment of the Court, although he is not able to be in Court to-day.

The interlocutor will probably run in this form: "Having "resumed consideration of the petition of the Coltness Iron "Company, dated March 10, 1880, with the amended case for the "petitioner, and heard counsel—Of new affirm the determination "of the Commissioners of the Middle Ward of Lanarkshire, "dated November 7, 1878, and decern; and appoint the clerk "to report this judgment to the House of Lords, in terms of the "order to that effect, of date August 1, 1879."

HOUSE OF LORDS.

COLTNESS IRON COMPANY *v.* BLACK (on remit).
21st and 22nd March 1881.

Sir F. Herschell, S.G., and *Benjamin, Q.C.,* for Appellants.—
The capital exhausted in the year by pit-working must be taken
into account as a deduction. According to ordinary trading
principles no profit is made until the whole cost of getting the
minerals has been allowed for. Profit means the increment, if
any, which exists after you have replaced the exhausted capital.
Until exhausted capital has been replaced profit does not begin
By 29th Vict. c. 36. sect. 8, mines are taken out of Schedule A.
and become assessable with other trading concerns under and by
the rules of Schedule D.

The Lord Advocate and the *Solicitor General for Scotland*
(*Crawford* with them) for the Crown.—The income tax is an
annual tax. There is no distinction in regard to the taxation of
perpetual and terminable interests. *Primâ facie,* the subject of
taxation, in the case of mines, is not profits, but annual value.
From 29th Vict. c. 36. s. 8., it does not follow that the assessment
of profits under Schedules A. and D. is to be made in the same
manner. Mines are not totally transferred to Schedule D. by
that Act, which preserves No. 3 of Schedule A., sect. 60,
5 & 6 Vict. c. 35., but introduces Schedule D. rules as regards
all other matters. A mine is not to be treated as a trade but as
a heritable subject.

JUDGMENT.

Tuesday, 7th April 1881.—*Earl Cairns.*—My Lords, this is an
appeal from the First Division of the Court of Sessions, in which the
Appellants, and Iron Company at Coltness, contend that in rating
for the property and income tax they ought not to be assessed
on a sum of 9,027*l.,* a portion of the gross proceeds of their mines
for the year ending the 5th April 1879. The description of this
sum of 9,027*l.,* upon which the Appellants contend that they
should not be rated as given in the case originally was this:—
The Coltness Iron Company, carrying on business at Coltness,
appealed against the assessment made on them under Schedule D.
of the Act 5th and 6th Victoria, caput 35, and subsequent Income
Tax Acts referring thereto, in respect of the profits arising from
their business for the year preceding, in so far as the said assessment includes a sum of 9,027*l.,* being the cost incurred by them
in sinking new pits, and for which they maintained they were not
assessable. The Coltness Iron Company stated, and it is the fact,
that for a number of years they have carried on business as coal
and iron masters, and have opened up several mineral fields,
sinking new pits at their own expense from time to time as the
old ones have become exhausted, and they submitted that in
ascertaining the profits on which they are liable to be assessed
under the said Act, there ought to be deducted from the gross

annual receipts derived from their business the sums expended
by them in sinking the said pits.

This and the other statement in the special case when the
appeal first came before your Lordships were not deemed by
your Lordships to be sufficiently explicit, and you remitted the
case for amendment. This amendment has now been made, and
I will read the statement as to this sum of 9,027l. in the
amended case. " The sum of 9,027l. claimed as a deduction from
" the assessment by the Appellants does not represent the cost
" of pit sinking during the year, but is a sum arrived at by
" calculating 2s. a ton on iron made, and a penny halfpenny a
" ton on coal sold during the year, it being estimated that this
" will properly represent the amount of capital expended on
" making bores and sinking pits which have been exhausted by
" the year's working. The cost of making bores and sinking pits
" is charged in the books of the Company to an account called
" ' sunk capital account,' and is written off annually by a sum
" computed at the respective rates where specified on the
" quantities of iron made and coal sold in the year as repre-
" senting the capital expended on pit sinking exhausted by the
" year's working. The working charges deducted and allowed
" in ascertaining the profits for assessment include the whole
" cost of getting and raising the minerals after the pits are sunk,
" and of manufacturing the metal, and selling the iron and coal,
" and the general expenses of the concern." It therefore now
appears that the statement in the case as it originally stood is
not sustained, and that the sum in question does not represent
the cost of pit sinking during the year of which the profits are
taken. I am not prepared to say that under the words of the
5th and 6th Victoria, chapter 35, a mine owner might not in
some cases be entitled to an allowance in respect of the cost of
sinking a pit by means of which pit the minerals are gotten
which are the source of profit for the year in which the pit was
sunk. I desire to reserve my opinion on that point until the
question arises, but in the present case the question is altogether
different. It is, as now explained, can a mine owner write off
and deduct from the gross earnings of his mine in a particular
year a sum to represent that year's depreciation of all the pits in
the mines whenever sunk. I am clearly of opinion that this
cannot be done. It may be proper for a trader or for a trading
company to perform in his or their books an operation of this
kind every year in order to judge of the sum that can in that
year be safely taken out of the trade and spent as trade profits.
But I am clearly of opinion that the owner of a mine cannot
quâ owner thus manipulate his accounts when the question is
under section 60 of the principal Act, what is the amount of
profits received from the mine in each of the five years upon
which the average is to be taken?

My Lords, I do not think this question is affected by the
29th Victoria, chapter 36. That Act provides that mines shall
be charged and assessed according to the rules prescribed by

Schedule D. of the principal Act so far as such rules are consistent with No. 3 of Schedule A. But the thing to be assessed remains the same.

Your Lordships were referred by the Appellants to a decision, viz., Knowles *v.* Macadam (*b*), in the Exchequer Division of the High Court of Justice in England (3 Law Reports, Exchequer Division 23), as an authority in their favour. Your Lordships are now sitting in appeal from the Court of Session, but even supposing that case were a Scotch authority I am bound to say that it is a decision which does not seem to me to be capable of being supported, and I could not advise your Lordships to follow it.

Lord Penzance.—My Lords, the arguments of the Appellants was based on the interpretation which they gave to the word "profit" in the Act. And it was contended that they could not be properly said to have made any profit out of their mines until a certain portion of the cost of making the bores and sinking the pits necessary to approach the mineral-bearing strata were deducted.

In a general and perhaps a strict and logical sense I think this is true, but it is also and equally true, I think, that the cost of the mineral strata themselves, whether they have been hired or bought, should be included in any calculation which had for its object the ascertainment of the actual profit obtained by the Company out of the entire adventure. So much for the prime cost of the mineral bed, so much for approaches to it in the shape of pits, so much for working it and getting the mineral to the surface, so much for getting the mineral to the market, and against all these the price obtained for the mineral sold; these would be the elements of a profit and loss account of an entire adventure of this nature. But is this the sense in which the word profit is used in the Act? I think not.

The intention of the Act, it is abundantly clear, was in Schedule A. to tax property. If a man had bought an estate the tax was intended to be paid by him on the annual value of that estate, without reference to where he got it, or how he got it, or how much he paid for it. So if a man built a house, or bought a house, he was intended to pay tax on the annual value of the house, no matter what it cost. Nor does anything turn upon the fact that the estate is a permanent and undecaying species of property, while the house is a species of property of a less durable kind; he was intended to pay tax upon it so long as it lasted.

What, then, is the case of a mine in the Schedule A., which is the Schedule applicable to property? A mine is in express terms included as a species of property, and is made the subject of a tax. The only question is how shall the annual value of this species of property be ascertained. It is to this object that the Rule No. III. found in section 60 of the Act is addressed. That

---

(*b*) *Ante,* p. 161.

rule assumes the ownership of the "mine" passes by altogether
the sum of money which it may have cost either in the way of
purchase or rent, and proceeds to describe the method of calculating its "annual value" to the owner thereof, and this it
declares shall be the average "profit" over a period of five years
"received therefrom." The words "profit received therefrom"
are here introduced to define the annual value of the thing which
is to be taxed, which is the "mine," and it could not I think be
intended that for the purpose of calculating " the annual value "
of a "mine," the original cost of the "mine" itself, or any part
of it, should be first deducted. On the contrary, the words
"profits received therefrom" in this connexion mean, I think,
the entire profits derived from the "mine," deducting the cost of
working it, but not deducting the cost of making it. I do not
think the subject is elucidated but rather confused by the illustration brought forward in argument of the merchant or trader
who spends a sum of money or who invests capital in the purchase of goods and sells them again at an advance in price. No
doubt in such a case the "profit" can only be ascertained by first
deducting the original cost of the goods. If a man spends 100*l.*
in the purchase of goods and. sells them for 140*l.* his profit is
not 140*l.*, but at most 40*l.* only.

But when such a matter as that is brought under the provisions
of this Act for taxation, the wide difference between it and the
present case is at once apparent. For the merchant or trader is
taxed in such a case not in respect of any "property" which he
possesses and of which he enjoys the fruits, but only upon the
profits which he realises annually in his trade, whereas the
owner of a "mine" is taxed in respect of that "mine" as a fixed
and realized "property," which belongs to him and from which
he reaps an annual benefit; and the words "annual value" or
"profit received" from that "property" are introduced into the
Statute, not as the subject of taxation, but only as the measure
of the taxation to which the "property" shall be subjected.

A pit sunk to approach the mineral underground is not unlike
a road made above ground from the pit's mouth to the highway
as a means of transporting the mineral to the market. If a man
were possessed of such a mine and such a road, it would be true
that as the mineral was gradually worked out the road and the
capital sunk in making it, would gradually be exhausted and lost,
but the decaying character of the property would not make it
the less subject to be taxed according to its annual value or the
profit obtained by using it as long as the mineral lasted.

This, I think, is the principle that runs through the entire Act,
and your Lordships could not, I think, sustain the present appeal
without introducing principles which would entirely subvert the
method of taxation which the Legislature intended, and according
to which this statute has hitherto been administered.

I agree that the judgment of the Court below should be
affirmed.

Lord Blackburn.—My Lords, this case was stated in order to be able to ask your Lordships to review the decision of the Court of Session in the case of Addie v. the Solicitor of Inland Revenue (2 Rettie 431), and reliance was placed on the decision of the Exchequer Division in Knowles v. Macadam (Law Reports, 3 Exchequer Division 23). Both of those decisions were pronounced at a time when there was no appeal against either, and as they were, I think, justly considered inconsistent with each other it is important that both should be brought under review.

The Coltness Company appealed against the assessment for the year 1878 in so far as the assessment includes a sum of 9.027*l.*, being the cost incurred by them in sinking new pits. It was thought that the statement of facts contained in the case was not sufficiently full to enable this House finally to dispose of the point of law on which its decision was asked, and it was directed that it should be amended, which was done, and the result shows that this was requisite; for the amended case, besides entering into various details as to the mode of pit sinking and working the mines in the Appellants' mineral field contains a statement as to what the 9,027*l.* consisted of, which, I think, could not have been collected from the statements in the original case.

I think it is not necessary to inquire what other points might possibly have been raised on the other facts, still less to decide them, if that statement shows that the sum of 9,027*l.* is not properly to be deducted from the assessment. I will read that statement. The sum of 9,027*l.* claimed as a deduction from the assessment by the Appellants does not represent the cost of pit sinking during the year, but is a sum arrived at by calculating two shillings a ton on iron made, and a penny-halfpenny a ton on coal sold during the year, it being estimated that this will properly represent the amount of capital expended on making bores and sinking pits which has been exhausted by the year's working. The cost of making bores and sinking pits is charged in the books of the Company to an account called "sunk capital account," and is written off annually by a sum computed at the respective rates above specified on the quantities of iron made and coal sold in the year as representing the capital expended on pit sinking exhausted by the year's working. The working charges deducted and allowed in ascertaining the profits for assessment include the whole cost of getting and raising the minerals after the pits are sunk, and of manufacturing the metal and selling the iron and coal, and the general expenses of the concern.

The phrase capital exhaused does not occur anywhere in the Income Tax Acts. It is taken from a passage in Mr. McCulloch, on Political Economy, where he says, "Profit must not be con-"founded with the produce of industry primarily received by "the capitalist. They really consist of the produce on its value "remaining to those who employ their capital in an Industrial

"undertaking after all their necessary payments have been
"deducted, and after the capital wasted and used in the under-
"taking has been replaced. If the produce derived from an
"undertaking after defraying the necessary outlay be insufficient
"to replace the capital exhausted, a loss has been incurred; if the
"capital is merely sufficient to replace the capital exhausted,
"there is no surplus, there is no loss, but there is no annual
"profit, and the greater the surplus is, the greater the
"profit."

I do not feel at all inclined to dispute the sufficiency of this
definition. I think that if a building society had taken a
building lease, and it became necessary at any time to ascertain
what profit or loss had been made by it from that lease, all the
monies expended in building houses would be placed on one side
of the account, and on the other all that had been received for
houses let or sold, and the value during the residue of the
building lease of the houses then remaining in the society's hands,
and that value would of course be less and less as the lease drew
nearer to an end; and if in the first year of the building lease a
house was built at a cost of, say, 10,000*l.*, and the profit or loss
on the lease had to be estimated when the residue of the building
lease was reduced to, say, 5 years, and the lease of the house for
those 5 years would sell for only, say, 5,000*l.* I do not think
it inaccurate to say that in computing the profit or loss on
the building lease 5,000*l.* would be allowed as capital invested
in building that house and now exhausted. But that is
certainly not the scheme of the income tax as far as regards
building leases, and other properties comprised in Schedule A.,
No. I.

The tax is imposed on the annual value of the block of
buildings which is to be taken at the rack-rent at which the
same are worth to let for the year.

By no process of reasoning could that rack-rent be made to
depend on the sum which has been expended in building the
house, or to be greater or less according as the building lease
was longer or shorter. Mines are not comprised in Schedule A.,
No. I., but in Schedule A., No. III., and the tax is imposed on
them by a different set of words certainly. And if the decision
in Knowles *v.* Macadam is correct, it is imposed on a radically
different principle. I have felt myself constrained to advise your
Lordships to say that the case of Knowles *v.* Macadam was
wrongly decided.

I think the question thus raised can hardly be decided without
examining at some, I fear tedious, length the enactments on the
construction of which it depends. No tax can be imposed on
the subject without words in an Act of Parliament clearly
showing an intention to lay a burden on him. But when that
intention is sufficiently shown, it is, I think, vain to speculate on
what would be the fairest and most equitable mode of levying
that tax. The effect of those framing a taxing Act is to grant
to Her Majesty a revenue; no doubt they would prefer if it

were possible to raise that revenue equally from all, and as that
cannot be done to raise it from those on whom the tax falls with
as little trouble and annoyance, and as equally as can be con-
trived; and when any enactments for the purpose can bear two
interpretations, it is reasonable to put that construction on them
which will produce these effects. But the object is to grant a
revenue at all events, even though a possible nearer approxi-
mation to equality may be sacrificed in order more easily and
certainly to raise that revenue; and I think the only safe rule
is to look at the words of the enactments, and see what is the
intention expressed by those words.

Before, however, proceeding to examine the words of the
Income Tax Acts, on which, in my opinion, everything depends,
I wish to point out that long before any income or property tax
was imposed for general revenue, the parochial authorities in
England raised a revenue for parochial purposes which was very
much in the nature of an income and property tax; and the
language used in the Income Tax Acts is such as to convince me
that the legislature had in their contemplation what had been
done in this branch of the law, which if not exactly in pari
materia, is at least an analogous subject. I think it more convenient to state briefly what was the state of the law as to rating
real property in general, and though by a very narrow construction the specific mention of coal mines was held to exclude all
other mines, coal mines, quarries, &c. in particular. By the
Statute of 43 Elizabeth, c. 2, the churchwardens and overseers of
the parish were empowered to raise by taxation of every inhabitant, parson, vicar, and others, and of every occupier of lands,
houses, tithes impropriate or proportions of tithes, coal mines, or
saleable underwoods in the said parish a sufficient sum. The
power to rate the inhabitants as such was put an end to by a
temporary Act 3 & 4 Vict. c. 89, continued from year to year,
and finally made perpetual by 37 & 38 Vict. c. 96. The power
to tax the occupiers of the species of property named in the Act
of Elizabeth continued.

In 1827 (King v. Attwood, 6 Barnewell and Cresswell, 277) a
case was stated for the Court of King's Bench, as to the principle
of rating of coal mines. Chief Justice Abbot delivered a Judgment which is so germane to the subject we are now considering,
that I will read the whole of it, as it is not long:—"We are all
" of opinion that the owner and occupier of a coal mine should be
" rated at such sum as it would let for and no more. As to the
" other points, the first was that the rate should not be imposed
" upon the coal produced, because that was part of the reality. It
" is the first time that such a proposition has ever been submitted,
" although many coal mines in various parts of the country have
" constantly been rated, and the argument in support of it is
" wholly untenable. The legislature has expressly made coal
" mines rateable, and they must be rated for what they produce,
" viz., the coals, slate quarries, and brick earth are also exhausted
" in a few years, but nevertheless the rate is always imposed on

" that which is produced. The other argument was, that the rate
" could not be imposed until the expense of planting the mine had
" been recouped. But I cannot discover any distinction between
" expenses incurred in bringing a mine to a productive state,
" and in building a house. The attempt to distinguish them is
" perfectly novel, and if a house is to be rated as soon as it is
" built and occupied, it must follow that a coal mine is rateable as
" soon as it is set to work and produces coal, although it may
" happen that the expense of sinking it may never be recovered.
" If the tenant of a mine expends money in making it more
" productive, that is the same as expending money in improving
" a farm or a house, in which cases the tenant is rateable for
" the improved value."

I do not say that what Lord Tenterden here lays down as to
the taxation of a coal mine is necessarily either just or expedient.
but though this case was decided after the earlier Income Tax
Acts, it was an authoritative declaration of what had been held
to be law before, and must have been well known to that large
proportion of the legislators who habitually acted at quarter
sessions.

The legislature in 1836, by 6th and 7th William IV. c. 96.
enacted that all poor rates shall be made " upon an estimate of
" the net annual value of the several hereditaments rated there-
" unto," that is to say, of the rent at which the same might
reasonably be expected to let from year to year free of all usual
tenants' rates and taxes, and tithe commutation rent tax, if any.
and deducting therefrom the probable average annual cost of the
repairs, assurances, and other expenses, if any, necessary to
maintain them in a state to command such rent: And in the
form of the rate prescribed there is to be in one column a statement of the " gross estimated rental, and in another of the
" rateable value."

The Act 5th and 6th Victoria, chapter 35, adopts without any
variations which affect this question the language of the former
Income Tax Act, 46 Geo. III., chapter 65. Before that there
had been an earlier Income Tax Act, 43 George III.. chapter 122,
from which there are changes, and I think some of those changes
throw light on what was the intention of the legislature in the
substituted enactments. The first Income Tax Act. 43 George
III., chapter 122, section 31, comprised in Schedule A. all lands,
tenements, hereditaments, or heritages, and enacted that for
them there shall be charged throughout Great Britain in respect
of the property thereof for every 20*s.* of the annual value thereof,
the sum of 1*s.*, and enacted that " the said duty shall be con-
" strued to extend to all manors and messuages, to all quarries
" of stone, slate, limestone, or chalk, mines of coal, tin, lead.
" copper, mundic, iron, and other mines, to all iron mills, furnaces,
" and other iron works, and other mills and engines of the like
" nature, to all salt springs or salt works, and many other things."

The legislature here classed together in one schedule properties,
such as agricultural land, which from their nature will continue

permanently to exist, and properties, such as quarries, which will COLTNESS
IRON
COMPANY r.
BLACK. certainly come to an end within a period longer or shorter, but the duration of which can be generally calculated, and properties such as iron works, which are real property, deriving their annual value from being ancillary to a trade. It imposed one tax at one rate upon them all, and gave one general rule that the annual value should be understood to be the rack rent, and it directed that the tax should be paid by the occupier, who might deduct a proportionate part from his rent; and by No. 3 there is allowed a deduction for repairs not exceeding five per cent. on the annual value of a dwelling-house, or two per cent. on the annual value of a farm. But there is not expressly, at least, any allowance made for repairs in respect of other kinds of real property, and the Schedule B. there is imposed in addition a tax on the occupier of all such properties (with some exceptions not material to be noticed); and the first of the rules for estimating the annual value of properties before described in Schedules A. and B. in England is that no such property shall be charged at less than the last poor rate, which shows that those who framed that Act were thinking of the analogous case of the parochial taxation for the relief of the poor. The statute 43 George III., chapter 122, also by section 84, imposes a duty by Schedule D. upon the annual profits inter alia of every trade, and by the rules therein the duty shall be computed upon a sum not less than the full amount of the profits upon a fair and just average of three years, without any other deduction than is hereafter allowed, and the third rule is no deductions shall be made on account of any sum expended on repairs of premises occupied for the purposes of such trade, nor for any sum expended for the supply, or repairs, or alteration of any utensils or articles employed for the purpose of such trade beyond the sum usually expended for such purpose, according to the average of three years. I conjecture that during the three years that elapsed between the passing of the 43 George III. and the passing of the 46 George III., chapter 65, experience had shown that there were difficulties in working this scheme, and that claims for deductions had been made, for whilst most of the provisions of the first Act were re-enacted, those to which I have above referred were all materially altered. It is not necessary to go through the 46 George III., chapter 65, for the provisions of that Act are re-enacted in the 5th and 6th Victoria, chapter 35, without any alteration which seems to me material to notice.

The third rule as to Schedule D., which I have above quoted, still continued to be negative in its form that no deductions should be made under several enumerated pretences, but the number of these was considerably increased, and why I do not know. Instead of saying that the duty should be imposed on a fair and just average of the amount of the profits for three years, it is imposed on the balance of such profits. I have not been able to discover any difference in the meaning of the two phrases.

C

The several rates and duties granted by the 5th and 6th Victoria, chapter 35, are imposed by section 1, Schedule A., for all lands, tenements, hereditaments, or heritages in Great Britain, shall be charged yearly " for every 20s. of the annual value thereof the sum of 7d." Then by section 60 the properties chargeable under Schedule A., instead of being as in statute 43 George III., chapter 122, treated altogether in one schedule, are treated of under numbers. By No. 1 (which gives the general rule which is the same as that which in 43 George III., chapter 122, was applied to all in Schedule A.), the annual value shall be understood to be the rent by the year at which the same are let at rack rent, if they have been let at rack rent within seven years before the assessment, but if the same are not so let at rack rent, then at the rack rent at which the same are worth to be let by the year, and by section 63, in addition to the duties to be charged under Schedule A., there shall be levied the duty, under Schedule B., on all properties to be charged according to the general rule in No. 1, with some exceptions not material to this case.

The rules which expressly gave power to allow for repairs a sum not exceeding a certain per-centage on the annual value of houses and farms are not re-enacted. Nor are the rules above quoted which refer to the poor rate in England as being the test of annual value. It is not material in this case to inquire whether the rack rent mentioned is to be measured by what in statutes 6 and 7 William IV., chapter 96, is called the gross estimated rental without making any allowance for those annual repairs which the tenant would certainly take into consideration when bidding that rent. It could not have been intended that the rack rent should be less that the rateable value.

No. 2 and No. 3 comprise properties which are comprised in the general description in Schedule A., but which it was not thought expedient to include in Schedule B., though in the first Income Tax Act they had been so-included. One would anticipate that the duty imposed on those would be on the rack rent which they would have been worth to let by the year, and something more in lieu of the duty imposed by Schedule B.; and as the duty imposed by the poor law and the duty imposed by the first Income Tax Act was precisely the same on properties like quarries which are terminable and properties which are permanent, one would expect that no distinction would now be made. Whether that is so or not must depend on the true construction of the words used, which with reference to No. 3 are these: " The annual value of all the properties herein-after " described shall be understood to be the full amount for one " year, or the average amount for one year, of the profits " received therefrom within the respective times herein limited," that is of quarries, &c., and what may be called miscellaneous properties, one year of mines, &c. five years. No definition is given of profits for one year. That is left to be ascertained as a matter on the construction of the Act. The rules which are contained in sections 60, 61, 62, and 64, relate to many things—as to the place where the duties shall be assessed, and the persons by whom they are to be assessed, and also as to many allowances to be made, but I can find nothing in them to throw any light on the construction of the words, "the full amount for "one year, or the average amount for one year of the profits "received therefrom within the respective times herein limited," that is, in some cases one year and in some five.

It may be convenient here to notice two arguments, not I think relied on by the Solicitor General in his argument at your Lordships' bar, though he had used them before the Exchequer Division in Knowles *v.* Macadam. It was said by Lord Cairns, in Gowan *v.* Christie (Law Reports 2, Scotch Appeals, 284), that a lease of mines is not in reality a lease at all in the sense in which we speak of an agricultural lease. There is no fruit; that is to say, there is no sowing and reaping in the ordinary sense of the term, and there are no periodical harvests. What we call a mineral lease is really, when properly considered, a sale out and out of a portion of the land. I think this is a perfectly accurate statement. But the argument that no income tax should be imposed on what is perhaps not quite accurately called rent reserved on a mineral lease, because it is a payment by instalments of the price of minerals forming part of the land (any more than on the price paid down in one sum for the out and out purchase of the minerals forming part of the land), is, I think, untenable. Even if it had not been as decided in the King *v.* Attwood (6 Barnewell and Cresswell 277), the constant course from the statute of Elizabeth downwards to construe an annual tax imposed on coal mines, quarries, and the like, as being imposed on that which is produced from them, I should say that no other construction could be placed on the 60th section of the 4th and 5th Victoria, chapter 35, especially after seeing in what manner the legislature in 43 George III., chapter 122, had dealt with them, though I think that the judgment of the Exchequer Division in Knowles *v.* Macadam (Law Reports 3, Exchequer Division 23) seems an authority to the contrary. From that judgment, however, to which I shall afterwards return, I must ask your Lordships to dissent.

It has also been sometimes argued that it is very unjust to tax at the same rate a terminable interest such as that in a mine which must at some time be worked out, and a fee simple interest which will endure so long as this world continues in its present state. I will not inquire whether this is just or not. There is much force in the argument on the other side, that if the interest is terminable, so is the tax, and will cease when the interest ceases; but whether just or not, there can be no doubt that the same annual charge is imposed upon a terminal annuity and on one in perpetuity, and, what seems harder, that the same annual charge is imposed upon a professional income earned by hard labour, often extending over many years before any return is got, and when earned precarious as depending on the health of the earner.

In the 5th and 6th Victoria, chapter 35, the different schedules were kept apart and complete in themselves, but I think
wherever there was any provision in any one of the schedules
that throws light on what is meant by annual value or annual
profits or capital, it may be very material in construing the
meaning of those words used in other parts of the Act. Thus, I
think, that the provision under the fifth head of No. 2, that an
allowance may be made from the amount to be taxed on fines,
if it be proved that such fines or any part thereof have been
applied as productive capital on which a profit has arisen or
will arise otherwise chargeable under this Act for the year in
which the assessment shall be made, "and the provision in
"Schedule D. that no deduction shall be made on account of any
"sum employed or intended to be employed as capital," neither
of which was in the 43 Geo. III. chap. 122, throw some light
on each other, and may fairly be referred to in inquiring what
is meant by "the average amount for one year of the profits
"received within the time limited." But Schedules A. and B.
were complete in themselves, and Schedule D., which was regulated by section 100, was complete in itself. The duties were,
however, assessed by different Commissioners, and in different
places. By the 29 Vict. c. 36, section 8, "The several and
"respective concerns described in No. III. of Schedule A. of
"5 and 6 Vict. c. 35, shall be charged and assessed to the duties
"hereby granted in the manner in the said No. III. mentioned
"according to the rules prescribed by Schedule D. of the said
"Act, so far as such rules are consistent with the said No. III.
"Provided, that the annual value or profit and gains arising from
"any railway shall be charged and assessed by the Commissioners
"for special purposes." In Knowles *v.* Macadam, Kelly C.B. says
"it is quite clear that section 8 of 29 Vict. c. 36, transfers the
"present case" (that of a coal mine) "from Schedule A. to
"Schedule D.;" and the judgment of the Barons in that case
seems to me to depend a good deal on this, as it seems to me,
erroneous assumption. I think that the duties are to be assessed
according to the rules in Schedule D., and consequently all the
anxiously devised provisions for keeping the rturns under
Schedule D. secret and confidential to be found from Section 100
to Section 131, are made in future to apply to returns for the
concerns described in No. III. of Schedule A., and any rule
expressed as to the mode of computing the balance of the profits
and gains during the period of three years given in Schedule D.,
which is not inconsistent with No. III., may perhaps be made
in future to apply to the mode of computing the annual profits
of properties chargeable under No. III., and I see that in Addie
v. Solicitor of Inland Revenue (2 Rettie 431), reliance is placed
on the judgment of the Lord President on the 3rd rule as to
concerns under the first case of Schedule D., that no deduction is
to be made "for any sum employed or intended to be employed
as capital." But I do not think reliance can be placed on this.
If from the nature of the concerns in No. III. an allowance ought

to be made for capital, then this rule should be rejected as COLTNESS
inconsistent with No. III. If no such allowance should be made, IRON
the rule is not required. COMPANY *v.*
BLACK.

In Forder *v.* Handyside (L.R. 1 Ex. Div. 233), the Exchequer
Division came to a decision as to repairs, estimated but not
actually incurred, which, whether it was right or wrong, is no
longer since the 41 Vict. c. 15. s. 12. to apply. And as there
is no question in the case at bar as to repairs, it is unnecessary
to inquire whether it was right or wrong.

If the effect of Section 8 of 29 Vict. was to transfer cases
in Schedule A. No. III. to Schedule D., it would change the
respective times on an average for which the profits were to be
assessed. Mines would be reduced from a five year period to a
three year period. Quarries and things of that sort would be
raised from a single year to three. I cannot think this was
either intended or expressed. But, on the assumption that it
had this effect, the Exchequer Division came in Knowles *v.*
Macadam to a very startling decision. In that case a company
had bought for a very large sum the minerals in beneficial
leaseholds of coal mines, having an average of 32 years to run,
and in freeholds. The decision of the Exchequer Division was
that the effect of transferring the mines, as they thought, from
Schedule A. to Schedule D., was to cause the company to be
assessed as persons carrying on the trade of vendors of coal who
had bought wholesale a large quantity of coal, not stored in
warehouses, but in the earth, and which they were going to sell
in the course of their trade, and that they ought to be assessed on
the principle of valuing the stock in trade, that is, the coals thus
stored in the earth, at the beginning of the three years, and
again valuing the stock at the end of the three years, and taking
the difference between them as being to be added to or deducted
from the net receipts during that period in estimating the
profits for the three years. The effect of this would be, that
though the mines were worked so as to produce a large profit
above the working expenses, yet if they were worked by a
purchaser, who had over-estimated the value of the minerals, and
paid such a price for them that he was a loser, no income tax
was to be paid in respect of those mines. That is a result
which never could have been intended by the legislature, and
if it follows by legitimate reasoning from the interpretation put
upon the 29 Vict. c. 36. s. 8., it seems to me a reductio ad
absurdum, showing that the interpretation was wrong.

I, therefore, advise your Lordships to hold that the decision in
Knowles *v.* Macadam was erroneous. I do not wish to lay
down any general proposition either that money expended in
sinking pits can never be in the nature of expenses incurred
within the five years, in working the coal so as to be properly
taken into account in estimating the profits made in that period,
or to say what, if any, the circumstances are under which it may
be done. That, I think, had better be left to be determined

COLTNESS
IRON
COMPANY r.
BLACK.

———

when the case arises. I think it enough to say that this sum of 9,027*l.* described in the case is not such as ought to be deducted.

The result is that, in my opinion, the Interlocutory below should be affirmed, and the Appeal dismissed.

Interlocutor affirmed, and Appeal dismissed with costs, except the costs incurred by reason of the remit.

PART XXI.

No. 47.—In the Court of Exchequer (Scotland).—First Division.
16th July 1880.

Banks (Surveyor of Taxes) *v.* Glasgow and South-Western Railway Company.

Inhabited House Duty.—A railway company occupies the ground floor and three other floors of a building as offices. The two uppermost floors are occupied by the same company, but for the purposes of, and in connexion with, a hotel of which the main body is another tenement under a separate roof. There is internal communication between the four lower and the two upper floors.

Held, *that the company is liable to Inhabited House Duty for the whole building.*

In re The Scottish Widows' Fund (No. 2), *followed.(a)*

At a meeting of Commissioners for General Purposes under the Property and Income Tax and Inhabited House Duty Acts, for the city of Glasgow, held at Glasgow upon the 19th day of April 1880, for the purpose of hearing and disposing of Appeals under the said Acts, for the year ending 5th April 1880.

The Glasgow and South-Western Railway Company appealed against an additional assessment for the year 1879-80 of 62*l.* 1*s.* 3*d.* made upon them for Inhabited House Duty,[*] at the rate of 9*d.* per £ on 1,655*l.*, the annual value of the premises at St. Enoch Station, Glasgow, occupied by the Appellants as general and other offices for the purpose of carrying on the business of a railway company. The premises in question are part of a tenement or building, consisting of six floors situated at St. Enoch Station aforesaid. The first four floors, from the ground or street floor inclusive, are solely and exclusively occupied by the Appellants as general and other offices, in connexion with, and for the purpose of carrying on the business of the railway company. The remaining two uppermost floors of said tenement or building are solely and exclusively occupied as a part of, and in connexion with, St. Enoch Station Hotel, also situated at St. Enoch Station aforesaid. The said hotel comprises, in addition to the said two uppermost floors of the foresaid tenement or building, another tenement or building attached to the former, and forming the main body of the hotel; but the said two tenements or buildings are distinct and independent, being under distinct and separate roofs. The entire hotel,

(Margin:) Banks *v.* Glasgow and South-Western Railway Company.

BANKS v.
GLASGOW
AND SOUTH-
WESTERN
RAILWAY
COMPANY.

inclusive of the said two uppermost floors of the tenement or building of which the premises, the subject of the assessment in question, are part, is also in the occupation of the Appellants, by whom the business of the hotel is carried on, and the Appellants have been assessed, and have paid, the sum of 163l. 15s. for Inhabited House Duty for the same year (1879-80) on the annual value of the said hotel, inclusive, as aforesaid, of the said two uppermost floors. There is internal communication between the first four floors of said tenement or building occupied as general and other offices and the two uppermost floors thereof occupied as part of the hotel, such communication being had by means of a staircase and hydraulic hoist, running from the ground or street floor to the said two uppermost floors, and which staircase and hoist also afford the means of external communication from the public street to the first four floors and the two uppermost floors in common. There is also a communication by a door between each of said two uppermost floors occupied as part of the hotel and the other tenement or building adjoining, of which the main body of the hotel consists. No person whatever inhabits, dwells, or abides in the portion of the said tenement or building occupied as general and other offices as aforesaid except in the day time only, and that for the purpose of carrying on the business of the Appellants: and no person whatever engaged in such portion of the said tenement or building inhabits, dwells, or abides in the other portion thereof occupied as part of the hotel, or in the other tenement or building adjoining, of which the main body of the hotel consists.

The Appellants contended—*First.* That the premises, the subject of the additional assessment in question, were exempted under the Acts 57 Geo. III. cap. 25, and 5 Geo. IV. cap. 44, or one or other of them, in respect said premises are part of a tenement or building whereof such part is occupied by the Appellants for the purpose of carrying on business within the meaning of said Acts, and the other part is in distinct and independent occupation by the Appellants as part of, and in connection with, the said hotel, and as such is charged to the said duties; and the Appellants referred to and founded on the " Customs and Inland Revenue Act " (1878), sect. 13, sub-sect. 1, as inferentially supporting their interpretation of the former Acts, and contended that inasmuch as sect. 13, sub-sect. 1, of the last-mentioned Act affords relief to an owner who is chargeable as constructive occupier under schedule B, Rule 6 of the Act 48 Geo. III. cap. 55, when, and in so far as, the building whereof he is owner is divided into, and let in different tenements or portions, and any of such tenements or portions is occupied solely for business purposes; so likewise an actual occupier of an entire building, whereof a portion is in distinct and independent occupation by him solely for business purposes, is entitled to relief in respect of such portion, the meaning and intent of the said first-mentioned Act being to place an owner chargeable to the said duties, as a constructive occupier on a footing of equality with an actual occupier similarly circumstanced, but not to operate relief to such an owner, if an actual occupier in similar circumstances would not be entitled to relief. *Second (Separatim)*, The premises, the subject of the additional assessment in question, being an assessable subject, within the meaning of the "Customs and Inland Revenue Act" (1878), sect. 13, sub-sect. 2, and as such, occupied solely for business purposes, they fall under the exemption in said sub-section contained.

The Surveyor of Taxes, Mr. John Henry Banks, contended, in support of ·the assessment, that the interpretation sought by the Appellants to be put on the Acts 57 Geo. III. cap. 25 and 5 Geo. IV. cap. 34 was not a correct interpretation so far as regards the exemption therein contained; and he further contended that, under the Act 48 Geo. III. cap. 55, Schedule B, Rules 3 and 5, the portion of the said tenement or building occupied by the Appellants as general and other offices for the purpose of their business must be valued with the other portion thereof occupied as part of, and in connection with, the hotel, in respect there is internal communication between the former and the latter portions of the said tenements or building, and between the latter portion thereof and the other tenement or building adjoining and attached thereto, of which the main body of the hotel consists.

The Surveyor, in support of the assessment, also referred to the case decided by the Judges in Scotland, where the Edinburgh and Glasgow Railway Company were held liable in an assessment for House Duty upon their station at Edinburgh, in consequence of the servants of the tenant of the refreshment rooms sleeping in a room attached to the refreshment rooms.

The Surveyor further maintained, that the section of the Act 41 Vict. cap. 13, sub-sect. 1, referred by the Appellants in support of their title to exemption, did not apply to the present case, as that clause provided for relief only where the premises are "divided into and let in, different tenements," and any of such tenements so let, are occupied "solely for the purpose of any trade " or business, or of any profession, or calling, by which the occu- " pier seeks a livelihood, or profit, or are unoccupied. In the present case, as the Glasgow and South-western Railway Company are occupiers of the whole tenements or building, including the portion thereof used as offices, as well as the part thereof occupied by them as a hotel, the offices must, in accordance with the Acts referred to, and the cases decided by Her Majesty's Judges, be valued and assessed together with the hotel, which is occupied as a dwelling-house.

The Commissioners sustained the appeal and granted the Appellants relief of the assessment, being of opinion that the premises, the subject of the additional assessment, in question fell within the exemption contained in the Acts founded on by the Appellants.

The surveyor expressed dissatisfaction with the determination of the Commissioners, as being erroneous in point of law, and

BANKS *v.* GLASGOW AND SOUTH-WESTERN RAILWAY COMPANY.

BANKS v.
GLASGOW
AND SOUTH-
WESTERN
RAILWAY
COMPANY.
___

having now required by notice in writing, a case to be stated for the opinion of the Court, in terms of the Act 37 & 38 Vict. cap. 16, sect. 9, the present case is stated and signed accordingly.

> JAS. HANNAN, } Commissioners.
> JAMES SCOTT, }

Glasgow, 4th June 1880.

Asher (*Pearson* with him) for the Railway Company admitted that the case of the Scottish Widows' Fund (b) governed the present case if the former had been properly argued, but he maintained that the 57 Geo. 3. c. 25. s. 1, and 5 Geo. 4. c. 44. s. 4,(c) had not been expounded to the Court and that those enactments gave relief in such cases.

16th July 1880.—*The Lord President,*—My Lords; it appears that the Glasgow and South-western Railway Company have two large tenements at their station in St. Enoch Square, in Glasgow, which are for the most part occupied together as a hotel. The two tenements stand close to one another, and the business of the hotel is carried on for the most part in one of these tenements, but the two upper floors of the other tenement also communicate with the rest of the hotel and are occupied as part of the hotel. The four lower storeys of that second tenement are occupied for purposes connected with the business of the railway company, apparently as warehouses or something of that kind. Now the question which is raised by this case is whether the Railway Company are liable for Inhabited House Duty on the whole of these two tenements, or whether that portion of one of them which is occupied for business purposes enjoys an exemption under the Acts of Parliament. At first sight, this case seemed to be clearly ruled by our judgment in the case of the Scottish Widows' Fund, and it was conceded that that judgment did rule the present if the judgment in the case of the Scottish Widows' Fund is sound and proceeds on a full consideration of the statutes. But it was maintained that there are clauses in some of the statutes conferring this exemption which were not brought under the notice of the Court, or at least were not properly expounded to the Court in argument in the case of the Scottish Widows' Fund. If that be so, it is certainly quite right that we should reconsider our judgment in the Scottish Widows' Fund case. But before adverting to the particular statutes which form the basis of the argument for the Railway Company, it is desirable to see how the case stands under the judgment of the Scottish Widows' Fund, or rather, what is the import and effect of the statutes applicable to a subject of this kind as fixed by our judgment in that case. Now it appears to me that a house, meaning thereby an entire tenement or building, may be placed in three different positions. It may be occupied by a variety of persons, the owner of the entire

___

(b) *Ante,* p. 247.
(c) These sections are set forth and explained in the judgment of the Lord President.

tenement letting out portions of it for different purposes to different tenants. That is one case. Another case is that the entire tenement may be divided into separate properties, and in that case it has always been the law that the separate properties are separately assessable to the Inhabited House Duty. But in the other case of the house being let out in portions to different tenants for different purposes, the law under the general Act, the 48th of George III., was that the owner of the entire tenement was held to be the occupier for the purposes of the Act, and was assessable to the Inhabited House Duty for the entire house or tenement. Then there is a third case, and that is the case of a house—by which of course I mean an entire tenement or building—belonging to one proprietor, and used and occupied by him for various purposes without being let out at all. Now, under the earlier statute, certainly whatever might be the purposes for which portions of the building were occupied, the owner would be assessable as the occupier of the entire tenement. Of that there can be no doubt. But certain changes have been made upon these rules of the early statute, and one statute in particular, the latest of all—the Act of 1878,—introduces some very important changes. It deals with the case of a house being let out by its owner in different portions to different tenants, and in certain circumstances grants relief for those portions of the house that are let out and occupied for business purposes. The other and earlier statutes, had before that given relief for separate tenements and separate parts of tenements belonging to different owners occupied exclusively for business purposes. But the case that is before us at present is the last case that I mentioned : the case of an entire house belonging to one proprietor but occupied by himself,—entirely occupied by himself, but different parts of it for different purposes. And the question comes to be whether that case is provided for by any of the statutes. There certainly is no provision for that case in the Act of 48 of George III., and it is just as little apparently contemplated in the latest statute of 1878. But the argument which was addressed to us was, that the 57th of George III., c. 25, followed by the 5th of George IV., c. 44, gives relief from the Inhabited House Duty for parts of tenements that are occupied for business purposes although the entire tenement may belong to one owner. If that is so, then our judgment in the case of the Scottish Widows' Fund is erroneous; but it depends entirely upon whether these two statutes are susceptible of the construction which is thus sought to be put upon them. Now, my Lords, I am of opinion that the 57th of George III., c. 25, does not contemplate the case of separate parts of tenements being relieved, the whole tenement being the property of one owner; and if that is the case with regard to the 57th of George III., I think it must be equally so in the case of the 5th of George IV., c. 44, which merely extends the provisions of the 57th of George III., in the manner which I shall immediately explain. But the language of the 57th of George III. is first to be considered. Now the first section of that statute

BANKS v.
GLASGOW
AND SOUTH-
WESTERN
RAILWAY
COMPANY.

proceeds upon a special preamble. It sets out the previous Act of the 48th of George III., and then it proceeds, "Whereas it has " become usual in cities and large towns and other places for one " and the same person or for each person where two or more persons " are in partnership, to occupy a dwelling-house or dwelling- " houses for their residence, and at the same time one or more sepa- " rate and distinct tenements or buildings or parts of tenements or " buildings for the purposes of trade, or as warehouses for lodging " goods, wares, or merchandise, or as shops and counting houses, " and to abide therein in the day time only for the purposes of " such trades respectively which have been charged with the " said recited duty,"—that is to say, the premises occupied for trade purposes only have been charged under the authority of the 48th George III. with the Inhabited House Duty,—" although " no person shall inherit or dwell therein in the night time, and " it is expedient in such cases to exempt from the said duties " such tenements or buildings or parts of tenements or buildings " as are or shall be solely employed for the purposes herein men- "tioned." Now I think in this preamble we find the key to the construction of the enactment. It is intended to give relief from taxation to something which has been previously subjected to taxation, and that is tenements or buildings, or parts of tene- ments or buildings which have been charged with the said recited duties. It is such only that are in contemplation of this clause of the statute. Now under the 48th of George III., no part of a tenement could be charged to the said recited duties unless it was a separate property. A tenement let out by its owner to different tenants for different purposes was charged as an entire tenement, and no part of that tenement was charged to the said recited duties. Therefore it follows of necessity that the parts of tene- ments which are here to be exempted or relieved are those parts of tenements which were charged with duty under the said recited Acts as parts of tenements, that is to say, parts of tene- ments belonging to separate owners. Now what is the enact- ment? " That from and after the 5th of April 1817 on due proof " made in the manner herein directed to the satisfaction of the " respective Commissioners acting in the execution of the said " recited Act, if any person or any number of persons in " partnership together respectively occupy a tenement or build- "ing or part of a tenement or building which shall have " previously been occupied for the purpose of residence wholly " as a house for the purposes of trade only or as a ware- " house for lodging goods, wares, or merchandise, or as a shop or " counting-house, no person inhabiting, dwelling, or abiding " therein except in the day time only for the purpose of such " trade, such person or each of such persons in partnership " respectively residing in a separate and distinct dwelling-house " or part of a dwelling-house charged to the duties under the said " Act, it shall be lawful for the Commissioners according to the " provisions of this Act to discharge the assessment made for that " year in respect of such tenement or building which shall be so

BANKS v.
GLASGOW
AND SOUTH-
WESTERN
RAILWAY
COMPANY.

"used for the purposes of trade, or be employed as a warehouse
"for the sole purpose of lodging goods, &c., anything in the said
"Act to the contrary notwithstanding." Then it is further
provided that this relief is to be given after the entire tenement
has been brought in as a subject of assessment, and the relief is
to be given upon due proof being made that the separate portions
of the tenement or the whole tenement itself is used exclusively
for the purposes of trade. The moment it ceases to be used for
the purposes of trade conclusively, the right to obtain the relief
comes to an end, and each year relief requires to be claimed under
the 2nd section of the Act upon due proof that the exclusive
occupation for the purposes of trade exists during that year.
Now, then, what is the result of all this? It seems to be that
the statute of the 57th of George III. did not intend to alter in
an indirect and almost unintelligible way the rule of the 48th of
George III., which provided that where tenements are let out or
occupied for different purposes, the whole tenement belonging to
one owner, the owner was no longer to be considered as the occupier and charged with the assessment. If it had been the purpose
of the statute to repeal that very important and very clearly
expressed rule of the old statute, it surely would have done so.
But instead of that all that is done, so far as I can see, is to take
up the subject of tenements, or parts of tenements, which, under
the 48th of George III., are assessable to the Inhabited House
Duty, and to deal with such tenements as are assessable to that
duty only. And, accordingly, when you come to look at what
parts of tenements are assessable under the 48th of George III.,
you find it to be parts of tenements belonging to different owners,
and nothing else. And thus the operation of the 57th of
George III. is limited in that way, and cannot possibly be held
to extend to such a case as the present, or to the analogous case
of part of a tenement being let out by the owner for different
purposes. I am, therefore, of opinion that the argument upon this
statute advanced on the part of the Railway Company fails
entirely. And if that be so, it is almost needless to say that he
derives no advantage from the 5th of George IV., because that
is merely extending to occupation for professional purposes the
exemption which was given in the other statute for trade
purposes. There are no doubt some very awkward expressions,
or forms of expression, in the 4th section of the 5th of George IV.,
but one of these, and almost the only one that creates the
slightest difficulty in reading the statute appears to me to be
simply a misprint, where, talking of the house in which the trader
or partner of a trading company dwells, it speaks of the dwelling-
house or part of the dwelling-house charged to the said duty.
The whole phrase, the whole sentence, is borrowed from the
earlier statute, and the change from the indefinite to the definite
article from " a " to " the," is just a plain mistake or misprint,—
I really do not know which. But anyone who reads that clause
I think must be satisfied that this is so. Now then, it seems to
me that that is an end of the case; because if the Railway Com-

BANKS v.
GLASGOW
AND SOUTH-
WESTERN
RAILWAY.
COMPANY.
——

pany can obtain no advantage from these two sections, they have nothing to say against the application of the judgment in the Scottish Widows' Fund case.

But it may be just as well to notice that the latest statute of all, that of 1878, seems to be quite inconsistent with the notion that these provisions, particularly the provision of the 57th of George III., was intended to have any of the effects attributed to it by the Railway Company. The first sub-section of section 13 relates to the case of a house being one property divided into and let in different tenements, and where some of such tenements are occupied solely for the purposes of any trade or business, or of any profession or calling by which the occupier seeks a livelihood or profit; and in that case the person chargeable as occupier of the house—that is, the owner of the entire house, shall be at liberty to give notice in writing at any time during the year of assessment to the surveyor, and upon certain proof, he is to obtain relief of a portion of the assessment corresponding to that part of his premises which is let out for trade purposes or for professional purposes. Now observe there that this last statute of 1878 continues in full force so far the rule of the Act of the 48th of George III. It still keeps the owner of the entire tenement as the person chargeable as occupier. There is no change in that respect. But according to the argument of the Railway Company, that change had been made in the meantime by the 57th of George III. by some language which certainly in its direct meaning does not effect any such purpose. But it seems to be contended that in some indirect and not very intelligible way the great fundamental rule of the 48th of George III., that the owner of the tenement shall be the person chargeable to the Inhabited House Duty, was put an end to. But here it remains in the year 1878 untouched, just as it was in the 48th of George III. Then when you come to the second sub-section another observation occurs which is very important. It deals with the case of a house or tenement occupied solely for trade purposes or professional purposes, although a caretaker shall dwell on the premises. Now that takes one back a little to the history of what occurred about the exemption of such premises. First of all, premises occupied for trade purposes were alone exempted by the 57th of George III. Then that exemption was extended to premises occupied for professional purposes, and then by the Act of 1869, the 32nd and 33rd of Victoria, there was an enactment to the effect that premises occupied for trade purposes should be exempt although a care-taker dwelt on the premises; but that statute did not allow a care-taker to dwell on the premises in the case of premises let for professional purposes. Now, observe what takes place here in the second sub-section. The third sub-section repeals that enactment about the caretaker in the Act of 1869, and it enacts that every house or tenement which is occupied solely for the purposes of trade or any profession or calling shall be exempted upon proof of the facts to the satisfaction of the Commissioners, and this exemption shall take effect although a servant or other person may dwell in such house or tenement for the protection thereof. Now observe that in this the existing enactment regarding the exemption of premises occupied for trade or professional purposes, there is no mention of a part of a tenement at all. So that if the mention of a part of a tenement is necessary in order to let in the contention of the Railway Company, that a part of their premises, being occupied for railway purposes, should be exempt, they could not get their exemption under this section, for there is nothing said about a part of a tenement at all. What would be the consequence? The consequence would be (if the argument is sound) that a part of a tenement belonging to one owner if occupied for trade purposes or for professional purposes, is exempt from taxation, but they would not be entitled to have a care-taker, and it would not be exempt if a care-taker dwelt therein, because that exemption depends entirely upon the Act of 1878. And there would be this strange anomaly, that while the Act of 1878 deals with the entire subject, and lays down rules which cover the entire subject of exemption, these trade purposes or professional purposes would exempt an entire house occupied for such purposes, even though a care-taker dwelt therein, but would not exempt a part of a tenement occupied for such purposes if a care-taker dwelt therein. Now, such anomalous results as that are, I think, sufficient in themselves to show that any construction of these earlier statutes that would lead to such results must be unsound.

Upon the whole matter I am very clearly of opinion that there is nothing in the two statutes which have been relied upon in the argument to interfere at all with the rule laid down in the case of the Scottish Widows' Fund.

Lord Deas.—I am certainly of opinion that this case is ruled by the case of the Scottish Widows' Fund and some other cases that were decided at the same time, and the only question, therefore, is whether the judgment in the case of the Scottish Widows' Fund and these other cases was sound. There are here four floors from the ground tenement upwards which are occupied entirely for other purposes than those of a hotel; but the Railway Company is proprietor of all these, and occupies the whole, and if the rule laid down in the case of the Scottish Widows' Fund is sound, it must necessarily occasionally include cases in which the proportions occupied for trade and business purposes are of an extent somewhat startling as compared with the portions occupied as a dwelling-house or hotel. That necessarily follows from the rule being a general one. But I am of opinion with your Lordship that these cases were rightly decided, and that that which is said to have been overlooked in the argument does not, when you look into the Act of Parliament, make any difference. And therefore I have no difficulty in coming to the same conclusion which your Lordship has come to, that these cases are applicable and that they were rightly decided.

BANKS v. GLASGOW AND SOUTH-WESTERN RAILWAY COMPANY.

BANKS v
GLASGOW
AND SOUTH-
WESTERN
RAILWAY
COMPANY.
—
against the decision in the Scottish Widows' Fund case entirely falls.

The Lord President.—Then we reverse the decision of the Commissioners and sustain the assessment.

No. 48.—In the High Court of Justice (Queen's Bench Division).
10th March 1881.

The Yorkshire Fire and Life Insurance
Company -   -   -   -   -   Appellants
and
Clayton (Surveyor of Taxes)   -   -   - Respondent.

Inhabited House Duty.—The term " different tenements," in sec. 13 (1) of 41 Vict. c. 15, means complete tenements occupied, or intended to be occupied, independently of each other. Per Lindley, J., the exemption does not apply where the owner occupies a part of the house himself.

YORKSHIRE
FIRE AND
LIFE
INSURANCE
COMPANY v.
CLAYTON.
—
At a Meeting of the Commissioners for the General Purposes of the Income Tax Acts and for executing the Acts relating to the Inhabited House Duties for the district of Hull, in the County of York, held at the Office of the Surveyor of Taxes, in the Town of Kingston-upon-Hull, on Thursday, the 27th day of February 1879, for the purpose of hearing this appeal.

The Yorkshire Fire and Life Insurance Company appealed against an assessment to the inhabited house duty of 450*l.* at 9*d.* in the pound in respect of the premises known as the "Yorkshire Buildings," situate in Lowgate, in the ward of St. Mary, Hull, for the year ending 5th April 1879.

The Company was represented by Mr. E. Gray, of the firm of W. and E. Gray, of York, the solicitors to the Company.

The premises in respect of which the assessment was made have been recently erected by the Appellants, and are occupied partly by the Appellants as offices, other portions by a banking company, traders and professional men for business purposes only, other portions by the curates of St. Mary's Church, Hull, for purely residential purposes, and the remainder by a caretaker and his wife, who clean the several portions used by the Appellants and let off as offices, and act as the domestic servants of the clergymen, each portion of the premises being accessible only by means of one common entrance and staircase.

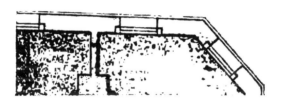

SE.

The Appellants claimed relief from the amount of duty charged YORKSHIRE in assessment, so as to confine the same to the portions of the FIRE AND LIFE premises used by the clergymen only under 41 Vict., cap. 15, INSURANCE COMPANY v. sec. 13, sub-sec. 1. CLAYTON.

In their appeal (amongst other arguments) the Appellants particularly called the attention of the Commissioners to the fact of the omission from the section in question of the words " being " distinct properties," which appear in the 14th Rule of 48 Geo. 3, cap. 55, and which were entirely relied on by Barons Bramwell and Cleasby in their judgment in the case, Attorney General v. Mutual Tontine Westminster Chambers Association (Limited), Law Reporter XXXIII., 181, a case quoted by the Commissioners in support of their view of this matter, Baron Cleasby stating that in his opinion the chambers of the association were " let in different tenements " within Rule 6 of the Act of Geo. 3, and that they were not distinct properties within Rule 14.

The Appellants also noticed the opening paragraph of the section, and urged that it must have been intended to effect some alteration in the existing law, and, if so, must apply to cases like the present, otherwise it would be practically re-enacting Rule 14 above mentioned.

The Commissioners decided that as portions of the premises were let off for residential purposes, without having a separate street entrance and staircase, and without being totally disconnected from the other portions of the building the whole of the premises were liable to the duty as one house or tenement inhabited by one person or family only under 48 Geo. 3, cap. 55, sched. B., and that the provision referred to in the Statute 41 Vict., cap. 15, sec. 13, sub-sec. 1, in nowise altered the law relating to inhabited house duties with respect to what is or what is not a house " divided into and let in different tenements," and accordingly confirmed the assessment.

Whereupon Mr. Gray, on behalf of the Appellants, declared his dissatisfaction with their decision, and duly required them to state and sign a case for the opinion of the Exchequer Division of the High Court of Justice, which we have stated and signed accordingly in pursuance of the 37 Vict., cap. 16, sec. 9.

J. G. W. WILLOWS, } Commissioners.
JOSEPH ATKINSON, }

Supplemental Case for the opinion of the Court under the 37 Vict. cap. 16. Part 3.

This Case having been referred to the Commissioners in order that the facts may be more fully stated, the Court having considered that it was not sufficiently informed as to the following particulars, viz. : —

YORKSHIRE
FIRE AND
LIFE
INSURANCE
COMPANY *r.*
CLAYTON.

(1.) " Whether the premises were divided within the meaning of the Act."

(2.) " Whether they were let within the meaning of the Act."

We, the undersigned, being two of the Commissioners for general purposes of the Income Tax Acts and for executing the Acts relating to the Inhabited House Duties for the District of Hull, in the county of York, do hereby state as an addition to the case as follows:—

The building in respect of which the assessment is made consists of

The Ground Floor. Occupied as offices by the Appellants, who are owners of the whole building.

Offices occupied by the York City and County Bank, and offices occupied by Mr. Clarke, civil engineer.

The First Floor. Offices occupied by Messrs. Beadle, Sykes, and Co., merchants, and Mr. Martin Samuelson, civil engineer.

The Second Floor. Rooms occupied as residences by the curates of St. Mary's Church, Hull, and by a caretaker.

It will therefore be seen that the Ground and First Floors are used as offices for business purposes only, and the Second Floor for residential purposes.

The building is to all intents and purposes one house, with one entrance to the street, and the offices open into a hall, passages, and staircase, which are common to all the tenants. Plans (which have been furnished by the Appellants) are annexed and show clearly the nature of the premises.

Two rooms on the Ground Floor, on the right-hand side of the entrance, are occupied as before stated by the Appellants, who are owners of the entire premises. The head offices of the Appellants are at York, and their offices in this building are occupied as a branch establishment by a local secretary and clerks, all of whom are in the employment of and are paid by salary by the Appellants.

The remainder of the offices on the Ground and First Floors, and the residences on the Second Floor, are let by the Company as previously stated.

The Building is rated to the poor as follows:—

Occupier.	Owner.	Description of Premises.	Gross estimated Value.	Rateable Value.
			£ s. d.	£ s. d.
—	York Fire Insurance Company.	Offices and club room.	450 0 0	
William Tyers Huffam, Secretary.	" "	Offices	60 0 0	
York City and County Bank.	" "	"	170 0 0	730 0 0
Beadle, Sykes & Co.	" "	"	190 0 0	
Clarke	" "	"	50 0 0	
Martin Samuelson	" "	"		
John Scott	" "	Rooms	40 0 0	

The first item in the rate is a separate and distinct house, occupied by the Hull Club, and is separately charged with Inhabited House Duty, and the assessment is not disputed, the remainder of the offices and rooms from the house in respect of which this case is stated.

The rateable value is charged in one sum, and the rates are paid by the Company, but each tenant repays to the Company the proportion due in respect of his share.

J. E. W. WILLOWS, } Commissioners.
JOSEPH ATKINSON,

Bigham, for the Appellants. The case comes within the very words of the statute 41 & 42 Vict. c. 150. 13 (1). The building is one property, and it is divided into and let in different tenements, some of which are occupied solely for purposes of trade or business, while others are occupied residentially.

Sir F. Herschell, S. G., for the Respondent. The relief was intended to apply to such cases as the Westminster Chambers (*d.*), where the block of buildings is divided into entirely separate tenements. The legislature has required that for the purposes of this section the house shall be not only let in, but also divided into, different tenements. In the Westminster Tontine case each tenant had his whole establishment, so to speak, within the house which he took, but the curates here are mere lodgers, waited upon by the care-taker, who is the servant of the landlord. Moreover, the house is not let in different tenements. The landlord occupies a part of it himself.

Bigham, in reply. I understand the point is that this house is not divided into different tenements.

[*Grove, J.* Or let in different tenements. *Solicitor-General.* The landlord occupies a part.]

Then the point is that as the whole of it is not let in different tenements, therefore it is not within the meaning of the Act; and the next point is that it is not divided into different tenements. The case clearly comes within the spirit of the Act, and it cannot be meant that all the different parts of the house are to be let.

[*Lindley, J.* Let or empty.]

The landlord by carrying on a business on the ground floor, increases the reason why the building should be exempt.

The whole of the building need not be let, because the section contemplates the possibility of a part not being let, and the Act does not say that if the part not let be occupied by the landlord, then the sub-section shall not apply.

The Solicitor-General drew attention to the plan of the second floor, showing that, with one exception, each room had a separate door opening on the landing or corridor.

NOTE.—*The following judgments were delivered before the passing of the Customs and Inland Revenue Act,* 1881, *which*

(*d.*) Attorney General *v.* Mutual Tontine Westminster Chambers Association, L.R., 10 Exch. 305 ; 1 Exch. Div. 469.

YORKSHIRE
FIRE AND
LIFE
INSURANCE
COMPANY *v.*
CLAYTON.

YORKSHIRE
FIRE AND
LIFE
INSURANCE
COMPANY v.
CLAYTON.

provides (sec. 24) that the words "servant or other person" in 41 & 42 Vict., chap. 15, sect. 13 (2), shall be deemed to mean a menial or domestic servant employed by the occupier, or a person of similar grade or description not otherwise employed by the occupier and engaged by him to dwell in the house or tenement solely for its protection.

Grove, J.—I do not say the section is free from difficulty, but upon the whole—and I think everything that can be said has been said by Mr. Bingham—our judgment ought to be for the Crown. I think, looking at it as far as I can judge not merely from the words, but the intention of this section, it was intended to apply to a house which was let in separate and distinct parts, something as chambers are let, so that the parts let were really perfectly in separate tenements inhabited by different occupiers, who had absolute and exclusive control over each separate part, having a common staircase, I will call it a common roadway to the house, and that in that case the taxation should not apply to those parts of the house so let, those "different tenements" (those are the words of the Act) which were so let for trade purposes. It is true that certain of the people inhabited this house, and others had certain rooms in the house for the purposes of trade, but I do not think the house is let in different tenements. The house must be substantially divided into, and let in, different tenements so as to constitute independent tenements. Here one whole floor is inhabited by persons who used it as a residential house, each of the rooms they inhabited, with one exception, opening by separate doors upon the staircase, two servants attend upon them, and as far as we know are exclusive attendants. It is not found they kept any other, and I suppose for three curates two servants would be sufficient, and those servants also act for the occupiers of the other rooms. They clean their offices, and do everything that a housemaid would do. They are not mere care-takers or watchers. They are not persons kept to watch a house at night, as a person resides in a gentleman's house when he goes into the country, or as the letter of chambers on a common staircase may leave a person during the long vacation to take care of the chambers, but they are daily occupied in the duties of ordinary servants. Therefore it appears to me that in one sense the whole of the house is to some extent residentially occupied. The question of there being servants may be a small matter, but it is to my mind quite separable and divisible from the position of a care-taker or watcher. I cannot, therefore, say that this house is within the fair meaning of these words let in different tenements, because there is nothing to show that each of those tenements is held as a different and separate holding, of which the persons have entire and absolute control irrespective of the whole of the remainder of the house. The words of the section when you come to analyse them are extremely difficult, and it is very difficult to give a consistent meaning to the whole of them.

I do not pretend to do so. I can only gather the sense of the YORKSHIRE section, and that appears to me to be the meaning of it. "Where "any house, being one property, shall be divided into and let in "different tenements, and any of such tenements are occupied "solely for the purposes of any trade or business," &c. I think that must mean that where the house is a house divided into separate and exclusive tenements, if I may use the term, then those tenements which are occupied for the purposes of trade shall be exempt. I rely more upon the finding of the case relative to the servants, although it is a small point, no doubt, but the line must be drawn somewhere. I think they show a common use of the house by the landlord, the curates and the other person occupying the house to that extent for residential purposes. I think, therefore, our judgment must be for the Crown.

Lindley, J.—I am of the same opinion. It is for the Appellant to bring himself within this exemption, and I do not think he has done so. The clause is obvious in its meaning. I do not think it does apply to a case where a landlord occupies any part of the house not as a caretaker, which might bring him within the section . (e) but for the purposes of residence or business. The difficulty about the word "let" is obvious. The only thing is, you must read the section in such a way as to give it a sensible effect. It contemplates the house being divided into tenements, and it contemplates a state of things in which the premises are not occupied. They may be let and some of the lessees not taken possession, but what I think is meant is this, that if the house is let, that is to say, intended to be let, habitually let, I do not think it includes the case of a house not intended to be let at all, and in which some of the property is occupied by the landlord. Sub-clause 2 would apply if the whole was let for the purposes of trade and the landlord only occupied it as a caretaker. I think this case comes within the first section. Then I confess I doubt whether these are different tenements within the meaning of the section. I do not think they are. It is difficult to say what a "different tenement" is, but my impression, which I get from the discussion in the Westminster and Tontine Association, is, that they are tenements complete in themselves, not a mere room opening on to a common staircase, that the tenements there were tenements which were complete in every sense, that is to say, they were suites of apartments, they were flats, they were houses on one floor instead of houses on several floors. Here we have only one set of rooms, some with external doors and some without. I do not think this house was divided into, and let in, different tenements, within the meaning of that section.

The Solicitor-General.—I ask for costs.

Grove, J.—Yes.

Judgment for the Respondent.

YORKSHIRE
FIRE AND
LIFE
INSURANCE
COMPANY v.
CLAYTON.

(e) *Vide* 44 Vict. c. 12. s. 24. and Note at p. 339.

7424

No. 49.—In the Court of Exchequer (Scotland).
11th March 1881.

In re Ainslie.

Inhabited House Duty. — *A farmhouse is not within* 41 & 42
Vict. c. 15. s. 13 (2).

In re Ainslie.   At Haddington, the 26th December 1880, at a Court held by
the Commissioners for general purposes for the County of
Haddington, acting in the execution of the Property and
Income Tax Acts, and the Inhabited House Duty Acts.

Robert Ainslie of Elvingston appealed against an assessment
of inhabited house duty at 6*d.* per 1*l.* on 28*l.*, being the annual
value of the farmhouse of Morham Mains belonging to him and
occupied by one of his farm servants, and against an assessment
of inhabited house duty at 6*d.* per 1*l.* on 24*l.*, being the annual
value of the farmhouse at Morhambank belonging to him, and
occupied by his farm steward or manager.

The houses in question are the farmhouses on the farms of
Morham Mains and Morhambank.   The farms were formerly
let to tenants who resided on the farms, occupying the houses in
question, and were charged to house duty.

Both farms are now in the occupation of the proprietor (the
Appellant), who resides at Elvingston, and the houses are occupied
by his servants and their families.

The Appellant claimed exemption under sect. 13, sub-sect. 2,
of the Act 41 Vict. cap. 15, which provides that any house or
tenement "occupied solely for the purposes of any trade or
"business, or of any profession or calling by which the occupier
"seeks a livelihood or profit, shall be exempted from the duties
"by the said Commissioners upon proof of the facts to their
"satisfaction, although a servant or other person may dwell
"therein for the protection thereof."   The case the Appellant
refers to in his appeal in support of his claim is that of the
Scottish Widows' Fund, 22nd January 1880, VII. Rettie, p. 491.

The Surveyor contended that the exemption referred to did
not apply to a farmhouse occupied as a dwelling-house, and
referred in support of his contention to the Act 48 George III.
cap. 55, and to the Act 14 & 15 Vict. cap. 36, and Schedule B.
appended thereto, where three classes of dwelling-houses are set
forth as liable to be charged at the rate of 6*d.* per 1*l.*, viz. : —

   1. Any dwelling-house occupied by any person in trade who.
      shall expose to sale and sell any goods, wares, or
      merchandise, in any shop or warehouse, being part of
      said dwelling-house and in the front or basement storey.

2. Any dwelling-house occupied by any person licensed to sell *InreAINSLI* beer, ale, wine, &c.; and

3. Any dwelling-house which shall be a farmhouse occupied by a *tenant or farm servant* and *bond fide* used for the purposes of husbandry only.

The surveyor maintained that the exemption granted by subsect. 2 of 41 Vict. cap. 15, applied only to the first of the three classes of house set forth—houses occupied by persons in trade.

The Commissioners dismissed the appeal, and confirmed the assessment on the grounds stated by the surveyor. The Appellant being dissatisfied with the decision of the Commissioners craved that a case might be stated for the opinion of the Court, which is done accordingly, and signed by the Commissioners the 22nd January 1881.

(Signed)   HEW DALRYMPLE,   } Commissioners.
    ,,   CHARLES J. SHIRREFF, }

Edinburgh, 11th March 1881.—I am of opinion that the determination of the Commissioners is right.

(Signed)   JOHN MARSHALL.

No. 50.—IN THE HIGH COURT OF JUSTICE (QUEEN'S BENCH DIVISION).

16th March 1881.

THE RYHOPE COAL COMPANY, LIMITED   -   -   Appellants
               and
FOYER, Surveyor of Taxes -   -   -   -   Respondent.

Income Tax.—The conversion of a private partnership into a Company with limited liability creates a succession by the Company within the meaning of the fourth rule of the first and second Cases of Schedule D. An extraordinary depression of trade may be a specific cause within the meaning of the latter part of that rule.

At a Meeting of the Commissioners for the General Purposes of the Income Tax Acts for the District of Easington Ward in the County of Durham, held at Sunderland in the said County on the 19th day of December 1876, for the purpose of hearing Appeals.

Mr. Charles Kidson, Secretary of the Ryhope Coal Company, Limited, appealed against an assessment under Schedule D. of the said Acts on the sum of 77,083*l.* in respect of the profits of the said Company for the year 1876, ending 5th April 1877 the

RYHOPE COAL COMPANY *v.* FOYER.

same being assessed on an average of the five preceding years. It being contended on behalf of the Company that it was only liable to pay on the computation of one year on the average of years on the average of profits from the date of its incorporation.

CASE.

1. The Ryhope Coal Company was an ordinary partnership formed on the 1st day of January 1856, for the purpose of working certain mines in the county of Durham, which they continued to do up to the 21st day of December 1875.

2. On the 21st day of December 1875 the then partners of the Ryhope Coal Company, by contract in writing, sold to the Ryhope Coal Company, Limited, the assets (subject to the liabilities) of the Ryhope Coal Company for the sum of 602,400l.

3. The Ryhope Coal Company, Limited, was incorporated on the 21st day of December 1875, for the purpose of taking over and carrying on the business of the Ryhope Coal Company with a capital of 652,600l. divided into 502 shares of 1,300l. each. The purchase money was to be paid by issuing to the partners of the Ryhope Coal Company the whole of the 502 shares (on each of which 1,200l. was to be written up as paid 502 by 1,200l. making the purchase money 602,400l.) in proportion to their shares in the Ryhope Coal Company.

4. The partners in the Ryhope Coal Company became holders of all the shares in the Ryhope Coal Company, Limited, according to their interest in the Ryhope Coal Company, and the only change effected was that the old partners were incorporated as a limited Company in which they held the same interest as in the old Company, but divided into partially paid-up shares. The working of the mines never ceased.

5. Since the 3rd day of August 1876, various changes have taken place in the shareholders of the Ryhope Coal Company, Limited, the said shares having been bought and sold.

6. It is agreed that should the Court decide that the Company is liable to pay on an average of five years, the amount assessed shall stand.

7. Under paragraph 2, No. III. of Schedule A. of 5 & 6 Vict. c. 35, the annual value of mines of coal, &c. was to be understood to be the full amount of profits for one year on an average of the five preceding years, subject to the provisions concerning mines contained in that Act.

8. One of such provisions is that the duty is to be charged on the person, Corporation, Company, or society of persons, whether corporate or not corporate, carrying on the concern or on their respective agents, treasurers, or other officers having the direction or management thereof, or being in the receipt of the profits thereof on the amount of the produce or value thereof, and before paying, rendering, or distributing the produce or the

value either between the different persons or members of the RYHOPE
Corporation, Company, or society engaged in the concern, or to COAL
the owner of the soil or property, or to any creditor or other COMPANY *v.*
person whatever having a claim in or out of the said profits. FOYER.

9. The Appellants admitted that the mines have not from
some unavoidable cause decreased, and are not decreasing in the
annual value thereof, and that consequently they could not and
did not claim any exceptional circumstances to entitle them to be
charged on a different basis from other mines, and the Commissioners thereupon decided that Rule 5 of No. III. (*f*) Schedule A.
of 5 & 6 Vict. c. 35, did not apply to this case.

10. By section 8 of 29 Vict. c. 36, it is enacted "that the
" several and respective concerns described in No. III. of
" Schedule A. of the said Act passed in the 5th and 6th years
" of Her Majesty's reign, chapter 35, shall be charged and
" assessed to the duties hereby granted (being the income tax
" duties) in the manner in the said No. III. mentioned according
" to the rules prescribed by Schedule D. of the said Act so far
" as such rules are consistent with the said No. III."

11. The first case under Schedule D. of 5 & 6 Vict. c. 35,
comprises the duties chargeable in respect of any trade, manufacture, or concern in the nature of trade and mines will
therefore come under that case.

12. By paragraph 1 of the rules of such first case, the duty
shall be computed on a sum not less than the full amount of the
balance of the profits or gains of such trade, manufacture,
adventure, or concern upon a fair and just average of three
years: Provided always, that in cases where the trade, manufacture, adventure or concern shall have been set up and commenced within the said period of three years, the computation
shall be made for one year on the average of the balance of the
profits and gains from the period of first setting up the same.
This paragraph will apply to mines, excepting that the average
will be five years instead of three.

13. By paragraph 4 of the rules applying to both cases under
Schedule D. of the said Act, it is enacted as follows: "If amongst
" any persons engaged, any trade, manufacture, adventure, or
" concern, or in any profession in partnership together, any
" change shall take place in any such partnership, either by
" death or dissolution of partnership as to all or any of the
" partners, or by admitting any other partner therein before
" the time of making the assessment or within the period for
" which the assessment ought to be made under that Act, or if
" any person shall have succeeded to any trade, manufacture,
" adventure, or concern, or any profession within such respective
" periods as aforesaid, the duty payable in respect of such
" partnership or of any such partners or any person succeeding
" to such profession, trade, manufacture, adventure, or concern,
" shall be computed and ascertained according to the profits and

---

(*f*) For No. III. read No. IV.

"gains of such business derived during the respective periods
"herein mentioned, notwithstanding such change therein or
"succession to such business as aforesaid."

14. The Commissioners were of opinion that the business of
the Ryhope Coal Company, Limited, is not a trade, manufacture
adventure, or concern, set up and commenced within the period
of five years within the meaning of the proviso of the Act cited
in paragraph 2 of this case. And further, having regard to the
fact that the Ryhope Coal Company, Limited, is formed to carry
on the business of the Ryhope Coal Company, and consists of
identically the same partners as the Ryhope Coal Company
consisted of, and to the fact that such partners have identically
the same interest in the new Company as in the old, they were
of opinion that the Ryhope Coal Company, Limited, is really,
and in fact, but a continuation of the Ryhope Coal Company
under another name, and is entitled to the benefit of the said
proviso, and therefore liable to be assessed on the average profits
of five years.

15. The Commissioners were also of opinion that as the mines
in question had been constantly working for more than five
years, such mines are liable under the Income Tax Acts to be
assessed on the profits on the average of five years irrespective of
the question of ownership.

16. The Commissioners were also of opinion, apart from the
fact that the Ryhope Coal Company, Limited, consists of the same
partners in the same interests as the Ryhope Coal Company, and
supposing such Ryhope Coal Company, Limited, to be a company
formed of altogether different persons from the Ryhope Coal
Company, then it comes within the meaning of the rule of the
Act cited in paragraph 13 of this case, as having succeeded to a
trade, manufacture, adventure, or concern, and is therefore
liable to an assessment on the average of the five preceding years.

17. The assessment on the average was accordingly confirmed,
whereupon the Appellants declared their dissatisfaction with the
determination as being erroneous in point of law, and duly
required the said Commissioners, by notice in writing, addressed
to their clerk, to state or sign a case for the opinion of the Court
according to the statute 37 Vict. c. 16. s. 9, which we have stated
and sign accordingly.

17a. *The profits and gains of the Appellants business have
fallen short since the 21st December 1875 from the following
specific causes, vizt. :—*

*The extraordinary depression in the iron and coal trades,
whereby the Appellants were unable to sell so large a
quantity of their coals as they had formerly been enabled
to do or obtain anything like so good a price for such coals.*

17b. *The following are the actual profits and gains of the
Appellants business since the 21st December 1875, vizt. :—*

*Profits and gains of the Appellants business
from the 21st December 1875 to the 31st De-* } £27,487 7 9
cember 1876 -   -   -   -   -

Whereas the profits and gains of the Ryhope Coal Company prior to the formation of the Ryhope Coal Company, Limited, from the 31st December 1874 to the 21st December 1875, were 58,889*l.* 16*s.* 9*d.*

RYHOPE COAL COMPANY *v.* FOYER.

18. The question for the opinion of the Court is whether the Ryhope Coal Company, Limited, is liable to pay duty in respect of its profits from the mines carried on by it on an average of the five preceding years, or whether, as contended by the Company, it is only liable to pay on a computation for one year on the average of the profits from its incorporation on the 21st day of December 1875.

Signed by us the said Commissioners on the 23rd day of April 1877.

H. R. A. JOHNSON.
C. MALING WEBSTER.

Henry Robert Allan Johnson, Esquire, one of the Commissioners who signed the case has since ceased to be a Commissioner.

This amendment in red ink (g) *is signed by us, two of the said Commissioners, and dated the 17th day of February* 1881.

C. MALING WEBSTER.
JOHN SCOTT.

Sir F. Herschell, S.G. (*A. L. Smith* with him), for the Appellants. The Commissioners acted on the ground that this Company was a mere continuation of the former Company. Our contention is that the Ryhope Coal Company, Limited, is an altogether different being from the old Ryhope Coal Company, which was a private partnership. The case is within the sixth rule of No. IV., Schedule A, and the profits should be estimated from the date of the possession by the new Company. Turning to Schedule D. to see the effect of 29 & 30 Vict. c. 36. s. 8, I say that this is a concern set up within the period of three years (first case of Schedule D, first rule), or, as it is here to be read, five years. Reads the fourth rule of Cases 1 and 2, Schedule D. If the contention on the other side were correct, that, under the first rule of Case 1, it matters not who is carrying on the trade so long as the trade goes on, you would not have found the fourth rule at all, because then it would have been already provided that, notwithstanding any change, the assessment should be on the average of three or five years, as the case may be, and therefore the existence of the fourth rule shows that I am right in my construction as to the former part. The next question is whether the Ryhope Coal Company, Limited, " succeeded " to the adventure or concern within the meaning of the fourth rule. I submit that they did not, and that the sale of the old partnership to this Company was not a succeeding. But even supposing that we are

(g) Here in italics.

within this rule, there comes the provision " unless such partners
" or such person succeeding . . . . shall prove . . . .
" that the profits and gains of such business have fallen short, or
" will fall short, from some specific cause . . . . since such
" change or succession took place, or by reason thereof." We
said that we could prove that our profits had fallen off from a
specific cause; and the Commissioners, to whom the case went
back on this point, find (Clause 17a) that from the extraordinary
depression in the iron and coal trades the profits had fallen from
58,889l. in the year before the transfer to the Company to
27,487l. in the following year; and yet they claim to assess us
on 77,083l. or rather less than three times the income made.
The fourth rule clearly implies that without it, where there had
been a change, the average would not be applicable, but while
it enacts that in certain cases the average is to be applied, it also
gives relief from the average, even in those cases, if what is there
mentioned be proved to the satisfaction of the Commissioners.
Now we have proved to the satisfaction of the Commissioners
that our profits fell short, and the Commissioners specify the
causes of that falling short. Therefore we come within the very
terms of that provision. To sum up my argument, I say that
we are within the sixth rule of No. IV., Schedule A., because
Schedule D. does not overrule it, and the two may be read
together. If that be not the case, I say that this is a concern
started within the three (or five) years, because otherwise you
could not apply the fourth rule of Cases 1 and 2, Schedule D.
Then I say that the fourth rule only applies to a change during
the year of assessment, or after that year and prior to the actual
assessment. Next I say that this is not a case of succeeding
within the meaning of the rule, and, lastly, that if we be within
the rule we have proved to the satisfaction of the Commissioners
that our profits have fallen short from a specific cause.

Sir H. James, A.G., (*Dicey* with him), for the Respondent.—
The eight section of 29 & 30 Vict. c. 36 enacts that the concerns in No. III. of Schedule A. are to be assessed "in the manner
" in the said No. III. mentioned, according to the rules prescribed
" by Schedule D. of the said Act, so far as such rules are consis-
" tent with the said No. III.," and therefore you must no longer
look at No. IV. of Schedule A. The rules prescribed by Schedule D. are substituted for No. IV., and you must look only at
No. III. and at Schedule D., but, if it were otherwise, could it be
alleged in this case that the accounts cannot be made out? The
accounts have been made out, and they exist. We now come to
the first case of Schedule D., and I submit that this concern—
this mine—has not been set up within three years. When the
Act says where the trade or concern shall have been set up it
refers to the business and not to the parties who carry it on.
This question is not what the individual is making, but what the
concern has been making, and the average of the past five years
is taken simply as evidence of the sum to be charged for the

coming year. On the formation of the limited Company there BYHOPS
COAL
COMPANY v.
FOYER. was no change whatever, except that the partners for their own convenience preferred a corporate existence. If the latter part of the fourth rule of Schedule D. takes the Appellants out of the first part of that rule, the effect is simply to leave them where they would be if the rule were not in the Act; but the Appellants contend that there has been no succession, and they would limit the words " shall have succeeded " to a succession by operation of law. What is the usual phrase on a transfer or sale of a business? It is, " Smith & Co., successors to Jones & Co." The words " shall have succeeded " apply to this case: but, say the Appellants, if they do we escape from them under the second part, because it has been found by the Commissioners that the profits have fallen off from a specific cause. This is a question of law as well as of fact. The Commissioners have found the falling off, and they have stated the cause which, I submit, is not a specific but a general cause, notwithstanding the decision of the Court of Session in Scotland in the case of the *Inland Revenue* v. *Farie* (h), where it was held that depression in the coal trade was a specific cause within the meaning of this rule. The Scotch Court also held that the three years' average in Schedule D. was not inconsistent with No. III. of Schedule A., a position which the Solicitor-General admits to be untenable. The 134th section of the 5 & 6 Vict. c. 35 also contains the expression ". specific cause " and throws light on its meaning. It says that where " any person . . . . shall cease . . . " to carry on the trade . . . . or shall die, or become bank- " rupt or insolvent before the end of the year for making such " assessment, or shall from any other specific cause to be deprived " of or lose the profits or gains," &c., then he or his executors can get relief. The words " specific cause " are to be read *ejusdem generis*, that it must be something having particular relation to that business and not a general depression of trade. Now look at the proviso to that 134th section. The meaning of the words " shall have succeeded " there cannot be limited to a succession of operation of the law, and why should those words have a different meaning in the fourth rule from what they have in this section. However, I can only rely on the fourth rule if the Crown fail on the other argument, that the business is the same business, and should be so assessed in accordance with No. III. of Schedule A.

A. L. Smith. for the Appellants, in reply.—The proviso to the fourth rule of Schedule D. (first and second cases) is in favour of the tax-payer, and to prevent his having to pay income tax on profits of which he had not the benefit; and it makes no differ- ence whether the specific cause of his not getting that benefit was the flooding of his mine so that he could not get his coal to the surface, or the fact that when he had got it to the surface he

---

(h) 16 Scottish L.R., 189.

could not sell it from depression of trade. The Attorney-General has left himself in this dilemma; either we are an adventure set up within the three years, or we are a succeeding Company.

[*Mr. Dicey.*—We say that you are the same Company.]

The private partnership has been dissolved; a limited liability Company has been formed, and its shares have been bought and sold in the market. It cannot be made out that the two companies are the same, and therefore the present Company is either a Company set up within the meaning of the first rule of Schedule D., or it is a Company which has succeeded within the fourth rule. The contention of the Crown can only be supported by your Lordships' decision that this is the self-same Company, and then I would ask how long is this Limited Company to remain the same as the old private partnership. Turning to Schedule A., the "Rules and Regulations respecting the said duties" are put in No. IV. for convenience instead of repeating them at the end of No. I., No. II., and No. III., but those rules are part and parcel of Nos. I., II., and III. The words " so far as such rules are consistent with the said No. III." mean with No. III. *plus* the rules of No. IV., because No. IV. is incorporated with Nos. I., II., and III. The provisions of the Act are framed with the object that the tax-payer shall not pay on more than he has received, and it appears on the special case that we have made 28,000*l.* instead of 77,000*l.*

19th March 1881.   *Grove, J.*—There was undoubtedly a change in the partnership, and a very important change, when the concern was converted from an ordinary partnership into a Limited Liability Company. The fourth rule of Cases 1 and 2, Schedule D., uses the words "as to all or any of the partners." It took place here as to all; and the Company having succeeded to their business the case comes within the first portion of this rule. Does it also come within the exception, "unless such " partners or such person succeeding to such business as afore- " said, shall prove, &c."? The Scotch Court, in the case which has been referred to, held that depression of trade was a "specific cause." In one sense I agree with them, except that I should put it thus, that depression of trade may be, but it is not necessarily, a specific cause. It must be, to my mind, to make it a specific cause, something unusual, exceptional, extraordinary. Here there was, to use the words of the Commissioners, an "extraordinary depression in the iron and coal trades," by which it is found that the profits of this concern are reduced to less than half of its former profits. I think, therefore, the Appellants come within that section, and are entitled to the benefits of it; and I think that the assessment should be on the profits and gains for one year. There are several points relied on by the

Appellants which have failed, and there should be no costs on either side.

Lindley, J.—By the 8th section of 29 Vict. c. 36, No. III. of Schedule A. is not touched, but you must substitute Schedule D. for the whole of No. IV., obeying the injunction that you must not make the substitution where it would be inconsistent with what is left of No. III.   Therefore wherever an average of three years is given in Schedule D. you must in the case of a mine read five, and with that basis you are to apply Schedule D. Turning to Schedule D., I say that this is not a concern " set " up and commenced " within the period of five years.   It is a new association carrying on an old trade.   We then pass to the fourth rule, and there appears to me to be precisely a case of succession within the meaning of this rule, so that *primâ facie* the five-year average would apply; but the Commissioners have found as a fact that from " the extraordinary depression in the " iron and coal trades " the profits have fallen off since the succession to the place, and the only question which remains is whether there is a " specific cause," and the Commissioners having found that it is, I am not prepared to say that it is not. The five-years' average, therefore, is gone, and the average must be taken from December 1875, the date when the Limited Company took over the concern.

Judgment for the Appellants, without costs.

No. 51.—IN THE HIGH COURT OF JUSTICE, QUEEN'S BENCH
DIVISION.
23rd March 1881.

HERMANN GUSTAV ERICHSEN (Representative of the Great
Northern Telegraph Company of Copenhagen) -   Appellant.

W. H. LAST (formerly Surveyor of Taxes)   -   Respondent.

Income Tax, Schedule D.—A foreign Company, domiciled abroad, had submarine cables in connexion with the United Kingdom, and other foreign cables not connected with the United Kingdom.   The Company, under an agreement with the Postmaster General, also has separate wires, worked by its own staff, between Aberdeen, Newcastle and London.   No profits were derived from the transmission of messages over these last-mentioned wires.   Held, that the Company exercises a trade in the United Kingdom, and is assessable on the net profit derived from the receipts here.

CASE stated under the Statute 37 Vict. cap. 16. sec. 9, by the
Commissioners for the general purposes of the Income Tax
Acts for the City of London, for the opinion of the High
Court of Justice.

. 1. The Great Northern Telegraph Company of Copenhagen is
a foreign Corporation, having its seat at Copenhagen, in Denmark,
and resident there.

2. The Company has three marine cables in connexion with
the United Kingdom, one at Peterhead, in Scotland, and two at
Newbiggin, near Newcastle. These cables are in connexion with
telegraph lines under the control of Her Majesty's Postmaster
General, at Aberdeen and Newcastle, and under and in pursuance
of the agreements set forth in the schedule hereto, or some of
them separate wires from Aberdeen to Newcastle and from Newcastle to London, have been provided by the Post Office for the
traffic passing over the Company's said cables to and from the
continent.

3. In accordance with the said agreement or some of them,
these separate wires are worked by the Company's staff and the
Company has workrooms with a staff of servants at Aberdeen
and Newcastle, and workrooms in Winchester Street in the city
of London, and the rents of the workrooms and salaries of the
staff, consisting of about forty clerks and electricians, are paid by
the Company.

4. Messages sent from this country to, say, Japan, pass over;
(1.) The lines of the Post Office in this country, (2.) Over the
said marine cables of the Company, (3.) Over land lines in
Denmark, belonging to the Danish Government, (4.) Cables in
the Baltic belonging to the Company, (5.) Land lines in Russia
belonging to the Russian Government, (6.) Cables east and south
of Russia belonging to the Company. Similarly messages from
this country to various parts of the world pass over the said
three marine cables of the Company, and subsequently over
cables and lines belonging to foreign Governments or to other
Companies, or over cables or lines belonging to the Company,
but having their commencement by attachment to cables or lines
not owned by the Company. A plan showing the cables and
lines of the Company is hereto annexed, and is to form part of
this Case; on such plan the cables and lines of the Company
are shown in blue ink and those belonging to foreign Governments and other Companies in red ink.

5. Under the international telegraph convention, to which the
British Government has adhered, the total charges from the
handing-in station in the United Kingdom to the place of destination abroad are, except as herein-after stated, collected and
received by the Post Office Telegraph Department, which retains
out of such total charges the sums due to it out of the said

agreements in respect of messages sent from the United Kingdom to abroad and received in the United Kingdom from abroad, and hands over the balance to the Company, which in its turn retains out of such balance the sum due to the Company in respect of the transmissions of messages over the cables and lines of the Company, and pays over the residue to the various Governments and Companies respectively entitled to the same.

6. By special arrangement with the Post Office, the Company receives payment direct from a few firms who desire to hand in their messages direct to the Company and accounts out of such receipts to the Post Office.

7. The expenses incurred by the Company in the transmission of messages over the said separate wires in the United Kingdom exceed the earnings received by the Company in respect of the same, and no profits are made by the Company from the use of the land lines in the United Kingdom.

8. At a meeting of the said Commissioners held in the Land Tax Room No. 3, Guildhall Buildings, in the city of London, on Thursday the 23rd day of May 1878, for the purpose of hearing appeals—

Mr. Herman Gustav Erichsen, representative of the Appellants, appealed against an assessment of forty thousand pounds (40,000l.) for the year 1876, ending 5th April 1877, under Schedule D. of the Income Tax Acts in respect of the profits of the business alleged to be carried on in the United Kingdom by the Agency of the Company.

9. It was contended for the Appellant that as no profits were derived from the transmission of the messages over the land lines used by the Company in the United Kingdom there were no profits made by the Company within the United Kingdom, and in these circumstances no liability to income tax attached to the Company. It was further contended for the Appellant through its agent that if liable at all the Company was only liable to be assessed in respect of the profits earned by the Company in the United Kingdom from the transmission of messages over the said three marine cables, and not further or otherwise.

10. The Respondent (the Surveyor of Taxes) admitted that the Great Northern Telegraph Company was a foreign Company domiciled in Copenhagen; but he contended that as its agency in this country despatched messages to the Company's offices in Aberdeen and Newcastle, and thence by its own cables from those places to Norway, Denmark, and Sweden, and from thence by the Company's own wires and the wires of foreign Governments to Russia, China, Japan, and India, and that as the entire charges of transmitting such messages from this country were paid by the senders and were received by the agency in London,

the amount so received being 70,000l. (seventy thousand pounds) per annum on the average of the years 1873, 1874, 1875 the Company through its agent was chargeable to income tax on the balance of profits or gains arising from the total sums received in this country from the transmission of messages.

11. The Commissioners present taking this view of the case, confirmed the assessment in respect of the entire profits of the agency calculated on the total sums received by the Company in this country, subject to the production of accounts showing the total receipts and expenditure in each year, whereupon the Appellant expressed his dissatisfaction with our decision as being erroneous in point of law, and duly required us to state and sign a case for the opinion of the Exchequer Division of the High Court of Justice, which we have stated and signed accordingly in pursuance of the said Act.

The question for the opinion of the Court is whether under the circumstances herein stated the Company is through its agent bound to make a return, and is chargeable to income tax, and if yea, upon what principle the annual profits of which the Company is bound to make a return, and on which it is chargeable to income tax are to be ascertained, or whether, as was contended for the Company, the Company is not bound to make a return and is not chargeable to income tax.

THOMAS HANKEY,
R. B. WHITESIDE,
BENJ. DOBREE,
W. C. FOWLER,

Commissioners of Income Tax for the City of London.

3, Guildhall Buildings,
January 30th, 1879.

SCHEDULE referred to in Paragraph 2 of Case for opinion of the Exchequer Division of the High Court of Justice.

AGREEMENT.

Entered into this 3rd day of November, 1868, between the Danish Norwegian English Telegraph Company, having their seat at Copenhagen, Denmark, herein-after called "The Danish Company," of the first part, Herman Gustav Erichsen, of Newcastle-upon-Tyne, merchant, the resident Director in this country of the Danish Company, duly authorised by the Board of Directors of that Company to act on their behalf with full legal powers, and binding the Company in accordance with the Articles of Association of the second part, and the United Kingdom Electric Tele-graph Company, Limited, having its chief office at Gresham House, in the city of London, herein-after called "The United Telegraph Company," of the third part. Whereas by an agreement dated the 17th day of January, 1868, made between the above Companies and signed by William Andrews, the secretary of the United Telegraph Company, for and on their behalf, and which Company is therein designated by the letter "A," and signed by Nathaniel J. Holmes, the then secretary and manager of and for and on behalf of the Danish Company, which is therein designated by the letter "B," the United Telegraph Company as "A," undertook to receive at and transmit from their several stations in Great Britain all messages or continental service passing through service, passing through the cables of "B," and "A," covenanted to provide a special direct wire (No. 6, B. W. G.) to meet the special wire and submarine cable wire to be laid by "B," as therein-after provided, exclusively for the traffic between Newcastle-upon-Tyne and London, in connexion with the through continental service of "B," and "A," covenanted to receive and convey every such message over their lines in Great Britain, and deliver the same within a radius of half a mile from their station for the uniform charge of one shilling, providing such message should not exceed 20 words, including address. And it was agreed that when such message should exceed 20 words, an additional charge of sixpence for every 10 words or fraction thereof should be maintained, and further, when the distance at which such message was required to be delivered exceeded the half mile radius, a sum for porterage in accordance with the usual scale charged by the other telegraph systems in Great Britain should be added to the original transmission of tariff of such message, and "A" further agreed to introduce the high speed automatic system of Wheatstone as the transmitting system over the special wire from Newcastle to London, provided that the royalty to be paid for the use of the same be the same as that paid by the Electric and International Telegraph Company for the use of the same system on their wire between Newcastle and London, so long as the instrument should prove efficient for the work to be performed, it being understood that should the number of messages of 20 words each, transmitted over the special circuit in connexion to the cables of "B" fall short of 30,000 per annum (interruptions in the continuity of the circuit between Newcastle and Copenhagen being excepted from the calculation), then "A" should be at liberty to make use of the special wire for public traffic other than the through continental service in connexion with "B" and "A," should be entitled to make use of such wire for inland messages during such breakage of continuity, and "B" undertook that the messages exchanged should number 30,000 per annum at the least, and "A" undertook and agreed to provide at the several stations all necessary staff and appliances for the speedy and efficient performance of the above-named inland transit, and as regarded the second parties to the said agreement, "B" agreed and covenanted with "A" as follows, that "B" should extend a special wire from the landing place of the cable in the vicinity of Newcastle-upon-Tyne, to the transmitting station of "A" in Newcastle, and "B" agreed and covenanted that all messages passed into the system of "A" under the agreement now in recital, should be exclusively in connexion with the continental service and cable transmissions, and that no message of local import as between local stations in Great Britain should be included under the terms of the agreement, and "B" covenanted to confine the continental service (that is the receipt and transmission of message through cables and circuits in connexion therewith), exclusively to the system, stations, lines, and circuits belonging to "A" for the term of their concession from the Danish Government, providing that such system should be maintained by "A" in proper and efficient condition, and "B" agreed that the local transmitting stations in connexion with the cable should be at Newcastle-upon-Tyne, and that the efficiency of the cable shore ends and other connexions should be efficiently maintained with all reasonable speed, wind and weather permitting, and "B" covenanted to maintain through the cables and circuits a high speed service on the automatic system equivalent to that attained on the land circuits of "A," due allowance being made for the difference in electrical condition between land lines and submarine cables employing the highest insulation (Hooper's core), and it was agreed between "A" and "B" that the statements of account and traffic receipts in connexion with the above inland and continental transmissions should be balanced on each side once a month, and that the accounts duly vouched should be paid over by "A" and "B" respectively. to their authorised agents or bankers therein after to be named.

And whereas the United Telegraph Company have in pursuance of the said agreement constructed and provided such special direct wire from Newcastle-upon-Tyne to London, as thereby stipulated, and do now receive and transmit the messages of the Danish Company in accordance with the said agreement; but the Danish Company have not extended any special or other wire from the landing-place of their cable in the vicinity of Newcastle-upon-Tyne to the United Telegraph Company's station at Newcastle in consequence of a company incorporated in this country, and called "The Danish Norwegian English Telegraph Company, Limited," herein-after called the said English Danish Company, having with the consent of the United Telegraph Company laid and constructed such a line from Newbiggin, in Northumberland, the landing-place of the Danish Company's cable to the station of the United Telegraph Company at Newcastle, aforesaid, whereby the extending of a special wire by the Danish Company has been rendered unnecessary. And whereas the United Telegraph Company have lately arranged with the said English Danish Company for the use of their said telegraph or line, subject to the payment of certain moneys and the performance of certain covenants and stipulations, and have agreed that the Danish Company shall be excused from extending such special wire as thereby agreed, and that the messages which were to have been thereby transmitted to the station of the United Telegraph Company at Newcastle shall in lieu thereof be transmitted by or through the telegraph or line so constructed by the said English Danish Company, as aforesaid, and that subject to such alteration and all alterations necessitated thereby the said herein-before mentioned agreement shall be confirmed and such further agreements made as herein-before mentioned, expressed, and contained. Now, therefore, these present witnesses, and they the several parties hereto do and each of them doth hereby ratify and confirm the said agreement of the 17th day of January, 1868, subject to the said alterations, and particularly they, the Danish Company, in consideration of the United Telegraph Company so excusing them, as aforesaid, do for themselves, their successors and assigns, and also the said Herman Gustav Erichsen on their behalf doth hereby confirm such agreement on the 17th January, 1868, and agree with the United Telegraph Company (in such agreement designated or referred to by the letter "A"). That the Danish Company, their successors and assigns, shall and will faithfully carry out, perform, and fulfil all and singular their part or parts of the same agreement (excepting the extending of such special wire from the landing-place of their said cable to Newcastle) and shall and will, in lieu and stead, duly and properly connect their cable or cables, and allow the same to be duly and properly connected with the telegraph or line constructed by the said English Danish Company, and from time to time duly maintain and allow to be maintained such connexions, and transmit all and every their messages to the United Telegraph Company station at [Newcastle by or through the telegraph or line so constructed by the said English Danish Company as aforesaid.

And further, the said Danish Company, their successors and assigns, shall not nor will either directly or indirectly transmit any of their continental messages to any of the stations or towns or places in which the United Company have stations through, along, or by means of any other telegraph or system than that of the United Telegraph Company. And also shall and will, whenever requested by the United Telegraph Company, enter into, make and execute all and every such acts, deeds, matters, and things whatsoever as may be considered necessary for carrying out the aforesaid agreement, as now altered or otherwise in respect of the matters and things therein and herein contained or referred to. And it is hereby further agreed and declared that the several provisions of the herein-before mentioned agreement of the 17th day of January, 1868, and of these presents, subject to the alterations hereby made, are extended to and shall henceforth be deemed and taken to relate and be applicable to and in respect of all cables, wires, and telegraphs which the Danish Company shall at any future time connect or cause to be connected with the shores of Great Britain and to all Continental messages transmitted along, through, or by the same in the same manner as the said agreement, and these presents relate to the cables, wires, and telegraph of the Danish Company in such agreement mentioned. And the said United Telegraph Company hereby covenant for themselves, their successors and assigns, that the United Telegraph Company shall and will (subject in the event of Her Majesty's Postmaster General purchasing the undertaking of the United Telegraph Company under the Telegraphs Act, 1868, to the approval of Her Majesty's Postmaster General for the time being) erect and maintain a special direct wire for every new cable so to be laid, as aforesaid, from the station of the United Telegraph Company nearest to the landing point of such new cable to London, and the United Telegraph Company shall in each and every month make out and furnish to the Danish Company a statement of the accounts and traffic receipts in connexion with the messages sent, received, and transmitted under or in pursuance of this agreement, and shall thereupon pay any moneys appearing thereby to be due and owing from them to the Danish Company, and the Danish Company shall once during every three months make out and furnish to the United Telegraph Company a statement of the accounts and traffic receipts in connexion with the messages sent, received, and transmitted under or in pursuance of this agreement, and shall thereupon pay any money appearing thereby to be due and owing from them to the United Company, and all such accounts not objected to within four calendar months after the same shall have been rendered shall be deemed to have been correct. This agreement shall continue in force until the expiration of the concession granted to the Danish Company by the Danish Government. AS

ERICHSEN r.
LAST.

WITNESS the common seals of the said Danish Company and the United Telegraph Company, and the hand of the said Hermann Gustav Erichsen the day and year

before written (Seal of the Danish Company) H. G. Erichsen (L.S.) (Seal of the United Telegraph Co.)

Board of Directors of the Danish Norwegian English Telegraph Company, C. A. Broberg, O. B. Suter, M. Levy, C. F. Tietgem, W. C. E. Sponneck. Witness to the signature of the within-named Hermann Gustav Erichsen, W. A. Harle, clerk to Messrs. Hodge and Harle, solicitors Newcastle-upon-Tyne. I, the undersigned Notary Public Royal, in and for this City and Royal Residence of Copenhagen, do hereby certify and attest that Mr. C. A. Broberg, Counsellor of State, merchant, Mr. O. B. Luke, Counsellor of State, merchant, Mr. M. Levy, Counsellor of State, Mr. C. F. Tietgen, Counsellor of State, Director of the Private Bank, and his Excellency Count W. C. E. Sponneck, Director of the National Bank, all personally known to me, have before me the said notary and the hereunto subscribing witnesses in their quality as Directors of the Danish Norwegian English Telegraph Company declared to have with their own hands signed the above agreement and to have caused the Seal of the said Company to be affixed. In witness whereof under my notarial firm the Seal of Office, Copenhagen, the 24th December 1868, W. C. L. Abrahams, Not. Pub.

(Stamp. 1868. 24/12. 48. W. C. L. Abrahams, Not. Pub.)

(L.S.) A. B. Witness fees and stamp 1 or dgy. 12 N. C. L. A. I hereby

certify that the above signature and seal are those of W. C. D. Abrahams, Esquire, Notary Public of this city, to whose attestation full faith and credit are due in and out of Court. In testimony whereof witness my hand and Seal of Office, British Consulate, Copenhagen, Decr. 24, 1868, C. W. Lange, Acting British Consul

(L.S.) fee five shillings.

CORRESPONDENCE constituting agreement between Great Northern Telegraph Company of Copenhagen and the Post Office.

"Great Northern Telegraph Company,
London Office,
"7, Great Winchester Street Buildings, E.C.,
7th July 1869.

"DEAR SIR,

"REFERRING to the conversation I had with you this morning, I beg to recapitulate the heads of an agreement to be entered into between the 'Post Office and 'this Company,' (as assignee of the Danish Norwegian English Telegraph Company' of Copenhagen,) in the event of the Money and Monopoly Bills being passed, viz., that—

"All messages for Denmark, Norway, and Sweden, are to be sent from England by the cables of this Company unless specially directed by the sender to go by another route.

"The same as regards messages for such parts of Russia as shall be named from time to time by the 'Russian Telegraph Administration.' As to all other messages in transit through Russia, the public to state the cable route from this country.

ERICHSEN v.
LAST.
———

"As regards messages for the United States of America and Canada, the public to state the route from this country.

"Requesting you to have the kindness to confirm this agreement.

"I remain, dear Sir,
"Yours faithfully,
(Signed)   "C. F. TIETGEN,
"Chairman of the Great Northern Telegraph Company of Copenhagen.

"Frank Ives Scudamore, Esq.,
"General Post Office."

———

"Telegraphs.

"General Post Office, London,
8th July 1869.

"SIR,

"I BEG leave to acknowledge the receipt of your letter of yesterday's date, and to state that you have correctly described the heads of an agreement proposed to be entered into between the 'Post Office and the Great Northern Telegraph 'Company,' (supposing that company to become the assignee of the 'Danish 'Norwegian English Telegraph Company' of Copenhagen,) when the transfer of the property of the United Kingdom Electric Telegraph Company' to the Post Office takes place, and to which agreement I have already assented on behalf of this department.

"I am, Sir,
"Your obedient servant,
(Signed)   F. J. SCUDAMORE.

"C. F. Tietgen, Esq.,
"Great Northern Telegraph Company of Copenhagen."

———

"Great Northern Telegraph Company.
"London Offices:
"7, Great Winchester Street Buildings,
26th January 1870.

'DEAR SIR,

"Thanking you for the obliging manner in which you received me to-day, I beg, for regularity's sake, to recapitulate the substance of our conversation.

"It was understood that my 'Company' should work their cables with their own staff. The Danish cable to be worked at Newcastle, the Norwegian at Peterhead.

"The question of how much the tariff should be reduced to be considered further by you, and I trust that you will find an early opportunity to give this matter your attention.

"On Friday I hope to be in Newcastle, and shall then, after having, with your permission, conferred with Mr. Mosley, make free to send you a plan of the arrangement I would propose.

"To Peterhead I have written, and shall by return of post have a description of the premises that would be suitable for the purpose, and shall submit the same for your approval.

"To Copenhagen I have wired, with a request that our staff should come over as soon as possible, but pending their arrival, and the fitting up of the respective working rooms, I suppose that you will have no objection to the cables being worked by the same United Kingdom clerks who have up to this been employed.

"I remain, dear Sir,
"Yours faithfully.
(Signed)   H. G. ERICHSEN.

"Frank Ives Scudamore, Esq.,
"General Post Office."

———

"Great Northern Telegraph Company.
"London Office:
"7, Great Winchester Street Buildings, E.C.,
25th March 1870.

"DEAR SIR,

"FOR regularity's sake I beg to recapitulate the several arrangements made when I had the pleasure of meeting you in Newcastle on the 19th instant.

"It was agreed that in consideration of the Danish, English, and Scotch Norwegian cables being worked by our own staff, the British terminal and transit rate should be reduced from one shilling to one franc per single message of 20 words.

"That should you desire it my Company is quite ready to have their own staff in your Central London station to work the wires to Newcastle and Peterhead or Aberdeen, subject to modification of terms.

"That if you desire it, I am ready to remove the Company's station from Peterhead to Aberdeen. On this matter an early definite reply would be very welcome.

"That if one of our cables or your wires leading to the same should be out of order, the traffic thus stopped to be sent by the other cable belonging to the Company.

"That you would order an alteration in the tariff for Swedish messages, which now erroneously stand at 7s. from London and 8s. from the provinces in lieu of 7s. from any station in the country.

"That you thought that Article 38 in staff instruction, (H. 4.) say the prefix clause might be understood with regard to Russian messages.

"That you would give instructions, that in future all messages handed over to our offices, are furnished with code time.

"That reclamations from abroad have to be sent direct to you from our office.

"That for matters of account you refer me to Mr. Chetwynd, the Receiver and Accountant-General.

"That I deposit my authority from the Company with you and this I now do as per enclosed.

"Requesting you kindly to acknowledge receipt of this letter and to confirm its contents.

"I remain, dear Sir,
"Yours faithfully,
(Signed)   H. G. ERICHSEN.

"Frank Ives Soudamore, Esq.,
"General Post Office."

ERICHSEN v.
LAST.

"Great Northern Telegraph Company,
"London Office,
"7, Great Winchester Street Buildings, E.C.
21st April 1871.

"SIR,
"As arranged with Mr. Baines when Mr. Tietgen and I had the pleasure to confer with him to-day on the subject of separate wires from Aberdeen to Newcastle and from Newcastle to London to be worked by this Company's own staff in connexion with their cables, I now beg to note down the heads of Agreement as made to-day.

"The Post Office undertakes to supply these wires not later than the 1st day of July 1871.

"The Company pays for the use of the same 5,500l. per annum besides 1d. (one penny) per message up to 200,000 messages per annum, and 2½d. (two-and-a half pence) per message for any number of messages above 200,000 per annum. This payment to include all expenses for collecting and delivering messages in the United Kingdom.

"The Post Office will, free of expense to the Company, supply a pneumatic tube from any of their Central Stations to the Company's Offices, at No. 7, Great Winchester Street Buildings, and will maintain the same.

"The Post Office will order four complete sets of Wheatstone's apparatus ; these to be paid for by the Company, but the same not to be subject to any Royalty charge.

"Requesting you to confirm this arrangement, I have only to add that it would be desirable to name a period over which the same should extend, and I shall feel obliged by your views on this subject.

"I am, Sir,
"F. I. Soudamore,   "Your most obedient servant,
"General Post Office."   (Signed)   H. G. ERICHSEN.

Registered No. 101,133.
Telegraphs.

"General Post Office, London,
"SIR,   April 26, 1871.
"IN reply to your letter of the 21st inst., setting forth the proposed heads of an Agreement between the Great Northern Telegraph Company and this Department, I beg leave to say that with the two undermentioned exceptions, the Department confirms the Heads of Agreement as laid down in your letter.

"1. In clause I. 'the Post Office will do its best to supply' instead of 'the Post-
'Office will supply.'

"I may state, however, that on the very day following your visit to this office, and
without waiting the receipt of the letter now under acknowledgment, orders were
given to the Engineer-in-Chief to proceed at once with the erection of the Aberdeen
wire, and to use his best endeavours so to arrange that the London as well as the
Aberdeen wire might be placed at your disposal at the date named.

"2. In Clause III. 'The Post Office will, free of expense, provide a tube from
'their Central Station for the time being' instead of 'from any of their Central
stations.'

"As regard the term of years I would suggest seven years as a desirable period
for the Agreement to run.

                         "I am, Sir,

                              "Your obedient servant,

"H. G. Erichsen, Esq.,   (Signed)   F. I. SCUDAMORE.
     "Great Northern Telegraph Company."

A. M. Bremner for the Appellant.—The Company being domiciled at Copenhagen is only liable to assessment for profits from
their trade exercised in the United Kingdom, but it is found in
the case that from its wires in the United Kingdom the Company
derives no profit. With regard to the cables which are wholly
abroad, the trade is not exercised here, and with regard to those
cables which touch the shore of this country, it must be held that
the Company carries on its business at Copenhagen, where its
chief office is.

Sir H. James, A.G., for the Respondent.—The Company does
not reside here, but it exercises a trade within the United Kingdom, and must be charged on the profits made by the exercise of
trade in the United Kingdom. The fact that a portion of the
contract made here has to be fulfilled abroad does not affect the
liability to duty on the profits made here.

Lindley, J.—I am of opinion that the contention of the
Appellants is not sustainable, that is to say, I am of opinion
that they are under the circumstances stated here liable to pay
duty in respect of such profits, if any, as accrued to them here
from carrying on their business in this Company.

Now the facts are shortly these. The Appellants, who I will
refer to as the Company, are resident, to use the expression, in
Denmark, and their principal place of business is there; and in
one sense they carry on their business there; they are resident there, they dwell there, and carry on their business there.
They have three cables which cross the German Ocean, which
are landed in the United Kingdom on the east coast. There
are three shore ends, and to that they have property there, and
whether much or little is another matter; to that extent they
have property, and that property whatever it is, is essential to
the transaction of their business. In addition to that they have
certain cables abroad, and in particular some property on the East
of Russia to Japan, the line of which we do not know. What is
done is, their messages are transmitted from this country say to
Japan; they are received by the Post Office authorities here and

are transmitted through these cables to which I have alluded which crosses the German Ocean. The money paid for those messages is paid in the first instance to the Post Office; they collect it, and then, as I understand, every year they account to the Company in this way: The Post Office deduct what is payable to them for the use of their lines for collecting or transmitting these messages to the German Ocean cables, and they hand over the balance of the gross receipts to the Company, and then the Company in their turn subdivide that; they pay certain portions of their gross receipts to the Danish Government and Russian Government for the use of their respective lines. That is no part of the profits of this Company; they merely transmit that, and no question arises about their being taxed upon these sums. Then there remains the balance, the net proceeds which include or partially include some profits, I do not say whether all profits: that is quite another matter.

Now that being the course of business, the first question we have to consider is, not whether the Company is or is not resident in the United Kingdom, but whether it does or does not receive profits or gains from some property in the United Kingdom or from some profession, trade, employment, or avocation exercised within it, because if it does it is chargeable with duty. It is said that it does not carry on business in the United Kingdom, and taking that expression generally I am rather disposed to accede to that view, that is to say, adopting the analogy between the railway case it has been decided that for the purpose of giving the County Court jurisdiction, the Great Western Railway Company, and the North Western Railway Company,. and so on, carry on business at Paddington and at Euston Square, and so I think that this Company carries on its business in that sense at Copenhagen and not here, but it does not follow that they do not in the language of this section receive any profits from any profession, trade, employment, or avocation exercised here. It is obvious they do. A great portion of their profits are derived here from the use of property belonging to them here, the shore ends of the cables, from the contracts entered into here from the transmission of messages received here and from the moneys collected here. It seems to me very strong to say that they receive nothing from any profession, trade. employment, or avocation exercised in the United Kingdom.

Now reliance has been placed upon certain cases on both sides. I do not think they help us much. The decisions to which the learned Attorney-General has referred, namely, the Ottoman Bank cases, were to my mind not cases similar to this. The Ottoman Bank has a branch bank in London, and they made profits at that branch bank. No questions arose as to the liability of the bank to pay income-tax in respect of those profits, but it was contended that they were resident here so as to have to pay upon all the profits they made at Constantinople, which is entirely another matter, and that was negatived. That case does not appear to me to touch this. Then *Gilbertson* v. *Ferguson* is a similar case arising, I think, in connexion with the same bank. Now Mr. Bremner on the other hand has relied upon the *Attorney-General* v. *Sully* in support of his proposition that this Company did not carry on business there. That was a case of this kind. There were certain persons, most of whom were resident in America, there was one partner who was resident here, and an attempt was made to make the partner' pay income tax on the whole profits of the firm. The answer was that they never received them here and no profits were received in this Company upon which income tax could be assessed except his share of the profits which was not in question. That case seems to be entirely distinguishable. I think the view is that this Company is taxable with income tax—that is to say, liable to pay duty, &c., for the transmission of telegraph messages from this country by the three cables landed in this country. How to ascertain those profits is quite another matter. That we are not asked nor do we know that such profits have accrued to them in that way which they ought to pay duty upon.

Williams, J.—I am of the same opinion. This Company, although not resident in the United Kingdom and carrying on its business at its head-quarters at Copenhagen, nevertheless exercises a trade within the United Kingdom, and that trade is the business of receiving and transmitting telegraph messages from England to distant parts of the world for reward. The contracts are made here, payment is demanded and made here for transmission to their destination. It seems to me that the ownership of the cables through which these messages are transmitted is wholly immaterial, or whether the Company own the cables or part of them, or hire them and pay tolls for the use of them, is quite beside the question altogether, and we can only enter into the question of whether profits have been realised or not. It seem to me that a trade is being carried on or transacted by them here on which profits may be realised, and on those profits it seems to me that they are liable to pay income tax.

Mathew, J.—I am of the same opinion. I cannot see that there is any practical difficulty in ascertaining what gains and profits are made by this Company through their English business, and on the gains and profits so made I think they were assessable.

Judgment for the Respondent, without costs.

No. 52.—IN THE HIGH COURT OF JUSTICE.—QUEEN'S BENCH
        DIVISION.   June 2nd, 1881.

CHAPMAN, Surveyor of Taxes   -   - Appellant.

and

THE ROYAL BANK OF SCOTLAND -   - Respondents.

*Inhabited House Duty.—Part of the ground floor and basement
    of a building structurally separated from the rest of the
    building by a party wall, having a separate door to the
    street, and without internal communication, held to be a
    separate house.*

*The words " divided into, and let in different tene-
    ments " in 41 Vict. c. 15. sec. 13 (1) require a real division.*

Yorkshire Fire and Life Insurance Company v. Clayton
        followed. (Ante. p. 336.)

*On the question whether 41 Vict. c. 15, sec. 13 (1) can
    apply where the landlord himself occupies one of several
    tenements into which a house is divided, the others being
    let for trade or professional purposes, or being actually
    unoccupied, the Court was not required to decide, but
    seemed to be divided in opinion.*

CASE stated under the Statute 37 Vict. cap. 16, sec. 9. the
    Commissioners for the General Purposes of the Income Tax
    for the City of London, for the opinion of the Exchequer
    Division of the High Court of Justice.

AT a meeting of the Commissioners for the General Purposes
    of the Income Tax Acts and for executing the Acts relating
    to the Inhabited House Duties for the City of London, held
    at the Land Tax Rooms, Guildhall Buildings, in the said
    City, on Thursday, the 17th July 1879.

The Royal Bank of Scotland, by its agent, Mr. St. Quintin,
appealed against an assessment to the Inhabited House Duties
for the year ending the 5th day of April 1879, of 6,000l. at 9d.
in the pound upon and being the full value of the whole of the
premises, No. 123, Bishopsgate Street, in the City of London,
and claimed exemption in respect of one portion of the said
premises under the Act 57 Geo. 3. cap. 25., and in respect of the
other portion under the Act 41 Vict. cap. 15. sec. 13.

The premises constituting No. 123, Bishopsgate Street, consist
of a basement, ground, and upper floors, with two separate main
entrances from the street as shown in the view of the front of
the building accompanying the Case.

The ground floor and basement of the building on the south side with entrance marked A on the ground plan herewith are in the occupation of the Respondents, and are used by them as a bank for the purpose of carrying on their business as bankers, and have no internal communication whatever with the rest of the building being separated by a party wall from the basement to the first floor.

The ground floor of the building on the north side is at present unoccupied.. The first and second floors which run over the whole of the premises are occupied by several traders, and used entirely for business purposes. The third floor is also let to and occupied by traders with the exception of two rooms, in the occupation of Mr. Dennistown, a clerk in the employ of the Respondents, who resides therein at night. The fourth floor is in the occupation of the housekeeper, wife, and family. The whole of the upper floors as well as the ground floor of the building on the north side is approached by entrance marked B. on plan.

The Respondents, the Royal Bank of Scotland, contend (1st) that the premises in their own occupation are so structurally severed from the rest of the building as to be a different tenement, and inasmuch as they are used for the purposes of trade only no person sleeping or dwelling therein at night time are exempt under the Act 57 Geo. 3. cap. 25.; that as regards the rest of the building that it came within the Statute 41 Vict. cap. 15. sec. 13, sub-section 1, as a house divided into and let in different tenements and that the assessment should be reduced to the value of such tenements as are otherwise occupied than for trade business, profession, or calling, by which the occupier seeks a livelihood or profit.

The surveyors referred to Exchequer Cases, No. 35, *in re* The Commercial Bank of Scotland (i), and contended that the whole was occupied as one building in one occupation and ownership, and that the occupation of the two rooms, rent free, by the bank clerk, must be regarded as the occupation of the bank itself. consequently the premises did not come under sub-section 1 of 41 Vict. cap. 15. sec. 2, as being "let in different tenements and "occupied solely for the purpose of business," but that the whole of the premises were liable to Inhabited House Duty.

The Commissioners were of opinion that the premises as divided, were so structurally severed as to form two distinct buildings, that the building or tenement in the occupation of the Royal Bank of Scotland was exempt from the Inhabited House Duty; that the other building, being let out in tenements. came within the Statute 41 Vict. cap. 15. sec. 13, sub-section 1, and reduced the assessment to the sum of 150l., being the annual value of the tenements occupied otherwise than for trade.

Whereupon the surveyor declared his dissatisfaction with their decision and duly required them to state and sign a case for the

opinion of the Exchequer Division of the High Court of Justice
which we have stated, and signed accordingly, in pursuance of
the 9th section of the 27 Vict. cap. 16.

THOMSON HANKEY,
R. B. WHITESIDE,
G. R. BENGOUGH,   } Commissioners.
HENRY POUND,

3, *Guildhall Buildings,*
October 16th, 1879.

Sir F. Herschell, S.G., for the Appellant.—With regard to the
part of the premises marked A on the plan the only question
is whether it is to be treated as a separate house or as part of
the one entire house. The whole is owned by the same persons,
and it all forms one building, and part A is merely a part of
the building marked B, it is *primâ facie* assessable, and those
who claim the exemption must show why it is ·exempt. The
house shut off from the rest of it. With regard to the rest of
41 Vict. c. 15 sec. 13. (1), was intended to meet the decision in
Attorney-General v. *The Mutual Tontine, Westminster Chambers,
Association.* (j) It requires that the house shall be structurally
divided into different tenements, not merely let in different
tenements, but "divided into, and let in, different tenements."
In the Westminster Tontine case each block or house was
divided into suites of rooms, and each suite was a separate
tenement, but here it is merely a letting of different rooms to
different persons, and if that were within the section so would
every lodging-house be within it. Again the whole house
should be let, but here a clerk of the bank occupies part as their
servant and his occupation is their occupation. Refers to

Yorkshire Fire and Life Insurance Company v. *Clayton.* (k).

Meadows White, Q.C., for the Respondents.—There is an
actual party-wall severing part A from the rest of the building.
There is a separate entrance door from the street, and there is no
communication whatever between the two parts.

[*Huddleston, B.*—In the case of *The Chartered Bank* v.
Wilson (l), you did establish that there was a separate house.]

·No, because there was a common entrance to the two parts
and a fire-proof doorway, which was only closed at night. As
to part B, the first question is whether it is divided into separate
tenements. I say that it is because it is let to different persons,
each of whom has exclusive rights against the persons whose
property the whole is. A structural division is not necessary,
but if your Lordships think that it is, I say that the door is a
sufficient structural division. Again, the section cannot mean

---

(j) L.R. 18 Exch., 305.   (k) *Ante,* p. 336.   (l) *Ante,* p. 179.

that all the different tenements are to be let because it provides for the want of an occupant. "The person chargeable as occupier" is the person who is to get the relief. It makes no difference if the owner or occupier lives in one of the rooms—the intention of the legislature was to give relief in respect of every tenement occupied for the purpose of a trade or profession.

Sir F. Herschell, S. G., in reply.—The words "the person chargeable as occupier" have reference to Rule VI. in 48 Geo. 3. c. 55. "Where any house shall be let in different storeys, tenements, &c., the landlord or owner shall be deemed the occupier of such dwelling-house, and shall be charged to the said duties." But in the Act of 41 Vict. you have not merely "let in" but divided into and let in." The distinction is the more important from the reference in the latter Act to "the person chargeable as occupier" under Rule VI., where the words "let in" only are used.

Huddleston, B.—In this case the Commissioners of Taxes had decided that the premises, 123, Bishopsgate Street, in which the Royal Bank of Scotland carried on their business, so far as those portions of the premises which were in the actual occupation of the Bank of Scotland were concerned, were not assessable: and they also held that the other portions of the premises were exempt under a statute of the present reign.

Now the first question which we have to consider is whether those premises on the basement floor entered by the door marked A upon the plan come within the meaning of "Inhabited house" under the statute of the 48th of Geo. 3. c. 55. The facts with reference to that as found in the case are these: that "the ground "floor and basement of the building on the south side, with "entrance marked A on the ground plan herewith, are in the "occupation of the Respondents, and are used by them as a "bank for the purpose of carrying on their business as bankers "and have no internal communication whatever with the rest "of the building being separated by a party wall from the base-"ment to the first floor." And the first question is whether premises so described are indeed an inhabited house. It was argued upon the part of the Crown that it was not an inhabited house, but that it was a portion of an inhabited house. It is very difficult to define or give any accurate definition of what a "house" is. We know perfectly well what it means. I should think a good definition to be that which one finds in the ordinary criminal books, where the question of burglary is treated, namely. "A permanent building in which the renter, or the owner and his family, dwells or lies." That will be for the purposes of burglary, but we may fairly read it, I think, "dwell or lie." It must not be a mere tent or booth, as in a market, although if it were a permanent building, only used for the purposes of sale, it would be held to be a dwelling-house, and in that respect that definition would include a room in a set of

chambers where there was no outer door. I find by reference to
the authorities upon that subject "that a room or lodging in a
"private house is the mansion for the time being of the lodger,
"if the owner doth not himself dwell in the house, or if he and
"the lodger enter by different outward doors; but if the owner
"himself lies in the house, and have but one outer door at which
"he and his lodger enters, such lodger seems only to be an
"inmate, and all the mansion to be part of one dwelling-house of
"the owner. This is a building structurally separated from all
the rest of the house, with an outer door, in which persons may
live if they choose, but which must in the legal and in the
ordinary parlance be to all intents and purposes a house; and
inasmuch as it is a house within the 48th Geo. 3. c. 55, and
occupied merely for the purposes of trade within the 57th of Geo. 3
c. 25, we think that it is exempt from the rating to inhabited
house duty. Then we have to consider the question with
reference to the other part of the premises. No doubt, following
the definition so far as I have been able to give it, of what is a
dwelling-house, the whole of the other part of the premises,
marked B, would be a dwelling-house; and as they are not
occupied exclusively for the purposes of trade within the last
statute which I referred to, they would be assessable; but it is
said that they are exempt in consequence of the provisions of
the 13th section of the 41 Vict. c. 15.

Now the onus of proving that they are exempt must lie upon
the Appellant, and to make them exempt he must show that the
house being one property was "divided into, and let in, different
tenements." I am very much inclined to agree myself with the
view taken of my brother Lindley and my brother Grove in the
case of *The Yorkshire Fire Office* v. *Clayton;* that the house must
be a house divided into and let in different tenements, and that
the whole house must be divided into separate tenements and let
in different tenements, and that if the owner occupy any portion
of those premises, the house would not be a house divided
into. and let in, different tenements within the meaning
of this 13th section. But it is not necessary that I should decide
absolutely that point, because it seems to me to be clear that
these premises marked B do not come within the 13th section.
I apprehend that that section contemplates the case of a house
which shall not only be let in different tenements, but shall be
divided into, that is divided into structurally different tenements,
as for instance the Westminster Tontine case to which we have
been referred, where there was an outer door, but all the floors
or tenements were structurally divided from the rest. A familiar
instance we know is where a house is let in flats; there is a
common staircase, but each tenement or flat is structurally
divided so as to form as it were a tenement of itself. That is
what was contemplated by the legislature in passing this Act of
Parliament. I agree with the Solicitor General that the object
of the first and second sections was to obviate the difficulty which
was created in consequence of the decision of the *Weavers Hall*

case (m), applicable to the second section, and the Westminster Tontine Association case as applicable to the first. Now if I am right in that view of the case, I proceed to consider what I find in this case to be the condition of these premises. "The ground " floor of the building on the north side is at present unoccupied. " The first and second floors, which run over the whole of the " premises, are occupied by several traders and used entirely for " business purposes." It may be that each room is occupied by separate persons, with no structural division from the others. It may be that several persons occupy one room, but there is nothing to indicate here that on the first and second floors that run over the premises the house is divided into (I rely upon those words of the section) different tenements. "The third floor is also let to " and occupied by traders, with the exception of two rooms in the occupation of Mr. Dennistown, a clerk in the employ of the " Respondents, who reside therein at night." The third floor therefore is not described as being divided into different tenements, and the same with regard to the fourth floor. I therefore think that these premises do not come within the meaning of the 13th section; that the house no doubt is one property; but that the portion of the premises not being divided into and let in different tenements does not come within the exception claimed in the 41st of Victoria, cap. 15. s. 13, and therefore that those portions of the premises are rateable.

Under those circumstances the order in this case made by the Commissioners must stand with reference to the portion of the premises marked A, but must be set aside with reference to the portions of the premises described as B.

Hawkins, J.—I am clearly of opinion that the Commissioners rightly relieved the Royal Bank of Scotland from the assessment so far as it related to that portion of the building occupied and used by them as a Bank. I refer to the portion of the building marked A upon the plan.

Now that portion of the building, No. 123, Bishopsgate Street, was as distinct and as much separated from the rest of the building as it was possible to be; and to my mind it falls very clearly within the exception of the 57 Geo. III. cap. 25. sec. I, as a house occupied wholly for the purposes of trade, and it falls also, if it were necessary to have recourse to the 41 Vict., within the second sub-section of section 13, as a house or tenement which is occupied solely for the purpose of any trade or business.

Now I do not pretend myself to attempt to give any definition of what is a "house." It seems to me that it is impossible to have any very satisfactory definition. But, certainly, I can conceive it impossible to say that that is not a house which is entirely and absolutely isolated from every other part of the building, so that no access can be had from it to the building, or from the rest of the building to it, but as a separate outer

(m) *Ante*, p. 15.

door upon the street; and I am rather fancying to myself what
would be the condition of things, supposing that that structure
which I call a house had stood alone and by itself, if it had been
one single room with a basement below made with substantial
walls all round it, and with a door opening on to the street.
Then could it be said that it was not a house? Supposing a man
chose to go and live in it; supposing he chose to carry on his
business and to live in it, how could it be said that if it stood
alone that it was not a house, there being no communication
with any other part of the building, and it being absolutely an
entirely distinct and separate property? Then, if that be so,
how can it make any difference, and how can it be the less a
house because the owner has thought fit to allow an adjoining
house to be built, and to be continued partly over it. It seems
to me impossible to say that if it is a house standing by itself,
it is rendered less a house because somebody has built the other
rooms over it, whether it be the same landlord or whether it
be somebody else, by the permission of the landlord. It is very
like the case of a house that we had in this Court the other day,
where two rooms or four rooms had been built over a portion of
a public house; it was not necessary to distinctly determine
whether that which was below was a house or not; but it is
like this case that they were totally and absolutely distinct
tenements, and with no communication from one to the other,
and that the lease of the rooms below could not be said to carry
with it the premises which were erected above. I think as far as
regards the portion of the premises used by the Bank, for the
purposes of their business, that portion is clearly exempt, whether
I take it under the one statute or under the other.

Now as to the rest of the building, I do not agree in the
conclusions arrived at by the Commissioners. I do not think it
necessary at all to discuss at length the authorities cited in the
Law Reports. 10th Exchequer. *The Attorney General* v. *The
Westminster Tontine Company*, and *Rusby* v. *Newson;* by the
former of which it was decided that although the building
was structurally divided into several distinct and separate
tenements, it must be assessed in its entirety as one building;
and its entire value, even though some of the distinct tenements
were unoccupied and unproductive; and by the latter it was
decided that if any, even the smallest portion of an entire
building was used for other than trade purposes, the whole
building was liable to the full assessment. It was to enable
owners of houses to obtain relief against these very obvious
hardships, that the 41 Vict. cap. 13. sect. 13 was passed, which
enabled the owners of houses, sub-letting tenements, to obtain
relief against this obvious hardship, subject to certain conditions contained in that section, those conditions being, first
of all, " Where any house being one property, shall be divided
" into, and let in, different tenements, and any of such tene-
" ments are occupied solely for the purposes of any trader or
" business, or of any profession or calling by which the occupier

"seeks a livelihood or profit, or are unoccupied, the person
"chargeable as occupier of the house shall be at liberty to give
"notice in writing at any time during the year of assessment
"to the surveyor of taxes for the parish or place in which the
"house is situate, stating therein the facts; and after the receipt
"of such notice by the surveyor, the Commissioners acting in
": the execution of the Acts relating to the inhabited house
"duties, shall, upon proof of the facts to their satisfaction, grant
"relief from the amount of duty charged in the assessment, so
"as to confine the same to the duty on the value according
"to which the house should in their opinion have been assessed
"if it had been a house comprising only the tenements other
"than such as are occupied as aforesaid, or are unoccupied."
Then the second sub-section does not in my judgment, bind the
residue of the house with which I am dealing; that is to say,
that portion of the building other than that occupied by the
Board. The second sub-section does not apply to that; nevertheless I may just as well read it for the purposes of one observation that is in my mind, "Every house or tenement which is
"occupied solely for the purposes of any trade or business, or of
"any profession or calling, by which the occupier seeks a
"livelihood or profit. shall be exempted from the duties by the
"said Commissioners upon proof of the facts to their satisfaction,
"and this exemption shall take effect although a servant or other
"person may dwell in such house or tenement for the protection
"thereof." It seems to me that this second sub-section applies
rather to a case in which a house is occupied, or a tenement is
occupied as one single tenement by a single occupier, solely for
the purpose of his trade or business; and it was intended in
reality to give relief to the occupier of such building who used
it for the purpose of his trade or business, notwithstanding the
fact that he might have a servant or housekeeper or other person
for the protection thereof. And of course, under this section, if
a man occupied the whole house, or occupied any portion of that
house for the purpose of residing in himself, it could not be said
that it was a house or tenement which was occupied solely for
the purpose of any trade or business, and it therefore clearly
would not come within that exemption. It is true that a person
might reside in the house, notwithstanding, for the purpose of
taking care of it as provided by this sub-section; but if used by
the owner as a dwelling-house, apart from the question of
servants and care-takers for himself, as well as carrying on his
business, it is quite clear that this house could not be protected
or exempted from the duties imposed by the statute which
imposes these duties.

Now that being so, let us consider what is the meaning of the
first sub-section, and what is it that is required by that section,
and under what circumstances is the person to be relieved; and
I think that we must also consider what were the hardships
which it was intended to relieve the owners of houses from,
certainly the two cases which I have mentioned, and which were

cited in the course of the argument, did point out an obvious
hardship upon the owners of property. Now in order to
provide against that hardship; the first sub-section says, "Where
"any house being one property shall be divided into and let in
"different tenements, and any of such tenements are occupied
"solely for the purposes of any trade or business, or of any pro-
"fession or calling by which the occupier seeks a livelihood or
"profit, or are unoccupied," then I have already read what is
to be done for the purpose of obtaining relief. So that it will be
seen that while the second sub-section applies to a house which
in its integrity is used for the purposes of trade the first sub-
section applies to a house which is divided into separate tenements to be occupied by different persons, and possibly some of
them for the purposes of professions, some for the purposes of
trade, and some even for residential purposes. But before exemption can be claimed, it is necessary that the house should be
divided into and let in different tenements. The question is,
what is the meaning of that first part of the sub-section? Mr.
White on the one hand contended that the exemption applied,
even though there was no actual structural division, but if there
was a letting of the portion of the house he said that the mere
letting of a separate portion of the house without any structural
division, would bring the occupier or owner of the house within
this part of the clause. "Where any house, being one property,
"shall be divided into and let in different tenements." To my
mind that contention cannot prevail. I must read these words
as they are here; and I must read them thus; that the house
must be divided into different tenements. Now how can a house
be divided into different tenements unless there is some structural
division? I am using the word "divided" here, having regard
to what I find in the Acts, and to the context. It strikes me
that there must be a structural division in the first place. But
what the structural division is to be is a very difficult thing to
lay down as a general rule. I do not apprehend that it is necessary that the divisions should be made in any particular way,
provided that there is an actual division of the house into different tenements, whether the division is effected by having a
brick wall, or whether it is effected by lath and plaster, or
whether the division is effected by match boarding, so long as
there is an actual division of the house into separate and different
tenements. I say, in my judgment, that it is sufficient to satisfy
the statute. But it must be a real division into separate tenements, so that anybody going to the premises, and going over
them, would say, that is one tenement, and that is another. It
would not do to say that there is to be only an imaginary line
which shall mark the holding of one man from the holding of
another; there must be a distinct tenement analogous to the sort
of division that we find in chambers, and in a great many of
those mercantile buildings which have been erected lately to such
a great extent throughout the City of London. It must be a
division of a tenement analogous to that, and it must be a tene-

ment let to an occupier otherwise than as an apartment; and I say, "otherwise than as an apartment," because I find in the Income Tax Act, in the 16th & 17th Vict. c. 34. sec. 36, that the language of the section is this: "any house or building let in "different apartments or tenements, and occupied by two or "more persons severally, shall nevertheless be charged to the "duty under this Act as one entire house or tenement," so that they recognise the distinction between a separate tenement and mere apartments; and therefore having regard to the legislation which has taken place upon the subject, I think it would be wrong to say that any division of the house would be sufficient; it must be a division of the house into that which can fairly and under all circumstances be considered as a distinct division of the house into separate tenements, so that each particular tenement may be occupied by the particular separate occupier of it as his own; that he may have full control over it, so as to be able to call himself for the time the possessor, if I may use the expression, of a little house within a house, so that he may be considered to be the occupier of a house within a house, having full control over it, subject only to the fact that his access to his particular portion of his house must be and is by some common staircase, or by some common passage or access. That being the case, first of all, has there been in this case any such structural division?

Now, I have looked very carefully through this case, and in reading the case I have borne in mind this, that *primâ facie* the duty is imposed upon the occupiers and owners of all houses, and the man who seeks to claim exemption from the payment of the duty must bring himself within the exemption clause. Now, in order to do that, it is necessary that there should be a division of the house into separate tenements.

Now let me see if there is any particle of evidence of the division of this house at all, and if there is no evidence of the division of the house at all, is there any evidence that it is divided into separate tenements or into separate apartments, the one applying to lodgers merely, people occupying lodgings in the house and the other to persons who have the control of such tenements as I have mentioned? Now, here we have a description of the premises. The first, I pass by altogether, because I have finished with the bank building itself. "The "ground floor of the building on the north side is at present "unoccupied." Whether it is divided or not, we know not. "The "first and second floors which run over the whole of the "premises are occupied by several traders and used entirely "for business purposes." Are the first and second floors subdivided at all? Are these several traders, persons who are using them, either in partnership together or for any common purpose, or each having the joint and several use of the property? There is nothing of the sort said. "The first and second floors "which run over the whole of the premises are occupied by "several traders, and used entirely for business purposes." All

Assuming that the house had been divided into a number of

several traders, and used entirely for business purposes." All that would be satisfied by simply continuing the floor without a division, and it being all occupied by the persons when they did occupy it, for the mere purposes of trade. "The third floor is "also let to and occupied by traders, with the exception of two "rooms" (not saying that the two rooms are subdivided into a different tenement) "in the occupation of Mr. Dennistoun, a "clerk in the employ of the Respondents, who resides therein at "night. The fourth floor in the occupation of the housekeeper, "wife and family. The whole of the upper floors, as well as the "ground floor of the building on the north side, is approached by "the entrance marked B on the plan." This is all that applies to the sub-division of this house into tenements, and if I were to confine my attention simply to the statement of the division of the house as appears upon this case, I have ample material for saying that this house is not subdivided in the way required by the first sub-section of section 13 of the 41st of Victoria. There is no proof that it is subdivided at all, except in so far as applies to these two rooms in the occupation of Mr. Dennistoun; therefore it could not fall within the exempting clause of sub-section 1.

That would be quite sufficient for me to give my judgment upon; and, indeed, upon that ground I have ventured to come to the conclusion that that portion of the premises is not exempt.

There is one part of the case, however, which was argued upon which it is not necessary to give formal judgment, but upon which I do desire to say a word. It was contended first of all that Mr. Dennistoun, being a clerk, in the service of the bank, who are really the owners of the whole of this house, and occupying two rooms, must be taken to be occupying those two rooms in the character of a servant or a clerk of or on behalf of the landlords. If he had resided in that portion of the bank which is separate from the rest of the building, and had resided there not as a mere caretaker, but as a clerk who received free rent as part of his salary or part of the remuneration he would have for his services, as a matter of course there would have been an end of the question, it could no longer be considered a house used solely for the purposes of trade. But the bank have nothing to do with that portion of the building, with which I am now dealing; they do not occupy themselves any portion of the building which is separated from their bank, or what I should call the residue of the larger building, which is said to have been let in separate tenements; they occupy no portion of that themselves. There is the coincidence, no doubt, that one of their clerks lives in two rooms, but how he comes to live there rent free, we have no proof at all; and certainly I cannot come to the conclusion, as a matter of fact, that he in that case is occupying on the part of the landlords any portion of the house so as to make the house occupied, partly by the landlord, together with these other tenements. I will assume, however, for the moment, that that could have been made good. Assuming that the house had been divided into a number of separate tenements, and that those separate tenements had been occupied by a number of different owners, and that one of those tenements had been occupied by Mr. Dennistoun as representing the landlord of the house, I am far from saying that I agree in the notion that the house would, because of that occupation simply, be rendered incapable of being exempted under this 13th section. I make this observation because I cannot myself at present, without much consideration, give my assent to that suggestion which is made by my brother Lindley, in his judgment in the case of *The Yorkshire Insurance Company*, in the Law Reports, 6 Queen's Bench Division, page 560. "I do not think," he says, "the clause applies to a case where a landlord "occupies any part of the house not as a caretaker which might "bring the case within the second sub-section, but for the "purpose of residence or business." Speaking for myself, I confess that at present I do not agree in that suggestion. It strikes me that the words of the first sub-section are rather against that view. Again, if the landlord is occupying for other purposes than business a part of the house the whole of the rest of which he uses for the purposes of trade, it is clear he would not be exempt under the second sub-section. But I am taking now the first sub-section, which says, "Where any house being one "property shall be divided into and let in different tenements, and "any of such tenements are occupied solely for the purposes of any "trade or business, or of any profession or calling by which the "occupier seeks a livelihood or profit or are unoccupied the person "chargeable as occupier of the house shall be at liberty to seek the "relief as provided here." The meaning of that is that the whole house must be let; it being one property it must be divided into and let in different tenements, and that if the landlord reserves to himself or occupies one single tenement in the house, the house cannot be said to be let, within the meaning of this section. I confess I think myself that that is rather against what was the intention of the Legislature. I think the intention of the Legislature, and I think we have it substantially expressed here, though not in very apt language, is this, that the house shall be one entire property; that it shall be sub-divided for the purpose of letting, and that substantially, the whole house must be let or be intended to be let. It would not do for the landlord to say I am going to occupy the whole of the house myself, and only sublet one portion of it; because there might be a difficulty there. Take this case. Supposing a landlord built a house, and built it with a hundred different tenements, ninety-nine of which could reasonably be made use of for business and trade, or professional purposes, and with one single tenement, the hundredth, which is at the top of the house, inapplicable for trade, and which the landlord himself occupies as nobody else will take it, I cannot myself come to the conclusion that the intention of the Legislature was to deprive him of the benefit that he otherwise would have by having his house divided and sublet in different tenements. I cannot think that it was the intention of the Legislature to deprive him of the benefit of that, simply because he occupied one single tenement himself for other purposes than for the purposes of trade. It is contended that if he even occupies it for the purposes of trade it prevents him claiming exemption. That is not the meaning of the Legislature. I need not decide it, and I only mention it because a difference of opinion exists upon the matter, and I should be very sorry to have it go forth that I gave any opinion of mine, for whatever it may be worth, in support of the proposition that such a state of things would disentitle the landlord from claiming the exemption.

The ground upon which I determine the case, as far as I go, is, as regards the first portion of the house, that it is occupied solely for the purposes of business, and therefore is distinctly exempt under both the Statutes to which I have referred. As regards the other portion of the house, there must be judgment for the Crown, because there is nothing to justify me in thinking or in coming to the conclusion that the house has been divided into, and let in separate tenements in the way mentioned in section 13, which alone can give exemption.

CHAPMAN v. THE ROYAL BANK OF SCOTLAND.

No. 53.—IN THE COURT OF EXCHEQUER (SCOTLAND).—FIRST DIVISION.

14th June 1881.

In re The Strathearn Hydropathic Establishment Company (Limited).

In re THE STRATHEARN HYDRO-PATHIC ESTABLISH-MENT.

Inhabited House Duty.—In a hydropathic establishment visitors are boarded and lodged. Some are patients receiving treatment under the advice of a resident physician, others are mere visitors not undergoing treatment. Both patients and other visitors are subject to the rules of the establishment. Held, that the proprietors are hotel-keepers within the meaning of section 31, 34 & 35 Vict. cap. 103, and are entitled to be charged at the lower rate of duty.

CASE for the opinion of the Court of Exchequer, stated under the provisions of "The Taxes Management Act, 1880," by the Commissioners for the General Purposes of the Property and Income Tax Acts, and for executing the Acts relating to inhabited house duty, for the Crieff District of the County of Perth, on the requisition of the Strathearn Hydropathic Establishment Company (Limited), Crieff.

In re THE
STRATHEARN
HYDRO-
PATHIC
ESTABLISH-
MENT.

AT a meeting of the Commissioners for the General Purposes
of the Property and Income Tax Acts, and for executing
the Acts relating to inhabited house duty, for the Crieff
district of the county of Perth, held at Crieff, on the 10th
day of February 1881, for the purpose of hearing and
disposing of appeals against the assessments made for the
year 1880-81.

The Strathearn Hydropathic Establishment Company
(Limited), appealed against an assessment of 36*l.* 7*s.* 6*d.*, being
inhabited house duty on 970*l.*, at the rate of 9*d.* in the pound,
made on them for the year ending Whitsunday, 1881, in respect
of their being occupiers of the Strathearn Hydropathic Establishment, at Crieff, and claimed to have the assessment restricted to
24*l.* 5*s.*, the duty on 970*l.*, at the rate of 6*d.* in the pound, on
the ground that they carry on in their establishment the
business of a hotel-keeper, or an inn-keeper, within the
meaning of sect. 31 of the Act 33 & 34 Vict. cap. 103. The
following facts were admitted by the parties at the Appeal
Court.

1. The company was incorporated in March 1869, as a limited
liability company, under the Companies Acts, 1862, "For the
"purpose of feuing, purchasing, leasing, or otherwise acquiring
"of lands and buildings or others, within the parishes of Crieff
"and Monsievaird, in the county of Perth or elsewhere, the
"erecting, fitting-up, furnishing, or maintaining thereon, of all
"necessary or convenient buildings and erections for a hydro-
"pathic establishment, together with baths, offices, and other
"buildings connected therewith; and also such branch esta-
"blishments (if any) as may be deemed expedient for carrying
"on the usual business of a hydropathic establishment."

2. In pursuance of the memorandum of association, the
company erected a large hydropathic establishment in the
vicinity of Crieff, which is the subject of this appeal, and have,
since the opening of the establishment in 1869, carried on the
usual business of a hydropathic establishment therein. There
has been no change in the articles of association, as regards the
objects for which the company was established, since the
company was first incorporated.

3. The object of the hydropathic establishment is the treatment, under the advice of a resident physician, of patients by
hydropathy, and for the boarding and lodging of them in the
establishment. The company board and lodge visitors who may
not desire to undergo hydropathic treatment.

4. The patients and visitors are subject to the strict rules of
the establishment. They are rung up in the morning at a fixed
hour. The meals are served only at certain fixed hours, and
any inmate sitting down to table, after grace is said, or making
allusion to hydropathic treatment during meals, is fined. Family
worship is held morning and evening. The front door is locked

IN RE THE
STRATHEARN
HYDRO-
PATHIC
ESTABLISH-
MENT.

at 10.30 P.M., and the gas turned off at 11 P.M., when perfect
quietness must be maintained by all.

5. By the rules and regulations of the company, which are
hung up in the bedrooms of the establishment, for the information
of the public, the officials of the company are empowered to
refuse admission and to send away such as they judge unsuitable.
No children under six years of age are admitted, except under
special arrangement.

6. The company board and lodge patients and visitors at a
certain fixed rate per day or per week. Visitors wishing to
invite a friend to the *table d'hôte*, or to spend the evening, require
to give notice at the office. The company decline to say that
they are bound to supply the travelling public with meals at odd
hours, but they stated they had never refused to do so.

7. The company have no signboard, and they have never, in
their official papers, nor in their advertisements to the public,
designated themselves as hotel-keepers or as inn-keepers, nor
their establishment as a hotel or an inn.

A printed copy of the regulations of the establishment is
attached thereto (*n*).

It was contended for the company that, as they hold themselves out to the public as providing board and entertainment
for the public, and do provide such board and entertainment,
they are carrying on, in the said house, the business of a hotel-
keeper, or an inn-keeper, in the terms of the Act. They also contended that, as in the case of *Ewing* v. *Campbells* (23rd Nov.
1877, 5 Rettie 230), such establishments were found to be subject
to the burdens and obligations to which hotels are liable, they
should also be entitled to the like relief.

Mr. ALEX BAIN, surveyor of taxes for the district, maintained—

1. That the Appellants, who carry on in their establishment
the business of hydropathic establishment keepers, do not come
within the scope of section 31 of the Customs and Inland Revenue
Act of 1871, which refers solely to persons carrying on in their
premises the business of "a hotel-keeper, or an inn-keeper, or
coffee-house keeper."

Until the passing of the last-mentioned Act, the only statute
regulating the rate per pound on which inhabited house duty
was chargeable was the Act of 14 & 15 Vict. cap. 36. By the
schedule attached to that Act, *all* inhabited houses liable to duty
were chargeable at the higher or ninepence rate of duty, except
certain classes of houses which were distinctly defined and
enumerated in the schedule. Among others chargeable at the
sixpence rate were dwelling-houses occupied by any persons who
shall be duly licensed by the laws in force to sell therein by
retail beer, ale, wine, or other liquors.

The Customs and Inland Revenue Act of 1871, 34 & 35 Vict.
cap. 103, under which the Appellants claim, extends the privilege
of being chargeable at the sixpence or lower rate of duty, to

---

(*n*) Being sufficiently set out in the case, they are not reprinted here.

In re THE
STRATHEARN
HYDRO-
PATHIC
ESTABLISH-
MENT.

inhabited houses occupied by persons carrying on therein the business of a hotel-keeper or an inn-keeper, or coffee-house keeper though not licensed to sell by retail beer, ale, &c. Here, again the houses intended to enjoy the benefit of the statute are carefully defined and restricted, and all others are necessarily excluded; the last-mentioned Act even enumerates severally " a hotel-keeper " and an " inn-keeper," which shows that these terms are used in their specific and not in their general sense. Had the Legislature intended that hydropathic establishments should be chargeable at the lower rate of duty, they would also have been distinctly specified and enumerated in the section.

2. The surveyor further maintained, that the Company's establishment was not a hotel or an inn; and that they did not carry on therein the business of hotel-keepers or inn-keepers within the meaning of the Customs and Inland Revenue Act of 1871.

In Chambers' *Etymological Dictionary* (edition of · 1878), a recent and reliable work, a hotel is defined as " a superior house " for the accommodation of strangers—an inn." and an inn as " a " house for the lodging and entertainment of travellers; " and the boarding and lodging of his guests appears to be the end and aim of a hotel-keeper. But, as shown by the statement of facts, the object of the Strathearn Hydropathic Establishment is the treatment, under· a resident medical physician, of patients by hydropathy, as well as the boarding and lodging them. The rules and regulations of the Company, and the facts found by the Commissioners, show that the cure of disease is the object of their establishment, and that the boarding and lodging of the patients and visitors is one of the curative means.

By their rules and regulations, which are hung up for the information of the public in every bedroom of the establishment, the Appellants especially reserve the right to refuse admission to, and to send away, such as they deem advisable. In said rules and regulations they also intimate that they decline to admit children under six years of age, except under special arrangement.

The Appellants decline to admit that they are bound to supply meals to the travelling public at any hour other than the fixed hours of the establishment.

The Appellants have not in their official papers nor in their advertisements to the public designated themselves as hotel-keepers or as inn-keepers, or their establishment as an hotel or an inn. They are incorporated for the express purpose of carrying on the usual business of a hydropathic establishment, which, as before shown, is not the business of a hotel-keeper, inn-keeper, or coffee-house keeper.

3. That the case of *Crum Ewing* v. *Campbells*, referred to by the Appellants, was from the facts and circumstances not applicable. The question here is, whether hotel-keeper, inn-keeper, or coffee-house keeper in the Revenue Statutes comprehends hydropathic establishment keeper? ·

The Commissioners being of opinion that the Appellants did not carry on the business of a hotel-keeper, or an inn-keeper in their establishment, within the meaning of the 31st section of the Act 34 & 35 Victoria, cap. 103, refused the appeal, and confirmed the assessment, whereupon the Appellants, being dissatisfied with our determination, declared their dissatisfaction, and have, within the statutory period, required us to state and sign a case for the opinion of the Court of Exchequer, which is hereby stated and signed accordingly.

The question of law for the opinion of the Court is, whether the Company carry on in their establishment the business of a hotel-keeper, or an inn-keeper, within the meaning of the 31st section of the Act 34 & 35 Victoria, cap. 103, so as to entitle them to have the assessment on them to inhabited house duty, made at the rate of sixpence in the pound?

Dated at Crieff the 15th day of April 1881.

HENRY CURR,
GEO. M. PORTEOUS, } *Commissioners.*

Shaw and *Macintosh* for the Appellants, and *Rutherford* for the Commissioners of Inland Revenue, having been heard

The Lord President.—By the statute which was passed in the year 1871, sec. 31, it is provided that for the future on " every " inhabited dwelling-house which . . . . is or shall be worth " the rent of 20*l*. or upwards by the year, which shall be " occupied by any person who shall carry on in the said dwell-" ing-house the business of a hotel-keeper or an inn-keeper or " coffee-house keeper, although not licensed to sell therein by " retail beer, ale, wine, or other liquors, there shall be charged " for every twenty-shillings of such annual value of any such " dwelling-house the sum of sixpence." Now this section in itself contains from the date of this statute the whole law applicable to the particular kind of hotel here mentioned, a hotel in which there is not a license to sell exciseable liquor; and therefore I think we may confine our attention to the construction of this particular clause. And upon that I observe in the first place, that if the dwelling-house be occupied by any person who shall carry on in the said dwelling-house the business of a hotel-keeper, he is to be charged only at the rate of 6*d*. per pound. It certainly is not necessary, in order to enable him to claim the lower rate, that he shall carry on no other business or no other occupation in that dwelling-house. He must carry on the business of a hotel-keeper there, but I should suppose that he might carry on another business also; and in many hotels which have licenses to sell exciseable liquors we know very well that the hotel-keeper carries on the business of a wine merchant as well as that of a hotel-keeper. That is quite a common thing; and I suppose where the hotel-keeper has a conscientious objection to selling exciseable liquors, he might deal in provisions, and that would not prevent him from being a hotel-keeper within the meaning of

In re The
Strathearn
Hydro-
pathic
Establish-
ment.

this action. Therefore the circumstances that the people who dwell in this house that we are dealing with, to a certain extent come there for medical treatment is, I think, not by any means conclusive as to its not being an hotel, or conclusive against the keepers of this establishment carrying on in the building the business of a hotel-keeper. Then, in the next place, it must be observed that the essential business of a hotel-keeper is entertaining guests at bed and board, and it certainly is very difficult to say that the Appellants in this case do not carry on that kind of business. Every person that comes to their house is entertained at bed and board. Some of them get in addition to that medical treatment, but that does not prevent them being the guests who use this house just as other persons use a hotel, viz., by sleeping and eating and drinking in it, and sleeping and eating and drinking nowhere else. So that the business carried on independent of and in addition to the medical treatment is undoubtedly of the nature of the business of a hotel-keeper. But then it is said that the rules and regulations of this establishment are such as no hotel-keeper could be allowed to make or to carry into effect, and that a hotel-keeper is bound to open his house to all lawful travellers unless there be any special objection to particular individuals who claim admission, that he is liable for the property of the persons in his establishment under the edict *Nautæ caupones*, and that the guests who resort to his house are not liable to have their liberty infringed or limited in the manner that is proposed in the regulations of this establishment. Now, in the first place, with regard to the obligations of a hotel-keeper to receive all lawful travellers, unless there is some special objection to individuals, I do not find in the regulations of this establishment anything at all inconsistent with that. It is said that the officials, by which of course is meant the persons who under the company are carrying on this business, have power to refuse admission and to send away such as they judge unsuitable, and that those suffering from infectious diseases or intoxication "cannot be received or allowed to remain in the establishment." It does not appear to me that that properly construed would enable the keepers of this establishment to refuse guests capriciously or maliciously; and every hotel-keeper must have a certain power of selecting his guests, or perhaps, to speak more precisely, of rejecting certain guests. He is bound to attend to the decency and order of his establishment. That is one of his obligations, and that would be inconsistent with admitting certain classes of guests. He is bound also to attend to the health of his guests and the salubrity of his house, and that would lead to his rejecting certain guests. He is bound also, I think, to exercise a discretion as to the class of people whom he will admit to his hotel. A man who is carrying on business as a hotel-keeper in a first-class establishment is not bound to admit to his hotel persons in every rank and condition of life. Sometimes persons in the condition of working men become, for the time, very rich and very extravagant. We have heard tales of navvies drinking up all the champagne, and eating all the spring chickens of a whole neighbourhood; and if any of that class of people presented themselves to a hotel-keeper of the character we are supposing, I cannot doubt that he would have a discretion to reject them because their manners and habits are not suitable to the class of people whom he receives. So that there is a pretty wide discretion in hotel-keepers as to rejecting guests that are not suitable, which are the very words used in this regulation; and I don't think, therefore, that that regulation is intended, or can be fairly construed as meaning anything more than the exercise of such a discretion as the law allows to every hotel-keeper. It is said farther that they don't admit their liability under the edict for the property of their guest. Now it does not appear to me to be at all material whether they admit that or not, because I should not have much difficulty in holding that they were liable under the edict if the case arose. Then as to all those little regulations about hours and the like, I cannot say that I think there is anything in that to show that this differs from the business of a hotel. I can quite understand a hotel-keeper saying to his guests and to the public. " My establishment is of such a limited character that I " cannot afford, and have not the means of giving dinners in " private apartments; you must all dine in the public room " when you come to, my hotel." I can quite understand that, and if he can say that, he can surely also fix the hour at which the dinners in the public apartments are to be prepared. People cannot expect to have a *table d'hôte* every hour of the day, or even for a great number of hours. They must be satisfied with one or perhaps two dinners being allowed in the course of a day in a hotel of that kind. Then, with reference to the fines, I must say that appears to me to be ridiculous. Whether they are in practice exacted we don't know, because the case does not tell us; but I am very clear of this, that if they were attempted to be exacted and were resisted, this hotel-keeper would have no means of enforcing them. And therefore I don't attach any importance to that. Upon the whole matter I cannot say that this company are not carrying on the business of hotel-keepers. They are carrying on the business of a hydropathic establishment, which may be represented as having for its primary use the cure of disease, but that is not inconsistent with carrying on in the same building, and with reference to the very same people who come there to have their diseases cured, the business of a hotel-keeper. I think therefore the determination of the justices is wrong, and that the rate should be reduced.

Lord Deas.—I confess I have had a good deal of difficulty about this case according as I directed my attention to one clause or another of the statute; but I have come latterly to think, that it all depends on section 31, and that as to the other clauses of the statute, they have very little to do with the question. Section 31 deals with inhabited dwelling-houses, and

In re THE
STRATHEARN
HYDRO-
PATHIC
ESTABLISH-
MENT.

In re THE
STRATHEARN
HYDRO-
PATHIC
ESTABLISH-
MENT.
___

it enacts that every one who lives in an inhabited dwelling-house,
if he carries on certain kinds of business, shall on that account,
and that account alone, pay sixpence in the pound in place of
ninepence. Now, this is undoubtedly an inhabited dwelling-
house, and I think it is hardly contested that if a party carries
on in his inhabited dwelling-house a temperance hotel, he is
liable only in sixpence. As your Lordship has observed, there
is no restriction upon a man who has an inhabited dwelling-
house as to what kind of other business he should carry on in
that dwelling-house. A hotel-keeper may also carry on the
business of letting horses and carriages, and that would not
make him liable for any higher rate than he would otherwise be
liable for. If that is the right construction of the statute, what
does it matter what kind of business it is that the party carries
on in his inhabited dwelling-house; and if he can carry on a
temperance hotel and only be liable at the rate of sixpence, I
think that comes very near the case of this hydropathic establishment. It comes more under the category of a temperance
hotel than any other; and, therefore, on the whole matter I
come to the same conclusion as your Lordship.

Lord Mure.—The words of section 31 are very broad. They
expressly provide that any person who shall carry on in the said
dwelling-house the business of a hotel-keeper, inn-keeper, or
coffee-house keeper, although not licensed to sell by retail intoxi-
cating liquors shall be assessed in the sum of 6d. per pound
instead of 9d. It extends to everyone who carries on the
business of a hotel-keeper, and I confess I have come to the same
conclusion as your Lordship. I do not see how it is possible to say
that what is carried on in this house, according to the admitted
facts of this case, is not in part at all events the business of
a hotel-keeper. People are received, and lodged there and fed,
and they are charged for that a certain sum. No doubt there
are certain specialities. They are said to be treated hydropathically. That is so, but the establishment is not exclusively
for that, because it is admitted that people go there who are not
so treated. It seems in fact to be a kind of temperance hotel,
where, besides conforming to the rule of abstaining from alcoholic
liquors, the guests are treated hydropathically by means of the
water cure; and I cannot see how that puts the case in a different
category from that of a hotel-keeper. I cannot see how that
can be maintained under the words of section 31; and although
there may be some rather absurd rules as it seems to me, I do not
think that they are so inconsistent with the carrying on of the
business of a hotel-keeper as to take the case out of the exemption in the 31st section.

Lord Shand.—Throughout the discussion in this case I thought
the question rather attended with difficulty and doubt, but at
the same time, having heard the reasons stated by your Lordships, I do not feel that I am in a position to differ from the

judgment which your Lordship proposes. If the case had been one in which the building had been exclusively devoted to the reception of guests for medical treatment, although an incident of that treatment was that they should be boarded and reside in the house, I should certainly have been of opinion that this was not in any reasonable sense within the meaning of section 31, a carrying on of the business of a hotel-keeper, inn-keeper, or coffee-house keeper. But it appears in the case that there is a very large class of persons coming there as visitors who do not want medical treatment, but who just come to a beautiful district to live for the time as people live in hotels in the country, paying for their rooms and for their board, or for separate meals if they choose to have them. In that respect undoubtedly the establishment is substantially of the same kind as a hotel. The difficulty I have felt in the case has arisen from the two circumstances, that I do think the rules leave some power in the hands of those who are managing this business to exclude guests as in their opinion unsuitable, and in addition to that, when guests are received, they are put under some very remarkable .restrictions which are not, I think, to be found in any hotel in this country. At the same time I am not disposed to give undue weight to that circumstance. The broad features of the case are, as your Lordship has put it, that people are there living temporarily in a house which is practically open to the public, and they are living in a hotel at bed and board, paying hotel charges or what may be represented as hotel charges; and therefore looking to the whole matter, I am not disposed to differ from the judgment which your Lordship proposes.

In re THE STRATHEARN HYDROPATHIC ESTABLISHMENT.

Judgment for the Appellants.

Lord President.—Find the Appellants entitled to expenses.

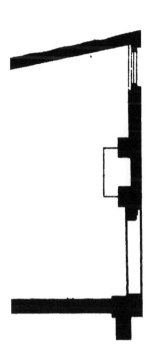

Part XXII.

No. 54.—In the Court of Appeal.
6th and 7th December 1881·

·The Mersey Docks and Harbour Board v. Lucas.*

Income Tax.—" Profits."—Statutory Restrictions.—Corporation.

The Mersey Docks and Harbour Board were constituted by Act of Parliament a corporation for the management of the Mersey Dock Estate. Under the Act the surplus revenue of the Board, which was derived from dock dues, &c., after payment of interest on moneys borrowed, was to be applied towards a sinking fund for the extinguishment of the principal moneys spent in the construction of the dock, and for no other purpose whatsoever.

Held (reversing the judgment of the Queen's Bench Division), that the surplus moneys which remained after payment of the expenses of earning the same, and which under the statute could only be applied in a particular manner for the purpose of reducing the past debt, were available as "profits," and could be assessed to the Income Tax.

Appeal by the Crown from a judgment of the Queen's Bench Division upon a Special Case, reported 50 Law J. Rep. Q·B. 449, where the facts and the material sections of the Acts of Parliament relied upon are fully set out.

The *Solicitor-General* (Sir *F. Herschell*, Q.C.) and *Dicey* for the Crown.

Bigham (with him *Benjamin*, Q.C.) for the Board.

The following cases were referred to in the course of the argument:—The Glasgow Corporation Water Commissioners v.· The Solicitor of Inland Revenue (1): The Attorney-General v. Black (2): The Mayor of Worcester v. The Assessment Committee of the Droitwich Union (3): The Mersey Docks and Harbour Board v. Cameron (4): The Queen v. The Churchwardens and Overseers of Chirton (5): and The Coltness Iron Company v. Black (6).

---

* Coram Jessel, M. R., Brett, L. J., and Cotton, L. J.
(1) Court of Session Cas. (4th ser.) vol. ii., page 706.
(2) 40 Law J. Rep. Exch. 194 ; Law Rep. 6, Exch. 78, 308.
(3) 46 Law J. Rep. M. C. 241 ; Law Rep. 2, Ex. D. 49.
(4) 20 Com. B. Rep. N. S. 56 ; 35 Law J. Rep. M. C. 1.
(5) 28 Law J. Rep. M. C. 131 ; 1 E. and E. 516 ; sub. nom. The Tyne Improvement Commissioners v. The Overseers of Chirton.
(6) Law Rep. App. Cas. 315.

IN THE HIGH COURT OF JUSTICE.

BETWEEN THE MERSEY DOCKS AND HARBOUR
BOARD   ...   .   Appellants,

and

JOSEPH GOLDSMITH LUCAS, Surveyor of Taxes Respondent.

CASE stated by the Commissioners for the general purposes of
The Income Tax Acts at Liverpool for the opinion of the
Court under "The Customs and Inland Revenue Act 1874"
(37 & 38 Victoria, chapter 16, section 9), as to the extent
of the liability of the Appellants to Income Tax.

1. The Appellants are the Mersey Docks and Harbour Board
or Corporation constituted by Act of Parliament for the management of the Mersey Dock Estate.   There are twenty-eight members of the Board, four of whom are appointed by the Mersey
Conservancy Commissioners, and the remainder are elected by
the dock ratepayers.

2. The estate of the Appellants consists of property at Liverpool and Birkenhead, and comprises wet docks, graving docks,
warehouses, quays, sheds, houses occupied by dock-masters and
other servants of the Board, lands acquired under the authority
of Parliament for dock purposes, workshops, cranes, machinery,
railways, and buildings used for and known as the dock offices.

3. The estate is vested in the Appellants by virtue of "The
"Mersey Docks and Harbour Act, 1857." There are no shareholders, nor are any persons individually interested in or entitled
to share the surplus, if any, that may arise from the working of
the estate.

4. A large part of the estate has been acquired and constructed
by means of money borrowed from time to time in that behalf
on the security of the rates herein-after mentioned under statutory powers.   These loans are represented by bonds of the Board
bearing interest.   The amount of the debt is about 14,000,000l.

5. The revenue of the Appellants is derived from the undermentioned sources, the assessment, collection, and application of
the same being directed and controlled by Act of Parliament.

1. Dock tonnage rate on ships entering into or leaving the
docks.

2. Dock dues on goods imported into or exported from the
port of Liverpool and brought into the docks or landed
at or deposited upon or carried over any of the Appellants'
quays, piers, landing stages, or land.

3. Town dues on goods imported into or exported from the port of Liverpool.

4. Anchorage dues on vessels anchoring in the Mersey.

5. Harbour rates paid by vessels entering or leaving the Mersey but not using the Appellants' docks.

6. Charges for unloading and housing in and delivering from the Appellants' warehouses goods from vessels.

7. Quay rents levied in respect of goods not removed by the owners from the quay within the prescribed time, and rents for quay spaces occupied by owners of goods by permission of the Board.

8. Rental of various properties belonging to the Board, and occupied for the storage of timber as shipbuilding yards, stores, coal-yards, &c.

9. Payments made by shipowners for the special appropriation to their use of quay space.

10. Charges made for the use of cranes and machinery and tolls levied for the use of the Appellants' dock railways.

6. Subject to certain provisions of "The Mersey Docks and Harbour Act, 1857," which are not material for the purposes of this case, and subject also to certain special directions hereinafter mentioned, the application of the revenue of the Appellants is governed by the 284th section of "The Mersey Dock Acts and Consolidation Act, 1858." In that Act (section 3) the word "rates" is defined as including "dock rates, tonnage rates, "graving-dock rates, harbour rates, wharf rates, warehouse rents, "town dues, anchorage dues, and other rates, and dues or pay-"ments in the nature thereof payable to the Board."

By the said 284th section it is provided as follows:—

"All the moneys which shall be collected, levied, borrowed, and raised or received by the Board under and by virtue of this Act or the said Act, the application of which may not be otherwise expressly directed, shall be applied by the Board in any order with respect to priority of such application as they shall deem expedient for the following purposes, some or all of them; that is to say,

"In Payment of all expenses and charges of collecting rates:

"In payment from time to time of all interest accruing due on moneys borrowed and to be borrowed, and in payment of the Mersey Docks' annuities herein-after authorized to be granted according to the respective priorities of such moneys and annuities under this Act:

"In the construction of works authorized to be erected, established, and maintained by the Board, and in supporting, maintaining, and repairing the same, and

in carrying into execution all the provisions of this
Act and of 'The Mersey Docks and Harbour Act,
1875: '

" And in the general management, conducting, securing,
preserving, improving, amending, maintaining, and
protecting the Mersey Dock Estate.

" And the residue or surplus of all such moneys which
shall remain after such application thereof as aforesaid
shall from time to time be applied in or towards the repayment of all principal moneys which shall have been
borrowed by or shall be due by the Board, and in or towards
the purchasing up and extinguishing of the Mersey Dock
annuities in the manner herein-after directed, until all such
principal moneys shall have been repaid, and all Mersey
Dock annuities shall have been purchased up and extinguished; and when by the means last mentioned all such
principal moneys shall have been repaid, and all such dock
annuities shall have been purchased up and extinguished,
then and in such case the Board shall, and they are hereby
required to lower and reduce the rates hereby authorised
to be taken; so far as the same can be done in the then state
of the docks, and leaving sufficient for the payment of the
expenses of collecting the rates, and the supporting, maintaining and repairing the docks, and the general management, conducting, securing, preserving, improving, amending, maintaining, and protecting the Mersey Dock estate."

And, " except as aforesaid, such moneys shall not be applied
by the Board for any other purpose whatsoever."

7. By the 285th section of the same Act it is provided as
follows:—

" Nothing in this Act contained shall alter or affect the
question of the liability of any of the docks or works vested
in the Board to parochial or local rates, but the same shall
in all respects be judged of and determined as if this Act
had not been passed."

8. The special directions as to the application of the revenue
of the estate, so far as they are material to this case, relate to the
application of moneys to a sinking fund for the repayment of the
principal moneys of the debt, and are contained in the 4th
section of "The Mersey Dock (Money) Act, 1859," which is as
follows:—

" In order to make provision for the repayment of the
principal moneys which have already been borrowed or
which may hereafter be borrowed by the Board under the
authority of Parliament, be it enacted, that after payment
in each year of all charges and expenses attending the collection of rates, or incidental thereto, or to the recovery
thereof, and after payment of all interest accruing due or
moneys for the time being forming a charge upon such rates,

and of the dock annuities authorised to be granted by the
Board, and after payment of all charges and expenses of
supporting, maintaining, and repairing the works authorised to be erected, established, and maintained by the Board,
and of the general management of the Mersey Dock estate,
and of all reasonable expenses necessary for conducting,
securing, preserving, improving, amending, maintaining,
and protecting the same, the Board shall yearly, and every
year subsequent to the 24th day of June, 1860, apply the
surplus, if any, of the rates which shall remain in their
hands after such payments as aforesaid, to the extent of
100,000l. or such less amount as the said surplus shall be
equal to, in or towards the repayment of some or any of the
principal moneys which shall then be due and owing on the
security of the rates, and which shall then have become due
and payable, and in the purchasing up and extinguishing
of the Mersey Dock annuities which may be then existing,
according to the respective priorities of such moneys and
annuities, until all principal moneys due on the security of
the rate shall have been repaid, and all Mersey Dock annuities shall have been purchased up and extinguished; and,
subject to the provisions herein contained, all rates and
other moneys which shall be collected, levied, borrowed,
and raised or received under or by virtue of the said recited
Acts, or either of them, or of this Act, the application of
which may not be otherwise expressly directed, shall and
may be applied by the Board according to the provisions for
that purpose contained in section 284 of ' The Mersey Dock
Acts Consolidation Act, 1858.' "

The word "rates" in the above section has the same meaning
as is assigned to it by "The Mersey Dock Acts Consolidation
Act, 1858."

9. The Appellants (as directed by the before-mentioned Act,
1857), make up year by year an account showing their total
receipts and expenditure, and the appropriation of the surplus
(if any) of the former over the latter. If, after payment of
interest on the debt, and providing for the prescribed sum to be
placed to the sinking fund account, there remains any balance to
the credit of the general account, the amount is carried forward to the next year's account, and employed for the general
purposes of the trust and in meeting accruing liabilities.

10. In the annual account which was made up to the 1st July
1872 the total amount of the net receipts of the Appellants was
697,964l.; and out of that sum, after providing for the payment
of interest on the debt, the sum of 100,000l. was placed to the
sinking fund account, and a surplus was carried forward to the
next year's account.

11. By the Act 36 & 37 Victoria, chapter 18, income tax at the
rate of threepence in the pound was imposed for the year commencing the 6th day of April 1873, in respect of all property,

profits, and gains mentioned or described as chargeable under
Schedules (A), (C), (D), or (E) of the Act 16 & 17 Victoria,
chapter 34, and all such provisions contained in any Act relating
to income tax as were in force on the 5th day of April 1873
were made applicable to the income tax so imposed.

The provisions of the Acts relating to income tax which have
the most material bearing upon the question in this case are
No. III. of Schedule (A) in section 60 of the Act 5 & 6 Victoria,
chapter 35, section 102 of the same Act, and section 8 of the
Act 29 & 30 Victoria, chapter 36.

No. III. of Schedule (A) contains the provisions following:—

"The annual value of all the properties herein-after
described shall be understood to be the full amount for one
year, or the average amount for one year, of the profits
received therefrom within the respective times herein
limited.

"1. • • • • • • • •

"2. • • • • • • • •

"3. Of ironworks, gasworks, saltsprings or works, alum
mines or works, waterworks, streams of water, canals, inland navigations, docks, drains and levels, fishings, rights
or markets and fairs, tolls, railways and other ways, bridges,
ferries, and other concerns of the like nature, from or arising
out of any lands, tenements, hereditaments, or heritages, on
the profits of the year preceding.

"The duty in each of the last three rules to be charged
on the person, corporation, company, or society of persons,
whether corporate or not corporate, carrying on the concern,
or on their respective agents, treasurers, or other officers
having the direction or management thereof, or being in the
receipt of the profits thereof, on the amount of the produce
or value thereof, and before paying, rendering, or distributing the produce or the value either between the different
persons or members of the corporation, company, or society
engaged in the concern, or to the owner of the soil or property, or to any creditor or other person whatever having a
claim on or out of the said profits; and all such persons,
corporations, companies, and societies respectively, shall
allow out of such produce or value a proportionate deduction of the duty so charged, and the said charge shall be
made on the said profits exclusively of any lands used or
occupied in or about the concern."

Section 102 of the Act 5 & 6 Victoria, chapter 35, is as
follows:—

"102. And be it enacted, that upon all annuities, yearly
interest of money, or other annual payments, whether such
payments shall be payable within or out of Great Britain,
either as a charge on any property of the person paying the

same by virtue of any deed or will or otherwise, or as a reservation thereout, or as a personal debt or obligation by virtue of any contract, or whether the same shall be received and payable half-yearly or at any shorter or more distant periods, there shall be charged for every twenty shillings of the annual amount thereof the sum of sevenpence, without deduction, according to and under and subject to the provisions by which the duty in the third case of Schedule (D) may be charged. Provided that in every case where the same shall be payable out of profits or gains brought into charge by virtue of this Act, no assessment shall be made upon the person entitled to such annuity, interest, or other annual payment, but the whole of such profits or gains shall be charged with duty on the person liable to such annual payment without distinguishing such annual payment, and the person so liable to make such annual payment whether out of the profits or gains charged with duty, or out of any annual payment liable to deduction, or from which a deduction hath been made, shall be authorised to deduct out of such annual payment at the rate of sevenpence for every twenty shillings of the amount thereof, and the person to whom such payment liable to deduction is to be made shall allow such deduction at the full rate of duty hereby directed to be charged upon the receipt of the residue of such money, and under the penalty herein-after contained; and the person charged to the said duties having made such deduction shall be acquitted and discharged of so much money as such deduction shall amount unto, as if the amount thereof had actually been paid unto the person to whom such payment shall have been due and payable. But in every case where any annual payment as aforesaid shall, by reason of the same being charged on any property or security in Ireland or in the British plantations, or in any other of Her Majesty's dominions, or on any foreign property or foreign security, or otherwise, be received or receivable without any such deduction as aforesaid; and in every case where any such payment shall be made from profits or gains not charged by this Act, or where any interest of money shall not be reserved or charged or payable for the period of one year, then and in every such case there shall be charged upon such interest, annuity, or other annual payment as aforesaid the duty before mentioned according to and under and subject to the several and respective provisions by which the duty in the third case of Schedule (D) may be charged.

"Provided always, that where any creditor on any rates or assessments not chargeable by this Act as profits shall be entitled to such interest, it shall be lawful to charge the proper officer having the management of the accounts with the duty payable on such interest, and every such officer shall be answerable for doing all acts, matters, and things

necessary to a due assessment of the said duties, and payment thereof, as if such rates or assessments were profits
chargeable under this Act, and such officer shall be in like
manner indemnified for all such Acts as if the said rates
and assessments were chargeable.''

Section 8 of the Act 29 and 30 Victoria, chapter 36, is as
follows:—

" 8. The several and respective concerns described in No. 3
Schedule (A) of the said Act passed in the 5th and 6th
years of Her Majesty's reign, chapter 35, shall be charged
and assessed to the duties hereby granted in the manner in
the said No. 3 mentioned according to the rules prescribed
by Schedule (D) of the said Act, so far as such rules are consistent with the said No. 3, provided that the annual value
or profits and gains arising from any railways shall be
charged and assessed by the Commissioners for special
purposes.''

12. In making a return for assessment of income tax by the
Commissioners acting under Schedule (D) for the year 1873-74,
the liability of the Appellants was stated at the amount due and
payable by them for interest on the debt during the year of
assessment, being the sum of 532,252l.

13. The Surveyor of Taxes, the Respondent, was dissatisfied
with the amount so stated in the return, and duly served a notice
of surcharge upon the Appellants.

By such surcharge the sum of 532,252l. was increased to the
sum of 697,964l. as the profits for the year preceding of the
concern under the management of the Appellants.

14. Notice of appeal against this surcharge was given by the
Appellants, and the appeal came on for hearing before the Commissioners in March, 1875.

15. Upon the hearing of the appeal it was contended on
behalf of the Appellants that their liability to income tax (if
any) did not extend beyond the sum which was paid as interest
upon the debt, and ought not to extend to the said sum of
100,000l. carried from the revenue to the sinking fund account,
or to the surplus carried forward to the next year's account. On
the other hand, it was contended on behalf of the Respondent
that under the provisions of the Income Tax Acts the Appellants
were liable to assessment to income tax in respect of the profits
arising or accruing to them from the concern under their
management, and not in respect of interest due or payable by
them, and that for the purpose of ascertaining the amount for
such assessment the total amount of their receipts should be
taken, from which there should be deducted the costs of working,
maintaining, and repairing the sources of revenue, but not the
interest payable upon the debt, nor the said sum of 100,000l.

16. The Commissioners concurred in the view put forward on
behalf of the Respondent, and having satisfied themselves that

allowance had been made in respect of rents for warehouses, &c., already charged under Number 1 of Schedule (A) confirmed the surcharge in the sum of 697,964l.

17. The Appellants expressed their dissatisfaction with the determination of the Commissioners as being erroneous in point of law, on the ground that in the circumstances herein stated no assessment could be made upon them in respect of any larger amount than the interest on their debt, and duly required the Commissioners to state and sign a case for the opinion of the Exchequer Division of the High Court of Justice according to the Act 37 & 38 Victoria, chapter 16;—which we have stated, and do now sign accordingly.

18. Either party is to be entitled to refer to and reply upon any of the provisions of the several Acts of Parliament relating to the Mersey Dock estate and to income tax, and the Court is to have power to draw inferences of fact.

> The question for the opinion of the Court is, whether the assessment made upon 697,964l. is the proper assessment; or whether it should have been made upon the sum of 532,525l., or upon any other and what sum.

EDWARD GIBBON,
Commissioner.

J. J. MYERS,
Commissioner.

6th December, 1881.

The Solicitor-General (Sir F. Herschell).—My Lords, this is an appeal from a judgment of the Divisional Court, who gave judgment in favour of the then Appellants, the Mersey Docks and Harbour Board, and I appear in support of that appeal against that judgment. It was a case stated by the Commissioners of Income Tax in Liverpool for the opinion of the Court. " The Appellants are the Mersey Docks and Harbour Board or " Corporation constituted by Act of Parliament for the manage- " ment of the Mersey Dock Estate. There are 28 members of " the Board, four of whom are appointed by the Mersey Con- " servancy Commissioners, and the remainder are elected by the " dock ratepayers. The estate of the Appellants consists of " property at Liverpool and Birkenhead." I may say, shortly, the point is, whether in respect of the surplus of receipts over expenditure, which we call profits, the Mersey Docks and Harbour Board are liable to income tax.

Lord Justice Brett.—They say not, because by Act of Parliament——

The Solicitor-General.—Because by Act of Parliament there is a provision how the money is to be applied. We say that is

immaterial; that that must mean subject to the limitation of the
liability to be taxed.

The Master of the Rolls.—That was prior to the Income Tax
Act, I suppose?

The Solicitor-General.—Yes, my Lord. The Income Tax Act
is a new Act annually; and that seems to have been one of the
errors into which the Court below fell; they treated this Act as
being subsequent to the Income Tax Act, whereas it was prior
to the Income Tax Act under which we are proceeding.

The Master of the Rolls.—But subsequent to other Acts.

The Solicitor-General.—But subsequent to other Acts, my
Lord.

The Master of the Rolls.—With which we have no concern.

The Solicitor-General.—Yes. I may say that, quite apart
from the amount of income tax claimed here, the question, having
regard to the ground of the decision below, is undoubtedly important.

The Master of the Rolls.—How does it affect the Income Tax
Acts,—the mode of application of the income.

The Solicitor-General.—I say it does not affect them at all.
The Court below thought it did affect them.

The Master of the Rolls.—I suppose a corporation can in no
sense enjoy income?

The Solicitor-General.—No. my Lord.

The Master of the Rolls.—It must apply it to some purpose
or other.

The Solicitor-General.—There is a decision in the Exchequer
Chamber, which is binding upon this Court, which clearly shows
that the fact that a corporation receives dues, and can apply
those dues only to the public purposes of the borough, does not
prevent them in any way being liable to income tax.

The Master of the Rolls.—In no case can a corporation avoid
income tax?

The Solicitor-General.—No, my Lord.

The Master of the Rolls.—Has there been any decision upon
the income tax, or upon the rates?

The Solicitor-General.—The case of the Attorney-General *v.*
Black, in the Exchequer, was a case upon the income tax. That
was a question with regard to the coal dues the corporation of
Brighton were entitled to. I say that there is a distinction
between the Attorney-General and Black in this case. I had
better give your Lordships the section of the Mersey Dock Act
upon which this question turns. It is the 284th section. I
may remind your Lordships—I daresay it will be in your recollection—that prior to the vesting in the Mersey Docks and
Harbour Board of these rates they were possessed by the corporation of Liverpool.

Lord Justice Brett.—They all went into the borough fund?

The Solicitor-General.—Yes, my Lord.

The Master of the Rolls.—I suppose it is not contended if there was not this special provision they must pay income tax. Is that one of the points?

The Solicitor-General.—Yes, I think they do contend that; but the ground of the decision in the Court below rests on the special provision in the 284th section, that the word " rates " shall be defined as including. " dock rates, tonnage rates, graving- " dock rates, harbour rates, wharf rates, warehouse rents, town " dues, anchorage dues, and other rates and dues, or payment in " the nature thereof, payable to the Board. By the said 284th " section it is provided as follows:—' All moneys which shall be " ' collected, levied, borrowed, and raised or received by the " ' Board under or by virtue of this Act or the said Act, the " ' application of which may not be otherwise expressly directed, " ' shall be applied by the Board in any order with respect to " ' priority of such application as they shall deem expedient for " ' the following purposes, some or all of them, that is to say, " ' in payment of all expenses and charges of collecting rates.' "

The Master of the Rolls.—What is the meaning of the word " expenses " there, because, as I understand, there is no other provision for the payment of their expenses?

The Solicitor-General.—No, none, my Lord.

The Master of the Rolls.—There must be a stop after expenses.

The Solicitor-General.—Yes, my Lord.

The Master of the Rolls.—It is not expenses for collecting the rates, but expenses of charging. Why is not the income tax an expense,—as much an expense as any other tax? I suppose they are liable to rates of any kind?

The Solicitor-General.—Yes, my Lord.

The Master of the Rolls.—How are they to pay them?

The Solicitor-General.—Under that. " Expenses " must include borough rates.

The Master of the Rolls.—There are, I suppose, expenses of repair.

Lord Justice Brett.—It may be said it required an express exception to bring that in.

The Master of the Rolls.—Is there any exemption of the docks being repaired?

Mr. Bigham.—Yes, my Lord, further on.

The Solicitor-General.—" In the construction of works autho- " rised to be erected, established, and maintained by the Board, " and in supporting, maintaining, and repairing the same, and " in carrying into execution all the provisions of this Act, and " of the ' Mersey Docks and Harbour Act, 1857,' and in the " general management, conducting, securing, preserving, im- " proving, amending, maintaining, and protecting the Mersey " Dock Estate."

Mr. Bigham.—No; the word " repairing " is in the previous paragraph.

The Master of the Rolls.—" In carrying into execution all the
" provisions of this Act." I suppose one of the provisions is to
pay their debts.

Lord Justice Brett.—They do not have debts, they have
bonds.

The Solicitor-General.—The first is, " In payment of all
" expenses and charges of collecting rates; in payment from
" time to time of all interest accruing due on moneys borrowed
" and to be borrowed, and in payment of the Mersey Docks
" annuities herein-after authorised to be granted according to
" the respective priorities of such moneys and annuities under
" this Act; in the construction of works authorised to be
" erected, established, and maintained by the Board, and in
" supporting, maintaining, and repairing the same, and in
" carrying into execution all the provisions of this Act, and of
" the Mersey Docks and Harbour Act, 1857, and in the general
" management, conducting, securing, preserving, improving,
" amending, maintaining, and protecting the Mersey Dock
" Estate; and the residue or surplus of all such moneys."

The Master of the Rolls.—Take the Queen's taxes. Were
there charges on houses at this time?

The Solicitor-General.—No, my Lord.

The Master of the Rolls.—How are they to pay them?

The Solicitor-General.—I suppose " in payment of all ex-
" penses."

The Master of the Rolls.—Then it carries income tax, if they
are liable to it?

The Solicitor-General.—Yes, my Lord. " And the residue or
" surplus of all such moneys which shall remain after such
" application thereof as aforesaid shall from time to time be
" applied in or towards the repayment of all principal moneys
" which shall have been borrowed by or shall be due by the
" Board, and in or towards the purchasing up and extinguishing
" of the Mersey Dock Annuities in the manner herein-after
" directed, until all such principal moneys shall have been repaid
" and all Mersey Dock annuities shall have been purchased up
" and extinguished; and when, by the means last mentioned, all
" such principal moneys shall have been repaid, and all such
" dock annuities shall have been purchased up and extinguished,
" then and in such case the Board shall and they are hereby
" required to lower and reduce the rates hereby authorised to
" be taken, so far as the same can be done in the then state
" of the docks, and leaving sufficient for the payment of the
" expenses of collecting the rates, and the supporting, main-
" taining, and repairing the docks, and the general management,
" conducting, securing, preserving, improving, amending, main-
" taining, and protecting the Mersey Dock Estate."

The Master of the Rolls.—I see there is a clause, " Nothing in
" this Act shall omit the rates." But is there anything as to
paying them?

The Solicitor-General.—No, my Lord. The explanation of that rate clause is, for many years great litigation went on between the dock authorities and the local authorities, whether they were liable to rates. It was found in the House of Lords they were liable to rates.

The Master of the Rolls.—All that is reserved is their liability?

The Solicitor-General.—Yes, my Lord.

The Master of the Rolls.—Income tax would come under "expenses."

The Solicitor-General.—Yes, my Lord.

The Master of the Rolls.—And so would the Queen's taxes?

The Solicitor-General.—Yes, my Lord.

The Master of the Rolls.—Was that point taken in the Court below?

The Solicitor-General.—Yes, my Lord.

The Master of the Rolls.—How do they deal with it?

The Solicitor-General.—This was one of their views, that you could not have profits taxable to the income tax.

The Master of the Rolls.—That is the other point; you say it was decided against you upon that ground.

The Solicitor-General.—They decided both grounds. Mr. Justice Lindley relied upon this provision, and what is contained at the end; " and except as aforesaid, such moneys shall not be " applied by the Board for any other purpose whatsoever."

The Master of the Rolls.—Would that cover the Queen's taxes and the assessed tax on the houses?

The Solicitor-General.—No. I gather, according to their view, there would be no liability to any such taxation, because they refer to the fact that their liability to the local rates was saved, and they draw from that inference it was not intended that anything else should be saved, and that therefore "expenses" must be read in relation to them.

The Master of the Rolls.—Did they say they were free from assessed taxes?

The Solicitor-General.—They did not say that, but I should say they took that view.

The Master of the Rolls.—I suppose they pay their taxes like other people?

The Solicitor-General.—Oh, yes. They relied a good deal on these negative words: " Except as aforesaid, such moneys shall " not be applied by the Board for any other purpose whatsoever;" and then, " Nothing in this Act contained shall alter or affect " the question of the liability of any of the docks or works " vested in the Board to parochial or local rates, but the same " shall in all respects be judged of and determined as if this " Act had not been passed. The special directions as to the " application of the revenue of the estate, so far as they are " material to this case, relate to the application of moneys to a

"sinking fund for the repayment of the principal moneys of the
"debt, and are contained in the 4th section of 'The Mersey
"Docks Money Act, 1859.'" And then it provides, "In order to
"make provision for the repayment of the principal moneys
"which have already been borrowed or which may hereafter be
"borrowed by the Board under the authority of Parliament,
"be it enacted, that after payment in each year of all charges
"and expenses attending the collection of rates, or incidental
"thereto or to the recovery thereof, and after payment of all
"interest accruing due on moneys for the time being forming
"a charge upon such rates, and of the dock annuities authorised
"to be granted by the Board, and after payment of all charges
"and expenses of supporting, maintaining, and repairing the
"works authorised to be erected, established, and maintained
"by the Board, and of the general management of the Mersey
"Dock Estate, and of all reasonable expenses necessary for con-
"ducting, securing, preserving, improving, amending, main-
"taining, and protecting the same, the Board shall yearly and
"every year subsequent to the 24th day of June 1860 apply
"the surplus, if any, of the rates which shall remain in their
"hands after such payments as aforesaid to the extent of
"100,000l., or such less amount as the said surplus shall be
"equal to, in or towards the repayment of some or any of the
"principal moneys which shall then be due and owing on the
"security of the rates, and which shall then have become due
"and payable, and in the purchasing up and extinguishing of
"the Mersey Dock annuities which may be then existing
"according to the respective priorities." I think that is all of
that section I need read. Then, "The Appellants, as directed
"by the before-mentioned Act, 1857, make up year by year
"an account showing their total receipts and expenditure, and
"the appropriation of the surplus (if any) of the former over
"the latter. If, after payment of interest on the debt, and
"providing for the prescribed sum to be placed to the sinking
"fund account, there remains any balance to the credit of the
"general account, the amount is carried forward to the next
"year's account and employed for the general purposes of the
"trust, and in meeting accruing liabilities. In the annual
"account which was made up to the 1st July 1872, the total
"amount of the net receipts of the Appellants was 697,964l.,
"and out of that sum, after providing for the payment of
"interest on the debt, the sum of 100,000l. was placed to the
"sinking fund account, and a surplus was carried forward to
"the next year's account. By the Act 36 & 37 Victoria,
"chapter 18, income tax at the rate of threepence in the pound
"was imposed for the year commencing the 6th day of April
"1873 in respect of all property, profits, and gains mentioned
"or described as chargeable under Schedules A, C, D, or E of
"the Act 16 and 17 Victoria, chapter 34." Then it proceeds
to quote the terms of the Income Tax Act in Schedule A. I do
not suppose it can be disputed for a moment that this is a
property which in itself naturally is taxable within the Income

Tax Acts; that is to say, apart from the persons by whom it is held, and the purpose to which it is to be applied, it is taxable.

The Master of the Rolls.—I do not think anybody would contend that the private owner of a dock could not be taxable.

The Solicitor-General.—No, my Lord; it would be impossible to contend so; and the value is to be ascertained by Rule 3, number 3, that is to say, it is to be the annual value of the profit of the preceding year. That is the language. The general rule, as your Lordships remember, is to take the annual value of lands and tenements, and so forth, and see what we will let for. That is not to apply to certain specified properties, such as docks. The annual value is to be taken to be the profit of the preceding year.

The Master of the Rolls.—You say the word " profits " in the Income Tax Act means surplus after paying interest.

The Solicitor-General.—Yes, my Lord.

The Master of the Rolls.—That it does not matter to what purpose their profits are applied.

The Solicitor-General.—Yes, and that the only exemptions are those in the Act, such as public hospitals. The mere fact that it is for a charitable purpose would not exempt it from the special provision.

The Master of the Rolls.—I know there has been a very strong contest about that exemption.

The Solicitor-General.—Then it sets out how the question arose; that they made the return returning only the amount which they paid in interest.

Lord Justice Brett.—The duty is as to 100,000*l.* or rather more, is not it?

The Solicitor-General.—Yes, my Lord. They paid only upon their interest they paid to the bondholders, that was 532,000*l.*; but their surplus was 697,000*l.*, and the surveyor of taxes contended the question in dispute should extend to 697,000*l.*; therefore the question in dispute is 165,000*l.*

Lord Justice Brett.—That was the sinking fund. What was the rest?

The Solicitor-General.—The rest was what they would carry over to the next year's balance.

Lord Justice Brett.—Do they say they are not to pay for that?

The Solicitor-General.—Yes, my Lord.

Lord Justice Brett.—There may be a distinction between the two sums.

The Solicitor-General.—Yes. They say there is no distinction. After paying the sinking fund it is to be applied in reducing their rates, and when the rates are dealt with they are to lower the rest, so that they would say there is no distinction between the two. The Legislature described how the surplus is to be applied. That is the question I have to address your Lordships upon.

Lord Justice Brett.—There are negative words.

The Solicitor-General.—Yes. "Except as aforesaid, such "moneys shall not be applied by the Board for any other "purpose whatsoever." Now, my Lords, I first of all submit that this is a property in its nature taxable. That, I suppose, could not be disputed for a moment. Next, that it is clear on the authorities that the fact that dues are to be received by a corporation who are trustees only for public purposes, and are trustees to apply it to those public purposes, does not prevent its being taxable to the income tax. Let me call your Lordship's attention to the decisions.

The Master of the Rolls.—Go to the Act of Parliament. What is there in the Act to exempt anybody?

The Solicitor-General.—There is nothing, my Lord. Your Lordship will find the only exemptions are number 6 in the rules, section 61 of the Act of the 5th and 6th Victoria, chapter 35.

The Master of the Rolls.—First, you must get the charging part.

The Solicitor-General.—First, I will give your Lordships the charging part. The charging part is in section 60.

Lord Justice Brett.—What is that statute?

The Solicitor-General.—I will not say this is the original statute, because there were prior Income Tax Acts in George the Third's time, but it is the Income Tax Act which has been re-enacted year by year, and section 60 says: "That the duties "hereby granted and contained in the said schedule marked A "shall be assessed and charged under the following rules," and so on. The first rule, No. 1, is "The annual value of lands, "tenements, hereditaments, or heritages charged under Schedule "A shall be understood to be the rent by the year at which "the same are let at rack rent, if the amount of such rent shall "have been fixed by agreement commencing within the period "of seven years preceding the fifth day of April next before "the time of making the assessment, but if the same are not so "let at rack rent, then at the rack rent at which the same are "worth to be let by the year; which rule shall be construed to "extend to all lands, tenements, hereditaments, or heritages, "capable of actual occupation, of whatever nature, and for "whatever purpose occupied or enjoyed, and of whatever value, "except the properties mentioned in No. 2 and No. 3 of this "schedule." That is the first general rule; it is beyond the annual value at which the land might be let at the rack rent. Then No. 3 is, "Rules for estimating the lands, tenements, "hereditaments, or heritages herein-after mentioned which are "not to be charged according to the preceding general rule. "The annual value of all the properties herein-after described "shall be understood to be the full amount for one year, or the "average amount for one year, of the profits received therefrom "within the respective times herein limited."

Lord Justice Brett.—What section is that?

The Solicitor-General.—That is the same section—rule 3 of section 60. Your Lordship knows it is assessed under Schedules A., B., C., and D., and Schedule A. commenced at section 60, and contains all the rules; and the rule under which this is to be assessed is rule No. 3 of No. 3. "Of iron works," and other things, "docks, drains, and levels, fishings, rights of markets "and fairs, tolls, railways and other ways, bridges, ferries, and "other concerns of the like nature from or arising out of the "lands, tenements, hereditaments, or heritages, on the profits "of the year preceding."

The Master of the Rolls.—Now go on.

The Solicitor-General.—"The duty in each of the last three "rules to be charged on the person, corporation, company, or "society of persons, whether corporate or not corporate, carrying "on the concern, or on their respective agents, treasurers, or "other officers having the direction or management thereof, or "being in receipt of the profits thereof on the amount of the "produce or value thereof, and before paying, rendering, or dis-"tributing the produce of the value either between the different "persons or members of the corporation, company, or society "engaged in the concern, or to the owner of the soil or property, "or to any creditor or other person whatever having a claim on "or out of the said profits; and all such persons, corporations, "companies, and societies respectively shall allow out of such "produce or value a proportionate deduction of the duties so "charged." That is, the persons to whom it is paid.

The Master of the Rolls.—You see, that makes it paid by the corporation carrying on the concern before paying the profits to anybody else.

The Solicitor-General.—Yes, My Lord.

The Master of the Rolls.—That is expressly enacted?

The Solicitor-General.—Yes, My Lord.

The Master of the Rolls.—In a subsequent part of the private Act you will say it repealed that?

The Solicitor-General.—Certainly; but I shall take a higher ground than that. I think it would be a very dangerous doctrine to admit, that any provision in the private Act of Parliament as to the way in which money is to be dealt with, excludes general legislation.

The Master of the Rolls.—It is a private Act, and does not affect the general law.

The Solicitor-General.—Yes. Your Lordship sees, when a private Act of that sort is passed, the parochial people may watch their interest, but there is no one to watch the interest of the Revenue. It is a very dangerous doctrine to which sanction is given by the Court below, that people, by getting a private Act of Parliament, could withdraw money from taxation by providing how money should be applied.

Lord Justice Brett.—The general Act does not repeal the principal words of the private Act, that is the rule, is not it?

The Solicitor-General.—Yes, if they were the words in the general Act or in the private Act. If they were inconsistent with one another, so that it was clear the two were in conflict, I agree it would be so.

The Master of the Rolls.—Suppose the word " expenses " was not there, you say " the income " meant the net income, and that they would not go to the inhabited house duty, because the Act directed the application of their income.

The Solicitor-General.—Quite so. It must be always subject to the general law as to general taxes, unless there are words excluding that. Unless the money is to be expended in a particular way, it must be subject to all general charges, unless the words exclude that.

Lord Justice Brett.—The question is, whether there are words here excluding it.

The Master of the Rolls.—The question is whether it does not mean net income.

Lord Justice Brett.—Suppose the word " expenses " does not include income tax,—" except as aforesaid, such moneys shall " not be applied for any other purpose whatsoever."

The Solicitor-General.—I should say, even if " expenses " did not include it, that that exception would be implied; that you would not read an Act of Parliament which really is procured by the parties, nobody watching the public interest; you would not read it as providing that they might in that way escape taxation unless there were express words protecting them.

The Master of the Rolls.—The Act regulates the rights of the creditors of the corporation as between themselves and the corporation?

The Solicitor-General.—Yes, my Lord.

Lord Justice Brett.—I should like you to define the word " expenses."

The Solicitor-General.—I have no hesitation in submitting it comes within the word " expenses," because I say it is clear this Act preserves the liability to parochial rates. There is no express provision for parochial rates, they must be intended. to be provided for somehow, and in payment of private expenses is the only way to describe them.

The Master of the Rolls.—It is the widest word known to the English Law.

The Solicitor-General.—Yes, my Lord.

Lord Justice Brett.—What you must answer is this: those who inserted that section must have supposed if it were not there the parochial taxes would be shut out by the negative words.

The Solicitor-General.—I should not assume that. Knowing what one knows of the way in which private Acts are conducted,

I should say that provision was there, because the local authorities were watching to get a clause put in to make it clear that their interests were not in any way affected.

Lord Justice Brett.—They would not leave them open to this argument.

The Solicitor-General.—No, my Lord; but, of course, nobody is interested in the general revenue in the way a local authority is. If that were so, you would want to have the Treasury represented in every fight about a private Bill. People would put into a private Bill provisions as to the payment of money, and say, "We have not provided for any way of paying our debts, "and therefore we cannot pay a tax to the country."

Lord Justice Brett.—Does not the solicitor to the Treasury watch the Bills?

The Solicitor-General.—No; it would be too tremendous a job. There are hundreds of Bills brought before the House every session which he considers he has no concern with, it is only affecting the private body.

The Master of the Rolls.—I am not saying whether you are bound at all. The question is, whether the Crown is bound by these Acts. If you are going to deprive the Crown of its right to tax, you must deprive it by so many words.

Lord Justice Brett.—The Crown has no right to tax, they are the grant to the Queen.

The Solicitor-General.—The General Act grants it to the Crown for all property of every description; and what you would be doing by the private Act would be to abstract part of the property.

The Master of the Rolls.—If there had been no arrangement between the Crown and Parliament for the disposal of the taxes they would be part of the general revenue of the Crown, just as the old aids, and so on, were in old times.

Lord Justice Brett.—You would have to argue it in this way: "The Legislature had declared this income was to be applied to "particular purposes, and to no other, and then afterwards "the same Legislature would make a general Act with regard "to income tax." Would the doctrine of the rights of the Crown come in, or would it come in the ordinary rule, that general words in a private Act do not override particular words in another Act?

The Solicitor-General.—They do not override general words; but this has nothing to do with taxing. This is a mode of taxing corporated property. Then came a taxing Act, which deals with corporate property, with certain exceptions, and this is not within those exceptions.

The Master of the Rolls.—There was at this time a taxing Act.

Lord Justice Brett.—If this private Act had been in terms "the corporation shall not pay any present or future income "tax——"

The Solicitor-General.—The Crown would then have given its assent to the thing itself. There is an Act expressly dealing with the revenue to which the Crown has given its assent.

The Master of the Rolls.—There are plenty of decisions on that. The Crown need not be named in so many words. We had a case under the Bankruptcy Act of that kind.

Mr. Bingham.—Yes, my Lord; that was the Postmaster-General in re Bonner.

The Master of the Rolls.—You will find it completely established that you cannot take away the right of the Crown, either without express words or equivalent words.

The Solicitor-General.—Yes, my Lord.

Lord Justice Cotton.—Does this prevent the application of the moneys in discharge of any liability not arising from their own contract, but from an external Act of Parliament? Is not it what contracts they are to enter into to be paid this money?

The Master of the Rolls.—Suppose a tort committed?

The Solicitor-General.—They have been held liable in *Jones v. The Mersey Docks.*

The Master of the Rolls.—If it is not under the word "expenses," under what word is it?

The Solicitor-General.—I see not under what they pay their servants if it is not under "expenses."

Lord Justice Brett.—I understand that argument; but it was the argument you were putting which frightened me. To say the taxes granted by Parliament are the property of the Crown, so as to bring in that thing, is a doctrine that startles me so strongly that I differ from it.

The Solicitor-General.—I do not think it necessary in this case, but I should most strenuously insist that by no private Act of Parliament could you, by expressly providing it should be applied in a particular way and no other, and even if you do not use the words payment of taxes, exclude the liability to tax.

The Master of the Rolls.—You know by history that some of the old aids granted to the Crown were so much hereditary to the Crown that the Crown granted them to subjects. The Humber dues were so granted.

The Solicitor-General.—Yes, my Lord.

Lord Justice Brett.—If we had been arguing this in the time of Queen Elizabeth I would not have stated my opinion, because my head might have been off, but I can now state my opinion.

The Solicitor-General.—I think that this can be determined on narrower grounds, because nobody can dispute that this Act can be applied in the way directed, after they have paid their ordinary debts, the debts of their servants, to officers, and their solicitor's bills.

The Master of the Rolls.—You say the intendment of the Act is not that the Corporation shall allow execution to go against their property.

The Solicitor-General.—No, my Lord.

The Master of the Rolls.—If they could not pay Queen's taxes or assessed taxes a levy can be made.

Lord Justice Brett.—It has been held they are liable.

The Solicitor-General.—Yes, that was in *Jones* v. *The Mersey Docks.* It was held they were liable.

The Master of the Rolls.—I must say for myself I prefer not to look at the sections. We may treat it it does not regulate their title as regards third parties by what I may call a title paramount.

The Solicitor-General.—That is my contention, my Lord, that it was a private Act, and was not intended to deal with such a question as the liability to taxation to property which undoubtedly comes within the general liability. Your Lordships will find in paragraph 8, the Act of 1859, in reference to expenses, is a little wider in its terms than the Act of 1857. It is in these terms, " All charges and expenses of supporting, main-" taining, and repairing the works authorised to be erected, " established, and maintained by the Board, and of the general " management of the Mersey Dock Estate, and of all reason-" able expenses necessary for conducting, securing, preserving, " improving, amending, maintaining, and protecting the same, " the Board shall yearly and every year—" I should submit that under those words they can certainly pay their taxes; that they would still come within those words. I forget whether I gave your Lordships the reference to the exempting clause.

The Master of the Rolls.—No.

The Solicitor-General.—It is number six.

The Master of the Rolls.—These words are very common, especially in Acts where the estates are vested in trustees to pay debts, nobody says anything about taxes.

The Solicitor-General.—And I find in Corporation Acts it is a common thing to find the corporate fund especially applied to such and such a purpose and no other; and yet if you look to those purposes one of them is not the payment of taxes; and your Lordships know in the General Municipal Corporations Act, with regard to the borough funds that are not especially appropriated, it is provided that the surplus shall be applied for the public benefit of the inhabitants and improvement of the borough. Several cases have arisen where they have tried to do something which the Court have held is not within the public benefit or improvement of the borough; there is a surplus of the borough fund after providing for all specific things, and then the Legislature have provided that surplus shall be charged under the direction of council for the benefit of the public and improvement of the borough. There was a case the other day when the Corporation gave an entertainment to General Grant when he came to Sunderland, and the question was raised whether that was for the benefit of the inhabitants; and there have been several cases where the Courts have held

(marginal note:) MERSEY DOCK AND HARBOUR BOARD *v.* LUCAS.

things have been outside the powers. I mean when you have these provisions as to how the money shall be spent it always means after payment of necessary expenses.

The Master of the Rolls.—What they are liable to authorise?

The Solicitor-General.—Yes, it is what they have to dispose of after discharging all legal liabilities.

The Master of the Rolls.—Yes, the words " to be applied to any purpose whatsoever " are only applied *inter se.*

The Solicitor-General.—I will now give your Lordship the exemption in the Income Tax Acts. They are contained in section 61. They exempt " any college or hall in any of the " universities in respect of the public buildings and offices " belonging to such college or hall, and not occupied by any " individual member thereof, or by any person paying rent for " the same." This is what one may call the public parts as distinguished from the private rooms. " And for the repairs of " the public buildings and offices of such college or hall, and the " gardens, walks, and grounds for recreation repaired and main- " tained by the funds of such college or hall." Then, " Or on " any hospital, public school, or almshouse in respect of the " public buildings, offices, and premises belonging to such hos- " pital, public school, or almshouse, and not occupied by any " individual officer or the master thereof." Then, " Any build- " ing the property of any literary or scientific institution used " solely for the purposes of such institution." And then, " Or " on the rents and profits of lands, tenements, hereditaments, " or heritages belonging to any hospital, public school, or alms- " house, or vested in trustees for charitable purposes so far as " the same are applied to charitable purposes." Those are the only exemptions.

The Master of the Rolls.—It is plain that the general words include everybody else.

The Solicitor-General.—Yes, and include those too but for the special allowance that is to be made. Of course in all those cases they would only have power to apply their funds to the purposes for which they are trustees.

The Master of the Rolls.—And frequently by Act of Parliament. Many of these charities are governed by Act of Parliament.

The Solicitor-General.—Yes, my Lord. Now I was going to call your Lordship's attention to the *Attorney-General* v. *Black* upon the point whether the funds would be taxable. That was in the Exchequer Chamber.

The Master of the Rolls.—Is there any distinction between an Act of Parliament directing it to be applied to a given purpose and any other?

The Solicitor-General.—No, my Lord.

The Master of the Rolls.—You exempt any other purpose?

The Solicitor-General.—Yes, and you can get by injunction the other purpose.

Lord Justice Brett.—I do not know whether you want to have the unanimous opinion of the Court, but if you do so you must satisfy every member of it.

The Solicitor-General.—I hope to do so. I will call your Lordship's attention to the *Attorney-General* v. *Black*, and I say there is no difference in principle applicable to this case. It is reported in the Law Reports, 6th Exchequer, at page 308, " By " 13th George III., chapter 34, a power was given to the Im- " provements Commissioners for Brighton to levy a duty of 6*d.* " on every chauldron of coals landed on the beach or brought " into the town for the purpose of erecting and maintaining " groyns, &c. against the sea. By subsequent Acts the duty " was continued and increased, and by 6 Geo. IV., chap. 179, it " was, together with rates which the Commissioners were em- " powered to levy, market tolls, &c., to form a common fund for " the general purposes of the Act, which included paving, light- " ing, watching, and the maintenance of groyns and other sea " works. Held (affirming the judgment of the Court below) " that the Corporation (who had succeeded to the rights of the " Commissioners) were liable to pay income tax in respect of the " coal duty." Now, the judgment was that of Mr. Justice " Byles, Mr. Justice Blackburn, Mr. Justice Keating, Mr. Justice Mellor, Mr. Justice Montague Smith, and Mr. Justice Lush. Mr. Justice Blackburn says this, and there is an observation of his Lordship's very much in point here, " The question is as to " the construction of the 5th and 6th Victoria, cap. 35." That is the income tax. The learned judge referred to section 60, Schedule A., that is the one we are dealing with, and section 100, Schedule D. " The words in this latter section are very exten- " sive. My brother Martin says, ' It seems impossible that any " ' net could be extended more widely; every possible source of " ' income seems included.' Not, however, that every kind of " income derived by a corporation in whatever way it may " come to them would be included in it. They would not be " liable except in respect of something of the same nature and " kind as what had been previously mentioned; not, for instance, " in respect of a borough rate, a poor rate, or a highway rate, " because these are not within the analogy of ' property or " ' profit ' previously described. The question then is whether " this particular income does come within the description of " ' property or profit,' and after listening attentively to the " argument for the Appellants, I have come to the conclusion " that it does. The mention of ' rights of markets and fairs ' " and ' tolls ' in Schedule A., No. III., shows the intention of the " Legislature to include in the general sweeping words of " Schedule D. sources of income similar to these. Harbour and " port dues, therefore, originally granted to the owners of the " ports being *ejusdem generis*, with market dues and tolls, " would be included in those general words. The question, " therefore, is whether the rate or duty in this case is of the " same sort or kind as harbour or port dues. I observe in

" passing that the fact of the proceeds of the rate being brought
" into a common fund, which also includes other kinds of income
" that are not subject to income tax, does not affect the question;
" for the true principle is that adopted in *Mersey Docks and
" Harbour Board* v. *Cameron,* that if the fund is in its nature
" subject to taxation, it remains so subject notwithstanding its
" proceeds are to be applied to public purposes, and the proceeds
" which are to be so applied are what remain after discharging
" the burden to which it is subject."

The Master of the Rolls.—Who is that?

The Solicitor-General.—Lord Blackburn in this case of the
Attorney-General v. *Black,* " That circumstance therefore fur-
" nishes no ground of distinction.   Taking this rate or duty
" then independently of that consideration it is strictly *ejusdem
" generis* with tolls and dues."   That was whether this rate was
a toll or due or was a highway rate.

Lord Justice Brett.—Is he dealing with a private Act or a
local Act which had negative words in it?

The Solicitor-General.—No; there were no negative words in
it, but there were positive words in it.

The Master of the Rolls.—I cannot see the distinction, that if
one were to be applied in the payment of A., a man might be
restrained by injunction from paying it to B.

The Solicitor-General.—The other judgments are to the same
effect.   Now, I say that case is undistinguishable from the
present.   There it was received by trustees, who were to apply
it to certain specified purposes.   True, it did not say to no other,
but it specified the purposes.   Therefore that is equal to saying
it was to apply to no other.

Lord Justice Brett.—This is all upon the supposition that the
income tax is not within the word " expenses."   Do you argue
it would be right to strike out of this Act of Parliament the
words " and except as aforesaid "?   That is, the application of
the money having been directed to particular things, " and, as
" aforesaid, such moneys shall not be applied by the Board for
" any other purpose whatsoever."

The Solicitor-General.—I should certainly say in the case I
am dealing with, I say in the case of a private Act dealing with
the application and distribution of moneys received by a corporation or private person, you could not be permitted so to
construe the words as to exclude the liability to a tax.

The Master of the Rolls.—Those words have a meaning.   They
are not meaningless.   They apply to a special Act providing for
purposes.   When you have an Act of Parliament directing all
the money to be applied to a certain thing, the words are absolutely meaningless, because the first words exhausted all the
money; but where the words will not exhaust all the money,—
and, in fact, you will find there is a surplus in this Act,—but
where there is an absolute disposition, that is, where it will

necessarily exhaust the fund, or there is a mode of disposition which must exhaust the fund, the words would be of no use, because the first words dispose of the whole.

Lord Justice Brett.—I put to you the case where there is a surplus.

The Solicitor-General.—I certainly should answer, given there was a surplus, if there were those prohibitory words, I should say you ought not to construe a private Act of Parliament so as to exclude the liability to pay debts.

The Master of 'the Rolls.—You say neither the affirmative words nor the negative words apply to liabilities paramount to the rights of the Corporation?

The Solicitor-General.—No, my Lord. I say that would be an unreasonable construction to put upon a private Act of Parliament, which, in many cases, is said to be a private bargain to which the Legislature has given its sanction. In *The Mersey Docks* v. *Cameron*, the case which Lord Blackburn refers to in his judgment in *The Attorney-General* v. *Black*, Lord Blackburn, in his opinion to the House, uses this language in delivering the judgment of himself and some of the other learned judges: " We think, in conformity with the decision in *The Tyne Com-* " *missioners* v. *Chirton*, that enactments directing that the " revenue should be applied to certain purposes and no others are " directory only, and mean that after all charges imposed by " law on the revenue have been discharged, the surplus or other " revenue which otherwise might have been disposed of at the " pleasure of the recipient shall be applied to these purposes."

The Master of the Rolls.—That is that very point.

The Solicitor-General.—That is that very point.

The Master of the Rolls.—That was the opinion given to the House of Lords on the part of the judges.

The Solicitor-General.—That was the opinion given to the House of Lords on the part of the judges, on the part of five of the judges.

The Master of the Rolls.—It is an authority.

The Solicitor-General.—Yes, my Lord. Now, there was another case which was relied upon by the learned judges in the Court below, and which, therefore, I ought to call to your Lordships' attention, the decisions in the Scotch cases. It is the case of the Glasgow Waterworks, the Income Tax Commissioners, and the Glasgow Corporation. It was before the Court of Session in Scotland. Under the Glasgow Corporation Waterworks Act there was power to raise certain funds for the purpose of bringing the water from Loch Katrine to Glasgow, and there was a power given to the Corporation to levy a rate upon every householder within the limits of Glasgow, whether he took water or not; a general rate on everybody for the purpose of providing funds. Then there was a provision that the moneys raised and received by the Corporation in respect of their waterworks should go, first, to the discharge of a sinking fund similar somewhat to this. Then it was alleged that there was a surplus of receipts over expenditure; that is to say, after paying their expenses there was a surplus, and the question was whether that was to be taxed to the income tax, and the Court of Session held it was not. The ground, as I say, on which they decided was this: that that was like any other rate,—like the highway rate or any other rate,—that it was not a payment for the use of the water, or a profit got by them,by the selling of the water; but there was a power to rate everybody in their limit in Glasgow, whether they took any water or not.

The Master of the Rolls.—It was a borough rate and not an income tax.

The Solicitor-General.—It was a borough rate and an income tax.. That was the ground of the decision, and that that was the ground of the decision will be apparent when the judgments are read. Under the Glasgow Corporation Act they had power to supply water to people outside their district. They only paid when they received the water, and the judges expressly reserved the point whether in respect of such a sum income tax would not be payable. Therefore the fact that they reserved that shows the ground they decide is not the ground that would govern this case, but that it was a borough rate.

Lord Justice Brett.—Did not they say it applied necessarily to a single borough by legislation?

The Solicitor-General.—It is true they relied upon that, or alluded to it, but that would equally have applied to the matter they left open.

The Master of the Rolls.—Were there any negative words?

The Solicitor-General.—No, my Lord.

The Master of the Rolls.—The case of Black is entirely negative.

The Solicitor-General.—Except so far as this was in the nature of a borough rate, I should say there was no distinction between it and Black.

Lord Justice Brett.—The ground of that decision was, that because the Legislature enacted the funds were to be applied to a sinking fund, therefore there was no income that could be taxed. It is against your view.

The Solicitor-General.—After stating the facts the Lord President says: " Now the sum of 17,032*l*. 15*s*., upon which the " charge is made under Schedule D. of the Income Tax Act, " comprehends the whole portion of the revenue of the Water " Commissioners, which is applied towards the formation of the " sinking fund in redemption of the annuities and mortgages in " the manner that I have already mentioned, and also the " balance, if any, which is carried forward to the following " year's account, to be applied as the Act directs in reducing " the domestic water rate, and the question is, whether income

" arising from this assessment which is appropriated to such
" purposes is assessable for income tax under Schedule· D. as
" profits of this water undertaking. I am humbly of opinion
" that it is not. It seems to me that this in an Act of Parlia-
" ment by which the citizens of Glasgow have undertaken,
" through this water corporation as their representatives, to
" assess themselves for a very important public purpose—a pur-
" pose very conducive to their own comfort and well-being—to
" obtain a good supply of water for the city. In so assessing
" themselves they had not in view certainly to make profit by
" the undertaking. On the contrary, what they have distinctly
" in view is, to pay money in order to obtain this particular
" benefit. They are not, therefore, trading in any commodity,
" nor are they entering into any undertaking for the use of
" property that is to be attended by a resulting profit, or a
" beneficial interest accruing to any individuals or to any cor-
" poration. The object of the assessment is to pay for bringing
" in the water, and when that is done, the assessment and the
" authority to levy it comes to an end. If, in the progress of
" the operation of this Act, the City of Glasgow is in so happy
" a condition that they can afford to reduce their assessments to
" a mere fraction of a penny, that must be done under the
" operation of the statute. If that fraction of a penny is suffi-
" cient to pay the current expenses of maintaining this Water
" Commission, and the works under their charge, and, I suppose,
" if by some wonderful scheme of good management they should
" so contrive that they would be able to get water for nothing
" by and by, then the right to levy assessment would come
" to an end altogether. But one thing at least is perfectly
" certain, that it is made matter of absolute statutory regulation
" that the expense of supplying this water, including all the
" various items of expenditure that I have already mentioned,
" and the revenue, are to be kept actually commensurate and
" equivalent, as near as possibly can be, and that being prac-
" tically impossible in every year, the way in which the same
" object is achieved is by carrying over any surplus of one year
" into the next year, and employing it in reducing the revenue
" for the next year. Now, it seems to me that it is not within the
" contemplation of Schedule D. of the Income Tax Act to
" charge any portion of a local rate raised for such a purpose as
" profit or as anything else, falling within that Schedule D. The
" case is entirely different from those that have been cited,
" which have been decided in the Court of Exchequer in England,
" because in those cases the statute which gave the right to
" levy the assessment did not impose it upon the citizens of
" the particular burgh or locality which obtained the Act. It
" was not an authority to the citizens of a particular locality to
" assess themselves. On the contrary, it was a right and privi-
" lege given to a particular corporation to assess everybody, the
" whole public, who happened to import in the one case coals
" into the burgh, and in another case to import something else.
" I forget what it was. But there it must be the corporation of

"the particular burgh, or the Commissioners—for it does not
"matter in the least degree what they were—were making a
"profit out of a tax levied upon the lieges generally, and were
"applying the proceeds of that tax for the benefit of the com-
"munity which they represénted; and, therefore, they were
"held, most justly, I think, to be making profit; no doubt, not
"for individual benefit, but for corporate benefit, and for the
"benefit of the community represented by the administrative
"body that levied the tax."

Lord Justice Brett.—Whose judgment is that?

The Solicitor-General.—That is the Lord President's judgment in the Court of Session.

Lord Justice Brett.—Was that judgment relied, upon by the
judges in the Court below?

The Solicitor-General.—Yes, my Lord.

The Master of the Rolls.—He distinguishes it from Black's
case?

The Solicitor-General.—He distinguishes it from Black's case.
It is taken in connexion with the fact that the rate is a local
rate levied upon everybody within the borough, and levied upon
everybody whether he uses the water or not.

Lord Justice Brett.—Were there other judges there?

The Solicitor-General.—Yes, my Lord.

Lord Justice Brett.—Did they give the same reasons?

The Solicitor-General.—Yes, my Lord. I should like to read
the next few lines. "I have only farther to say that if any
"attempt had been made here to discriminate between that por-
"tion of the revenue which arises from the rates levied within
"the limits of compulsory supply, and that portion of the
"revenue which is raised in the districts beyond the limits of
"compulsory supply, I should have been very glad to attend to
"any grounds which might have been urged for such a distinc-
"tion. It was said, no doubt in argument, but rather by way
"of illustration of the general claim than anything else, that
"this corporation does, in a certain sense, trade in water, and
"sell it to those people who are outside the limits of compulsory
"supply; that it is matter of traffic with them, and what they
"derive from them in the shape of rates may perhaps be fairly
"represented as coming within the denomination of profit, of
"revenue derived from the use of a certain subject of which
"they are the administrators. But it appears to me that that
"question does not arise here. We have not before us the
"means of seeing what the result of the transactions between
"the Water Commissioners and the persons beyond the limits
"of compulsory supply are or have been. We do not know
"that any surplus has arisen from these transactions." So
that although if they had got money from the outside supply,
they would equally have been bound to apply it to the sinking
fund, they do not say that is conclusive, they say it may be a

different case. I submit to your Lordships when you read
that judgment of the Court of Session so far from infringing
upon the case of *The Attorney-General* v. *Black*, they entirely
accept it, and they deal with that case upon wholly different
grounds. I think, my Lords, that is all I have to address to
your Lordships in this case, and I have now only to call the
attention of your Lordships to the judgment of the Court below.
Mr. Justice Grove says, "I am of opinion that the Appellants
"are entitled to our judgment. The question arises really
"under the provisions of certain Acts of Parliament. There
"are three Mersey Dock Acts, one for 1857, which states the
"general character of the Mersey Dock Act, which I need not
"go through, and also states from what source the revenue of
"the Mersey Docks Harbour, or that body from whom the
"Mersey Docks have been derived, 'tonnage, dock dues,' &c.,
"all of which by section 6 are denominated thus: they are to
"include dock rates, tonnage rates, graving dock rates, wharf
"'rates,' and several others which I need not enumerate. Then
"by the 284th section of that Act, it is provided in what way
"the moneys which shall be collected, levied, borrowed, and
"raised under or by virtue of either of the two Acts shall be
"used, and then it points out the manner in which they shall be
"used. The payment of moneys borrowed in the construc-
"tion of works, and in the general management, conducting,
"securing, preserving, improving, amending, and maintaining
"the Mersey Dock Estate, and then it provides, &c.—it is upon
"this the question mainly turns, that the residue or surplus
"of all such moneys which shall remain after such application
"thereof as aforesaid shall from time to time be applied in or
"towards the repayment of all principal moneys, which shall
"have been borrowed, &c., and the repayment of the annuities
"'In manner herein-after directed, until all such principal
"'moneys shall have been repaid, and all Mersey Dock An-
"'nuities shall have been purchased up and extinguished, and
"'when, by the means last mentioned, all such principal moneys
"'shall have been repaid, and all such dock annuities shall
"'have been purchased up and extinguished, then and in such
"'case the Board shall and they are hereby required to lower
"'and reduce the rates hereby authorised to be taken, so far
"'as the same can be done in the then state of the docks, and
"'leaving sufficient for the payment of the expenses of collect-
"'ing the rates, and the supporting, maintaining, and repairing
"'of the docks, and the general management, conducting,
"'securing, preserving, improving, amending, maintaining, and
"'protecting the Mersey Dock Estate.' Then came these words,
"'and, except as aforesaid, such moneys shall not be applied
"'by the Board for any other purpose whatever.' Now, here
"the Appellants are willing to pay, and it is assumed that they
"will pay income tax upon the interest which they pay to
"the lenders of certain money and to certain annuities. They
"do not pay that income tax upon the profits which they them-
"selves receive, but they pay it as interest due by the person

" who receives a profit in the shape of interest upon their
" bonds or an annuity."   I do not think I need read that.
" Upon that there is no dispute in this case, but then the
" question is, are they liable to pay income tax upon this surplus,
" which is beyond all those moneys which are paid in the reduc-
" tion or redemption of their debt, and paid in the expense of
" maintaining and carrying on the undertaking, and the argu-
" ment of the Appellant is that that is in no sense profit to
" them, that they do not get anything out of it in any sense
" for themselves, nor do they get it as a body receiving a fund
" and exercising their vocation, if I may use the expression, in
" its distribution, or being able to distribute it for the purpose
" of its being beneficial to the body whom they represent, but
" here they got nothing at all.   The money is, as fast as it is
" received, practically appropriated by the statute itself to a
" particular use, and that, therefore, they never get any profit,
" and if it can be said, they nominally received it into their
" hands, and in that sense it can be called a profit, it is a profit
" which by force of the statute must immediately pass out of
" their hands, and therefore it is not a profit within the sense
" of the Income Tax Acts, upon which the Respondents rely.
" Now I am of opinion that is the correct construction of the
" different clauses of the Act.   In addition to this section, the
" one in the Act of 1858, there is a section of the Act of 1859,
" which says ' that the Board shall yearly, and in every year,
" ' subsequent to the 24th June, apply the surplus, if any, of
" ' the rates which shall remain in their hands, after such pay-
" ' ments as aforesaid, to the extent of 100,000l.,' that is the
" maximum, ' or such less amount as the said surplus shall be
" ' equal to, in, or towards the repayment of some or any of the
" ' principal moneys which shall then be due and owing to the
" ' security of the rates, and which shall then have become due
" ' and payable in the purchasing up and extinguishing of the
" ' Mersey Dock Annuities, which may be then existing, accord-
" ' ing to the respective parts of such moneys and annuities until
" ' all principal moneys shall be repaid,' and so on, I need not
" read that in full, ' and subject to the provisions herein con-
" ' tained, all rates and other moneys which shall be collected,
" ' levied, borrowed, and raised or received under or by virtue of
" ' the said recited Acts, or either of them, or of this Act, the
" ' application of which may not be otherwise expressly directed
" ' shall and may be applied by the Board, according to the pro-
" ' visions for that purpose contained in section 284 of the Act of
" ' 1858,' if I may put it shortly.   Therefore, the residue of this
" surplus fund includes this surplus fund itself, after having
" devoted it to paying or buying up all those annuities and those
" debts which they owe to the persons who have lent the money,
" whether on bond or in the shape of annuities, or in any other
" way, they are to apply as directed in the 284th section of
" the Act of 1858, and that directs, as I have already read,
" ' that they shall and are hereby required to lower and reduce
" ' the rates and, except as aforesaid, such money shall not be

" ' applied for any other purpose whatsoever.' Now, reading
" that Act by itself, I must say I should have no doubt, and
" indeed at first I had the greatest possible difficulty in seeing
" what the arguments were against the Appellants, because it
" seemed to me an absolute and imperative statutory applica-
" tion of the money, and that therefore the money could not
" fairly be called profits in the hands of the person receiving
" it, because they were directed to use it for a certain purpose
" mentioned in the Act, and directed expressly by the Act not
" to apply it for any other purpose whatsoever.   Then it is
" said that that direction is subject to paying Government duties
" and subject to paying income tax, and certainly in words it
" is not so subject, but it is said in the case of the *Attorney-*
" *General* v. *Black* it was held there (though I may say there
" was nothing like the prohibitory clause which there is in this
" Act, to say nothing of other differences)."

The Master of the Rolls.—The opinion you read of Lord
Blackburn was not read to them.

The Solicitor-General.—I will not be quite sure. I think it
was. We had it at the time we quoted the *Mersey Docks* v.
Cameron.

The Master of the Rolls.—That is not the case.

The Solicitor-General.—My impression would be that it was,
but I should not like to pledge myself.

Mr. Bingham.—I think, with all deference to my learned
friend, it was not read.

The Master of the Rolls.—I should assume so. If it had been
read, I do not think Mr. Justice Grove would have passed it
over in that way.

Mr. Bingham.—I have had the advantage of reading the
Solicitor-General's observations.

The Solicitor-General.—" There being there a certain surplus
" which went over for the taxpayers generally it was subject
" to income tax. Then, as I understand, it was held on the
" ground, among others, it goes to a part of the common fund,
" that part of the profit of the Corporation of Brighton which
" was to be used for all purposes to which they may appropriate
" it, and that is a distinction which was taken in a subsequent
" case, the case of the Corporation of Glasgow, much more
" similar to the present case than the case of the *Attorney-*
" *General* v. *Black*, though not so strong as the present case,
" as far as I have gathered from it, because in that case there
" were no such prohibitory words as here occur at the end of
" the 284th section that, ' except as aforesaid such moneys shall
" ' not be applied by the Board for any other purpose what-
" ' soever,' but there the words were (I do not know whether
" I have taken them all down), that the surplus should be
" applied in reducing a domestic rate or water-rate. It was
" a water company of a public nature, and the surplus was to

" be applied in reducing the domestic water rate. The Court
" there held that that was not liable to income tax, and that
" it was distinguishable from the previous case of the *Attorney-*
" *General* v. *Lloyd*; on the ground, here, there was a statutory
" provision, and that the surplus was not to be applied at the
" discretion of any body of people, or for the particular benefit
" of any body of people, but there was an absolute statutory
" discretion, and it appears to me that, assuming that case to
" be good law, and it is not disputed by the Solicitor-General,
" this case is *à fortiori*." I do not dispute the case in the
Scotch courts being good law, but I dispute that that was
entirely the ground upon which that proceeds, and had so
disputed strenuously in the Court below. " It is considerably
" stronger in favour of the Appellants, because in this case there
" are the very strong words. First of all the 284th section
" points out what the exact surplus is by stating what are the
" previous things to be deducted from it, ' and shall remain
" ' after such application thereof as aforesaid.' That is an
" enumeration of all the applications of the moneys that then
" shall be applied in the way directed, and amongst those
" modes one is, coupling the two Acts together, that the surplus
" fund shall be, after paying the debts, and paying those things
" required, ' that the Board shall and are hereby required to
" ' lower and reduce the rates hereby authorised to be taken, so
" ' far as the same can be done in the then state of the docks,
" ' leaving sufficient for the payment of the expenses of collecting
" ' the rates, and of supporting, maintaining, and repairing the
" ' docks, and the general management and conducting, securing,
" ' preserving, improving, amending, maintaining, and protect-
" ' ing the Mersey Dock Estate,' and then come still stronger
" words, ' and except as aforesaid such moneys shall not be
" ' applied by the Board for any other purpose whatever.' Now,
" I cannot see if the Glasgow case is good law that this is not a
" very much stronger case, because this had all the elements that
" were in the Glasgow case, and it has plus those this
" prohibitory clause." I say it differs in the one essential
element on which the Glasgow case rested, " except as afore-
" said such moneys shall not be applied by the Board for any
" other purpose whatsoever. Then the answer is as applied to
" those words, parochial taxes have been held, if I may use the
" expression, to take precedence of the statute directing the
" application." That shows, so far, that, whether we read the
passage or not, we called attention to the fact of the decision in
the *Mersey Docks* v. *Cameron*. " I am not sure the words have
" the same strength as these, but at all events that seems to be
" meant in this very statute, because in this following section
" it does not exempt parochial rates."

The Master of the Rolls.—He relies on the negative words.

The Solicitor-General.—Yes, my Lord. " Nothing in this Act
" contained shall alter or affect the question of the liability of
" any of the docks or works vested in the Board to parochial or

"local rates, but the same shall in all respects be judged of and
"determined as if this Act had not been passed."

Lord Justice Brett.—As to your quoting the Cameron case in
the report in the Law Journal, it is not cited in the argument
on either side.

The Solicitor-General.—We certainly referred to it.

Lord Justice Cotton.—In the Report in the Law Times which
I have, you are stated to have cited it.

Lord Justice Brett.—That is decisive.

The Solicitor-General.—"It therefore makes it still stronger,
"because if the Act, or those who framed it, have decided to
"exempt income tax, when it intended to make an exemption
"it makes it from the general exemptive words ' parochial rates,'
"and therefore as it knew what it ought to say," (I call your
Lordship's attention to this:) "with respect to parochial or local
"rates it would have applied an equal exemption with regard to
"income tax. It does nothing of the sort. It therefore uses
"prohibitory words, giving one exception without giving any
"other. Therefore, not merely on the authority of the Glasgow
"case, but on the much stronger authority, if I may say so, of
"the statute itself, it appears to me the income tax is not
"excepted from the negative words, and that therefore there is
"no income tax due, for that would be, in my judgment, appli-
"cation by the Board for some other purpose. The words
"expressly exclude it, and therefore the Appellants are entitled
"to judgment." Then Mr. Justice Lindley says, "I am of the
"same opinion. *Primâ facie* I think the Solicitor-General's
"argument is well founded; that is to say, in looking to the
"Queen's Tax Act alone, the word ' profits ' in that Act means
"what profits ordinarily mean; namely, the excess of expendi-
"ture over the expenditure necessary to make the income. And
"I think he is right in his second proposition, that when you
"have profits in that sense, income tax is payable in respect of
"them. But after all, when you have several Acts of Parliament
"to construe, you must construe them, and construe them to-
"gether; and this case is reduced to a very simple problem.
"There is a general Act of Parliament imposing income tax on
"such profits as I have mentioned; there is a special Act of
"Parliament passed subsequently to the general Act of Parlia-
"ment." That is a misapprehension. "There is a general Act
"of Parliament imposing income tax on such profits as I have
"mentioned; there is a special Act of Parliament passed subse-
"quently to the general Act of Parliament, and which says
"how certain moneys and certain receipts are to be applied."

Lord Justice Brett.—I do not know whether that is a slip,
because in this report he says, "Now there is a general Act
"passed since the special Act."

The Solicitor-General.—I am reading the shorthand note.
"There is a general Act of Parliament imposing Income Tax on

" such profits as I have mentioned; there is a special Act of
" Parliament passed subsequently to the general Act of Parlia-
" ment, and which says how certain moneys and certain receipts
" are to be applied, and says negatively that those moneys so
" received shall not be applied in any other way."

Lord Justice Brett.—It is this report which is wrong.

The Solicitor-General.—Yes, my Lord. "To make it plainer
" still there is a provision which is to the effect that nothing in
" that Act contained shall exempt this Board from liability to
" parochial or local rates. All we have to do is to construe
" those Acts of Parliament, and it appears to me it is quite im-
" possible to hold the combined effect of the three special Acts
" of Parliament and the Income Tax Act is to make income
" tax payable out of these receipts, or any portion of them. I
" rely on the special words of this Act of Parliament; the autho-
" rities do not appear to me to throw much light upon it."

The Master of the Rolls.—It is plain you did not read that
passage of Lord Blackburn's judgment.

The Solicitor-General.—"The Scotch case, whether you take
" the case of the Gas Works, or the other one, turned on Acts of
" Parliament which have not got those negative words; and
" without those words, and without the express provision, the
" Gas Works case might be applicable, or even, perhaps, the
" other. I do not pause to say which would be most applicable,
" but rely entirely on the special wording of this special Act of
" Parliament, which appear to me inconsistent with the theory
" that income tax is payable, and therefore there will be judg-
" ment for the Appellants."

Lord Justice Brett.—The reporter of the Law Journal has put
this note at the bottom of the case: "See the Mayor of Wor-
" cester and the Assessment Committee of the Droitwich Union."
Does that mean it is inconsistent with that case, or what? Perhaps Mr. Dicey will look it up.

Mr. Dicey.—Yes, my Lord, I will look it up.

The Solicitor-General.—That must have been a poor rate case,
not an income tax case, by being the Assessment Committee of
the Droitwich Union.

7th December 1881.

Mr. Dicey.—I will go at once to the point which I think is
the main point urged against us in the argument yesterday,
—the question as to the effect of this restrictive clause, as I may
call it, in the Mersey Docks Act. The intention of the clause
seems to me to be really this: In the first place, the Mersey
Docks and Harbour Board are directed to expend their money
in certain particular ways, and in no other way; and there is a

further provision, which must be taken with it, that nothing is to affect the question of the liability of the docks in regard to parochial or local rates.

The Master of the Rolls.—I do not see that that section has any direct bearing upon the matter. There is no greater fallacy in construing Acts of Parliament than to say, because there is a provision protecting A. therefore B. is not protected.

Mr. Dicey.—That is the view we take. If your Lordships are satisfied upon that I will not dwell upon it further.

Lord Justice Brett.—You must not take it that we are satisfied.

Mr. Dicey.—I put it in two ways; in the first place, putting aside the question about the word "expenses"——

The Master of the Rolls.—As to the word "expenses," the thing is quite clear. There is no stop after "expenses." I thought, yesterday, that "expenses" was to be read as if standing by itself, but it is the expenses with respect to the rate.

Mr. Dicey.—If your Lordship will allow me, I will put my two points. It does not seem to me that Lord Justice Brett is satisfied as I should wish him to be satisfied.

Lord Justice Brett.—What is the section of the Mersey Docks and Harbour Act?

Mr. Dicey.—Sections 284 and 285. First, I put aside altogether the question of expenses.

The Master of the Rolls.—As far as I am concerned, it appears to me to be quite plain as regards "expenses." There is no stop after the word "expenses"; it runs on in one sentence; it means the expenses of collecting the rates.

Mr. Dicey.—I shall have a word to say about expenses, but I put that aside for the present.

Lord Justice Brett.—I have not looked at the Act. Which is the Act, and which is the section?

Mr. Dicey.—The Mersey Docks Act, 1858. It is in paragraph 6 of the case. The 284th section provides——

Lord Justice Brett.—What is the No. of the Act of the Queen?

Mr. Dicey.—The 21st and 22nd of Victoria, chapter 92, sections 284 and 285.

Lord Justice Cotton.—At present I take the same view as the Master of the Rolls, that "expenses" in the first of these two clauses only refers to the expenses of collecting; that it means the expenses of collecting the rates.

Mr. Dicey.—At present I will not refer to the question of expenses.

The Master of the Rolls.—If you look at it you will see that it is payment of all the expenses and charges of collecting the rates; you cannot make a sentence of it by putting a stop after the word "expenses."

Mr. Dicey.—I will not go into the question of expenses at present. This first clause, clause 284, is nothing more than that kind of direction between parties as to the way in which a fund is to be appropriated, of which you find constant specimens in these local Acts. You will find in some local Acts you are to expend money in such and such a way, and not otherwise, and in other local Acts you will find the words " in no other manner whatsoever."

The Master of the Rolls.—What do you think the words " general management " include?—" general management, conducting, securing, preserving, improving, amending, maintaining, and protecting the Mersey Dock Estate."

Mr. Dicey.—I should say that those words include all the expenses which by law the persons were bound to incur.

The Master of the Rolls.—If it does not mean that, the Board would be in this difficulty : suppose the land tax has to be paid, under what words do you pay it if you do not pay it under those words ? or a tithe-rent charge.

Mr. Dicey.—Just so.

The Master of the Rolls.—Or the costs of an action against the Board.

Mr. Dicey.—That very question has been decided against them.

The Master of the Rolls.—Unless it is under those words they cannot pay it at all.

Lord Justice Cotton.—As I understand the judgment of the Judges in the Court below, they say, not that the Mersey Dock and Harbour Board cannot pay it if it is payable, but that because the Act provides how the surplus is to be dealt with, there is no profit on which income tax can be charged ; that seems to be their reasoning.

Mr. Dicey.—That is not precisely the way I should have put it.

Lord Justice Cotton.—Mr. Justice Lindley says, as a rule profit is the difference between the gross revenue and the expenses ; but it cannot be here, because the surplus is to be dealt with in a particular way. I do not give any opinion about it, but that seems to be the reasoning.

Mr. Dicey.—Allow me to distinguish two different points. Two points were before the Court : One, the main one, that the Mersey Docks and Harbour Board could not be called upon to pay income tax, on account of this clause, which excludes the payment of income tax. Another point was, that there was no profit, properly speaking, made by the Board. Dealing with the first point, I am now endeavouring to show that this clause does not in any way preclude the payment of income tax.

Lord Justice Brett.—As to the word " expenses," I do not see that it is so excessively clear ; it is capable of reading " in " payment of all expenses, and in payment of all charges of " collecting rates." I do not say that that is the right way of reading it, but it is capable of being so read.

Mr. Dicey.—I shall take what advantage I can of that construction, but I confine myself to this point at present, that the words do not prevent the Mersey Dock and Harbour Board from paying income tax.

The Master of the Rolls.—You claim the benefit of what Lord Blackburn says?

Mr. Dicey.—Yes. Though it is expressed with more verbiage in this Act, there is no more said than is said in endless local Acts, where the Corporation are to expend money under such and such heads of expenditure, and not otherwise; the words "and not otherwise" cover quite as much as the more lengthy provisions of this Act. If you take the thing without the 285th section, it is simply and solely the case of certain expenditure being provided for by the Act as might be provided for under a trust deed or under any agreement between the parties. To add after the provision that the money is to be spent in such and such ways, the words "and not otherwise," I confess, seems to me rather unmeaning, because it would be the same thing if you said in such ways, without the words "and not otherwise." Then I come to my second point, and I take section 285, which we must read together with 284. Section 285 is simply a saving clause which I cannot account for in a moment. "Nothing in this "Act contained shall alter or affect the question of the liability "of any of the docks or works vested in the Board to parochial "or local rates, but the same shall in all respects be judged of "and determined as if this Act had not been passed." That clause is merely one of these saving clauses which would have no effect; and the most you can say for it is that it shows that a doubt existed in the mind of the draftsman whether something in these clauses might not affect the liability to local rates.

The Master of the Rolls.—There was a burning question at that time about that.

Mr. Dicey.—Yes. The reason he put it in was that there was a question at that very moment. Therefore, the argument seems to be this: that because an over-cautious draftsman put this in, we are to read it as though he had in effect said, Because I save local rates I repeal the liability to all taxes,—not income tax only, but all taxes.

Lord Justice Brett.—What was the question which you say was pending or burning?

Mr. Dicey.—The question which was then burning was the very question ultimately decided in Cameron *v.* The Mersey Docks and Harbour Board, namely the liability of this class of property to rates.

The Master of the Rolls.—To be rated at all?

Mr. Dicey.—Yes. That brings me to another point, about profits.

The Master of the Rolls.—What this section meant was this, that the mode of disposition of the property shall not affect the pending question as to liability to be rated; that is all.

Mr. Dicey.—Quite so. That leads me to the second point, about profits.

Lord Justice Brett.—If that pending question did not depend on this Act, then this saving clause does not affect it. It is,

" Nothing in this Act contained shall alter or affect the question
" of the liability of any of the docks to parochial or local rates."

Mr. Dicey.—The pending question might have been affected
by this Act. Allow me to refer to the point referred to last
night. One question with the draftsman was the question of
disposition, and he thought that principle laid down by Lord
Blackburn not being made clear, possibly those provisions as to
the mode of disposition might affect the question which had
already been raised as to liability to poor rates. I ask your
Lordships to put together what is very important for our case,—
four cases which have a very distinct bearing upon one another,
and which taken together answer the question about' both
disposition and profits. One of those cases is the Queen v. the
Churchwardens of Charlton, reported in 28th Law Journal,
Magistrates' cases, p. 131. I read first the headnote: "The
" Tyne Improvement Commissioners were empowered by Act of
" Parliament to make and maintain the Northumberland Docks,
" and to borrow money upon the security of the rates and dues.
" The rates and dues were ordered to be applied, first, in
" payment of the expenses of managing and maintaining the
" docks; next in paying the interest of the money borrowed;
" next in creating a sinking fund for the purpose of paying off
" the money borrowed, and, if there were any surplus afterwards,
" the rates were to be lowered to that extent." That was a very
similar case to our present one: " The Commissioners were also
" authorised, after the payment of the expenses above mentioned,
" and after the extinction of the debt for money borrowed, to
" set apart a sum of money annually to be applied in defraying
" extraordinary repairs, &c.; and whenever there was any
" surplus the Commissioners were to lower the rates and dues
" so as to reduce them to the annual amount of the expenses of
" the management, maintenance, and working of the docks.
" The docks having been built were used by the shipping fre-
" quenting the Tyne, and the rates and dues had amounted to
" as much as 10,000l. a year. Held, that the Commissioners
" were liable to be rated for the occupation of the docks." The
date of the decision in that case is January 26th, 1859. Therefore that particular case must have been pending and before the
draftsman's mind, or the question must have been pending,
at the time these Acts of 1857 and 1858 were drawn. I, therefore, in answer to Lord Justice Brett, say that, no doubt, this
clause must be read in this way: Whereas there is at present a
question as to whether poor rates are payable in cases where the
expenses are to be applied in a particular way; therefore, that
nothing in this Act shall affect the question already raised.
And you cannot in such a saving provision legitimately draw the
further inference that because all question as to liability to local
rates is saved, therefore this Act is to be read as though it exempted from liability to income tax and not only income tax,
but, logically, if it exempts from income tax, it exempts from
payment of every tax except those particular rates saved in the

clause. I will leave that point there. I hope I have made it intelligible. Then with the Queen v. the Overseers of Cherton, I would ask your Lordships to combine the following cases, all of which have been cited except one, but I think they should be taken in combination together. The next is the leading case on the subject, Jones v. The Mersey Docks and Harbour Board, House of Lords cases. I cite it from the 35th Law Journal, House of Lords, Magistrates' cases, page 1. It is in that case that we get the two principles governing this case laid down.

Lord Justice Brett.—When was that decided?

Mr. Dicey.—It seems to have been argued in 1864, and re-argued in 1865. In this case of Jones v. The Mersey Docks, these very persons were concerned.

Lord Justice Brett.—What was the argument in the Chirton case? That they were not liable to be rated? Why?

Mr. Dicey.—Partly because of the nature of the property, and partly because of the nature of the appropriation. I am particularly anxious to take these cases together; their combined effect is stronger than any one of them taken alone. In the Mersey Docks case we have this dictum or rather doctrine laid down by the present Lord Blackburn:

Lord Justice Brett.—I should have thought you relied upon that case for the other purpose too.

Mr. Dicey.—Yes, I do. The case covers the whole ground and the whole point before your Lordships. The two questions run one into the other. The doctrine laid down in that case was cited last night. It is in these words "We think, in con-"formity "—(I am particularly anxious that these words should be noticed)—" We think, in conformity with the decision in the "Tyne Commissioners v. Chirton" (that is the case that I have read), "that enactments directing that the revenue shall be "applied to certain purposes, and no other, are directory only, "and mean that after all charges imposed by law on the revenue "have been discharged, the surplus or free revenue which other-"wise might have been disposed of at the pleasure of the recipi-"ents should be applied to these purposes." That is the doctrine laid down by Lord Blackburn as representing four other judges.

The Master of the Rolls.—Will you read the exact words again?

Mr. Dicey.—"That enactments directing that the revenue "shall be applied to certain purposes, and no other, are directory "only, and mean that after all charges imposed by law on the "revenue have been discharged the surplus or free revenue "which otherwise might have been disposed of at the pleasure "of the recipients should be applied to these purposes;" and he refers to the Chirton case, considering that that case did decide the question as to the application of revenue.

The Master of the Rolls.—He says the section applies to that which would be otherwise disposable?

Mr. Dicey.—Yes, that is our contention. I am dwelling more upon the question of profits. Here was a case about profits.

The Master of the Rolls.—I do not at present see how, on the contention of the Mersey Board, they can pay rent. Suppose the land to be subject to a fee-farm rent.

Mr. Dicey.—I see the whole difficulty, and with one more reference I will make a few more observations upon it. Black's case was placed before your Lordships yesterday; that affirms again the doctrine laid down by the House of Lords in this case of Cameron *v.* The Mersey Docks and Harbour Board.

Lord Justice Brett.—What were the negative words in Cameron's case? I see Mr. Justice Crompton in the Chirton case said, " Then it is said that the clauses in the Act exclude pay- " ment of poor rates, but I do not think that that is so. The " Birkenhead case goes this length,—that where there is a clause " enabling the trustees to lower the tolls from time to time as " far as they can be lowered, it is not sufficient to exclude the " liability to pay poor rates, unless there be also words appro- " priating the funds in such a way as to exclude the payment " of such rates." That leaves the whole question open.

Mr. Dicey.—No. I venture to say respectfully it does not, for this reason: In the Chirton case (the decision in which was referred to with approval) there are the words " not otherwise." I think that is so. I do not wish to pledge myself to it. I see the clause in the Act in that case provides specifically for what may be paid.

Lord Justice Brett.—It provides specifically for what may be paid, and then says if there is more money than will pay these specific things the rates are to be lowered.

Mr. Dicey.—Yes. The construction I am putting is the same as that put by Lord Blackburn as giving the doctrine of the case, " That enactments directing that the revenue shall be applied to " certain purposes and no other; "—from which I infer, and I think I rightly infer, that Lord Blackburn held that it was precisely the same thing, and logically and rightly the same thing, whether you say such moneys shall be paid on such specific subjects, or whether you add the words " not otherwise." At any rate the provisions of this Act go not a whit logically further than those words " not otherwise "; and I say that such expressions as those are rife in local Acts. This tremendous effect must follow, if the argument of our opponents is to have any weight, that the Mersey Docks and Harbour Board are exempted from liability to every general tax imposed by Parlia-ment, whether before the time that the private Act passed, or after the time. It will not do to draw any distinction between before and after, because this particular Income Tax Act passed subsequently to their local Act.

Lord Justice Brett.—I do not see the unfairness or injustice of exempting these docks from public burdens. It was that if they were to be exempted from poor rates, it was very unjust to the parish in which they were, because for public purposes the docks were built upon land taken away from that parish which otherwise would be paying rates to the parish. It was thought that was very unfair with regard to the parish; with regard to the whole county I do not see the same unfairness.

Mr. Dicey.—I was not arguing on the unfairness, though all these exemptions narrow the area of taxation, and make it worse upon others.

The Master of the Rolls.—I do not know what right Liverpool has to tax the whole country for the maintenance of its docks. If they do not pay income tax they are taxing the whole country to that extent for the benefit of their docks.

Lord Justice Brett.—The point I put to you is this: that the surface occupied by the Liverpool docks, as compared with the parish of Liverpool, is very different to the space occupied by the Liverpool docks as compared with the whole of England.

Mr. Dicey.—Of course I admit that.

The Master of the Rolls.—The same principle applies. On what theory is the whole country to pay towards the maintenance of the docks at Liverpool?

Mr. Dicey.—Let me put this point. There are certain other docks in the county besides Liverpool. Let us take the Bristol docks. Suppose that in a corresponding clause in the Bristol Dock Act the draftsman omitted to put in the words "not otherwise," while those words were found in the Liverpool Act; what an astounding effect it would produce if the contention of our opponents is to prevail,—that whereas the Bristol docks paid income tax, the Liverpool docks did not pay it,—wholly from the words which are constantly used or not used by the draftsman merely as so much verbiage.

Lord Justice Brett.—I do not know that you are right in assuming those words to be introduced by the draftsman; it may be that they were put in in Parliament upon a most lengthened and solemn discussion; we do not know. To say that they are the words of the draftsman seems to me not a proper mode of construing an Act of Parliament.

Mr. Dicey.—I will say the Legislature instead of the draftsman.

The Master of the Rolls.—Is not this argument open to you: that a direction to pay A. B. has exactly the same effect, whether it is to pay A. B. and not otherwise, or to pay A. B. without the words "not otherwise." Your argument, good or bad, is that those words are pure surplusage?

Mr. Dicey.—Yes.

The Master of the Rolls.—The same words constantly occur in Acts of Parliament relating to other docks, you say.

Mr. Dicey.—That is my contention; I do not know that I need go so far.

Lord Justice Brett.—If you had used the argument which has been suggested by my Lord, I could not have made the observa-

tion to you that I did. I was making that observation to you
upon the argument which you were using.

Mr. Dicey.—Quite so. I did not put my argument in the
happiest form, but I am willing to adopt the form put by my
Lord. It really does sum up upon that point, what I intended
to say,—which was this, that if the full force and effect contended for were given to these words, it might produce very considerable injustice as between different docks. Before I sit down
I will call your Lordships' attention to one other case,—that is,
the case of the Coltness Iron Company v. Black, House of Lords,
Scotch cases, in the last June number of the Law Reports,
page 315. This case has no direct bearing on the particular
point I am arguing, but it has a very strong indirect bearing.
The direct decision in the case is that mines come within
Schedule A., and certain questions are dealt with as to how
profits on mines are to be computed. The indirect bearing that
that case has upon my present point is, that Lord Blackburn
throughout bases his argument upon the similarity, I may
almost say identity, between the rules as to income tax and the
rules as to poor rate. His view in this case, as in the case I cited
before, the Chorlton case, is that where you have profits, where
you have items which are taxable in the hands of bodies of this
kind under the poor rate, so you have the same items taxable
under the income tax. I do not press the argument further, but
I think that throws very great light upon the whole thing as
showing that in estimating whether there are profits you are to
look not at whether a particular person derives profits, but
whether the concern is a thing that brings in an excess of
receipts. Here I would sit down, but that Lord Justice Brett
asked me a question about the Cameron case last night.

Lord Justice Brett.—I asked you this about the Cameron
case. You have cited the proposition contained in the advice to
the House of Lords of Lord Blackburn,—no doubt a very high
authority; but did any of the other judges give a contrary
opinion?

Mr. Dicey.—One of the other judges, Mr. Justice Byles, did
not agree with the whole of the judges. I venture to think Lord
Blackburn was followed by the House of Lords.

Lord Justice Brett.—In that part of what he said, was he?

Mr. Dicey.—Not a word was said criticising that part of it.
No doubt that proposition was not re-stated in his Lordship's
judgment, but the opinion of the House of Lords was arrived at
after that proposition had been laid down by Lord Blackburn.
I do not put it as the decision of the House of Lords.

The Master of the Rolls.—It is not a decision of the House of
Lords.

Mr. Dicey.—I should not be arguing here if it was a decision
of the House of Lords.

The Master of the Rolls.—You are entitled to say this, that
the House of Lords decided with the majority of the judges.

Mr. Dicey.—They spoke in terms of approval of this particular judgment. One of their Lordships says, " I think it not worth " while going minutely through it."

The Master of the Rolls.—You may say it is an authority which we may follow; it is not necessarily an authority which we must follow.

Mr. Dicey.—Yes.

The Master of the Rolls.—Can you give me the reference to that case in the Appeal Court last year about the right of the Crown to issue an extent under the Bankruptcy Act?

Mr. Bingham.—The case of *re* Bolland, 8th and 9th Chancery Division.

The Master of the Rolls.—I am not going to decide this case on the ground of the decision in that case, but I am going to look at it.

Mr. Dicey.—Your Lordship asked me to look at a case last night, which is a case to some extent against us; it is the case of the Mayor and Aldermen of Worcester *v.* the Assessment Committee of Droitwich. It is to be found in Law Reports, 2nd Exchequer Division, page 49, " Where land is used for a " public purpose, and the occupiers thereof are prevented by " statute from deriving the full pecuniary benefit which it is " capable of producing, the land is to be rated to the poor with " reference to the amount of profit actually made, and not with " reference to the amount which might be secured by the occu- " piers if they were not subject to restrictions. The Local Board " of Health for W. erected and occupied works for the purpose of " supplying the inhabitants thereof with water. The works " were situate within the parish of C. In order to benefit the " inhabitants of W. the local board made the scale of charges so " low as to leave a profit far less than would have accrued to a " company carrying on the works as a commercial undertaking. " In adopting the scale of charges above mentioned, the local " board intended to carry out those provisions of the Public " Health Act, 1848, the object of which was to insure a supply " of water at a low price for sanitary purposes. The assessment " committee of the D. Union, within which the parish of C. was " situate. by a valuation list assessed the local board at a rate- " able value of 1,400l. issued upon the amount which might " have been earned by a trading company carrying on the " waterworks for their own benefit. The local board claimed to " be assessed at a rateable value of 540l. based upon the profit " actually earned by them. Held, affirming the judgment of the " Court of Appeal from Inferior Courts, that the Assessment of " 1,400l. was wrong. and that the local board were liable to be " assessed at 540l. only; for, under the provisions of the Public " Health Act, 1848," they could not make rates of an amount " more than sufficient to enable them to maintain the water- " works. and they could not be assessed only with reference to " the profit actually earned." I shall have an opportunity of reply of addressing any further arguments to your Lordships that may appear to me to be necessary. No doubt the case for our opponents will be put in the most attractive way by my learned friend.

Mr. Bigham.—In this case Mr. Benjamin leads me; but he is not here at present. I hope he will be here in time to address your Lordships. In the meantime I propose, as far as I am able, to deal with the two points that appear to me to be the only points in the case; and I shall have to deal more fully with the point which the Solicitor-General and Mr. Dicey have not addressed themselves to particularly, namely, whether these are profits at all.

The Master of the Rolls.—Why are they not profits? Why are not the surplus of receipts profits at all?

Mr. Bigham.—That is the question I am about to address myself to. I hope I shall be able to persuade you that these are not profits. Your Lordship asks me at once to assume that they are not profits. I hope I shall satisfy your Lordship that they are not profits.

Lord Justice Brett.—Then there are no profits?

Mr. Bigham.—There are no profits. There are two points in the case, and only two. First, are these profits within the meaning of the Income Tax Acts?—that is the first question. The second question is this: If they are profits, is there anything in the special Acts of Parliament which exempt the Mersey Dock Board from the payment of a tax upon profits?

The Master of the Rolls.—Are not the profits of a dock the excess of receipts from the dock over expenditure?

Mr. Bigham.—Let me, before answering that question, go step by step. First, I admit that if this dock were opened by a private individual not governed by any statutory obligations and his receipts by way of tolls were greater than his expenditure, he would be bound to pay income tax upon the surplus.

The Master of the Rolls.—As profits?

Mr. Bigham.—As profits.

The Master of the Rolls.—What I asked was, what were the profits of a dock? Suppose a statute taxes the profits of a dock, whoever receives them.

Mr. Bigham.—The docks make no profits; it is the individual who owns the dock that makes the profits.

The Master of the Rolls.—If a dock is to be taxed on the profits of that dock, whoever receives them, it may be a private owner, or it may not.

Mr. Bigham.—A person who works a dock for himself or for somebody else earns a profit.

The Master of the Rolls.—Suppose he works it for a charity.

Mr. Bigham.—I do not know that it matters whom he works it for; the question is, does he earn a profit within the meaning of the Act?

The Master of the Rolls.—If by working the dock he gets a profit, it does not matter for whom that profit is applied. Is that a proposition you are willing to accede to?

Mr. Bigham.—I will not accede to that at present.

The Master of the Rolls.—I do not recommend you to do so.

Mr. Bigham.—I do not at present accede to it. I have only to deal with the case before the Court, and I confine myself to that case. The first question is, are these profits?

The Master of the Rolls.—They are the profits of working the docks; you cannot deny that.

Mr. Bigham.—Your Lordship says so. I think your Lordship begs the whole question by saying that they are profits at all. I say they are not profits, for the reasons I am going to give. I admit that the ordinary test of profits is this: Is the receipt more than the expenditure; if it is, the difference is profit. That is the ordinary test; and if this case had no peculiar circumstances attending it, the ordinary test might be applied to it, and the surplus would be profits. But first let me draw your Lordship's attention to the way in which this Board is constituted. There are a number of trustees elected by the very persons who pay these rates; and my proposition is this, that this money which is collected over and above the expenditure——

The Master of the Rolls.—Are you right that the trustees are elected by the persons who pay the rates?

Mr. Bigham.—Certainly.

The Master of the Rolls.—What rates?

Mr. Bigham.—The dock rates.

The Master of the Rolls.—Are they?

Mr. Bigham.—Certainly. There are four nominated members.

The Master of the Rolls.—Nominated by a certain body?

Mr. Bigham.—Nominated by the Mersey Conservancy Commissioners. The case states, "The Appellants are the Mersey "Docks and Harbour Board or Corporation, constituted by Act "of Parliament for the management of the Mersey Dock estate. "There are 28 members of the Board, four of whom are ap- "pointed by the Mersey Conservancy Commissioners, and the "remainder are elected by the dock ratepayers." I can point out to your Lordships the section of the Act of Parliament under which they are elected.

Lord Justice Brett.—What are the dock ratepayers?

Mr. Bigham.—The different merchants, principally in Liverpool, though they may be elsewhere, who pay rates.

The Master of the Rolls.—Does the shipowner pay the rates?

Mr. Bigham.—Yes, certainly.

The Master of the Rolls.—Where do you find that the persons who pay the rates elect the trustees?

Mr. Bigham.—It is stated in the case. That is sufficient authority.

The Master of the Rolls.—Where do you find it in the case?

Mr. Bigham.—In the first paragraph.

The Master of the Rolls.—It does not appear to be in the Act of 1858.

Mr. Bigham.—It is not in that Act, but in the Act of 1857, which is an earlier Act.

The Master of the Rolls.—I have the Act of 1857 before me.

Mr. Bigham.—Section 8 of the Act of 1857 says, "The " elective members of the Provisional Board shall be chosen by " the dock ratepayers for the time being qualified, in pursuance " of the Act of the 15th of Her present Majesty, chapter 64, to " vote for the 12 members of the committee for the affairs of the " estate of the trustees of the Liverpool Docks, by the said Act " directed to be appointed by dock ratepayers."

The Master of the Rolls.—Then it is not the dock ratepayers, but a certain portion of them.

Mr. Bigham.—No.   With deference, this first Act of 1857 vested the docks in certain trustees, and then provided that the trustees were to be elected from time to time.   I cannot tell how, or for what periods.

The Master of the Rolls.—It is the Act of 1852.

Mr. Bigham.—They are elected from time to time by the dock ratepayers.

The Master of the Rolls.—Who are the dock ratepayers?

Mr. Bigham.—There is a register kept of those persons who pay dock rates.   They are entitled, if they choose, to get their names put upon that dock register; and having got their names upon the register, they are entitled to vote for members of the Dock Board.

The Master of the Rolls.—Is that so?   Is anybody who pays rates entitled to put his name upon that register,—the owner of a foreign ship coming in, for instance?   It cannot be.

Mr. Bigham.—Anybody who pays rates.

The Master of the Rolls.—Is that really so.   Let me see the Act of Parliament.   I cannot take that.

Mr. Bigham.—Your Lordship has the Act before you, I think.

The Master of the Rolls.—It does not say what dock ratepayers.   It can only be some of them.

Lord Justice Brett.—Is there anything in the interpretation clause to say what a dock ratepayer is?

Mr. Bigham.—I am told by a very high authority that the dock trustees are elected by persons who pay dock rates in Liverpool, of course in respect of the Liverpool docks, and who are resident in this country.   If they pay to the Mersey Dock and Harbour Board dock rates, they are entitled, though they are foreigners, if they be resident in this country, to elect members.

The Master of the Rolls.—If they are resident in the country generally?

Mr. Bigham.—Yes, in the country generally. They are entitled to vote in the annual election of members to this Board. That is what I am told.

The Master of the Rolls.—We will take that to be so.

Lord Justice Brett.—There are people who pay the rates who are not on the register.

The Master of the Rolls.—All the foreigners who do not reside here who pay dock rates?

Lord Justice Brett.—Owners of foreign ships?

Mr. Bigham.—I daresay those persons employ people in Liverpool to pay the rates. I presume that the persons who pay rates for those persons in foreign countries are registered as electors. The rates have to be paid in Liverpool. They must be paid by somebody in Liverpool; and I presume that a dock-ratepayer in Liverpool, whether he pays for a person out of the country or not, is entitled to vote for members of the Dock Board.

The Master of the Rolls.—The dock ratepayers elect the majority of the trustees.

Mr. Bigham.—They elect 24 out of the 28. I take it step by step. First, I say these are not profits, because the surplus is provided by those for whom these gentlemen are trustees. The ratepayers themselves provide the surplus, and, as your Lordship said yesterday, a man cannot make a profit out of himself. I say that the trustees of the Liverpool Docks are in other words the dock ratepayers. Let me give an illustration of what I mean. I say it is an analogous case. Suppose a number of merchants in the City of London, for their own convenience say, We will buy a warehouse, we have not the money to buy it with, therefore we will borrow the money with which to buy it; in that warehouse we will keep our goods, and we will appoint A, one of our number, to manage it, and it shall be managed on this principle: He shall charge us just as much for warehousing our goods in that warehouse as will meet the annual expenditure of keeping the warehouse in order; at the end of the year, in order to wipe off the debt which we have incurred in starting the warehouse, we will have a whip round and charge ten per cent. upon the amount of the contribution which we have paid. Could it be said that the ten per cent. that Mr. A. received over and above the rents which really met the expenditure was profit which he or anybody else was earning?

The Master of the Rolls.—Do you put it this way; that if half a dozen persons combine to keep a warehouse for the purpose of warehousing only their own goods, they do not get a profit if they do not warehouse their goods equally? If they warehouse them equally I can understand that each does not get a profit out of the other, but if they warehouse them unequally there is a profit. Suppose six people kept a warehouse, and only one warehoused his goods, and they charged him warehouse rates which exceeded the expenses, the five would get a profit out of him.

Mr. Bigham.—That is not my case.

The Master of the Rolls.—In the case you put you do not suppose that each warehouses his goods in the same proportion.

Mr. Bigham.—No.

The Master of the Rolls.—There is no equality of warehousing in the case you put.

Mr. Bigham.—No, but if I state my case properly there is no profit. Suppose that five merchants take a warrehouse for their own convenience, and they buy it with borrowed money, and they say A shall work this warehouse for us. Simply for convenience we appoint one man to look after it; he shall find out what it costs to keep the men there, pay the taxes, and do the necessary repairs. Each of us will put such goods as we choose in it, and we shall be charged by A a proportion in accordance with the quantity of goods which we put in it; we shall be charged each such a sum as will at the end of the year cover the outgoings. If nobody uses the warehouse but B he will be the only one to pay any rent; if B, C, and D put in different quantities they must pay a proportionate amount for rent; but we also agree that at the end of the year we shall each contribute ten per cent. of whatever the rent may be which we have already paid, and that ten per cent. shall be used to pay off the debt which we have incurred in buying the warehouse. Is that a profit?

The Master of the Rolls.—Ten per cent. on what?

Mr. Bigham.—On the amount they have been called on to pay for the twelve months.

The Master of the Rolls.—An additional sum.

Mr. Bigham.—Yes.

The Master of the Rolls.—The profit would be the excess of the amount received from the persons who deposited the goods over the expenditure. A contribution by five people, however estimated, is not a profit.

Mr. Bigham.—Your Lordship does not accept my hypothesis. I begin with this: that A, who has the management of the warehouse, is to charge no more on the whole of the five persons than the expenses.

The Master of the Rolls.—Then there is no profit, because the expenses equal the receipts.

Lord Justice Cotton.—Does not your argument assume that the ratepayers are a body consisting always of the same persons?

Mr. Bigham.—No, I do not think it does. When I come to call your Lordship's attention to the Scotch case——

The Master of the Rolls.—At present I do not see any profits. If the man charges no more than the expenses there are no profits.

Mr. Bigham.—I put this. Having charged no more than the expenses by agreement among them' A says B's proportion of the expenses which he has to pay in respect of rent is 100*l.*, but by agreement I am to add 10*l.* on to that, being the proportion he is to contribute on the debt due by the warehouse. Then the result of that is that A, managing the warehouse, not only receives all the expenditure, but he receives ten per cent. more, being the sum which those five persons contribute towards paying off the debt. Is that a profit?

The Master of the Rolls.—Yes, it is. If each of those persons only pays in respect of his goods, and if he pays ten per cent. not as an equal contribution but over and above the rent for warehousing his goods the others make a profit, because according to your theory they are equally liable to pay the debt, but they make that man pay a larger proportion of the debt, that is a profit to them.

Mr. Bigham.—That difficulty is easily got over in this way, they are to contribute 10 per cent. each on the amount of their respective rents.

The Master of the Rolls.—It is an additional charge on the goods.

Mr. Bigham.—No.

The Master of the Rolls.—The man who does not send any goods to the warehouse pays nothing.

Mr. Bigham.—It is not an additional charge on the goods.

The Master of the Rolls.—If the man pays 10 per cent. upon the amount of warehouse rental in respect of the goods sent to be warehoused, it is the same thing as an additional charge on the goods sent—it is in respect of the goods he sends that he is charged.

Mr. Bigham.—Let me put it in another way. I see I have confused it a little by the way I have put it, let me put it in another way.

The Master of the Rolls.—At present I do not see that there is no profit. I daresay you will make me see it.

Lord Justice Brett.—You say in the hypothetical case you put there is no profit.

Mr. Bigham.—Yes.

Lord Justice Brett.—When you come to apply that case to this you will have to show that it is like it.

Mr. Bigham.—Yes.

The Master of the Rolls.—At present I am not able to assent to your hypothetical case.

Mr. Bigham.—I begin with my hypothetical case, unless I make that clear I am afraid it would be no use applying that case to the case before me, therefore I want first to show that in the case I am putting there would be no profit.

Lord Justice Brett.—My Lord pointed out that in the case as you put it up to this time some of the six persons would make a profit, though the others would not.

Mr. Bigham.—Let me put it this way. Suppose that A in managing the warehouse is to charge each of the five men so much as will cover the expenditure, but there is an agreement that at the end of the year they shall each contribute and pay into the hands of A an equal sum each towards the payment off of the debt, would that be profit.

The Master of the Rolls.—That is to say, quite irrespective of warehousing.

Lord Justice Brett.—That would not be profit.

Mr. Bigham.—What is the difference between that case and the one I have just put, where instead of A being entitled to receive a fixed sum from each of them they agree among themselves that in proportion to the extent that each of them has used the warehouse for 12 months they shall each contribute towards paying off the debt.

The Master of the Rolls.—That is payment in respect of user of the warehouse. The man who does not use the warehouse gets payment from the man who does. That is a profit from the use of the warehouse.

Lord Justice Brett.—It is a profit to some of them, it is a profit to those who have not put anything in the warehouse, they get the advantage of the use of the warehouse by the others.

Mr. Bigham.—The fallacy there is this. Let me ask you to look at the five or six different persons as if they were one entity,—as if it were a partnership,—would they then have made a profit?

The Master of the Rolls.—As I said yesterday, a man cannot make a profit of himself. If he only uses his own warehouse he makes no profit—that is your difficulty.

Mr. Bigham.—The point I want to make clear is this. The Mersey Dock and Harbour Trustees are simply representatives for convenience sake of the Mersey Dock ratepayers.

The Master of the Rolls.—There is another body appoints four of them.

Mr. Bigham.—There are four of them appointed, for what purpose I do not know,—four of them, it is true, are appointed by the Mersey Conservancy Commissioners,—but one can easily suppose why they are appointed. They have, I suppose, to perform certain duties; to take care that the harbour is kept in proper order.

The Master of the Rolls.—They are appointed by the public.

Mr. Bigham.—They are appointed on behalf of the public; perhaps they are appointed to see that the harbour is kept in proper order; still the body who are receiving these rates are in fact the ratepayers who themselves are paying the rates.

The Master of the Rolls.—No, only some of them. Even if that was not so they do not pay equally.

Mr. Bigham.—I do not know that it matters whether they. pay equally or not.

The Master of the Rolls.—It makes all the difference, because if you charge rates all round only on the quantity of goods brought in, and the man who brings in a large quantity of goods, though he has only the same vote as the man who brings in a small quantity, pays a larger sum for rates, then the other men make a profit.

Mr. Bigham.—The dock ratepayer is simply a member of the Corporation.

Lord Justice Brett.—Who are incorporated? Not the ratepayers.

Mr. Bigham.—No; I say the Corporation is, for convenience sake, put there as representing the ratepayers.

The Master of the Rolls.—Even supposing there were no Mersey Dock and Harbour Board, if it were a Corporation elected by the ratepayers, and they charged the ratepayers unequally, the difference would be profits.

Mr. Bigham.—Profits derived from what?

The Master of the Rolls.—The people who pay the rates. They pay more for rates than the expenditure.

Mr. Bigham.—Received by whom?

The Master of the Rolls.—Received by the manager of the Corporation.

Mr. Bigham.—It is received by the same persons who pay.

Lord Justice Brett.—The Corporation are not the ratepayers.

The Master of the Rolls.—And even if they were, it is not received by the same persons who pay, because it is not divided in the same proportions. One pays 1,000*l.* and another 10*l.*; the 1,000*l.* is paid to the Corporation, but it is not equally divided between the ratepayers. The Corporation are not trustees for the ratepayers to divide the surplus in proportion to what they pay. That is the fallacy of the whole thing.

Lord Justice Brett.—In order to make this case like your supposed case, you must make the Corporation the same thing as the ratepayers, whereas it is not.

Mr. Bigham.—I admit that it is necessary that I should make the Corporation the same.

The Master of the Rolls.—They are not the same people; they do not pay in the same proportions. One ratepayer may pay 1,000*l.*, and another 10*l.*

Mr. Bigham.—That appears to me to have been the case in the Scotch case which the Solicitor-General referred to yesterday. There the ratepayers in Glasgow——

The Master of the Rolls.—State first the principle before you state the case.

Mr. Bigham.—The principle, I understand, to be this, that the water rate imposed there was imposed by the ratepayers upon themselves. I submit that that was the principle, and that being so it was not a profit at all.

The Master of the Rolls.—With deference to you, as I understand the case, it was this; that there was no water rate at all

7425   D 2

but a general rate paid by the people of Glasgow. It was not a
water rate; if it had been it might have been a different case.

Mr. Bigham.—Every person in Glasgow, whether he used the
water or not, was liable.

The Master of the Rolls.—It was not a water rate, but a
general rate.

Mr. Bigham.—Still the persons who did pay paid unequally.

The Master of the Rolls.—As it was a general rate upon the
town there was no benefit from the water. I take it that the
distinction is this, that where it is a water rate, and the receipts
exceed the expenditure on the water, it is profit, but if it is a
general rate you cannot tell whether there is any profit or not,
because a man who takes the water does pay more than a
man who does not take the water; there is no profit on the use
of the water.

Mr. Bigham.—You make a profit in the sense in which your
Lordship puts the definition of " profits."

The Master of the Rolls.—Not upon the water. It is a general
rate. If everybody living in Glasgow had to pay the rate whether
he took the water or not it was not a profit on the use of the
water.

Mr. Bigham.—It was a profit from the working of the waterworks; it was a profit in the sense in which your Lordship
defines it.

The Master of the Rolls.—No. The Glasgow Corporation
levied a borough rate, and supplied its inhabitants who wanted
it with water. There is no profit from a borough rate; it is a
tax.

Mr. Bigham.—It is a tax, but the Lord President puts it this
way. He says: " It seems to me that this is an Act of Par-
" liament by which the citizens of Glasgow have undertaken,
" through this Water Corporation as their representatives, to
" assess themselves for a very important public purpose,—a pur-
" pose very conducive to their own comfort and well-being,—to
" obtain a good supply of water for the city." What did the
persons who did not get the water get?

The Master of the Rolls.—Nothing. They may have got the
benefit of the cleaning of the streets.

Mr. Bigham.—They got something more; they had the right
to require the water.

The Master of the Rolls.—Still, that is not a profit. Suppose
the city of Glasgow do as some other cities and towns do, that
is to say, supply gas and water to their inhabitants and charge
it all in a borough rate, that is not profit; they levy as much
rate as is wanted for the purpose of their expenditure.

Mr. Bigham.—If that is not profit, why is this?

The Master of the Rolls.—Because they do not charge for the
gas or the water. They levy a tax upon everybody, whether he
takes it or not. They supply water and gas to those who want it
at the public expense.

Mr. Bigham.—In the same way we find that many persons who bring their ships to Liverpool have to pay particular kinds of dues whether they get the particular benefits to which those due are applied or not.

The Master of the Rolls.—I will put it in another way. The Municipality taxes its citizens for such a sum as it wants for its expenses, and it supplies to any citizen who wants it, gas and water. There is no profit there, because they do not make any charge, upon that theory, for gas, for they give it for nothing, but they defray the expenses by means of a general tax. That is the theory of that case.

Lord Justice Cotton.—Was not the point in that case this? If it was profit it was not profit within the Act, which charged profit arising from certain things,—amongst other things water, —but not from the borough rate. The Act charged certain profits arising from certain property.

Mr. Bigham.—Let me follow that. The Act charged profits arising from certain property, which would include the waterworks.

Lord Justice Cotton.—As I understand the decision, it was that this was not a profit arising from the waterworks. It was a borough rate, and though it was more than sufficient for the purpose required, it was not profit arising from the waterworks, but from something else.

Mr. Bigham.—Is that so?

Lord Justice Cotton.—The profit arising from charging persons other by borough rate was, as I understand, deducted, because that was profit arising from the waterworks.

Mr. Bigham.—Is that so? In that case the waterworks commissioners were a body appointed for the purpose of erecting these waterworks, and for the purpose of levying the rate to be paid by all the inhabitants in Glasgow for the benefits which the waterworks were expected to confer. The inhabitants paid those rates. The fact that they did not avail themselves of the benefit which the waterworks commissioners were capable of offering to them did not free them from the liability to pay. They had still to pay, but they had the advantage of being able to call for the benefit.

The Master of the Rolls.—Is that so? Is not it exactly the same thing as a School Board rate? You have a Board that levies a school rate upon everybody in the district, but keeps school gratis for anybody. Do they make any profit in keeping the schools? Put "waterworks" for "schools" and you have the same point.

Mr. Bigham.—I fail to see——

The Master of the Rolls.—Or put "bread" for "schools." A poor rate is levied on a district so that all the needy shall come and be fed. The Union no doubt keep a bakehouse in which to bake the bread. Is there a profit from keeping the bakehouse?

Mr. Bigham.—No, there is a loss.

The Master of the Rolls.—It is the same thing the moment you have a general rate. Supposing you have a water rate on the district, and the water is to be supplied to anybody who asks for it—half of the people may have wells and they do not ask for the water, the other half take the water—is that a profit to the waterworks? That is the case you have to deal with.

Mr. Bigham.—If there is no profit in that case I say why is there a profit in the Mersey Docks case?

The Master of the Rolls.—Because, as I take it, there is a profit from carrying on the docks. The profit may be applied to a public purpose, but it is a fallacy to suppose that nobody receives it. When we talk of a public purpose somebody gets the benefit of it. The profit is received.

Lord Justice Brett.—In the Scotch case a distinction is drawn on that very ground. The Lord President says, at page 49: "The case is entirely different from those which have been cited, "which have been decided in the Court of Exchequer in "England, because in those cases the statute which gave the "right to levy the assessment did not impose it upon the "citizens of the particular burgh or locality which obtained "the Act. It was not an authority to the citizens of a particular "locality to assess themselves. On the contrary, it was a right "and privilege given to a particular corporation to assess every- "body." He says in the English cases it was a profit to the corporation, in other cases there was no profit.

Mr. Bigham.—That is a distinction upon which I rely.

The Master of the Rolls.—Profit being the difference between receipts and expenditure, if your receipts do not arise from property how could there be a profit upon that property? If the receipts arise from the general taxation of the district, irrespective of profit, you cannot take the expenditure from those receipts and make a profit.

Mr. Bigham.—Why not?

The Master of the Rolls.—Because they are not profits from the works. Take the case I put to you. Take the case of a parish that has a right to tax every inhabitant of the parish in order to supply the parishioners with water; half of the parishioners have wells and do not take the water, the other half take as much as they want. Where is the profit to the waterworks? On the contrary, it is a loss, because they have supplied the water gratis to everybody.

Mr. Bigham.—Your Lordship begins by assuming that there is some water rate.

The Master of the Rolls.—There is a rate for the purpose of enabling the vestry to supply the parishioners with water. It is a water rate in that sense.

Mr. Bigham.—Why is not it a profit?

The Master of the Rolls.—Because there is a loss to the water-works. They supply everybody gratis in the case I put.

Mr. Bigham.—What is the difference in principle between
selling water at so much a gallon and selling unascertained
quantities in exchange for a rate?

The Master of the Rolls.—You do not sell unascertained
quantities in exchange for a rate. The people who take the
water pay only a small proportion of the rate.

Mr. Bigham.—All the people pay for the benefit which they
are entitled to ask for if they choose to ask for it.

The Master of the Rolls.—That is not the point. They may
pay ten times as much as the water costs. You tax them
whether they take it or not. Then there is no profit.

Mr. Bigham.—So in the case of the Mersey Docks.

The Master of the Rolls.—No; there the excess of tolls over
the expenses is profit. There you charge specifically for a
certain thing—it is a rent for the use of the docks. The difference between what you receive and your expenses is the profit of
the dock.

Mr. Bigham.—I do not like to argue a point upon which it is
obvious that the Court is against me.

Lord Justice Cotton.—I understand you have been charged
under Schedule A. That is a charge on property—that is, it is
a charge on the property of the docks,—but the only reference to
profits is for the purpose of ascertaining the amount to be
charged; it is a mode of ascertaining the annual value of the
hereditament, the docks. It seems to me that you have been
dealing with it as if it was a profit from trade carried on. The
real question is what, under the Act, is the annual value of the
docks for the purpose of being assessed to property tax. The
Act authorises the levying under Schedule A., "For all
" lands, tenements, and hereditaments or heritages in Great
" Britain, for every twenty shillings of the annual value thereof,
" the sum of sevenpence." Then rule No. III. (because it is not
under No. I.) is, "The annual value of all the properties herein-
" after described shall be understood to be the full amount for
" one year, or the average amount for one year, of the profits
" received therefrom within the respective times herein limited."
Why is not the surplus of receipts over the expenditure received
from these docks "profit received therefrom" within the meaning of these two clauses of the Act of Parliament as a mode of
ascertaining what is the annual value of the docks.

Mr. Bigham.—I begin with this proposition, that " profits "
must mean profits received from some person other than those
persons who are supposed to earn them.

Lord Justice Cotton.—I call your attention to that because
I thought you were arguing as if it were profits arising from
trade. The question is whether the assessing of profits is only
a mode of ascertaining the annual value of the dock in respect
of the property of which a certain charge is made.

Mr. Bigham.—I do not know that I follow the difficulty.

Side note: MERSEY DOCK AND HARBOUR BOARD v. LUCAS.

[ERSEY
)OOK AND
LABBOUR
JOARD *.
/UCAS.
——

Lord Justice Cotton.—I do not give any opinion at present, but it struck me that we had been arguing a matter not decisive of the question. The question is, what is the annual value of these docks. That is to be ascertained by the annual profits. But does not profits there mean the difference between the working expenses and the receipts.

The Master of the Rolls.—I think that you will find that it is so. The word "profits" in this part of the schedule is used in the legal sense in which we talk of "rents, issues, and profits" of land. It is a perfectly well-known legal term. The three words used to be used, "rents, issues, and profits." If you look at the schedule you will see that it is so. What is to be estimated? It is the annual value of the thing itself. The first rule is: "The annual value of lands, tenements, hereditaments, "or heritages charged under Schedule A. shall be understood to "be the rent by the year." That is the annual value. Then comes II.: "Rules for estimating the lands, tenements, heredita- "ments," and so on, "which are not to be charged according to "the preceding general rule." "The annual value of all the "properties herein-after described shall be understood to be "the full amount for one year, or the average amount for one "year of the profits received therefrom." You have the word "profits" there: "First, of all tithes if taken in kind." That is not profits in the sense of trade profits, but in the legal sense in which we talk of rents, issues, and profits. Those are not trade profits. Then, "Second, of all dues and money payments in "right of the church, or by endowment, or in lieu of tithes, not "being tithes arising from land, and of all teinds in Scotland." Those are profits. The word "profit" is used in the legal sense of the word, as meaning the profits of land.

Lord Justice Cotton.—Or the return from it?

The Master of the Rolls.—Yes. Then: "Third. Of all tithes "arising from lands, if compounded for, and of all rents and "other money payments in lieu of tithes," and so on, "on the "amount of such composition, rent, or payment for one year "preceding." The word "profits" is throughout used in that sense. Then we come to No. 5: "Of all fines received in con- "sideration of any demise of lands or tenements on the amount "so received in the year preceding by or on account of the "party," and so on. Then comes No. 6: "Of all other profits "arising from lands, tenements, hereditaments, or heritages not "in the actual possession or occupation of the party to be "charged." There again the word "profits" is used in the legal sense not as meaning profits of trade, but profits arising from land.

Lord Justice Cotton.—Rule No. III. is the one that applies to docks.

The Master of the Rolls.—Now I come to No. III. "The "annual value," that is what we have to find out, "of all the "properties herein-after described shall be understood to be "the full amount for one year, or the average amount for one ·: year, of the profits received therefrom." That is the mode of finding out the annual value of these lands. The words " profits received therefrom " are used in the same sense as they are used with respect to property in No. II., that is to say, the amount of receipts over expenditure. Look at the rule with regard to quarries: " Of quarries of stone, slate, limestone, or " chalk, on the amount of profits in the preceding year; " that is to say, what the stone, slate, or chalk is sold for.

Mr. Bigham.—But does that meet the point?

The Master of the Rolls.—If you look at the next part of the section you will find out how the duty is to be charged. It is a totally different thing. You first find out the value on which the duty is to be charged; then the duty in each of the last three rules is to be charged in this way.

Mr. Bigham.—It is to be charged upon the corporation.

The Master of the Rolls.—If the corporation let lands at a rack rent under Rule I., or if tithes are received in kind or compounded under Rule II., or if profits are received from quarries, or works, or docks under Rule III., they are to be charged in the same way. There is no distinction.

Mr. Bigham.—The duty is to be charged on the corporation.

Lord Justice Brett.—What do you argue about profits? I understood you to say that there were no profits. If there are no profits, there cannot be any profits received.

Lord Justice Cotton.—I understood your argument to be this: that no man can make a profit from himself, and therefore, if the persons who contribute towards the surplus are the corporation in another shape, they cannot make a profit of themselves. I call your attention to this, whether that is the true test here. Is not the true test here the annual value of the docks; that is to say, what is the difference between the annual expenditure and the receipts?

The Master of the Rolls.—It is the annual value of the dock that you are to ascertain under this section.

Lord Justice Cotton.—Your argument was very ingenious, and therefore I thought I would put that point to you.

Mr. Bigham.—Let me deal with the words "annual value." If we stopped there, and ascertained the annual value of this property, it would be rated. I cannot tell at what sum, but the Act specifies what the annual value is to be. It is to be the profits received. Now we get back to my first proposition, that a man cannot receive profits from himself.

The Master of the Rolls.—That is a mistake; it is " received therefrom." Look at No. 1, and look at No. 2.

Mr. Bigham.—If he occupies the premises himself, he does not get a rent. If he works the docks himself for his own ships, and for nothing else——

The Master of the Rolls.—If he occupies himself he pays under Schedule D. He pays on the value of the thing, whether he occupies himself or not.

Mr. Bigham.—I do not know how that may be.

The Master of the Rolls.—If you occupy anything yourself, you pay the tax.

Mr. Bigham.—I pay inhabited house duty.

The Master of the Rolls.—And property tax also.

Mr. Bigham.—Yes, I pay property tax. Still, I put this as a proposition, that the dock ratepayers are, if I may use the expression, crystallised into and represented by the dock trustees; that they are themselves using their own property, and that they cannot therefore be said to make a profit out of it at all. If you look at the Attorney-General *v.* Black, you will see the difference between that case and this, and I think the difference is pointed out in the judgments. There the Corporation of Brighton were receiving dues from every person who might bring coals into the port, and they were at liberty to apply the due so received to their own general purposes. That is to say, there was one body paying on the one hand, and another body receiving on the other hand, and the persons who were receiving were entitled to deal with the things for their own benefit. So there was a distinction between that case and this. I say here there is not one body paying on the one hand, and another receiving on the other. It is all one body contributing towards paying off the debt on this dock, and therefore the difference between receipts and expenditure is not profit. I do not know whether I have dealt with the difficulty,—I am not quite sure that I understand it,—put by Lord Justice Cotton.

Lord Justice Cotton.—You say there is not profit because the persons who receive and the persons who pay are the ratepayers. During the existing year the trustees may have been elected by an entirely different body to those who elected them in the preceding year. The trustees are elected by those ratepayers on the books who may not have been ratepayers, and probably were not, during the preceding year in which the rates were paid. I thought your whole argument was proceeding on the assumption that the ratepayers elected were the same as the ratepayers who paid the rates.

Mr. Bigham.—No.

Lord Justice Cotton.—If you do not say that, I do not see how your proposition applies at all.

Mr. Bigham.—I say that the ratepayers are a shifting body, continually changing, changing every year when the register is made up. But take the Scotch case; assume that the persons who paid the rate there were continually moving.

Lord Justice Cotton.—That case was not decided upon the principle you were trying to introduce here. It was decided on the ground that the excess of rates received over expenditure is not a profit; that if it is a profit at all, which I do not say it is, it is not a profit assessable under the Income Tax Act. Therefore that has not anything to do with this case of profits arising from using a dock, where you have to ascertain the annual value of the dock on the property of which the tax is to be paid.

Mr. Bigham.—Let me draw your Lordship's attention to what I think are the facts in the Glasgow case and how they coincide with the facts in our case, and then try to show, if I can, that the principle upon which the judgment in that case is based is the principle for which I contend.   In the Glasgow case the magistrates of the City of Glasgow, who, I suppose, are elected as magistrates usually are, took power to acquire the Glasgow waterworks, and for that purpose they were authorised to borrow money, the money so borrowed to be applied in paying the expense of purchasing and executing the works; and they were required to furnish the City of Glasgow with a supply of water.   To provide for the annual expenses connected with the carrying on of the undertaking the Commissioners were empowered, first, to levy a rate from the occupiers of all dwelling-houses within the municipal boundary, which rate was laid on according to the rental of the dwelling-houses; and, secondly, a public water rate on the full annual value of all premises, not dwelling-houses only, but every kind of premises within the limits; and as regards the limits of compulsory supply those rates were payable whether the inhabitants of the district within those limits used the water or not.   Therefore you have, first of all, an Act of Parliament by which these magistrates, elected presumably by a shifting body, namely, the burgesses of the City of Glasgow, had rights conferred upon them for the purpose of borrowing money to buy these waterworks.   Then they had powers conferred upon them to levy a rate upon all the occupiers of dwelling-houses within the municipal boundaries—a shifting body again,—and they had a right to levy a general rate of one penny in the £ on the full annual value of all the dwelling-houses.   Then they were entitled to levy a rate upon persons who resided beyond the limits who might choose to use the water.   Then it was provided that the rates thus raised, whether within the limits of compulsory supply or beyond them, were to be applied, in the first place, for the payment of current annual expenses of keeping up the undertaking and conducting the supply of water to the City;—in short, all ordinary current expenses.   They were also applicable, of course, to the payment of interest upon the money borrowed on mortgage, and to the payment of the annuities which have been granted to the shareholders of the old water companies.   There is a further provision that after the lapse of 10 years there shall be a sum, at the rate of 1*l.* per cent. upon the total amount of the money borrowed upon mortgage, paid over into a sinking fund for the redemption of that debt, and after the lapse of 20 years a sum of 30*s.* per cent. was to be paid over into the sinking fund for the same purpose.   If, after providing for all those purposes, there was any surplus of the income for any year, the Water Commissioners were required to apply it in making a reduction on the amount of the domestic water rate for the next year.   The facts appear to be so far almost identical with the facts here, except that I see there is one distinction, but a distinction that appears to me to be not very valuable as creating a difference; the distinction is this, that in the Glasgow case there is a liability upon all persons, whether they take water or not, to pay. I do not know why, because some persons are bound to pay though they do not take the water, that should alter the principle upon which the case is decided. Then, those being the facts, it was said in argument, "The question in the present case comes to be whether the "monies dedicated to the erection" (*reading from the argument*).

The Master of the Rolls.—You are reading us the points again.

Mr. Bigham.—I want to show what the points put before the court were, and then show your Lordships the decision. That shows your Lordships what the nature of the argument was. Then the Lord President in his judgment says this: "It seems to "me that this is an Act of Parliament by which the citizens of "Glasgow have undertaken, through this water company as "their representatives, to assess themselves for a very important "public purpose,—a purpose very conducive to their own com- "fort and well-being,—to obtain a good supply of water for the "city. In so assessing themselves they had not in view certainly "to make profit by the undertaking. On the contrary, what they "have distinctly in view is to pay money in order to obtain this "particular benefit. They are not, therefore, trading in any "commodity."

The Master of the Rolls.—Nor are they entering into any undertaking for the use of property that is to be attended by a resulting profit, or a beneficial interest accruing to any indi- viduals or to any corporation.

Mr. Bigham.—I read the whole of that sentence: "In so "assessing themselves they had not in view certainly to make "profit by the undertaking. On the contrary, what they have "distinctly in view is to pay money in order to obtain this "particular benefit." I say in our case this surplus is to obtain a benefit for the ratepayers.

Lord Justice Brett.—We are not bound by that decision of the judges in Scotland, though we listen to it with great respect. We listen to it in order to try and collect from it the prin- ciple upon which they acted. It is no use to say that they decided upon anything but the principle which they themselves enunciate.

Mr. Bigham.—I put it forward for that purpose.

Lord Justice Brett.—They say distinctly that in that case it was not any charge for the use of water, or any imposition in respect of the use of water, but was a charge upon all the in- habitants, quite irrespective of the question of water, and they distinguish it upon that ground from the English cases. There was no water receipt.

The Master of the Rolls.—They gave it to everybody.

Lord Justice Brett.—There was no trade at all in the water.

The Master of the Rolls.—As I understand that case, it was quite possible that a man received the water who paid nothing;

that is to say, that a previous ratepayer may have paid his rates and then gone away, and a fresh tenant come into the house who never paid any, and left before the rates became due. That is quite possible. Such a man might pay nothing, and his next-door neighbour who did not want water might be paying the rate.

Mr. Bigham.—That might be.

The Master of the Rolls.—It is a curious thing, but it appears to me that they not only never made a profit by the waterworks but that they made a loss.

Mr. Bigham.—That is a view of the case that I can scarcely accept. It seems to me that if they received money from the water rate which they are entitled to levy by virtue of the Act which gave them these waterworks and the right to work them, the carrying on of the waterworks undertaking could not be said to be a loss.

Lord Justice Brett.—You said it could not be said, but do not these judges say so?

The Master of the Rolls.—What do you say to this: a power to a water company to tax the county of Middlesex to supply water to the city of London.

Lord Justice Brett.—When that happy day arrives when the Government will buy up all the water companies in London and impose a water rate, we will try and define the Scotch case.

Mr. Bigham.—Then Lord Deas puts it this way: the corporation is the mere instrument of the ratepayers; there is no rule, therefore, to say that the corporation can make a profit. That again is applying the principle, as it appears to me, that a man cannot make a profit out of himself.

The Master of the Rolls.—I am afraid that some of the learned Lords of Session did not quite distinguish between the different schedules; Schedule A. relates to the annual value of lands or works.

Mr. Bigham.—Now, my Lord, I do not think I can say anything more upon that point. The next question is, assuming that these are profits within the meaning of the section of the Act, whether the Legislature has not thought proper to say something which is equivalent to directing that we shall not apply them to the purpose to which the Crown contend that we are to apply them. The object, I suppose, of this statute was to take care that the docks were freed as much as possible from taxation and imposts of all kinds, so as to encourage trade; and so the Act said you shall charge no more than absolutely necessary for keeping down the debt and paying the expenses. It is done for the encouragement of trade; that is the great object that was in view when this Act was passed; the object was to protect and encourage trade.

Lord Justice Brett.—Whose object?

Mr. Bigham.—The object of the Legislature.

Lord Justice Brett.—Not the object of the Mersey Docks and Harbour Board; their object was to get profits.

Mr. Bigham.—No; with deference, they were not to get any profit.

Lord Justice Brett.—Their object was to get sufficient profits to pay the expenses of the docks.

Mr. Bigham.—The only object of the Act was to take care that the shipping coming to the port of Liverpool should be free as far as possible from any impositions which might be in the nature of a tax upon trade. That was the object of this Act, as I submit. At the same time the Legislature said, inasmuch as a debt must be incurred we will take care that provision is made for that debt; and the Legislature say, your rates shall be only such rates as it will be necessary for you to charge for the purpose of paying your expenses, plus sufficient to make reasonable provision towards the reduction of the debt. That was the object of the statute.

The Master of the Rolls.—What does reduction of debt mean? Money laid out for the purchase of the lands on which the docks are made? For whose benefit?

Mr. Bigham.—For the benefit of persons trading with this port.

The Master of the Rolls.—That is, you make a profit which is to be laid out in the purchase of land for the benefit of persons trading to Liverpool. You apply your profit to buy lands to make docks?

Mr. Bigham.—That is, we tax those persons who use the docks by something more than is necessary to pay the expenses.

The Master of the Rolls.—You must not use the word "tax" in that connection in the sense in which the word is used when we speak of taxes imposed by the paramount authority. You do not tax those who use the dock; you only charge them rates.

Mr. Bigham.—This is a tax in this sense: The dock ratepayers have to pay rates to cover the expenses, and to contribute towards a sinking fund. It is a tax in this sense; it is an obligation to pay the impost which the statute imposed upon those who use the docks.

The Master of the Rolls.—I am speaking of a dock rate.

Mr. Bigham.—I am speaking of a dock rate, because the dock rate is a thing which goes not only to pay the expenses, but to provide a sinking fund.

The Master of the Rolls.—It is a payment made by the person who uses the dock; he may use the dock, or not use it.

Mr. Bigham.—I do not use the word "tax" in the sense in which it is used when we are speaking of Imperial taxes.

The Master of the Rolls.—It is a toll.

Mr. Bigham.—It is an obligation to pay, by statute, upon those persons who use the docks.

Lord Justice Brett.—The only act of the Legislature with regard to the amount of rates was to limit them. If there had

not been a limitation as to the amount of tolls to be taken, MERSEY
DOCK AND
HARBOUR
BOARD v.
LUCAS.
they might have charged a ship any amount.

Mr. Bigham.—Yes. In another way that shows the object
of the Act. The object of the Act was to take away burdens
upon trade, to prevent its being placed under onerous and improper burdens; the object of the Legislature was to limit what
these people might charge, and to say the trade of this country
is to be as free as possible, and these ships which use these docks,
which we regard as part of the machinery of working the trade,
are to be relieved from all unnecessary obligations; therefore
we pass this Act of Parliament, by which there is an obligation
upon the persons using the docks to pay rates which will meet
the expenditure, and provide a surplus to go towards a sinking
fund. That was the object of the Legislature. Therefore
I do not think it unreasonable to say that the Legislature also
thought, when they passed this Act, that the persons using
the dock should be liable to pay for nothing else than those
particular things for which, according to our contention, the
docks were entitled to make the charge. I say that, in putting
in this restrictive clause, as to how the money was to be applied,
and how it was not to be applied, the Legislature may very well
have intended that the income tax should not form one of the
things by which these persons should indirectly in that way be
burdened in the carrying on of their trade. I suppose every
merchant in Liverpool contributes something towards the income
tax, and possibly it was thought that it was not necessary that
these docks should also contribute. Let us see what the words
of the Act are, and let us see if they are not sufficiently strong
to take away the obligation imposed on the general public by
the Income Tax Act. I will not argue this at any length. I
feel the force of what has been said by Lord Blackburn in this
case of Cameron v. The Mersey Docks and Harbour Board, and
therefore all I propose to do is to draw your Lordships' attention to the words of two or three sections to show how strong
they are as limiting the way in which the money is to be
applied. First, the 284th section says, "All the moneys that
"shall be collected, levied, borrowed, and raised or received by
"the Board under or by virtue of this Act or the said Act,
"the application of which may not be otherwise expressly
"directed, shall be applied by the Board in any order with
"respect to priority of such application as they shall deem
"expedient for the following purposes:" the first is "in pay-
"ment of all expenses and charges of collecting rates." It seems
to me that that means what it says—the expenses and charges
of collecting the rates; and that the words "or charges" must
be read as supplementing "expenses." So that the first thing
you have to do is to pay the costs and expenses of the machinery
for collecting the rates, the salaries of the men that collect the
rates and so on. Next, you are to pay interest upon the money
you borrow; the next thing you have to do is "to pay the cost
"incurred in the construction of the works, and in supporting,
"maintaining, and repairing the same," viz., the works, "and

"in carrying into execution all the provisions of this Act."
There is no provision in the Act that says we are to pay income
tax, and therefore the obligation to pay income tax does not
come under those words, "and the general management, con-
"ducting, securing, preserving, improving, amending, main-
"taining, and protecting,"—what?—"the Dock Estate." Is
payment of income tax comprised under money spent in the
"management of the estate," or "conducting" it, "securing" it
or "preserving" it, or "improving" it, or "amending" it, or
"maintaining" it, or "protecting" it?' I submit not. Then it
goes on to say what shall be done with the surplus. The surplus
"shall be from time to time applied in or towards the repayment
"of all principal moneys which shall have been borrowed," and
in purchasing up dock annuities, and then the rates are to be
reduced. Then, in order to make quite certain that the moneys
are to be applied in no other way whatever, the Legislature
have put in these express words at the end of the sentence
"Except as aforesaid, such moneys,"—and by "such moneys,"
I suppose, is meant the whole receipts received by the Dock
"Except as aforesaid, such moneys,"—and by "such moneys,"
"other purpose whatsoever." If words can be strong, those
words surely are. We are told first what we shall apply the
moneys to, and those provisions do not cover the purpose to
which it is contended by the Crown in this case the moneys
are to be applied. And then when you come to the end of
the section you find the express provision that "except as afore-
"said, such moneys shall not be applied by the Board for any
"other purposes whatsoever."

Lord Justice Brett.—Do you say that under those words, if
it had not been for the introduction of the next section, the
Dock Board would not have been liable to pay the poor rate?

Mr. Bigham.—It appears to me to be clear that the person
who drafted this Act thought, as I contend now, that if the
legislation was left in the state in which it is by the 284th section, the liability to pay poor rates might be gone; he thought
that to be the effect of legislation if it stopped there. I suppose
the overseers of Liverpool came in when this Act was being
passed, and said we must have a section in, otherwise this will
take away the liability to poor rates.

The Master of the Rolls.—Then they were wrong, that is all.

Mr. Bigham.—Your Lordship says they were wrong, but at
present I show that somebody else, besides the Respondents in
this case, evidently thought that the Act had the effect which
we are contending for.

Lord Justice Brett.—Why do you put it on the draftsman;
why not say the Legislature? It may have been put in by the
House of Lords.

The Master of the Rolls.—Whoever put it in put it in *ex abundante cautela*. It is a very common thing to put in clauses
which are unnecessary *ex abundante cautela*.

Mr. Bigham.—It may have been put in for that reason. Caution would not have been required to be exercised unless the statute was capable of the meaning I contend for.

Lord Justice Brett.—Suppose that next section, which says that nothing is to affect the liability of the Dock Board to local rates, were not in, how would you have applied the decision in the case of Cameron to this case? You would have said, notwithstanding that case, they were not liable to pay poor rates.

Mr. Bigham.—I do not know that this Act was in existence.

The Master of the Rolls.—I will tell you why I say the overseers were wrong. There cannot be a doubt about it. If you look at the 284th section, it says, " Subject to the provisions of " the Mersey Docks and Harbour Act, 1857, all moneys shall " be applied," and so on.

Mr. Bigham.—To begin with, your Lordship must read the whole of that.

The Master of the Rolls.—It is " subject to the provisions of " that Act " all the moneys shall be applied.

Mr. Bigham.—I ask your Lordship to read the statement in the case " subject to certain provisions of the Mersey Docks and " Harbour Act, 1857, which are not material for the purposes " of this case."

The Master of the Rolls.—But I think they are. I am not going to take your case as deciding that point. I think they are very material on this question of whether it was necessary to introduce that section about liability to poor rates. I know that is in your case, but it appears to me erroneous. Will you be kind enough to look at sections 26 and 27 of the Mersey Docks and Harbour Act, 1857? You will find there that the property is vested in the Board, but, " subject to all charges and liabilities " affecting the same." How do you get rid of those " charges " and " liabilities " ? Is not the poor rate a " liability affecting " the same " ?

Mr. Bigham.—I do not know that it is.

The Master of the Rolls.—You are not bound to know, but I ask you the question.

Mr. Bigham.—I say no.

The Master of the Rolls.—Is land tax " a liability affecting " the same " ?

Mr. Bigham.—If your Lordship asks me what "subject to " all charges and liabilities affecting the same " means, I say I do not think the person who drafted that section or the Legislature had in contemplation taxes at all.

The Master of the Rolls.—It is every charge and liability. It uses the largest words known to the law. That is the expression used in the Bankruptcy Act.

Lord Justice Brett.—Do you say it is admitted in the case that those sections of the previous Act are not material?

Mr. Bigham.—It says so in so many words.

Lord Justice Brett.—Are we not bound by the statements in the case?

The Master of the Rolls.—We may consider the effect of former legislation.

Lord Justice Brett.—I think we should hear the Solicitor-General upon this.

Mr. Solicitor-General.—I have not looked at the provisions of the former Act; I do not think it necessary to do so.

The Master of the Rolls.—We are not precluded from referring to previous legislation by statements in the case as to law.

Mr. Solicitor-General.—I think permission is given in the case to either of us to refer to any Act of Parliament. "Either "party is to be entitled to refer to and reply upon any of the "provisions of the several Acts of Parliament relating to the "Mersey Dock estate."

The Master of the Rolls.—On this point of liability to poor rate it appears to me very material to refer to the former Act. The property is vested in the Board subject to all charges and liabilities affecting the same. I cannot understand why all rates are not charges affecting the property just as much as fee-farm rents.

Mr. Bigham.—At present I say what I think was meant by those words, "subject to all charges and liabilities affecting the "same," was this, the debts due in respect of money borrowed.

The Master of the Rolls.—How do you deal with the words "liabilities affecting the same"?

Mr. Bigham.—I take that to mean "liabilities in the working "of the concern."

The Master of the Rolls.—Why is not land tax, or poor rate, or tithe-rent charge, included under the word "liabilities"; is there any legal definition of the word liabilities to exclude them?

Mr. Bigham.—If this point is to be regarded as of any importance at all, or to be taken into consideration, I confess I have not looked at it or considered it, and I thought it immaterial to refer to that former Act, because we had agreed that it was not material.

The Master of the Rolls.—It is a very small point, it is only an answer to your suggestion that there was a difficulty about poor rates. I do not see it myself.

Mr. Bigham.—If your Lordship says that your Lordship does not think it is necessary to rely upon the earlier Act for the purpose of deciding the case, it is not necessary for me to deal with the point. I repeat again what I have said that there are express provisions as to how the money is to be applied, and this direct provision, that the moneys are to be applied to no other purpose whatsoever. Then, going to the next point, the Legislature—I will not say the draughtsman, but the Legislature—evidently contemplated that if——

The Master of the Rolls.—Do you or not contend that, under these words, you would be exempt from land tax if not otherwise charged?

Mr. Bigham.—If it is necessary that I should contend it, of course I should contend it. If it is a parallel case—I am not prepared to say whether or not it is—if it is a parallel case, I must admit it. If it is not a parallel case,—and I do not know whether it is or not,—I do not admit it.

Lord Justice Brett.—Your argument goes the length of saying that no general tax of any kind whatever can be payable by this Corporation.

Mr. Bigham.—It appears to me that it does involve that proposition.

The Master of the Rolls.—Do you get rid of all taxes? Do you get rid of the Church too?. What do you say to tithe-rent-charge?

Mr. Bigham.—I do not know what the remedies are in the case of non-payment of tithes.

The Master of the Rolls.—They are levied by distress.

Mr. Bigham.—It might be necessary for the "protection" of our property that we should pay for it. It might be that the payment of the tithe-rentcharge would come within the words "for the "purpose of protecting the estate."

The Master of the Rolls.—If you can pay tithe-rentcharge to protect your property you can also pay Queen's taxes on the same principle.

Mr. Bigham.—Whether it involves the contention that we are free from all taxes or not, it is sufficient for me at present to say that the exemption for which I contend covers the tax in question.

Lord Justice Brett.—If your argument necessarily involves that you are free from the payment of all taxes, it is a *reductio ad absurdam*, perhaps. You cannot escape from having to consider whether your argument does not carry you a certain length.

Mr. Bigham.—I do not at the moment know whether the income tax can be distrained for, whether there are any means of taking the staiths or the land or property in execution for payment of the tax.

* *Mr. Solicitor-General.*—I am told that that is the mode of recovery under Schedule A.

Lord Justice Brett.—Your point was, if I understood you, in order to escape from the difficulty put to you, that they might pay in order to avoid a distress; but if your construction of this section is right, where is that power to pay in order to avoid a distress?

The Master of the Rolls.—The right to distrain is given in express terms by the third section of the Income Tax Act.

MERSEY
DOCK AND
HARBOUR
BOARD *v.*
LUCAS.

Mr. Bigham, answering Lord Justice Brett.—I say this, one of the purposes to which the money is to be applied is in the general management, conducting, securing, preserving, improving, amending, maintaining, and protecting the estate, and it occurred to me that it might be said, that if the land was liable to be distrained if the Dock Board did not pay the tax they might pay it in order to protect them from distress.

Lord Justice Brett.—Then if there is anything in the last point to put to you that Queen's taxes can be distrained for in the same manner, you are not helped very much by your argument that they might pay to "protect" the estate.

Mr. Bigham.—If Queen's taxes can be distrained for, the argument is not good for anything.

The Master of the Rolls.—If you look at the third section, income tax is payable like assessed taxes. "All the powers, "authorities, rules, regulations, directions, penalties, clauses, "and matters contained in the former Acts are to have full "force and effect."

Mr. Solicitor-General.— And subsequently there was an Act called the Taxes Management Act, which gives the remedy of distress for any of the Tax Acts.

The Master of the Rolls.—That third section is express. If your argument as to the protection of the property against distress is worth anything, it would apply to all taxes.

Mr. Bigham.—I take it it is so. If the Solicitor-General says that income tax can be distrained for, of course, the observation I was making does not apply.

Lord Justice Brett.—Then you withdraw it?

Mr. Bigham.—Yes.

The Master of the Rolls.—Your argument was that you might protect your waggons and horses against distress?

Mr. Bigham.—Yes, and my argument does not apply, the law being as the Solicitor-General tells me it is, that is to say, I understand that income tax can be distrained for. I was saying that tithe-rentcharge might be payable because it would be distrained for, and therefore it would be necessary to pay it in order to protect the estate; of course the observation I made falls to the ground. I see the force of the observation as to other taxes, and I see the difficulty.

The Master of the Rolls.—You cannot escape from what Lord Justice Brett put, that if the argument is good for anything it exempts you from all those taxes.

Mr. Bigham.—I am not sure that that was not the object of the legislature in passing this statute.

The Master of the Rolls.—Where assessed taxes were not in force before this Act passed?

Mr. Bigham.—Yes.

The Master of the Rolls.—You say that the words exempt you from all assessed taxes?

Mr. Bigham.—It appears to me so.

Lord Justice Brett.—If you give any other force to these negative words than is given in the opinion of Lord Blackburn, if anything that could be charged by anybody against this Corporation has by accident escaped from some mis-description, you would not be liable?

Mr. Bigham.—Yes.

Lord Justice Brett.—Does not that show that the opinion of Lord Blackburn, besides its being the opinion of the four judges given on the direct case, is right?

Mr. Bigham.—I told your Lordship, in the face of that opinion of course I had great difficulty.

Lord Justice Brett.—Does not Lord Chelmsford's judgment which is the most elaborate opinion of all the judgments in the House of Lords, really adopt that view?

Mr. Bigham.—I think none of their Lordships deal with the point at all.

Mr. Solicitor-General.—They say the rates are payable, notwithstanding that they do not rest it upon that clause preserving the rights of the parishes. That, I think, is the judgment.

Lord Justice Brett.—I think, in discussing the former decisions, Lord Campbell adopts the view of Lord Blackburn upon this very point.

Mr. Bigham.—In conclusion, I do not think I can do more than refer to the judgments of the Judges in the Court below.

Lord Justice Brett.—We have had them read.

Mr. Bigham.—I will ask your Lordships to allow me to refer to the judgment of Mr. Justice Lindley; it is very short, and it puts the point in as clear language as it can be put. He says: " I am of the same opinion. *Primâ facie*, I think the Solicitor-" General's argument is well-founded, that is, to say, in looking " at the Income Tax Act alone, the word 'profits' means the " excess of income over the expenditure necessary to meet the " income. I also think that he is right in his second proposition, " that when you have profits in that sense income tax is payable " in respect of them. We have, however, three Acts of Par-" liament to construe, and we must construe them together. " The present case is reduced to a very simple problem. There " is a general Act of Parliament imposing income tax on such " profits as I have mentioned; then there is the Mersey Docks " Act, 1859, passed subsequently to the general Act, which " provides how certain moneys and receipts are to be applied, " and then it says, incidentally, that the moneys so received " shall not be applied in any other way. To make it plainer. " still, there is a provision to the effect that nothing in the Act " contained shall exempt the Board from liability to parochial " or local taxes. All we have to do is to construe those Acts " of Parliament, and it seems to me impossible to hold that the " combined effect of the three special Acts and the Income Tax " Act is to make income tax payable out of these receipts or " any portion of them. I rely entirely on the special words of

" the Act of Parliament, for the authorities cited do not appear
" to me to throw much light upon the subject. The Scotch
" case turned on Acts of Parliament which did not contain these
" negative words. I rely entirely on the special wording of the
" special Act, which appears to me to be inconsistent with the
" argument that income tax is payable."

Lord Justice Brett.—I gather from that that he relied entirely
upon those negative words.

Mr. Bigham.—Yes. The reason I read this judgment was
because I thought it put in as plain language as it could be put
the contention I was putting forward upon this point. I have
endeavoured to put before your Lordships as clearly as I can the
two points upon which we rely; viz., first, that these are not
profits, because they are really paid by the persons who themselves are supposed to derive the benefit; and secondly, I say
even if they are profits the legislature has thought fit by these
very express words to relieve trade from the payment of this
tax, and possibly other taxes also; and therefore I submit that
the judgment of the Court below was right.

REPLY.

Mr. Solicitor-General.—A very few words in reply upon this
case. The matter is now fully before your Lordships. I
submit, and in fact that is the view taken by one of the Judges
in the Court below, that, *primâ facie*, apart from anything
peculiar in the wording of this Act, with reference to the application of the income, these docks are taxable under Schedule A.,
and the proper mode of arriving at their annual value is to
ascertain what the profits were, that is, the surplus of receipts
over expenditure, in the preceding year. Mr. Justice Lindley
appears to have conceded me that in the Court below. Therefore
you have an Act of Parliament making all docks taxable under
Schedule A., *primâ facie* therefore including this, like every
other dock. That being so, it rests upon those who contest their
liability to show you that they are freed from it. This particular
general taxing Act is an Act passed, be it observed, subsequently
to this private Act of the Mersey Docks and Harbour Board.
Therefore, my learned friend has to contend, because an Act had
been passed dealing with the application of the funds of the
Corporation, saying what they were to do with their receipts,
that they are to be exempt from a subsequent general taxing Act
which in terms taxes docks of which this is one, and which taxes
a corporation carrying on docks of which this Corporation is
one, that they are exempt from that subsequent general taxing
Act applicable to them by reason of this prior Act, which provides how they are to deal with receipts and expenditure.

The Master of the Rolls.—Have you stated that quite strongly
enough?

Mr. Solicitor-General.—It seemed to me to be strong enough
for my purpose.

The Master of the Rolls.—If you look at the Income Tax Act 5th and 6th Victoria, I think it is a great deal stronger. When you look at the third rule you find these words, "the duty in "each of the last three rules to be charged on the person, cor- "poration," and so on, in priority "to the owner of the soil or "property or any creditor or other person whatever having a "claim on or out of the said profits, and all such persons, corpo- "rations," and so on "shall allow out of such produce or value "a proportionate deduction of the duty so charged, and the said "charge shall be made on the said profits, exclusive of any lands "used or occupied in or about the concern."

Mr. Solicitor-General.—I was going to quote those words.

The Master of the Rolls.—The Income Tax Act, by which those rules were enforced, was a subsequent Act to that of the Mersey Docks and Harbour Board. Mr. Justice Lindley seemed to think it was prior.

Mr. Solicitor-General.—I was going to point out, that before applying the produce this is made a first charge, before they do anything else with it, by this subsequent Act. Therefore, you have a general Act taxing docks, of which this was one, in a particular way, and providing that the tax shall be a first charge upon the produce of the docks.

The Master of the Rolls.—Destroying the right of the creditor or other person who would have a prior claim?

Mr. Solicitor-General.—Yes, therefore what is to be contended is, though it destroys the right of the creditor, though it makes it a first charge on the produce even to the prejudice of the creditors, nevertheless this prior Act, which provided for the distribution and the mode in which the earnings should be dealt with, set aside, for the benefit of this Corporation, the provision in the general taxing Act.

Lord Justice Brett.—If I understood Mr. Bigham's argument, it was that this dock is not a dock within the statute, because it is not a dock from which any profits can be received.

Mr. Solicitor-General.—That is the other point. I will say a word upon that presently. I am dealing with the last point first. I say it was conceded to me by one of the Judges that this was a dock earning profits within the meaning of the Act, and *primâ facie* taxable. Mr. Justice Lindley only gave judgment against the Crown on the ground of the provision as to the mode in which the income was to be expended. I was dealing with that point first, and I was putting this question: that the docks being made *primâ facie* taxable, as they are, and the tax being made a first charge before the produce is distri- buted, how can it be that a prior Act of Parliament, merely dealing with what you are to do with your income, should relieve you from liability under a subsequent general Act which imposes a tax on this subject matter and makes that tax a first charge upon the produce? That is my answer to that point. Beyond that I contend that the words in the 284th section are not sufficient to give the exemption that is contended for. I say you must read the words of the 284th section "and in the general management, conducting, securing, preserving," and so on, as covering such a charge as this, otherwise I want to know how they are to pay the wages of any of the dockmen, for example.

The Master of the Rolls.—The words are "general management."

Mr. Solicitor-General.—"Management" of what? If by "management of the estate" you include the management of your dock business, then, I say it would include taxes, just in the same way. Why should my learned friend only exclude taxes from payments in respect of the general management, conducting, securing, and so on of the estate. If the section includes expenses incurred in the general management of the dock business, then there is no reason why it should not include the payment of your taxes like any other expenses. The trustees who are to manage the estate must not only pay the debts but the taxes like any other debts ; it is one of the expenses of management, and one which is taxable. The dock trustees must pay their taxes like any other debt or liability incurred in carrying on the business. The words are rather curious—"and in the "general management, conducting, securing, preserving, im- "proving, amending, maintaining, and protecting the Mersey "Dock Estate." First you begin with "management," and then you go on "conducting, securing," and so on. What is the meaning of "general management"? I say of the dock business, you cannot read "the general management of the dock estate," it is not grammar.

The Master of the Rolls.—Perhaps in what you are arguing now you are rather wasting time. I have looked at the previous Act, and I find that there are provisions in the previous Act enabling the new board to exercise all the powers of the old board, including the payment of wages and everything else ; it is the 30th section, "All powers, rights, and privileges what- "ever of the old board devolve upon the new board,"—that means working the dock and carrying on the business.

Mr. Solicitor-General.—I should certainly have submitted that the "general management" and "conducting" of the Mersey Dock Estate means the business they carry on as dock trustees, and that it includes every expense to which they are chargeable as trustees carrying on the concern.

Lord Justice Brett.—Either under the words "general management" or under the word "conducting"?

Mr. Solicitor-General.—Yes, you conduct a dock business ; you do not conduct an estate. Therefore, the words "general management" and "conducting" apply to the dock business. Then, if so, those words include all expenses necessary for that purpose ; amongst others, the payment of taxes. Therefore, I do not admit that it is excluded by those words ; but even if the Act were so construed, I say that it cannot exempt the Mersey Dock and Harbour Board from the operation of the subsequent general taxing Act, which makes the tax a first charge upon the property of a corporation owning docks. As regards the question whether these are profits taxable, I apprehend that this is a dock.

Lord Justice Brett.—Would you carry that so far as to say, that if the negative words were construed against you, that is to say, if the prohibitive enactment against paying anything but those things that are mentioned were construed against you to the extent of saying that those things did not comprise income tax, still a general Act passed subsequently would override such an exemption.

Mr. Solicitor-General.—Yes. A general taxing Act · which came subsequently and imposed a tax would compel you, without special words of exemption, to pay that tax, even though a prior Act exempted you from payment of it.

Lord Justice Brett.—Suppose in a private Act there were positive words which said that a corporation shall not be liable to pay any general tax which may now exist or which may hereafter be imposed ?

Mr. Solicitor-General.—Then possibly, or probably, the words of a general taxing Act passed afterwards might not affect it.

Master of the Rolls.—Does not the same rule with regard to general words apply to a taxing Act as to every other one ?

Mr. Solicitor-General.—These are general words too; you have general words in the private Act.

Lord Justice Brett.—I was putting to you, if the construction was against you on the words of the private Act, whether you would contend that a subsequent general Act would override the enactments of the private Act.

Mr. Solicitor-General.—Of course, if these words in this private Act were to be construed as if they had been, "except as "aforesaid, such moneys shall not be applied by the Board for "any other purpose whatsoever, including even the purposes of "paying any taxes," it would have been a much more serious question whether a subsequent Act got rid of that exemption from paying general taxes, but that is not the case here.· You have merely the general words to be applied to those purposes and no other. Then you have the subsequent general taxing Act, which imposes upon such subject matters as this a tax, and the question is, can the Mersey Dock and Harbour Board get rid of the operation of the subsequent Act by such general words as these which they are relying upon,—general words in a private Act, not a special provision relating to taxation, but mere general words of this description.

Lord Justice Brett.—I cannot see that these words are general words; they seem to me to be as particular as words can be.

Mr. Solicitor-General.—They are general words as regards taxes; they do not point to taxes specially; they merely say you shall be limited in the application of your funds to certain purposes ; but it is quite consistent with that to say : you never-theless may be made liable to income tax, and that may be made a prior charge on the application of the income, because the two Acts are dealing with two different subject matters. An obli-gation imposed by a subsequent statute dealing with another subject matter is not got rid of by a previous provision which is not dealing specifically with taxation at all, but merely with the disposition of the funds of the Dock Board. First of all it would be a most unreasonable construction of this section to construe it as excluding all power to pay these taxes, and I contend against that construction. Take the case of a railway company taxable on profits, and an Act is passed, when it has got into embarrassment, which provides that all its profits shall be applied in payment of certain debentures till the debentures are entirely discharged. Could it be said that it would not be taxable to income tax? The purpose of that provision is *alio intuitu* altogether; it is to provide what they shall do with the money they get—it is not to relieve them from taxation. I do not suppose that it would be contended, in the case I put, that the profits would not be taxable. As regards the question whether these are profits, it would be difficult to entertain a doubt that they are profits within the meaning of Schedule A., Rule III.

Lord Justice Brett.—They are profits in the hands of the Corporation.

Mr. Solicitor-General.—They are profits in the hands of the Corporation. The thing taxable is the docks, the measure of taxation is the annual profits in the preceding year ; " profits " meaning excess of income over expenditure. The thing itself is taxable. On these grounds I submit that the judgment below is wrong, and ought to be reversed.

JUDGMENT.

The Master of the Rolls.—This is an Appeal from the Decision of the Divisional Court to the effect that Income Tax was not payable by the Respondents—The Mersey Dock Board, and the questions that we have to consider may be divided conveniently into two ; first of all whether any profits within the meaning of the Income Tax Act are earned at all by this Board ; and secondly, if that point be decided against the Respondents, whether the terms of their local Act are such as to exempt them from any liability to pay the tax, which, but for those special provisions would be chargeable. As regards the first point, I must say I have so clear an opinion upon it that I cannot bring myself to believe there is any doubt about it whatever. Of course l am only expressing the state of my own mind, and upon that point l may observe that it is quite clear also that

at least one of the Judges, if not both, who gave the judgment MERSEY
appealed from were of the same opinion as I am, namely, that DOCK AND
these are profits taxable under the Income Tax Act. HARBOUR
BOARD v.

Now, I should like before going into that question of profits LUCAS.
to say a word or two about the constitution of this Board,
because I think that a great deal of the argument of the
Respondent rested upon a very insecure foundation as to facts.
This Board is not a mere dock board, but it is a board with
very large powers indeed. It is a board of conservancy of the
River Mersey, and it is also a pilot board. I may refer to the
31st, the 32nd, and the 33rd sections of the Act of 1857 to show
that these additional powers belong to this Board, and that it
is constituted not merely for the management of the docks but
for other important public purposes. Then by 26th and 27th
sections of the Act of 1857, certain property real and personal
at Birkenhead, and all docks, lights, buoys, &c. at Liverpool, are
vested in the new Board "subject to all charges and liabilities
"affecting the same," and various powers and liabilities are
conferred and imposed upon the Board, especially by sections
30 and 34; the latter of which; after providing for the salary
of an acting Conservator says, that "all other expenses which
"are now incurred or payable by the Corporation in respect of
"the Conservancy of the Mersey shall be paid and borne by
"the Board." That is the position of the Board. Having
ascertained what the position of the Board is, I go to their
special Act to show what they are to do with their money.
The Special Act, which was passed in 1858 (284th section)
shows that all moneys which shall be collected, levied, &c. by
the Board "under or by virtue of this Act or the Act of 1857"
(that includes all their dock rates) "shall be applied by the
"Board 'first' in payment of all expenses and charges of
"collecting rates." Then "in payment from time to time of all
"interest accruing due on moneys borrowed and in payment
"of the Mersey Docks Annuities." Then in the construction of
certain works. Then comes these words, "and in carrying into
"execution all the provisions of this Act, and of the Mersey
"Docks and Harbour Act, 1857." Therefore the Act says you
may spend your money in carrying all those things into execution, and that includes the working of the dock as well as the
maintenance of the navigation, the duties of conservancy, the
duties of pilot board, the removing of sunken vessels, and various
other things.

Then come the words "and in the general management, con-
"ducting, securing, preserving, improving, amending, maintain-
"ing, and protecting the Mersey Dock Estate." These words
relate to the Mersey Dock Estate, and do not include the working
of the docks, which is provided for under the prior words of the
section. Then we come to the words, "and the residue or surplus
"of all such moneys which shall remain after such application"
are to be applied in the formation of a sinking fund; and
"except as aforesaid, such moneys shall not be applied by the
"Board for any other purpose whatsoever." There is only one

other section which it is necessary to refer to, it is section 285, which provides that "nothing in this Act contained shall alter " or affect the question of the liability of any of the docks or " works vested in the Board to parochial or local rates." The question is, what is the meaning of these sections and that embraces the second point raised as regards the liability to pay income tax, if such tax was otherwise payable by the Board, but for the existence of section 284. It appears to me upon the words of that section " subject," (of course), " to the provisions " of the former Act," that whatever tax was properly payable under the former Act is still payable, and there is nothing in this Act to discharge them from their liability to pay such taxes. But I do not rest my judgment upon that ground alone, because if there had been no such provision in the former Act, and no such reference to the former Act as is contained in the 284th section of the Act of 1858, I should have arrived at the same conclusion. I think that conclusion may be arrived at first of all on general grounds applicable to all similar local Acts. I cannot express them better, and I should not wish to express them better, than they are expressed by the present Lord Blackburn, then Mr. Justice Blackburn, in the case of the Mersey Docks v. Cameron, that, " enactments directing that the revenue shall be " applied to certain purposes and no other are directory only " (he is speaking of local Acts,) " and are to be read that after all " charges imposed by law upon the revenue have been dis- " charged, the surplus, or free revenue, which otherwise might " have been disposed of at the pleasure of the recipients, shall be " applied to those purposes." Now, that applies, I think, to all local Acts, and there is very good reason why it should apply. The persons obtaining these local Acts are not checked by the public, they are not checked by representatives of the kingdom at large, and it is a reasonable thing to say that they are dealing with their own property, and not with the public right to obtain payment of taxes from that property, or in respect of it. That would put an end to the whole argument on the part of the Conservancy Board, whatever the words of the section might have been. It is immaterial, therefore, whether the words "shall not " be applied for any other purpose whatsoever" are or are not in the Act, because if the Act deals only with what I will call the legally available surplus at the time the Act passed, it could not absolve the Board from liability to pay taxes, if such liability then existed. There is another ground which I think would govern this case. This tax is granted to the Crown, and it is part of the prerogative of the Crown that it is not bound by any local Acts of Parliament (with certain exceptions, which need not be mentioned here, because they do not apply to this local Act), unless named or expressly referred to in the Act. The prerogative of the Crown has nothing to do with the mode of applying the tax.

Formerly the sovereign had control over the revenues, and applied them both to public and private purposes. It was as much the duty of the sovereign then, if I may so, as it is now, to apply the public revenues to public purposes, and the only difference now is that those public purposes are defined and controlled by Parliament, whereas such was not formerly the case. It has been held by the Court of Appeal that the privilege of the Crown in this respect applies to the postal services (in the case of the Postmaster-General v. Benham)[*] on that ground; and there seems to be as much reason for applying this doctrine to the case of the Crown when the revenue received is applicable to public purposes as when it is applicable to the private purposes of the sovereign, because the public at large require this protection. The private purposes of the sovereign might be looked after by some officer appointed for the purpose, but when you come to the interest of the public there is, as a general rule, no one to look after it. Therefore it is most material that the attention of those who act on behalf of the public should be drawn to the provisions of any local or private Act which affect the rights of the Crown. However, it is not necessary to rest my judgment upon this ground, because the second ground is sufficient to support the view that this local Act of Parliament does not relieve the Board from liability to pay income tax.

There is another ground upon which also I should have come to the same conclusion. The Income Tax Act in question is subsequent in date to the local Act (this point appears to have escaped notice in the Court below), and, assuming that my view of the operation of the local Act was not correct I should still hold that that provision of the local Act was to the necessary extent repealed by the special provisions of the Taxing Act, which refers back to the 3rd rule of Schedule A., sect. 60, 5 and 6 Vict., chapter 35. In this case the income is to be paid into a sinking fund for the benefit of the creditors, and then there is an enactment which says that this tax subsequently imposed shall be paid before and in priority to any creditors or other person having a claim on the profits. The words "any "creditor or other person" includes everybody in the kingdom, and would, in my opinion, be sufficient to make this tax a prior charge, even if the construction of the local Act had been different from what I take it to be. For these reasons I consider that there is nothing to exempt this Corporation from paying the tax if it can be levied.

I now go to the other point, is it leviable? It is said to be, and truly said to be a tax upon profits, and it was argued on behalf of the Conservancy Board that these were not profits at all. First of all, let us consider what the meaning of the word "profits" in the Income Tax Acts is, because the word "profits" is used in law in rather a different way to that in which it is used in common parlance. We constantly in law talk of profits of land. The old conveyances used to talk of the rents, issues, and profits of land, but those profits are what you get out of the

---

[*] 48 Law Journal Reports, p. 84 ; Law Reports, 10 Ch. D. 595.

land after deducting the expenses of getting them. The profits
of a farm in that sense are not quite the same as the profits of
the farmer, but may be fairly described as the net produce of the
land. It is plain that that is the meaning to be attributed to
the word in the 2nd and 3rd rules in Schedule A. The profits
mentioned in Rule 2 are not the profits of a person, they are
"profits arising from lands." And an examination of that rule
shows that the word "profits" is used in its technical sense.
Then we come to Rule 3, under which this tax is charged, " Rules
" for estimating the lands, tenements, hereditaments, or heritages
" herein-after mentioned which are not to be charged according
" to the preceding general rule." The annual value of all the
properties herein-after described (the tax being on the annual
value) "shall be understood to be the full amount for one year,
" or the average amount for one year of the profits received"
(that is, from the properties) within the respective times herein
limited. The word is here used in exactly the same sense as
that I have already mentioned. The profit may be received from
the property in a rather different way, but it is the amount got
from the property minus the cost of getting it. These observations apply to the properties described in the two first clauses of
the rule. Then we come to the thing sought to be charged,
viz., ironworks, gasworks, salt springs or works, alum mines or
works, waterworks, streams of water, canals, inland navigations,
docks, and other concerns of the like nature, which under clause
three are to be charged on the profits of the year preceding. Now
of what kind are the profits? On a dock or a navigation you
get tolls or dock rates; those are what you receive from the
docks, and you deduct from them the expenses of carrying on the
docks, and you get the net proceeds, and those are the "profits"
mentioned in the Act. I have no doubt, therefore, that the
moment you find that the amount received for the dock rates
exceeds the expenses, the difference is "profits" within the
meaning of the section.

Then the next question is: Who is to pay the duty? Having
ascertained what the profits are, the statute says that, "The
" duty in each of the last three rules is to be charged on the
" person or corporation carrying on the concern." Now this
board, being a corporation carrying on the concern, are to pay
duty upon these profits. It is immaterial under this part of
the section whether any other person is beneficially interested
or to what purpose the profits are applied. A suggestion has
been made that the word "profits" is not the correct one where
the net proceeds, which I call profits, are applicable to public or
charitable purposes. But there is nothing to support that
suggestion in the Act which treats "profits" as the thing earned
from the carrying on of the concern; the Act does not regard
either the person who carries on the concern, except for the
purpose of saying who shall pay the tax, or the purposes to
which those profits are applied, except in certain cases. Thus,
we find in No. 6 certain allowances are made for privileged
persons who would otherwise be within the previous section or

rule. For instance, colleges, halls in universities, hospitals, and public schools, and almshouses are exempt; so also all trustees for charitable purposes are exempt to the extent to which the rents are applied to such charitable purposes; and this shows that had it not been for these exemptions they would have been liable to pay on the profits, though in the ordinary sense of the word as used in trade they took nothing, because they were all expended in charitable purposes. The Attorney-General v. Black is an authority to show that that is the true construction of the Act, but what was the argument on the other side? It was this: That a man cannot make a profit by selling to himself, and so far I agree. But it was then said that because 24 members of this Mersey Dock Board are elected by the ratepayers—the remaining four being appointed by the conservators—the ratepayers are to be treated as persons who pay the rates to their own nominees, so that if they pay too much the surplus is to go to them; and is not therefore a profit earned by carrying on the concern. Even if that is the meaning of the word "profits" the argument would be unsound, because as I have already pointed out, this Mersey Dock Board is created for certain public purposes besides those of carrying on the docks, and moreover it is not composed exclusively of nominees of the ratepayers, because four out of the 28 members are appointed by the conservators. In addition, the ratepayers who elect the board and the ratepayers who pay the rates are not the same persons, and the persons to pay the rates one year might not be exactly the same persons who would pay them the next year. So that an entirely new body of ratepayers might arise during the next year who would have taken no part in the election of the members of the board, and consequently the profits earned by the Board by charging a larger sum than the expenses, do not belong to the ratepayers in any sense. Therefore that part of the argument fails because it is not the fact that the persons who pay the rates are the same as those who elect the Board, and even if that were the fact this would not be the less a profit, because it is not a sum paid by one man to another. For these reasons I think the decision of the Court below cannot be maintained, and the appeal must be allowed.

Lord Justice Brett.—I am also of opinion that this appeal must be allowed. The question is whether the Mersey Docks and Harbour Board, which is a corporation, is bound to make a return under the Income Tax Acts, and whether it is bound to pay the income tax. On behalf of the Crown it is urged that this Corporation is bound to do so by virtue of the 5th and 6th of Victoria, chapter 35, because that statute enacts generally that persons who are owners of or in possession of a dock shall pay income tax upon the profits actually received therefrom, that the word "profits" there means the difference between what is actually received for the use of the docks and the expense of maintaining the docks; that this Corporation did receive money for the use of the docks, and were subject to pay the expenses incident to the earning of that money, and that therefore they were liable to pay income tax on such profits.

It was also argued on behalf of the Crown that the Mersey Docks and Harbour Board Consolidation Act, 1858, did not contain any enactment which in express terms relieved the Dock Board from liability to pay such a tax; and that even if it did contain such an enactment the Mersey Docks Board would still be liable to pay the tax, because the general taxing Act was passed after the Act of 1858. Another ground, which was suggested by the Master of the Rolls in his judgment—and I think it is my duty to say whether I agree to it or not—is that, because any relief from this tax is not named expressly in this private Act the Crown is not bound by it. As regards the question whether, assuming that the private Act did relieve this Corporation from the payment of income tax, the general words of a subsequent Act would make them liable, I say, with deference, but giving it as my clear opinion, that the subsequent Act did not impose this tax upon this Corporation.

A taxing Act is to be construed upon the same principles and by the same rules as any other Act, and the rule to be applied is, that if the particular provisions of the private Act absolved this Corporation from paying this tax, then the general words of the subsequent Act would not impose that tax, and would not repeal the provisions of the private Act. Therefore, I could not agree to the judgment of my Lord upon that ground. And with regard to the first suggestion, I again, with great deference, differ, and say that there is no prerogative of the Crown whatever with regard to taxes until those taxes have been granted by Parliament, and the question being whether this tax has been granted by Parliament so as to impose it upon this Corporation, the ordinary construction of the Act could not be limited by asserting in any way any prerogative of the Crown. But it does seem to me that this general Act, provided there is nothing in the private Act which takes this Corporation out of its operation, does impose a tax upon the difference between the receipts for the use of the docks and the expenses of maintaining them. The question is not what is the annual value of the docks, as in the case of poor rates, where the annual value of the property is not determined by what the person in possession of that property receives a year, but by a hypothetical proposition as to what a responsible tenant would pay for the property if he held it upon a lease from year to year. The Income Tax Act takes the present case out of that doctrine, and provides that the annual value under this Act shall be the full amount for one year, or the average for one year of the profits received therefrom. If in this there were no profits in fact, then there would be no tax.

It was not argued on behalf of this Corporation that upon the true construction of the 5th and 6th of Victoria, chapter 35, the word "profits" would have any other meaning than its ordinary meaning as applied to a trade or business, viz., the difference

between the receipts and the expenses incurred in order to obtain MERSEY
those receipts, but it was argued that by reason of the constitu- DOCK AND
tion of this Corporation under the Mersey Docks and Harbour BOARD v.
Acts, there were not any profits received, and that if there were LUCAS.
any profits received in the sense of there being a difference between the actual receipts and the expenditure, that under the
Mersey Docks and Harbour Act, 1858, this Corporation was
absolved from paying any tax; but after careful consideration I
cannot agree with that argument. It was said in the first place
that no profits at all were earned or received, because this Corporation and the ratepayers are identical, and therefore, the
money which is received by the Corporation is money which
is really paid by the ratepayers and is not profit at all, but
merely a contribution between the same persons.

Two hypothetical cases were put—first, where there was
nothing but contribution between the parties, and secondly,
where there was a receipt of that which might fairly be called
"profits." In the latter case there would have been a difficulty
in making all the parties pay income tax, because some of them
would have received no profit at all; and in the former case
there could have been no tax to be paid, because it was all con-
·tribution. But Mr. Bigham has failed to bring this case within
the two hypothetical cases. Here the Mersey Docks and Harbour Board is authorised to receive the rates, and the ratepayers
are not the same people as that corporation. The analogy,
therefore, fails. The Corporation are in possession of the docks,
and are the persons who maintain them, who receive money for
their use, and who incur the expense of maintaining them in
order to earn those receipts; therefore, they are persons within
the meaning of the general Act who are liable to make a return
and to pay income tax, if not otherwise relieved by the special
Act. But it was said that the Corporation was relieved from
liability to pay this tax because their special Act has directed
affirmatively that they are to make certain payments, and then
negatively declares that the moneys are not to be applied for any
other purpose whatsoever. It seems to me that the liability to
pay income tax is included in the affirmative enactments of that
statute; and I should be sorry to base my judgment upon any
former Acts referred to in this present statute, and which have
not been brought before us, especially as it is stated in the case,
and admitted by counsel on both sides, that those Acts were not
material to the present case. I do not, however, say that they
might not give these affirmative powers by reference, but I think
there is enough on the face of this Act to impose this liability.
The Act itself, amongst other things, provides that the Corporation may pay for the carrying into execution of all the
provisions of the Act, and then the 31st section gives·them
power to pay everything which an ordinary dock board would
have to pay; and even if that were not so, I am inclined to
agree with the Solicitor-General, that such a tax as this might
be included under the words "and in the general management

"and conducting, &c. the Mersey Dock Estate," including also
the Mersey Dock concern. The Act, therefore, by this affirmative enactment seems to empower the Board to pay all taxes,
including the income tax.

Mr. Bigham, however, relies upon the negative part of the
section, which says that "except as aforesaid such moneys shall
"not be applied by the Board for any other purpose whatsoever."
Now, if what I have said about the affirmative parts of this
section be true, then this negative part does not apply to what
is contained in those affirmative parts, because the affirmative
power and direction to pay these taxes would be pointed at by
the words "except as aforesaid," and there would be no prohibi-
tion against paying them.   Besides, if I were of opinion that
these words were not directory but were prohibitory, and that
the power to pay these taxes was not contained in the former
part of the statute, I should agree with Mr. Bigham that there
were no profits received by this Corporation which could be
brought within the later Income Tax Act, and that this Corporation is not a corporation in possession of a dock within the
meaning of the general Act which imposes income tax.   I also
think that the proposition which was enunciated by Lord Blackburn on behalf of the judges in the House of Lords in the
Mersey Docks *v.* Cameron is a true proposition, and one which
was really adopted by the House of Lords in the judgment of
Lord Chelmsford.   I am of opinion that the words at the end
of section 284 are merely directory and not prohibitory words ;
and therefore there is nothing which takes this Corporation in
respect of these docks out of the general rule.   Consequently
they are within the general Act, and must pay income tax upon
receipts to be ascertained according to the ordinary rules applying to a trading company, namely, upon the difference between
the receipts arising from the dock dues and the expenses of
earning those receipts, including, amongst other expenses, this
very income tax which they are bound to pay.   I do not think
that the Glasgow Waterworks case applies here, but I think, if
I may say so with deference, that it was rightly decided upon
the facts then before the Court.

Lord Justice Cotton.—In this case the Commissioners have
held that the Mersey Dock Board are liable to be surcharged by
a sum which represents the net receipts from the dock, and the
question is whether they are right in that.   I will first consider
whether, independently of sections 284 and 285 of the Special
Act of the Mersey Dock Board of 1858 they are liable to be so
charged.   The Income Tax Act under which the Board is
sought to be charged was passed subsequently to the Mersey
Docks Act of 1858, but it refers back to the 5th and 6th Victoria
chapter 35, Schedule A., which gives for "all lands, tenements,
"and hereditaments in Great Britain in respect of the property
"thereof for every twenty shillings of the annual value thereof
"the sum of sevenpence."   We have, however, to determine the
annual value in respect of which the Board are to be charged by

reference to another portion of the Act, and general rules are
there given for estimating the value of the lands, tenements, or
hereditaments mentioned in Schedule A.

It is only necessary to refer to that portion of No. III. which
relates to the property, namely, "docks," in respect of which the
Board are sought to be charged. That rule says, "the annual
"value of all the properties herein-after described shall be
"understood to be the full amount for one year of the profits
"received therefrom within the respective times herein limited."
It was urged that in this case there could be no profits, because
the persons who contribute that from which the net income
arises are the persons to whose nominees the money is paid, and
that, therefore, as a man cannot make profit out of himself, there
is no profit in this case. Now, even assuming that the whole
of the Board is nominated by the ratepayers, and that their
nominees are to be considered as being the same persons as themselves, the persons who nominate the Board are not the same as
those who in each year pay the rates from which the net income
arises, because they are persons who are on a certain list of
voters which does not include all those who in any year pay
rates, nor all the persons who in the particular year when the
assessment is made pay the same to the Board, who are said to
be their nominees. But, in my opinion, it is not necessary to
advert to that, for we must consider what is meant in this
section of the Income Tax Act by the word "profits." The
profits here do not accrue, as under Schedule D., to any person,
but are "profits received" from real property, the annual value
of which is to be ascertained by reference to another portion of
the Act. In my opinion, the word "profits" means the difference between the gross sums received from that property and the
expenses of receiving those sums; in other words, the net receipt
from that property in any particular year. I also am of opinion,
without entering into that question more fully, that there are
profits here do not accrue, as under Schedule D., to any person,
the Act, without reference to the purposes to which they are to be
applied.

But then it was said that, nevertheless, there are provisions
in the special Act which precluded the Board from being charged
under the Income Tax Act. The special Act was not passed in
order to give certain powers and exemptions to the Board, but
as is shown by the recital in that Act, to consolidate Acts which
existed previous to the year 1857, and to regulate the charges to
be made by the Board to give them power to raise certain
further sums of money. Independently of that, it was an Act
dealing with the powers of the Board as regards those from
whom they were to receive rates, and their rights as against
those persons.

In dealing with a private Act like this which is intended to
give to a body constituted for certain purposes additional powers,
one must treat the clauses if they do prohibit the revenues of
that body from being applied in any other way but those

specified in the Act, and those did not include taxes not as being
intended to deprive the Crown of the right to collect those taxes,
but as dealing with the application by that Board of such
revenues as they had after paying the obligations which Parliament may have put upon them. It would be a wrong construction (even if there are no words in the Act of Parliament which
authorised the payment of this tax) to say that general words
in such an Act take away the right to collect for public purposes
any tax which otherwise would be chargeable against that body.
That being so, I am not careful to consider whether there are
in the previous parts of section 284 terms that would authorise
the Board to apply any of their revenues towards the payment
of this tax. Even if there were not any such provision the
words "such moneys shall not be applied by the Board for any
other purpose whatsoever" cannot be taken to prevent the collection of taxes which the Board would be otherwise liable in
respect of property which they hold. Section 5 of the Act of
1858 moreover shows that it was not intended that the Board
should be exempted from taxes which the general public would
have to bear but for this Act. That section which deals with
land tax, assumes that while the docks are being made and
before they are made, the land might not be sufficient to provide
for the assessment, and it provides during that period for the
Board paying the deficiency, but it leaves untouched what is to
be done afterwards, because afterwards when the docks were
made undoubtedly the land would be sufficient to pay the assessment. That assumes as clearly as possible that there is no exemption by section 284 from any taxes which otherwise the
Board would be liable to pay.

The principle upon which I base my judgment is that the
general terms contained in such an Act are not to be taken to
exempt a body to whom it has given certain powers for certain
purposes from the general public burden of paying taxes.

Appeal allowed.

LONDON:
PRINTED UNDER THE AUTHORITY OF HIS MAJESTY'S
STATIONERY OFFICE
BY DARLING & SON, LIMITED, BACON STREET, E.

1916.

Part XXIII.

No. 55.—In the Court of Exchequer (Scotland).

First Division.

November 25, 1881.

RUSSELL (Surveyor of Taxes) v. COUTTS.

Inhabited House Duty.—A solicitor (in partnership) and stamp distributor (sole) occupies, for purposes of business and residence, a block of buildings separately entered in Valuation Roll, but with internal communication.

HELD—(1.) *That whole block is liable to Inhabited House Duty. (2.) That the house is not "divided into and let in different tenements" (41 Vict. c. 15. s. 13) by reason of the firm occupying rooms as offices.*

At an adjourned Meeting of the Commissioners for the general purposes of the Income Tax Acts, and for executing the Acts relating to the Inhabited House Duties for the County of Banff, held at Banff on the 16th day of February 1881.

Mr. William Coutts, solicitor, and distributor of stamps and collector of taxes at Banff, appealed against an assessment of 2l. 12s. 6d., made upon him for Inhabited House Duty, for the year commencing on the 24th Day of May 1880, at the rate of 9d. per 1l. on 70l., the *cumulo* value of a dwelling-house and business offices situated in Low Street, Banff, of which he is proprietor, holding the haill subjects under the same title.

The Commissioners found the following facts to be proved:—

1. The subjects are entered in the Valuation Roll of the burgh of Banff for the year 1880–81 as under:—

Description of Subject.	Proprietor.	Occupier.	Annual Value.
			£ s. d.
No. 968. House, stable, and garden, 30A.	William Coutts, solicitor.	Same	35 0 0
„ 969. Law offices ...	Do.	Coutts & Morrison, solicitors.	20 0 0
„ 970. Stamp office, 30 ...	Do.	William Coutts	15 0 0

2. The premises which form the subject of appeal form two sides of a square, which may be called respectively the back

A

and the wing. The back consists of two storeys and sunk flat; and the wing, which was built at a subsequent date, of two storeys. The roofs of the back and wing are on the same level, but are totally unconnected, except by an ordinary metal gutter, which is common to both.

3. The premises are occupied in the following manner, viz :—

		£	s.	d.
(a)	The whole of the back, and a bedroom, bath-room, and w.c., forming the back part of the upper storey of the wing, as the private residence of Mr. Coutts. Annual value -	35	0	0
(b)	The front part of the upper storey of the wing and landing there, of considerable size, and the back part of the ground floor of the wing and w.c., and passage thereto, as the writing offices of William Coutts and Morrison, solicitors, under a deed of copartnery, dated 29th March 1879, for five years from 31st March 1879, in which it is provided that before striking a copartnery balance each year there shall be charged against the business rent of the offices 20*l.*, and taxes effeiring thereto. The annual value of this part is - - - - - - -	20	0	0
(c)	The front part of the ground floor of the wing, by Mr. Coutts himself, as a stamp and tax office. Annual value - - -	15	0	0
	Total value of block - - £70	0	0

4. The appellant is a partner of the firm of William Coutts and Morrison. Mr. James Morrison, the other partner, resides in another part of the town.

5. In the bedroom in the wing is a bolt in connection with the lock of the safe in the stamp and tax office, which was used to control this lock when the office in question was used as a bank office ; but this bolt has not been used since Mr. Coutts ceased to be the bank agent, eight years ago.

6. There are three principal entrances to the premises : one in the back, the principal entrance to the private residence; one in the interior angle of the back and wing, leading to the writing offices occupied by William Coutts and Morrison ; and one from the street end of the wing, leading into the stamp and tax office. From the stamp and tax office there is a door leading into the passage to the w.c. mentioned under head 3 (b), and from this passage there is another door by which access can be had into another passage which leads into the writing offices on the ground floor. From this last-mentioned passage a stair leads up to the landing on the second floor, and from this landing at the top of this stair there is a door leading into the bed-

room before mentioned, and from this bedroom there is another RUSSELL (SURVEYOR OF TAXES) *v.* COUTTS. passage to the main portion of the private residence. There is thus the means of internal communication throughout the whole building ; but it is impossible to pass from the dwelling-house to the stamp office, or *vice versâ*, without passing through the premises let to Messrs. William. Coutts and Morrison, or leaving by the main entrance of one place, and entering by that of the other.

7. Mr. Coutts has reserved no right to use the entrance to Messrs. William Coutts and Morrison's writing offices, or the lobby, as means of access, either to his private residence or to the stamp office. Neither the firm, nor the individual partners thereof as such, have any right to use the entrance leading from the landing at the top of the stair to the private residence, nor have they the right to use the entrance from the passage to the stamp office ; and, in point of fact, these entrances are not used for the business purposes of the firm, but only occasionally by Mr. Coutts, during the pleasure of his firm, for his personal convenience out of office hours.

Mr. Coutts contended that the assessment should be reduced to that on 35*l.*, the annual value of his private residence, on the ground—(1) that the writing offices occupied by William Coutts and Morrison, and the stamp and tax office occupied by himself, being each a separate place of business, occupied by separate and distinct persons, and the stamp office not being attached to the dwelling-house, and having no communication with it without passing through the subjects let as writing offices to the firm of William Coutts and Morrison, by the passages and stair mentioned under head 6, neither could in any sense be held as part of his dwelling-house ; and (2) that the whole business being one property, divided into and let or used in different tenements, the portion occupied solely for the purpose of the profession or calling of the occupiers is not liable to the duty, but is exempt by sub-section 1 of 41 Vict. cap. 15, section 13.

On the other hand, the surveyor, Mr. Russell, contended—(1) that in the eye of the law the whole block of buildings is one inhabited dwelling-house, and that, apart from any special exemption, the assessment fell to be made upon the full *cumulo* value ; that the Act 14 & 15 Vict. cap. 36., under which the assessment is made, referred back for the rules of charge to the Act 48 Geo. 3. cap. 55., and that the present case fell under Rules I. and V. of Schedule B. of this latter Act ; and (2) that the special exemption founded on under sub-section 1 of 41 Vict. cap. 15. sec. 13, plainly had reference to houses which fell to be assessed under Rule VI. of Schedule B. of 48 Geo. 3. cap. 55., and that the premises in question are not let in such a manner as to bring the whole house within the scope of this Rule VI., or the writing offices within the exemption ·in sub-section 1 of 41 Vict. cap. 15. sect. 13.

Authorities quoted : (1) for Mr. Coutts—*The Glasgow Coal Exchange Company, Limited,* decided 18th March 1879, No. 33

of Exchequer Cases; and also decision by Commissioners of
Banffshire, in *Crown* v. *Allan*, in 1879, acquiesced in by the
Crown. (2) for the Crown, Nos. 2599, 2781, and 2782 English
Cases, and Nos. 27, 29, 35, and 40 of Exchequer Cases.

After hearing parties, the Commissioners sustained the appeal
as to the writing offices occupied by William Coutts and
Morrison, but refused it as to the stamp and tax office, thus
reducing the assessment to the duty on 50*l.*

With this decision, in so far as it excluded the writing offices,
the Surveyor declared his dissatisfaction; and Mr. Coutts, in so
far as the decision included the stamp offices, also declared his
dissatisfaction; and in terms of section 59 of 43 & 44 Vict.
cap. 19. both parties craved a case for the opinion of the
Court, which is here stated accordingly.

W. G. SCOTT MONCRIEFF, *Cr.*
JOHN HANNAY, *Cr.*

1st Division, Wednesday, 14th December 1881.

Counsel having been heard—

The Lord President.—I confess I think the precise facts as to
the occupation of this inhabited house belonging to Mr. Coutts
are better discovered from the plans than from the case. The
statements in the case are not very clear and distinct to my
mind, but the plans are perfectly so. This is one inhabited
house, which is the property of Mr. Coutts, but it is occupied in
different ways. A portion of it is occupied as a dwelling-house
by Mr. Coutts himself, another portion of it is occupied as a
stamp office by Mr. Coutts, and a third portion of it is occupied
by Mr. Coutts and his partner, Mr. Morrison, as writing
chambers. Now these are all parts of the same inhabited house,
and it is past all dispute that they communicate with one
another. It is said, indeed, that the doors of communication are
so arranged that Mr. Coutts only can use these different doors
of communication. The dwelling-house on the upper storey
extends beyond what it does upon the ground floor. Upon the
ground floor it is confined to what is called the old house, but
in the upper storey it extends not only over the whole house but
over the back part of the new house. The back part of the new
house below that portion occupied as part of the
dwelling-house is occupied as part of the writing chambers of Coutts and Morrison, and the front portion is occupied
as the stamp office. On the upper floor over the stamp office
there are three additional rooms occupied by Coutts and
Morrison's writing chambers. On the ground floor there is a
door of communication opening from the stamp office into the
premises of Messrs. Coutts and Morrison, and by means of a
staircase from that passage there is a communication to the
whole of the upper storey of what is called the new house; and
there is a door of communication between that portion of the

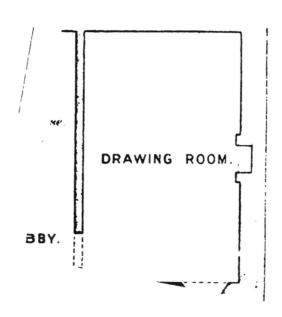

house which is occupied as part of Mr. Coutts' dwelling-house RUSSELL
and the front portion of it, which is occupied by Coutts and (SURVEYOR OF TAXES) v.
Morrison's writing chambers. So that, as far as Mr. Coutts COUTTS.
is concerned, he may enter by any one of the entries from the
street, and being once within this inhabited house he can pass,
by means of these various doors and passages, to any part of the
entire house.

Now the first question comes to be, whether the stamp office
is within the exemption contemplated in the second sub-section
of section 13, of the Act of 1878. That provides "that every
"house or tenement which is occupied solely for the purposes
"of any trade or business or of any profession or calling by
"which the occupier seeks a livelihood or profit" shall be
exempted from the duty. Mr. Coutts maintains that he
occupies this stamp office for the purpose of his business as a
distributor of stamps, and that it is within the meaning of this
sub-section a house or tenement occupied solely for that purpose.
My Lords, that is a contention which I think it is impossible to
sustain. It is not a house or tenement within the meaning of
that sub-section, but it is simply a room in the inhabited house
belonging to and occupied by Mr. Coutts, and such a room is
not within the meaning of that sub-section. That seems to me
to be too clear to require any further statement or argument.

The other question regards a part of the inhabited house
occupied by Messrs. Coutts and Morrison as writing chambers.
Now it is said that this is within the meaning of the first
sub-section a part of a divided house let as a different tenement;
and the case depends entirely upon the construction of the
words in that first sub-section. It has been said that this
sub-section (1) is very difficult of construction, and particularly
that there is a great difficulty in fixing precisely the meaning
of the word "tenement" or "different tenements." My Lords,
I confess I do not experience that difficulty at all, because I find
it solved by going back to the original statute which imposed
the duty upon inhabited houses. I find the word used there
in such a way as to make it perfectly clear what is meant by it.
The sixth article of Schedule B. of the 48th of Geo. 3. provides
that where any house shall be let in different storeys, tenements,
lodgings, or landings, there the owner of the entire house shall
be deemed to be the occupier of the whole, although it is
occupied separately by different persons. Now the word
"tenements" there occurs in connection with storeys, lodgings,
or landings; and certainly, to a Scotch lawyer, whatever it may
do to anybody else, that at once suggests the mode in which
houses are occupied in those large buildings that we have in
Edinburgh and other towns, where the different tenements are
approached by a common stair. The 14th Article of that same
schedule provides that where any dwelling-house shall be
divided into different tenements, being distinct properties, then
they may be separately assessed in the duty. It is plain, therefore, from these two articles taken together that the meaning of

the word " tenement " in this statute is a part of a house so
divided and separated as to be capable of being a distinct
property or a distinct subject of lease. Now if that is not a
sufficient definition of the word " tenement " I am afraid we
shall require another. But it enables me to construe without
difficulty this first sub-section. The sub-section is, no doubt,
expressed in rather a cramped way, and it is elliptical a good
deal ; but, reading it more at large, I should say the meaning of
it is this,—to bring a case within the exemption there must be a
house belonging to one owner, so structurally divided into
different tenements as to be capable of being separately owned or
separately let, and these different tenements, must be either all
separately let, or all for the time unoccupied, or some of them
separately let, and some of them for the time unoccupied. I
think that exhausts the whole words and meaning of the
sub-section. Now the only question in the present case is
whether we have got in the possession or occupation of Messrs.
Coutts and Morrison a separate or different tenement, separately
let within the meaning of these words ; and I think the facts of
the case do not amount to such a separation of these rooms of
the inhabited house belonging to Mr. Coutts as to make it a
separate tenement, and so within the exemption. It appears to
me that Mr. Coutts is really in the occupation of the whole of
this inhabited house ; he has access to every part of it. No
doubt he occupies some of the rooms jointly with his partner in
business, Mr. Morrison, and that is all that can be said about it.
There is the form of a rent paid by the firm of Coutts and
Morrison to Mr. Coutts. That is all quite right ; but paying a
rent for the occupation of two or three rooms in my house
will not constitute these rooms into a separate tenement unless
there is that structural division which makes a separate tenement such as could be the subject of a separate property or a
separate lease ; and here we certainly have nothing of that kind.
Whether the circumstance of Mr. Coutts being in the occupation
himself of a part of the inhabited house, even supposing that it
were divided structurally into separate tenements, would prevent
the application of this clause, I desire to give no opinion, because
I do not think it is at all necessary for the decision of this case ;
and one cannot help seeing that there must be difficulty in that
question, because learned Judges in the other end of the island
have differed upon it ; but it is not all necessary for the judgment in this case.

I am for altering the determination of the Commissioners in
so far as concerns Messrs. Coutts and Morrison, and affirming
the rest of their determination.

Lord Mure.—I have come to the same conclusion. On the
admitted facts of the case as explained in the Appeal, it appears
to me that the house originally was one inhabited house belonging to Mr. Coutts,—built at different times, but built, as far as
we can see, by Mr. Coutts as the proprietor, and apparently from
the plans intended to be occupied by him. What is called the

old house was built first, but on the back wing being built a considerable portion of it, as shown by the plan, was connected with the old house and with the bedroom flat of the old house, and is at present so occupied by the proprietor. On the plan it is shown distinctly that there is a bedroom, a dressing-room, watercloset and bath, and a passage connecting them with the upper flat of the old original house, and in that Mr. Coutts now lives. The rest of the same flat or wing is occupied by Mr. Coutts and his partner as their writing offices, and there is a door of communication between the two. That is shown on the plan. Coutts and Morrison's offices are immediately above the stamp office, and they communicate by a private door leading to the passage of the bedroom flat. The lower part of that back wing is also occupied by the firm, with the exception of a room or two rooms which are occupied by Mr. Coutts as his stamp office, and which communicate with the premises of the firm by a door, which he can use when he likes ; and although there may be no positive agreement between the firm and him about the use of a door of communication between the bedroom flat and the part of the same flat occupied as offices, it is stated in the case that he occasionally uses them both. Now, in these circumstances, it appears to me that Mr. Coutts is actually occupying his own house, and occupying the stamp office as part of his own house ; and I cannot see that they fall under sub-division 2. of section 13., because it is not, in the view that I take of the facts, a separate tenement in the sense of sub-division 2. That, according to my recollection, is in principle substantially the same question as was raised about the Glasgow and South-western Railway Company (o) as to the premises occupied by them partly as a hotel and partly for their own offices.

The remaining point is, whether under sub-division 1. the premises occupied by the firm can be said to come within that section. Now I think they do not come within that section, because I cannot hold that where premises of that sort have a door which is in frequent use as a means of communication between them and the other part of his house,—I cannot hold that that is a structural division in the sense which is necessary to make a distinct and separate tenement of that description. I think the whole arrangement is one by which the proprietor lives in a part of the house, for the greater part of it is his dwelling-house, and has his private stamp office and his business premises in the same house occupied by himself, although these business premises may be in point of fact let to the firm of which he himself is a member.

Lord Shand.—I concur in the opinions which your Lordships have delivered. It appears to me, in the first place, to be clear that this old house, and the wing which has been built as an addition to it, form one house or tenement. It is true that in building the wing as an addition to the house there appears to have been no communication opened between the old house and the wing on the ground floor, but when we turn to the plans of the upper floor we find that there is an important passage connecting the upper floors, so as, I think, to make them one house. The purpose of that passage was to enlarge the old house by providing as an addition to it upstairs a bedroom, dressing-room, and watercloset and bath, and these are all occupied by Mr. Coutts now as part of his house. I observe it is stated in the case that the roofs of the back and wing are on the same level, but are totally unconnected except by an ordinary metal gutter, which is common to both; but I do not think that makes any substantial difference. It is just the case of an old house having had an addition built to it; and although the roofs are only connected by a common metal gutter, I think this is substantially a house which is in the same position as if it were all under one roof. That being so, there are two questions raised;—first in regard to the stamp office, and secondly in regard to the office or rooms occupied by Messrs. Coutts and Morrison; and I think these ought to be taken separately.

In regard to the stamp office, it is true that the direct entrance to the stamp office is separate from that to the house, although it is also true that from the upper floor of the house, by means of internal doors of communication, Mr. Coutts can go from his dwelling-house, through the passages connecting his dwelling-house and the other parts of his premises, to the stamp office without going inside. But in regard to the stamp office, the exemption is claimed, not under sub-section 1st, but under sub-section 2nd, of section 13 of the Act of 1878. It is clear that sub-section 1. would not avail Mr. Coutts in this question, because it cannot be said that the stamp office is a part of that which I have called one house or building which has been let by him. He has not let the stamp office. He is himself the occupant of the house and of the stamp office. The question, and the only question, for determination upon this part of case is, whether sub-section 2. gives the exemption. Now that sub-section provides that every house or tenement which is occupied solely for the purposes of any trade or business or of any profession or calling by which the occupier seeks a livelihood shall be exempted from the duties. What I have already said seems to me to exclude the application of that section. It appears to me that this is one house or tenement, for the reasons I explained at the outset; and if they be one house or tenement, then it is not occupied solely for the purposes of Mr. Coutts' profession or calling, because he occupies part of it as his dwelling-house, and part of it as his stamp office. And therefore it appears to me that this sub-section does not apply. I may say that I am also of opinion that the case is directly ruled by that of the Scottish Widows' Fund (*p*). In that case there was an entirely separate entrance to the dwelling-house above the Widows' Fund Office, which dwelling-house was

---

(*p*) *Ante*, p. 247.

occupied by one of the clerks of the office ; the remainder of the RUSSELL building,—by much the larger part of it,—was occupied for (SURVEYOR business purposes ; and the argument maintained was that the COUTTS. large part of the building occupied for business purposes was within the meaning of sub-section 2. a house or tenement by itself, occupied solely for the business of the society. But we were unanimously of opinion that that part of the house or tenement occupied for business was not a house or tenement by itself, but that the whole building must be taken as a house or tenement, and we therefore held that it was not made out that that whole house or tenement was occupied solely for the purposes of the trade or business. It therefore appears to me that that is a direct authority upon this question.

There remains the question as to Messrs. Coutts and Morrison's office, consisting of several rooms on the first floor and rooms upon the second floor of the wing attached to the house. It has been argued that in no possible view can there be exemption on account of Coutts and Morrison's offices, because in order to let in sub-section 1. the whole property must be divided into and let in different tenements, and that in this case it appears that Mr. Coutts, the proprietor himself, occupies the house in which he dwells, and the stamp office, and therefore this sub-section cannot apply to the case. As your Lordship has observed, that raises a question upon which a difference of opinion has occurred amongst eminent judges in England, and I shall not express any opinion upon it. I shall only say this, that upon the argument which we have heard on these cases I am not satisfied at this moment that the circumstance that the proprietor himself occupies part of the building would exclude sub-section 1.; and if it were necessary to determine that point in the Crown's favour in order to decide this question, I should not be prepared at this moment so to decide. But assuming for the purposes of this case that sub-section 1. does apply to a case where part of a house or building has been divided into and let in different tenements, I am of opinion that in this case Mr. Coutts cannot get the benefit of this sub-section. If it had appeared or been the fact that the doors of communication shown on these plans as existing on the first and second floors of this building had been built up or permanently closed, I should have been of opinion that the exemption did apply to the part of the premises occupied by Coutts and Morrison ; for in that case we should have had these premises with a separate entrance of their own, which admitted the partners of that firm, and their clerks and people going there on business, and no one else, to the portion of the building given off to Coutts and Morrison. There would, in my opinion, in that case have been such structural division in this building as amounted to the creation of a different tenement let to Coutts and Morrison by Mr. Coutts. But it makes all the difference, I think, that there is not that permanent structural division. We have here, in the first place, a door of communication between the upper part of this dwelling-house and the passage leading into Coutts and Morrison's office, and we have in addition another door of communication between the stamp office and the passage on the ground floor which again leads into Coutts and Morrison's offices both downstairs and above. I do not say that that second door of communication is of the same importance in this case as the upper one which connects the dwelling-house with the offices; and it may be that if the door of communication from the dwelling-house to the offices had been permanently closed, that would have been enough to make the case one for exemption. But, as it is, I think the case does not come within sub-section 1. as being a house,—one property divided into and let in different tenements,—because there is not a structural division which would make the offices of Coutts and Morrison a different tenement. It is said no doubt in this case that the passage or communication is only used occasionally by Mr. Coutts during the pleasure of his firm, for his personal convenience, and out of office hours. It is extremely difficult to accept that, or to see why a door of communication of that kind should be used out of office hours when it must be of much more convenience to Mr. Coutts during the day and during office hours; but even taking it so, the passage is available at all hours of the day; and that being so, it appears to me that you cannot predicate of Coutts and Morrison's office that it is a separate tenement structurally divided from the house. Upon that ground I agree with your Lordships in holding that sub-section 1. does not apply. And I may just observe that if we were to hold in this case that this door of communication which may be used by Mr. Coutts at any time, and I assume is used by him only, or persons in his house, but if the existence of such a door as this were not held as a communication which distinguished the case from a structural division, I do not know where in other cases it would be possible to draw the line. We should have other cases in which a door of this kind existed, and was used all day long, it might be, or where two or three such doors were used, and the same argument would apply. I think the line must simply be drawn by looking at the particular premises, and ascertaining whether they are so structurally shut off from the rest of the building occupied as to form an entirely separate tenement of itself, and I do not think Coutts and Morrison's office is in that position.

Lord President.—Reverse the determination of the Commissioners in so far as they sustain the Appeal as to the writing chambers occupied by Coutts and Morrison; *quoad ultra* affirm the determination.

No. 56.—IN THE SUPREME COURT OF JUDICATURE ; before the
Court of Appeal at Westminster, 6th December, 1881.

YORKSHIRE FIRE AND LIFE INSURANCE COMPANY *v.*
CLAYTON, Surveyor of Taxes.

*Inhabited house duty.—A house which is let in separate offices
and rooms, but which has merely the ordinary structural
division of different floors and separate rooms, does not fall
within section 13 (1) of the Act 41 Vict. c. 15.*

This was an appeal from the decision of the Divisional Court.
The facts are set forth in the case and supplemental case stated
for the opinion of the Divisional Court, and printed at pp. 336–
339 *ante.*

Lumley Smith, Q.C. (for the Appellants, the Insurance Company).—The Act has not said that there shall be a structural
division.   I define a tenement to be any room or set of rooms
separately held in such a way that the occupier has exclusive
possession of control.   To take the words of Lord Blackburne in
the Queen *v.* St. George's Union, it would depend upon whether
there was a separate demise, or merely an agreement to allow the
tenant to come in while the occupation remained in the landlord.   If the landlord has not the right of getting in, then it is a
tenement.   The word applies as much to a single room as to a
structurally separate part of the house, if the room is demised
in such a way as to give complete control to the tenant.

Jessel, M.R.—The question is what "divided into" means.
It is not only "let in different tenements," but "divided into."—

Lumley Smith.—The moment you part with the control of a
part of your house, you divide it.   The act of turning a portion
into a tenement divides it.

Jessel, M.R.—It is impossible, according to your argument, to
let it in different tenements without dividing it.   Then the
word "divided" is superfluous.

Lumley Smith.—It may be superfluous.

Bigham, for the Appellant.—" Divided into different tenements " means divided not by means of any structure, but by
virtue of an agreement or otherwise ; divided in such a way that
the holder has an exclusive control over the part of which he is
tenant.   The words "divided into" may not be superfluous.   A
house which the landlord owns and lets in lodgings is "let in
different tenements ; " but when the landlord gives up the
exclusive control of portions of the house, then the thing is
divided into different tenements within the meaning of the
Act.

Lord Justice Brett.—Suppose we say "let in tenements " did
not apply to lodging-houses ?

Bigham.—Where a man lets a dining-room and drawing-room
why are not these tenements ?

YORKSHIRE
FIRE AND
LIFE INSUR-
ANCE CO. *v.*
CLAYTON
(SURVEYOR
OF TAXES).

YORKSHIRE
FIRE AND
LIFE INSUR-
ANCE CO. v.
CLAYTON
(SURVEYOR
OF TAXES).

Lord Justice Brett.—They have never been so called in any legal or common phraseology. When you take a lodger to lodge with you, he has no tenement at all.

JUDGMENT.

The Master of the Rolls.—This is one of those cases which I agree is fairly open to argument. I have no complaint to make, either of the appeal being brought, or of the length of argument adduced in support of the appeal. The real question we have to decide is, whether we can properly overrule the Court below, which has put an interpretation on section 13. of the 41st Vict.,— a section which is not very easy to be interpreted. The section standing alone, without having regard to the previous legisla- tion and to the previous course of decisions, would be almost beyond interpretation ; but, having regard to that previous legislation and previous course of decisions, I think we can fairly put a meaning to it substantially the same as that which was adopted by Mr. Justice Lindley in his judgment in the Court below. Under the old Acts an entire house occupied for business or trade purposes was exempt ; afterwards an entire house occupied partly for business purposes and partly for pro- fessional purposes was exempt ; and by the 6th rule of Schedule B. of the 48 Geo. 3., chapter 55., I find this :—" Where any " house shall be let in different stories, tenements, lodgings, or " landings, and shall be inhabited by two or more persons or " families, the same shall nevertheless be subject to and shall " in like manner be charged with the same duties as if such " house or tenement was inhabited by one person or family only." Now the use of the word " tenement " in the latter part of what I have read means " the house," because what the Legislature are speaking of is the house. The " house " is to be let, " and the " landlord or owner shall be deemed the occupier of such dwell- " ing-house, and shall be charged with such duties." Then there is a provision that if the landlord is not within the district of the collector, or does not pay, the occupier shall be liable. The first question to decide is, what is the meaning of the words " let in different stories, tenements, or landings." Now, one can give a different meaning to each of those words. A story of a house is one thing. A " tenement " means a separate house. Its ordinary meaning is clear ; but, in order to avoid any doubt, I have sent for an old edition of Tomline's Dictionary, and I find it so stated there. " Tenement signifies " properly a house or homestall, but more largely it comprehends " not only houses but all corporeal inheritances which are holden " of another, and all inheritances issuing out of or exercised with " the same." Therefore we have the primary and the secondary meaning of the word. It is obvious that its meaning in this section and in this rule cannot be the secondary meaning ; it must be the first. Therefore the word "tenement" is used as what is in law a house, although it is at the same time part of a house. It may be both;—an illustration of which is given in the well-known case relating to chambers in the Temple, in the time of Charles II., where a tenement was held in law to be a house, although in fact it was a set of chambers in a house in the Temple. Well, that being so, we have a distinct meaning for these words in the rule. I understand the word "tenement" in this collocation to mean a legal house as distinguished from an ordinary house. We may have a legal house divided into two or three stories, or it may be only a part of a storey. Then a landing is a different thing. A landing is generally only a portion of a storey, or it may not be a portion of a storey at all, but it may be a landing between two stories, generally called by builders a half-landing. Therefore we have words that are quite distinct, and I think there can be no doubt as to the meaning to be attached to them. Then, that being so, we get an Act of Parliament following the decision in the case of the Attorney-General *v.* The Mutual Tontine Westminster Chambers Association (*q*). · That decision was this, that although a large house was divided into a number of little houses, the large house was liable to the tax quite irrespective of the small houses which it contained. Then an Act is passed which, it is alleged by the Crown, and I think rightly alleged, was to get rid of the hardship caused by that decision, because as these were separate legal houses, let separately, held at separate rents, they were within the principle of the exemption by which houses occupied for business purposes were excused from taxation. If it was intended to go further, and to say that every part of a house, although not a separate house or a separate tenement in law, should have a separate taxation, one does not see on what principle the owner of a house who occupied the lower part for business purposes, and the upper part as a residence, should not be exempted to the extent to which the house was occupied for business purposes. It would be a most singular result of legislation if the owners of two adjoining houses who chose to cross tenancies,—that is to say, if A occupied the lower part of B's house, and B occupied the lower part of A's house,—should be exempt from taxation as regards the lower part of these houses. I cannot understand that. Again, having before one the 6th Rule of the Schedule to the Act of the 48th George 3rd, one cannot help noticing that the words stories, lodgings, or landings, are not repeated. A few lines from the commencement of the Rule, the word "tenements" only is used ; the word "tenements" having by its collocation in that Rule a definite meaning. Now what are the words of the section on which this question arises ? " Where " any house being one property shall be divided into and let " in different tenements, and any of such tenements are " occupied solely for the purposes of any trade or business,

YORKSHIRE FIRE AND LIFE INSURANCE CO. *v.* CLAYTON (SURVEYOR OF TAXES).

YORKSHIRE
FIRE AND
LIFE INSUR-
ANCE CO. *v.*
CLAYTON
(SURVEYOR
OF TAXES).

" or of any profession or calling by which the occupier seeks a
" livelihood or profit, or are unoccupied, the person chargeable
" as the occupier of the house " (it is not the actual occupier)
" may give notice in writing to the surveyor of taxes," and then
the tax shall be remitted on the parts so occupied. Now it
appears to me that the argument of the Appellants entirely
throws aside the word " divided," because the argument of the
Appellants is this,—the moment you get separate tenements,
that is to say, separate holdings, from that moment you get a
tenancy which divides the houses into tenements, and thereby
creates the state of things pointed out in the section. But the
same result would follow if you left out the word " divide."
Although I agree it is not always possible to give a meaning to
words used in an Act of Parliament, of course as a general rule
when we find words like this it is right to give the supposed
meaning to the words, and not to treat them as surplusage, if
such a meaning can be fairly given to them. Now a meaning
can be fairly given to them if you read the word " tenement " to
be not that which is held in tenure, but that which is a house,
that is, that which in law is a house ; and if you so read it, the
whole enactment becomes perfectly intelligible. It means this :—
A new state of things has arisen. Formerly houses were built
each on one piece of ground, each house occupying a separate
site. In modern times a practice has grown up of putting
separate houses one above the other, so that they are all super-
imposed upon the same site or piece of ground. They are com-
monly called houses built in separate flats or in separate stories ;
but for all legal purposes, and for all ordinary usage purposes,
they are separate houses. Each house has a separate door, is
separately let, is separately occupied, and has no connection or
relation with those above it or below it, except deriving support
from the house instead of from the ground below. Now, if that
be so, the Legislature might well say a house so situate should
enjoy the same advantages as a house which stood by itself on a
piece of ground, and did not rest upon any substructure. Then
it is all intelligible. The Legislature have said, " We will
" extend the same class of taxation to this new sort of house as
" applied to the old houses." It existed in the Inns of Court, but
that was provided for separately. It did not exist in the case of
houses built in flats, as they had not come into common use,
and the Legislature therefore said, " Now we find this sort of
" houses getting into common use we will extend the same class
" of taxation to that sort of house as we extended to the old
" houses." It appears to me that that is the fair meaning of
the section, and it gives a meaning not only to every word, but
fairly carries out the object of the Legislature ; which, it appears
to me, we should entirely frustrate if we gave the enlarged
meaning that is suggested on the part of the Appellants. For
these reasons I think the decision of the Court below was right,
and ought to be affirmed.

Lord Justice Brett.—The right mode of reading the first part of this section, which is the one we have to construe, seems to me beyond doubt. It is to be read as if it was thus written: "Where any house being one property shall be divided into "different tenements, and let in different tenements," and the other stipulations are fulfilled, then the result shall take place. There are two words used which to my mind are used in somewhat different senses. The section is, "where any house "shall be divided into different tenements :" it is not, "where "any house shall be divided into different houses." And the first thing one has to think of is, why was that distinction made, and what is the meaning of the first word "house," and what is the meaning of the second word "tenement." The first word "house" must mean a house which shall be divided—divided into different tenements. Then I think that the word "tenements" there was used in order to comprise several different kinds of things into which a house may be divided. "House" in the first part does not mean "dwelling-house." That is obvious. If the Legislature had put in the second part of the sentence "houses" instead of "tenements," it might have been said it would not apply to those things to which I think it would apply, that is, to shops or offices or warehouses. It might have been said those are not houses, they are known in ordinary parlance by different names, and therefore the word "tenement" was intended to comprise all of those things into which a house that can be divided may be divided. What we have first then to construe is "shall be divided into different tenements," that is, into different houses, or different offices, or different shops, or different warehouses. It seems to me that the meaning of that is that the house may be so structurally arranged that it may be used or actually occupied, as people in ordinary parlance would say, as a man's own house, or own office, or own shop, or own warehouse ; that is to say, that the tenement which is spoken of in the second part of the sentence is a part of the house so structurally arranged that it may be used or actually occupied, as people in ordinary parlance would say, as a man's own house, or his own shop, or his own office, or his own warehouse. That, I take it, is the meaning of "divided into "different tenements." It is not sufficient to fulfil this statute to say that it is divided into such different tenements, it must also be let in such different tenements. Therefore you must have a house composed of these different tenements. But it is not enough to say, it is let in different tenements ; it must also be divided into different tenements. It might have been difficult to come to this conclusion if one did not know what the state of the law was as to the taxation of houses at the time of this Act of Parliament was passed ; but it is an ordinary well-known rule or canon of construction that you have a right, in order to construe an Act of Parliament to take into account the state of the law and the state of judicial decisions at the time the Act of Parliament was passed. We find that there had been decisions that such divisions of buildings or houses

YORKSHIRE
FIRE AND
LIFE INSUR-
ANCE CO. v.
CLAYTON
(SURVEYOR
OF TAXES).

YORKSHIRE
FIRE AND
LIFE INSUR-
ANCE CO. *v.*
CLAYTON
(SURVEYOR
OF TAXES).

as have been spoken of,—namely into chambers, such as in the Temple, or into different flats, as in Victoria Street, or by other modes of dividing houses (not necessarily always vertical divisions, there might be horizontal divisions which anybody would say divided the house structurally so that it might be occupied by different people, each part of it as their own house, or as their own office, their own shop, or their own warehouse),—did not free the house from liability to be rated as an entire house. We find that there had been many decisions, certainly in the Revising Courts and in the Common Pleas, as to such matters as chambers. We find that there had been that decision in what has been called the Tontine case, to the accuracy of which decision I have nothing to say, because it has been decided by an authority which here we cannot dispute, to the accuracy of which therefore I bow with submission. We find that it had been held that such a building as those in Victoria Street was one house, and that although by structure each flat of it could be used as a separate house, and although by the letting each part of it was used and let as a separate house, yet nevertheless for the purpose of the inhabited house duty the whole was to be considered as one house, although for the purpose of registration and the franchise each of the flats might have been held to be a separate house. And I say, bowing with submission to that judicial decision, and looking at it, and applying the words of this section to that state of the law and decisions, it seems to me clear that this section was passed in order to meet such a case as that, and cases similar to that, and to say that, notwithstanding that decision, yet in such cases, and in such houses the law so declared should be altered, and that in such houses, if the other parts of this section were fulfilled, there should be relief from the tax. The words therefore are entirely fulfilled when we bear in mind that the section was passed to meet such a case. If you try, as has been tried here, to carry it beyond such a case, you are immediately driven, as has been shown, to strike out a part of this section, namely, to strike out the words "divided into." That is contrary to the rule of construction unless you are obliged to do it. You are not, when you come to consider the state of the law and the decisions, obliged to do it here; therefore you are obliged to give a meaning to those words, and that meaning is satisfied by what I have enunciated. Therefore in any case such as the flats in Victoria Street this section applies. It may apply to other things, but, as I said before, it is not necessary now to decide in what other cases it would apply. The question is, whether it applies to the case now before us.

Now the case before us is the case of a house which, although at the beginning of the argument it was suggested that it was different from an ordinary house, nobody now, I think, can fairly say it is at all different in structure and arrangement from any ordinary house; and therefore, if the Act of Parliament applies to this house, it must apply to every house; and if it is to be applied to this house, you must strike out the words "divided into," and give no meaning to them. In this case it seems to me clear that this house is beyond the dividing line, and far beyond it. It is one, therefore, to which this section does not apply, and in respect to which, therefore, however let, there can be no exemption, because this house has not been divided.

Lord Justice Cotton.—The first question one has to consider is, whether these words, "where any house shall be divided into and let in different tenements," require that there should be some physical division of the house, so as to make separate portions of it, to be treated as separate tenements, or whether a separate letting and a separate holding is sufficient to satisfy the words of the Act. To hold that "shall be divided into and let in different tenements" means "let" simply, would be entirely altering the words of this section, and it would be departing in a very gross way from the rule of construction, that if there is an ordinary meaning which can be given to words, that meaning shall be given to them. I think, therefore, one cannot say that these words are satisfied where there is a letting of a house not having a structural division into separate holdings. If it had been the intention of the Legislature to cover such a case as that, it would have been easy to have said, "Where a house being one property shall be let in separate portions." But that is not what the section says. Now, what is the meaning of "shall be divided into different tenements"? Of course one need not deal with all possible cases that may arise, but one must have before one what there is here. Here there is no division of the house except that which exists in all houses, of different floors and separate rooms. And really the argument went to this, that wherever a house had rooms, which of course could be let separately, there the words "shall be divided into different tenements" would apply to it. If that had been the intention, it would have been easy so to have framed the clause. I think, without going more fully into the case, "shall be divided into different tenements" must mean shall be so constructed as to have various portions used for the purposes of separate occupation, for the purposes of trade, or for professional purposes. Here there is not that division in the structure of the house, and therefore, in my opinion, this house is not within the exception in the Act of Parliament.

Appeal dismissed with costs.

PART XXIV

No. 57.—COURT OF EXCHEQUER, SCOTLAND.—SECOND
DIVISION.

July 6, November 4 and 18, 1880.

CALEDONIAN RAILWAY COMPANY v. BANKS (Surveyor
of Taxes).

Income Tax.—Wear and tear of plant and machinery. *Com-*
missioners refused to grant an allowance under section 12, 41 Vict.
cap. 15., on the ground that there was no diminution of value within
the meaning of the section, the sums allowed in respect of repairs and
renewals having been sufficient to meet the loss by wear and tear.
They also refused to grant any allowance under that section for
depreciation of new plant which had not yet been in need of repair.
Decision of the Commissioners was confirmed. Per LORD GIFFORD.
The Company cannot get deduction for deterioration twice over,
first by deducting the actual expense of repair and renewal, and
then by deducting an additional estimate for the same thing.
Nor will it do, as the Railway Company urge, to make a distinction between old and new plant, and to deal with the old plant in
one way and with the new in another. I think the same principle
must be applied to both.

CALEDONIAN
RAILWAY
COMPANY v.
BANKS.

At a meeting of the Special Commissioners, held at Glasgow on
the 26th February, 1880, for the purpose of hearing appeals
under the Income Tax Acts for the year ending on the
5th April, 1880, Mr. George Galbraith, accountant, and
Mr. George Jackson attended on behalf of the Caledonian
Railway Company to appeal against an assessment of
1,323,304*l.* in respect of the profits of the concern carried
on by the Company.

(2.) The Special Commissioners in estimating the amount of
assessable profits for 1879-80, based their charge on the profits
of the preceding year, as shown by the Company's printed
accounts for the two half-years ended 31st July, 1878, and 31st
January, 1879.

(3.) The Special Commissioners, on reference to these accounts,
found charged against capital the sum expended on working
stock up to the 31st January, 1878, to be 4,806,012*l.*, and that
during the half-year ending 31st July, 1878, there was expended
on working stock 86,355*l.*, making the sum expended up to the
31st July, 1878, 4,892,367*l.* on working stock.

year, which only amounted to 2¼ per cent. of the cost, and that this arose from the fact of the large amount of new plant having been *added* (not replaced), which new plant, though actually depreciating at the rate of 4½ per cent. per annum, required little or no repair during the first 5¼ years of its existence. The whole plant is kept up to the standard of its being worth 75 per cent. of its original cost, but until the new plant has depreciated to the extent of 25 per cent. (that is during the first 5¼ years of its life) it requires no substantial repairs. The cost of *additional* new plant during the 5¼ years prior to 31st January, 1879, was 1,096,534*l*. and 4½ per cent. of that sum amounts to 49,344*l*.

(15.) The Company contended that they were entitled to the deduction claimed under the 12th section of the Customs and Inland Revenue Act of 1878, it representing the diminished value by reason of wear and tear during the year.

(16.) It is stated that the assessor appointed by Her Majesty under the Valuation of Lands (Scotland) Act, 1854, in ascertaining the yearly value of railways, takes the gross revenue from all sources. From that he deducts the working expenses and one half of the cost incurred for maintenance of way (the latter allowed under section 3 of 30 & 31 Vict. c. 80). From the net revenue thus arrived at a further deduction of 25 per cent. of the present value of the plant is made. The present value is assumed to be 75 per cent. of its original cost; and the 25 per cent. of deduction consists of 5 per cent. of interest on the money invested in the plant, 5 per cent. for the deterioration of the plant, 12 per cent. for tenants' profits, and 3 per cent. to cover accidents and incidents. After these are deducted the residue represents the yearly value of the heritable subject. In calculating the interest on the capital invested in the plant, the railway companies claimed that the interest should be calculated on the original or actual cost, but the assessor maintained that the plant was liable to deterioration, and that the interest should be calculated on its present or diminished value, which he estimated at 75 per cent. of its original cost, and this view was confirmed on appeal by the Lord Ordinary. The annual value of the appellants' undertaking as fixed by the assessor under the Act for the year ending 31st January, 1879, was 654,785*l*.

(17.) The Company do not recognise any distinction in principle between the plant employed in earning revenue, which is taken as the basis of the annual value of the undertaking, and the same plant employed in earning the profits as carriers, for the purpose of assessment under the Income Tax Acts.

(18.) The Special Commissioners, having duly considered the Company's claim, confirmed the assessment in the sum of 1,323,304*l*.

(19.) They considered that, in arriving at the amount on which the assessment was to be made, by reference to the Company's printed half-yearly accounts for the year preceding, the full sums stated in the accounts for the two half years ended 31st July, 1878, and 31st January, 1879, to have been expended in the maintenance, repair, renewal, and reconstruction of the Company's machinery and plant had been admitted as deductions therefrom, as well as the sum of 20,837*l.* set aside from revenue on account of plant not yet renewed, carried to the credit of the rolling stock renewal fund, for value of plant not replaced at 31st January, 1879. CALEDONIAN RAILWAY COMPANY *v.* BANKS.

(20.) That the whole of the sums stated to have been thus expended year by year in maintenance, repair, and renewals have been duly allowed as deductions in estimating the profits liable to be assessed from year to year, as well as the full sum at the credit of the rolling stock renewal fund, and will hereafter continue to be yearly allowed in estimating the assessable profits.

(21.) That inasmuch as any diminution in value by reason of wear and tear during the year upon which the assessment was founded has been met by the allowances before detailed, it is not just or reasonable that any further deduction should be allowed by reference to the provisions contained in section 12 of the Customs and Inland Revenue Act, 1878.

The assessments of railways are, according to the terms of No. III. Schedule A. of the Act 5 & 6 Vict. cap. 35, by computation of the profits of the preceding year.

It is the diminished value by reason of wear and tear for the year to which section 12 of the Customs and Inland Revenue Act, 1878, relates. The year referred to in that section, so far as respects a concern assessable on the profits of the preceding year must be the preceding year, and the comparison, in order to arrive at the diminished value of the machinery and plant, is between the value thereof in that year and the value in the year before it.

(22.) That the statement in the Railway Company's accounts of the value of the machinery and plant must be held as the Company's estimate of the actual value of such as a going concern; that the effect of the allowance by the Commissioners for repairs and renewals is to keep up the value to the same amount, and this being so, diminished value by reason of wear and tear does not exist. If a per-centage on the value were to be allowed as a deduction from the profits and gains representing the diminished value by reason of wear and tear of the machinery and plant, then the deduction for repairs and renewals should not be allowed. To allow deduction of the cost of renewals and repairs as in this case and also a per-centage for diminished value by reason of wear and tear would be to allow twice deduction for the same thing.

Section 12 of the Customs and Inland Revenue Act, 1878, allows such deduction as the Commissioners shall think just and reasonable as representing the diminished value, by reason of wear and tear during the year, of any machinery or plant used for the purposes of the concern. Diminished value would seem to be fact, and the judgment of what is a just and reasonable deduction in respect of it is committed to the Commissioners.

CALEDONIAN
RAILWAY
COMPANY &
BANKS.
——

(23.) Mr. Galbraith, on behalf of the Company, expressed his
dissatisfaction with the decision of the Special Commissioners,
and by letter of the 8th March, 1880, the Company demanded a
case for the opinion of the Exchequer Court of Scotland, under
the provisions of the Customs and Inland Revenue Act, 1874,
which we hereby state and sign accordingly.

R. M. LYNCH,   }   Special
D. O'CONNELL, } Commissioners.

Somerset House, London.
3rd June, 1880.

6 July 1880.   *Johnstone*, for the Appellants (the Railway Company).—The
first claim is to have a deduction allowed for deterioration of the
whole of the machinery and plant belonging to the Company.
The Act of 1878 (41 Vict. c. 15. s. 12) expressly sanctions such
an allowance. It is impossible to keep the value of the plant up
to cost price. The annual expenditure in repairs and renewals
only keeps it up to 75 per cent. of cost price, therefore 25 per
cent. has been consumed. The actual expense of repairs and
renewals was allowed by the Act 5 & 6 Vict. c. 35. I say the
Act of 1878 gives something in addition, and it is described as
something for depreciation during the year.

The alternative claim for an allowance at 4½ per cent. on the
cost of additional new plant added during the last 5½ years.
When new engines are added, not replacements, when the concern is increased by a new branch railway being opened and
additional engines being brought in, for the first few years those
engines require little or no repair. The actual capital of those
engines is consumed till it comes down to 75 per cent. While it
is coming down to that standard capital is consumed and worked
out entirely, and therefore we are entitled to that in addition to
what is required to keep the plant generally up to 75 per cent.

Balfour (S.G.), for the Respondents.—The Company's claim
cannot prevail unless it can be shown that there was diminished
value by reason of wear and tear during the year. An allowance
in respect of the fall of the whole plant from 100 per cent. to 75
per cent. is simply out of the question, because that fall took
place before last year. The amount of the deduction for depreciation is left to the judgment of the Commissioners, and unless
it can be shown that they have gone against some principle, the
amount of the deduction is a matter the Court cannot go into.
In a case where the plant is kept up by repairs and renewals to
the condition in which it was at the beginning of the year there
can be no room for deduction.

The Company is not entitled to the alternative deduction
claimed. Some of the plant is in the first 5½ years of its life,
and is therefore worth more than the average of 75 per cent.
but other plant is in the last 5½ years of its life, and worth less
than the average. The whole of the plant, new as well as old,
is taken into account in estimating the average.

Kinnear, for the Appellants.—Actual expenditure upon repairs and renewals does not represent the whole depreciation in value of machinery and plant. If it did, the actual value of a going company which had been some years in existence would equal its prime cost. The allowance granted by the Commissioners in this case is nothing but the money actually expended upon repairs and renewals, and a sum of 20,000*l.* not yet actually expended, but set aside to meet renewals which have become necessary. This would all have fallen under the original Act. Did then the Act of 1878 mean to give nothing at all?

Balfour (S.G.).—It depends on the state of the fact in each particular case whether the Act 41 Vict. comes into play or not. If plant is depreciating each year without being restored or renewed there is necessity and room for the Act, but if there has been repair and renewal of corresponding amount to the depreciation during the year the Act has no place, because the depreciation has been made up already.

In this case the Commissioners find as a matter of fact that there is no diminished value which has not been met by the sums allowed for repairs and renewals.

Cur. adv. vult.

After further hearing of counsel—

Lord Justice Clerk.—This is a case stated by the Special Commissioners of Income Tax in a question as to the assessment for income tax of the Caledonian Railway. The Commissioners having confirmed the assessment, and the Caledonian Railway Company having demanded a case, the case now before your Lordships has been prepared and presented for that purpose. The kind of question that we have to decide in regard to the mode in which the income derived from carrying on a trading concern like the Caledonian Railway Company is to be estimated is one of course with which we are not generally familiar, and that fact has rendered the discussion and the consideration of it somewhat difficult.

The case stated by the Special Commissioners for our opinion, divested of arithmetical details, which do not affect the matter, raises a very simple issue. The object of the calculations explained in the case is to exhibit the process by which the amount of assessable income realised by the Caledonian Railway Company for the year 1879-80 has been ascertained. The principle which underlies the process is of course to ascertain the amount of clear profit realised by this commercial concern within the year, and to determine this (which really is at the very root of the matter) all the outgoings which are necessary to attain the sum of gross profit must of course be deducted from that sum before the clear or assessable value of the income for the year can be arrived at. The material appliances used by this

CALEDONIAN RAILWAY COMPANY *v.* BANKS.

18 Nov. 1880.

trading company in order to create net incomes or profits, which are the subjects of the tax, are (apart from the general expenses of management), first, permanent way, stations, and other fixed property, forming what is popularly called the line of railway; and, secondly, the plant or rolling stock, consisting of locomotive engines, carriages, waggons, implement, and the like. The present case relates entirely to the mode of estimating the amount which ought year by year to be deducted from gross profits as representing the outlay on plant necessary to enable the Company as a trading concern to realise them. This was originally regulated by Schedule D. of the Income Tax Act of 1842, which provided what deductions were, and what were not, to be allowed in the case of expenditure on plant. The clause of the statute is printed, and I need not read it at length. It was contained in the original Income Tax Act of 1842, and provides in the 3rd sub-section that in estimating the balance of profits and gains chargeable under Schedule D., or for the purpose of assessing the duty thereon, "no sum shall be set against "or deducted from, or allowed to be set against or deducted "from, such profits or gains, on account of any sum expended "for repairs of premises, &c., ... nor for any sum ex-"pended for the supply or repairs or alterations of any imple-"ments, utensils, or articles employed for the purpose of such "trade . . . . beyond the sum usually expended for such "purposes according to an average of three years preceding the "year in which such assessment shall be made." That sub-stantially is the principle upon which from 1842 down to 1878 this calculation was made.

This statement contained in the case exhibits in some detail the process by which the Commissioners of Income Tax endeavoured to apply practically the statutory provisions. Railway profits cannot be realised without the constant use of the rolling stock, and as this use necessarily deteriorates the plant and diminishes its value as a means of producing profit it requires repair and renewal. The Commissioners have allowed deductions for repairs and renewal. The only complaint now made by the Caledonian Railway Company to which their claim is restricted relates to additional plant said to have been furnished during the five years prior to January, 1879, and is founded on the provisions of the 12th section of the Income Tax Act of 1878. What they now demand is that they shall be allowed the value of what they allege to be the wear and tear upon additional plant furnished by the Railway Company for the five years prior to the year 1879. That, they say, has not been allowed for by an allowance for repairs or renewals, because there have been no repairs or renewals, but they say the plant is older than it was, and therefore its value must be depreciated by the use for the five years; and they found that upon the 12th clause of the statute of 1878—the 41st of the Queen, c. 15—which runs thus—"Notwithstanding any provision to the contrary contained in "any Act relating to income tax, the Commissioners for General "or Special Purposes shall, in assessing the profits or gains of

" any trade, manufacture, adventure, or concern in the nature
" of trade chargeable under Schedule D., or the profits of any
" concern chargeable by reference to the rules of that schedule
" allow such deduction as they may think just and reasonable as
" representing the diminished value by reason of wear and tear
" during the year of any machinery or plant used for the purposes
" of the concern, and belonging to the person or company by
" whom the concern is carried on; and for the purposes of this
" provision, where machinery or plant is let to the person or
" company by whom the concern is carried on upon such terms
" that the person or company is bound to maintain the machinery
" or plant and deliver over the same in good condition at the
" end of the term of the lease, such machinery or plant shall be
" deemed to belong to such person or company."

Unquestionably this was a clause intended to alter and to
extend in favour of the person or company assessed the provisions of the Act of 1842, and of Schedule D. thereto annexed.
About that there can be no doubt at all, because it allows and
enjoins the Commissioners to make a deduction which certainly
was not allowed by the original Income Tax Act. It is, however, to be such a deduction as they may think just and reasonable, as representing the diminished value by reason of wear and
tear. Now, that being the nature of the claim, which arises
simply in this way, that neither repairs nor renewals of plant
are the foundation for it, but additional plant contributed or
furnished during the five years prior to January, 1879, the question is, whether the Commissioners were bound to make allowances for the wear and tear on that plant? The Railway Company complain that as far as this plant is concerned, while its
value has been diminished by wear and tear during the five
years in question, no allowance has been made on this head
by the Commissioners in terms of the Statute. As a matter of
fact, I take the last statement to be true. The Commissioners
have made no allowance for the diminution of the value of this
plant during the five years in question, while it cannot be disputed that after a period of use the engines and carriages are not
and probably cannot be as valuable a commodity for sale as
they were when new. There are some grounds to which the
Commissioners have appealed as supporting their determination
in the confirmation of the assessment to which I attach no importance at all, and I think it is unfortunate that they are stated
as grounds for judgment—if they are so stated, about which I
have some doubt. The first was, that a sum of 20,000l.. to
which we were referred was an equivalent allowance on this
head; but it seems to me that the sum has no connexion whatever with the question raised in this case. That sum of 20,000l.
was properly made a subject of deduction upon its own merits.
It was a sum withdrawn from profits, and therefore not clear
profits, and set apart to meet a prospective demand for renewal,
and was not therefore an allowance for past wear and tear in
any sense whatever. Neither do I think it could be successfully

contended that this 12th section was sufficiently carried out by the allowance already referred to for renewals, if it appeared as matter of fact that there had been a diminution of value in regard to any part of the plant which these allowances did not cover; for the clause in question certainly meant to go beyond the deductions allowed in the Act of 1842. But I am nevertheless unable under this case to give the Caledonian Railway Company the redress which they ask for. I think the Commissioners were entitled to hold and that their judgment proceeds on that footing, that the value of the additional plant in question was not diminished by wear and tear during the five years in question, and they do so find in express terms in the words of their judgment, and I am not prepared to review or alter their decision on that question of fact. The ground on which the Special Commissioners seem to have proceeded is the alleged and assumed fact that during the first five years of the life of a railway locomotive or carriage it requires no repairs, and is therefore of the same value—that is, capable of earning the same amount of income as when it was new. That manifestly is a principle quite capable of being maintained, and, in my apprehension, it is sound. The view seems to be this—the whole expenditure in repairs and renewal of old plant has been allowed for, and as there is no diminution by wear and tear in the value of new additional plant for the first five years in the sense of producing profit, that is to say, the plant requires no repairs to enable it to produce the same amount of profit that it did at first, then it is clear that from first to last the plant has been in the position that it was at starting, and is capable therefore of producing the same amount of profit by the same outlay, and no more. If the Commissioners assumed that the expression "diminished value" in the 12th section of the Act of 1878 signifies value for the purpose for which it was intended in a going concern, I cannot say they were wrong in so holding. I do not think that the words had any reference to the value of the plant as merchantable or marketable articles, because its capacity to earn income constitutes its sole value to the Railway Company, and is the only quality contemplated under the statutes relating to the taxation of income. I am the more confirmed in this impression by the terms of the second part of the first paragraph of the 12th section, relative to the valuation of plant in the hands of a tenant under an obligation to restore it to the owner in as good condition as it was when he received it. By the terms of this section such plant is to be held to belong to the tenant, and is to be settled with for income tax on precisely the same principles as it would have been if he had been the proprietor, but it is plain enough that if the plant is restored as it was by the tenant under such a contract within the first five years of its existence, assuming that no repairs or renewals are required during that period, his obligation is fulfilled, and he could have no possible interest in the marketable value of an article which he had no power to sell. But even if these things were not so, I must say that, looking to the terms of the 12th section of the Act.

of 1878, I should feel very great difficulty in interfering with the result at which the Commissioners have arrived. They have held, following out the wide discretion vested in them by the statute, that no wear and tear has taken place in this plant for which any allowance would be just and reasonable. I cannot see how we can review that conclusion. If, indeed, we were satisfied that the Commissioners had misread the statute, and had not applied their minds to the question, we might have sent the case back to them for consideration, obviously. But I am satisfied that they have applied their minds very directly to the question, and have come deliberately to the conclusion that the plant had suffered no diminution in value in the sense intended by the statute, but was of as much value to the Company, and was capable of producing with the same outlay the same amount of profit, as it had been at any former period. The plant, it will be observed, was not five and a half years old at the termination of the period.

I am therefore disposed to refuse the appeal, and confirm the judgment of the Commissioners. It may be asked, in this view, what is the real meaning and intendment of this 12th section of the statute? I do not know that I should be able to give a very clear response to that question without more practical knowledge than is disclosed or is to be derived from this case. But I can understand that there may be plant deteriorated after the five years by wear and tear on which no sum has been expended for repairs or renewals within the period of assessment, and probably the Income Tax Commissioners had felt themselves hampered before the passing of the statute by the very stringent words of Schedule D. of the Act of 1848. But that is more speculative than anything else. Meantime, I am not prepared to alter, and therefore I propose that we should confirm, the judgment of the Commissioners.

Lord Gifford.—I concur in the opinion which your Lordship has expressed, and will confine myself to a very few additional or supplementary observations.

This is an appeal against a determination of the Special Commissioners under the Income Tax Acts assessing the profits of the Caledonian Railway Company for the year 1879-80 at the sum of 1,323,304*l.* The appeal to this Court at the Court of Exchequer in Scotland is taken under the 9th and 10th sections of the statute 37 Vict. c. 16., known as the Customs and Inland Revenue Act, 1874. By the 9th section of that Act it is made competent to the railway company or party assessed, " if dis- " satisfied with the determination of the Commissioners, as being " erroneous in point of law, to declare " dissatisfaction therewith, and to require the Commissioners to state and sign a case for the opinion of the Court thereon. It is provided that the case shall set forth " the facts and the determination," and that it shall be transmitted to this Court for decision.

From these provisions it appears that it is only on proper questions of law that there is any appeal to this Court as the Court of Exchequer in Scotland. All review upon questions of fact which are to be ascertained by evidence of any kind is excluded, review being allowed only upon pure and proper questions of law; and, in order that the law and the fact may be kept entirely separate, it is provided that the case to be stated by the Commissioners shall "set forth the facts"—that is, shall specify all the matters of fact upon which the legal determination proceeds—and shall also set forth "the determination"—that is, the decision in law—which the Commissioners have pronounced upon the facts proved or admitted before them; and it is this determination, so far as proceeding upon grounds of law, which alone is the subject of appeal to this Court.

As explained at the bar, the whole legal question really turns upon the legal import and effect of the 12th section of the statute 41 Vict., c. 15, known as "The Customs and Inland Revenue "Act, 1878." This section 12 provides—"Notwithstanding any "provision to the contrary contained in any Act relating to "income tax, the Commissioners for General or Special Pur- "poses shall, in assessing the profits or gains of any trade, manu- "facture, adventure, or concern in the nature of trade, charge- "able under Schedule (D.), or the profits of any concern charge- "able by reference to the rules of that schedule, allow such "deduction as they may think just and reasonable, as represent- "ing the diminished value by reason of wear and tear during the "year of any machinery or plant used for the purposes of the "concern and belonging to the person or company by whom the "concern is carried on." The statute goes on to provide for cases of machinery and plant being let on lease or otherwise, or held under condition of maintenance in good condition, but the substance of the enactment is that in estimating profits deductions shall be given for tear and wear of plant and machinery— that is, an allowance spread over a reasonable number of years, which will enable the trader to keep up his plant, and replace it when it is worn out.

Now, the complaint of the Railway Company is that they have not received allowance or deduction from profits, or have not received sufficient allowance or sufficient deduction from profits for what they call depreciation upon rolling stock and machinery, and they claim as additional deductions from the estimated profits for the year in question either, first, a sum of 185,391l. as the deterioration of their whole plant for the year in question, 1879-80—(no doubt this first claim was given up at the bar, but it is important to keep in view that in the case before us this claim stands on the same footing as the alternative claim, which is alternatively)—second, deduction of a sum of 49,344l. being 4½ per cent. of the cost of additional new plant added during the last five and a half years. The question of law sought to be raised by the Railway Company is, whether they are entitled in point of law to deduction from the assessed amount of their income and profits of one or other of the above sums in respect CALEDONIAN
RAILWAY
COMPANY v.
BANKS. (I take the words of the Act) "of the diminished value by reason " of wear and tear during the year of their machinery or plant." The statute requires that the diminished value shall be occasioned by reason of wear and tear, and it must be wear and tear " during the year " in question.

Now, the first point to observe is that this special case does not state what the diminished value of the plant is by reason of wear and tear during the year in question. This is a question of fact, and was a question for the Commissioners, and not for this Court, and so, even if the Railway Company are entitled in law to an estimated deduction for wear and tear there are no materials before the Court for fixing such deduction, and the reason of this is obvious. The Special Commissioners, at the instance of the Railway Company, or at least with their consent, have fixed the deduction for wear and tear on a different principle altogether from that contemplated in the Act of 1878. Instead of attempting to fix "diminished value by reason of wear and " tear during the year," they have allowed the Company deduction of the actual sums expended by them for repairs and renewals, amounting to 253,389*l.*, and, as it is stated and certified by the Railway Company themselves that by the expenditure of this sum the whole plant has been maintained in good working order and repair this sum may fairly be taken as making up the whole deterioration which the wear and tear of the year has occasioned. The view taken by both parties seems to me to have been fair and reasonable. Instead of the Commissioners guessing at probable deterioration, by taking per-centages or round sums, which is necessarily a rough mode of getting at the result, they have taken the Company's own plan of calculation, namely, taking the actual sums expended in repairing and renewing the plant, and this although the renewed plant was better and more expensive than that which was worn out. This is perfectly fair, and the plan over a series of years will be perfectly equitable. The Caledonian Railway is a continuing Company with perpetual duration, and if it receives deductions over a series of years for the actual expense of repairs and renewals, so as to keep up its plant in undiminished efficiency this will be better than any mere guess or estimate which the Commissioner could make. The Railway Company will get deduction for their actual expenditure, instead of a mere estimate of what their expenditure would probably be. At all events this is the view upon which the assessment has been made, and there are no materials for throwing this assessment aside and making it up anew upon another principle. The Railway Company themselves do not complain of this. They accept—indeed it appeared from the argument that they asked—deduction of the whole cost of repairing and renewing their plant, and this has been allowed, and they decline to go back upon this, but they ask an additional deduction on a different principle altogether, and they claim both deductions cumulatively.

It seems to me quite clear, as the Commissioners observe, that the Railway Company cannot get deduction for deterioration twice over—first, by deducting the actual expenses of repair and renewal, and then by deducting an additional estimate sum for the same thing. Nor will it do, as the Railway Company urge, to make a distinction between old and new plant, and to deal with the old plant in one way and with the new in another. I think the same principle must be applied to both.

Still further, the assessment has been made in entire accordance with the Railway Company's own accounts. In striking their annual profits so as to fix the sum divisible as dividend, the Railway Company have gone upon actual expenditure, and not upon a mere estimate of probable wear and tear. I see no reason why the income tax to Government should not be fixed upon the same principle as that which determines the dividend to the proprietors, and prima facie it seems very anomalous that the Railway Company implies the admission that, for the year in realised a certain sum of profit, which they propose to divide as dividend, and should yet maintain, as in a question of taxation, that their real profit is a much less sum. The contention of the Railway Company implies the admission that for the year in question, they are paying dividend to some extent out of capital. Surely no complaint can be made if the Railway Company pay income tax only upon what they themselves divide as dividend or net profit, and upon which they get back or retain from their shareholders precisely the income tax which they have paid.

At all events, I am perfectly clear that this case does not contain the materials necessary to enable the Court to interfere with the determination of the Commissioners. For example, there is no finding in point of fact of what the average life of the plant is, but a mere statement by the Railway Company that it was about 22 years, but if a slump or estimated deterioration is to be taken, founded upon the life of the plant, this life of the plant must be found as a matter of fact by the Commissioners. Indeed the Commissioners must themselves, in the case supposed, fix in figures the deduction for wear and tear for the year. This they have not done, and they were never asked to do so. Without such finding the Court cannot give effect to the claim.

The statute seems to regard deterioration from wear and tear during the year as the true criterion, and this answers another objection of the Railway Company, that upon new or added plant there is little deterioration during the first five and a half years of its existence. If this be so, then the statute only allows little deduction. It is actual deterioration only that is to be taken into account.

On the whole, I am for affirming the determination of the Commissioners. If the Railway Company want the assessment made upon a different principle—that is, upon estimated wear and tear, and not upon actual wear and tear—they must be entitled to insist on this last. Counsel at the bar stated that they did not seek to open up the assessment altogether, but only CALEDONIAN RAILWAY COMPANY v. BANKS claimed an additional deduction. If the principle of the statute of 1878 is sought to be applied I think the whole assessment must be reviewed, and the question raised in a different form. I would humbly suggest for the consideration of the Railway Company, however, whether the actual expenditure will not give a more equitable result than any mere estimate could, especially as the actual cost is the criterion adopted in their own accounts.

Lord Young concurred.

The Court dismissed the appeal.

No. 58.—IN THE COURT OF APPEAL.

May 9 and 10, 1881.

GILBERTSON and others *v.* FERGUSSON (Surveyor of Taxes).

Income Tax. Foreign dividends. The dividends of a foreign bank are payable either at its London agency or abroad, at the option of the Shareholder. The agency receives no remittance from abroad to pay the dividends claimed in London, because it holds in its hands the agency profits, and these are sufficient for the purpose.

Held, *that the London paid dividends are entrusted to the agency for payment within the meaning of section 10, 16 & 17 Vict. c. 34.; but in assessing the dividends an allowance should be granted in respect of that portion which arises from the previously taxed profits of the English agency.*

GILBERTSON *v.* FERGUSSON.

CASE.

Stated for the opinion of the Court by the Commissioners for the Special Purposes of the Income Tax Acts under the Act 37 & 38 Vict. c. 16. as to Income Tax assessed under Schedule D.

1. The question for the opinion of the Court is whether any portion of the profits made out of the United Kingdom by a Turkish Corporation carrying on business in Constantinople, London, and elsewhere, under the name of the Imperial Ottoman

GILBERTSON *v.* FERGUSSON.

Bank, and not actually remitted to the United Kingdom, is, as profits, or as forming part of dividends paid in the United Kingdom, the subject of assessment to income tax under Schedule D. of the Act 16 & 17 Vict. c. 34. in the circumstances herein-after appearing, and, if any, then whether either of the assessments for the year 1874–75, which have been made by the Commissioners for Special Purposes on the appellant has been made upon the right principle or upon what principle an assessment should have been made.

2. The Commissioners for Special Purposes conceive that it is convenient and advisable to set forth in the first instance the enactments, or the substance of the enactments, which have an especial bearing upon the question.

3. By the Act 16 & 17 Vict. c. 34 certain duties are granted to Her Majesty upon profits arising from property, professions, trades and offices (*inter alia*), section 2.

SCHEDULE D.

For, and in respect of the annual profits or gains arising or accruing to any person residing within the United Kingdom, from any profession, trade, employment, or vocation, whether the same shall respectively be carried on in the United Kingdom or elsewhere.

And for and in respect of the annual profits or gains arising or accruing to any person whatever, whether a subject of Her Majesty or not, although not resident in the United Kingdom, from any profession, trade, employment, or vocation exercised within the United Kingdom.

[*Paragraphs 4 to 18 of the case cite the following provisions of the Income Tax Acts :—16 & 17 Vict. c. 34. s. 5; 5 & 6 Vict. c. 35. ss. 23, 40, 41, 44, 51, 53, 54, 100 (Schedule D.), Rules 1 and 2 of the first case, and No. 3 of the rules apply to the first and second cases, 111, 113, 118, and nine following sections, 131, 132, and 192.*]

19. By the Act 5 & 6 Vict. c. 80. s. 2 all persons entrusted with the payment of annuities or any dividends or shares of annuities payable out of the revenue of any foreign state to any persons, corporations, companies, or societies in Great Britain, or acting therein as agents or in any other character, shall without further notice or demand thereof, deliver or cause to be delivered into the head office for stamps and taxes in England an account in writing. containing the names and residences, and a description of the annuities, dividends, and shares entrusted to them for payment, within one calendar month after the same shall have been required by public notice in the "London Gazette," and shall also on demand by the inspector authorised for that purpose by the Commissioners of Stamps and Taxes deliver or cause to be delivered to him for the use of the said Commissioners for Special Purposes true and perfect accounts of the amount of

GILBERTSON
v.
FERGUSSON.

the annuities, dividends, and shares payable by them respectively, and the said Commissioners for Special Purposes shall make an assessment thereon, giving notice of the amount of such assessment to the respective persons intrusted with such payments, who shall respectively pay the duty on the said annuities, dividends, and shares on behalf of the persons, corporations, and companies entitled unto the same out of the moneys in their hands.

20. By the Act 16 & 17 Vict. c. 34. s. 10 the provisions of the last-mentioned Act for the assessing and charging the duties on dividends and shares of annuities payable out of the revenue of any foreign State shall be extended to the assessing and charging of the duties by the now stating Act, granted as well on such dividends and shares of annuities as aforesaid as on all interest, dividends, or other annual payments payable out of or in respect of the stocks, funds, or shares of any foreign company, society, adventure, or concern, or in respect of any securities given by or on account of any such company, society, adventures, or concern, and which said interest, dividends, or annual payments have been or shall be intrusted · to any person in the United Kingdom for payment to any persons, corporations, companies, or societies in the United Kingdom, and all persons intrusted with the payment of any such interest, dividends, or other annual payments as aforesaid in the United Kingdom, or acting therein as agents, or in any other character, shall do and perform all such acts, matters, and things in order to the assessing and charging and paying of the said duties on all such interest, dividends, and other annual payments as aforesaid, as by the said Act of 5 & 6 Vict. c. 80. persons intrusted with the payment of annuities of any dividends or shares of annuities are required to do and perform.

21. By a series of subsequent Acts the duties of income tax granted by the Act 16 & 17 Vict. c. 34. have been continued at various rates until the present time. The Act imposing the duty for the year ending on the 5th April, 1875, was the Customs and Inland Revenue Act, 1874 (37 & 38 Vict. c. 16.).

22. Towards the close of the year 1862 the Ottoman Bank of London, which was a banking Company established in London, and carrying on business there with a branch at Constantinople, arranged to transfer its business to the Imperial Ottoman Bank, which was a Turkish corporation incorporated according to the laws of Turkey by a firman of the Sultan.

23. The transfer of the business was completed in the beginning of the year 1863 by the issue of shares in the capital of the Imperial Ottoman Bank to the amount of 250,000l. to the shareholders of the Ottoman Bank of London, and the business in London of the Imperial Ottoman Bank as bankers was then commenced in London under the management of the London members of the committee, herein-after referred to, in the premises theretofore occupied by the Ottoman Bank of London; the remainder of the capital was subscribed in Constantinople,

Paris, London, and other places. Immediately on the formation of the Imperial Ottoman Bank preparations were made to commence business in Constantinople, and it actually commenced business there on the 1st June, 1863.

24. The affairs of the Imperial Ottoman Bank (herein-after called the bank) were then and until the 17th February, 1875, continued to be regulated by a concession from the Government of Turkey and certain statutes. A new concession was granted, and new statutes were passed on the last-mentioned day, but the position of the bank, so far as the question in this case is concerned, is not thereby affected. A translation of the original concession and statutes will be found in the Appendix to this case.

25. By the original concession the bank is a State bank for the Ottoman Empire, and is established subject to the general laws of the Empire, with its seat fixed at Constantinople, and power to establish branches and agencies at other places, and it is provided that the bank shall be administered at Constantinople by a board of two or three members, and a council of administrators of three members, both to be named by a committee, chosen by the London and Paris founders, and this committee is to have power in conformity with the statutes to guide, control, and superintend the operations of the bank.

26. By the statutes above referred to it is declared that the bank is formed for the purpose of carrying into effect the privilege of the bank as defined in the concession, and the operations to be undertaken are defined in accordance with the concession. The capital of the bank is divided into shares of 500 francs, or 20l. each, and the liability of the shareholders is limited to the amount of their shares. There is no register of shares, but, according to the provisions of the statutes, all the certificates of shares are made out to bearer, and the shares themselves are transferable by delivery of the certificates, and the dividends payable thereupon are repayable at the option of the holders at Constantinople, Paris, or London by means of coupons attached to the certificates.

27. By the statutes the administration of the bank in Constantinople is confided to a director general, one or two assistant directors, and a council of administration of three directors. These are appointed by a committee of from 20 to 25 members, of whom 10 at least must be English, or resident in England, and 10 at least French, or resident in France, and each member of the council and of the committee must deposit in the treasury of the bank 100 shares therein, which are to remain unalienable during his continuance in office. This committee has the general guidance, control, and superintendence of the operations of the bank, and its members are elected by the general meeting of shareholders. The statutes further require that the committee shall meet four times a year alternately in London and Paris, and the committee has, in fact, met and still does meet sometimes in London and sometimes in Paris. The execution of the

decisions of the committee and the more immediate supervision of the affairs of the bank is assigned under the statutes to a sub-committee appointed by a general committee, consisting of eight members, of whom four are chosen from the English and four from the French section of the general committee.

28. It is provided by the statutes that the English members of the committee shall be charged under the control of the sub-committee with the management of the London Agency of the bank, and since the early part of 1863, when the business of the bank in London commenced until the present time, the London business of the bank, being the ordinary business of bankers, has been carried on under the management of the English members of the committee in premises in the City of London.

29. It is provided by the statutes that the annual general meetings of the shareholders in the bank, and all extraordinary general meetings, shall be held at such places as the committee shall fix, and at the annual general meetings the report of the committee on the state of affairs of the bank is received, the accounts are discussed, approved, or rejected, the dividends are fixed and declared, and members of the committee are elected. The general meetings have in fact always been and still are held in London.

30. According to the translation of the statutes furnished to the Commissioners for Special Purposes Articles 41 and 42 of these statutes are in the terms following:—

"Article 41. At the end of each of the Company's years a general inventory of the assets and liabilities is drawn up by the sub-committee and confirmed by the committee. The accounts are submitted to the general meeting, who approves or rejects and fixes the dividends after having heard the report of the committee.

"Article 42. The net proceeds after deducting all expenses constitute the profits. Out of these profits there is taken, in the first instance, annually—

"1st. Five per cent. on the capital of the shares issued to be distributed among the shareholders by way of dividend on account.

"2nd. Ten per cent. of the profits for the reserve fund.

"The surplus is divided in the proportions of, nine-tenths for the shares by way of dividend, the remaining one-tenth is divided into moieties, of which one is for the founders and the other for the members of the committee and the administrative council.

"The part coming to the founders in the division of the annual profits and in the reserve fund shall be in the proportions fixed by their private agreements represented by special certificates whose form the committee shall determine; the payment of the dividends voted by the general meeting is made at the times fixed by the committee."

31. In relation to an assessment in respect of the profits and gains of the bank for the year ending 5th April, 1872, it was contended on the part of the Commissioners of Inland Revenue that the bank as a person residing in the United Kingdom was bound under the Income Tax Acts to make a return in respect of all its annual profits and gains, whether made in the United Kingdom or elsewhere, and was chargeable to income tax thereon under Schedule D., but upon a special case stated to test the validity of that contention the Court of Exchequer held that the bank could not be regarded as residing in the United Kingdom.

The case is, the "Attorney-General v. Alexander and others," and is reported in Law Reports, 10 Exchequer, page 20.

32. On or about the 16th day of November, 1875, two returns for income tax for the year ending the 5th of April, 1875, were made by the appellant, one being in respect of the English profits of the bank, and the other being in respect of the dividends of the bank.

The return in respect of the English profits was as follows:—

"The Imperial Ottoman Bank (London Agency.)

"Return for income tax on English profits for the year 1874-75.

"I hereby on behalf of myself and the other persons constituting the London Agency of the Imperial Ottoman Bank made the following returns in respect of the assessment to be made for income tax under Schedule D. for the year ending 5th April, 1875.

"The London Agency act in the character of agents for the Imperial Ottoman Bank, which resides at Constantinople, in the Empire of Turkey.

"The said London Agency consists of the following persons:—

"Mr. James Alexander, 10, King's Arms Yard, E.C.
"The Honourable Thomas Charles Bruce, 42, Hill Street, Berkeley Square.
"Mr. George Thomas Clark, Dowlais, Merthyr.
"Sir William Richard Drake, 46, Parliament Street, S.W.
"Mr. Edward Gilbertson, 8, Upper Phillimore Gardens, W.
"Mr. Pascoe Dupre Grenfell, Bartholomew House, E.C.
"Sir Charles Henry Mills, Bart., 67, Lombard Street, E.C.
"Mr. Lachlan Mackintosh Rate, 60, Threadneedle Street, E.C.
"Mr. John Stewart, 13, Curzon Street, May Fair, W.

"The amounts of profits and gains accruing to the bank from the trade of banker exercised within Great Britain, viz., at London, for the year ending 5th April, 1875, computed on a just and fair average of three years ending the 31st December, 1873, the last-mentioned day being the day on which the accounts of the said bank have been usually made up, is 81,477l. 14s. 8d.

"The London Agency of the bank do not make any return of the profits accruing to the bank from business carried on by the bank elsewhere than in the United Kingdom, the Court of Exchequer having decided that such profits are not chargeable.

"I declare that the foregoing declaration is true, and that the same is fully stated upon every description of property and profits in respect of which the London Agency is chargeable under Schedule D; of 5 & 6 Vict. c. 35., estimated to the best of my judgment and belief according to the directions and rules of the Acts relating thereto.

"The London Agency desire to be assessed upon this return by the Special Commissioners of Income Tax.

"Dated this 16th day of November, 1875.

"E. GILBERTSON."

The return in respect of the dividends of the bank was as follows :—

"The Imperial Ottoman Bank (London Agency).

"Return of amount of dividends chargeable to income tax under 16 & 17 Vict. c. 34. s. 10 for the year 1874-75.

"In pursuance of the demand of Mr. J. Mayhew, the inspector authorised for that purpose by the Commissioners of Inland Revenue, and in pursuance of the statute 16 & 17 Vict. c. 34 s. 10, I hereby, on behalf of myself and the other persons constituting the London Agency of the Imperial Ottoman Bank, deliver to the said Inspector, for the use of the Commissioners for Special Purposes mentioned in the said schedule, the underwritten account, being a true and perfect account of the matters and things, of which an account is required to be delivered ·by the above-mentioned section, for the year ending 5th April, 1875; that is to say,

"There were no interest, dividends, or other annual payments payable out of or in respect of the stocks, funds, or shares of the said Imperial Ottoman Bank, and (within the meaning of the said Act) intrusted to the said London Agency for payment to persons, corporations, companies, or societies, in the United Kingdom, and payable by the said London Agency, for the year ending 5th April, 1875.

"Dated this 16th day of November, 1875.

"E. GILBERTSON."

33. The appellant who signed the above returns, and the other nine persons therein named or referred to, and who are therein described as the London Agency, were and are the English members of the committee, and charged with the management of the London Agency of the bank.

34. Before and at the time when the above returns were transmitted to the surveyor of taxes (the respondent) the secretary of the London Agency furnished a statement, showing how the sum

of 81,477*l*. 14*s*. 8*d*., mentioned in the return in respect of the English profits, was arrived at, such statement being as follows:—

The English profits for the year ending—

				£	*s.*	*d.*
31st December 1871, were	...	...	...	69,118	1	0
,, 1872	...	...	...	76,070	18	10
1873	...	...	...	99,244	4	4
				3)244,433	4	2
Return for 1874-5	...			81,477	14	8

and a further statement of the amounts of dividends paid in England out of the profits of the bank in the course of the financial years 1871-72, 1872-3, 1873-4, and 1874-75, and such amounts were thereby shown to be respectively 164,344*l*. 10*s*., 189,694*l*. 10*s*., 169,081*l*. 2*s*., and 98,322*l*. 10*s*. It was also thereby shown that in the year 1871-72 there was in the hands of the London Agency money derived from profits made in England amounting to 69,118*l*. 1*s*., which the agency applied towards payment of the said dividends, and that the amount to make up the said sum of 164,344*l*. 10*s*., viz., 95,226*l*. 9*s*., was remitted from abroad out of the foreign profits of the bank; that in the year 1872-73 the amounts so applied and remitted respectively were 76,070*l*. 18*s*. 10*d*., and 113,623*l*. 11*s*. 2*d*.; that in the year 1873-74 the amounts so applied and remitted respectively were 99,244*l*. 4*s*. 4*d*. and 69,836*l*. 17*s*. 8*d*., and that in the year 1874-75 the amount of English profits being in excess of the amount required for the dividends payable in England no remittance from abroad out of foreign profits were required or made towards payment of the said sum of 98,322*l*. 10*s*.

The secretary also furnished copies of the annual reports for the years 1871, 1872, 1873, and 1874, which will be found in the Appendix to this case.

35. The Commissioners for Special Purposes in the first instance made an assessment for the year 1874-75 (herein-after called the assessment on English profits) in respect of the profits of the bank upon the sum of 81,477*l*. 14*s*. 8*d*. for the English profits in conformity with the return, and duty was charged upon that sum accordingly. This assessment was not objected to, and no question arises upon it.

The Commissioners then proceeded to consider the return in respect of the dividends of the bank, and were of opinion that in making that return the appellant had taken an erroneous view of the liability of the English Committee with reference to the provisions of section 10 of the Act 16 & 17 Vict. c. 34., and having no information as to the proportion of the said sum of 98,322*l*. 10*s*. paid in dividends in England in the year 1874-75 which represented English profits, and had been included in the assessment on English profits, they made an assessment (herein- GILBERTSO after called the assessment on dividends) upon the whole of the FERGUSSON said sum of 98,322*l.* 10*s.*

In giving notice to the appellant of the assessment on divi-deñds the Commissioners left the English members of the com-mittee to prove upon appeal what amount should be deducted as having been included in the assessment on the English profits.

36. The appellant on behalf of the English members of the committee of the London Agency appealed against the assess-ment on dividends to the Commissioners for Special Purposes, and upon the hearing of the appeal on the 14th day of January, 1876, it was stated by the Commissioners that in case section 10 of the Act 16 & 17 Vict. c. 34. was inapplicable to the bank, or did not in circumstances warrant any assessment on dividends, they should, under the authority vested in them by law, make an assessment under the provisions of the third rule applicable to the two first cases of Schedule D., in section 100 of the last-mentioned Act in addition to the assessment on English profits so as to cover the foreign profits of the bank to the extent to which in the opinion of the Commissioners they were liable to income tax. It was, therefore, arranged between the Commis-sioners and the appellant that the hearing of the appeal should be adjourned, and that the Commissioners should forthwith make such assessment in respect of foreign profits as they should think proper as an alternative assessment, and that an appeal there-from, and the previous appeal so adjourned, should come on for hearing on the same day.

37. On the 20th day of January, 1876, the Commissioners for Special Purposes made an assessment (herein-after called the assessment on general profits) upon the sum of 115,935*l.*, which they ascertained to be the amount on an average of the three preceding years of the proportion of the foreign profits distri-buted in dividends in England, and which sum, with the addi-tion of the said sum of 81,477*l.* 14*s.* 8*d.*, the amount of the assessment on English profits, amounted to a total assessment in respect of profits of 197,412*l.* 14*s.* 8*d.*

The way in which the Commissioners arrived at the foregoing result is shown by the following statement of account :—

		£
1871.	Total dividend paid in England and abroad	273,375
	Dividend paid in England	164,344
	English profits	69,118

As 273,375 : 69,118 : : 164,334 : 41,551
  Subtract the 4th term   41,551

	£
Portion of English dividend composed of foreign profits	122,793
English profits	69,118
Total profits assessable	191,911

1872. Total dividend paid in England and abroad — 283,500

Dividend paid in England 189,694

English profits 76,070

As 283,500 : 76,070 : : 189,694 : 50,899
Subtract 4th term — 50,899

Portion of English dividend composed of foreign profits	138,795
English profits	76,070
Total profits assessable	214,865

1873. Total dividend paid in England and abroad — 202,500

Dividends paid in England 169,081

English profits 99,244

As 202,500 : 99,244 : : 169,089 : 82,865
Subtract 4th term — 82,865

	£
Portion of English dividend composed of foreign profits	86,216
English profits	99,244
Total profits assessable	185,460

Total profits assessable for 1871	...	...	191,911
,, ,, 1872	...	...	214,865
,, ,, 1873	...	...	185,460
			3)592,236
Average for assessment	...	...	197,412

In making the said assessment the Commissioners regarded all the shareholders in the bank, who were resident in England, as carrying on business in England and abroad jointly with the shareholders resident abroad, and the English committee, as the accountable and chargeable persons under the provisions contained in the third rule applicable to the two first cases of Schedule D. in section 100 of the Act 5 & 6 Vict. c. 35. in respect of the profits of the bank, so far as they were liable to income tax.

38. On the same day on which the assessment on general profits was made, the Commissioners for Special Purposes sent a notice thereof, addressed to the appellant and the other English members of the Committee, which was in the following terms:—

" Take notice that the Commissioners for the Special Purposes of the Income Tax Acts, by virtue of the power and authority vested in them by the said Acts, have made an assessment on you as representing the London Agency of the Imperial Ottoman Bank, and on the part of yourselves and all other the shareholders or members, in or of the said bank, for the profits of the said bank arising in the United Kingdom, and so much of the profits of the said bank arising out of the United Kingdom, as is subject to income tax under the said Acts, in the sum of 197,412*l.* 14*s.* 8*d.*

" The above sum includes the sum of 81,777*l.* 14*s.* 8*d.* returned for assessment on the part of the London Agency, and the duty now charged in addition to the duty previously charged in respect of the said sum of 81,477*l.* 14*s.* 8*d.* amounts to 966*l.* 2*s.* 6*d.*

" Dated this 20th day of January, 1876."

39. Upon the receipt of the said notice, the appellant signified his intention to appeal to the Commissioners for Special Purposes against the assessment on general profits, and on the 26th day of January, 1876, that appeal and the adjourned appeal against the assessment on dividends came on for hearing.

40. At such hearing it was stated on the part of the appellant that no technical objection was or would be taken to the assessments or the mode in which they had been made, but that objection was taken upon the simple ground that the whole liability of the appellant and the other English members of the committee, either as representing the London Agency of the bank, or on the part of themselves and the other shareholders, in the bank in respect of income tax upon the profits of the bank, had been discharged by the assessment for the English profits and the payment of income tax upon that sum. In support of that objection it was alleged that it was decided by the Court of Exchequer in the case of the Attorney-General *v.* Alexander that the bank was chargeable to income tax in respect of the English profits only, and that the bank could not be regarded otherwise than as a person residing out of the United Kingdom and carrying on business in the United Kingdom through an agent. It was further urged that the bank having a foreign incorporation must be regarded as a corporate body or entity for all purposes connected with the income tax, and that the Commissioners for Special Purposes had no power to make any assessment upon the shareholders in the bank in respect of these

dividends or shares of the profits thereof. It was further urged
that the provisions of the Income Tax Acts, with the exception
of the provisions contained in section 10 of the Act 16 & 17 Vict.
c. 34. were such as to restrict the obligation of the agent of a
foreign corporation to make a return of profits of the corporation
to a return of the profits made in the United Kingdom, and consequently to restrict the charge of income tax to the profits so
made. It was further urged that inasmuch as all dividends paid
in the United Kingdom in the year 1874-75 were paid out of
English profits retained by the English members of the committee for the purpose, no dividends payable on the shares of
the bank were intrusted to such members or any person for
payment in the United Kingdom, and that consequently no
return could be called for and no assessment could be made by
reference to the said section 10 of the Act 16 & 17 Vict. c. 34.

41. It was submitted on the part of the respondent that in
the case of the Attorney-General v. Alexander, the Court of
Exchequer decided nothing more than that the bank was not
chargeable as a person residing in the United Kingdom.

With respect to the assessment on general profits it was urged
on the part of the respondent that, where persons (some of whom
reside while the others do not reside in the United Kingdom)
carry on a concern jointly in the United Kingdom and elsewhere, the annual profits arising to such persons from the concern are chargeable, Schedule D. of the Act 16 & 17 Vict. c. 34.
and the third rule applicable to the first two cases of Schedule D.,
as stated in section 100 of the Act 5 & 6 Vict. c. 35. And that
the fact of such persons having formed themselves into a body
which has been incorporated by a firman of the Sultan does not
diminish their liability or deprive the Crown of the Income tax
which would have been payable if there had been no such incorporation. It was also urged that whatever may have been
the effect of the Turkish incorporation, it was not such as to
bring the bank within the meaning of the expression "bodies
politic or corporate," in section 40 or section 192 of the Act
5 & 6 Vict. c. 35., or to make the bank chargeable as a company
or corporation under the general provisions of the Income Tax
Acts.

With respect to the alternative assessment, viz., the assessment on dividends made with reference to section 10 of the Act
16 & 17 Vict. c. 34., it was urged on the part of the respondent
that the appropriation by the English members of the committee
of the whole of the English profits to the payment of dividends
to a certain class of shareholders, viz.. those whose dividends
were paid in London, could not have the effect of depriving the
Crown of income tax upon so much of the foreign profits as
must be considered to have formed part of such dividends. It
was also submitted that the construction of the said section 10,
for which the appellant contended, viz., the limitation of the
expression "dividends intrusted" to moneys actually remitted
by the bank from abroad for distribution in dividends in London,

was manifestly opposed to the intention of the legislature in the application of the section to the case of a foreign corporation, carrying on business and making profits in the United Kingdom and abroad.

42. The Commissioners for Special Purposes concurred in the views put forward on behalf of the respondent, and upon consideration of the general question involved in the alternative assessments, were of opinion that the contention on the part of the appellant that the assessment on English profits was to be regarded as embracing and satisfying the whole liability of the appellant and the other members of the English committee in every aspect of the case could not be supported in point of law in the state of facts which has been herein-before set forth, because the practical result of yielding to such contention would be to free from income tax either the portion of the foreign profits which should be regarded as forming part of each dividend paid to a shareholder in the United Kingdom or the portion of the English profits which should be regarded as forming part of each dividend paid to a shareholder abroad.

The Commissioners, therefore, were of opinion that one of the two assessments, viz., the assessment on dividends, and the assessment on general profits were right, and, inasmuch as it was the desire of the persons who represented the appellant and the Crown at the hearing of the combined appeals that all the points affecting the liability to income tax should be brought before the Court upon a case to be stated, they determined to confirm the two alternative assessments.

43. The assessments were accordingly confirmed, whereupon the appellant expressed his dissatisfaction with the determination of the Commissioners for Special Purposes as being erroneous in point of law, on the ground that, in the circumstances herein stated, no portion of the foreign profits of the bank is the subject of assessment to income tax on the appellant and the other English members of the committee for the year ending 5th April, 1875, and duly required the Commissioners to state and sign a case for the opinion of the Exchequer Division of the High Court of Justice according to the Act 37 & 38 Vict. c. 16. which we have stated and do now sign accordingly.

R. M. LYNCH. } Commissioners for the
SUDLEY.   } Special Purposes of the
               } Income Tax Acts.

24th May, 1876.

The case was argued in the Exchequer Division (r) on 28th February, 1st and 3rd March, 1879, and on 4th July, 1879, judgment was delivered. The assessment on profits (para. 37 of the case) was held to be bad; but the majority of the Court (*Kelly*, C.B., dissenting) held that the assessment on dividends (para. 35) was based upon the right principle, in so far as it assessed so

GILBERTSON
v.
FERGUSSON

(r) L.R., 5 Ex. D. 57.

much of the profits of the bank, intrusted to the Committee for payment of dividends in the United Kingdom, as was not shown by a proper return on the part of the bank to arise from profits made in the United Kingdom. The appellant, on behalf of the London Agency, appealed from this decision.

9th and 10th May, 1881.

Matthews, Q.C. (*Bosanquet* with him), for the appellants:— Schedule D. of the Act of 16 & 17 Vict. c. 34. establishes two classes of persons liable to be taxed, namely, residents in the United Kingdom and non-residents. A resident is to be charged in respect of all profits wheresoever acquired, and a non-resident only in respect of profits acquired in the United Kingdom. In Attorney-General v. Alexander (*s*) it is laid down that the Imperial Ottoman Bank is a person residing abroad, and liable therefore, under Schedule D, to be assessed for the whole of the profits made in England, and not liable in respect of foreign profits.

Then comes the question what further liability is imposed upon the bank by section 10 of the Act 16 and 17 Vict. c. 34. That is really the whole question in this case. That section says that if an agent in this country is intrusted with the payment of dividends of a foreign corporation to people in the United Kingdom, he must deduct income tax from the dividends, and pay it to the Government. I contend that section applies only to sums remitted from abroad to pay dividends here. The bank pays income tax to start with upon its whole English profits; these profits are distributed in dividends in England, and ought not to pay the tax twice, first as profits and then as dividends. Then, if in addition to those English profits we get any sums intrusted to us from abroad to distribute in dividends here we pay also upon that sum; but this year (1874-5) we have been intrusted with no funds except the English profits which have been more than sufficient to pay all the dividends claimed in London.

[*Bramwell, L.J.*—Supposing you make 1,000*l.* in England and 1,000*l.* in Constantinople, and supposing the shares are equally held in England and Turkey, then you say you pay on nothing more than 1,000*l.*]

Then I say we pay on nothing more.

[*Bramwell, L.J.*—The tax on the 1,000*l.* would be deducted from the dividends of the English shareholders; the Turk therefore would pay no tax although he has derived a profit from business carried on in England, the dividend being made up of profits made in England and Turkey.]

This is not a case of taxation of individual shareholders. If you could catch the Turkish shareholders and bring them within the jurisdiction it may be that you might tax each individual. But this is a question of taxing the bank; in Sully's case (*t*) although a partner in England was liable to be taxed for his share of the profits of the firm, it was held that the firm itself was not taxable.

Dicey (Sir John Holker, Q.C., with him) for the respondent.— The principle of the Income Tax Acts with reference to the persons to be charged is contained in the schedules; the remainder of the Acts describe the machinery by which those persons are to be got at. Schedule D. charges two classes of profits, firstly, profits made in the United Kingdom to whomsoever paid, and secondly, all profits wherever arising payable to persons in the United Kingdom. In accordance with this principle income tax would be payable in the case of the Imperial Ottoman Bank, firstly, on the whole of the English profits, and secondly, on the portion of the dividends paid to persons resident in England which arises from foreign profits. It is said that the English dividends are paid out of English profits, but it matters not whence the actual money paid away was obtained, the essential fact is that the dividend accrues, not merely from English profits, but from foreign profits also.

This being the principle of liability the next point for consideration is the mode of assessment. After the course the case has taken we mainly rely for the present on the assessment on dividends under section 10, 16 & 17 Vict. c. 34. That section creates no additional liability to income tax. Under the earlier Act (5 & 6 Vict. c. 35.) the bank would first have had to pay on the whole of its English profits, and then the individual shareholders would have made a return of their dividends, although they might in fairness have claimed a reduction in respect of the portion of the dividends which had already paid tax as English profits. But section 10, instead of relying on the conscience of the individual recipient of dividends of a foreign company, authorises an assessment upon the agent intrusted with the payment of the dividends. A person who undertakes to pay dividends is intrusted with the payment thereof within the meaning of the section. In the present case the English Agency was intrusted with the payment of the dividends and did actually pay them, the English profits being left in their hands for that purpose.

Although relying mainly on the assessment under section 10, the respondent, if their Lordships should not approve the order of the Court of Exchequer, would say that the alternative assessment on general profits (para. 37 of the case) was right.

Matthews, Q.C., in reply.

(*t*) 4 H. & N. 769, and in error 5 H. & N. 711 ; 29 L.J. (Ex.) 164.

GILBERTSON
v.
FERGUSSON.

Bramwell, L.J.—I think this judgment should be affirmed, and although the order may require a verbal alteration, I think the substance of it should be retained. I agree with the judgment of my brothers Pollock and Huddleston, and with the reasons they give. With great submission to the late Lord Chief Baron, and with great respect for his opinion, I think he has misunderstood the effect of the contention of the Crown in the first part of his judgment.

It seems to me that the substance of the claim which the Crown is making is this, to assess the dividends received in England. Take the case of the shares being equally held in England and Constantinople, and take it that the profits are equal in England and Constantinople, say, 1,000*l*. in each place. Now the Crown says, " assess the dividends received in England, " because the persons who receive the dividends are English or " persons residing in England," and so this case is under one of the classes in Schedule D. Then the Crown says, " assess so " much of the Turk's dividends as he receives out of the profits " made in England." Then if the proportions and profits are what I have said, equal in England and Turkey, the Turk will receive 500*l*. out of the English profits. Therefore upon the whole the Crown says that of the profits made by this bank, supposing they were made in the proportions I have mentioned, three-fourths ought to be assessed to income tax. That is the contention of the Crown, and I have no misgiving on the subject that that is right in substance, and I have heard no argument that it is not. On the contrary, it has been conceded that in the case put of two partners, one living abroad and the other in England, and making equal profits and having equal shares, three-fourths of the profits would be taxed in England. It seems to me that that is not susceptible of doubt. Supposing there was only one partner who lived abroad, the whole of his profit made in England would be assessable in England, and because he has got a partner residing here, and consequently only gets half of that profit, there is no reason why the duty should not still be paid. Then there is another illustration, suppose there was one dividend in the course of the year on English profits, and other dividend in the course of the year upon Turkish profits, I do not see how it could be contested that the whole of the English profits should be subject to income tax, and that the English shareholders' share of the profits that were made in Turkey must be subject to income tax. It seems to me, therefore, that the substance of the Crown's contention is correct, and cannot be controverted.

Then the question is whether the machinery is enough. I think it is; I think it comes within the meaning of section 10 of 16 & 17 Vict. c. 34., the expression there, " acting therein as " agents or in any other character," is most general and comprehensive. There is another case that might be put. Supposing there was a branch at Liverpool, and supposing the agent for the payment of the dividends was in London, it is quite certain that a return must be made showing the whole of the dividends paid in England, and showing also the profits made in Liverpool, and I think that this would be done under the words of section 10, and so that no dividend receiver in England would be made to pay the tax twice over. In the present case this London Agency are persons who have the duty to pay or who are instructed to pay dividends on the shares of the Turkish company, to the extent only to which those shares are held in England, and to the extent only of the worth of the profit made out of those shares abroad, so that they are not intrusted to pay to the English shareholders the English profits within the meaning of the Act of Parliament, but to pay to the English shareholders the Turkish profits. I think that in that way the very language of the Act of Parliament may be made to work out justly and properly. I think, therefore, the judgment below is right and should be affirmed.

Brett, L.J.—I agree with Mr. Dicey that the questions here are first, who are the persons intended to be charged ultimately with the income tax; and next, what is the machinery by which those persons are to be got at?

I think that the first question is to be determined by Schedule D. of 16 & 17 Vict. c. 34. The profits dealt with by that schedule are the profits arising from business carried on in England, and the profits arising from business carried on abroad. The income tax is to be levied on all profits in such first part, and on so much of those in the second as would accrue to persons residing in England. That divides the profits into two classes.

But when one comes to the profits which have been dealt with in this case, namely, the profits earned by this Ottoman Bank, and which are to be distributed in dividends by that bank, they are not two profits but one indivisible profit, so far as the bank is concerned, which the bank divides within itself. It is a profit arising partly from business carried on in England and partly from business carried on in Turkey, but within the bank it is one profit and one profit only, and which is to be divided in dividends. But when one comes to apply the income tax to it the statute obliges one to divide that profit into two. Each person resident in England, who is to receive a dividend out of that profit, receives part of such dividend in respect of profit arising from business carried on in England, and part in respect of profit arising from business carried on in Turkey. Now the profit which is dealt with by the income tax in the present case is distributed by an agent in England, who is the appellant, that agent has to make a return, and it seems to me that by virtue of that statute he is bound to make a return of the whole amount of profit earned in England, and also of all the dividends payable in England. By the statute the Government are entitled to receive the income tax upon all the profits made in respect of the business carried on in England, and also

GILBERTSON
v.
FERGUSSON.

O

beyond that on all dividends paid in England, whether in respect
of profits made in England or in Turkey. Now it may be
true that there are no specific words in this statute which point
out that the Government are not to receive the tax twice over,
but it would be so clearly unjust and obviously contrary to the
meaning of the statute that the Government should have the
tax payable twice over by the same person in respect of the
same thing, that I should say it was a necessary implication that
that could not be right.

Therefore, if part of the dividends in respect of which the
income tax is payable is also in respect of profits earned from a
business in England, the tax on that part would have to be paid
twice over, which ought not to be; and as to that, there should
be a deduction. In respect, however, of so much of the dividends
payable in England as is derived from profits from business
carried on in Turkey, it is not paid twice over, and consequently
as to that there ought not to be any deduction at all. That
being so, it seems to me that the order of the Divisional Court is
in substance correct. That order points out the true principle,
which is, that in respect of so much of the dividend as is payable out of the profits from the business carried on in England,
the income tax is to be paid, not twice, but only once, but that
the income tax is also to be paid in respect of so much of the
dividend which is paid in England from the profits of business
carried on in Turkey. It may be that the order requires a
verbal alteration, because it has used the word " profits " instead
of " dividends " at the beginning, but that is so slight that it
really makes no substantial alteration. The principle of the
judgments of Baron Pollock and Baron Huddleston seems to me
to be correct, and it is that principle which has now to be upheld.

Whether it is properly worked out by the rule of three sum
stated in the case I know not, and do not care. That is a matter
for an accountant more than for a court of law.

The judgment below does not deal with that, but directs that
the principle which is to be carried out, shall be carried out by
some manipulation or other correctly, and that seems to me to
be the judgment we ought to give now. The judgment below,
therefore, is substantially affirmed.

Cotton, L.J.—The English Agency has been called upon to
pay, and there is no doubt that they are liable to pay income tax
on the profits made by the business carried on by that agency in
England. The question arises how far, if at all, they are liable
to pay duty in respect of dividends from profits made by the bank
in Turkey, which are paid in England to the shareholders of the
bank, and, as I understand, these dividends are payable by
coupons to bearer, and any person in England may receive his
dividends and have them payable here. When a corporation
carries on its business in more than one place the dividends are
not a share of the profits arising on the transactions in any one

place, but of the profits made by the entire business of the corpo- GILBERTSON
ration, and unless for any purpose it is necessary to analyse the *v.*
source from which the dividends arise, it must be taken that the FERGUSSON.
dividends are not paid out of any particular fund, but out of the
sum which, on the whole transactions of the corporation, is the
profits during the year. Suppose the English branch to make
large profits, and the bank in Turkey a large loss, or, on the other
hand, the English branch make a loss and the bank at Constantinople to make a large profit, it cannot be said because the
shareholders are residing in one country or the other that they
get their dividends in respect of the profits of any particular
country, but in respect of profits of the entire transactions of
the company taking it as a whole, and when we look at the
statutes of this bank there is nothing at all to take them out of
the general rule; there is nothing about profits in England
and profits in Constantinople, or anything to show how far or out
of what profits dividends to the shareholders in any particular
country are to be paid. Now the Act by Schedule D. charges
income tax upon the profits which are paid to persons resident
in England, and on the profits made in England by persons,
which include corporations, whether resident in England or
not. It must be conceded that if there are any shareholders
who reside in England and receive dividends there they are
chargeable under the Act, and are bound to make a return and
pay the tax on what they so receive. There is no exception in
their case in respect of so much of their dividends as is attributable to or arising in respect of profits made in England, but I
take it there would be this implied exception, that when duty is
charged as against the person in one part of the Act he is not to
be charged again under another part applying no doubt in terms
to him, but intended to include those who have not been charged
under the preceding part. Of course section 10 of 16 & 17 Vict.
c. 34. is the section, if any, on which the English Agency ought
to be made chargeable. I quite agree we ought not to put a
strained construction upon that section in order to make liable to
taxation that which would not otherwise be liable, but I think it
is now settled that in construing these Revenue Acts, as well as
other Acts, we ought to give a fair and reasonable construction,
and not to lean in favour of one side or the other on the ground
that it is a tax imposed upon the subject, and therefore ought not
to be enforced unless it comes clearly within the words. That
is the rule which had been laid down by the House of Lords in
regard to the Succession Duty Acts, and I think it is a correct
rule.

Now first, this 10th section is not, in my opinion, a clause
imposing on the bank or the English Agency on behalf of the
bank a liability to pay duty in respect of profits coming to them,
but it is a mode of collecting the duty which would be chargeable on the persons who are to receive the dividends. The
liability of the agent to pay may be different from his liability
to make a return. I think, having regard to section 2 of 5 & 6

Vict. c. 80., that the liability of the agent to pay only arises when
he has received money to pay, and that payment is to be made by
him out of moneys in his hands; but that is an entirely different
question from his liability and duty to make a return of dividends which he is intrusted to pay, and we do find in that second
section express words that he is to make a return of, *inter alia*,
the dividends, the payments of which are intrusted to him. It
may be said that payment of the dividends is not intrusted to
him until he gets the money to pay them. That may be so, but
then still the question arises when the dividend is intrusted to
him, is he or is he not to pay the duty. It is a fallacy, in my
opinion, to say that these dividends are payable out of English
profits which have already paid duty. The dividends are payable
in respect of all profits, and although the shareholders would be
entitled to say as against the Crown, part of this is attributable
to English profits, and we have already paid duty in respect of
that, yet part of it, in my opinion, is attributable to and must
be taken as payable in respect of profits accruing from business
in Constantinople and therefore it cannot be said that duty has
been already paid in respect of that part of the dividend because
duty has been paid on the English profits, and those profits
appear to exceed or equal the amount of dividends which is paid
to the shareholders in England. It is said, and it strikes me as
a difficulty, that there is no provision here enabling any of the
shareholders to get back or to enable the English Agency to
make an exception in their return in respect of that proportion of
the dividend which is to be attributable to English profits; but
that can only be dealt with in this way, that where the dividend
has already been taxed then, by the necessary implication of the
statute, the duty is not again to be paid upon it, and therefore
the exception must be allowed, which is provided for by the
order made by the Court below, that a return is to be made and
duty is to be paid except so far as the dividend is shown by a
proper return on the part of the bank to arise from profits made
in the United Kingdom which has already been charged with
the duty.

In my opinion, therefore, the judgment of the Court below is
right, but I would suggest that the order should be altered by
stating that it " is based upon the right principle of assessing, in
" so far as it assesses so much of the dividends intrusted to the
" committee for payment in the United Kingdom as is not
" shown by a proper return on the part of the bank, to arise from
" profits made in the United Kingdom." It is put in the order
as drawn up at present, " in so far as it assesses so much of the
" profits of the bank," and, in my opinion, it is not necessary to
show that it is profits. Whatever dividend they are intrusted to
pay, of that, in my opinion, a return is to be made, and on that,
in my opinion, duty is to be paid, unless so far as it is shown
that that dividend arises from or is payable in respect of profits
made in the United Kingdom.

Bramwell, L.J.—I wish to add that our judgment does not make the profits of the bank pay a larger income tax than they ought to pay, even supposing the objection raised on the part of the appellant to be well founded; because the income tax ought to be upon the English profits, and the shareholders ought also to pay the tax on what they receive from the Turkish profits. The only result, if we had not so decided, would have been, as it seems to me, that the bank, when it paid its English shareholders, would have paid them with a deduction of the income tax on their proportion of the English profits but without any such deduction on their proportion of the Turkish profits, and then each such shareholder would have had on his return to the Income Tax Commissioners to have charged himself in respect of the dividends received by him on which he had not paid tax.

Judgment of the Divisional Court affirmed.

GILBERTSON
v.
FERGUSON.

No. 59.—IN THE COURT OF APPEAL.

April 19, 1883.

ALEXANDRIA WATER COMPANY, LIMITED, *v.* MUSGRAVE.
(Surveyor of Taxes).

ALEXANDRIA
WATER CO.
v. MUSGRAVE.

Income Tax.—Debenture interest paid by an English Company, whose works and property are at Alexandria, to Debenture Holders residing in Egypt, not an allowable deduction from the assessment upon the Company's profits.

This was an appeal by the Water Company from a decision of the Queen's Bench Division on 23rd May, 1882, when *Grove* and *North*, J.J., delivered judgment in favour of the Crown with costs.

The case stated for the opinion of Court was as follows:—

At a meeting of the Commissioners for Special Purposes, held at Somerset House on January 19th, 1881, for the purpose of hearing appeals under the Income Tax Acts for the year ending the 5th April, 1881, Mr. Basil Martineau attended, and appealed on behalf of the Alexandria Water Company, Limited, against an assessment of 25,600*l.* made in respect of the profits of the Company by the District Commissioners for the parish of St. Margaret's, Westminster, in the county of Middlesex.

Accounts were furnished and are attached hereto, (u) together with copy of debenture bond and coupon, and form part of the case.

The Company claimed as a deduction from the sum assessed the amount of 7,695*l.*, being interest on debenture bonds paid to foreigners residing in Egypt.

The Special Commissioners decided that the Company being an English Company were liable to pay income tax on the whole profits of the concern, irrespective of the manner and places in which such profits were distributed, and they confirmed the assessment in the sum of 25,600*l.*

The Company have, through their solicitors, required the Special Commissioners to state and sign a case for the opinion of the High Court of Justice, which we have stated, and do now sign accordingly.

Dated at Somerset House, London, this 8th day of October, 1881.

R. M. LYNCH, } Special Commissioners
D. O'CONNELL, }   of the Income Tax.

The debenture bond referred to was worded as follows:—

The Alexandria Water Company, Limited, in consideration of the sum of 100*l.* sterling paid to them by

of

the said   hereby covenant with
                                                     his executors
and administrators, to pay for him, his executors, administrators, or assigns, or to the bearer hereof, on the 30th April, 1884, at the bankers of the Company, the sum of 100*l.* sterling, and also, until repayment of the said principal sum, to pay by way of interest to the bearer of every coupon hereto annexed, at the time and place (v) in such coupon mentioned, such sum of money as in such coupon appears. And the said Company do hereby charge with the aforesaid payments the waterworks, undertaking, lands, canals, plant, machinery, works, property, and effects, both present and future, of the said Company, to the intent that this security and the other securities forming part of the abovementioned sum of 225,000*l.*, or so much thereof as shall for the time being be issued, may rank equally as a first charge upon the said waterworks, undertaking, lands, canals, plant, machinery, works, property, and effects, but so that the same may be a floating security, not hindering any sale, exchange, or lease of the said waterworks, lands, canals, or other property, or any part thereof, or the receipt or payment of any moneys, or any other dealings in the course of the business of the said Company, but attaching to the premises leased, and the proceeds of any sale or exchange, and the lands or other property purchased therewith, or with any moneys of the Company. Provided always that the bearer of these presents, or of any of the Coupons hereto annexed, shall be entitled to the payment of the money intended to be secured by such respective instrument, without being affected by any right of set off or

---

(u) It has not been thought necessary to print the accounts for this report.
(v) The coupons were payable to the bankers of the Company in London or Alexandria.

ALEXANDRI.
WATER CO.
v.MUSGRAVI

other right or equity of the said Company, against the said , the original or any intermediate holder of such respective instrument, and that the receipt of the bearer shall be an effectual discharge for such money, and the Company or person paying such money shall not be bound to inquire into the title of the bearer, or to take notice of any trust affecting such money, or be affected by express notice of any equity which may then be subsisting in relation to the title of the bearer, or to the instrument presented for payment, or the money intended to be thereby secured. And the Company do hereby for themselves and their successors, covenant with the said his executors and administrators, that the Company will, from time to time as may be necessary, by registration in the proper Bureau des Hypothèques of a proper Acte de Convention, and by all such other means as the law of Egypt may require, well and effectually charge by way of mortgage or hypothèque all the said waterworks and undertaking for supplying the City of Alexandria, in Egypt, with water, and all other for the time being the real property and chattels real of the Company in Egypt, and all other for the time being the property of the Company for which such registration is required, with the payment of the moneys intended to be hereby secured, and will, from time to time as may be necessary, do all other acts necessary for giving full effect to the security intended to be hereby given, and for securing the payment of the principal sums, and interest payable under this debenture, and the other debentures, for the said sum of 225,000l., or so much thereof as shall for the time being be issued.

> Given under the Common Seal of the said Company, the 31st day of July 1879.

Directors.

Secretary.

Charles, Q.C. (*Radcliffe* with him), for the appellant.—Where a Company carrying on business abroad, having all its property abroad, and earning its profits abroad, pays interest in full to debenture holders resident abroad, they are not liable to income tax on those payments. A foreigner resident in Alexandria and receiving interest on a debt there would incur no liability to the income tax. A Company paying interest on debentures is charged in respect of such interest merely as a collector for Government; the real person aimed at is the recipient of the interest, and, therefore, when the recipient would not be liable neither should the Company be charged.

The Crown relies upon the 4th rule of Case I., Schedule D., section 100, 5 & 6 Vict. c. 35., which forbids any deduction in respect of interest payable out of profits and gains; but this debenture interest is not payable out of profits and gains; it is a charge upon the whole property of the Company, and would have to be paid whether there were any profits or not.

Moreover, rule 4 is repeated, amplified, and explained by a later section of the same Act (s. 159), which limits its operation to cases where the income tax paid in respect of the interest can be deducted upon payment of the interest to the persons entitled

thereto, and section 102 supports the argument that the operation of rule 4 was intended to be limited in this manner; in
the present case the Company do not and could not deduct
income tax upon payment of the interest in question.

In the court below it was argued for the Crown that in the
Income Tax Act of 1806 (w) the clauses corresponding to rule 4
and section 159, (x) each contained an exception in favour of
interest of debts due to foreigners not resident in Great Britain
or any other of Her Majesty's dominions, and that in the Act of
Victoria the exception has been omitted; but the exception
referred to was different in two respects from the one I am
contending for; in one sense it was broader, inasmuch as it
covered interest arising from property in England; in another
sense narrower, because it applied only to foreigners.

Herschell (S.G.), for the respondent, was not called upon.

Brett (M.R.).—It seems to me we must affirm the decision of
the Divisional Court.

Now, the first point seems to me to be, what is it that this
Company desire should be done? The Company claims as a
deduction from the sum assessed the amount of 7,695*l.*, being
interest on debenture bonds to be paid to foreigners residing in
Egypt. Therefore the complaint of the Company is, that
although they admit that they are liable to be assessed to the
income tax, they have been assessed upon a wrong amount; that
is to say, that in assessing the amount, something ought to have
been deducted which had not been deducted. Now, what is that
which they say ought to have been deducted in assessing the
amount? It is interest payable on certain debentures. Now,
out of what is that payment to be made? It is a payment of
interest on debentures, that is, a payment of interest on money
borrowed by the Company. Out of what can such a Company
pay? The only fund out of which such a Company can pay is
the money they receive by way of water rents. What is the
money which they receive by way of water rents? It is that
which the Company gains by its trade, not its net profits, but
that which it gains; it is a gain by the Company, out of which
this is to be paid. It is true that by the words of the debenture,
and by the construction of the debenture, the debenture holder
has another security, that is, if he is not paid his annual interest
he has the security of the property of the Company to fall back
upon; but his annual income is paid out of that fund, which is
the only fund that the Company has in its hands to pay with,
that is, part of its gains. Therefore, what the Company is contending for is, that in estimating the amount of the profits and
gains for the purpose of assessment a deduction shall be made
on account of certain annual interest which is payable out of
its gains. But then, it being admitted that the Company is to

(w) 46 Geo. III. c. 65.   (x) ss. 112 and 198.

be assessed, the only contest being upon what amount, you have ALEXANDER
WATER CO.
v. MUSGRAVE the 4th rule of section 100, which says, that in estimating that which is the subject matter of estimation in this very case no deduction may be made on account of any annual interest payable out of such profits or gains.   If, therefore, this annual interest which this Company now contends ought to be deducted were deducted, it would be in direct contradiction to the grammatical reading and the ordinary plain English reading of the 4th rule in the 100th section—in plain contradiction, I say—to the ordinary grammatical construction and to the ordinary English meaning of those words.   Therefore the case comes to be this, is there anything in the statute, 5 & 6 Vict. c. 35., which entitles the Court to read that 4th rule in section 100 in any other than its ordinary grammatical construction or according to the ordinary meaning of it in the English language?

Now, it is said that section 102 enables and obliges the Court to read it otherwise than according to its ordinary construction, but section 102 does not apply to the same operation or to the same time.   Section 102 applies to operations which all come into play to be executed or to be performed after all that it stated in section 100 has been fulfilled.   Under those circumstances it seems to me we cannot read anything from section 102 into section 100.

Well, with regard to the 159th section, that may, and does, probably, apply to the same time; but, as was pointed out by my Brother Bowen, it seems to me that there is nothing in section 159 which you can read into the 4th rule of section 100, so as to limit its operation.   Mr. Charles's argument, therefore, seems to be reduced to one of hardship.   Well, I do not deny that, assuming that the Company cannot get payment from the foreign bondholder or debenture holder, there is a hardship.   I, for myself, am unwilling to give an opinion whether the foreign debenture holder can be made to repay the Company.   I am unwilling to say that, because it seems hard to say that against the foreign debenture holder, who is not here.   I have, I confess, a strong suspicion that those who drew this Act meant, as far as English legislation can, to make him liable, and I am not prepared to say that there is anything contrary to natural justice in making him pay if he lends his money to an English Company to be paid out of the profits and gains of that English Company, but it seems to me that, whether the foreign debenture holder can be made to pay or not; in this sense, whether the Company in paying the foreign debenture holder, can or cannot deduct from him, is immaterial.   If they can, there is not hardship if they cannot, there is a hardship, but that hardship is imposed upon them by the plain terms of the Act.   I confess that I rather incline to think that there is a great force in that which was relied upon by Mr. Justice Grove, namely the difference between this latter statute, and the former statute as to this very point and the probable reason why, as given by him, any words of limitation are omitted from this statute.   I agree myself with the judgment which was given by Mr. Justice Grove, and substantially with the reasons which he gives. I do not observe that he mentions section 100, but I cannot help thinking that his judgment is really founded upon the true and proper reading of section 100 in the way which I have stated.

My Brother Cotton, I think, agrees with the result of what I have said, but from the unfortunate state of the weather he is unable to express himself in audible terms.

Bowen (L.J.).—I am of the same opinion, and have nothing to add to what the Master of the Rolls has said.

Appeal dismissed with costs.

No. 60.—COURT OF EXCHEQUER (SCOTLAND).—FIRST
DIVISION.

May 19, 1883.

WILSON (Surveyor of Taxes) *v.* FASSON.

Inhabited House Duty. Exemption. House within precincts of an infirmary, wherein the Medical Superintendent is required to dwell, not by statute as in Jepson v. Gribble, (y) but by minute of the Managers and by the exigencies of the hospital,—

Held, *That the house was a necessary part of the infirmary, and therefore exempt under Case IV., Sched. B. 48 Geo. 3, c. 55.*

At a meeting of the Commissioners for executing the Acts relating to the Inhabited House Duties for the county of Edinburgh, held at Edinburgh, the 13th day of November, 1882,—

Charles H. Fasson, Deputy Surgeon-General, Superintendent of the Royal Infirmary, Edinburgh, appealed against the charge of 2*l.* 5*s.* made upon him for inhabited house duty, at the rate of 9*d.* per £ on 60*l.*, the annual value of a dwelling-house occupied by him within the precincts of the Royal infirmary grounds, for the year ending 25th May, 1882.

The house, which is self-contained and occupied by Mr. Fasson and his family, is a part of the infirmary buildings, but is separate and distinct from the infirmary itself, it being distant about 30 yards from the nearest point of it. There is an entrance to

(y) Ante, p. 78.

the house by the principal gate of the infirmary in Lauriston
Place, but there is also a private entrance for the superintendent
and his family from the Meadow Walk, a public thoroughfare,
though for foot passengers only.   There is nothing in the constitution of the Royal Infirmary, although there is a resolution and
a regulation as herein-after stated adopted 30th October, 1876,
which requires the superintendent to reside within the precincts
of the infirmary.

Previous to the appointment of Mr. Fasson to the office of
superintendent on 18th December, 1871, the offices of treasurer
and superintendent were combined in one person, Mr. M'Dougall,
who resided in the old infirmary.

The managers, at their meeting of 17th April, 1871, approved of
the report of their committee on expenditure, which recom-
mended the separation of these offices, the duties of the former
superintendent as treasurer requiring him to keep the accounts
and to perform the duties relative to the extensive money transactions of the infirmary, and to carry on the correspondence with
parochial boards and others regarding patients.

The managers, in their minute of 23rd October, 1871, resolved
to advertise for a medical superintendent; and in their minute
of 30th October, 1871, the terms of the advertisement are given,
which set forth, *inter alia*, that the managers having resolved to
separate the offices of treasurer and superintendent, a qualified
and efficient gentleman was required to fill the latter office; that
he would have the general control of the whole establishment,
and be answerable to the managers for the proper working of
every department; that a medical education would be a recom-
mendation; that he would not be required to sleep in the infirmary until it was removed to the new site; that the salary
would be 420*l*., with 80*l*. until a house should be provided.

The former superintendent, Mr. M'Dougall, who, after Mr.
Fasson's appointment, held the office of treasurer only, continued
to reside in the old infirmary until October, 1879, when the new
infirmary was opened.   During the same period Mr. Fasson
resided at Merchiston, his duties being attended to by Mr.
M'Dougall when Mr. Fasson's absence rendered this necessary.

On 16th October, 1876, the building, house, and finance com-
mittees of the managers adopted a joint report, in which they
" came to the unanimous conclusion that the superintendent
" should be required to live within the infirmary grounds, and
" that a suitable residence should be provided for him there."
They came to this conclusion, *inter alia*, on the following grounds
(as the report bears):—" The experience of the last four years
" seems to the committee to have proved that the duties of
" superintendent cannot be efficiently and in their entireness
" carried out unless he resides at the infirmary.   He cannot,
" living at a distance, exercise constant supervision and control
" over the large staff of a great establishment such as the new
" infirmary; he cannot be at all times easily accessible to those

"who may have occasion to apply to him for advice or assist-
"ance; he cannot conveniently, especially at night, visit from
"time to time the wards to see that matters are properly con-
"ducted; he cannot take effectual cognisance of the stores, nor,
"in short, can he keep himself continuously acquainted with
"the whole working of the institution, for which he is answer-
"able to the managers." The managers, by their minute of
30th October, 1876, adopted the said report, and resolved that
the building committee be instructed to provide a suitable house
for the superintendent on the new site; and this was accordingly
done. Mr. Fasson removed to the house so provided for him on
or about 1st October, 1879, and he has since resided there, his
allowance for a house being discontinued.

The Appellant contended that the house occupied by him,
being part of the infirmary buildings, and occupied by him in
his official capacity as superintendent of the Royal Infirmary,
fell under Case IV. of the Exemptions, Schedule B. of the Act
48 Geo. 3. c. 55., which exempts from inhabited house duty
"any hospital, charity school, or house provided for the recep-
"tion or relief of poor persons," and which exemption is still
continued in force by the Act 14 & 15 Vict. c. 36.

The appellant further contended that his case was ruled by
the decision of the judges in the Exchequer (England) case,
Jepson v. Gribble, as reported in the Exchequer cases, Income
Tax and Inhabited House Duties, Part V., No. 16, in which the
resident medical superintendent of a lunatic asylum was held
not to be liable for inhabited house duty, in respect of the house
provided for him separate and detached from, but within the
grounds of the asylum.

Mr. Andrew Wilson, surveyor of taxes, contended that, but for
the exemption relied upon by the appellant, the whole of the
infirmary buildings would, under the Act 14 & 15 Vict. c. 36,
be chargeable; that the exemption was meant to prevent such a
result, but that it was straining it to hold it as applicable to the
family dwelling-house of the superintendent, in which patients
are neither received nor treated. The fact that the house being
situated within the grounds of the infirmary might affect its
annual value (which is not objected to), but could not constitute
a right to exemption. The surveyor further contended that a
material difference existed between this case and that of Jepson
v. Gribble, inasmuch as in that case it was provided by statute
16 & 17 Vict. c. 97.) that the medical superintendent shall be
resident in the asylum, whereas in this case no such obligation
exists either under a statute or the constitution of the Royal
Infirmary.

We, the Commissioners, having regard to the decision by the
judges in the Exchequer (England) Case, No. 16, above referred
to, sustained the appeal, and granted relief from the assessment
to inhabited house duty. The surveyor expressed his dissatisfaction with our decision, and craved that a case might be stated

for the opinion of the Court, and which is hereby stated accordingly.

WILSON v.
PASSON.

JAMES S. FRASER TYTLER.

J. GIBSON THOMSON.

Counsel having been heard,—

The Lord President.—My Lords, the simple question before
us is whether the medical superintendent's house in the Royal
Infirmary in Edinburgh is part of that hospital within the meaning of the exemption in the 48th of George III., which exempts
from the inhabited house duty "any hospital, charity school,
" or house provided for the reception or relief of poor persons."
Now, apart from authority altogether, I must say I think the
case admits of very little doubt. The hospital with which we
have to deal is, as we all know, a very large establishment. I
am not aware how many beds it contains now, but it must be one
of the largest hospitals in the kingdom. And *primâ facie* I
think any one would say it is absolutely necessary that the
medical superintendent of that institution should reside within
the walls of the institution. Accordingly we find that the
managers of the infirmary when they got possession of their new
building, which is much more extensive than their old building,
came to a resolution in terms of a report of a committee on the
16th of October, 1876, that "the experience of the last four years
" seems to the committee to have proved that the duties of
" superintendent cannot be efficiently, and in their entireness
" carried out unless he resides at the infirmary. He cannot,
" living at a distance, exercise constant supervision and control
" over the large staff of a great establishment such as the new
" infirmary; he cannot be at all times easily accessible to those
" who may have occasion to apply to him for advice or assist-
" ance; he cannot conveniently, especially at night, visit from
" time to time the wards to see that matters are properly con-
" ducted; he cannot take effectual cognisance of the stores, nor,
" in short, can he keep himself continuously acquainted with the
" whole working of the institution, for which he is answerable
" to the managers." It is not said in this case, nor has it been
suggested in argument, that the managers were wrong, or that
they did not adopt a step which was as they thought absolutely
necessary for the proper working of the institution under their
administration. If it be necessary, as I think nobody will doubt,
that the medical superintendent should be enabled from time to
time at night and throughout the night to visit the wards, does
that not create an absolute necessity for his being resident on the
premises? It is impossible, if we take the statement of the
managers as being consistent with fact, to doubt for one moment
that what they have done is absolutely necessary for the well-
being of this institution. Now then, if it be necessary that the
medical superintendent should be resident at the hospital, as it
is expressed, what does it matter whether the rooms which he

WILSON v.
FASSON.
———

occupies are connected with the main body of the hospital by a covered passage or consist of a separate house still within the grounds and walls of the infirmary itself. I don't think this is a technical question at all. We have sometimes had very nice technical questions arising on statutes as to what forms part of a house, but there is no such question arising here. The simple question before us is one which I agree with Chief Baron Kelly (z) in the case that has been cited, is to be looked at with the eye of common sense; is this in fair common sense a part of the hospital? I think it is a necessary part of the hospital, and I do not think the hospital could go on or be administered without it, and therefore the necessity is of the highest possible kind. We are told it is not a statutory necessity. I admit that, but I don't see the relevancy of it. The circumstance of a resident superintendent being required by a statute would not make his house a part of the building of the asylum or hospital a bit more than if it becomes necessary for other reasons. The requirement of the statute is no doubt one necessity, but the absolute requirement of the exigencies of the hospital itself is just as strong a necessity and makes the building in my humble opinion just as much a part of the hospital as if it had been required by statute. I think the case of Jepson v. Gribble (a) and the previous case of Congreve and the overseers of Upton (b) are strong authorities in support of the view which I am now stating; but I desire to give my opinion upon the broad question that is presented on the face of this case disclosing the facts, without reference to authority at all, and upon the merits of that question I entertain no doubt.

Lord Deas.—I am entirely of the same opinion. The question is, is this part of the hospital? I don't think that depends upon whether it is made by statute part of the hospital or not. It is still a part of the hospital clearly and imperatively whether there is a statutory provision on the subject or not; and I think that all the cases we have had before us go to support that proposition. It is argued that if the building for the medical superintendent were a part of the hospital, a building for the chaplain of the hospital must be so also. I don't think that follows at all. The duties of the two officers may be equally important, but they are not equally connected with the purpose of the hospital. The duties of the chaplain relate to the next world; the duties of the medical superintendent relate to this world; and apart altogether from questions of importance the one is certainly much more immediate than the other. Therefore, there is no use arguing that if the one were held to be a part of the hospital the others must be so. I have no doubt whatever that it is of no consequence that the necessity arises from a statutory condition. The question is whether, in point of fact, this is a part of the

---

(z) *Ante*, p. 80.   (a) *Ante*, p. 78.
(b) 4 B. & S. 857 ; 33 L. J (N. S.) (M. C.) 83.

hospital. Now it is not only a part of the hospital but it is a necessary part of it. It could not be dispensed with. We need no authority at all about it, and I would be of the same opinion with your Lordship upon a mere statement of the case that this is a part of the hospital. The managers have so held, but I don't go upon the fact that the managers have so held, for I think that apart altogether from the managers' finding it is a part of the hospital and a necessary part of the hospital. I am clearly of opinion that the exemption applies.

Lord Mure.—I have no difficulty in concurring with your Lordships. I think that by the minute which has been read it is made absolutely necessary that this gentleman should live within the precincts of the infirmary, and that being made clear by the regulations of the managers, it is in my opinion just as necessary that he should be there as it was in the English case, where the Act of Parliament said he was to live there. They have the power of fixing where he is to reside; they have fixed on this house within the precincts of the infirmary, and therefore I think he is residing in a house which is exempt from duty.

Appeal dismissed, with expenses.

No. 61.—COURT OF EXCHEQUER (SCOTLAND).—FIRST DIVISION.

July 7, 1883.

CORKE (Surveyor of Taxes) *v.* BRIMS.

Inhabited House Duty. Tenements. Two houses with internal communication are let to various occupiers and used partly as offices and partly as a residence. The street door of one house opens into a vestibule from which two doors lead into the offices; and another door opens into the lobby of the residential portion, and affords the only means of entrance into the residence. The house falls within section 13 (1) of the Act 41 Vict. c. 15.

Russell *v.* Coutts (c) and Yorkshire Fire and Life Insurance Co. *v.* Clayton (d) distinguished.

(c) *Ante*, p. 469.   (d) *Ante*, pp. 356 and 479.

At a meeting of the Commissioners for the general purposes of the Income Tax and Inhabited House Duties for the county of Caithness, held at Wick on the 6th day of November, 1882, Mr. James Brims, solicitor and bank agent, Thurso, appealed against an assessment of 1l. 10s. made upon him for inhabited house duty for the year 1882-83, at the rate of 9d. per £ on 40l., the *cumulo* value of certain premises situated in Thurso, of which he is owner.

The premises consist of—

1. Bank offices rented by the Bank of Scotland—Messrs. Brims (the owner) and Mackay, joint-agents—at 20l. per annum.

2. House occupied by Mr. Alexander Mackay, one of the agents, at a rental of 10l.

3. Writing offices occupied by the aforesaid Messrs. Brims and Mackay, solicitors, at a rental of 10l.

The premises comprise two houses,—one containing the bank office and houses, and the other the law offices, communicating as shown by the annexed plan. In the place on the plan marked A—B there is a door between the bank and the lobby, but this door has from the first been kept locked and nailed up, and has never been used as a means of communication. The house is partly over and partly behind the bank.

The bank authorities only rent the bank offices, Mr. Mackay himself renting the house; it being quite optional, so far as the agreement with the bank is concerned, whether his house should be in the same building as the bank office.

Mr. Brims stated that his own private dwelling-house was situated at a distance from the premises in question, and that he was assessed for inhabited house duty in respect thereof, and pointed out that, though there was internal communication between the bank office and the bank consulting room, and between the bank consulting room and the writing offices occupied by Messrs. Brims and Mackay, there was no internal communication between the dwelling-house occupied by Mr. Mackay, and the other part of the premises, except that access to the house was by a common entrance from the street, which also gave access to the offices rented by the bank, and that there was no communication otherwise. He also pointed out that the dwelling-house might be occupied by any person not connected with the bank, or with Messrs. Brims and Mackay, and that the annexed plan showed that there was a separate entrance from the street to the writing offices. Mr. Brims further stated that the occupation by him of any part of the premises was as a partner of the firm of Messrs. Brims and Mackay, and not as an individual. He therefore contended that the premises charged consisted of the three separate tenements, capable of being, and were actually, let to separate tenants, that the bank offices and law offices were used solely for business or professional purposes and consequently were exempt under section 13 of 41 Vict. c. 15., and that the residence being under 20l. in value was not liable.

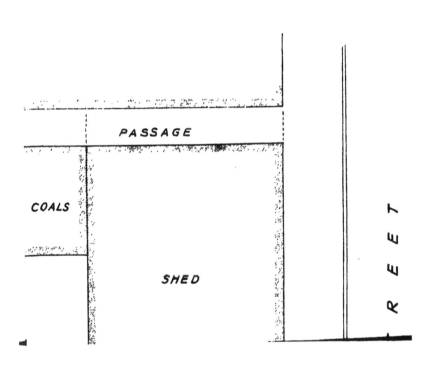

CORKE v.
BRIMS.

The surveyor of taxes, Mr. B. Corke, contended (1) that there being internal communication throughout the whole premises, as shown by the plan, they were to be looked upon as one house let to different persons, and chargeable on the landlord under Rule 6 of 48 Geo. 3. c. 55., Schedule B.; and (2) that 41 Vict. c. 15. s. 13 did not apply, as in consequence of the internal communication the lettings could not be held to be "different tenements" in the meaning of the Act. In support of this contention he referred to the Judges' remarks in Exchequer Court Cases, Nos. 48, 52, and 55, where it was laid down that the different tenements must be structurally divided, which was not the case here, where there was internal communication throughout.

The surveyor also referred to the fact that the landlord occupied part of the premises himself, and drew attention to the Judges' remarks on a similar point in case No. 48, and pointed out that the fact that Mr. Brims paid house duty elsewhere did not affect the liability of these premises.

After hearing parties, the Commissioners sustained the appeal, with which decision the surveyor expressed his dissatisfaction, and craved a case for the opinion of the High Court, which is here stated accordingly.

WILL. MACKAY.
DAVID SINCLAIR.

Counsel for the Appellant having been heard and counsel for the Respondent not having been called on :—

Lord President.—My Lords, there are three separate occupations of the house in this case. One is a bank office, which is occupied by Messrs. Brims and Mackay as joint agents for the Bank of Scotland, at a rent of 20l.; the second is writing chambers, occupied by the same firm, as solicitors, at a rent of 10l.; and the third is a dwelling-house or place of residence occupied by Mr. Alexander Mackay, one of the partners of Brims and Mackay, at a rent of 10l. Now, the only question of the slightest importance here is whether the part of the house occupied by Mr. Mackay as a dwelling-house is a separate tenement within the meaning of the statute, because if it be separate, then there can be no assessment, such as is proposed by the surveyor of taxes here, for, whether the other two portions namely, the bank offices and the writing chambers, are considered as separate or one, they are plainly occupied for the purposes of business, and therefore are exempt; and, therefore, if it be a separate tenement the house occupied by Mr. Mackay is also exempt. The whole point, therefore, is whether Mr. Mackay's house is really a separate tenement. The case of Russell *v.* Coutts (e) which is mainly relied on by the surveyor here, is essentially different,

---

(e) *Ante*, p. 469.

in this respect: that in that case, when Mr. Coutts entered from
the street into the house occupied by him he had means, without
coming out of his door again, of ranging over the entire buildings. There was no physical division of the entire premises
into separate parts in such a way that when he was in one part
of the premises he could not get access to the other. Once
entered by the street door, he had the means of going into
every room in the entire building. Now, in the present case
Mr. Mackay, who occupies a dwelling-house here, has an entirely
separate door of entrance to his house. It is not, indeed, immediately from the street that the door has an entrance. There is
a small lobby or vestibule from which three doors open, one into
the bank only; another into the bank consulting room, and the
third, which is in the centre, is the outer door of Mr. Mackay's
house; and when he has once entered in at that door and shut
it behind him he cannot obtain access from the premises in which
he finds himself to any other part of the building, except that
which is occupied by him as his residence. Now, one would
think the distinction between the two cases is so perfectly obvious
upon that simple statement that it is in vain to say that the
one case is parallel with the other. I am clear that Russell
and Coutts is an authority in support of the determination of
the Commissioners here as being a judgment requiring for its
basis the very thing that is wanting in this case. Now, I confess that is so very clear to my mind, after the frequent occasions
we have had to examine the statutes regulating the inhabited
house duty, that I should not have thought it worth while to
say more on the subject than simply to point out the distinction
between this case and the case of Russel v. Coutts, but Mr.
Lorimer has brought under our notice a judgment by the Court
of Appeal in England in the case of the Yorkshire Fire and Life
Insurance Company (f) and in so far as the facts of that case are
concerned, it appears to me that the judgment could be nothing
else than it was. I find it distinctly stated there that the
building in respect of which the assessment was made consisted
of several floors; one floor was occupied as offices by the appellants, who were owners of the building. There were also offices
occupied by a bank and other offices occupied by a civil engineer.
The first floor was occupied by a firm of merchants and a civil
engineer, and the second floor consisted of rooms occupied as
residences by the curates of St. Mary's Church, Hull, and by a
caretaker. Now, when you compare that statement with the
plans which were produced along with the case, nothing could
be clearer than this, that that house which contained all these
different occupations was a house which had one common entrance from the street, and when once you entered that door from
the street every part of the house was open to you; that is to say,
nothing stood in your way, except the doors of the particular
rooms that were occupied by the different persons described as

---

(f) *Ante*, pp. 336 and 479.

bank agents and engineers, and dwellers, and so forth; and in the second floor, which was very much relied upon by Mr. Lorimer in arguing the case, the plan shows distinctly that when you go up the stair to that second floor there is just a series of sitting-rooms and bed-rooms, each having its door opening into the common passage or staircase. A more thoroughly undivided house, in so far as physical division is concerned, it is almost impossible to conceive. Therefore, the principle of that case is, I think, entirely in accordance with the judgments which we have hitherto pronounced upon these Acts of Parliament. No doubt there are some things said and quoted from the opinions of the judges which, I confess, I should not be very willing to accept as a thoroughly sound exposition of some of the clauses of the statute, but I cannot think that that alters the nature of the case as an authority upon the statute. Certainly, it is only in one or two opinions of the learned judges that these expressions occur, and there is one of the learned judges, Lord Justice Cotton, whose opinion, I think, explains the principle of this construction of the statute in a very clear and satisfactory manner. He says, "What one has to consider," &c. [*reads*]. Now, if that is an accurate description of the case that was before the Court it certainly can have no application here; and it is quite plain, I think, notwithstanding some of the expressions to which I have referred, that the judgment of the Court did not really go beyond this, that they could not hold the exemption to apply where the only division that existed was that which exists in all houses of different floors and separate rooms. In the present case there is as plainly a separate dwelling-house here as there is in the numerous large lands in the city of Edinburgh, and in other Scotch towns where flats constitute separate dwelling-houses, and half flats constitute separate dwelling-houses entering from a common stair by separate doors, each forming the door of entrance to the house occupied by one particular tenant or proprietor, or, be it observed, these divisions are of such a nature that there is no difficulty in the proprietorship of each separate portion of the tenement being different altogether. But in the case with which the Court of Appeal were dealing, the case of the Yorkshire Fire and Life Insurance Company, that would have been altogether different. You cannot say that a room in a house, where the only division is what exists in all houses where there are separate floors and separate rooms, each room with its own door, is a separate tenement, and that appears to me to be the true test as to whether a part of a large house of this kind is or is not within the fair meaning of the statute a separate tenement. I am, therefore, for affirming the determination of the Commissioners.

Lord Deas.—I was not present at the discussion in Russell and Coutts, but I quite agree with the principle upon which your Lordships decided that case. I think this case is quite different, and after the statement of the case and the explanations we have had of the plan. I am of opinion that the decision

D

which your Lordship proposes to pronounce in this case is
altogether correct. I do not think there is any reason to make
any further remark upon the case.

Lord Mure.—I concur in thinking that this case is quite
different from that of Russell and Coutts which has been referred
to. I see there we were all unanimous in the opinion that the
case was one in which it was open to Coutts to get to every
part of the premises by doors connected with his dwelling-house,
and that in point of fact he did so when ever it suited his convenience. Now, in the present case, it is shown in the plan
that this vestibule has at one side of it the bank office; at the
other side the consulting office of the bank, and these are let
to the Bank of Scotland, and you cannot get from either of the
rooms of the bank, as they are at present fitted up, into the
house occupied by Mr. Mackay except by going through the
vestibule, in which there is a house door leading into the lobby
of Mr. Mackay's house by a separate entrance altogether. That
is quite distinct from the case of Coutts. I think it is a separate tenement in these circumstances, and that the bank and
consulting room are let as a separate tenement in the fair sense
and meaning of the statute. Looking into the opinions given
in the Yorkshire Fire and Life Insurance Company referred to,
it seems to me that the judges there took the view expressed by
Justice Grove, who says—"The house must be substantially
"divided and let in different tenements so as to constitute inde-
"pendent tenements." Now, when these rooms are let to the
Bank of Scotland and the house is let to Mr. Mackay, I think
the house is so arranged that it becomes an independent tenement in the sense indicated by Mr. Justice Grove. Then he
says again—"Where there is a house divided into separate and
exclusive tenements," &c. [*Reads*]. (*g*). Now these are exclusive tenements in this case. In fact, Mr. Mackay, being one of
the bank agents, must get to his house by different means from
what he gets to the premises let to the bank, and it is a separate tenement in that way. I agree in the result at which your
Lordships have arrived.

Lord Shand.—I am of the same opinion. The question is
whether this is a case in which the party is entitled to the exemption provided by sub-section 1 of section 13 of the statute
of 1878, and the decision of the question depends upon whether
the Court is in a position to affirm that this house, though one
property, is divided and let in different tenements, certain of
which tenements are occupied exclusively for the purpose of a
business or profession. Now, I think, looking to the arrangements of these premises and the divisions which exist separating
the business premises from the dwelling-house, the property is
one which is not only let in different tenements, but is divided
into different tenements, and I think the distinguishing feature

---

(*g*) *Ante*, p. 341.

of the case is that after the entry to the vestibule, which no doubt is common to the dwelling-house and the business premises, the dwelling-house is entirely shut from the business premises by means of a street door of its own which completely incloses and divides it from the rest of the building. The case is entirely different from that of Coutts, because there is no internal door of communication here as there by where a person once inside the dwelling-house might range over the whole premises. If, indeed, the door AB shown upon the plan in this case, which has been permanently closed, had been a door which was open and used, the case would have been different, but the fact that that door is shut and that thereby anyone entering the business premises is confined to these alone and cannot get into the dwelling-house above without entering by the proper entrance door for these premises, completely distinguishes the two cases. In regard to the Yorkshire case, I have only to say that I think there is a clear distinction between it and the present. In the case of the Yorkshire Insurance Company there were no doubt separate holdings. The premises on the second floor and third floor were let to separate tenants—parts of them —but though there were separate holdings there was no division such as the statute requires. There was no physical or structural division of any kind. Here there is a physical or structural division consisting of the front door of the dwelling-house which shuts it off from everything else. It appears to me that the circumstances that you have that structural difference clearly distinguishes the case from that of the Yorkshire Insurance Company, and I am therefore of opinion with your Lordships that the decision of the Commissioners was right.

Judgment for the respondent, with expenses.

No. 62.—IN THE COURT OF APPEAL.—DECEMBER 6, 1881.
ERICHSEN v. LAST (Surveyor of Taxes).

This case came before the Court upon the appeal of Erichsen from the decision of the Divisional Court, reported at page 351, *ante*. The judges (*Jessel*, M.R., *Brett*, and *Cotton*, L.J.J.) affirmed the decision of the Queen's Bench Division (*vide* L.R. 8 Q.B.D. 414).

INDEX.

Abbreviations : H. of L. = House of Lords.
      "   C.A.   = Court of Appeal.
      "   C.E.E. = Court of Exchequer, England.
      "   C.E.S. = Court of Exchequer, Scotland.
      "   E.D.   = Exchequer Division, England.
      "   Q.B.D. = Queen's Bench Division, England.

Note.—Two cases reported in this volume have been omitted from the Income Tax portion of the Index, viz. :—

Knowles v. *McAdam* (p. 161), over-ruled by the H. of L. in the case of *Coltness Iron Co.* v. *Black* (p. 287); and

Clerk v. *Commissioners of Supply for Dumfries*, over-ruled by the H. of L. in the recent case of *Coomber* v. *Justices of Berks*, which will shortly be reported.

Also the following cases have been omitted from the Inhabited House Duty portion of the Index :—

which turned mainly on the construction of the words "servant or other person" in 41 Vict. c. 15. s. 13 (2), the meaning of which has been subsequently defined by 44 Vict. c. 12. s. 24.

Income Tax.

ABROAD.—English Company carrying on business abroad. *See* RESIDENCE—*Company.*

ALLOWANCE under the Income Tax Acts. *See* DEDUCTION FROM PROFITS.

ANNUAL GIFT to Scotch Minister by his friends, chiefly Members of the Congregation. *See* OFFICE—*Schedule E.*

AVERAGE.—Partnership converted into Company. *See* SUCCESSION.
      Slate Quarry worked underground. *See* QUARRY.

BENEFICIAL OCCUPATION.—Official Residence of Police Superintendent. *See* Occupier.

BREWER paying premiums for Leases of Public Houses *See* DEDUCTION OF PROFITS.—*Premiums.*

BUILDINGS.—Depreciation. *See* DEDUCTION FROM PROFITS—*Depreciation.*

BUSINESS CHANGING HANDS. *See* SUCCESSION

Inhabited House Duty.

F

*This case was dealt with under Rule III. The question whether the banking house was "a shop or a warehouse" within the meaning of Rule III. was not submitted to, or dealt with by, the Court in this case.

Lightning Source UK Ltd.
Milton Keynes UK
UKHW02f2239230818
327720UK00011B/431/P